MW01251312

Cyberlife!

Cyberlife!

PUBLISHING

201 West 103rd Street
Indianapolis, Indiana 46290

COPYRIGHT © 1994 BY SAMS PUBLISHING

FIRST EDITION

All rights reserved. No part of this book shall be reproduced, stored in a retrieval system, or transmitted by any means, electronic, mechanical, photocopying, recording, or otherwise, without written permission from the publisher. No patent liability is assumed with respect to the use of the information contained herein. Although every precaution has been taken in the preparation of this book, the publisher and author assume no responsibility for errors or omissions. Neither is any liability assumed for damages resulting from the use of the information contained herein. For information, address Sams Publishing, 201 W. 103rd St., Indianapolis, IN 46290.

International Standard Book Number: 0-672-30491-0

Library of Congress Catalog Card Number: 94-66639

97 96 95 94   4   3   2   1

Interpretation of the printing code: the rightmost double-digit number is the year of the book's printing; the rightmost single digit, the number of the book's printing. For example, a printing code of 94-1 shows that the first printing of the book occurred in 1994.

Composed in Goudy and MCPdigital by Macmillan Computer Publishing

Printed in the United States of America

TRADEMARKS

All terms mentioned in this book that are known to be trademarks or service marks have been appropriately capitalized. Sams Publishing cannot attest to the accuracy of this information. Use of a term in this book should not be regarded as affecting the validity of any trademark or service mark. StereoGraphics is a registered trademark and CrystalEyes is a trademark of the StereoGraphics Corporation. Graphisoft is a registered trademark of Graphisoft U.S. Inc. Leverage is a trademark of CLS Inc. VActors is a trademark of Simgraphics Engineering.

PUBLISHER

Richard K. Swadley

ACQUISITIONS MANAGER

Stacy Hiquet

MANAGING EDITOR

Cindy Morrow

ACQUISITIONS EDITOR

Gregory S. Croy

DEVELOPMENT EDITORS

L. Angelique Brittingham
Dean Miller

SOFTWARE DEVELOPMENT SPECIALIST

Keith Davenport

PRODUCTION EDITOR

James Grass

EDITORS

Marla Abraham
Rosie Piga
Joe Williams

EDITORIAL COORDINATOR

Bill Whitmer

EDITORIAL ASSISTANTS

Carol Ackerman
Sharon Cox
Lynette Quinn

MARKETING MANAGER

Gregg Bushyeager

COVER DESIGNER

Tim Amrhein

BOOK DESIGNER

Alyssa Yesh

DIRECTOR OF PRODUCTION AND MANUFACTURING

Jeff Valler

IMPRINT MANAGER

Juli Cook

MANUFACTURING COORDINATOR

Paul Gilchrist

PRODUCTION ANALYSTS

Angela D. Bannon
Dennis Clay Hager
Mary Beth Wakefield

GRAPHICS IMAGE SPECIALISTS

Brad Dixon
Jason Hand
Clint Lahnen
Dennis Sheehan
Craig Small

PRODUCTION

Georgiana Briggs
Mona Brown
Elaine Brush
Mary Ann Cosby
Elaine Crabtree
Rob Falco
Kimberly K. Hannel
Louisa Klucznik
Wendy Ott
Brian-Kent Proffitt
Kim Scott
Susan Shepard
Scott Tullis
Holly Wittenberg

INDEXER

Charlotte Clapp

Overview

Contents

PART II   CONNECTION SPACES

About the Authors

David E. Day has been writing about computers and high-tech gadgets for more than 20 years. His first work was for a large computer company, where he helped launch two major products (one an international success, the other only a dim memory). He specializes in desktop publishing, recently wrote a book on fonts and desktop applications for Macmillan/Alpha Books, and has written nationally published magazine articles.

Dave also prepares marketing materials and brochures. He programs and develops projects for microcomputers, and he participated in creating the first true laptop PC marketed in the United States. He has also instructed and lectured widely on various computer applications.

He's also an active amateur radio operator, and directs emergency communications for his county of residence. He's a volunteer Emergency Medical Technician and holds a private pilot's license. He's an avid backpacker; he has climbed in the U.S. and Canada and has summited the 48 higher peaks of New Hampshire. Dave is the proud father of a bright and active 6-year-old.

David Galbraith was born in Scotland in 1966 and currently lives in London. He trained as an architect and worked for Sir Norman Foster (who made his name designing Hong Kong and Shanghai bank headquarters, and now is working on the Reichstag in Berlin). Galbraith recently has been working in set design for Fisher Park (whose work ranges from sets for rock concerts, including the U2 Zoo TV tour and the current Rolling Stones and Pink Floyd sets, to projects for multimedia theater). Galbraith last year co-founded Realtime Anywhere, which works on projects ranging from the production of realtime 3-D graphics for a banking system to an automated means of "setting out" on building sites directly from CAD. His e-mail address, for correspondence about *Cyberlife!*, is *anyone@anywhere.com*.

Stuart Harris has extensive experience in TV production and post-production, in providing both equipment and technical expertise. Harris is a veteran of science specials, such as the BBC's *The Ascent of Man*, *Connections*, and four major specials on space topics. He also has worked on selected programming for *NOVA* and *Horizons*. He is interested in writing and mass media, and is an expert with IBM PC computer hardware, DOS, assembly language, and BASIC.

• •

Anne Hart, 52, of San Diego, California, is a full-time book author, columnist, and cartoonist specializing in books on virtual reality, multimedia, career development, and personality-type issues. She has authored 40 books.

Her latest books include *Ways to Make Money with Your Video Camera*, *How to Write for the New Media*, *The Video Resource Book*, and books on MBTI personality types, including *Pick Your Mate by Personality Type*, all published by Tiare Publications, Lake Geneva, Wisconsin. She also has authored *Winning Resumes for Computer Personnel*, published by Barron's Educational Series, Inc., Hauppauge, New York, which details how to write resumes for jobs in virtual reality, multimedia, and interactive media.

Hart holds a master's degree and bachelor's degrees in creative and professional writing emphasis from SDSU and NYU, and she has had coursework in computer graphics, multimedia, scriptwriting, and fine art. She writes up to four books a year and articles on virtual reality and multimedia for national columns.

Rick Leinecker has been writing books, articles, and software since 1985. His list of published games includes GrandMaster Chess, BridgeMaster, Trump Castle 3, and The Cardinal of the Kremlin. Besides occasional appearances in *Dr. Dobbs*, he writes a regular column, features, and reviews for *Compute* magazine.

Former jobs include High School Band Director at South Miami Senior High, Director of Programming and Online Services at Compute Publications, and Director of Technology at IntraCorp, Inc. He currently teaches math and computers at Reidsville Senior High School in Reidsville, North Carolina.

Kelly D. Lucas, 34, is a resident of San Jose, California. He was born and reared in Topeka, Kansas. Immediately after high school, he enlisted and served for 14 years in the U.S. Marine Corps. During this time, he served as a Cryptographic technician in Japan and North Carolina, and later served as a technical controller, which included a tour in Saudi Arabia (Desert Shield/Desert Storm 1990-91). He is currently working as a technical support engineer for McAfee Associates, and recently toured South America to present virus and antivirus technology in seminars and trade shows.

HP Newquist is a writer who has covered the business of artificial intelligence for more than a decade. He was the founding editor of *AI Trends*, the first business publication devoted solely to the commercial aspects of AI, and more than 100 of his articles have appeared in magazines and journals around the world. His expertise in the field of thinking machines has been cited by publications ranging from the *Wall Street Journal* and *Forbes* to *Newsweek*, *USA Today*, and *The New York Times*. Newquist has served as chairman of a number of conferences on advanced technology and consults with major corporations on the development and application of critical new technologies.

He and his family live in Scottsdale, Arizona.

• •

Charles Ostman has spent more than 20 years working with electronics, physics, and computers, including eight years at Lawrence Berkeley Laboratory at the University of California, Berkeley. He currently is a member of Nanothinc, a San Francisco-based nanotechnology focus and development support group that is interested in furthering both the support of the various technologies and related industries, and in developing a general public awareness of the subject.

Ostman also is an author/technical editor for several technology and "future culture" publications, including *Midnight Engineering*, a 70,000 national circulation technical trade journal for the software/technical product development industry, and *Mondo 2000*, a Berkeley-based, worldwide-circulated technology "culture" journal.

Daniel W. Rasmus lives in Laguna Hills, California, from which he commutes more than three hours a day to act as a senior systems engineer in a major aerospace company. When Rasmus is at home he spends most of his free time with his wife, Janet, and two daughters, Rachel and Alyssa.

He has, however, found time to write more than 130 articles and present several papers to major conferences. Rasmus is the Western Regional Editor for *Manufacturing Systems Magazine*, the AI and Objects Columnist for *Object Magazine*, and a contributing editor to *PC AI*. He has contributed in the past to *Byte*, *MacUser*, *MacWeek*, *The Office*, *Mondo 2000*, *Wired*, and several other publications.

Rasmus currently is working on several books.

• •

Dr. **Donald Rose** was born in a log cabin in midtown Manhattan (or in a hospital, one of the two; he's not sure which because that memory is a bit hazy). He eventually moved to Florida and received his B.A. in Economics from the Univer-

sity of Florida, after which he decided to head west (because he was a young man). At the University of California–Irvine, he received his M.S. and a Ph.D. in Computer Science, specializing in artificial intelligence (AI)—the art and science of making machines think (like his smart toaster, which somehow is able to set off the smoke alarm when the toast is done). Rose has published more than a dozen technical papers on various areas of AI, and has lectured internationally on the subject.

Today, Rose consults in AI and other computer topics, and is also a writer on science-related matters. His new book, *Minding Your Cybermanners,*—a fun guide to Internet etiquette and manners—comes out in October 1994 (from Alpha Books, another fine Macmillian company).

Rose's other technical interests include artificial life (especially genetic algorithms) and virtual reality. Rose's non-science interests include screenwriting (required by law in his home city of Los Angeles) and live performance (guitar/vocals, comedy, and combinations of both).

He'd also love to host an all-science talk show one day, if anyone would listen.

Paul M. and **Mary J. Summitt** have been married since January 1991. Together, they have three children, Catherine, Michael, and Jaclyn, and are going to be grandparents in December 1994.

Paul served four years in the U.S. Marine Corps as a television production specialist. He has worked at a variety of radio and television stations in both news and production positions, and has a B.S. in Radio/Television and a master's degree in Mass Communication from Arkansas State University. He is currently working on his dissertation in Communication with the University of Missouri-Columbia and is the Director of Broadcasting and an assistant professor in communication at Pittsburg State University.

Mary has a B.S. in broadcasting from Lincoln University and is currently a graduate teaching assistant working on a master's degree in Public Relations at Pittsburg State University. Individually and together, Paul and Mary have presented research at a variety of national and international conferences. The topics have ranged from the future of radio and the impact of television on the Vietnam conflict to creating a virtual newsroom and communication in cyberspace. They have published articles in *Current Notes* and in *Vietnam Magazine,* as well as being the principal writers for the user manual for VR Basic.

Paul and Mary are both avid readers and love to travel. Their current research interests concern Quantum theoretical applications involving communication in cyberspace.

Valerie Promise (previously known as Valerie Bloch) is a writer on state-of-the-art topics, technical and otherwise. On the technical side, her credits include contributions to computer books, manuals for software, and feature stories for the *San Jose Business Journal*. She is also the author of a soon-to-be-published, yet-to-be-titled compendium of techniques for transcending negative feelings about anything, and another soon-to-be-published work provisionally entitled *The Liberal Arts Guide to High-Tech Careers*. A photographer by training, Promise is starting a line of photographic postcards and notecards. She lives in the San Francisco Bay Area with her daughter, Ariel.

Christopher Van Buren has been in the computer industry for almost 10 years—first in education, teaching computer basics of educational technology, and then as a writer and editor for a computer book publisher. He has also worked as a contract writer on projects involving computer hardware and software in such industries as banking and semiconductor testing and was instrumental in writing the first Epson FX-80 user's manual for Epson America, Inc. Van Buren was also editor and publisher of several computer newsletters involving desktop publishing, Microsoft Works, and AppleWorks. He has written or co-written several computer books and has published articles for major computer magazines, including *A+*, *Compute*, *The Computer Buyer's Guide*, and *Call A.P.P.L.E.* He has a B.A. in English from San Diego State University and has won awards from computer groups and technical societies for his user manuals.

Introduction

The computer has changed everything. Sales clerks no longer count out change, reacting instead with blind acceptance of the change total reflected in red LEDs on their cash register. Movies like *Jurassic Park* are populated by computer-generated characters. Pinball and pool give way to Super Mario Brothers and Mortal Kombat. We can talk, draw, and brainstorm over a computer network instead of driving to meet our colleagues face-to-face. We don't type; we fine-tune our phrases and punctuation with word processing. Our cars are tuned by computers and our food is cooked in computer-controlled ovens or microwaves. Minutes and hours sweep or scroll by, governed not by mechanics, but by the pulse of silicon. Our images of the cosmos return to Earth in streams of ones and zeros, finding false color and digital enhancements on the computers at JPL. We rediscover our ancestry and similarities from DNA, sequenced and mapped with the assistance of computers. We read computer-typeset books, we read computerized books, and we submit term papers via e-mail. We even flirt and frolic, and sometimes get married, via computer.

The computer has changed everything. The world is a different place even for those without access to computer technology. Computers and related technology have profoundly influenced culture. They have added new words to our slang. They have transformed our perception of need. From personal e-mail to developing a new business plan, everything is supposed to be faster, more colorful, and more polished.

This book explores the boundaries where the inhumanity of the industrial revolution meets the humanity of the information revolution. In the industrial revolution machines augmented our muscles, helping us to build great cities and vast farms, and escape into the sky. The information revolution is much more subtle. It helps us build larger cities, grow better crops in smaller spaces, and move past the sky toward the stars. The physical manifestations of the information revolution become increasingly integrated with personal and professional life.

The effects too, of computers, are more subtle. Whereas it is clear a man cannot construct a new housing tract without the aid of scoopers and bulldozers, tractors and cranes, it is not so clear that the finances or the design for that project require a computer. Yet we use the computer because it allows multiple iterations of design, checks tolerances, automatically balances statements, creates 3-D walkthroughs before the first two-by-four is nailed, displays a color-coded site topology, creates sales brochures, verifies financing qualifications, manages loan documentation, and prints welcome letters for new residents; all of the activities potentially running on a single tool, a single computer.

And we take for granted the computer's ability to support us. We no longer figure the cost benefit of doing those activities on drafting boards, ledger pads, and typewriters. Even if we need more than one computer, we will do the work with a computer. The amount of time needed to perform these activities seems intuitively less with computers. Even when you add new activities like 3-D walkthroughs, the overall process is more efficient, more engaging, and in the long run, costs less to perform.

And so with each keystroke, with each glance at our digital watch, with each mouse movement or phone call to our automated bank response system, we move closer and closer to symbiosis with our technology. Already all of the financial institutions, from the local bank to Wall Street and the Nikkei, depend on computers. They do not just use them; they require them. The overwhelming complexity of the financial systems and the interaction between banks, investors, and governments make it impossible to process financial transactions without computers.

And it was the computer that transformed financial interactions from piles of paper to explicit, realtime links. Most large transactions today take place without real money exchanging hands. Even in our personal lives the automatic deposit has removed the step of taking our check to the bank to process the deposit. Our pay becomes a journal entry from our employer to our bank. Only the digital balances change, not the stacks of money in the vault or the bags of coins; the only thing that changes are the digits in our computer records.

You all knew those things without my telling you, didn't you? You knew how pervasive computers have become. If that is true, look at this book as a check point to verify your assumptions. If not, read it as an awakening resource book. It is no longer possible to succeed with an industrial revolutionary mind in the age of information. It is questionable if you will even be able to live in the near future without some knowledge of computers. Interactive television and telephones thrust computers into the home. Rather than hopping into the industrial revolutionary car to pick up your industrial revolutionary videotape, it is likely you will receive a digital movie within minutes of requesting it from a computer at your cable company.

But that is the simple stuff. The hard stuff will come in job competition and general standards of living. People without computer knowledge will be forced to take less and less sophisticated service jobs, driving down their standard of living. People with knowledge of computers will become the new middle class, if not the new aristocracy. They will control the wealth, the technology, and the content. Look at the highest-paid executives and the richest people in America. Bill Gates, CEO of Microsoft, dominates the technology landscape with Microsoft Windows and a smorgasbord of supporting players from word processing to children's software. And Michael Eisner—Chairman and President of The Walt Disney Company—has more control of popular content than anyone else in the world. Two of the wealthiest men in America. Software and content.

So this is a book about recognizing the future. And it is a book about tools. From working with schools to creating an overhead presentation at work, there is, or will be, an expectation of computer knowledge. Beyond that, their will be an expectation of mastery. The mastery of language will evolve into the mastery of layout and image. It will no longer be sufficient to just publish a memo. Digital archives will trace a version and store it for quick retrieval. Perhaps the memo will be the seed for conversation in a groupware product.

Our assumptions about work and entertainment, music and literature change with the computer. The beautiful flute playing on the latest CD is not a flute at all, but a synthesizer mimicking a flute. And our literature is slowly moving from paper to computer, and with that shift, linking words and phrases and ideas to each other. The essential linearity of paper becoming obsolete except in short bursts of linear thought woven into webs of digitally represented knowledge.

The computer has changed everything. We live in a time of profound change. The pace of life is quickening. Our ability to cope with those changes is stretching our abilities as human beings. Our technology is driving the pace. "If we can access, then, it must be important." So when technology drives us, we use technology to manage technology. As human beings, we adapt, as we always have, to the changing conditions of the planet. This time, instead of an Ice Age, we adapt to the expansion of our own knowledge by expanding our minds.

And into that world generated from information, we bring all of our frailties and greatness. We create new forms of music and literature and art. And we seek companionship and play. We even create pets and allies that crystallize our imagination or extend our wishes.

This book is about more than cyberspace. It is about a profound shift in our place. A shift precipitated by us. It is about adapting to a future where the distinction between digital and physical becomes nearly meaningless. Where the boundaries blur between imagination and the possible. Everything is possible in the memory of a computer. And so we will try everything and go everywhere. It is that inclination that we add to the equation.

Computers are doing things today their inventors could not imagine. In the 1950s, a slim 2KB of hard-wired memory barely held enough information to add up columns of numbers. Virtual reality systems demand huge amounts of memory and speedy processors to render what does not exist so that it does.

This is a book of implications. If you are a corporate executive, mailroom clerk, paper salesman, housewife, or teacher, the computer will change the way you do what you do. In some cases whole categories of activities will disappear; in others new skills will be required. Read this book as a transition between the physical and the digital. It is all about a world totally dependent on electricity. A world that ceases to exist at the flip of a power switch. So we leave the power running. This book, however, requires no power. It is fully self-contained. Read it and absorb it. Each chapter will mean something to your present or your future. Contemplate the implications—and remember, once you power up, you can never power down again.

PART

• •

I

Cyberart

Computers as the Vehicle for the New Art

The diversification offered by computer communication hints at the possibility of a new culture for the 21st century. This will mimic what has only been possible in large cities, where people of minority groups or interests have been able to create fringe communities. What cyberspace offers is a chance for communities to grow independently, without a central location or leadership structure around which to coalesce.

chapter 1
by David Galbraith

The traditionally analogous world of art, literature, film, and music is currently being replaced by a superficially similar—but conceptually different—digital counterpart. Simultaneously, a digital culture is evolving with pioneers from the new Wired-West: a band of techno-savvy mavericks, dubbed cyberpunks, who are mapping a new virtual territory created by the exponential growth in computer networks. Passive art forms promise to be replaced by wholly interactive alternatives as the interface between people and computers becomes progressively more intuitive and the speed at which computers communicate with one another increases. The hard and fast logic of the computer is being harnessed in a truly creative fashion and is propelling not only an information revolution but a potentially cultural one.

In the last few years, the image of computer users has been transformed from social inadequacy to radical chic, and the notion of a cyberculture has captured the spirit of the moment, stimulating a rash of media interest from the *Wall Street Journal* to a myriad of "alternative culture" 'zines. J. David Bolter, author of Turing's biography, wrote in 1982 when the possibilities of computers as an artistic tool were far less obvious, "...it makes sense to regard the computer as a technological paradigm for the science, the philosophy, even the art of the coming generation." The computer is fast becoming the cultural paradigm of our age.

● ●

In the last few years, the image of computer users has been transformed from social inadequacy to radical chic, and the notion of a cyberculture has captured the spirit of the moment.

Some claim that since the science fiction authors who first envisaged the concept of a cyberculture have largely withdrawn from the arena, the idea is defunct. William Gibson may have coined the term "cyberspace" (a fact that he says "they" will never let him forget), but as a proponent of the ideas the term embodies, his involvement stops there. (He only recently disposed of his aging Apple II.) Science fiction is, however, a reliable benchmark for the development of a cyberstyle, if not an integral part in its development; and the portrayal of computing technology in science fiction has mirrored the evolution of computers themselves, from inaccessible machines residing in sterile, air-conditioned rooms to familiar household products available to almost everyone. In the 1960s, before there was a technoculture, the fictional depiction of technology reflected its clinical environment. Technology, in general, was depicted as being antiseptic, and computers as cold and inhuman. The starship Enterprise was clean and plastic (and the planets they visited all bore an uncanny resemblance to Southern California), Spock had the mind of a computer, and he was scientifically gifted but emotionally retarded. Later, in Stanley Kubrick's *2001*, a real computer called HAL (an acronym derived from the letters that precede the letters IBM in the alphabet) spoke slowly and precisely and showed little trace of feeling. *Alien* was the first film to suggest that space could be dirty, but it wasn't until *Blade Runner* that the depiction of the fusion of technology and the organic chaos of a futuristic L.A. (that Philip K. Dick had written about) gave us the first seminal glimpse of what has subsequently developed into a cyberstyle—an idea of a computer-driven culture that has only recently transcended the realm of fiction to become a practical reality.

THE NETWORK

The development of the new virtual travel parallels the development of transportation at the beginning of the century. If mainframes are the steam trains of the computer world, then personal computers are its automobiles (and perhaps laptops its motorcycles).

Trains enabled people to travel great distances in relative comfort, with a predictable journey time, and at speeds impossible on horseback. (Some Victorians even thought that travelling faster than 40 mph would lead to asphyxiation.) Trains forced people to travel a fixed route, however, and new towns often had to be close to the railroad. Consider that in a country as vast as Canada, nearly all of its population lives within a thin strip of development that straddles either side of the railway line that traverses it.

In the 1960s, computing was rather like train travel—only more ascetic. Logging on to a terminal, you were restricted in where you could go. These restrictions were set by men in white coats, supplicant to a transistor-God who resided in a futuristic, air-conditioned clean room. Computers were sold by men who wore gray suits and worked for companies like IBM. Buying a computer required large amounts of capital. Not surprisingly, few were actually bought. Computers were inaccessible, sterile, and inhuman, and their portrayal in the culture reflected this.

The motor car did not suffer from the same restrictions as the steam train. With a car, you could travel anywhere and anytime. Whereas once they were the domain of mechanically minded enthusiasts, cars have become an integral part of world culture. In America, the automobile became *the* symbol of its culture and character, from the quintessential capitalist Henry Ford, to the first teenage rebel, James Dean. Visit the Guggenheim Museum and American culture barely whispers through the relics of Euro-

Shortly after the invention of the telephone, an anonymous American mayor made what he thought was a daring suggestion: "One day every town will have one."

pean modernism; but witness a '58 Cadillac prowling through Vegas at night with the liquid reflections of multicolored neon flowing over 20 feet of chrome and steel, and culture kicks you in the teeth. Car travel has become part of the American dream. Cars have infiltrated American artistic culture throughout this century—just as computers will infiltrate the culture of the next century.

The development of the personal computer has liberated millions of users from the restrictions of large mainframe computers, giving them the same kind of increased freedom that cars provided 80 years ago. Like the car, personal computing started out in the garages of enthusiasts and has ended up as part of everyday life. Computers have been humanized and a computer culture has proliferated.

Ironically, as the highways of America become increasingly gridlocked, shattering the image of the open road as a symbol of freedom, Americans find themselves shackled by their cars, as predicted by Marshall McLuhan. In response, a new alternative culture has arisen that revolves around the opening of a vast new digital highway, a place where the message is the medium. Jack Kerouac has been succeeded by William Gibson, and computers have become the vehicles for the new culture.

Figuratively speaking, computers around the world are nodding and shaking their heads, billions of times a second, over thousands of miles, turning human thoughts, sound, and imagery into trillions of bits of Morse code. All information is being turned into the most basic language of all—the binary code of Yes/No—and as such, any type of information, sound, image, and text can be transmitted over the same infrastructure.

At first glance, a digitized picture, film, or sound may seem no different from its analog counterpart. The difference, however, has ramifications that will destroy our perception of what is "real."

The digital version of the real world can be ripped to shreds and reassembled in any form imaginable. (An analog signal is a reproduction, whereas an analog-to-digital conversion is by necessity a reconstruction.) Furthermore, a digital reconstruction is based upon the language of a machine that manipulates symbols in a purely logical manner (first hinted at by Alan Turing in 1936). The implication is that the original input can be altered by any programmable algorithm to produce a completely different result. This is why something like the Rodney King video footage will not be admissible court evidence in the not-too-distant future, and how dinosaurs have been seemingly brought to life on film after millions of years of extinction.

A change as fundamental as the communications revolution often generates its initial interest outside the mainstream of society. When the Well, the computer network arm of the *Whole Earth Review*, was set up in 1985, it was assumed that its users would come mainly from the business sector. Instead, the Well has become a world-famous melting pot for the free exchange of the fringe ideas of the counterculture. At the same time, a new generation of businessmen has been spawned from this fringe. The designer of Lotus 1-2-3, for example, was a teacher of transcendental meditation. The most powerful of all the new breed, Bill Gates, was first branded a computer nerd, before kicking sand in the face of the media by building a business empire as frighteningly large as the fictional Tyrell Corporation in *Blade Runner*.

It makes sense to think of the pioneers of the digital terrain in terms of the old "Wild West." This is a newly colonized space where prospectors have yet to make their fortunes and where freedom prevails. Ironically, however, some of those who are communicating via modem, in a space where contacts are made through mutual interest rather than geographical proximity, are typing to friends they could shout at over the backyard fence. Many of the best freestyle Net-surfers could crawl out from behind their screens and meet their cyberspace counterparts in the glorious California sunshine and catch some real waves. The cyber lifestyle is characterized not just as an American culture but a West Coast American culture. The travelers of the digital highways are the descendants of those who first used the railroad in the 19th century and who later removed the trolleys in L.A. to ensure the success of the highway system. What is certain is that the impact of computers on culture, although most visible in and around the Computer Holy Land of Silicon Valley, will rapidly spread around the world and change its character as it does so.

Potentially among the first digitally networked nations are the old Soviet Bloc countries of Eastern Europe, where antiquated telephone systems will require total replacement with up-to-date technology. In India, a country where the existing media is heavily censored, there has been an explosive interest in deregulated satellite television. An alien culture is being beamed in from space, as tens of thousands of dishes point toward satellites over the Far East. If the arrival of a digital network is embraced by the younger generation as enthusiastically as the satellite technology has been, it will have an even greater cultural impact.

Wired journalist Neal Stephenson predicts that the biggest potential market for the adoption of a digital culture is China, the world's fastest-growing economy. In China, the cyberculture will evolve into something quite different from the West Coast American idiom. A form of "communal" capitalism has evolved, so successful that the Chinese government would have fallen into bankruptcy were it not for taxes raised from the new capitalism. It is a province where businesses are set up with little more than the ubiquitous pager and cellphone, where technology is adopted and integrated into society so easily that it is conspicuous only to an outsider. Street corners bristle with cellphone users and antennae reach out from every rooftop; beneath the streets, cabling defies the official border with Hong Kong, tapping into the networks of China's wealthy neighbor. Software piracy goes hand in hand with the sale of fake Cartiers and Lacoste T-shirts. (Microsoft has even opened an office in Hong Kong with the futile aim of curbing software piracy in Asia.) Chinese society lends itself to the concept of computer networking, according to Stephenson: "In network jargon, the Chinese are distributed....Instead of moving stuff around in large hunks on trucks and trains, they move it around in tiny little hunks on bicycles....The packet switching system that makes things like the Internet work would be immediately familiar to the Chinese."

Despite the Chinese acceptance of communications technology, computers themselves have yet to be treated as much more than glorified adding machines. There is no cyberculture in China yet. The reason for this is undoubtedly the crippling handicap of the Chinese writing system. As Stephenson illustrates: "The most popular system of text entry works like this: the user types in the Pinyin version of a word (that is, its spelling in the Roman alphabet). All of the Hanzi characters so transliterated then appear on the screen—sometimes there can be dozens—and the user chooses the desired one by punching in its number on the list. Then it appears on the screen—sort of. CRTs don't have enough resolution to display the more complicated characters, so the screen fonts consist of simplified versions, and the reader has to puzzle out the identity of a character from its context."

The Chinese are hampered by a word-based character set in the same way that the Romans were hampered by their lack of a symbol for zero. But the Romans took over the world without a rational system of counting. Who knows what will happen when keyboards give way to pen interfaces and speech synthesis, removing the final impediment to the easy use of computers throughout Asia?

The likelihood of a truly global computer culture has ironically been made possible by a communications system first developed by the military. Today that system has become the vast collection of interconnected networks known as the Internet (or simply, the Net). Far from its present altruistic, non-profit, private-sector, academic image, the Internet's foundations were the Department of Defense's Advanced Research Projects Agency network, or ARPAnet. It was started with the aim of sending information that was split up into small chunks, or "packets," which could be sent across a network by leapfrogging from one computer to another. The idea was that in the event of a nuclear war, if part of the network went down, the information could reroute itself. Even by official, conservative estimates, the Net is growing at the incredible rate of 10 percent a month. If the Net continues to spread at its current rate, it will reach every person on Earth by the year 2005.

According to Howard Rheingold, editor of the *Whole Earth Review*, the Net "may eventually be seen in retrospect as a narrow window of historical opportunity, when people either acted or failed to act effectively to regain control over communication technologies." Major corporations believe the Internet is too important a phenomenon to be overlooked. It is an entirely new medium with the potential for both commercial broadcasting and advertising. A high-bandwidth version of the Internet could be used for pay-per-view videos and direct marketing.

Some view this personalized media optimistically, as an opportunity for increased choice. User Bryon Larson suggests, in an article posted on CompuServe, that the scale of the services offered will necessarily involve large business conglomerates formed by mergers of media and communication companies. "Forms of income require that a private communication company appeal to the greatest number of people in each market. Even so-called niche markets need to be of a critical size before companies find it profitable to provide specialized services. What this portends is an acceleration, not an abatement, of the trend toward mindless, lowest-common-denominator, programming." Whatever the result, services such as video-on-demand require the use of spectacularly advanced networking technologies to save the trip to the local video store. This technology could be used far more imaginatively to get people to interact with each other. As journalist Mark Edwards points out: "If computer networks are tough enough to survive nuclear war, maybe the virtual communities that have developed on them will even be able to survive the onslaught of the mega-corporations."

If the liberal character of the Net is preserved, it will create an important cultural precedent. Mass media in the 20th century created the first-ever truly popular culture. The diversification offered by computer communication hints at the possibility of a new culture for the 21st century. This will mimic what has only been possible in large cities, where people of minority groups or interests have been able to create fringe communities. What cyberspace offers is a chance for communities to grow independently, without a central location or leadership structure around which to coalesce. This, coupled with the acceleration of change and the increased fragmentation of society, will promote in the future a diversified culture comprised of a multitude of fringe or minority groups.

Removal of the need for immediate geographical proximity for the rapid exchange of ideas may contribute to a reduction in the size of existing cities to that of their pre-industrial counterparts. The possibility of teleworking may preserve endangered rural communities. The orderly gridiron layout of New York and the hierarchical layout of old Peking, which reflected implicitly the method of transferring goods and ideas within those places, have been replaced by a complex miniature network of laser-etched pathways on a microchip city the size of a fingernail.

- -

The orderly gridiron layout of New York and the hierarchical layout of old Peking, which reflected implicitly the method of transferring goods and ideas within those places, have been replaced by a complex miniature network of laser-etched pathways on a microchip city the size of a fingernail.

- -

The character of computer communication exemplified by the largely text-based communication on the Internet will change dramatically as the bandwidth increases. Data-communication speeds are currently limited by the use of copper cable as a transmission medium and by the conversion of digital signals into analog tones that are passed onto the existing telephone network. While larger organizations have for a long time used dedicated lines for higher-speed transmissions, none of these have even approached the speeds that will become commonplace as existing networks are replaced by optical fiber. In September 1993, Nippon Telegraph and Telephone managed to transmit a 100-gigabits-per-second signal (the equivalent of over 500 copies of the Bible) over a distance of 50 kilometers.

When data is transmitted optically, at the speed of light, the bottleneck occurs at the connection end. Present-day electronic processing collapses at speeds of more than 50 gigabits per second, because in a semiconductor, the electrons move at speeds that are significantly slower than the speed of light. As speeds increase, networks will move away from merely transmitting conventional text documents. The whole notion of documents will be transformed to include sound, images, and video, which will give them qualities impossible with paper.

It is ironic that in the computer age the ideal of the paperless office has become increasingly less attainable. Computer transmission of text documents has produced an *increase* in paper, as people routinely print out electronically transmitted documents. This situation may change, however, as multimedia documents, which can only exist in electronic form, become the norm, and the screens on which they are read approach the quality and portability of printed matter.

Current architectural projects in Britain and France to rehouse the ever-growing collections of their national libraries are in danger of becoming white elephants. In the past 20 years, a project to build a new British Library has become obsolete as the process of technological change has accelerated at a far greater rate than the rate of construction of the building. The expense of housing the books themselves in the center of London has reduced the potential of creating a work of art to read them in. (Already a branch of the British Library that deals with the distribution of copies of documents in the collection accounts for over half of the library's business.) By converting the books into electronic

form, both as full text and as high-resolution image files, researchers could gain better access to materials from anywhere in the world—and could do so at the same time that others access the material. A virtual library provides a better repository for existing work, and a compatible medium for the electronic documents of the future.

• •

THE INTERFACE

The ease and fluency with which people are able to utilize the computer as a creative tool are increasing rapidly as the interface between humans and computers fuses, becoming more transparent and allowing intuitive expression.

The analog mode is the way we perceive the real world. Any form of computer art eventually ends up as analog output, whether it be the variation in the voltage of the electron gun driving a screen, the current driving a loudspeaker, or the light reflected off a sheet of paper. The method in which we communicate with the computer also depends on a conversion from the analog of the real world to the digital data of the computer's memory. As interfaces have become more sophisticated, the ability to use them in a less rigid, more fluent way has increased. This has largely been due to input methods that emulate the analog nature of the real world. A pressure-sensitive stylus that produces a continuously variable line behaves more like a real pencil and allows the computer artist genuine expression. Likewise, a computer-linked keyboard that changes the amplitude of a sound according to how hard a key is struck can produce a sound with as much depth as a piano, unlike the static, harpsichord-like feel of less-sophisticated interfaces.

Probably the most familiar man-machine interface of all is the car. As Andrew McCarthy points out, the interface remains roughly the same, no matter what car is being driven: "When I enter a car anywhere around the world, I am greeted with a familiar interface and I know without a second thought how to start up the vehicle and drive away."

When you drive a car, you are bombarded with sensory feedback that enables you to drive it safely. You can feel if you are going too fast by the pressure exerted on your body, you can monitor the presence of other cars by their sound, or the view around, and feel if you are braking too hard to stop. For a computer simulation to appear real, it must utilize an interface that allows for the same senses we use when handling real-world objects. These sensations have been divided into six major categories: vision; cognition; motor preparation (the anticipation of the weight of an object before it is picked up); tactile feedback; kinesthesis (internal sense of orientation); and closed-loop muscular adaptation (muscular control).

An early computer simulation would have only allowed manipulation of the car by typing in numbers representing speed, acceleration, and so forth. Subsequently, a crude two-dimensional representation of a cartoon-like graphic of the car would allow simple, visual manipulation of the car. There are now arcade games that allow a 3-D environment to be "driven through," with hydraulics beneath the seat to simulate inertial pressures. Game development is so advanced that it now produces simulations that are more accurate than some commercial simulators used for pilot training.

Currently, computer operating systems have progressed beyond the simple character level to the familiar 2-D icon/windows approach. Microsoft, secure in the knowledge that it will not be taken to the courts again as it was by Apple in 1988, will produce a version of Windows that will be almost identical to the Apple operating system, which had its origins in research done at Xerox PARC. (PARC predicted in the 1970s that millions of people would use mice and icons.) What eventually will happen is that a 3-D representation analogous to the real world, instead of just the desktop, will supersede the current interface. Again the pioneering work in this field is being done at Xerox PARC. Research teams there have tackled the problem of navigating through complex file structures via a variety of 3-D approaches. The most interesting of these involves a 3-D, chandelier-like lattice of files and file connections that can be spun around and manipulated like a real-world object, enabling files to be selected more quickly than from a standard filing cabinet.

A call to Dell support staff by a customer who couldn't get his computer to fax anything, resulted in 40 minutes of troubleshooting. The technician finally realized that the customer was trying to fax a document by holding it against the screen and hitting the send key. (Reported in the Wall Street Journal.*)*

This points toward an interface that is based around virtual reality—a series of 3-D objects in a computer-generated, virtual environment—which mimics the real world.

The essential hardware elements to immerse oneself totally in a virtual world are a head-mounted display (HMD) to view it, and a Dataglove to touch things within it. Although the Dataglove was invented in 1981 by Thomas Zimmerman, the HMD dates back to 1965, when Ivan Sutherland was the first to propose a virtual-reality system as a means to develop a seamless interface. Later Tom Furness and a team at Wright-Patterson Air Force Base developed a sophisticated HMD for use by pilots. The first time the HMD and Dataglove were combined was in a system designed by Michael McGreevy at NASA's Ames Research Center. With this setup, NASA proposed uses for dealing with "hazardous or scale-sensitive situations." In other words, by developing a tele-robot and a virtual reconstruction of its environment, NASA could use this system to construct a space station, including the manipulation of very large or very small objects, from within the relative safety of the space shuttle.

Mark Weisner, head of the Computer Science Lab at Xerox PARC, thinks that virtual reality, however important it is to games, entertainment, architecture, design, and scientific visualization, will not soon become the norm for the way we interact with computers. One problem is that VR will not be able to produce a sufficiently realistic simulation of real life, at a sufficiently reasonable cost, for it to be convincing. The invention of a personal Holodeck, such as that in *Star Trek: The Next Generation*, may be a long way off. The main objection Weisner has with the use of a VR interface in the computers we use every day is that VR takes us into the world of the computer instead of seamlessly integrating the computer into

our world. Weisner looks forward to a day when computers will be ubiquitous and their interfaces so user-friendly as to be almost transparent. These computers will be integrated with the way we think and operate to produce a flawless human-computer symbiosis. According to Weisner, they will not be mere data-processing tools but "mind augmentors."

To this end, the recent products prototyped at Xerox PARC exemplify this philosophy. Labeled "pads" and "tabs," they consist of tiny badge-like tabs and larger, slate-sized pads, a bit like current PDAs such as the Newton. The idea is that personal information, such as a list of the badge-wearer's files and software, will be contained within the tabs. When the wearer of one of these approaches any pad within an office, an infrared link between the two will custom-configure the pad for the tab wearer's usage. What this means is that the hardware itself (the pad) need not belong to any one particular individual but can be a shared item that can be left around, somewhat like an ordinary pen and paper. This has a nice ring to it, rather like the white bicycles of Amsterdam, which were once left around the city for communal use. (Unfortunately, however, they were all stolen!)

Another current branch of research at PARC takes as its inspiration the evolution of Multi User Dungeons (MUDs) on the Net. Pavel Curtis has examined the way MUDs are used as meeting places and how the sophistication of them has included the development of group programming languages to enable the development of new fantasy worlds. He has developed MOO, which stands for "MUD Object Oriented" (quite possibly the first two-level acronym). He envisions this being used as a tool kit to create a virtual environment for people to meet and exchange ideas with each other in cyberspace.

What is special about Xerox PARC is that it is looking into the overall effects of these developments on both computers and society. John Seely Brown, director of PARC, says this research is part of an emerging "ecology of communications." By involving people with skills across the spectrum, from the development of new materials to the social sciences, it has provided a base for some of the most original and thought-provoking research. The somewhat tragic consequence of being on the cutting edge of technology is that many of the ideas that first originated there were later made commercially successful by others. It was at Xerox that some of the first work was done on graphic screens, icon interfaces, Local Area Networks, and Object Oriented Programming; and it was there that the world's first true personal computer was developed, the Xerox Alto. As Alan Kay, a PARC employee puts it, "One phrase became PARC's hallmark: The easiest way to predict the future is to invent it."

Looking toward the future, there are several scarcely believable interfaces being developed. The Human Interface Laboratory at the University of Washington State is developing a system in which an image is laser-scanned directly onto the retina at a resolution approaching human vision. A similar system exists in the United Kingdom, where it is a classified project of the military. According to Robert J. Stone, Technical Manager of the National Advanced Robotics Research Centre (Salford,

UK): "Work has been under way for some 10 years now attempting to link brain electrical potentials (electroencephalography) with cognitive and motor behavior. It is now possible to utilize specific brain waves to select menu items."

THE PRODUCT

The major difference between photography or film and a traditional painting is that the former are reproduced art forms; there is not necessarily one single original and—in the case of film—not necessarily one author. Of course, painters, such as Rembrandt, could have teams of people working on pictures, rather like contemporary architectural practices, and still leave historians today to quibble about which paintings are authentic. The myth of authorship is easiest to hide in a medium in which the final output can be signed off by the artist. Appropriated imagery, taken from popular culture, has confused the traditional collectors who still want to buy it. There are countless people who bought Pop Art thinking they possessed an original. The original cartoon strips that Roy Lichtenstein traced are better composed and more fluently drawn than his versions. One poor, deluded soul even coughed up money for the instructions to create a copy of an installation by

Sol Le Witt. Much modern art collecting has become glorified autograph hunting, and much of the art hanging in galleries is no more relevant today than is the supreme art form of the Ancient Greeks: lyre playing.

Unfortunately, the use of the computer in art presents the traditionalists with a further dilemma: a photograph, although reproducible, is not repeatable. It is the capture of an instant in time that is unlikely to be repeated. The steps taken in the construction of a piece of computer art, in whatever medium—sound or vision—can be repeated by recording them in a macro-like manner. A common bit of anti-computer-art bigotry is the idea that computer art can be created by clicking a button randomly and coming back after a cup of coffee to see the result. It can, of course, but it usually looks or sounds like junk. Playwright Tom Stoppard suggests: "Craft is art without imagination and modern art is imagination without craft." However, just because a computer can automate procedures that previously would have been done by hand does not mean that computer art entails inherently less production craft than its analog equivalent. There are almost limitless ways in which computer art can be distorted and refined to produce a result that is exactly how the artist intends. The creation of computer art is often a complex and difficult process involving both imagination and skill.

The ability of the computer to dissect and reassemble data has been used to enhance existing art forms in a way that suggests an entirely new medium. This is no different from the evolution of early silent film, which looked more melodramatic and theater-like than the film of today. The possibility of close-ups, which is impossible in the theater, gives film an intimacy that requires a different approach to acting. Floppy-disk pornography and the neon-lit ultra-violence of the computer arcade are not much different from the earliest forms of cinema, which largely existed as an end-of-the-pier titillation. It is inevitable that computer-generated art will follow the same pattern as the cinema and mature into a sophisticated art form offering more than gimmickry. What computers offer is a chance to create an imitation of the real world. The level of sophistication of this imitation will surely improve. At the moment, however, both computer-generated art and music rarely produce a sufficient level of realism to avoid being self-consciously the work of a machine.

Computer-generated art can be divided into three notional categories: the surreal, the hyperreal, and the impossible. The majority of computer sound and imagery today falls into the first category and is obviously synthetic. Limitations in the technology of computers have meant that graphics have been

When some Disney animation stills were recently sold at auction, there were two versions of drawings, each bearing the Disney signature but in different handwriting. The world-famous, instantly recognizable signature turned out to be drawn by someone else in the Disney office. The authentic Walt Disney signature looked different. The real one fetched less money.

At the moment, however, both computer-generated art and music rarely produce a sufficient level of realism to avoid being self-consciously the work of a machine.

cartoon-like and music robotic. Until now, attempts to create realism in computer art have resulted in the crass and the kitsch. The most rewarding computer art has been that which has accepted the current limitations of the technology to produce sound and imagery that bear an unmistakable stamp of artificiality. Computers rarely create convincingly sophisticated textures like wood, or sounds as rich as ethnic instruments. What computers are good at is generating artificial versions of man-made objects and man-made sounds. The most convincing computer models use plastic textures and primary colors and the best synth sounds and electronic noises. Attempts at photo-realistic renderings of natural scenes and electronic imitations of real instruments often give "cheesy" results that lack the depth of the real thing—the equivalent of a photograph of a sunset.

Self-conscious "techno" art hit the dance floors and magazine pages more than 10 years ago with bands such as Yello and Kraftwerk and the graphic design of Neville Brody. In 1988, it caught the imagination of the rave generation, a pill-popping, fluorescent-clad, fringe culture, convulsing 120 times a minute to an electronically sampled house beat. In a curious role reversal, music was being created in the living room to be listened to on the dance floor. Adenoidal adolescents from council estates in Hackney, London, created club hits with little more than an Amiga. At the same time, desktop publishing hit the magazine world with the release of PageMaker, and a myriad of underground magazines were launched, with multiple stretched fonts and distorted layouts. The release of Photoshop made available the kind of image-editing and photo-retouching capabilities that were previously only available to those who could afford a high-end system such as a Quantel Paintbox. While the transient worlds of clubs and magazines were buzzing with computer-generated art, in true pop-culture fashion the concert halls and mainstream art galleries were devoid of any real influence. For instance, nothing that has emanated from IRCAM, the electronics-packed basement of the Pompidou Centre, dedicated to institutionalized musical research, has captured the public imagination.

What computers do particularly well is allow layering of multiple sounds or images. Computers enable images to be cropped, and sound to be sampled, and an intricate lattice of overlapping sound and transparent imagery to be woven. The technique of collage has been taken to a new level where sounds and images can be plucked from their surroundings and seamlessly pasted, repeated, distorted, altered and reassembled—*reconstruction* rather than deconstruction.

In music, one of the most obvious examples of the layered approach is ambient music by bands such as the Orb, who have created an "architectural" soundscape that draws influences from Phillip Glass and John Adams. The idea of ambient music was coined by Brian Eno in 1975, while he was lying ill in bed, listening to 18th century harp music emanating from a badly tuned radio, with the TV on in the background. He realized that the music was combining with the other sounds in the room to create a specific atmosphere or ambience. The same layered approach translated to graphic design, particularly with the work of Terry Jones, the first editor of *i-D* magazine in London. Jones' early experiments with distorted Polaroids and photocopied imagery, layered and mixed with type, were followed by experiments in computer layout and post-production video work. April Greiman, a leading figure in New Wave graphic design, adopted the use of computer techniques as director of the visual-communication program at the California Institute of the Arts. Her work employs the flexibility of computer layout to alter two-dimensional space for the multiple layering of text and graphics.

Mixed media 2-D drawings can be easily assembled using Photoshop to collage hand drawn and photo-graphic elements, as in this detail section of a recent scheme for a fabric-lined, hollow-core tower.

While the worlds of graphic design and dance music have exploited the computer to generate a highly stylized, computer-enhanced art form, special-effects houses have had the resources to produce images that are indistinguishable from reality. One firm in particular, Industrial Light and Magic, has teamed up with hardware manufacturer Silicon Graphics to produce animation in films such as *Jurassic Park* which is so realistic that it hardly bears any trace of a computer signature. Once such a level of realism becomes commonplace, the merits of the work will depend not on the gee-whizzery of the technical skills, but on the subtlety and creativity of the product. This type of work has transcended the day-glo, the artificial, to produce a simulacrum that is as rich and varied as the real world around us. The concept of the artificial as a world inhabited by primary colors and synthetic sounds has been rendered meaningless. Computers can contribute to an art form that is more natural, organic, and ultimately more human.

A simple 3-D model of a set design can be constructed in a couple of days on a PC, using software such as 3D Studio.

What was needed to allow the possibility of re-creating natural objects on a computer was an algorithm to generate them. That is exactly what happened when Benoit Mandelbrot of IBM plotted the results of repeated transformations of a single quadratic equation. He discovered organic-looking shapes of infinite complexity, which he called fractals. He had discovered how to recreate the geometry of nature in a fractal landscape that obeys the same rules as the real thing. This was a secret that was at its core so simple, but which required the fast, repetitive processes of computing to be revealed. Fractals, above all, have become a symbol of the potential of computers to create new imagery that would not have been possible by other means.

If it is possible to create an exact replica of reality, the obvious question is: Why would you want to, if it is less than utopian? Would you want to be stuck in a broken elevator in a virtual South Bronx? The logical extension of computer-generated art and the use of virtual reality is to create places that are limited only by the imagination, and which need not even obey real physical laws. The ideas that Lewis Carroll toyed with in literature could be faithfully recreated in digital form. You or I could become a shrinking Alice. The scale at which we perceive the world could be altered. Astrophysicists with enormous egos could give themselves the mass and size of galaxies, explore distortions of time and space, and experience non-Euclidean geometry. All with an analogous sensory feedback (a force could be given a sound or color, and so forth), capable of soliciting intuitive understanding. Weaklings could inhabit a world where Newton's laws were reversed, where they could beat Sylvester Stallone unconscious with a feather.

What really makes computer art so different from other media is the potential for interactivity and non-linearity. Most traditional art is passive entertainment for the spectator. Film, theater, dance, music, photography, and painting all engage the spectator but don't allow alteration or change of direction. The only art form that involves any real interactivity is literature. With a book or a magazine, you can read what you want when you want.

The logical extension of computer-generated art and the use of virtual reality is to create places that are limited only by the imagination, and which need not even obey real physical laws.

The building block for all interactive computer art is hypertext. Hypertext has a single but profound difference from printed text—it is non-linear. When you read a novel, you may be able to skip bits and you don't have to read it at once, but inevitably you can only read it in one direction, from start to finish. Magazines can go one step toward being non-linear; there can be fragments of information, pictures, and running captions, but the overall effect of the linkage between the different parts, like the paper itself, is two-dimensional. Hypertext allows a framework of linkages with a three-dimentional feel, which can be of infinite complexity and size, and which requires interaction to step between each link. This is what Brian Eno calls "a 3-D lattice of cause and effect." By extending the principles of hypertext to include other forms of information than text, you get the concept of hypermedia.

There is some confusion at the heart of many discussions about interactive art. Journalists haven't realized that it has to be a truly digital medium. With a few simple rules you can create a very large number of possibilities. From the few rules of chess, there are more than 10^{120} possible games. Since this is more than the number of atoms in the known universe, it is impossible to create a computer chess program that works by storing every possible game in its memory. You can, however, program a computer to play chess, with varying degrees of success, using the few simple rules, and therefore a relatively small amount of memory. The same principle can be applied to interactive art. Suppose, for example, we want to create a simple interactive music program to select a piece of music. Mozart wrote a waltz with 16 bars. There are 11 variations of each of the first 14 bars and two variations of one of the other bars, giving a total of 2×11^{14} possible pieces of music. To be able to select any one of the possible pieces of music if it were stored on vinyl in a jukebox would require 760 trillion records. If, however, the sound was to be re-created digitally, by a synthesizer, the program to create any of the possible choices of music would fit on one floppy disk. In any interactive art where there is significant choice, the sound or vision would have to be digitally created.

Many artists who are desperate to jump on the multimedia bandwagon have concocted products that are not truly interactive or which are merely conventional art forms strung together randomly to produce an interactive experience that is no different from a passive one. Billy Idol produced an album called *Cyberpunk*, which came with a floppy disk that includes little more than a lyric sheet. Peter Gabriel, on the other hand, has given us a first glimpse at what may be possible with a truly interactive format. Each of the audio tracks on his *Xplora* disk is accompanied by Quick Time video, and there is the opportunity for the listener to try some remixing. On the same disk is a description of the WOMAD festival and stills of ethnic instruments that you can simulate by clicking with a mouse. By using technology to promote ethnic music, Gabriel is displaying what he sees as the humanizing aspect of technology, which he wishes to develop. To this end he has started up a multimedia enterprise in a suitably low-tech English village.

Despite the hype and the occasional glimpses of brilliance from various computer artists around the world, no one has yet produced a seminal, interactive work of art. Most computer games fall short because they have rigid goals, tend to be realistic instead of abstract, and don't allow you to indulge yourself for "art's" sake. The interactive art released by such well-funded performers as Peter Gabriel is traditional art in an interactive guise, not truly interactive art. Interactive art, when it finally happens, will be unlike any medium that has ever come before it.

Computers in Literature and the Arts

chapter 2
by David E. Day

A book can't reach out and grab your attention like a computer can. A computer can tickle your interest with sound and motion and words. It can turn a collection of paragraphs into a mother lode of references by leading you to all the passages that are related and all the concepts that cluster together—which gives you a better understanding of what you're seeing.

THE BOOK

There's something wonderful about a good book.

It's pure utility—a very compact and portable source of knowledge and entertainment. You can take it to the classroom or the office—even to the beach. You can easily shuffle between multiple passages, inserting paper bookmarks to mark you way (or even defacing the book by turning the page corners down). If you're like me, you may sometimes choose to read it from back to front.

A book feels good. Crisp, supple pages that slide under your fingers and turn with a snap and a smell of ink (and sometimes, distantly, a smell of printing solvents).

Books are available almost everywhere, in myriad varieties. And they're eminently affordable.

So why would anybody want to replace a book with a clunky computer, a complicated electronic gadget that is guaranteed to give you eyestrain and technical frustration?

For one thing, a book can't reach out and grab your attention like a computer can. A computer can tickle your interest with sound and motion and words. It can turn a collection of paragraphs into a mother lode of references by leading you to all the passages that are related and all the concepts that cluster together— which gives you a better understanding of what you're seeing.

A multimedia presentation on computer can transport you to a place or time, give you a guided tour through a museum, and provide insights with sound and animation. You can be in touch (however abstractly) with experts who can ease your passage through experiences you might otherwise never have. Because the experience is interactive, you participate in the process in your own time, at your own pace, in your own style. When used creatively, technology can be a true stimulant to imagination and not the anesthetic it's often reputed to be.

The technology required to do all this isn't as portable as a book—at least not today. There are, of course laptop computers, and even some portable electronic books. They're a little larger and probably more expensive then you'd like. But we're now only in the dawn of this technology; true electronic literature will soon come into its own.

So please remember to distinguish the advantages of electronic literature from the relatively clumsy tools that now deliver it.

If you want to approximate the cozy, personal sense of curling up with a good book, consider a laptop or "notebook" computer. These are small, they are battery-powered for portability, and they can weigh under four pounds. You pay for portability, however; and if you get a laptop with a color display, you'll pay a lot more.

The one or two novel "electronic book" devices on the market are currently limited in display quality and in the number of available titles. They don't include sound and other effective multimedia features. In a few years, there will be affordable products like these with full-color, high-quality displays, sound, smooth animation, and vast libraries from which to choose.

If you just can't wait and you want to experience electronic literature today, you will need the appropriate hardware configuration. Most titles require a multimedia IBM-compatible computer. This means you need, at a minimum, a 386DX (much better, a 486-based) PC with at least 4MB of RAM. You also need a VGA display, a mouse, and a sound card with speakers. The operating environment is Microsoft Windows 3.1 unless otherwise indicated. Titles on CD-ROM require a CD-ROM drive, which should be double-speed with at least a 64KB cache.

ENCYCLOPEDIAS

When was the last time you used an encyclopedia? It's the "Swiss Army knife" of reference documents— useful but a bit cumbersome. Encyclopedias take a lot of space, they're heavy, they cost a lot, and some of their contents are inevitably irrelevant as soon as you receive them. What's more, the information you seek may be spread among several volumes. (Remember that school report when you had to cover the floor with those ponderous books, each full of paper slips marking entries of interest? Or, just as likely, you grew up without your own set of up-to-date encyclopedias, and you had to trek to the library for the reference material you needed.)

Encyclopedias are real "naturals" for computer enhancement. They're replete with words, pictures, and graphics, and their cross-disciplinary content benefits from the kind of indexing available through hypertext links.

A printed encyclopedia might give you some words about Borneo, show some natives in traditional dress, and throw in a map to put the place in perspective. A multimedia encyclopedia, on the other hand, can let the natives dance for you in those colorful costumes, let you hear the lap of water on the war canoes, and make the map show not merely the island's global position but the realities of life and geography there.

This elaborate vision of a multimedia encyclopedia hasn't been fully achieved by the current offerings, but they come close. Products available right now offer exciting benefits to help you learn about the world quickly and accurately. They're compact, convenient, and affordable. Best of all, they're fun. In the following sections I'll review the major product lines that offer sights, sounds, and motion along with fast information search and retrieval.

> **Encyclopedias are real "naturals" for computer enhancement. They're replete with words, pictures, and graphics, and their cross-disciplinary content benefits from the kind of indexing available through hypertext links.**

COMPTON'S INTERACTIVE ENCYCLOPEDIA 1994

[CD-ROM for Windows; requires multimedia PC]

Compton's Interactive Encyclopedia is widely distributed as one component of product "bundles." Thus it is commonly included with CD-ROM drives and multimedia upgrade kits. (Compton's is actually another arm of Encyclopedia Britannica.) It's a single CD-ROM that includes brief articles about thousands of topics—basically a mini-encyclopedia. It also includes a world atlas.

(Because Compton's claims to have pioneered much of the technology used in its interactive CD-ROM encyclopedia, it is currently requesting licensing fees from other manufacturers of similar products.)

Compton's is far more than a simple desktop reference. It contains text, pictures, graphics, sounds, narrated slide shows, some video "movie" shorts, and even a few animations. The quality of the sounds, slides, and movies, however, varies from fair to good, mostly because of the limitations of the technology.

Different people have different styles of finding information, even when the source material is formally structured. The following are some techniques you can use to help Compton's find what you're looking for. For this example I'm going to seek some information about Borneo, probably an esoteric topic for most Americans, but still one you'd be likely to find in any encyclopedia. There are several different methods you can use to locate the same article.

Here's one method of looking up Borneo: the "Topic Tree." It's a "branching" approach that starts with very general topics (including geography, history, literature, mathematics, and others). It continues branching to ever-more specific topics. I choose "Geography" and Compton's gives me a list of geographic features. From that list, I choose "East Indies," because I happen to know that Borneo is in that region of the world. Compton's finds an article about the East Indies, which includes a reference to Borneo.

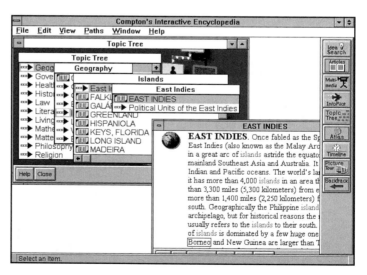

Compton's Interactive Encyclopedia Topic Tree.

If I want more detail, I can simply click the word "Borneo." Instead, I use another variation of this approach by choosing "Political Units of the East Indies" to get the Borneo article.

Here's another approach: I know Borneo is an island. I choose the "Ideas Search" and look for the word "island," which I enter in the search box. Compton's instantly finds 67 island topics (including "New YorkManhattan"). By scrolling through the list, I am quickly able to find the island group I want (East Indies) and the same article as before.

Let's just cut to the specific topic we want. If I want Borneo, I look for Borneo. Here, I use the "Articles" search, and enter the word "borneo" (don't worry about capital letters). Now I find an article that tells me something new— that Borneo is the Earth's third-largest island.

In the left margin of this article, I see an icon of a globe and another of a camera. If I click the globe, Compton's finds me a map from the atlas. (More on that later.) If I click on the camera, Compton's shows me a picture of life in Borneo.

Compton's Interactive Encyclopedia Topics search.

Compton's Articles search.

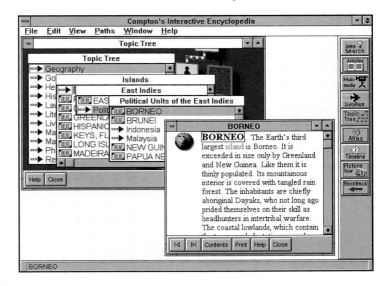

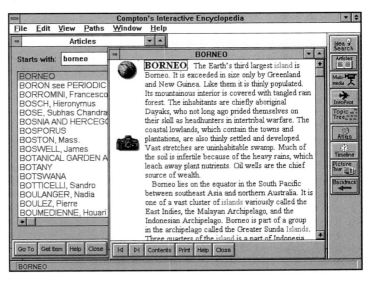

Compton's provides a powerful way of retrieving an entire cluster of Borneo-related material using the "InfoPilot." Once you select a topic, it is surrounded with a group of windows representing related articles. To the right of the InfoPilot, I've opened an "Expand Article" window. This window is in effect a "map" of the position of each story in the cluster at left. I simply click any button to select the story I want to read.

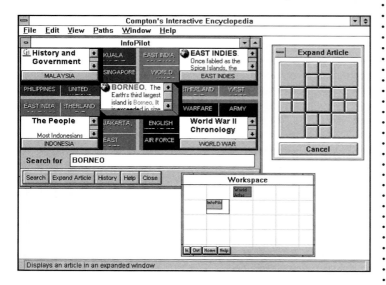

Compton's InfoPilot.

That window at the bottom is another unusual tool that helps you assemble the stories you want to use in your report. (You are writing a report about Borneo, aren't you?) It creates a very large workspace where you can "spread out" the articles—in columns or rows by category if you want. The workspace is, in effect, an expandable electronic desktop. To look at a specific article, you simply drag it from its box into the single viewing box (the one with the outline at center). As you drag the article, it comes into view in the main display. (This is easier done than described.)

Highlighted words in these articles are hypertext or cross-linked references. Click any of them, and you're transported to either a definition or a related article for more information.

Let's now look at the atlas. I searched for places beginning with "born...", and dragged the map into view. There's Borneo—right between Malaysia and the Philippines, and just south of Cambodia. Although I haven't shown it, you can also view a monochrome photo of primitive native life on the island. A world timeline display is also available to help you put that country in historical perspective.

Compton's Encylopedia World Atlas.

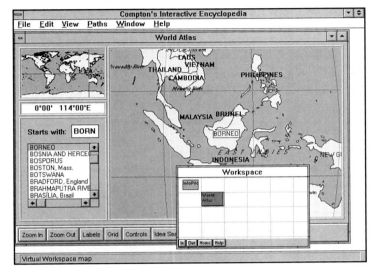

Borneo doesn't interest everybody, so how about a subject that's probably had a more direct impact on American life: civil rights. You'd expect broad coverage, and you get it. For example, from the atlas, I assembled a montage of windows representing material I discovered when I searched for "civil rights." Clockwise from bottom left, there's an article on civil rights; a photo of a civil-rights march led by Dr. Martin Luther King, Jr., with an inset video movie of the march (including an audio narrative); and three other photos related to the civil-rights movement (including captions).

Except for the video, a printed encyclopedia might be able to give you this level of content and detail. But you'd never have this kind of access to the material or such control over its presentation and assembly into a report. With Compton's, you can also print a copy of any text, graphic, or even a photograph (with the right printer).

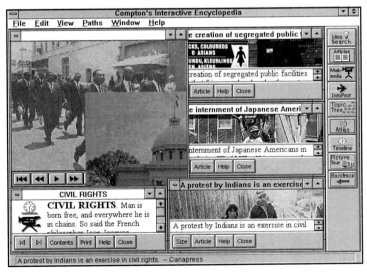

The encyclopedia's civil rights search results.

MICROSOFT ENCARTA 1994

[CD-ROM for Windows; requires multimedia PC]

Microsoft has introduced a broad and growing line of consumer computer products in its Home product line, most of which is available on CD-ROM. Encarta is one such product; you'll be seeing others elsewhere in this book.

Encarta 1994 is Microsoft's stylish and competent multimedia CD-ROM encyclopedia, the flagship of the Home line and a clear upgrade from previous releases. This single CD-ROM contains an astounding 26,000 articles containing 9 million words, 8 hours of sound, and over 100 video "movies." It also has over 8,000 graphics of various kinds (photos, illustrations, and maps), a dictionary, a thesaurus, and a timeline.

You can search and display this huge mass of information using a broad collection of access tools. Topics are linked to others using 25,000 cross-referenced "hot links" that bring you to the related materials.

. . . .

Let's start with the 20-foot-long graphic timeline display, which is one of several search techniques.

I'll start in the middle, with so-called "modern" times, in the first millennium AD. The earth at this time is really hopping. Christianity is just beginning, the Jews are defending a fortress called Masada from the Romans, the volcano Vesuvius erupts and buries Pompeii and Herculaneum, black Africans in the Sudan form the soon-to-be empire of Nubia, the Mayans are building a sophisticated civilization in Guatemala, and China develops paper based on mulberry bark. In central Mexico, Teotihuacán—the first known city in the Western hemisphere—is founded. (When I clicked the little globe symbol, the small map popped out to identify the region for me.) To access all this interesting material, all I have to do is click the timeline icons and read the articles that pop onto the screen.

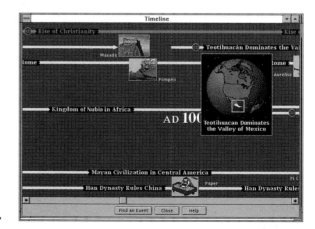

Microsoft Encarta's Timeline.

You can imagine how complex the timeline gets as it approaches the present. The breakup of the Soviet Union is featured (a good sign that this encyclopedia is up-to-date), and there's a philosophic essay called "The Future as History."

But let's not forget Borneo. I looked it up by searching for the word in the Contents, and I was rewarded with a screen featuritg text, a color photo, an Islands topic, and a little camera icon. Click that, and your display fills with a photo about diamond mining.

As you scroll through the story, another small photo—this one of native village life—pops up automatically at bottom left.

If I use the "Find" box to search for the word "Borneo," Encarta lists 44 related entries. I see entires related to people, animals, and places, including an entry for Brunei, one of the countries that inhabits this enormous island. I click that word, and I see an article, the country's flag, and a window with a slider on it. When I click on the slider's right arrow, Encarta plays Brunei's national anthem for me, a full 45 seconds of synthesized music.

To aid weary eyes, there is a special feature called a "zoom text" button at the bottom of the article. When I click it, the text enlarges, becomes bold, and fills the screen.

Encarta's contents search.

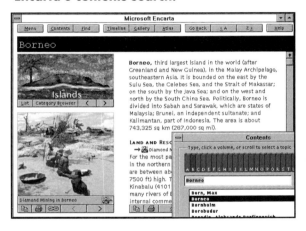

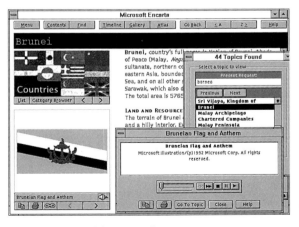

Encarta's Find box and "Borneo."

I click a "history" button, and an extended history article pops up, along with a color shot of one of the most exotic castles (mosques) I've ever seen, complete with genuine gold trim. (In the miniature view, you can see only a stone ceremonial barge that graces the water in front of the mosque. Yes, stone.) When I ask to "Find a Place," a map with tiny Brunei appears. By clicking on the country itself, I get another window that offers to pronounce the country name and lead me to more information. Not bad for a few mouse clicks!

Let's see what Encarta has to say about civil rights. Using the Contents button at the top of the screen, I scroll through the "C" listings to find my subject. A general article appears, with the first of several photos—this one of the U.S. Bill of Rights. The Law category window at top left enables me to explore the larger topic further if I wish.

Every word that's highlighted represents a reference to another article or definition. Encarta has tens of thousands of these hypertext cross-references. Click one and the new article instantly pops up. If you like, you can search further or return to the previous material.

Encarta's history and "Find a Place" functions.

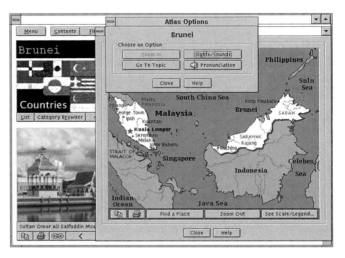

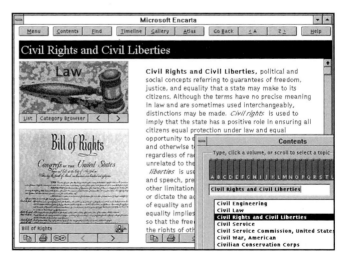

Encarta's Civil Rights contents.

If I use the "Find" button to search for the topic by entering "civil rights" in a box, Encarta delivers, in seconds, no less then 478 topics. I scroll down to "King, Martin Luther, Jr.," click the name, and an article about Dr. King appears, with a "People" category browser and a small photo. For a closer look, I click the speaker icon, and the photo fills the screen. I click the right arrow at bottom and hear a recording of the well-known, "I have a dream" speech.

Every word that's highlighted represents a reference to another article or definition. Encarta has tens of thousands of these hypertext cross-references. Click one and the new article instantly pops up. If you like, you can search further or return to the previous material.

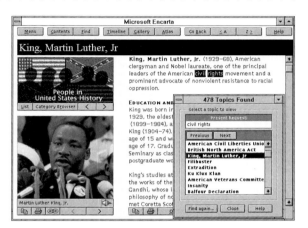

Microsoft Encarta finds "civil rights."

Martin Luther King's "I have a dream...".

Not only does Encarta have thousands of articles, graphics, and photographs, but it has more than 1,000 sound bites, 95 animations, and 32 video clips (short movies). Let's select one: I'll use the "Find" box to search for the "solar system" and request to list only animations. The computer returns an article titled "Movements of the Planets...," which contains a miniature drawing of the solar system. If you click the icon at the bottom, the picture fills the screen and you can run an animation of the solar system. Each of the planets circles the sun with its proper rotation period, and you can start and stop the motion at will. Talk about control!

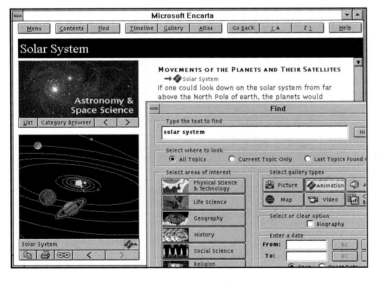

Encarta's solar-system animation.

Microsoft has also championed a feature it calls "Wizards." These are tools that guide you through an application. Encarta's Wizard is a sequence of forms you can fill out to help you narrow your search for topics. It works well and is almost fun.

To solidify its usefulness as a general reference, Encarta includes a dictionary and thesaurus.

BRITANNICA
[CD-ROM to be released]

Encyclopedia Britannica has long been considered the premier publication among world encyclopedias. However, its collection of authoritative and carefully-written entries on a vast array of topics represents a daunting multimedia packaging problem.

For educational institutions, Britannica produces an online version of its encyclopedia. It's not multimedia, but it does allow fast topic searches. It requires a massive database system on a big computer.

For the home market, Britannica will soon release on CD-ROM what amounts to an extract and index of their printed volumes. Even packaging this extract required innovative research to find a way to condense many million of words into a relatively small storage device. It's not multimedia, and it is only intended to be an adjunct to the printed version of the encyclopedia. You will not be able to buy it separately.

Britannica isn't saying exactly what its future consumer offerings will be like, but it seems firmly committed to the venerable distribution method of printed encyclopedias.

. . . .

TRADITIONAL LITERATURE ON THE COMPUTER

CMC COMPLETE SHERLOCK HOLMES

[CD-ROM for DOS or Macintosh]

Some of the most widely read mystery stories in the world are the Sherlock Holmes books, by Sir Arthur Conan Doyle. These books represent a veritable lifetime of work; work that almost had a life of its own. For years Conan Doyle wanted to abandon writing these tales, but his reading public wouldn't hear of it. Finally, he created a plot that "wrote out" his hero, by having him mysteriously disappear, and presumably die. (Later, however, he resurrected his hero, much to the delight of the reading public.)

This CD-ROM by Creative Multimedia Corporation contains all the words of all the stories in Conan Doyle's long series. It's arranged in a database. You can search for any title or any word and print it out if you want. The organization is formal. When you pick *The Hound of the Baskervilles*, all the chapters are listed, and when you select a line, the story text appears.

This is a no-frills product whose major benefits accrue from its publication on CD-ROM, which gives you the entire work in a very compact form. And you can search for a topic anywhere in any of the Sherlock Holmes books—something that would be almost impossible any other way.

I went directly to Chapter 12, "Death on the Moor," of this old mystery chestnut. The text is in a plain font, in a wide, full-screen format; nothing fancy, but readable.

As you're reading the story, you can also view a few old illustrations, including the original cuts from early printings of the book. Press a function key, select a drawing, and it fills the screen. This is an interesting adjunct to the printed text. There are also selections of physician Conan Doyle's medical journals, which add an interesting perspective on the author.

Note:

CMC also publishes a similar CD-ROM that includes the complete works of William Shakespeare. Besides his plays, it includes the full text of all the poems and sonnets. This title uses the same menu and search format as the Sherlock Holmes CD. The Shakespeare CD lets you search for any text in any of the works. It includes both British and American versions of the text and is available for both IBM-compatible PCs and the Macintosh.

INTERACTIVE LITERATURE

CMC BEYOND THE WALL OF STARS

[CD-ROM for Multimedia Windows 3.1]

It's hard to tell if Beyond the Wall of Stars is a story or a game. It's billed as a multimedia adventure story, but it uses a lot of game-like special effects. It's loaded with lots of color, 3-D animations, voices, sound effects, and combined photos and graphics. A lot of text screens are included also—enough to make it sometimes appear to be an animated book.

This is one story that's truly interactive; the reader is built into it from the first. Your mission as part of a stalwart crew is to travel from your base planet to one in a distant galaxy, bringing much-needed help. You decide on the crew's leader and can make yourself available as backup leader.

The story unfolds as a series of still images with embedded animations of spaceships, people, or details. You turn electronic pages to continue the adventure. The embedding is a clever way to add motion effects without using full-motion video (which takes a lot of memory space, costs a lot to develop, and is less than convincing to watch on many PCs).

Pressed into service as leader, you're confronted with choices, which branch the story in various directions and help determine the outcome. As with so many real-life choices, yours must be made using a lot of instinct and without much objective information to help you. It's a rich adventure, complete with good guys, bad guys, mysteries, and monsters. Real or imagined danger is lurking everywhere.

An interactive choice in Beyond the Wall of Stars.

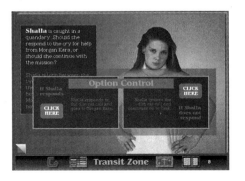

The previous figure shows you about to help Shalla decide whether to respond to a distress call from a passing planet that will deflect you from your goal. As any pilot or sailor knows, a distress call supersedes all other priorities. (Naturally, this propels you into a heap of trouble.)

Once Shalla sends a team to the planet's surface to check out the distress, you're chased around by various mean and ugly critters. Soon you're confronted with another choice: Take the cave on the left, toward the ominous blue light, or take the one on the right, which is dull and dark. Not wanting to be dull, you chose left. (Naturally, this propels you into a heap of trouble.)

Submerged in the story line is a sort of value-testing that I found variously intriguing or tacky (depending on my mood). Here's one example: Confronted with a potentially nasty opponent, and given the choice of using force, deception, or understanding to counter the threat, I was politically correct and chose understanding. (Naturally, this propels us into a blissful state of grace.)

At the end of each of the four chapters, you "graduate" to the next segment (unless of course you've made some truly bad decisions). There's no real end to this tale—at least not in this CD. Your final message is (you guessed it): "To be continued." If you want to be part of the thrilling conclusion, you must buy one or more sequel CD-ROMs.

Your mission as part of a stalwart crew is to travel from your base planet to one in a distant galaxy, bringing much-needed help. You decide on the crew's leader and can make yourself available as backup leader.

Another choice in Beyond the Wall of Stars.

Yet another choice in Beyond the Wall of Stars.

ART ON THE COMPUTER

MUSEUM TOURS/ART COLLECTIONS

When was the last time you went to a museum? Once in a while, a special exhibit brings out thousands of spectators (many of us recall the King Tutanhkamen tour), but that's an exception. No wonder—you have to pack up the kids, drive to the city, find a place to park, buy tickets, and wait in line. Sometimes the exhibits are shrouded in a gloomy light, and you can't buy popcorn or even sit down.

Multimedia is changing all that. Without leaving home, you can get close to priceless works of art, view them at your own pace, and even enlist an expert tour guide to put them into historical perspective. Current software titles let you look at photo reproductions of these artworks and often experience related sights and sounds. In the future, you'll be able to "walk through" a gallery, see objects in three dimensions, and "chat" with a group of art experts.

Perhaps no technology can ever replace a face-to-face encounter with a masterful painting or sculpture. But for many of us, these products offer the next best thing: easy access.

MICROSOFT ART GALLERY

[CD-ROM for Windows or Macintosh; requires multimedia PC]

One of Microsoft's Home product line, the Art Gallery, is a tour of London's National Gallery. It contains more than 2,000 works by Western European artists dating from the 13th century to the present. You'll find 750 artists, including such masters as Van Gogh, Raphael, Titian, da Vinci, and Rembrandt.

You can search for paintings in several ways: By the artist's name, by time and place, and by type of work in one of six broad categories. You can also read more than 5,000 text pages containing more than a million words, including over 700 biographies of the featured artists.

You can also experience four presentation "tours" on various aspects of paintings, each with a spoken narrative. Each tour is like a slide show, but with added text and multiple art displays. Unlike some tours, you can stop at any time and peruse the paintings in more detail or ramble off in pursuit of your own interests. These tours even employ animations to clarify points about perspective, composition, alteration, restoration, and other details. You probably wouldn't find that depth of coverage on most museum trips.

Let's start the tour that addresses the elements of composition and perspective, and break away when we are attracted to a particular artist's work. (Breaking away is completely acceptable here.) We stop for discussion at a painting called "The Martyrdom of St. Sebastian," shown in the next illustration. Our virtual guide explains symmetry in a series of narrations and employs some animated overlays to show how elements in this work are combined.

The next work, by the 17th century French artist Claude Gellèe, illustrates perspective. An animation shows how the type of perspective employed here relies on horizontal line elements that can be drawn out to meet at a single point in the distance (the "vanishing point"). One of Claude's innovations was to use the sun as his central unifying element.

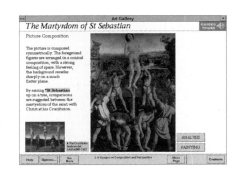

A painting shown during the Microsoft Art Gallery tour on composition.

A tour's focus on composition and perspective.

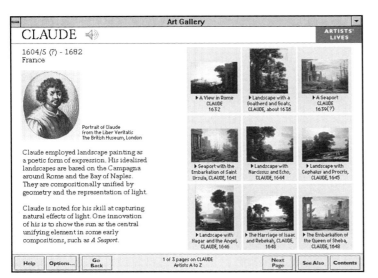

Microsoft Art Gallery's section on Claude Gellée.

The gallery's historical atlas and timeline.

I was so struck by Claude's rich and dramatic use of light and color that I decided to leave my tour at this point and explore this artist more fully. I simply clicked on the highlighted word "Claude" in the text, and was rewarded with a page showing most of his works in the collection. If I click on any of these small photos, I get a full-screen copy of the work and text, as you see here. If I click on the little speaker icon, I can hear his name pronounced. I can also go on to more pages.

All the highlighted words are "hot links" to more articles on the topic, or to definitions. Experiment freely by clicking them; you can always return to the tour if you like.

If you'd care to look through the collection by time or place, choose the historical atlas. You'll find a time line at the bottom of the map. Click there, and that single period is denoted on the map. Simply click a callout to view the art from that location.

To get closer, you can enlarge a work to fill the screen by clicking a control button. However, you can't "zoom in" at will on a painting's detail—a feature that would be useful if you'd like to learn about color mixing or brush strokes.

I hope you enjoyed your visit. (Personally, I would prefer to see more cultural and political cross-references, including some music, dance, and literature.)

CREATIVE MULTIMEDIA COMPLETE AUDUBON

[CD-ROM for DOS; VGA monitor and sound card recommended]

John James Audubon was America's premier 19th century "technical illustrator" of wildlife. He made far-ranging treks across North America to gather animals and plants, study them, and produce faithful depictions. His legacy is a collection of wonderfully accurate and attractive drawings preserved in lithograph, as well as a set of exacting journals on his field research.

Creative Multimedia has produced two multimedia CD-ROMs of Audubon's work, one on birds, the other on mammals. Each is a complete Octavo edition, with more than 150 plates (photos of Audubon's original lithographs), as well as the complete text of his journals.

There are several advantages to this multimedia publication. You can search for any title or category of animal; you can choose the art, text, or both; and you even can briefly hear the animal. You can see an index of the first 50 mammal lithographs; an asterisk indicates that there's an associated sound as well.

Audubon's Mammals, plates 1-49.

I have discovered first-hand how much realism a little sound can add. I am an avid backpacker, and several times I have encountered bears while walking solo in the West. So, I decided to search Audubon for "bears," and I quickly discovered the Cinnamon bear. I'd left the volume up a tad high on my sound card, and when two big bears appeared on screen accompanied by a very lively snorting, the hairs on the back of my neck went straight up. It instantly brought me back to a certain very dark night in the North Cascades. (Perhaps you'd rather begin your adventure by listening to a chipmunk or even one of the many gentle bird chirps on the Audubon's Birds CD-ROM.)

Audubon's journal entries add a fascinating dimension to his lithographs. They are very workmanlike and unsentimental. If you're looking for Bambi, you won't find him here. For instance, you can view part of Audubon's journal about the Cinnamon (or Black) bear. He takes the then-recent Lewis and Clark expedition to task for the insufficiency of their reports on this animal.

Audubon's Cinnamon bear journal entry.

CREATING ART ON THE COMPUTER

You may be inclined to create masterpieces of your own rather than merely view them or read about them. I'll show you some new computer applications that utilize incredibly realistic synthetic art materials that afford you a wonderful freedom to experiment and innovate. Electronic art has gone far beyond mere simulation to become a genre in its own right.

Traditional art media have a permanence that's both a great asset and a daunting barrier, especially to the neophyte. When you touch a pen to paper or put oil upon a canvas, your marks are there to taunt or delight you for a long time. If you "touch" a mouse or stylus to an "electronic canvas," you'll find it's easy to make adjustments in position, size, color, and proportion. And there's no cleanup. Now your children can try their hand at art with complete freedom and without the stigma of waste and failure. It's a wonderful boon for art education and entertainment.

When you're ready, you can print your masterpiece (or send the computer file to a service bureau to have slides or prints made). Or you can delete part or all of it and try again until you're satisfied. You can also easily mix media without the usual mechanical restrictions. You can use existing graphics or photographs as part of your composition, borrow textures, and even save the best of your brush strokes for next time.

When you touch a pen to paper or put oil upon a canvas, your marks are there to taunt or delight you for a long time. If you "touch" a mouse or stylus to an "electronic canvas," you'll find it's easy to make adjustments in position, size, color, and proportion. And there's no cleanup.

Note:

A few words about the technology. Applications that simulate art materials require fast computers. You'll also want a large, accurate-color, high-resolution display monitor, and you need a good pointing device, such as a pressure-sensitive tablet with stylus, to faithfully record hand movements. More on these later.

The technology employed by the following products won't give you the "feel" of pen on paper or brush on canvas, nor the rich odors of oils and turpentine and gesso. But you may be surprised how closely the "look" can be simulated. It's a useful tradeoff to gain the convenience and latitude to innovate. (Besides, sniffing turpentine may be hazardous to your health.)

ALDUS INTELLIDRAW
[Diskette for Windows 3.1]

Intellidraw was one of the first products to feature "smart shapes," shapes that automatically adjust or adapt to your drawing. Although Intellidraw is primarily an illustration program, this novel feature makes it a landmark product, worthy of mention.

FRACTAL DESIGN FRACTAL PAINTER/X2 V2.0
[Diskette for Windows 3.1]

You say you've always wanted to "do" some art but didn't know where to start? You're a kid and your mom doesn't want you to mess up the house? You've been an artist for years and you want to try new ways of combining media? Well, Fractal Painter is one computer art tool that can do it all.

Painter is actually sold as two products: Painter itself and the "X2" add-on that gives you floating "objects." Floating objects are images that can be created and edited separately and combined to form a single composition that can be taken apart again as you like. (These two products will likely be merged into one program in the near future.)

This illustration shows some of the incredibly large selection of "tools" that Fractal Painter gives you. In creating a computerized *object d'art*, you make the same choices you might make with actual media. First, you start with the kind of paper to use. (Fractal gives you nine to choose from.) Then you choose your weapons: There are 14 groups of "brushes," each with multiple variants; six basic brush shapes whose size and angle you can select; and seven brush "looks" that control how the brush will lay down pigment. (Some brush types can even apply multiple colors at once.)

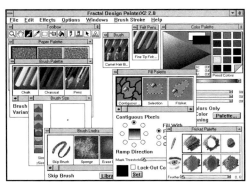

Fractal Painter 2.0's tool windows.

And then there is color. There are 14 color palettes of 15 swatches each, with myriad variants. You can use standardized colors, assemble your own palettes, or restrict yourself to only the colors that can be printed on your particular printer. If you use color fills (single colors or textures that occupy a defined area), you can select among five palettes to control that effect.

You can choose one or more "lights" to be cast on your painting surface at any angle and with any color you choose. You'll immediately see the result on your electronic canvas.

Several more control windows let you customize the brush effects to your own hand stroke and to the media, and then to save the settings for future use. You can also use Painter to import a scanned image or clip-art into your work. And you can import additional textures, brush looks, and other effects from libraries as you need them.

You say you have too many windows on your screen? There's no room for the artwork itself? No problem. You can "tear off" selected paper, brush palette, and looks windows, and then close the main control windows. From the Brush Palette, I tore off two small windows (shown at top center in the illustration) for camel-hair brushes and felt-tip pens. Just click one of these windows to change your drawing implement as you work.

I think you'll be astounded at how well Painter simulates real art materials, especially the way the different media interact with each other and with paper or canvas. On the other hand, you can also combine media in ways that are impossible in real life. For instance, you can use acrylic, oil, markers, and water in the same composition in the same hour.

Just as in real life, when you paint with water colors in Fractal Painter, the colors "puddle out" from the wet brush and soak into the paper. (Puddling is completely adjustable, of course.) If you overbrush, the color builds up, and if you use another color, the hues blend in a very realistic way.

Want to soften and blend water-based media even more? You can load a brush with water, and paint with that. To "lock in" your brush strokes, you can "dry" them, which prevents later colorants from mixing in. Some effects are even contrary to nature. For example, you can selectively erase watercolor brush strokes (unless you made them "dry," of course). Try doing that with an actual wet brush! (For maximum control over brush strokes and effects, you'll need to use a pressure-sensitive tablet.)

Fractal Design makes a more basic art-sketching product called Dabbler that works well with a simple tablet or even a mouse. (You can even buy a bundled product that combines Dabbler with a tablet by Kurta.) Instead of displaying art tools as complex windows (which, a bit intimidating for younger, budding artists), Dabbler hides them in wooden drawers. With a mouse click, a wooden drawer slides open; then click again on one of the exposed colorful icons.

FAUVE MATISSE V1.25

[Diskette for Windows 3.1]

Another capable painting application is Fauve Matisse, which gives you many of the same tools as Fractal Painter /X2.

Matisse includes some unusual and interesting filters, including a complex "convolution" method of creating your own special effects. You can also add optional plug-in filters for even more effects.

You get a good selection of brushes, brush shapes, and slider-adjusted options to produce an enormous number of variations. A color selector palette lets you choose between 16 million hues. (Even though your eye can distinguish them, you'll need a good quality display board and monitor to see them.)

For refined control over brush strokes, you'll want to use a pressure-sensitive tablet.

Matisse lets you work with floating objects (the same feature that the X2 extension package adds to Fractal Painter). This means you can develop a composite drawing from multiple elements; each element can be separately moved and modified.

You say you're not a fine artist, but you'd like to use the effects? Import a photo or drawing into Matisse, and select "Auto Paint." Watch while the application applies "brush strokes" to modify the image to give it the "feel" of a painting. And that brings us to the subject of image enhancing tools.

Import a photo or drawing into Matisse, and select "Auto Paint." Watch while the application applies "brush strokes" to modify the image to give it the "feel" of a painting.

IMAGE-ENHANCING TOOLS

Much of the graphic material surrounding us is in photo images. The tools I'll describe let you work with any image that is available to your computer as a pattern of dots (a bitmap).

If you'd like to use your own photos as a basis for computer graphics, you can use a scanner to enter them directly into the computer, or you can have them stored by Kodak on a Photo CD to be imported into your composition. Alternatively, you might select any of thousands of "stock photo" images now sold in CD-ROM format. Another source is an electronic camera, which is a relatively rare item now but guaranteed to be common and popular in a few years. With the right equipment, you can even extract still images from your videotaped movies or from live TV.

The following are some powerful applications that can disprove the old adage that "pictures don't lie." With a little patience, you can selectively modify any aspect of an image, including its color, brightness, contrast, and any shapes within it. You can revise history by removing undesirables from your family album or wrinkles from a face. You can even transport your viewer from reality into futuristic dimensions that never could exist.

You can revise history by removing undesirables from your family album or wrinkles from a face. You can even transport your viewer from reality into futuristic dimensions that never could exist.

ADOBE PHOTOSHOP V2.5

[CD-ROM or diskette for Windows 3.1 or Macintosh; Windows version includes Kai's Power Tools 1.0]

A premier image-enhancement and illustration product, Photoshop lets you create and edit both the shape and the color of the elements within an image. With its filters, you can create a wide variety of special effects. Using an included accessory called Kai's Power Tools (discussed later), you can add exotic textures and other effects. With Photoshop you get import and export features and filters that enable you to work with almost any kind of image files including those of video (NTSC) images.

You can import and export images in a wide variety of types and even scan them directly in. You can combine portions from multiple images as objects and seamlessly combine them into one, or delete or extract a portion of any image for use elsewhere. Photoshop is also an electronic darkroom. You can mask or "dodge" any part of an image to selectively correct color, contrast, and brightness. If you're going to publish the image, you can create and edit four-color separations, including traps (a printing technique).

MICROGRAFX PICTUREPUBLISHER 4.0 AND 5.0

[CD-ROM or diskette for Windows 3.1]

Strictly speaking, PicturePublisher is a graphics-arts editing tool. It lets you select an image, resize, trim, and shape it, adjust its color and lighting dynamics, add special effects, and print it.

It's like a complete color darkroom with masterful retouching tools. PicturePublisher gives you powerful artistic control over a picture's rendering.

One interesting use for such image-editing products is selective retouching. For example, if you have a family photo with someone in it who's literally no longer "part of the picture," you can delete that blemish from the past. You simply replace the image of the person with a section of background or even with another person.

I used this feature recently to "repair" a photo of our local town hall. It's a nice old brick edifice, but it is surrounded with the trappings of modern life, such as telephone wires, street signs, and a fire hydrant. I was able to eliminate all of them by carefully blending in background samples from around the same areas, using a process called "cloning." Pretty slick.

You can combine separate picture elements from various sources into a composite. Each element remains a separate "object" that retains a separate identity for editing; the objects can be stacked on the composite in any order you like, and with more or less transparency.

One of PicturePublisher's more powerful tools is its set of printer controls. You can select from many setups and (for Postscript printers) choose advanced color controls.

For each printer, you can select a color calibration that can be fine-tuned to give the best possible results for the kind of scenes and paper you're using. If you have a scanner, you can print a special calibration image, then scan it in, and PicturePublisher will analyze and adjust the image tones.

HSC KAI'S POWER TOOLS V2.0 AND BRYCE

[Diskette for Windows 3.1; VGA monitor required]

Sometimes you might like some dramatic special effects that aren't part of a basic application. HSC Software makes a product called Kai's Power Tools that you can add to Fractal Painter, Adobe Photoshop, and other graphics products. It gives you a whole range of exotic and often surreal effects that you can apply to whatever art, illustrations, or photos you have open in those applications. Its "bag of tricks" includes powerful filters, color controls, and other effects, including artificial textures (called fractals) that mimic natural or organic forms.

Power Tools extends the visual space to simulations of three dimensions. You control special lighting, shading, and perspective effects that create and enhance the extra dimension.

One of Kai's tools, shown here, is called the Gradient Designer. You can use it to apply very complex gradations of color and light to an existing image. This figure shows the stylish control panel for Gradient Designer. A cone-shaped color gradient has been applied to the photo at lower left. Various control windows let you select density, position, direction, and shape of the gradient.

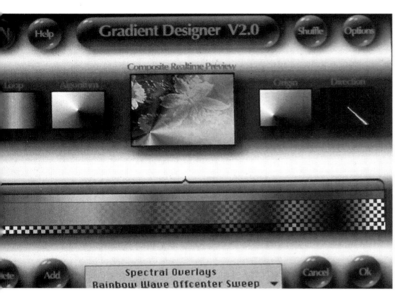

An HSC product called Bryce (recently made available for the Macintosh) lets you create artificial 3-D-style landscapes, including mountains, skies, land surfaces, and other textures. Named after Utah's breathtaking Bryce Canyon, it renders amazingly realistic, yet often surreal, artificial environments. Even metals, rocks, sand, water, and waves can be produced—complete with surface effects such as erosion or polishing. (Yes, you can polish water and erode a wave if you want to.)

Kai's Power Tools with the Gradient Designer in use.

HSC Bryce with artificial terrain (available only for the Macintosh).

3-D/Multimedia
Applications

If your artistic fancy takes you beyond the flat page and you want 3-D effects and possibly animation or full-motion computer video, the following new products can do the trick. The incredible power to produce convincing solid-like objects extends art into the realm of sculpture, at least visually.

These applications require a very fast computer with a math coprocessor and lots of memory (RAM); I would suggest, as a minimum, a 486DX33 with 8MB of RAM. That's because three-dimensional images are created using many math calculations and consume lots of storage space. You'll also want a hardware-accelerated display board and a large color monitor with 800×600 resolution or higher.

Until very recently, this kind of processing power was only available on the kind of large, expensive computers found in professional animation studios. Now you can find it in almost any department store. The applications themselves are, for the first time, affordable to the serious graphic artist.

Later in this chapter, I'll discuss some similar, but even more powerful applications, whose features make them more suited to developing full, broadcast-quality video animations or electronic "movies."

CALIGARI'S TRUESPACE

[Floppy diskette for Windows; included CD-ROM containing extra textures and objects]

trueSpace is a complete 3-D modeling and animation application that lets you make realistic-looking on-screen "sculptures." It was the first of its kind to let you work in full perspective in real time. You can see the outline of your object change while you build and modify it.

(One remaining limitation of PC-based 3-D modeling is that figure shapes often must revert to "wire-frames"— line segments outlining the shapes—while you create them. They don't reveal the other visual aspects— surface texture, color, lighting, or animation—until you've done the modeling stage.)

Basic shapes ("primitives"), such as spheres and cubes, are provided as building blocks for your 3-D model. You can combine and edit primitives by rotating or distorting to get any imaginable figure. Simply grab an object with a mouse and move, rotate, or change its shape anywhere in 3-D space, then watch the effects. You can even "extrude" a shape through a deformation lattice to squeeze it into any overall form. If you animate this process, it results in a kind of morphing effect.

trueSpace also lets you create three-dimensional text from any TrueType font.

To paint the 3-D surface, you select the material, its color, and its shading attributes, and then apply it to any part of the solid. You can also adjust opacity, add shadows, and even blur or fog the image. At the bottom of the workspace is a library of some of the many provided materials, including rock, glass, wood and metals. In this example, I chose granite and applied it to my truncated cone.

You can add reflections and refractions to simulate different materials and lighting effects. I added a spotlight light source, which trueSpace indicates as a sort of fuzzy spider shown here above and to the left of the cone. That's what creates the subtle glint on the granite surface. You can add single or multiple lights from any direction, and with any color or brightness.

You can edit any of the path positions step by step and change speeds. There's even a "camera" icon you can place in the scene whose view appears in a window; that way, you can "watch" the object or animation from any selected position.

Once the object is complete and the animation is drawn (if you want it), TrueSpace will render the work—that is, make it ready for viewing. This process converts the drawing into one or more still graphics or a real-time video movie that can be played on the monitor or recorded on videotape.

VISUAL SOFTWARE'S VISUAL REALITY FOR WINDOWS

[Floppy diskette for Windows 3.1; included CD-ROMs containing clip-art and textures]

Visual Reality is a 3-D graphics and animation product that's really a collection of five coordinated applications: Visual Image, Visual Model, Visual Font, RenderizeLive, and Visual Player. An included clip-art library on CD-ROM includes business-related, ready-to-use, solid objects, and another library of textures contains materials, finishes, and building materials.

Visual Image is an image editor that enables you to combine photos or other graphics, and then modify their color and appearance. Each combined element remains a separate graphic object for later changes. Visual Model is the 3-D object creation tool; it lets you model solids and combine shapes and materials from the libraries. The resulting design is presented to RenderizeLive

A Visual Reality composite design.

for 3-D photo-realistic rendering and animation in full color—in effect, a video production.

Although objects themselves can't be animated, you can take a "camera" on a visual walk through your synthetic scene.

Visual Font uses a Windows TrueType font to generate extruded 3-D text shapes that you can add to a scene. And Visual Player is an animation player for a RenderizeLive production.

The visual results of this design sequence can be stunning. This example, provided by Visual Software, shows a composite design with solids, text, textures, and photo images.

By using the Visual Reality applications to combine objects and backgrounds, it's possible to create complete artificial landscapes—such as a rendered bridge superimposed on a photo of lower Manhattan.

A bridge scene created by Visual Software's Visual Reality. Courtesy of Frederic Bertrand, of Compugraf, Brussels, Belgium.

Virtual Reality's Vistapro 3.0 for Windows

[CD-ROM for Windows 3.1; also available for DOS and Macintosh]

If your designs require photorealistic artificial landscapes, look at Vistapro. It creates full-color, 3-D landscapes, some that are based on real places and some that don't exist. You can also add roads, buildings, bodies of water, weather effects, trees, roads, and buildings.

You can extract scenes from more than 4,600 included landscapes, which are drawn from the U.S. Geological Survey and NASA. These include all of the United States (including several national parks and mountains at high resolution), several well-known mountains around the world, and most of the surface of Mars. (Some of the Mars terrain and a viewer are also sold separately by Virtual Reality as Mars Explorer.)

You can modify the terrain, or build your own, and add fractal texturing and dynamic lighting effects. Then you can choose one of several vehicles to transport you through the scene, draw a flight path with your mouse, and start your adventure. Capture your armchair flyover using a variable camera lens, and save it as an animation. Play it back with an included viewer (with CD audio if you like).

An included tool lets you create "morph" transitions between scene variations (lighting, tree growth) or between two completely different scenes. Vistapro can even generate the twin images needed for true stereoscopic viewing.

This illustration shows a mountain range, complete with vertical pillars of rock, eroded faces, snow, and grassy slopes.

Vistapro's mountain range.

Another scene of mountains, but this one a bit more gentle, is shown next. In the back, a caldera is depressed into steep basalt cliffs. Closer, there are patchwork quilts of brown earth or grasses. Dotted everywhere are conifers pointing sharply skyward, and mixed beneath them are some deciduous trees like maple or oak.

Next, you can see a whirling nebula bursting with a hot core of gas and new stars being born. In the foreground, a cratered orb is on one side, and a plume of luminous red and dark-black matter (perhaps the remnants of an exploding star) on the other. In the background, some spiral galaxies hang like celestial pinwheels.

Vistapro's mountains with foliage.

Vistapro's celestial pudding.

DRAWING DEVICES

MICE

Many manufacturers produce computer mice—the universal pointing device for graphical environments. Other pointing gadgets are also on the market, including trackballs and touch-sensitive displays. None of them has the broad appeal that mice have gained. A mouse is excellent for choosing menu items, drawing simple lines, and moving windows. It's a rather clumsy tool, however, for sketching, drawing curved lines, or simulating pen or brush strokes.

A mouse is an example of a relative pointing device; that is, it can't tell your computer where it is on a surface—only how far it's moved from its original position. Tablets (described shortly) are absolute devices. They signal exactly where on their flat, active surface you've pointed. They also can be pressure-sensitive, responding to the force you put on their electronic stylus. Absolute positioning and touch sensitivity are essential for many kinds of drawing and painting.

One of the most widely available mice is the Microsoft Mouse, which was recently released in an improved design. Logitech markets several mice, ranging from one for kids that looks like a bewhiskered little mouse to a radio-operated model that frees you from the annoyance of a cord.

TABLETS

If you're going to draw complex freehand shapes—especially if you're going to do artwork with simulated pen or brush strokes—you'll need a tablet. Although a mouse is fine for choosing menu options and drawing straight lines, it just doesn't translate your hand motions well enough for art applications.

A tablet is, in effect, an electronic canvas—a drawing surface with a pen-like wand. When you "draw" using the wand, your motions are translated into positions that are conveyed to your display screen. You can use a tablet to replace a mouse, whether to select menu options, simply draw lines, or to "paint."

Here are the basic tablet features: resolution, size, and pressure-sensitivity. Resolution is a measure of how many points in every inch the tablet can distinguish; most tablets give you an adequate 400 per inch or more. Tablets are either small (used to replace a mouse as a pointing device) or page-size: 6×8 to 12×18 inch is common.

A pressure-sensitive tablet tells your drawing application how hard you're pushing on the wand. You'll definitely want that feature if you're trying to simulate the natural effects of, say, brush strokes on canvas. (Many tablets are not pressure-sensitive because they are used for computer-aided design or drafting, for which this extra-cost feature isn't needed.)

The following are a few examples of quality tablets available from Kurta—a well-known and respected vendor.

Kurta PenMouse

PenMouse is a light, 4×5-inch electronic "easel," a low-cost graphics tablet that fits easily on most any computer desk. Its wand is wireless. You can use it as an electronic pen, pencil, or brush to make drawings or sketches, even to sign letters. It also replaces your mouse for pointing, highlighting, or moving around a display.

PenMouse is a serial device, and works with either the Macintosh or IBM-compatible PCs. It is intended for a window-type graphics environment. You can also buy it bundled with Fractal Design's Dabbler, which is an entry-level drawing and painting application. PenMouse is intended as a mouse replacement and isn't pressure-sensitive.

Kurta XGT Tablet

If you're a serious computer-graphics artist, you need a full-featured tablet such as this one. A new design from Kurta, the XGT has a full 256 levels of pressure sensitivity. It also includes a wireless electronic pen, which does away with restrictive cables. The XGT is available in three sizes—6×8, 12×12, and 12×18 inches—to fit your size needs for electronic "paper" or "canvas." Twelve function buttons across the top give you control over menu and setup features.

The XGT is a serial device and includes drivers to replace your mouse for both DOS and Windows environments. Various optional cursor pointing devices can replace the pen, to allow exact entry of positions on a drawing. These options are typically used for drafting.

Kurta's PenMouse.

Kurta's XGT pressure-sensitive tablet.

Kurta VTS-5 VideoTablet

Here's one of the most intriguing tablet designs yet devised: An electronic pointing surface integrated with an LCD display. It's like being able to draw on your computer' monitor, with none of the distraction of pointing in one place and seeing the results in quite another.

Imagine being able to display a sketch or drawing, then touchup or copy parts of it in freehand, just as though you were working on a paper print. You might also use the VTS-5 to hand-annotate a document or mark-up an illustration. Or you can use it like a "super mouse" to select from a complex menu or list; you can point quickly and directly at any text or icon displayed on the LCD screen.

This technology has a few limitations, at least at the present time. The LCD is a 64-level monochrome display, and the tablet isn't touch-sensitive. To upgrade both those features would price this unit out of the current market.

Kurta's VTS-5 LCD tablet.

INTERACTIVE MUSIC

There are many products available today that can teach you about music, whether as a listener or as budding composer. The following sections describe some of the more prominent music-education software products on the market today. (The latest technology in computer-generated music is described in more detail in Chapter 25, "Cybermusic.")

MICROSOFT MULTIMEDIA MOZART

[CD-ROM for Windows 3.1]

Here is one of the most engaging ways to learn about the major concert-music composers, with an interactive guided tour of the music.

Microsoft has contracted with the Voyager Company for several multimedia interactive titles included in its Home product line. Each covers a single major work of Mozart, Beethoven, Stravinsky, Richard Strauss, and others as a springboard to a deeper exploration of the artist's life and work. The titles share several features: A complete musical work with a full listing of all its sections, a thorough history of the composer and the period, a discussion of instruments, and a musical game to test what you've learned.

Mozart is one of the most beloved of concert-music composers; this title highlights the "Dissonant Quartet"—his String Quartet in C-major K.465—performed by the Angeles Quartet. Before we get to the music, let's view some of the background material. You'll find highlighted "jump words" sprinkled throughout the text. Click the phrase "string quartet," and the definition pops up. You can also choose words from an extended glossary.

You'll find a helpful section describing the instruments that compose a string quartet, with text and nicely illustrated examples. Click any component of a musical instrument, and a detailed photo of the part pops up with a good explanation.

Now that you know something about the instruments, you may want some details on the composition and construction of this work. For instnace, you can view a description of the anatomy of the third movement. There's a commentary with a structural outline at the bottom. If you want to hear the music that is being described, click the arrow and it plays. Follow the highlighted section that keeps track of your place.

The narrative text follows the music to provide explanatory details. If there's a word whose meaning isn't quite clear, click it, and a window pops up with a helpful definition. And the music plays on.

Mozart was a child prodigy who lived a life almost exclusively dominated by music. He was, of course, widely acclaimed. Yet he often felt misunderstood and unfulfilled. (Don't we all?)

MICROSOFT MULTIMEDIA BEETHOVEN

[CD-ROM for Windows 3.1]

This title covers Beethoven's "Ninth Symphony"—one of the most awe-inspiring works ever written by a composer. Called "The Symphony of a Thousand," it's a work of grand proportions that requires both a greatly expanded orchestra and many voices. This recording features the Viennese State Opera with the Viennese Philharmonic and some internationally known soloists.

In two hours with this CD, I felt I had learned more about Beethoven, his life, and this symphony than I'd ever thought possible. Once you begin a close reading—the performance accompanied with written narration—you're given an expert tour through all the nuances of this work. Your guide is music scholar, professor, and pianist, Robert Winter.

Want to absorb the music a little at a time? Just click the Play Page button, and the music plays only through the current section. Or click Play Through for non-stop listening. You can move to any part of the symphony by clicking the item on the section list you want or on the Movement button at the bottom.

In two hours with this CD, I felt I had learned more about Beethoven, his life, and this symphony than I'd ever thought possible.

On this CD, you'll find an absorbing musical game that plays musical segments and examples and asks you to identify them in various ways. The CD also includes a bibliography and other background material. I found myself fascinated with the very complete history of Beethoven, his music, and his age. Here's one poignant point: Beethoven began to lose his hearing and could no longer perform on the piano by 1814. Soon he could carry on conversations with his friends only by having them write their replies in notebooks. He tried many ways to overcome this malady, including wearing hearing trumpets.

Beethoven wrote this, his last symphony, after he became totally deaf. When the symphony was first performed in 1824, he had to be turned to the audience to realize their warm applause of acceptance. You can also see a handbill for that performance, with a description of the responsibility the composer was required to assume in order to mount it.

MICROSOFT MULTIMEDIA STRAVINSKY

[CD-ROM for Windows 3.1]

Igor Stravinsky is the only modern composer included in this series. He lived until 1971, and this major work, "Le Sacre de Printemps" ("The Rites of Spring") is a ballet suite first performed in 1913. It's a dramatic and fast-paced composition, full of shifting rhythms, dissonance, and harsh dynamics.

It's a fascinating yet difficult composition to understand, and this title from Microsoft is a fine example of the educational value of multimedia. You get an intensive, self-paced introduction to the music that would be hard to exceed with anything other than a college-level course. Robert Winter is again your expert tour guide on this interactive exploration. He also narrates this recording, which is by the Ochestre Symphonique de Montreal.

You'll find a long section in Multimedia Stravinsky called "The Rite as Dance." It explains clearly and with great detail the influences and attitudes Stravinsky brought to the composition. It also explains the long and somewhat torturous history of live performances of "Le Sacre" by various ballet troupes.

You can also view some of Stravinsky's personal notes on the work. Not only did audiences react strongly to the work, the premiere was greeted with such an uproar of protest from the listeners that much of the performance was drowned out.

As you listen to the music, a running narrative keeps you informed of the details. A button click takes you to an explanation of "The Rite as Dance"— the choreographic element of the work. Another button brings you a window with more details of the music. A "closer look" describes a horn passage (a component of "The Ritual of the Rival Tribes" in Part One).

. . . .

You can also view some of Stravinsky's personal notes on the work. Not only did audiences react strongly to the work, the premiere was greeted with such an uproar of protest from the listeners that much of the performance was drowned out.

. . . .

Here's what you'd see about "The Ritual of the Rival Tribes" if you click the Listening button: An incredibly thorough explanation of the music's internal structure. You can follow easily because each section is highlighted as the music plays.

MICROSOFT MUSICAL INSTRUMENTS OF THE WORLD

[CD-ROM for Windows 3.1]

As you can see, technology and the arts have become complementary. Whether you are learning about art or creating it, you can now use the multimedia capabilities of modern computers to explore the manifold possibilities of literature, painting, music—indeed, the whole spectrum of experience as expressed and refined by the human imagination.

Every region of the world has its unique instruments, developed and played by the local citizens. From the very primitive Australian bull-roarer to the modern violin, each has a special tonality and musical history. Using this nicely packaged multimedia guide, you can identify a variety of musical instruments by region and actually hear them play. On this CD, most of the pictures of the instruments are interactive icons or "hotboxes." Using the product is fun and intuitive. You can click the picture to learn more about the instrument.

Part of the CD is like an atlas with a twist: The maps are marked with instruments instead of cities. Start with the world map, click a region, and another window pops up with a regional map. Featured instruments are shown in their place of origin. Click the little speaker to hear one play. Or click the instrument itself to get more details.

One way to experience the instrument collection on this CD is to click the "Random" button at the top of the screen. It introduces you to the sights and sounds of each instrument in no particular order.

I decided to be a bit more focused and investigate Australia's didjeridu—a very primitive horn played by aboriginal tribesmen. A click on the small instrument picture brought up a window with a write-up on the instrument and a large photo with callouts.

If you click the "Types" icon, you're transported to a description of the instrument's category. Believe it or not, the didjeridu is considered a trumpet; it consists of a tube with a mouthpiece (and no reed). An illustration includes the family of trumpets and shows that the didjeridu is probably the most primitive of all.

You can also learn about those instruments that are played in groups, including chamber groups, orchestras, and even rock 'n' roll bands. I clicked an icon for rock 'n' roll bands and got a window with a description and pictures of the featured instruments.

As you can see, technology and the arts have become complementary. Whether you are learning about art or creating it, you can now use the multimedia capabilities of modern computers to explore the manifold possibilities of literature, painting, music—indeed, the whole spectrum of experience as expressed and refined by the human imagination.

Virtual Architecture

chapter 3
by Anne Hart

Virtual architecture reaches into hard-to-see spaces or creates them. It projects the viewer to a different location in real time. Architectural simulation sells the illusion of control, not escape. Do architects simply want to create graphics at higher resolution for fewer dollars? Or are they also looking for the wormhole entrance into cyberspace?

With virtual reality, architects and planners can see a commmunity develop before their eyes. Courtesy of StereoGraphics Corp.

Virtual reality (VR) can be a strong tool in the hands of the poor. One noteworthy example is how VR is democratizing architecture, by giving individuals and communities more choices before they actually spend money on blueprints and construction. The challenge of virtual architecture is to find unique, new ways to use it as a communicaton medium between humans and machines that can transcend the limitations of space, time, and matter.

Virtual architecture reaches into hard-to-see spaces or creates them. It projects the viewer to a different location in real time. Architectural simulation sells the illusion of control, not escape. Do architects simply want to create graphics at higher resolution for fewer dollars? Or are they also looking for the wormhole entrance into cyberspace (which can be defined as "the place where you are when you're calling Tonga from Coney Island")?

Communities and neighborhoods can be rebuilt in virtual reality, as a test model or simulation. Courtesy of William Jepson.

VR also enables the detailed design of specific streets and buildings. Courtesy of William Jepson.

How many ways can architects use virtual reality? The two primary goals of virtual architecture are

- To make hard-to-understand representations easier to read and use by the interactive viewer, and
- To democratize neighborhood planning by involving residents in their own community's design.

On the community level, virtual architecture is about using feedback from the residents, walking them through simulations and models before the malls, subways, businesses, and housing developments are actually built. It includes using employees' suggestions to rebuild the workplace by transporting workers through simulated models of their changes or designs. Virtual environments are affordable, adaptable, and wide open for barter, rental, or time-share.

Prospective home buyers use VR to tour new housing. *Courtesy of Vream.*

Interior design can be altered on a whim. *Courtesy of Vream.*

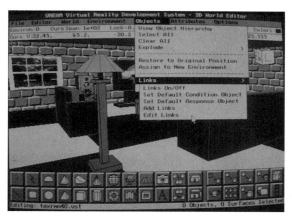

A prospective buyer can select from a variety of housing features. *Courtesy of Vream.*

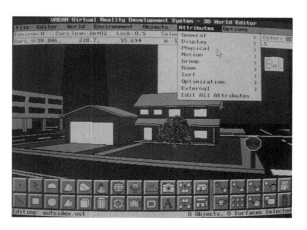

According to Stephen R. Ellis, head of the Spatial Perception and Advanced Displays Lab, Aerospace Human Factors Division, at NASA, virtual reality is not a clearly-defined concept. It is more of a buzzword than anything, and virtual architecture is just an extension of the desktop metaphor. Ellis reported that "virtual environment displays represent a three-dimensional generalization of the two-dimensional 'desk-top' metaphor." (Ellis holds a Ph.D. in psychology from McGill University.)

To the architect, the VR environment may be experienced either from what Ellis calls "egocentric" or "exocentric" viewpoints. Architects concerned with issues of cost and performance want their clients to appear to actually be inside the unique environment or to have total control over a "you are here" symbol where they can see themselves represented in the virtual architecture experience.

The goal of virtual architecture is to be as usable, concrete, and personal an experience of spatial relations as reality itself. Virtual reality thus provides an opportunity to study how the mind becomes oriented to a new world as well as to a new media.

Virtual architecture plays off of our sense of the organic nature of physical space. Someday a virtual-reality machine is going to visit distant planets, and the VR robots will send back images of reality that will be close to what a human would experience.

Virtual reality helped NASA put an end to the troubles with the Hubble Space Telescope when Lockheed Research Labs developed an opto-mechanical prototype for NASA's recent repair mission to the orbiting Hubble. The full-color, three-dimensional VR prototype of Costar enabled scientists to test the $50 billion instrument to make sure it wouldn't collide with parts of Hubble's Wide Field/Planetary Camera.

Story Musgrave, the astronaut who helped design the equipment and space suits for the shuttle's extravehicular activity (EVA), predicts that in the future a new kind of virtual reality will replace the kind of simulations that are done now.

He recently told *Omni* magazine, "If it's going to replace simulations we do, like in the water tank, virtual reality must represent an anthropomorphic suit relationship and turn that into a single organism." (The Hubble designers used VR for testing and verification, which helped to establish what positions Hubble's remote arm could assume during the spacewalk repair sessions.)

In virtual environments, it's only one small step from designing the cockpits of space vehicles to adapting the results of virtual reality for urban renewal or residential development. Thus the relevant question becomes, how can virtual architecture become as affordable as it is adaptable?

• •

The goal of virtual architecture is to be as usable, concrete, and personal an experience of spatial relations as reality itself. Virtual reality thus provides an opportunity to study how the mind becomes oriented to a new world as well as to a new media.

• •

"If architects can't afford high-end VR equipment, then a number of architects or a society can raise funds, chip in together, and rent or time-share the equipment as urban residential and business renewal projects arise," says A. Joan Levine, an interior designer and a talent manager for creative contingency professionals in architecture and interior design. Levine, of San Diego, free-lances for architects around the world in virtual reality, time-sharing VR equipment.

"Most architects use 3-D modeling or animation as a lower-cost alternative to high-end virtual reality. Few architects run cooperatives to time-share higher-end VR equipment during its downtime," Levine explained. "It's time to create affordable ways of using VR so it's accessible to all designers."

Time-shared virtual-reality studios are referred to in the industry as "multiuser dungeons" (a term used recently in *Omni* magazine science fiction) or "multiuser cells" (a term used by architectural animators).

"You don't have to be city-bound or rich," Levine adds.

"You can still use the high-end equipment only when you need it, until high-end VR prices come down by the end of this decade. Of course, there's always the chance that your client will pay expenses for VR-tool time-share rentals. Or you could write a proposal for a grant from your city."

Levine believes in garage VR.

"I can buy an inexpensive 14-ounce, head-mounted display, such as CyberEye, [and] affordable interactive virtual reality for my IBM 486 PC from VREAM for under $500. Or I can alternate with 3D-Ware, a virtual reality toolkit that uses my standard VGA card.

"Where I learn the latest news on garage VR fastest is at the virtual-reality expos," Levine explains.

Levine's daughter, Annee, is a free-lance, home-based grant-proposal writer, specializing in developing grant requests for academics to use virtual reality to create such things as models of future cities, re-creations of destroyed cities, and simulations of new medical, scientific, and urban designs.

CrystalEyes enables PC users to view three-dimensional images at home. *Courtesy of StereoGraphics Corp.*

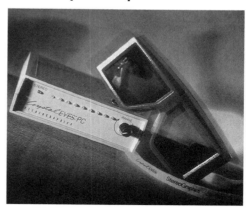

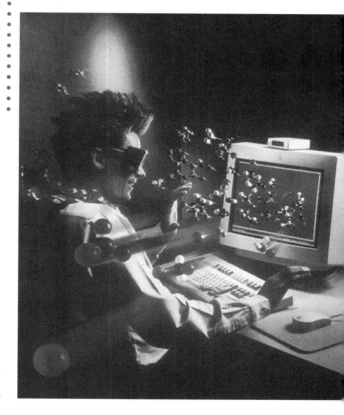

CrystalEyes produces a true 3-D image.
Courtesy of StereoGraphics Corp.

The eyewear is broadly applicable to a wide variety of desktop VR markets. *Courtesy of StereoGraphics Corp.*

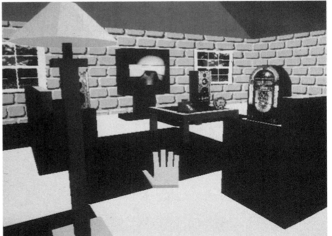

The market for games which use 3-D products is growing. *Courtesy of StereoGraphics Corp.*

Reality software enables a user to enter a virtual reality room. *Courtesy of Vream.*

"City money is out there waiting for you," Annee explained. "Grants from any large city to fund education for virtual reality architectural development is poised and ready to be given to urban developers, architects, and academics.

"It's up to the individual architecture, urban design, landscape, or computer-science professors to hire a grant proposal writer who knows something about architecture or urban development to tell the city why it should grant money for modeling cities in real time."

During the Los Angeles riots of 1992, virtual reality enthusiasts sat quietly in their multiuser dungeons, cells, basements, and studios, videotaping the looting and fires shown on television that destroyed some of the poorest neighborhoods in Los Angeles. (Architects and urban designers can quickly become avid virtual realists.)

A quick way to rebuild neighborhoods or cities is by first creating models and simulations through which viewers can walk or fly. Virtual architects aspire to work in an environment where the computer and keyboard disappear, where they will have total immersion in an artificial world rather than mere three-dimensional modeling on a computer screen.

. . . .
Virtual architects aspire to work in an environment where the computer and keyboard disappear, where they will have total immersion in an artificial world rather than mere three-dimensional modeling on a computer screen.
. . . .

The major impediment right now is the cost of high-end virtual architecture. By the end of the decade, prices will surely come down. In the meantime, simulations are being done at a more reasonable cost by interactive simulation or—at the lowest-cost end—with 3-D modeling and imaging.

Levels of detail can be enhanced.

Courtesy of Vream.

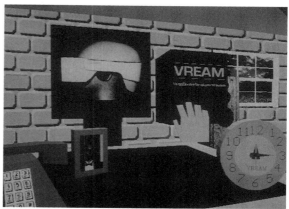

Reality software enables fully interactive textured virtual worlds to be created. *Courtesy of Vream.*

USING VR TO EMPOWER DIVERSE POPULATIONS

Today, architects and urban designers can use virtual reality or three-dimensional interactive modeling and simulation to empower populations of diverse ethnic, economic, or cultural backgrounds to share in the planning of their neighborhoods.

The city of Los Angeles recently provided a $175,000 grant to fund the Urban Simulation Environment. Now the residents of the poor, mostly Hispanic immigrant neighborhood of Pico-Union will have the power of virtual reality in their own hands. And they will contribute significantly to designing their own virtual-reality neighborhood.

The purpose of the urban planning simulation system is to give neighborhood residents a strong and interactive voice in city planning. The public will walk through three-dimensional new streets, stores, shopping malls, and parks. Virtual architecture can even help in the design and development of transportation systems, such as subways.

In the Urban Simulation Environment, the screen doesn't disappear such that the person walking through is immersed in 360 degrees of an artificial world. Instead, interactive images in real time are shown on a large TV screen or on a high-speed graphics terminal. Readable city plans are shown so residents can make suggestions for changes.

This high-tech project, whose purpose is to democratize how neighborhoods around the world use urban-planning models and simulations, was brainstormed by academia. It's the creation of students and 12 volunteer professors of the University of California, Los Angeles, graduate school of Architecture and Urban Planning. The project has an ambitious goal—to make the world a kinder and gentler place.

The complex blueprints and charts used by architects and urban planners usually are hard to understand for the person in the street who wants a strong, individual, and interactive voice in planning neighborhood communities. The creators of the simulation realized that architects needed to bring their engines down to the solid earth of reality so the individual in the street can understand and interact with complex representations used on designs.

Virtual reality is critical for exterior design.

Courtesy of William Jepson.

Involving the residents of neighborhoods in planning their own communities is a fresh approach. There is a brash, urban edginess to the process that adds a discordant but not altogether unwelcome note. And the vigor of the virtual revolution will ultimately help drive down the price of the technology.

Virtual architecture can bring technology to the layman. With the Urban Simulation Environment, residents don't have to worry about interacting with complexity. According to project director William Jepson, the television format is readily understandable to the public.

Any interactive simulation has to be user-friendly for the residents of a community; yet ironically it was an advanced military flight-simulation reality engine that inspired the creation of the Urban Simulation Environment. (The "reality engine" is a high-speed image processor. It merges and stores huge amounts of visual and sonic data from videotape, including geographic information systems, textual databases, and a variety of other resources.)

VR can help architects design entire blocks or individual businesses. *Courtesy of William Jepson.*

Individual streets can be designed and fully textured. *Courtesy of William Jepson.*

From **Defense Dollars** to **Virtual Architecture**

When the cold war ended, one of the first places defense conversion program funds went was into virtual architecture and VR-based law enforcement.

As billions of government dollars are funnelled away from weaponry and into so-called defense-conversion programs, funding for grants may become available for unique projects. Researchers are looking for more ways to apply battlefield robotic technology to urban and forensic architecture.

For example, architects can design simulations of "smart" buildings, which interact with their occupants to control such environmental factors as energy use and traffic flow. In transportation, forensic architects and industrial designers can experiment with such things as spikes embedded in retractable panels beneath roads, which can be raised by remote control to blow out tires during high-speed police chases. Architects and SWAT teams work together in forensic virtual architecture when virtual robots drill through walls to feed in fiber-optic tubing for surveillance.

When the cold war ended, one of the first places defense conversion program funds went was into virtual architecture and VR-based law enforcement. Research is now being done at national laboratories that a decade ago were used to build nuclear zappers. As defense contracts nearly ground to a halt, military defense equipment had to be re-designed for commercial purposes.

In fiscal 1994, almost $2.7 million in VR-related grants were awarded to private firms, architectural and design companies, virtual reality businesses, police groups, and four national laboratories through the National Institute of Justice, the research branch of the U.S. Department of Justice. The federal agency wants the money to help develop equipment that protects police and subdues suspects without killing. Architects, designers, engineers, and scientists are using some of the grant money to go into police departments to get expert advice on how to better protect officers on the street.

Architects and scientists at the Idaho National Engineering Laboratory are working on devices for stopping fugitive cars with little or no police pursuit, using mechanisms that formerly disabled military tanks. The application shuts off a car's ignition from a distance. Federal grant money also is being used at the Lawrence Livermore National Laboratory in the San Francisco Bay Area to refine a computer-aided machine mounted on a police car that can trace the trajectory of sniper fire.

WILL GARAGE VR DEMOCRATIZE ARCHITECTURE?

Socially correct virtual reality includes "garage VR"—lower-end virtual reality and 3-D modeling that is affordable to personal-computer owners. Garage VR is increasingly popular because people are seeking low-cost solutions to complex imaging and design problems and one of the biggest stumbling blocks to the home-based VR lab remains the cost.

Independent architects hope they won't have to wait a decade before the cost of high-end VR comes down to a level that the average PC owner can afford. Home-based virtual architects generally need a concept demonstration to get funded. Architects thus find themselves in a catch-22 maze: To get money, they must have a concept demonstration, but they need an expensive VR system to create the demonstration before they can ask for the money. In many cases, the problem is solved by low-cost garage virtual architecture.

The best garage-VR reference publication for low-end PC users is *PCVR Magazine*, published in Stoughton, Wisconsin. Also very helpful is the book *Garage Virtual Reality*, by Linda Jacobson, from Sams Publishing.

Independent architects hope they won't have to wait a decade before the cost of high-end VR comes down to a level that the average PC owner can afford.

WHAT DO YOU WANT AND WHERE DO YOU WANT IT?

Another way to democratize architecture is by using interactive multimedia to give individual home buyers more choices. Real-estate developers and residential construction companies can now employ simple interactive multimedia or complex virtual architecture as part of their overall planning, construction, and marketing process.

Virtual real estate's biggest selling point is customization. In other words, VR can be used to design houses to order. People will buy houses that don't yet exist if they can decide from the outset what they want and where they want it.

How does one sell a house that is not yet built? With these new technologies, potential home buyers who can't walk through the actual units can still look at the units in either virtual real estate or interactive media. Then, if they like what they see, they can customize the interiors according to their own tastes. It's beyond showing two-dimensional artist's sketches and relying on the buyer's ability to fantasize—the way unbuilt houses have been sold for the past century.

In San Francisco's Potrero Hill district, six artist's lofts, 24 residential lofts, 24 condominiums, and 10 houses needed to be pre-sold before they were built. The project's developer—the McKenzie, Rose and Holliday Company—commissioned Neo House Multimedia of Burlingame, California, to build a kiosk that enabled home buyers to see the future units. Buyers also could customize the interiors by selecting carpets, wall colors, and countertops.

Potential buyers could change their selections by pushing a button. Neo House used photographs from another of the company's developments as the basis for the computerized image. They used Photoshop and Director software to make color and texture selections available to the prospective buyers of the units.

Agents can also use these virtual technologies to show a furnished model in order to sell the display furnishings rather than the house itself.

At the high end of virtual real-estate technology, prospective residents can walk or fly through total simulations, immersed in new cultural activities, businesses, restaurants, ethnic gourmet groceries, churches, schools, arts facilities, and other components of the surrounding environment. Virtual architecture may also be used to plan the preservation of historical sites.

At the high end of virtual real-estate technology, prospective residents can walk or fly through total simulations, immersed in new cultural activities, businesses, restaurants, ethnic gourmet groceries, churches, schools, arts facilities, and other components of the surrounding environment.

Neo House Multimedia gave prospective house buyers a computerized palette of potential colors and styles. *Courtesy of Neo House Multimedia.*

THE STEREOSCOPIC DIMENSION

Stereo viewing offers a new dimension to architects who want to tell a story or enhance the illusion of a simulated environment. The term "3-D CAD" is really the projected image of a 3-D database displayed on a flat screen. In standard 2-D rendering, designers can rotate and reposition objects on a screen, but the flat screen forces the designer to imagine the object's depth. Real 3-D CAD occurs when the objects are viewed in 3-D stereo.

You may recall the 3-D horror movies of the 1950s that required audiences to don special glasses to experience the 3-D effect. Today, a new generation of stereoscopic products enable users to experience a sense of depth on a computer monitor, often without any special apparatus.

Stereoscopic CAD gives the user binocular vision from a flat screen by delivering one slightly different image to each eye. The images are alternated in rapid succession. The brain fuses the two images into one, resulting in the sense of depth we call stereopsis.

The virtual architect can use such 3-D virtual prototypes as StereoGraphics' CrystalEyes eyewear or CrystalEyes PC to facilitate architectural "walk-through" demonstrations or to give a presentation that has all the elements of a convincing "story." Architects on the cutting edge are combining interactive three-dimensional modeling, imaging, animation, narrative text, and walk-through graphics to create the most effective presentations.

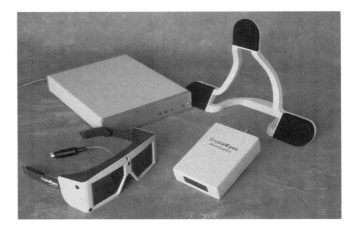

CrystalEyes systems are accepted as the industry standard for stereo viewing. *Courtesy of StereoGraphics Corp.*

Users can enter the desktop virtual world with a minimum of hardware. *Courtesy of StereoGraphics Corp.*

VR innovations offer superior functionality for creating and manipulating 3-D objects. *Courtesy of StereoGraphics Corp.*

Virtual reality has found uses in the medical profession. *Courtesy of StereoGraphics Corp.*

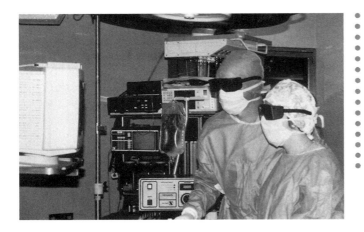

VR hardware is becoming an increasingly common sight in the operating room. *Courtesy of StereoGraphics Corp.*

THE ARCHITECT AS ANIMATOR AND STORYTELLER

With 3-D imaging and architectural animation, educators and history buffs can visit virtual ancient structures, virtual museums, or virtual recreations of historic events. Astronomy enthusiasts can use virtual simulations to examine structural ruins on other planets, such as NASA's famous photo of the "face on Mars," or (with permission), Richard Hoagland's startling videos and photos of ancient ruined crystal domes on the moon.

Andrew McClary is both an architect and a computer animator who has re-created ancient structures in three-dimensional computer animation. He has simulated neolithic, Egyptian, Greek, and Roman period structures in a CD-ROM entitled Exploring Ancient Architecture, from Medio Multimedia, Inc., of Redmond, WA. In McClary's CD-ROM software, the viewer can also access optional narrative features.

Virtual reality also can be used to create virtual architectural museums. Students studying how a Roman temple was built or what's inside the pyramids of Egypt may not be able to afford to visit the actual sites, but with virtual architecture, a student can visit the reconstructed site to see how it was built thousands of years ago and then travel through time to see how it was weathered each year into the ruin it is today.

McClary's self-guided, 3-D animated "virtual tour" of seven famous architectural marvels offers time-travel walk-throughs for those fascinated by the architecture of ancient civilizations. The "interactive documentary" model encourages exploration and discovery.

Each building was meticulously recreated by the award-winning architectural animator with sophisticated 3-D, computer-aided design (CAD), and animation programs. Each architectural period contains a slide show with a narrated overview written by Dr. Bruce Meyer, a noted architecture professor at Ball State University.

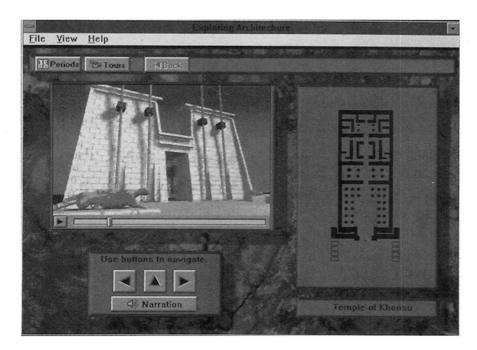

SHARING THE VIRTUAL ENVIRONMENT

Currently, the best model for virtual architectural and art museums exists at Carnegie-Mellon University in Pittsburgh. Their virtual art museum is networked so that users can experience total immersion in a digital representation of the ancient Egyptian Temple of Horus, which was built between 300 BC and 300 AD.

A virtual museum like the one at CMU adds another dimension to remote education (so-called distance learning) on a network. Viewers use a head-mounted display and jiggle a joystick to navigate from the exterior of the virtual art and architecture museum into the lobby and then into the Temple of Horus Gallery.

Outside the temple, the viewers experience the open-air courtyard. Sculptures and murals are interactive. Inside the inner sanctuary, viewers can experience the ambience of ancient Egypt.

Three virtual tour guides document the history of the temple. The space is modeled accurately. Rooms feature giant columns and open ceilings. In October, 1994, the virtual exhibition is slated to open at the Solomon R. Guggenheim Museum SoHo, in New York.

Carl Loeffler and Lynn Holden developed the virtual temple at the Studio for Creative Inquiry at Carnegie-Mellon. Loeffler is project director for telecommunications and virtual reality. He contributed the technical expertise. Holden, an Egyptologist, authenticated the architectural and anthropological details.

The virtual museum uses a distributed client/server architecture, enabling unlimited numbers of viewers to interact in the same virtual environment.

Is the virtual museum a symbol of what future museums will be like—a form of interactive entertainment as distance learning? Will the future virtual museum be available to everyone—architects, students, and the public—online? Who will put virtual museums on the Internet? The developers look at the virtual museum as a point of departure, a starting gate. Who in virtual architecture will pick up this idea and expand it further? Why not develop other virtual architecture museums for a variety of ancient cultures, religious groups, and ethnicities?

Will rabbis create a virtual museum of ancient and modern Jewish culture? Will priests and ministers create one for Christianity? How about a virtual architecture museum for Native American structures? To what extent can distance teachers use virtual museums to enhance remote learning or armchair travel? Will it be available for home-bound senior citizens and the physically challenged who can't travel, or for children too young to visit actual sites?

Architects can use broadcast equipment to offer virtual architecture as entertainment, as distance-teaching courseware, or as a shared video conferencing environment. They can broadcast to specific neighborhoods and communities. By telling a good story with a strong visual component, the virtual architect creates an unprecedented tool for education—or sales.

WHEN ARCHITECTS BUILD A STORY

Virtual architects can use the proven trade-show demonstrator's techniques to capture an audience and involve an entire convention hall of viewers. A compelling narrative in conjunction with strong designs can captivate people, take them to a new place, make them anticipate additional information, show them a product's benefits and advantages, and leave them feeling uplifted at the end. It is a logical evolution of economics and technology for direct-response telemarketing tools to be used in producing interactive infomercial videos and trade-show product demonstration tours.

Virtual entertainment and architecture thus create more projects for free-lance interactive multimedia and virtual-reality scriptwriters and for animators who work with architects as independent contractors.

How then does an architect visually construct a story that will keep the viewer's attention long enough to present the entire work? First you outline what you want to say—and why you want to say it.

Imagery alone cannot define and solve problems within the average person's seven-minute attention span while watching video. A good story will define and solve the problem. It will offer benefits and advantages, just like a successful direct response television infomercial.

VIRSCRIPTORS AND CONTENT WRITERS

In the multimedia industry, VR scriptwriters are called *virscriptors* or *content writers*. As a long-time multimedia scriptwriter and creative director, I recently collaborated with a team of architects and animators on a script project that illustrated the importance—and the potential difficulty—of constructing a compelling narrative. The clients wanted a dramatization incorporating 12 problems that were to be stated and solved in a 28 1/2 minute direct response television infomercial with 400 cuts and montages. The project also involved the creation of a CD-ROM containing video on how to prevent teenage dating violence, domestic violence, and abuse of the elderly.

The script emphasized benefits and advantages of preventing violence and abuse and told in a compelling story. When I work on a project like this, I use StoryVision software (created by StoryVision, of Santa Monica, CA), for creating "worlds" in interactive media scripts. And I use and highly recommend the Leverage Multimedia Scripting Language for designs that need the flexibility of a full-featured scripting language in a professional development environment. (CLS, Inc., St. Petersburg, FL.)

DEFINING THE PROBLEM FOR VIEWERS

Virtual architecture can show us how to navigate maps—both literal and conceptual—with less difficulty. Virtual architecture can teach us how to see patterns in everything, how to connect them to create something new, or how to reconstruct them to make something useful from what had been taken for granted.

Even without a scriptwriter, virtual architects can offer fantastic imagery. A good content writer will point out to the architect that flying through the models and simulations might very well show the viewer that the problem was solved, but that to compel the viewer to stick with the story, the architect needs to define the problem to the viewer and show sequentially, step-by-step, why and how the architect solved that problem.

If a concrete step is missing, the viewer will feel at a loss or experience "missing time." The viewer won't be able to navigate the map. A good VR scriptwriter thus learns to think in four dimensions—in both space and time.

An architect, by nature, recognizes patterns and can make giant, intuitive leaps. There is always a conceptual dimension to a process or structure that an architect will understand but that the layman viewer will not see until it's made manifest. Thus it is incumbent on the architect—and the scriptwriter—to show the viewer concrete, step-by-step solutions and to explain the benefits and advantages of each.

Having the concrete detail organized in a step-by-step manner, showing the problem and each detail of the solution, makes for a compelling story in virtual architecture, whether the goal is entertainment, education, demonstration, or marketing.

The most important point to remember in creating virtual architecture is that the architect, by nature, sees patterns in everything. The viewer, however, has to be taught to do this.

HOW TO SEE PATTERNS IN EVERYTHING

By stating the problem before showing how to solve it, by teaching the viewer to see patterns and make intuitive leaps, you can design a story that will involve the viewer until the end.

Ask yourself: What are you trying to say? If you can say it in a sentence of 10 words or less, you can produce a compelling, high-concept story told in virtual animation and narrative text, with viewer involvement and interaction.

For instance, if the point of your project is to involve poor, non-English speaking immigrants in the planning and design of their riot-torn community, you would certainly want much more than a fly through. You would want to involve the viewers more directly, to incorporate their suggestions and show them why those suggestions would or would not work. At its most dynamic, virtual architecture is a kind of dialogue, whether between humans and machines or between architects and clients.

TELEPRESENCE

Virtual architects have a powerful tool in telepresence, a form of VR that uses video cameras and remote microphones to project the viewer into a different location in real time. NASA Ames is using telepresence for planetary exploration. Architects use telepresence to see inside building structures not visible to the eye.

Telepresence is also used by architects who design hospitals and by medical-product designers who create surgical instruments operated by robotic control. Telepresence in surgical procedures enables doctors to see inside patients' bodies and organs.

Architects can apply the same principles to seeing inside of structures to inspect whether they are sound. Telepresence will play a big part in the future of virtual reality.

By matching the human agent with a contact surface, telepresence can help the virtual architect adapt a design to the different needs of different individuals—for instance, by measuring the accessibility of an area for physically-challenged people.

VIRTUAL ARCHITECTURE FOR THE PHYSICALLY CHALLENGED

The virtual architect must be sensitive to the particular needs of a client, especially for the physically challenged. For instance, a suitable VR simulation for a wheelchair user must keep a single point of view above ground level or from the height of the wheelchair. When designed with sensitivity, virtual rehabilitation enables a disabled person to drive a wheelchair through buildings, buses, and across streets in the same way the individual would move while actually commuting from home to the workplace.

To do this, the rehabilitation architect hooks up a disabled person's wheelchair to a VR system. The rehabilitation architect then creates a complete model of how the person in the wheelchair moves through a house, office, or entire city. Architectural models of buildings and interiors of homes, even gardens, can be simulated in three dimensions through VR.

Its usefulness is in creating designs that give wheelchair-based people better access to buildings, public transportation, and streets. Rollers underneath a wheelchair feed information to a computer, which creates, controls, and manages the VR simulations.

Architects can also use VR systems that track the progress of a handicapped commuter going to and from work. VR tracking that measures movement and control enables physically-challenged people to monitor their progress. At a rehabilitation center, a VPL DataSuit can help track a person's entire body movements for use in rehabilitation programs.

In the world beyond the hospital, virtual architects can help people with disabilities by redesigning the buildings they frequently navigate in wheelchairs. At the Hines Rehabilitation and R&D Center in Chicago, Dr. John Trimble and Ted Morris have developed a wheelchair simulator using Sense8 software to test building designs for wheelchair accessibility.

The Americans with Disabilities Act requires buildings and public spaces to accommodate the handicapped commuter. Virtual architecture makes it easier to test the designs using 3-D imaging, modeling, or simulations.

In the past, architects had to build bulky cardboard models and try to navigate wheelchairs through the huge mazes. Or wheelchair users were asked to express their needs verbally or in writing instead of illustrating them visually.

Blueprints are hard to draft based on verbal statements. Now that virtual architecture is possible, designers download computer-generated floor plans from software.

Buildings are tested by having the VR program use a real wheelchair installed on a platform that transfers the wheel movement into navigational data for the personal computer. Virtual architects don goggles and a VPL DataGlove to navigate the building.

The researchers test how accessible the shelves, doors, and drawers are for the wheelchair commuter. Using width parameters, the virtual wheelchair is prevented from passing through doorways that are too narrow. The system also can be used by businesses and schools who need to construct public bathrooms with doors wide enough and toilets high enough to accommodate the wheelchair user.

As buildings are tested for accessibility by virtual reality simulations, the architects find themselves immersed in the world of the physically-challenged wheelchair rider, or in the virtual world of the sight impaired or deaf person, the person who uses crutches or a walker, or the elderly person who can no longer climb stairs or step from a too-high bus step to the curb.

Virtual architecture teaches designers what it feels like to enter the world of the handicapped and see it from a wheelchair. Virtual architecture research is also addressing the needs of the aging, who need more accessible buildings and transportation.

Home imaging systems are now available to educate the physically challenged on transportation and building facilities. Virtual architecture is thus rapidly being integrated with medical simulation research.

Companies such as Boeing, Rockwell, Sense8, and others—including NASA—are helping architects involved in the rehabilitation field. Virtual architecture must continue to integrate industrial, instructional, and medical simulations in order to design functional buildings that are accessible to people with a variety of disabilities. Not only must buildings be accessible to people in wheelchairs, but elevators and computers in the workplace must be available by touch to the blind or multi-handicapped worker.

● ● ● ● ● ● ● ● ● ● ● ● ● ● ● ●

Virtual architecture teaches designers what it feels like to enter the world of the handicapped and see it from a wheelchair. Virtual architecture research is also addressing the needs of the aging, who need more accessible buildings and transportation.

VIRTUAL THERAPY FOR ACROPHOBICS

The Kaiser-Permanente Medical Group in Marin County, California, has developed a trial VR system for the treatment of patients with a fear of heights. In a ground-breaking study headed by Dr. Ralph Lamson, "virtual therapy" was shown to help more than 90 percent of participants reach their self-assigned treatment goals, such as walking over a narrow plank and crossing a suspension bridge spanning a deep gorge.

Dr. Lamson used Division's virtual environment-authoring software, PROVISION 100, to design a study that would determine the effects of immersing individuals in a computer-generated virtual environment in which they encounter the perception of depth and height. dVISE, Division's virtual-environment software, was used to develop a virtual world with a café, an elevated patio, and a plank leading from the patio to a bridge. Surrounding hills and water filled out the scene. Surfaces were given realistic textures, lighting, and shading.

Clients immersed in the believable environment moved through the scene, looking in all directions, exploring as they would in the real world. They walked to the edge of the plank and bridge as they looked below.

After encountering virtual heights and depths, participants then faced two real-world obstacles—such as driving across a bridge and riding a glass-enclosed elevator while viewing the surroundings.

Virtual reality has thus proved itself useful in treating phobias. According to Dr. Lamson, virtual architecture has clear advantages for helping those with environmental fears.

"Virtual therapy gives the individual an opportunity to approach the object they fear in a virtual environment," Lamson explained. "Being immersed in a virtual, feared situation is very close to reality. After the virtual therapy, participants feel as if they already have had a success in overcoming their fear. This is a strong confidence builder."

EXOTIC VIRTUAL ARCHITECTURE ON COMMONPLACE VHS VIDEO

You don't have to be an architect, physician, or scientist to use virtual architecture to make the world a better, friendlier, or safer place. Mindy Rosenblatt, owner of archiTREK, of Santa Barbara, CA, isn't an architect. She creates breathtaking computerized 3-D ArchiCAD architectural renderings and images on videotape for environmental impact reports and other projects.

One of the first times that animation became an integral part of the environmental review process was with an environmental-impact report

Rosenblatt did for the Samarkand retirement community in Santa Barbara. It proved to be both literally and figuratively ground-breaking.

Existing condition of a development site. *Courtesy of archiTREK.*

Rosenblatt runs a service bureau for architects, developers, planners, environmental consultants, builders, and for anyone wanting to see what an architectural project will look like before it exists. She creates fully-animated flybys, drivebys, and walk-throughs of a wide variety of projects, homes, and developments. The images are put on VHS videotape for easy home or office VCR viewing.

"I have found that few architectural firms can afford the resources or time to train their staff to produce high-end animation," Rosenblatt says. "By using independent firms such as archiTREK, even small architectural offices or individuals can access the valuable, visual resource animation provides."

Most people involved in designing and building find that plans are hard to visualize. Certainly it's difficult to visualize a house plan that doesn't exist. Decorators can't visualize well how a tiny patch of fabric will look when spread on the four walls of a large, sunny room if the room hasn't been built.

"I would tell interior designers to photograph the patch of fabric," Rosenblatt says, "have the photos scanned at Advanced Digital Imaging (ADI) onto a Photo CD master disc, then show clients how different fabric samples can change the feel and perception of the rooms."

A client may have a certain design in mind, but even scale models based on architects' blueprints don't guarantee the outcome. Virtual architecture makes it easier to visualize buildings from blueprints and to view them in their context. For instance, a simulated hotel is placed against an actual street and city background.

"I take the blueprint information, insert it into a CAD program, and construct a 3-D model," she explains. "I can take any texture or pattern and map it onto any surface in my 3-D image."

Rosenblatt can map almost anything into her drawings.

"I take pictures with a 35mm camera of images that no one else is going to photograph, like walls, roofs, floors, trees, bark, asphalt, gravel, and grass," she says. The film goes to Advanced Digital Imaging (ADI) in Fort Collins, Colorado, to be processed. It is then digitized onto Kodak Photo CD master discs.

Two days later, she has the compact discs, each of which holds up to 100 high-resolution images. This approach avoids the system-memory problems that might be caused by scanning the images directly into a PC. Kodak Photo CD technology takes the worry out of

How the site would look after development. _Courtesy of archiTREK._

memory-intensive graphics. Drivebys can take more than 2,400 frames of animation, with each frame containing one megabyte of data. Rosenblatt's two Macintosh Quadra 950 and 700 computers have up to 5 gigabytes of hard-disk memory.

What newer 3-D technology offers to interior decorators and designers, animators, renderers, and architectural support personnel is a set of better tools to map different textures onto architectural plans using computer simulation. Investors and civic planning commissions want a cost-effective way to see how projects will look before a lot of money is spent, and architects want a way to present realistic-looking proposals on VHS videotape. Because the resulting images can be transferred indefinitely to increasingly more sophisticated technology, Rosenblatt says, "you leave a mark for future generations."

VIRTUAL CREATION VERSUS MULTIMEDIA

Architects want new media concepts for less money. The people that architects sell to want a better environment to live in.

Everybody wants the illusion of control, which is precisely what architectural simulation sells. Garage VR, guerrilla marketing tactics, 3-D modeling, imaging, interactive media, and animation software are tools with the same ultimate ambition.

The differences between standard multimedia and virtual architecture are both economic and conceptual. In a multimedia presentation, a viewer watches a small square of videotape on a computer screen while listening to sound and reading narrative text. In high-end virtual reality, a viewer assembles complex 3-D

ArchiCAD has built-in tools to photorender and animate walk-throughs and fly-bys. *Courtesy of Graphisoft U.S., Inc.*

Modeled and rendered in ArchiCAD.

environments or navigates through territory, without having to stare at a computer screen and touch a keyboard.

Virtual architecture is merging with the animation industry. Both are potentially important community services seeking new applications while cranking out virtual 'Toon Towns. The visionaries in the architecture and animation industries want to create better worlds, but they want to do it on a shoestring budget. As a result, most architectural VR systems still have problems simulating realistic depth perception.

Macintosh, Power Macintosh, and Windows users can use architectural VR. *Courtesy of Graphisoft U.S., Inc.*

Modeled and rendered using ArchiCAD 4.5

Architectural VR tools include 2-D and 3-D drawings, initial design, and visualization. *Courtesy of Graphisoft U.S., Inc.*

Individual rooms and features can be designed with architectural VR. *Courtesy of Graphisoft U.S., Inc.*

In high-end virtual reality, a user can assemble complex environments. *Courtesy of Graphisoft U.S., Inc.*

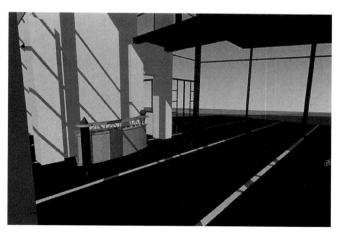

VR visionaries want to create better worlds. *Courtesy of Graphisoft U.S., Inc.*

TOWARD HIGH-RESOLUTION VIRTUAL ARCHITECTURE

You'd have to be crazy to balance a 10-pound head-mounted display on the bridge of your nose for hours at a time just to see what very-high resolution VR looks like. Architects are concerned that if they use the really high-end VR wherein the viewer is totally immersed in an environment, the viewer won't be able to accurately judge the distances. The viewer's perception will be skewed because people usually don't experience architecture by flying past buildings.

Virtual architecture is supposed to normalize VR by imitating human perception. Architects are supposed to have people walk through a room as they would do at home.

Generating and reproducing accurate information about human physiology is a prerequisite for effective virtual architecture. The images and information coming out of the new virtual architecture must match a person's perceptual system; therefore, virtual architecture must accommodate—and mimic—the senses. Matching the user's needs with the technology, allowing the user to keep a single point of view above ground level, and simulating realistic movement must remain important goals for the VR industry.

"Immersive media closely matches the human perceptual system," according to Rick Zobel of North Carolina State University's Virtual Environment Laboratory, "in terms of understanding what it means to walk through a building.

"As a direct participant," Zobel reported, "you can see what's above. If you're walking through a room in front of a screen, you must tell the viewpoint to show what's above your eye level."

· ·

A HISTORY AND SOME CURRENTS OF VIRTUAL ARCHITECTURE

In the recent past, some architects feared that virtual reality would dramatically alter structural design by bringing about architecture by "mob rule." According to architectural historian/researcher James Vincent of San Diego, the argument goes something like this:

"Would you trust building design to the person who has to live in that cramped house within that high-crime neighborhood, and work in that high-unemployment community?

"The person you're asking feedback from is part of the same body-piercing mob in the street who yelled incessantly, '1-2-3-jump' to the suicide leaper on top of that high-rise roof. Is that whose suggestions and directions you want to guide your architectural designs?"

Does the answer lie in politically-correct virtual architecture?

"If we have human resource managers asking for ways to make better use of employee suggestions, then architects must do the same," Vincent emphasizes. "People involved in their own residential and urban community planning want the power to control their world—virtual and real.

"Crowds out of control in their community can commandeer a virtual 'build it' game and play the frustration out of their systems by escaping to environments," he adds.

"It's the idealist's world, where action replaces hope," Vincent confesses. "Virtual architecture has a history of hiring experts with doctorates in psychology and ergonomics to design simulated environments. The field is so new, it's wide open.

"You don't need heavy experience in the computer industry to break into virtual architecture by serving architects in a variety of ways, such as creating animation or writing environmental impact reports. Anthropologists, science-fiction writers with master's degrees in creative writing, and archaeologists are often hired to develop those reports.

"Everyone hopes someone with money is listening to their architectural needs," Vincent says. "The history of virtual architecture is all about the need to control and manipulate those with money and power into helping communities get back some semblance of control over their home neighborhoods and nearby worksites. Look at what evolved historically from lampblack and the drafting table: Software that sells reality as escape."

At first there were only two-dimensional perspective drawings made by architect's drafters at a table. With the advent of the personal computer in the early eighties, AutoCad and other 3-D representations enabled architects and architectural drafters to use computer-aided design (CAD) to model finished designs.

Digital Technology became the first major developer for VR. As the control of the old analog machines of the seventies was taken over by digital circuits in the nineties, the computer's ability to control video made it an ideal medium for architects trying to build simulated cities or create virtual worlds in great detail.

Architects wanted a software that would enable 2-D and 3-D drawings, initial design, visualization, bill-of-materials, and working drawings. Contemporaneous with the advent of CAD software, animation software became available to AMIGA, MAC, and PC owners.

Since the eighties, entertainment-animation giants have looked overseas for animators, artists, and programmers who are willing to work for a cheaper wage than their American counterparts.

By the late nineties, will virtual architecture also turn to third-world countries, Asia, or Europe in search of low-cost creative labor? Since the mid-eighties, the number of college-level training programs in virtual reality, animation, and interactive multimedia production has dramatically increased. Will industry be willing or able to absorb all the new graduates trained in virtual architecture?

Two-user plant design. *Courtesy of Division Inc.*

Two-user office design. *Courtesy of Division, Inc.*

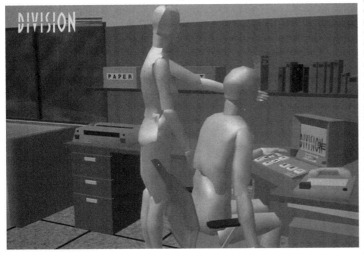

The CIBC Training Center.
Courtesy of Lightscape Technologies, Inc.

In the late eighties and early nineties, multimedia using graphics, text, video, and sound on CD-ROM flooded the PC market, creating the home-based electronic desktop publishing and desktop video industries, including the phenomenon of the home-based computerized rendering business serving architects, designers, developers, and animators.

The mid-nineties have brought garage VR and immersive virtual reality at a variety of levels and costs. CD-ROM databases of images, textures and animations have recently become available, such as AutoDesk's four-CD collection of sample image files for architectural, mechanical, landscaping, automotive, and corporate marketing applications.

Very high-end integrated software is now available for VR applications, such as Graphisoft's ArchiCAD, which is the only dedicated architectural software that has built-in tools to photorender and animate walk-throughs and fly throughs.

Compact video discs have enhanced virtual architecture's broadcastability. High-resolution sound and video have fulfilled a public demand to experience urban architecture as animated entertainment.

Jerusalem City Hall. *Courtesy of Lightscape Technologies, Inc.*

The University of Western Ontario. *Courtesy of Lightscape Technologies, Inc.*

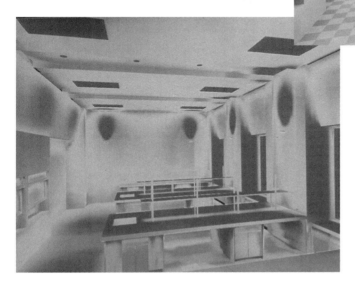

Pseudo-color rendering of the previous image, showing illumination levels. *Courtesy of Lightscape Technologies, Inc.*

Unity Temple, which was designed by Frank Lloyd Wright in 1904. *Courtesy of Lightscape Technologies, Inc.*

The Ontario Legislature Building. *Courtesy of Lightscape Technologies, Inc.*

Architects can now use video compact discs to bring to neighborhoods complex blueprints and visual representations. In 1994, Texas Instruments introduced a set of chips that it hopes will make video compact discs as common as audio CDs. Big-name movie companies, such as MGM, Paramount, and Columbia, and major record companies plan to offer Video CD products in the near future. Watch for the first hardware in your favorite electronics store; it will be audio CD players featuring Video CD. You can play your audio CDs on Video CD players, too.

By the early nineties, software-authoring tools enabled users to put narrative text on CD-ROM or disk to simplify complex blueprints and obtain feedback through interactive media. Interactive media and high-end virtual reality, both of which are spin-offs of space-industry training simulations, filtered down to PC users.

The publishing industry responded with a proliferation of magazines dedicated to VR, interactivity, and multimedia users at all levels. Four million CD-ROM discs are expected to be sold in 1994, double the two million sold in 1993.

The MultiMedia Bookstore in Findlay, Ohio, predicts that by 1999, 45 million CD-ROM discs will be in use. Already architects place their screen shots (slides) on CD-ROM discs as well as on videotape.

The next generation of virtual architects is seeking ever-cheaper ways to immerse the viewer. It is still looking to the space industry for more advanced spin-offs of simulations, and it is still guided by these three principles:

- To find new ways to make the keyboard and computer screen disappear.
- To go where people cannot.
- To make learning more fun.

THE FUTURE: WHO'S WATCHING THE WATCHERS?

As VR technology becomes smaller, cheaper and more commonplace, people will be projected into seemingly unreachable locations. They will travel inside buildings, pipes, microscopes, or arteries to make necessary repairs. They will travel across continents or across time itself to browse, select, fix, enjoy, and buy. Someday, home-shopping channels will link with virtual architecture to help people choose and customize their environments. Supercomputers will be connected to living-room entertainment centers.

But there are serious questions about virtual architecture that futurists, trend forecasters, industrial anthropologists, psychologists, science-fiction writers, and venture capitalists are only now starting to ask: Where is virtual architecture heading? What is its "prime directive?" What is its place in the cyberlife?

Teams of futurists, including myself, are being assembled to study virtual architecture from a psychological and anthropological perspective. Will virtual architecture become a new international language? Are we whatever our virtual architecture makes us? Will it lead us to a kinder and gentler world, or to enslavement by a centralized bureaucracy? Where does the virtual task force go for coffee?

No one is watching the watchers. We have to watch ourselves. Ironically, the brave new world of virtual reality reminds us that we're scarcely removed from our paleolithic past. If the technology is not used as a tool of our evolution and eduction, it could well become an agent of our extinction.

Virtual Reality

chapter 4
by Valerie Promise and
Christopher Van Buren

Virtual reality is, or promises to be, the ultimate computer experience.

VR: WHAT IT IS

Imagine a computer interface that looks like real life, sounds like real life, and even feels like real life. Imagine a technology so life-like that you can operate it without a manual.

Such a technology has been emerging over the last couple of decades, but it has only become a commercially viable possibility in the 1990s. It is called *virtual reality* (or VR). The term "virtual," as used here, is a technical term that typically refers to a software simulation. (In computerese, you can have virtual memory, virtual disks, virtual devices, and so on.)

Virtual reality is a make-believe environment that you relate to intuitively, just as you relate to the real world. All the processing still happens inside a plain, old desktop computer, but in state-of-the-art virtual reality applications, the "central command post" has input and output devices that enable human beings to interact with it in a more human, less machine-like way.

For instance, if you are moving through a virtual reality environment and you want to go forward, you simply place one foot in front of the other. If you want to look at something above your head, you look up. If you want to pick something up, you curl your fingers around it and apply upward force.

Even when special input and output devices are not used, the design of a good VR application invites the user to treat the rendered environment it as if it were "real life" outside the computer.

Besides the user-friendly interface, another hallmark of virtual reality is that it's interactive. As a user, you're not just along for the ride; rather, you're an active participant, and sometimes even the master of all you survey. The objective of this interactivity can be education, entertainment, or telepresence—transplanting your consciousness to a location where you're not physically able to be, such as the inside of a human pancreas or the surface of Mars.

WORKING IN CYBERSPACE

VR is more than just a potential arcade amusement. For instance, one promising application of VR technology is in surgery. Programmers can create a computer representation of the human heart and apply it to a dummy, on which medical students could perform practice bypass operations.

In state-of-the-art VR, special input/output devices create the experience of being immersed in a separate realm. The computer can accept input from the user's body via tracking devices, such as a helmet, goggles, gloves, a belt, shoes, or any combination of these. Electrosensitive elements within these implements track the movements of the corresponding parts of the body. One of the ways they do this is by sensing the activity of the different muscle groups. Gloves have sensors between each of the fingers and on top of the knuckles to register the degree to which the fingers spread or bend.

Some companies are even working on complete bodysuits that will detect the user's slightest movements.

However, not every application needs to have such a sophisticated interface. In fact, it's possible—and more practical—to run such applications with the technology that most end-users have been exposed to for so many years: the monitor and the mouse. This makes sense in applications where manual dexterity is not the point, where users are not learning to do things with their hands. For instance, if you're using a program that helps you design a house, you don't need to learn how to put up drywall or install wiring.

The CyberGlove, by Virtual Technologies of Palo Alto, CA. *Courtesy of Virtual Technologies.*

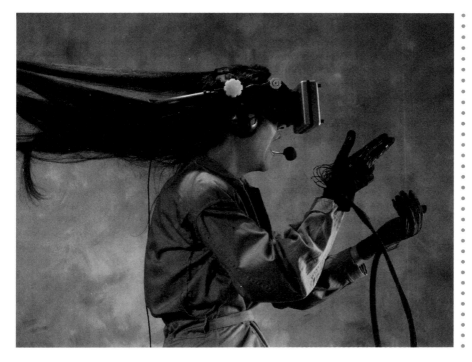

A user immersed in the Virtual Interactive Environment Workstation (VIEW) at NASA Ames Research Center in Mountain View, CA. *Courtesy of NASA.*

When a medical student is practicing surgery, however, manual dexterity is precisely the point. A virtual reality application could feature a very realistic model of the human heart. It could be animated, so that it would actually behave like a heart, with atria and ventricles contracting and releasing in a regular rhythm. The surgeon would have the typical surgeon's-eye view of the heart. Because this would be surgical practice, input would come from datagloves, which, like a mouse, take input from the user and translate it into electrical signals the computer understands.

The surgeon puts on a helmet and visor through which she can see a lifelike view of the beating heart in the open chest of a surgical patient. Now, as the surgeon moves her hand forward, the representation of her hand on the screen (inside the helmet) also moves forward. She looks down and sees an area of the chest lateral to the incision (since she's standing at the patient's side). She turns her head to one side and sees the patient's abdomen. She looks to the other side and sees the patient's neck and head.

She can pick up some surgical thread—perhaps by uttering a spoken command into a microphone—and tie off blood vessels that mustn't be active during this procedure. She can pick up a scalpel or scissors to make different kinds of cuts. In every case, her actions will produce exactly the same results as they would on a real operating table.

Best of all, the patient always survives.

In this scenario, the virtual environment mimics the persective of a human being. But the same program could be configured from the point of view of a red blood cell as it navigates through the chambers of the heart and courses through the blood vessels of the body.

THE BRAVE NEW WORLD OF VIRTUAL REALITY

The technological foundation of virtual reality was originally developed to deal with life-and-death scenarios of a different sort. During World War II, military trainers noticed that if novice pilots survived five missions, they were far more likely to survive the whole war. The idea occurred to them that the first five flights could be make-believe ones, utilizing computer simulation. Rookie pilots could be fastened into equipment that imitated the look and feel of a real flight. In those early days, a lot of it had nothing to do with computers, but even today, such simulators are still on active duty at NASA's Ames Research Center in Mountain View, CA.

Today there are distinct levels of what we call virtual reality. Some purveyors of VR products, including Autodesk of Sausalito, CA, believe that the greatest impact of the new technology can be achieved with the standard monitor-and-mouse setup. On the other end of the spectrum, VR can require a total immersion, and its input and output devices can be quite effective in cutting off the user from receiving sensory stimulation from the outside world.

But what is it that makes virtual reality such a trendy topic today, even before the technology is completely reliable and accessible?

I call it technological manifest destiny. Just as Americans in the 19th century thought it was God's will for America to spread itself from sea to shining sea, no matter what the cost, the modern sensibility craves technological evolution, without necessarily giving any thought to its place in the ultimate social scheme of things. Just as we *had* to create the automobile, the personal computer, the atomic bomb, and the Home Shopping Network, so too we are compelled to develop virtual reality, merely because we *can*.

Virtual reality is, or promises to be, the ultimate computer experience. In the unfolding of time, we've used technology to automate almost every aspect of our lives. However, up until now, the interfaces (such as the conversations between us and our machines) have not been intuitive. We've had to operate the machines by whatever method the engineers dictated, and we've had to learn separately for each machine. A VCR has a different interface from a toaster oven, which has a different interface from a washing machine, which has a different interface from a photocopier, and so on. Now, with virtual reality, we can put the automated functions together with our intuition, the way we always did things before the Industrial Revolution. Ultimately, there promises to be a seamless merging between the natural and the digitized.

At least in theory, the new technology promises great benefits for all of us, from the most sophisticated to the most technologically illiterate.

THE SCOPE OF THE TECHNOLOGY

At the high end of the technology, one of the markets most poised for developing VR applications is engineering and architecture. CAD (computer-aided design) has revolutionized architecture and engineering, but until recently, something was still missing: three-dimensionality. After all, engineers and architects design three-dimensional products, and that third dimension is not one that can be overlooked. That is why, after creating a design on paper, an architect or engineer produces a model as kind of a dry run. But model-building takes time, and if you want to make a substantial adjustment, the whole model has to be built all over again. With a virtual reality setup—such as Autodesk's CyberCAD—the designer and client can experience three-dimensionality, not just in miniature, but as a virtual environment through which they can seem to walk or even fly.

Autodesk's CyberCAD lets you "walk" or "fly" around a location as you build it, using only a mouse and monitor. *Courtesy of Autodesk.*

Frank Lloyd Wright's "Fallingwater" house is demonstrated as an interactive application. These perspectives show the details of living room furniture and exterior design, including texture maps. *Courtesy of Laura and Alex Sanchez.*

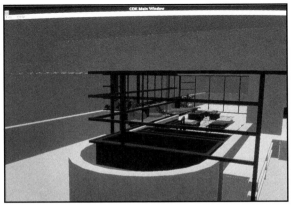

Many software developers have come up with very specialized uses for this technology. For instance, you can buy packages that enable you to design your own bathroom or landscape a piece of property. These software packages often come with prefabricated virtual objects, such as toilets and stoves and rosebushes. You choose the object you want, and then place it where you want. (These are not bodily-immersion simulators, so you will not be picking up a 200-lb. virtual toilet.) You could, if you wanted to, stack four toilets on top of each other, or perch a stove in the branches of your rosebush.

Working in a larger scale is even more impressive. In a famous demonstration at the Massachusetts Institute of Technology's Media Lab in 1981, researchers put together a project called the Aspen Movie Map. In it, you could navigate around Aspen, CO, as if you were driving a car through it, having the same choices at each intersection that you would have if you were driving. Although the imagery was collected on video disk, giving it a much higher resolution than the standard VR fare, it's surprising that this landmark project

This exterior perspective of "Fallingwater" house highlights some of the architectural details of this highly accurate model. *Courtesy of Laura and Alex Sanchez.*

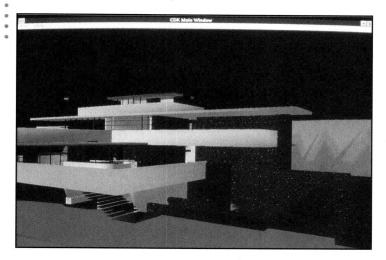

This perspective view highlights some of the interior details of the model, such as wall-to-wall carpeting. *Courtesy of Laura and Alex Sanchez.*

hasn't had many imitators by now—surely there's a fortune to be made in this kind of armchair travel.

At the simpler end of the spectrum, virtual reality can be applied to just about any training situation you can imagine. You can train post office workers to sort mail, or baseball players to improve their batting, or Taco Bell workers to sprinkle cheese over tostadas.

One author has suggested the possibility of having high-school and college students do their biology-lab dissections on virtual animals. That would make a lot of people—and animals—very happy. (Look, Ma, no formaldehyde!) You could dissect the same virtual animal over and over again. (In real life, this is only possible with salamanders—who can regrow severed tails—and even then, not on the same day.)

Procedures that are ordinarily messy or resource-intensive are good candidates for virtual reality training sessions. Cars could be accompanied by virtual reality software that would let the owner practice changing the virtual oil before attempting the real thing. An aspiring soufflé maker could bake up a virtual soufflé and learn to avoid slamming the virtual oven door.

THE SENSORY COMPONENTS OF VR

The question arises: Can you taste a virtual soufflé? Sorry, no go. Not even a virtual brussel sprout.

Virtual reality has a long way to go before it comes close to approximating the reality we know and love.

Visual perception has been translated fairly well into virtual reality applications and exceptionally well on computer screens in general. Resolution (the measure of how crisp the picture is) is still not nearly as good in a head-mounted display as it is on a standard desktop monitor. The more you pay, the better it gets, but inevitably you give up some acuity in the pursuit of three-dimensional immersion. (A top-of-the-line virtual reality helmet sells today for about $100,000.)

In VR applications, there is also a tradeoff between visual detail and the speed of rendering. This may not be readily apparent, but when you drag an object across a computer display, or even scroll down in a document, you are, in effect, creating your own movie. The computer must redraw the object in its new position, often several times over. It does this pixel by pixel, with a total of hundreds of thousands, or even millions, of pixels per screen. If that sounds like a resource-intensive task, it is. Because virtual reality is set up to respond to you just as a real-life environment would, the speed of response is of critical importance, while the complexity of the image is secondary. Images must be kept simple in order to be manipulated quickly. That's why all the pictures you see of virtual reality environments are so abstracted. (In static applications, the computer can easily reproduce an image with the complexity of a Rembrandt.)

In the auditory realm, voice synthesis—that is, a computer's ability to read text aloud in a preprogrammed voice—has been around for a while. Voice recognition, however, is still in its infancy. Apple Computer Co., when it was working on a voice-recognition project, once distributed T-shirts that said on the front, "I helped Apple wreck a nice beach" (showing a shoreline littered with apple cores), and on the back, "I helped Apple recognize speech." Not only do the real-life speech habits of human beings befuddle computers, but, to a computer, one voice is puzzlingly different from the next. In those rare applications where voice recognition is being used today, the program must be custom-tailored to recognize the voice of its "master."

Some progress is being made in the tactile and kinesthetic capabilities of VR. While we're still far from the day when we can revel in the warmth of virtual sunshine on our upturned

Virtual reality has a long way to go before it comes close to approximating the reality we know and love.

faces or the crunchy texture of fall leaves beneath our feet, input and output devices are increasingly sensitive to fluctuations in weight, volume, force, gravity, density, and the like. NASA's Virtual Planetary Exploration (VPE) program, for instance, gives the user a sense of the reduced gravity of the moon and other planetary surfaces. NASA also has a wind environment where you can actually *see* a representation of wind as it pushes against a surface.

With the Autodesk demo called Chain, the balls are endowed with mass and density. They are strung together on an invisible string, which acts like a spring. If you "ping" one of the balls, it will simulate real-life ball behavior under similar circumstances. It will bounce into the other balls, which also start moving, then bounce back, with all of the balls returning to their resting state within a few seconds.

You can change the gravitational force on the balls so they behave as they might on the moon, or you can make them entirely weightless. You can detach the string from one of the posts, and watch the balls fall down (if there's gravity) or watch them move toward the opposite post (if there's no gravity).

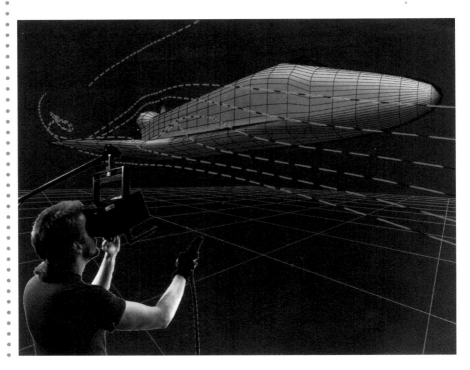

A visual representation of aerodynamics. *Courtesy of NASA.*

An Autodesk demo called Chain, created with Autodesk's Cyberspace Developers' Kit. The user can interactively control a lot of the balls' behavior. *Courtesy of Autodesk.*

Virtual billiards from a ball's-eye perspective. *Courtesy of Autodesk.*

Likewise, with a virtual billiards game, complex physical interaction must be programmed in. In the billiards application, you can experience the principles of collision detection, conservation of momentum, angle of reflection, and function at work.

At this point, in the strictest sense, taste and smell are out of the picture entirely. In a less strict sense, they can nonetheless be included in the virtual environment, by non-digital means. In 1961, filmmaker Mort Heilig introduced Sensorama, a self-contained, arcade-type "theatre" designed for an audience of one, which, in addition to other sensory experiences, injected aromas into the viewing environment. None of the Sensorama configuration used computers. Nowadays, a computer could trigger a machine to release an odor when needed, but a computer cannot actually create an odor, because an odor is a molecule that makes physical contact with the user's olfactory apparatus. The same obstacle applies to taste sensations. (Conceivably, in the sophisticated future, the computer could be connected to electrodes on the person's scalp, which could stimulate the exact region of the brain that creates the experience of a particular smell or taste. Our experiences, after all, happen inside our brains. Sensory organs are just the avenue that directs the information into it.)

THINGS UNDREAMED OF

Virtual reality can do more than just imitate the existing world. New media with new attributes inevitably generate their own new applications, applications that could not have been imagined in the old order. Photography is not just an improvement on painting. Movies are not just a portable form of theatre. Digital synthesizers are not just a means of amplifying or reproducing traditional musical instruments. Thus, 20 or 50 years from now, people reading books such as this will be chuckling to themselves at how benighted their predecessors were, that we didn't see the obvious application of _____ (fill in the blank) in our discussion of virtual reality.

One application that expands virtual reality into a whole other dimension is called telepresence. This means that, in a way, you can be where you're not; that is, you can act upon an environment in which you're not physically present. This is different from, say, astral projection, and it takes a lot more hardware. In NASA's case, it can be done with robots. The robot talks to your desktop computer via an interchange of signals—probably transmitted to and from a satellite. You, through your input devices, can pick up rocks on the lunar surface and stow them in your spacecraft; you can move around the lunar surface at will, assessing the environment through the robot's "eyes" (video cameras) and other sensors; you can manipulate instruments that analyze the lunar environment. Simultaneously, you can be back at your desk near Moffett Field, accessing the database in an effort to categorize your findings.

Similarly, you could do Rome.

Telepresence, like video teleconferencing, can be used to link you remotely with friends, family, and associates. Unlike video teleconferencing, telepresence enables you to project a fantasy self, if you like. You create a representation of yourself in someone else's cyberspace—and vice versa—with which to interact.

In shared cyberspace, you and your associates can manipulate the virtual environment, drinking virtual beer at a virtual bar, listening to virtual music from a virtual band, and avoiding virtual police as you virtually drive home under the virtual influence.

The frivolity of the preceding scenario notwithstanding, it is not unthinkable that people in the future who are beset with addictions might be able to create a reality of their choosing in cyberspace, even one that mimicked their favorite drug state, with no danger of cirrhosis of the liver, midnight munchies, or other assorted physiological woes. Of course, the VR junkie would still be stuck with an addictive personality. (Maybe there will be a market for a virtual 12-step program.)

In shared cyberspace, you and your associates can manipulate the virtual environment, drinking virtual beer at a virtual bar, listening to virtual music from a virtual band, and avoiding virtual police as you virtually drive home under the virtual influence.

ART FOR ART'S SAKE

As with other art forms, designing a virtual environment is an opportunity to create and develop an alternative reality that reflects your imaginative powers. You can create a world where the ground is up and the sky is down, where the stars come out during the day, where all objects are transparent, and where cars drive smoothly on square wheels. These possibilities are available even now.

Unlike with most other art forms, the world you create can be interactive. It can function like participatory theatre, in equal collaboration with others. Or, you can create a relatively stable and controlled theatrical environment, with prescribed characters interacting in cyberspace according to the will of the artist/designer. Even existing plays could be transliterated into this new medium.

Likewise, playwrights and directors could use cyberspace as a development tool that would help them position characters and props on a stage before committing their ideas to paper or involving the labor of real actors and a stage crew.

DON'T BLAME ME—
I'M JUST A COMPUTER

In creating a virtual world, you can apply as much imagination as you want, but you must still be specific in your instructions to the computer. When you design a virtual space, you need to include in your program some basic laws of physical reality. For instance, say you've got a geometric form on your screen, and you're enabling the user to fly around it. Unless you tell the computer otherwise, the user can also fly right through that form. You might have done very well in describing—by mathematical equations—what the surface is supposed to look like, but you need to also specify what it should act like. In this instance, you might want to build in something called *collision detection*, so that the computer branches to another routine when the insertion point intersects with the surface. With collision detection, you can describe what will happen if you ("you" being the entity represented by the cursor) bounce. Should you stick? Should you smash the geometric form into tiny pieces? Should you send it sailing off into the far reaches of cyberspace, like a billiard ball? In other words, you need to describe the properties of the form and of its surface.

Another interesting characteristic of forms in cyberspace is one-sided rendering. This means that if you create a form with an inside and an outside, only the outside is available to experience (assuming that you created the form from the perspective of someone standing outside and looking in). Say you make a wigwam or teepee, which is basically a cone. You, as the user, sail through the door—or through the wall, if there isn't any collision detection—and you see...nothing. It won't automatically look like the inside of a teepee. If you want it to look like the inside of a teepee, you have to tell the computer.

Then there's the *clipping plane*. Objects in cyberspace are allowed to travel only so far, and then they hit a wall. Actually, they don't hit the wall—they sink into the wall, without making any cracks in it. They just slide right on through, into the primal cybersoup. Therefore, it is necessary that the programmer specify the dimensions of the virtual space.

The user's movement through the space is also prescribed in the programming. Bodily-immersion VR can mimic real life, but there often isn't a one-to-one correspondence. If you move your hand forward an inch in physical reality, it might or might not move forward an inch in the virtual environment. It might move a quarter-inch, it might move a foot. It's something like trying to park vehicles of different sizes—you might know the right moves, but you have to scale them up or down to accommodate the size of the vehicle. Similarly, you, as a user, have to scale your bodily movements to fit the dynamics of the new space. And the programmer, conversely, needs to map the space as well as possible to the intuitive movements of the body.

When you're using a standard mouse, you're faced with the need to collapse many dimensions of movement into the limited number of functions available on the mouse (between one and four, depending on whether your computer accepts input from any of the secondary mouse buttons). In many applications, for instance, you move forward in the space not by moving the mouse forward on the desk, but by clicking the left mouse button. Moving the mouse to one side or the other rotates you in that direction—so that you're seeing from a different perspective—rather than moving you laterally along a line. Looking up or down is accomplished by moving the mouse forward or backward, respectively.

However, there are now three-dimensional mice on the market that let you move in "six degrees of freedom," which means that, besides moving linearly along the x, y, and z axes, you can also roll from side to side, pitch backward and forward, and yaw, or spin, around the vertical axis. This gives you great freedom of movement from a small handheld device, which enables you to move more intuitively than is possible with a standard mouse, yet more simply than can be done with a head-mounted display.

• •

STALKING THE DEADLY DACTYL

New realities can be designed for the realm of entertainment as well as art. Virtual reality is now becoming established in the consumer entertainment market, with installations such as Edison Brothers Entertainment's Dactyl Nightmare, a glorified video arcade game that permits two players to compete against each other—and a menacing pterodactyl—in cyberspace. Dactyl Nightmare is not a very portable setup. Each player stands inside his or her own pod and dons a head-mounted display. The input device is a gun-like object. As a player, you find yourself in a dreamscape, kind of an abstracted palatial environment with no walls and only the dark "sky" above. You can navigate around this space by turning 360 degrees inside your pod, and you can move forward or backward by using the hand control. You can also use the hand control as a gun, to shoot at your enemy—the other player—or the ever-menacing pterodactyl.

Some VR-based, role-playing games are especially engaging. In BattleTech, players are grouped in teams of four. The "cockpit" features over 100 controls (not all of which are necessary), which allows plenty of room for growth as players become more competent with the game.

In England, a game called Legend Quest appeals to a somewhat high-brow audience. The characters and dynamics are based on Jungian archetypes—wizards and warriors—rather than twentieth-century commandoes. The game utilizes a quest motif and rewards cooperation among the four players instead of having them shoot each other up, as most video games tend to do. Each player picks a character; the suspension of disbelief is augmented by electronics that transform the player's voice into the character's. Participants in Legend Quest can become lifetime members; with membership they receive a smart-key memory chip that stores all of their previous activities in the game and enables them to resume play from where they left off. For some players, it's much more than a game—it's a way of life.

LOOKING DOWN THE ROAD

Virtual reality is a technology that is still in its infancy, but it offers a phenomenal spectrum of possibilities. It figures to transform not just the way we interact with machines, but the way we interact with each other and with ourselves. Despite the hype, the revolutionary impact will be very real. How could it not be, when VR will enable us to create a reality—or many realities—exactly as we want it?

Consider a typical day in the ultra-virtualized world of the future. You start your day by video teleconferencing with your best friend in London, whose birthday it happens to be. No longer is the applicable motto "Long distance—the next best thing to being there." Now it's "Long distance—you *are* there." One good thing about life in the virtual world is that one set of apparel can suit you for every occasion. You slip on your ultra-sensitive data suit, complete with dainty cap and whisper-thin gloves, and you are ready to be transported.

No virtual reality system is complete without a virtual assistant to convey your needs and activities to Central Intelligence (really just your basic CPU), remembering your preferences as it does

so. If you wanted to, you could lease your assistant from any of the old flat-screen movies or TV shows, so that your assistant looked and acted like Big Bird from *Sesame Street*; Glinda, the Good Witch of the North from *The Wizard of Oz*: or E.T. But, because you are loathe to pay a premium just to be fashionable, you've decided to go with homemade and have your mom (or her virtual image) do it all for you.

When you put on your goggles, the virtual room looks just like your den, only "Mom" is sitting in a virtual armchair by a virtual bookcase, awaiting your instructions. You could have just as easily set the default environment to the North Pole or a street corner in Bombay, but that's the sort of thing beginners do. VR adepts tend to keep it simple and straightforward.

"Mom," you say, "call Regina." (In VR, you don't have to say "please.")

Mom checks to make sure you're ready. "All set?" she asks. If you say yes, you'll be telepresenced just as you are.

However, you might want to make some cosmetic adjustments. "Not yet," you say, "Give me my fairy godmother costume." Then you decide to change the ambience. "Give me Cinderella's ballroom." Your virtual room quickly morphs into a palatial ballroom, complete with waltzing characters. "OK. Now."

The phone rings through to London and Regina picks up. She knows what she's getting into because a sophisticated form of caller ID projects your virtual environment through to her virtual telephone monitor screen, along with the requisite bio-data. Regina answers, simultaneously agreeing, by pressing a virtual button, to be telepresenced into the space you've created for her. You can't talk for too long, but you take her out to the virtual garden and set off virtual fireworks in honor of her birthday.

Shortly afterward, back in your own virtual room and no longer a fairy godmother, you attend to the business of the day. You need to do some banking transactions, so you telepresence yourself to your virtual bank—which looks exactly as it does in real life. Transactions are managed by voice commands, and you have the satisfaction of handling virtual money that has all the right presidents (or celebrities) on the right denominations.

Similarly, you telepresence to the library to do some research. This time, Mom travels with you, because you need a research assistant who's conversant with your needs. Mom remembers dozens of different ways to search for the information you need, so for each search, she automatically cross-references a list of seven or eight synonyms of the keyword.

In the course of your research, you come across a reference to ancient Mediterranean blown glass, and you wonder how it was made. Fortunately, at this library a virtual hands-on experience is yours for the asking. There you are, in an ancient glass factory, with the master ready to show you how it's done. You only get one demonstration, but you can repeat it ad infinitum. When you're ready, you can try it yourself. You select the virtual ingredients for the virtual mixture, dip the virtual rod into the virtual goop, and blow. If you don't get the mixture right, the master's voice says, "That needs more stirring." As you blow, the master encourages you, breath by breath.

It turns out that you're a natural. You love what you've created; but unfortunately, there's some virtual bureaucracy in your way. You can't take your virtual piece home with you, because the programmer hasn't made objects of that sort detachable from the experience. (It's due for a fix next month, though.)

As long as you're browsing through antiquity, you decide that you might as well stroll through ancient Jerusalem. It's pretty well mapped out—although, unfortunately, a lot of it is based on conjecture—so that you can wander at will among the narrow, winding streets and encounter the same cultural and geographical phenomena you would have seen had you been alive at that time. In this particular VR experience, you can go to the marketplace and bring some goodies back "home." (Why go travelling if you can't bring back souvenirs?)

The Jerusalem marketplace reminds you that you need to do some regular American shopping. "Let's go home, Mom," you suggest. Then it's on to the virtual mall, where you just point and click at appealing items in order to make purchases. Sadly, it takes a whole day for them to be delivered to your physical door. (The impulse loses its thrill when you don't own the thing immediately after you buy it.)

You've had enough—you're "virtualed" out. You've been reading and hearing reports about how spending too much time in virtual reality causes brain damage; but you are willing to put up with some minor risks for the convenience of moving around from continent to continent and century to century, at will. Besides, if your brain gets damaged, it's a simple matter for doctors to telepresence themselves into the brain and repair it, neuron by neuron.

Is this scenario farfetched? Probably. From a practical perspective, the technology will eventually let us know what it does best and in what areas it makes sense to deploy it. It's far more likely that virtual reality will alter just a few significant corners of our experience, rather than our whole lives. Whatever the results, let the games begin!

T3-D echnology

chapter 5

by Valerie Promise and
Christopher Van Buren

**Although 3-D has plenty
of applications in adver-
tising and video games,
cinema is the medium in
which a new technology
is apt to make its stron-
gest impression on the
public.**

INTRODUCTION

Three-dimensional imaging technology is as close as your television. It's one of those technologies that has crept up on us unawares, and its developments have been so evolutionary that we often don't even realize that we're seeing it. A natural outgrowth of static computer graphics, 3-D is now more significant for its animation capabilities than for giving depth to still images.

3-D imaging enables computers to create images that look convincingly three-dimensional, whether still or animated. Besides being able to generate scenes that accurately simulate real life, 3-D can also model the world of the imagination. It can also meld the two—for example, by animating the scanned-in image of a movie star or other celebrity. (Finally, a way to make politicians behave the way we want them to!)

The technical elements of 3-D technology have been with us for some time, but only recently, with the advent of more powerful computers, has 3-D become financially accessible.

Although 3-D has plenty of applications in advertising and video games, cinema is the medium in which a new technology is apt to make its strongest impression on the public.

CHARACTERISTICS OF 3-D

Three-dimensional technology is a whole different animal from two-dimensional computer graphics. State-of-the-art 3-D requires a specialized design process from the outset.

Some features that distinguish 3-D include:

- *Wire-frame* construction, followed by the *rendering*, or filling in, of surfaces and textures
- Use of "camera positions" to create the impression of a traditional film or video approach

- Use of simulated lights to replicate real-life lighting conditions

- An overall attempt at superrealism (although the present technology lends itself better to uniform regular surfaces)

- Use of the computer to generate animation sequences from *key frames*, where the artist specifies the starting frame and the ending frame, and the computer fills in everything in between

Two main reasons why 3-D technology has become so popular are (1) it reduces labor and thus potentially saves money, and (2) the designer can conjure images straight from the wilderness of the imagination and make them breathtakingly real. As a viable commercial technique, though, 3-D is still in its infancy. Consider that there are typically 24 frames per *second* in a standard film. It can take hours of computer time to render, or compile, *each frame*. The number of frames in a feature-length film would be 24 frames/sec×60 sec/min×120 minutes. (Of course, you wouldn't be rendering all of those frames, because you would use the computer to create many of them from the *key frames* that you specify.)

Filming in 3-D has the added advantage of *not* being real, and therefore of particular usefulness in scenes where people and property get blown to smithereens, tossed from tall buildings, or shot out of cannons. (Look Ma, no lawsuits!)

Traditionally when a movie depicted, say, a city being blown up, studio technicians would create a scale model of the scene, which would then be shot with an appropriate lens to make it look like a real city. And then they would actually trash it, burn it, fry it, whatever—at considerable cost and logistical effort.

But now such an effect can be achieved much more impressively in a computer fantasyland.

Filming in 3-D has the added advantage of *not* being real, and therefore of particular usefulness in scenes where people and property get blown to smithereens, tossed from tall buildings, or shot out of cannons. (Look Ma, no lawsuits!)

Advertisers love three-dimensional technology. It can provide an exciting personality to such a dull household object as a bottle of mouthwash. In a battle with bad breath, Listerine emerges heroic. You'll never take mouthwash for granted again.

With 3-D imaging, a designer can endow a previously lifeless object, such as a mouthwash bottle, with personality and pizzazz. *Courtesy of Pixar.*

HOW A 3-D SCENE IS CONSTRUCTED

Three-dimensional scenes can be created in the following ways. In each case, the scenes are created on a frame-by-frame basis. They can then be animated after they are constructed.

- *Modeling* creates three-dimensional shapes from scratch, starting with wire-frame geometric primitives and working outward to the surface.

- *Lofting* pulls a two-dimensional, wire-frame computer image into the third dimension.

- *Digitizing* is used to scan in the spatial coordinates of an actor or object (from sensors attached to the actor or object), which can later be manipulated.

- *Fractal algorithms* use mathematical formulas to generate randomized textures that can be used for backgrounds such as mountains, rocks, or foliage.

- *Particle systems* are collections of dots that can be moved around to convey the image of flowing water, blowing snow, drifting sand, and the like.

- *Metaballs* (not to be confused with meatballs) are something like the spheres you find in the geometric-primitives collection (described forthwith), but behave more like gels than like solids. Their main application is in simulating the human face via the organic-looking curves that can be obtained from this technology.

The ground-up process of 3-D animation starts with *geometric primitives*, or basic shapes, such as cones, spheres, cubes, and so on. They are called "primitives" because their proportions can be expressed by relatively simple mathematical equations. When you change the value of a variable in the equation, the shape on the screen changes correspondingly.

The computer handles this sort of operation very smoothly. However, once a surface texture is applied (later on), the image will include bitmapping, which means a description of the position and color of each *pixel* (that is, each dot on the screen) to a total of hundreds of thousands or even millions.

Next, you make the shapes look more like real life by using *Boolean operations*, which is a way of adding or subtracting forms geometrically. For instance, you could create the six faces of a die (that's the singular of "dice") by subtracting spheres (or portions of their surfaces) from each of the six faces of a cube. This process has very little in common with line drawing.

During the steps of the process, the objects continue to be handled in their wire-frame modality. This is comparable to the construction of a building, wherein the frame is constructed before any of the covering materials are applied.

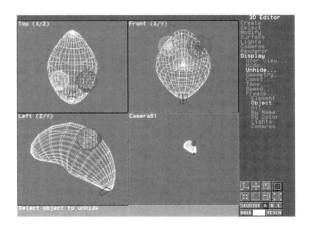

Wire-frame construction: the building blocks of 3-D technology. Objects (components of pictures) are shown in different colors to make them easier to work with. *Courtesy of Roger A. Rose, Cogswell Polytechnical College.*

Boolean operations let you customize geometric primitives into irregular, real-life shapes. Here, Boolean subtraction is used to make a dent in the creature's snout. *Courtesy of Roger A. Rose, Cogswell Polytechnical College.*

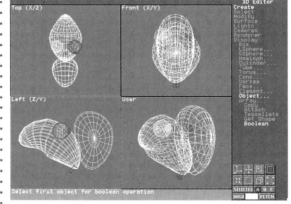

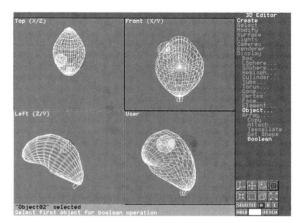

Although you might find it hard to translate the lines, angles, and arcs of a wire-frame drawing into, say, Santa Claus and his reindeer in your mind's eye, the wire-frame technique uses only a fraction of the computer resources that it would take to process a more fully rendered depiction of the same objects.

Alternately, your first step could be converting a two-dimensional image into a three-dimensional one. The task before you would then be to describe to the computer just how the shape should be filled out, what sort of depth it should have, and so on. In Autodesk's 3D Studio (a popular software used by high-end videographers), some of the options at this point include twisting, scaling, teetering, or beveling the shape, or even transforming it into a helix.

After the objects have been specified, surface textures are applied to the objects in a scene. Many programs contain a prefabricated list of materials—such as green glass, red plastic, wood inlay,

Two-dimensional figures can be "lofted" into three-dimensional equivalents, according to your specifications. *Courtesy of Roger A. Rose, Cogswell Polytechnical College.*

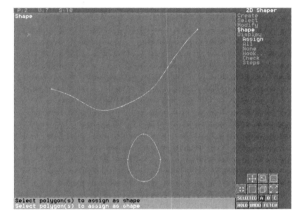

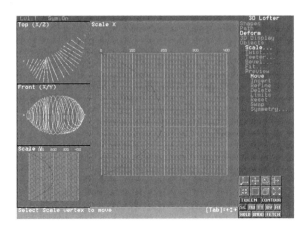

silver, copper, and chrome—which you can select to apply to your object with a couple of mouse clicks. Or you can create your own surface material by specifying what color it should be, how transparent or opaque it should be, how shiny or dull it should be, and what pattern it should display. As with many other parts of the animation process, plug-in modules are often available that provide you with whole libraries of textures that pick up where the freebies that came with the program leave off. Sometimes you can also edit the existing textures to customize the look you want. You also specify what the surface texture will be at this step in the process, but you never actually see the texture applied to the objects until the final rendering. Juggling all this information around in the computer's memory while you are still working on the scene would slow down processing speed tremendously.

After all of the objects are constructed, you assemble them into a scene that a camera, and ultimately an audience, will view. This step is comparable to assembling the actors and props on a movie set. When all are collected in one place, you (the *de facto* director) bring in the cameras and lights.

Selecting and positioning the camera and lights are the next steps. Three-dimensional animation software is capable of simulating most, if not all, of the capabilities of a movie camera. The most significant of these, of course, is the choice of lenses, or more accurately, lens lengths. As in still and motion-

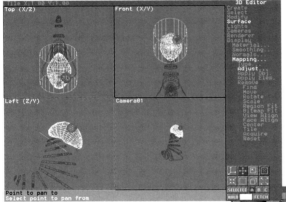

Libraries of surface materials let you easily layer real-life textures onto a wire-frame construction. *Courtesy of Roger A. Rose, Cogswell Polytechnical College.*

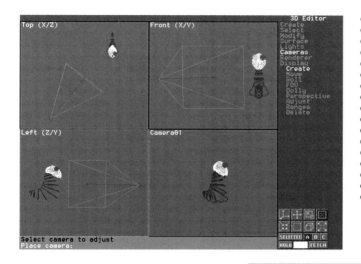

It's easy to position camera and lights by sliding them along the x, y, and z axes. Courtesy of Roger A. Rose, Cogswell Polytechnical College.

picture photography, the longer the lens, the more "telephoto" capacity it has; the shorter the lens, the more "wide-angle" capacity it has.

Also, you can control the depth of field, which means how much of the scene—measured from front to back—is in focus. A photographer or cinematographer will use a shallow depth of field in order to emphasize one element within a larger scene. For instance, you can have an actor's face be in focus, but the background may be a blur.

In standard moviemaking, there is usually more than one camera on the scene. A number of camera viewpoints are used to heighten interest and to create the effect of omniscience—that is, viewers are put in the position of seeing the scene from several angles, which has the effect of drawing them in, of engaging them. In the earliest filmmaking efforts,

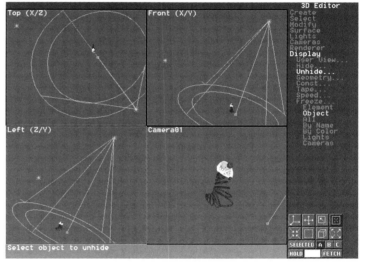

only one camera was used, from the point of view of someone watching a theatrical play in an audience. Soon, directors realized that having more than one point of view was something that distinguished this new medium from all others.

Although you can have more than one

camera position per frame in 3-D computer animation, scenes from other camera viewpoints are added during the editing process.

Lighting affects mood and emphasis. In theater, film, and video, lighting designers are artists in their own right—in effect, they paint with light. Rarely, if ever, does a scene rely on one light, even when the scene is supposed to be simulating light from the sun or a single light bulb. A complex configuration may be needed to convey the most simple effect. Typically, the designer will use one main light and several fills. This way, the designer can simulate everything from high-noon desert glare to midnight haunted-house shadows.

First, the lights are positioned to get the scene into the right ballpark. Then, for each light, you choose the brightness and the type of light source. Lights can be ambient (a general, overall lightedness, such as on a cloudy day), distant (all lit up, but from the same direction, like the sun), omni (an omnidirectional source, like a standard light bulb) or spot (a point source that's aimed directly at a subject, and nowhere else on the scene, like studio lighting).

You can place gels over the lights (digitally speaking, of course) to create a warmer or cooler effect. Some 3-D programs also include special-effects features for lights and shadows, like the light casting shadows through the windowpane.

And finally, there's the rendering phase. Most of the grunt work up until this point has been on the part of humans. Now it's the computer's turn to huff and puff. Rendering collects and makes sense of all the information you've so far input pertaining to the scene: the size, shape, and relative positions of the objects; the mathematical effect of the camera viewpoint on these components; and the calculation of the color and brightness of each of hundreds of thousands of pixels based upon the information about the surface materials and the settings of the light sources. One frame of 3-D imaging can thus contain about 1MB of information.

It can take an hour or more to render each frame—and that's on speedy, state-of-the-art computer systems. If you were doing this in your garage, it could take all night.

The bulk of the computer's task involves calculating the light for each pixel, based on the specifications you've set for the lights. In real life, lighting is a complex proposition, especially indoor lighting, wherein a number of sources illuminate each object from different directions. An animation director uses comparable lights in an animated scene to achieve a believable look. Multiple light sources translate into complex equations for the computer to calculate. It takes lots of number-crunching for the computer to create a thing of beauty.

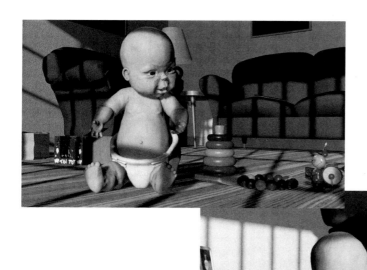

3-D lighting capabilities create the effect of sun streaming through a windowpane in Pixar's *Tin Toy*, a short, computer-animated film. *Courtesy of Pixar.*

When the rendering is done, you come out with a single frame. Of course, if you are creating a still image, say, for a magazine spread, one frame might be all you need.

As you might imagine, shortening the rendering time is one of the major challenges—very likely *the* major challenge—confronting 3-D software developers today.

To create an animation sequence, you create *key frames* for each of the pivotal moments. You then use the animation software to create the in-betweens— the frames interpolated between two consecutive key frames. For instance, say you are working on an animation of

a person walking. In one key frame, the right foot is all the way forward, and the left foot is all the way back. To complete that step, you need to pull the left foot forward and past the right. So the second key frame could be the point where the left foot crosses the right, or where the left foot hits the ground in front of the right.

Thus, you pick the starting and ending frames, select the objects (or parts of them) that are to be moved, and describe the movement and specify the number of frames to the computer. The object can be moved along a line, along a trajectory, or in a circle; it can be rotated, scaled, squashed, or twisted.

The finished scene—the results of the rendering operation. *Courtesy of Roger A. Rose, Cogswell Polytechnical College.*

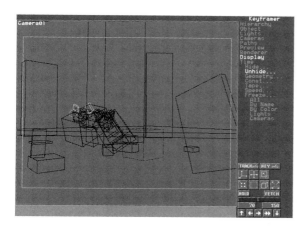

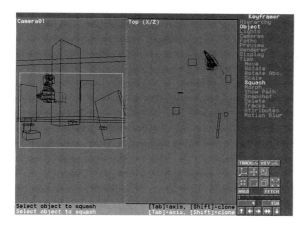

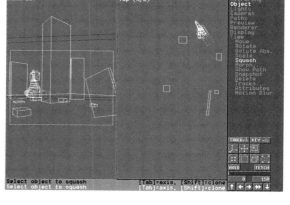

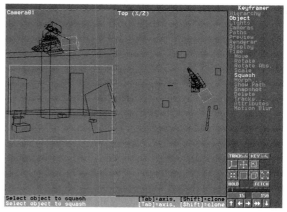

• • • • • • • • • • • • •

**The animation of a flea jump. 3D Studio
translates all objects into single rectangles
during this phase of the process, enabling
the computer to move as fast as possible.
*Courtesy of Roger A. Rose, Cogswell
Polytechnical College.***

A spectacular transition effect called *morphing* can be achieved with some animation software. Morphing was brought to public awareness in Michael Jackson's *Black and White* video, the Exxon commercial of a tiger morphing into a car, and in the motion picture *Terminator 2*. Morphing picks up where traditional film dissolves leave off. You can pick two frames totally unrelated in subject matter and have the first image transform, over the number of frames you choose, into the second image. A tiger thus can become a car. According to the current wisdom, the technique works best when the two objects occupy similar space on the screen.

Animation can be used to instantly "grow" houses on a hilllside. *Courtesy of Autodesk.*

The objects in the scene are not the only elements that may be subject to animation. The camera and lights may also be animated. The camera can be made to zoom in and out, pan from side to side, or be hoisted up from eye level to sky level for an aerial shot.

Likewise, the lights can be made to move. You could easily simulate the rising and/or setting of the sun, or the passage of clouds across the sky—even a solar eclipse.

At this point, the lion's share of the work is done. In fact, if you were just using the technology for a computer presentation, you would just need a bit of polishing up. However, if the animation were destined for film or video, you would need to use some sort of transfer technology to get the images from the computer onto film or videotape.

What's wrong with this picture? 3-D computer animation lets you easily combine some very incongruous elements for a humorous effect. *Courtesy of Pixar, Knickknack, 1989.*

THE HISTORY OF 3-D TECHNOLOGY

Efforts to simulate three-dimensional reality on a two-dimensional surface have a venerable history, and most of the techniques were around long before computers.

In painting, Pablo Picasso tried to simulate the 3-D experience with cubism, by depicting many simultaneous views of the same subject on one flat canvas. While in actuality this was just the opposite of 3-D technology, it fulfilled the same ambition—to have art mirror life.

In film, 3-D viewing was heralded in the 1950s as an idea whose time had come. Movie-goers flocked to theaters to watch such 3-D films as *House of Wax* with special 3-D glasses—at least for a while. But it seemed that the mere existence of the technology was not enough to popularize it. It had to be better integrated within the standards of quality art—a challenge that is no less critical today than it was way back when.

Walt Disney has always been in the forefront of animation technology. In time for a 1939 screening of the painstakingly-produced *Snow White*, Disney developed a multiplane camera. This allowed a layering of picture planes, which, when tracked with this camera, would convey the illusion of depth. It took advantage of the principle of parallax, which posits that nearby objects appear to shift in relation to distant objects when the observer's point of view changes.

(Despite advances in all of its supporting technologies, animation in any form has always been a precise, labor-intensive proposition—and is likely to remain that way.)

Efforts to simulate three-dimensional reality on a two-dimensional surface have a venerable history, and most of the techniques were around long before computers.

Where It's Going

Three-dimensional animation is a medium with several distinct applications—as an artform, as a special-effects enhancement, as a component of virtual reality—each of which has a promising future.

3-D Animation as Artform

Animation has long been an artform in its own right. The first feature-length, computer-generated 3-D movie, produced by Pixar, is scheduled for release in 1995. It's been in the works for several years. But while not featuring any ground-breaking technological advances, the scope of the work alone makes it remarkable.

As with any new medium, the organic evolution of the medium itself will reveal new possibilities. Computer-generated imagery must not be seen merely as a way to automate the drudge work of traditional animation.

From an artist's point of view, the most promising thing about 3-D computer animation is that the material being animated need not have any relation to life as we know it. *Jurassic Park* is a good example of this, where computer-generated dinosaurs were seamlessly integrated with shots of real, live human beings.

Likewise, animators can create entire characters in the computer, possibly even based on the physical appearance of long-dead actors. (This could put an end to tedious talent searches.) As with the dinosaurs in *Jurassic Park*, the computer creations could convincingly share the set with flesh-and-blood actors.

Taking this still further, 3-D computer animation lends itself well to science fiction, where the laws of physical reality may be broken at will. Or, we could get some insight into how the laws of physics operate in locales other than planet Earth. (Maybe it's time for a sitcom set in the heart of a black hole.)

So far, this chapter has mainly focused on the use of 3-D animation in movies. Compared to other potential venues for arts-related technical advances, movies certainly do draw the biggest box office.

But we mustn't overlook the likelihood that three-dimensional computer imagery will be used in art-for-art's-sake applications, especially in gallery installations. In such a setting, it would be possible to have viewers take a more interactive role in authoring the animation. Imagine, for instance, a museum display that scanned the movements of yourself or a companion, fed the digitized signals into a computer, and then enabled you to resculpt the image of your body on the screen. The digitized You could then be made to interact with other characters in the program. This sort of application borders a bit on virtual reality, as discussed in Chapter 4, "Virtual Reality."

3-D TECHNOLOGY ON THE FILM SET

3-D technology continues to play a supporting role in movies. The uses range from eye-popping special effects such as simulations of outer space all the way down to such nuts-and-bolts types of tasks as stunt-wire removal in action movies.

The available 3-D technology has already revolutionized the wire-removal business. In action movies, the "action" gets off the ground by means of strong but nearly invisible wires that support characters in flying, floating, or landing on the ground. If these wires turn out to be visible on the proofs, they can easily be removed by digitizing the image and then manipulating it (or parts of it) to achieve the desired result. This has been estimated to be 80-percent cheaper than reshooting the scene.

Part of the PC revolution is in the democratization of such processes. With software programs such as Adobe PhotoShop, anyone with a desktop computer can achieve professional results. The wide availability of the right stuff with which to do the job has the effect of bringing down both the price of the service and the time it takes to get the job done. Thus, we have the possibility of 3-D film studio in every technologically correct home. It might be just the thing for doctoring up those home videos.

Mama said there would be days like this... or maybe we need some stronger debugging tools! *Courtesy of Roger A. Rose, Cogswell Polytechnical College.*

3-D AND
VIRTUAL REALITY

Three-dimensional imaging is a natural complement to the virtual reality industry. Virtual reality in its current form uses very low-quality graphics. The reason for this is that it takes so long to render each frame, a user could grow gray waiting for one's virtual hand to grasp a precisely-rendered virtual object in cyberspace. By stripping away the details, the time needed for rendering an object in virtual reality is a fraction of that consumed for a comparable frame in a movie.

Thus, most virtual reality developers have elected to prioritize speed over image quality. (There's not much of a choice, really, since part of the excitement about virtual reality is that its speed of response mimics real life.) Still, the visionaries within the virtual reality community look forward to the day when a virtual building has a wooden or brick-like texture; when you not only can choose to take a stroll in cyberspace, but the stroll can be taken in morning light, high-noon glare, or San Francisco fog; and when you can see that the low-swooping pterodactyl in the Dactyl Nightmare game has caked blood on its matted feathers.

By all reckoning, we're going to see a lot *more* of this technology before we see anything radically different. As noted previously, the fundamental technological capabilities have been with us for some time and are only now becoming cost-effective. The market can take some time to absorb this influx of new graphics before unfolding to the next level of either aesthetics or technological development. But eventually 3-D imaging will be upon us like a herd of stampeding velociraptors.

Mystical experiences can be commonplace in cyberspace. *Courtesy of Glenn Melonhorst and Autodesk.*

Robots are a natural for 3-D computer animation. *Courtesy of Vince Parker, Cogswell Polytechnical College.*

PART II

Connection Spaces

L ife in the Virtual Village

chapter 6

by Donald Rose, Ph.D.

You put on a nice outfit, go to the mall, buy a CD and a book, withdraw some money from the bank, cruise to the local cool hangout to chat with a few friends, mail a letter to the President—then you logout. You've just spent an hour in a virtual village—and never left your home.

You put on a nice outfit, go to the mall, buy a CD and a book, withdraw some money from the bank, cruise to the local cool hangout to chat with a few friends, mail a letter to the President—then you logout. You've just spent an hour in a virtual village—and never left your home.

This scenario is not completely possible today, but it will be soon—and some aspects of this potential cyberday can already be achieved. Welcome to the Virtual Village, an electronic version (or perhaps augmentation is a more appropriate description) of the "global village" concept, popularized by media visionary and author Marshall McLuhan.

Writer and cyberexpert Howard Rheingold describes the experience of interacting in a virtual village in a way that many people would agree with. A member of such an electronic tribe can take part "... in a wide-ranging, intellectually stimulating, professionally rewarding, and often intensely emotional exchange with dozens of new friends and hundreds of colleagues." Although one may be physically located in an isolated room, one's mental domain can be "linked with a worldwide collection of like-minded (and not-so-like-minded) souls." The interactions are considered "virtual" because the members of the village enjoy a proximity that is not measurable in physical space, but rather is an electronic proximity provided by light-speed communication devices, such as the telephone and the (modem-enhanced) computer.

But the human-to-human interactions described by Rheingold will make up only one part of daily life in a virtual village. As the preceding scenario suggests, one may do many things that require no communication with other humans. For example, agents that represent real people might be on one or both ends of a virtual encounter. An example would be human-like ATPs (automated teller personas) in lieu of the real world's ATMs (automated teller machines). (See

Chapter 16, "Intelligent Agents," for more on these types of intelligent entities.)

We may be convinced that a kind of virtual village already exists, but how will a more complete vision of it be implemented? What are the relevant issues to face when building this village, as well as the data highways that will connect the village's various huts and caves? Furthermore, how will a true (more advanced, more complete) virtual village affect interpersonal interactions and social concerns in the coming years? This chapter will focus on two main concepts vital to answering these questions: the Internet and Virtual Reality.

THE INTERNET

Some people can't stop talking about the information superhighway. It was arguably the biggest media buzzword of 1993. For others, however, the information superhighway already exists—at least in part—in the form of a giant global entity known as the Internet.

The Internet, or "the net" as some prefer to nickname it, can be viewed as a communications conduit linking users from all over the world. To many users, the Internet is viewed and utilized as a text-based version of the worldwide phone system. For instance, a net user (or "netter") can send an electronic version of mail to anyone that has an Internet account, just as someone can phone anyone else in the world that has a phone "account."

The Internet began life as the ARPAnet, a loose collection of users from the relatively limited community of universities, government workers, and commercial businesses. What began as a means for this select group to communicate ideas in an easier and speedier manner has only recently caught on as a ubiquitous popular global phenomenon. If this last sentence sounds quite similar to the events that happened after the invention of the printing press, you are right; there exist many parallels between that invention for increased communication and today's Internet explosion. Both historical cases illustrate a simple fact: once a convenience is invented, it is only a matter of time before everyone wants to use it. And when everyone wants something, it's almost impossible to keep them from getting it! Ironically, the same government that created the ARPAnet is now increasingly concerned with managing or controlling the resultant Internet, as we will discuss later.

One reason many are already referring to the Internet as the first (or, more forcefully, the only viable) information superhighway is its vast size. One present estimate puts the Internet's contents at "over 3 million freely accessible programs and files." In addition, the net "connects more than 38,000 Internet Protocol (or TCP/IP) computer networks, 135 countries, [and] 10 to 20 million people," according to author Michael Strangelove, in *Online Access* magazine.

Perhaps more daunting is the recent *acceleration* in the net's size. Some call it "the fastest growing form of communication in history," and one estimate for the year 1998 puts e-mail exchange via the Internet at 100 million people, according to *Online Access*. Another source estimates that the number of European users increased seven-fold from 1993 to 1994. In addition, total global usage "was 5 million at the beginning of 1993, 20 million in January 1994, and is expected to be 100 million in 1995. The rate of use of the World Wide Web and Mosaic (two features of the

Internet discussed later in this chapter) is currently rising at 11 percent *per week*," according to *Kaleidospace*.

Another way to view the Internet is as "a worldwide network of computer networks ... comprised of thousands of separately administered networks of many sizes and types. Each of these networks is comprised of as many as tens of thousands of computers ... [with] the total number of individual users ... in the millions. This high level of connectivity fosters an unparalleled degree of communication, collaboration, resource sharing, and information access. In the United States, the National Science Foundation Network (NSFNet) comprises the

. . . .

Some people can't stop talking about the information superhighway. It was arguably the biggest media buzzword of 1993. For others, however, the information superhighway already exists—at least in part—in the form of a giant global entity known as the Internet.

. . . .

Internet 'backbone' (a very high-speed network that connects key regions across the country)," according to the digest *Internet Basics*.

It may seem to be a miracle that the Internet can manage to efficiently connect computers worldwide—and that so many different people and organizations can agree on how they are to communicate. To understand some of the process, note that "[c]onnections can consist of any of a variety of communication media or methods: metal wires, microwave links, packet radio, or fiber optic cables." Furthermore, such connections "are usually established within areas or regions by the particular networking organization with authority or economic interest in that area. For example, a university academic department may lay Ethernet cable to connect its personal computers and workstations into a local area network (LAN), which is then connected to the cables the campus laid to connect its buildings together, which is then linked to cables laid by a regional network, which itself ties into the NSFNet backbone, the infrastructure for which was funded by the U.S. Government. Therefore, the path between any two points on the Internet often traverses physical connections that are administered by a variety of independent authorities," according to *Internet Basics*. Somehow the whole mess works.

INTERNET FEATURES

(OR, WHAT CAN I DO ON THE NET AND HOW?)

Here's a quick sample of some of the tasks people can and do accomplish *today*—or have accomplished in the past—by utilizing the Internet:

- Send messages to the President and Vice-President and other famous people, and actually get replies, some even well-thought-out.
- Buy books—and just about everything else, too.
- Distribute electronic pamphlets, magazines, and journals. (Remember that a minor revolution occurred when Martin Luther discovered the paper version of pamphlets.)
- Chat with several people scattered across the globe, without paying long-distance phone charges.
- Download erotic images to one's home computer. Upload shareware or freeware programs for other users to access.
- Solicit money for get-rich-quick propositions. Rant back at the senders of these solicitations.
- Censor messages. Rant at these censors. Or applaud them.
- Discuss world issues of the day, or the news. Or just complain.
- Ask questions. Get answers. Or get harassed for wasting bandwidth asking stupid questions, then are advised to "get the FAQs." (Translation: read a prewritten list of Frequently Asked Questions for the subject you asked about.)
- Construct and send damaging viruses to other computers, crippling them (which is what happened in the 1980s). Send instructions on how to fix virus problems or guard against them (which also happened in the 1980s).
- Inform the world about a government coup attempt when other media may be temporarily incapacitated. (Remember the Soviet Union?)

Keep in mind this is a tiny subset of what you can do, and this does not take into account new features being implemented on a continuing basis. And as more people gain access to the Internet, the potential for profit grows. This potential provides an even greater incentive for additional money to pour into net ventures, which will eventually be used to provide even more services, which leads to even greater attraction for users, and so on. One can begin to understand why Internet growth has been so phenomenal in recent years.

Now let's take a look at some of the Internet features that enable the above tasks, and others we have not yet mentioned, to occur. The following passage, from *Internet Basics*, provides an excellent overview of some main Internet features:

"Electronic mail, or *e-mail*, is a fast, easy, and inexpensive way to communicate with other Internet users around the world. In addition, it is possible for Internet users to exchange e-mail with users of other independent networks such as CompuServe, Applelink, the WELL, and others. Internet users often find that the expanded capability to communicate with colleagues around the world leads to important new sources of information, collaboration, and professional development.

"Besides basic correspondence between two network users, e-mail presents additional opportunities for communication. Through various methods for distributing e-mail messages to lists of 'subscribers,' e-mail supports electronic discussions on a wide range of topics. These discussions bring together like-minded individuals who use such forums for discussing common problems, sharing solutions, and arguing issues.

"Another type of electronic communication that is growing in popularity is the electronic journal, or '*e-journal*.' Although some e-journals require certain types of software and hardware to display each issue, most e-journals are distributed to a list of subscribers as an e-mail text message, either complete as one issue, or retrievable at the article level by mailing a command to a software program that automatically sends the appropriate file. The very definition of a 'journal' is undergoing change in the electronic environment, as e-journal publishers experiment with different publication models (e.g. sending articles out individually as soon as they are ready rather than waiting until a group of articles are gathered for an 'issue').

"Remote login (*rlogin*) is the ability of a computer user in one location to establish an online connection with another computer elsewhere. Once a connection is established with a remote computer, the user can use that remote system as if their computer were a hard-wired terminal of that system. Within the TCP/IP protocol suite, this facility is called *Telnet*. Utilizing Telnet, an Internet user can establish connections with a multitude of bibliographic databases (primarily library catalogs), campus information systems of various universities, full-text databases, data files (e.g. statistics, oceanographic data, meteorologic data, geographic data, etc.), and other online services. Many of these systems are available for any Internet user to access and use without an account.

"What makes this application truly remarkable is that ease and speed of access are not dependent upon proximity. An Internet user can connect to a system on the other side of the globe as easily as (and generally not much slower than) he or she can connect to a system in the next building. In addition, since many Internet users are not at present charged for their network use by their institutions, or at least are not charged by the level of their use, cost is often not a significant inhibitor of usage. Therefore, the barriers of distance, time-and cost, which are often significant when using other forms of electronic communication, can be reduced in the Internet environment. A compensating disadvantage is that initial costs for Inter-net connection can be high, and access can be technically demanding.

"Another application of the Internet is the ability to transfer files from one Internet-connected computer to another. This function is provided by the File Transfer Protocol (*FTP*) of the TCP/IP protocol suite. In a method similar to using Telnet, network users initiate an online connection with another Internet computer via FTP. But unlike Telnet, this online con-nection can perform only functions related to locating and transferring files. This includes the ability to change directories, list files, retrieve files, etc.

"Types of files that can be transferred using FTP include virtually every kind of file that can be stored on a computer: text files, software programs, graphic images, sounds, files formatted for particular software programs (e.g., files with word processing formatting instructions), and others. Many computer administrators have set aside portions of their machines to offer files for anyone on the Internet to retrieve. These archive sites support 'anonymous' logins that do not require an account to access, and therefore are called anonymous FTP sites. To locate files, Internet users can use the *Archie* service, which indexes files from over 900 separate anonymous FTP sites, according to *Crossing the Internet Threshold: An Instructional Handbook*."

The three basic Internet applications of electronic mail, remote login, and file transfer are also building blocks of more sophisticated applications that usually offer increased functionality and ease of network use. Tools such as *Gopher*, *WAIS*, and *World Wide Web* go beyond the three basic Internet functions to make information on the network easier to locate and use. Gopher is a project of the University of Minnesota that uses a series of menus to organize and automate access to information and other online systems wherever they reside on the Internet. The Wide Area Information Servers (WAIS) project of Thinking Machines, Apple Computer, Dow Jones & Co., and KPMG Peat Marwick seeks to provide a common interface to a multitude of Internet databases. World Wide Web is a hypertext interface to Internet information resources that was developed at CERN in Switzerland. This trend toward more powerful, user-friendly, networked information resource access systems is likely to continue as the Internet grows and matures.

Note that, in addition to sending one or more messages to a pre-defined group, one can also post messages to *electronic bulletin boards* (or bboards). As the name implies, bboard messages, once posted, are readable by anyone who can access that bboard. This differs from e-mail, which usually is visible only to the sender and receiver(s). The main Internet bulletin board universe is known as *Usenet*, and the number of topics covered by Usenet bboards—now several thousand—includes everything from artificial intelligence to alternative sex. The huge number of bboards evolved in part because any group of netters can form a new bboard if they have enough critical mass—and, of course, it is not hard to fathom how millions of people will find thousands of subjects to talk about.

As mentioned, Archie is a program growing in popularity because it allows users to search the net's list of millions of files (which have a total size of over 11 gigabytes), and can e-mail you the result of such a search. After Archie has found the requested files that interest you, you can send an *FTPMail* message to a remote server on Archie's reply list and request the desired files. If they are indeed present on the remote server, the files will then be e-mailed to you to process as you like. For instance, you might download some of them to your home computer for further processing.

Text is today's most common "infocurrency" mainly because it takes the least amount of digital "space" or "bandwidth" to represent. However, pictures and sound are already becoming more commonplace on the net.

A relatively recent phenomenon is a piece of software called *Mosaic*. This name may conjure up an image of patchwork visual fragments, a set of small pieces that, when viewed altogether, make a unified whole. In a metaphorical sense, the Mosaic program fits this description. At its core are graphical screen documents that are a collection of information pieces (often words, but sometimes images, video, or sound clips), which together form a whole (such as a page with a unified theme, like a home page from which a hypertext search can begin).

Unlike a real physical mosaic, this patchwork's pieces can lead to other collections of information. For instance, click a home page's active hypertext words and other pages can be accessed, even if these new pages are physically stored on other computers elsewhere in the Internet cyberverse. Currently, a very fast (and expensive) connection to the net is required to avoid the frustratingly long waits that can ensue when Mosaic is used on a Macintosh—where many use this program because a free Mac version is readily available. This public domain version is provided by the National Center for Supercomputing Applications (NCSA) in Champaign-Urbana, Illinois. In fact, many netters access NCSA Mosaic from Internet storage sites (such as remote servers). Mosaic is currently the most popular client interface for accessing the WWW and, in terms of Internet traffic and use, is one of the fastest-growing applications in the world. Its ability to access and display so many different kinds of information from disparate global sources means it has great potential for innovative uses in the future. The WWW has the

potential to emerge as a multimedia platform that could compete with—and even overtake—the highly-touted CD-ROM.

So now we have seen how information can be manipulated, searched, and accessed via the Internet. But what *kinds of information* are generally present on the net? Text is the standard, the most common kind of information available online today. But an important point for the future is that *any* information one can represent in digital form can be stored on and accessed from the net. Text is today's most common "infocurrency" mainly because it takes the least amount of digital "space" or "bandwidth" to represent. However, pictures and sound are already becoming more commonplace on the net. Video, which encompasses both pictures and sound and does so many times per second (30 for full motion video), requires a great deal more storage. But even video is starting to be included in Internet communications, partly due to advances in compression technologies (in which redundant parts of visual or aural elements are eliminated or stored in a smaller form, then uncompressed when accessed). The combination of less expensive storage plus faster processors will hasten the arrival of video as an integral part of the net. When video truly arrives at a reasonable cost, look for an even more explosive growth in Internet interest by the public.

The combination of less expensive storage plus faster processors will hasten the arrival of video as an integral part of the net. When video truly arrives at a reasonable cost, look for an even more explosive growth in Internet interest by the public.

SMALLER NETWORKS, ONLINE SERVICES, AND INTERNET ON-RAMPS

No other network in the world matches the size or traffic of the Internet. However, there are many smaller networks—online services that users with a computer and modem can access, but which are not technically a piece of the Internet infrastructure. For example, CompuServe, America OnLine (or AOL), Delphi, GEnie, and thousands of other regional bulletin board services (BBSs) around the world fall in this class. For those millions of folks who cannot get free Internet accounts at a school or workplace (as I did when in graduate school), these services often provide the first or only on-ramps to the virtual village, or perhaps a kind of suburbs in relation to the Internet metropolis. These services help ensure that the virtual village can be a universally shared experience.

However, some say the Internet is in the process of gobbling up all the other networks, BBSs, and online services—and in some sense these people are correct. Certainly all these major online services, plus the majority of other BBSs, are converging in some areas with the Internet behemoth; for example, most now provide e-mail access to the net. Doing this allows a user of AOL, for example, to send e-mail to anyone with an Internet address, and vice versa.

While all of these services provide the means to use Internet e-mail, for some people this is their only on-ramp to the net. However, this state of affairs is rapidly changing. Delphi, for example, has been offering "full Internet" for many months, which includes FTP, Telnet, Gopher, WWW, WAIS, and even a few others in addition to e-mail. Not far behind in the major online group is AOL, which recently augmented its Internet e-mail access with Gopher and WAIS. Some of the other major services are not far behind, and many "non-major" net players (services not as huge but up-and-coming) such as Netcom, Kaiwan, Digital Express Group, and the Entertainment and Consumer Network are offering full Internet. These latter services often undercut the bigger players in price and restrictions. For example, Netcom and Kaiwan allow unlimited access time at no extra charge over their fixed monthly cost. This fee structure is similar to that of most pay-cable-TV services and unlike those of the bigger net players—which usually charge hourly fees when one uses up a monthly or daily quota of access time.

. . . .

E-mail has grown even more useful lately thanks to services like "information droids," which are servers that distribute info on demand based on e-mail messages you send to these droids.

. . . .

But don't despair if you only have e-mail access to the Internet. E-mail has grown even more useful lately thanks to services like "information droids," which are servers that distribute info on demand based on e-mail messages you send to these droids. For example, *Wired* magazine, whose growth and recognition is partially paralleling that of the Internet, provides text articles from its hardcopy issues, available via e-mail from its info droid. In addition, the company has started an online magazine called *HotWIRED* that appears *only* on the net. Third, *Wired* now has a WWW site, where text and graphics and sound can be accessed.

Eventually, all magazines could provide online equivalents, which contain all of the same information as their paper versions but exist on the Internet. Some could even become supersets of their hardcopy counterparts, since added features like video clips and additional comments that would not appear in print could be incorporated on the net.

SOCIOLOGICAL ISSUES IN THE VIRTUAL VILLAGE

Once you figure out how to access the Internet, what to do on it, and where to go for information sources, welcome to the next level: how to best interact with others in your virtual village. In other words, issues related to appropriate etiquette and manners eventually surface when the technical details are mastered.

Some discover this fact by accident, such as after posting a question to a Usenet bboard that everyone and his uncle has asked before; several other bboard users then might respond angrily, with soiled language and advice that includes "read the FAQ." Several things have just occurred. For one thing, you have just been *flamed*— an event loosely defined as a message that vents strong emotions or feelings about a certain issue. In addition, you will realize that FAQ is one of many abbreviations or acronyms commonplace on the net; in this case, FAQ means Frequently Asked Questions. The flame here teaches you a generalizable lesson: that reading the FAQ for any bboard you ask a question on will often answer your question, plus usually quite a few more. New netters can easily and quickly learn by others' past experience.

Of course, some people never learn. "Junk e-mail" has become a growing problem on the Internet. Such junk can take the form of messages sent directly to those on someone's mailing list, or messages posted to Usenet or other bboards. Many of the latter involve get-rich-quick schemes and occasionally even those that will make you rich slowly. And slowly is the operative word here because such junk e-mail bogs down any searches one makes within the net's already massive collection of information.

Junk e-mail is one of many reasons that an increasing number of netters are following the lead of Microsoft leader Bill Gates, who filters his e-mail so only the important items get his attention. Filtering can be achieved by hiring a human to search for files you find relevant, by downloading e-mail and manually searching the saved file for relevant keywords, or even by constructing artificial agents for this task (see Chapter

"Junk e-mail" has become a growing problem on the Internet. Such junk can take the form of messages sent directly to those on someone's mailing list, or messages posted to Usenet or other bboards. Many of the latter involve get-rich-quick schemes and occasionally even those that will make you rich slowly.

16 for more explanation of these useful software entities). Junk faxes were outlawed by Congress when fax usage skyrocketed during the last decade. Can junk e-mail legislation be far behind?

Although all of the above items are important to address, the larger social question we should address here is this: do people act differently when they interact in the Internet? Generally, the answer is yes. I personally experienced an interesting effect over a decade ago as a graduate student, comparing e-mail to face-to-face communication. One of my professors was very shy when he talked to someone in person, but was very bold—even funny or forceful—when he sent people e-mail messages. In general, netters react like this quite often, communicating in a manner that does not match the way they talk face-to-face. On average, people act bolder, feeling freer to communicate within the virtual village, probably because both visual and aural elements have been abstracted away, which reduces psychological pressures.

Another recent example involves the widow of Nirvana's Kurt Cobain, Courtney Love, who has never granted a live interview, yet did agree to speak to fans via AOL chats. In addition, she has been regularly posting notes to bulletin boards on AOL. Why did she exhibit freer expression over Internet? Probably because celebrities and others in the spotlight can avoid direct harassment, can avoid being put on the spot or on a deadline; the worst that can happen is a pile of e-mail, which can easily be filtered or discarded at the user's whim. Replies to fans, or deletion of unwanted messages, can be done on one's own time, at one's choosing, under one's full control, according to the *Los Angeles Times*.

In addition, there is the option to post some messages using "code names," a practice Love and others have used. The use of code names to preserve anonymity is a practice many "easily recognizable" or "known" people do on the net. Although this practice can be viewed as further increasing the virtual distance from other virtual villagers, it often becomes necessary in order to avoid excessive e-mail (sometimes hitting the delete key can get to be too much) or even virtual harassment. The use of code names then leads to the question of online personas. In the virtual village, your persona is always virtual, so you have options. It can inherit all your real attributes—or you can *try on a different persona*. Like a different sexual presence.

In general, gender issues have become increasingly important as net usage among the masses has increased. *Newsweek* recently ran a cover story that dealt with,

> In the virtual village, your persona is always virtual, so you have options. It can inherit all your real attributes—or you can *try on a different persona*. Like a different sexual presence.

among other things, e-mail differences between the sexes. One conclusion was that the "sexist ruts and gender conflicts" present in real life tend to transfer over to net life as well, and that the virtual village is far from an online Eden. Another example of gender etiquette disrespect was provided by a young lady who recently told me she is constantly "hit on" by guys on the net, simply because her net name (handle) is female. Some might say that code names could provide a temporary solution for her, but others would exclaim that even this small infringement on one's freedom violates the spirit of freedom the net is supposed to embody.

In the near future, the notion of alternate-sex code names might take on an even wider scope, even take the form of entire alternate personas complete with visual and aural elements. An oft-cited example involves users of the Habitat system, a fairly simple yet intriguing virtual world where one could enter a kind of "gender room" to create and don a persona for use on the system. Yet even the use of simple changed-sex code names has led some netters to experience a marked difference in tone (such as through online chats or e-mail) than was felt when interacting as the original sex. Through this use of code names or more elaborate mechanisms, it appears we will all soon be capable of playing Tootsie or Mrs. Doubtfire—or, like the character Pat from *Saturday Night Live*, playing neutral.

Assuming for now that most readers only have an e-mail address as their persona, how can someone convey nuance in the virtual village? How can one emote as one would in a real encounter? One way is by using *emoticons*. That is, icons that exhibit a form of emotion that the user is feeling (or perhaps just wishes to indicate). If I am trying to tell a joke, or say a sentence tongue in cheek, I can end with a smiley face, like this :) but notice you must read it sideways (a limitation of character design on modern keyboards).

Many variations of the traditional smiley have been spawned, of course. Like its opposite for conveying sadness :(or even something akin to anger >:(you get the idea. Going beyond emotions, some services are starting to offer additional means to convey nuance in virtual messaging. For example, the Millenium Online service is courting users with the promise of choices for e-mail fonts, font sizes, even music.

Another means to convey a kind of virtual style is to adorn one's e-mail with *signatures*. These typically come at the end of each message a user sends and can be as simple or complex as the user desires. One could gain an education just from all the quotes people often leave in these signatures. Some users even replicate art by arranging appropriate patterns of characters.

Speaking of pictures, it should be noted that it is not considered as tacky to send erotic pictures to someone via e-mail as it would using regular mail, partly because such pictures would only be a representation (for instance, binary code which, when properly translated, produces pictures). However, it is of sociological interest to note that as of December 5, 1993, the most popular

VIRTUAL REALITY AND THE INTERNET

Unless you have been living in a cave the past half-decade, you've at least heard of virtual reality, or VR. This technology should ultimately prove a good marriage partner for the Internet and the arena of global networks in bringing the potential of the virtual village to full fruition. For example, using the Internet to transmit virtual worlds that are then viewed and manipulated by users is a logical step. Or, another (perhaps more efficient) option would let users have predefined or generic worlds already loaded on their home or work computers, while the net would be used to transmit commands that execute changes in these worlds rather than the worlds themselves.

Some folks are already working on variants of these scenarios. For example, David Mitchell created the Diasper Virtual Reality Network which, according to Communications Industries Report, enables users to "send and receive video images while communicating online." Users can include video images in e-mail or bulletin board communications. The future goal is to enable users to connect goggles or other VR viewing devices to their PC, which can interface with the DVR network—a kind of "desktop virtual reality."

Another new company pursuing related goals is Knowledge Adventure Worlds, a startup venture spun off from Knowledge Adventure. KA-Worlds is pushing a three-dimensional virtual world that operates solely on one's home computer. These worlds are very fast and easy to navigate. You see a representation (or "avatar") of others as they navigate the system, and they in turn can see your avatar. Users can exchange text messages, which graphically follow the avatars that said them as they move. Despite its stand-alone PC operating environment, the company's ultimate goal is to have these worlds serve as front-ends for online services, which leads once again to the ubiquitous Internet.

Usenet newsgroup in the world (when the groups were ordered by traffic volume) was "*alt.binaries.pictures.erotica*," with an estimated 280,000 readers worldwide and recent traffic of roughly 24 megabytes per month. In true virtual village style, I ascertained these entertaining tidbits from the e-mail signature of someone's Usenet post. So it must be true, right?

Well, perhaps, but this does brings up another important point. As the Internet and other conduits that make up the burgeoning virtual village speed the transfer and manipulation of information, will the tests, checks, and balances that are the hallmarks of journalism and accurate communication keep up? Let us hope so. For example, I could have e-mailed the user whose signature I quoted above, in order to verify the information provided by him (or her—the user's handle was generic, as non-gender-revealing as Pat), but then I had too many other messages to read and send to do so. And since user handles are only *virtual* names and can easily conceal one's real identity, it is all too easy to conceal the true source of information. So what's the lesson, the moral, to learn here? Stay tuned.

Cybermalls are also coming into virtual reality with increasing rapidity. The University of California at San Diego, in tandem with the San Diego Supercomputer Center, "[came] up with a virtual reality system called In the Bag that is designed to make shopping from your living room a more familiar experience." The system enables users to "wander through various 3D mall stores, select merchandise, and drop the selected [items] into a depicted shopping bag," according to the *Los Angeles Times*. The bag here is analogous to the avatar in the earlier KA-Worlds paradigm and is manipulated by the user's cyberglove. A space ball and liquid crystal display glasses are also used by shoppers within this system.

Another approach to combining VR and the Internet is to settle for less complex VR worlds, such as those that paint images within the user's mind rather than on a screen or inside a helmet. That is, fully text-based virtual worlds. MOO's (Multiuser Object-Oriented environments) and MUD's (Multi User Dimensions) are two related examples of text-based VR already widely used on the Internet. One popular MOO, with over 600 regular users from around the globe in its virtual community, is called BayMOO, most likely named because the heart of the system is physically located near the San Francisco Bay. According to BayMOO, once logged in, a user finds a world of virtual objects including rooms, objects, and communication tools. And yes, even other people.

The BayMOO users can either explore in isolation, or get into the virtual village spirit to exchange ideas, socialize, and collaborate on "virtual building projects." Entire worlds can be created and enjoyed by people who have never physically met and likely never will. Note that words are the virtual coin of the realm in systems such as BayMOO; they not only express ideas and emotions, but actually make things happen. Like magic, words in these text-based VR systems conjure actions. The mental images created in the minds of MOO and MUD users are probably more realistic and inspiring than the graphics inside any current VR helmet.

A related version of virtual reality is provided by online chat sessions. AOL and other online services often provide these mini-town-meetings, a form of teleconference that are mainly text-only. Many celebrities have taken advantage of these online discussion forums to address their fans, answer questions, and give advice. As mentioned earlier, famous folk often feel less threatened or time-pressured when using the Internet to chat with fan groups, just as many find e-mail preferable to phone or live interactions. In addition, the ability to talk to many at once in an organized, controlled fashion provides an additional attraction.

Another kind of chat that runs solely on the Internet is *IRC*, or Internet Relay Chat. Once on the net, anyone can use IRC, assuming one's on-ramp to the net provides this service. IRC is a

Famous folk often feel less threatened or time-pressured when using the Internet to chat with fan groups, just as many find e-mail preferable to phone or live interactions.

network-wide service that can be provided to all systems affiliated or connected with the net. Anyone who is logged in can choose to form a "Channel" or "Chat Room," and make it either public or private. They can also limit the number of people attending or make it by invitation only. One could think of IRC as a kind of virtual CB radio, except that on the net the number of channels to talk on is theoretically unlimited. For now, IRC is basically a text-only service, but future netplanners see IRC blossoming into the next generation of teleconferencing.

For now, however, IRC is not the easiest tool to use. As one user describes IRC, "It is as difficult to get used to as learning another language; ... until you are familiar with it, it is awkward. You need to learn a number of basic commands and get used to having a conversation without all of the subtle cues provided in face-to-face or even voice-only conversations. If more than two people are involved, they had better all know the etiquette and nuances of group conversation. The way to learn this is get online and try it out, either by joining in on existing chats or forming your own, perhaps arranging to meet a friend."

Other alternatives to IRC and the big online chat services also exist. For example, a service called Worldlink enables users of many smaller BBSs to engage in live nationwide chats around the clock.

CENSORSHIP, PRIVACY, ENCRYPTION, AND FREEDOM

What does a BBS or Usenet bboard moderator do when someone says something that offends another user, or posts classified information or other data that is not "appropriate?" The field of cybersecurity and cybercensorship is rapidly growing in importance. In recent months, the Prodigy service caught flak from many of its users for censoring some messages; many of these disgruntled users subsequently left the service for Prodigy's competitors. However, it may be difficult to judge the true response to such actions, since there could always be a "silent majority" of satisfied but nonvocal users happy with Prodigy's policing policy. Perhaps the public should be polled as to their thoughts on cybercensorship.

A better answer may come by drawing on an analogy to TV and film, institutions that either police themselves or are governed by independent agencies. It seems high time for the Internet and other BBSs to join in the debate these fields are engaged in—especially since all of these fields are converging at warp speed anyway.

What does a BBS or Usenet bboard moderator do when someone says something that offends another user, or posts classified information or other data that is not "appropriate?" The field of cybersecurity and cybercensorship is rapidly growing in importance.

Of course, as in real life, subjects like security and safety are bound to arise for virtual villagers. By definition, hackers try to get into places they are not supposed to. This means that programmers will keep developing programs to defend virtual communities from unwanted penetration. Perhaps this is why "Internet firewalls" is one of the hottest buzzphrases in the field today.

Not only is the Internet the cause of debates on computer crime, but the net is even having an effect on crimes committed in the real world. For example, the West Valley Bureau of the Los Angeles Police Department is using a new computer BBS to help citizens "reach out and arrest someone." Although the system is "primarily geared toward West Valley residents ... anyone with a computer and a modem can call in and participate." Known as the Community Policing BBS (CP-BBS), it "provides a variety of services to the public, including home security tips, community alerts, and the ability to communicate directly with local police in a public forum." Under consideration are "plans for a guest log-in so tips can be left anonymously," which could provide citizens with a means "to report ongoing non-emergency crimes." The new service gives police "the ability to distribute a digital image of a suspect, along with the suspect's description, in a form that can be downloaded and displayed on your computer. The photo or sketch can be updated as needed, along with community alerts if the suspect has been seen in the area." In addition, the BBS should prove useful, perhaps even essential, during emergencies. Services like these could serve as a store of information such as damage, casualty, and insurance reports, collected from many sources that have access to the BBS, according to the *Los Angeles Times*.

However, note that this new service has already given rise to a privacy versus protection debate. For example, the BBS requires users to answer a "standard questionnaire," consisting of queries not unlike those of many other BBSs. In this case, however, this private personal information is being given to the police, a prospect some users are already expressing uneasiness about. For their part, the police insist this data "is used only to determine the access level of the caller and to periodically verify the caller's identity on future BBS accesses," said Bauman.

What will the majority of virtual villagers think of services such as the CP-BBS? Some might claim that the loss of privacy caused by required questionnaires is a necessary sacrifice to help protect society and catch criminals. Others claim that this amount of privacy loss is not worth such protection, especially since statistics proving the protection level of any new service take time to gather.

The bottom line is that we haven't reached bottom yet. There are no easy answers in sight, but as the debate unfolds we will hopefully gain new insights and find partial, even complete, solutions to appease both sides of the privacy-protection debate.

FUTURE ISSUES

What will a typical day be like in tomorrow's virtual village? The scenario offered at the start of this chapter may only come about in the *far* future if legal and ethical answers cannot keep pace with technical advances and convergences.

Or perhaps the earlier scenario will soon look limited in retrospect. For example, it is possible that planetary exploration will eventually widen the scope of the evolving virtual village. NASA Ames Research Center, as well as private companies, are already investigating the use of VR to explore virtual landscapes, but thus far these virtual trips have been based solely on preexisting data. What about live real-time telepresence? In this approach, anyone could be linked up to a craft and see what the craft sees, by transmission of data to one's VR gear via the Internet or phone networks. Of course, there would be delays due to signal transmission time requirements, but using this setup for telepresence on the moon would result in a negligible delay, and its proximity also makes it the likely first testing ground for such a system. These and other related projects would mean that anyone could be a weekend explorer, and the virtual village would be expanded to a degree only limited by the goals we give our spacecraft surrogates, our virtual eyes and ears to the planets and stars.

More mundane down-to-earth issues, such as the future cost of Internet features and other virtual village elements, are still not resolved. As mentioned previously, multiperson global chats can often be done essentially for free, or at least require no extra cost beyond a minimal monthly Internet access charge. Will phone companies, the losing competitors in this case, lobby Washington to slap fees on such chats? Or will the government simply act regardless of any lobby and enact fees in order to reap taxes from them? Will chats be subject to the same potential for eavesdropping as phone conversations, or will these backdoor capabilities be increased? No one has answers to these questions yet, but assembling a complete ranked set of the most important ones should be the next goal to be achieved. Of course, these issues have been, and will continue to be, active topics on online chats.

The government might also want to get involved in regulating the Internet or other online services because of potential changes the virtual village may inflict on existing real-world institutions. For example, software packages already exist for creating virtual personalized newspapers that could render pulp-based printed papers obsolete. (A program called Journalist can now automatically call the Prodigy service and, based on user preferences regarding content and design, can print or display a paper the way the user desires.) This development is one of many that have led futurist and author Michael Crichton, in *Wired*, to warn that the current "Mediasaurus" may be endangered, perhaps even headed for extinction due to the coming radical changes in our notions of mass media. No matter what government or other institutions attempt in order to cope with potential real-world changes caused by virtual village growth, the changes are destined to occur anyway. Perhaps they will be slowed, but their inception seems inevitable.

The invention of the printing press may have transferred information from the hands of the few to the hands of the many, but the virtual village will give the many the means for limitless manipulation of this information—plus the higher-order *meta-information* structures and procedures required to manage it all. At least this is the hope of many, who may prove more powerful than the few.

SUMMARY AND CONCLUSIONS

The virtual village is already here, but not everyone has been initiated into the tribe yet. This new village's main lifeline, the Internet, is growing extremely fast. Better to get on the on-ramp now, either to get a jump on your competitors (if you have them) or to begin expanding your horizons.

It's hard to believe, but Alexander Graham Bell actually had a difficult time selling his telephone because pre-phone people couldn't envision the need for it. Don't make the same mistake with the Internet! It will create a new revolution, equal to or greater than that of Bell's little item. The Internet has the potential to do everything the phone can do, plus a whole lot more.

In conclusion—get thee to the Internet. Any way, anyhow—and be anywhere, now.

RESOURCES

Although a comprehensive Internet resource list is not feasible for this addendum, the following items provide a smattering of assorted information readers should find intriguing, even helpful.

First, you should note that the standard format for Internet addresses is *<user-handle>@<service-name>.<service-type>*. For example, Bill Clinton's address is *President@whitehouse.gov*, the *gov* indicating that the address is a government site or service. Commercial services end in *.com*, educational sites end in *.edu*, and most other organizations (those that are non-profit) end in *.org*. Some addresses may have more than two words after the @ sign, some may have hyphenated phrases, some (like CompuServe) have two numbers on the left of the @ separated by a period, but the general format always stays the same. By the way, writing the President is almost guaranteed to result in a boring reply; remember, virtual form letters are even easier to create than real ones!

To subscribe to the *HotWIRED* mailing list discussed earlier, send a message to *infodroid@wired.com* with the message *subscribe hotwired* in the body of the message. To get off the list, do the same—except substitute *unsubscribe* for *subscribe*.

Another *Wired* development involves Internet etiquette. According to the *HotWIRED* 1.06 online newsletter of June 3, 1994, "The September issue (2.09) of [the hardcopy version of] *Wired* magazine will include a new attachment to Net Surf—the "Netiquette" column. This addition to the *Wired* pages will provide us an opportunity to deal with, and inform our readers of, the common and not-so-common net.errors and irritations that occur out on the digital waves—all with a dash of humor. (Think of it as a twisted "Dear Abby" for net nerds.) Got a gripe? Forward it to *<netiquette@wired.com>*. And don't post with your mouth full.

Interested in topics such as privacy, laws, and litigation? Subscribe to the *CUD: Computer Underground Digest.* Articles on these and other topics can be received by sending e-mail to *listserv@uiucvmd.bitnet* with the following single line in the message body: *SUB CUDIGEST <your name>.* If you want even more information pertaining to security and encryption issues, and don't mind wading through "thousands of threads about everything from comp.eff.talk (Electronic Frontier Foundation) to comp.security.pgp [Pretty Good Protection, the infamous public domain encryption program]," send e-mail to *dtangent@defcon.org* for details.

Eager to jump on the exploding Mosaic bandwagon? A version for the Macintosh as well as for Microsoft Windows can be obtained via FTP. One machine that stores the program has the address *ftp.ncsa.uiuc.edu* and the appropriate file(s) can be found by searching in the directory */Mosaic/.*

To try out BayMOO's text-based virtual reality, get onto the Internet and, at the system prompt, enter the following: *telnet mud.crl.com* 8888. Then explore. Connecting is free. If you want a character, send e-mail to *blast@crl.com* and give the desired character name. After getting your character, login and type help communication or help movement for basic information and advice. If you still wish to ask questions, type *@who,* page whomever is currently logged into the system, and ask for help.

MecklerWeb is a new organization devoted to business pursuits on the Internet. Call 1-800-MECKLER for more information.

Finally, we return to the subject of CompuServe, with a tip for those who use this service or communicate with those who do. To convert a CompuServe address to an Internet address, replace the comma with a period and add

@compuserve.com to the end. For example, the CompuServe address *71043,3616* would become the Internet address *71043.3616@ compuserve.com*. By the way, that's Barry Diller's address, in case you want to write and ask him what "QVC" stands for.

Most other online services have similar translation schemes that lead to the standard "*<user-handle>@<service-name>.<service-type>*" format for Internet addresses.

Here are some numbers and addresses to inquire further about some net services mentioned earlier:

- Netcom: 800-501-8649.
- Delphi: 800-695-4005
  Dial by modem to 800-365-4636
  E-mail *INFO@delphi.com*
- America OnLine (AOL):
  800-827-6364
- Prodigy: 800-PRODIGY
- Kaiwan: 714-638-2139
  Fax: 714-638-0455
  E-mail: *info@kaiwan.com*
- Digital Express Group:
  800-99-DIGEX
  E-mail: *info@orange.digex.net*
- CompuServe: 800-848-8990
- GEnie: 800-638-9636
- ECN: 310-204-6006

Many will also find *freenets* of extreme interest, especially since they provide a broad collection of net services for little or no cost, an excellent means of getting one's feet wet on the net. One of the newest freenets is in one of the most populous regions: Los Angeles. Use your modem to dial 818-776-5000 to get access. Visits are free, or you can become a registered user (with full access) for a mere $10.

Finally, you can even send *me* e-mail: *drose@pro-palmtree.socal.com* (for questions, or just to say you're a fan). Speaking of fans, I've got to go fan the virtual fire, so I can see you—see you in the virtual village.

B

BSs: The Home Brew Component of Cyberspace

chapter 7

y Rick Leinecker

My first BBS was destroyed by a disgruntled former co-sysop who, before things hit the fan, changed an inactive user's status to full sysop status. That meant that this user, who rarely logged on, could do virtually anything. One morning at 3 a.m. I awoke to the sound of a grinding printer, running continuously because there were no files left on the disk. This former helper had logged on as the inactive user and deleted all of the system's files.

THE LOCAL ALTERNATIVE: BBSs

Prodigy and CompuServe advertisements seem to be everywhere. You hear about the Internet in the news on a daily basis. These giants in the information superhighway, though, can be rather intimidating, especially for newcomers to telecommunications.

The big boys have plenty of baby brothers. These are smaller operations known as bulletin board services (BBSs). They're most often run by individuals or small groups of people. The equipment is usually rudimentary. Even an old IBM XT will suffice for a basic BBS. Since BBSs are accessed mostly by local callers, the regulars are people who live in the same area. This fosters a sense of community that is hard to discern on the larger services.

For years, BBSs have been the backbone that serviced the needs of many telecommuters. In the early 1980s, entire communities of computer enthusiasts were held together by local BBSs. Many people today who are industry leaders spent endless late-night hours in front of their computer screens communicating with other like-minded people via BBSs. Today, some of my most valuable and prominent contacts are those I met while online during that period.

. . . .

Neighborhood boards offer some attractive advantages:

- They're local calls, so you don't have to pay for long-distance phone charges.
- It's easy to register. All you usually have to do is answer some simple questions after logging on to obtain an account.
- BBSs are usually free. Even those that charge fees cost far less per month than the commercial services.
- You'll meet people online who are in your area who might become valuable contacts and resources in the future.
- BBSs can react quickly to member needs.
- A BBS can be built around a particular theme or subject in which you hold a special interest. This kind of information and exchange of ideas might not be readily available anywhere else.

. . . .

Most BBS software offers the kind of features you'd expect. You get full e-mail capabilities, software upload and download areas, conferences, information retrieval sections, and sysop-customizable areas. (Sysop—pronounced "siss-op"—is short for "system operator," the administrator of the bulletin board.)

It takes some time to find the BBSs in your area, and even more time to sort out the ones you really like. The best way to start is by asking friends what systems they call and enjoy. Many systems have lists of other BBSs, so once you log on to one system, you can get an entire list of active systems. Many times the lists you get are commented and will help you decide which ones to call first.

There are also several small newspapers, both locally and nationally, that list BBS advertisements. Try to find a copy of Micro Times or Computer Currents. They'll list a fair number of BBSs, many of which may be in your area. Computer Shopper often has BBS lists categorized by states. These lists are reasonably current, as opposed to ones obtained from other BBSs, which may not be reliable. BBSs come and go, and you may find a fair percentage of the telephone numbers disconnected when you call.

If you have a CompuServe account, you can find an extensive list of BBS numbers. Type GO IBMBBS to get to the IBM Bulletin Board Forum. Once there, set to the BBS Listing library. Use the browse function to find listings that interest you. The most current and comprehensive file as of this publication date is named USB123.ZIP and contains hundreds of American BBSs. If you have a GEnie account, you can get to the BBS section by typing BBS. If you're on America Online, use the keyword BBS to find the section on the BBS topic.

. . . .

There are a few disadvantages, though, to small BBSs:

- They don't have as much downloadable software and information available as do the commercial services.
- They usually have a daily time limit for user access.
- Since they're usually run from PCs, they can crash and be down for a considerable amount of time. Many times when this happens, you'll have to reapply for an account.
- There's always a chance that an unscrupulous sysop may read your e-mail.
- With a commercial service, you know the rules. On a BBS, the sysop can interpret things as he or she sees fit.

. . . .

BBS ETIQUETTE

It's a good idea to observe some general rules when accessing BBSs. Always be polite and considerate of other users. Never be a negative influence. Cooperate with the sysop's requests so that the service will be the best it can be.

But there are others. I once ran across a tongue-in-cheek set of BBS rules. While humorous, these rules cover the major areas of proper BBS behavior:

1. Thou shalt love thy BBS with all thy heart and all thy bytes.
2. Thou shalt remember thy name and thy password.
3. Thou shalt not POST IN ALL CAPS!
4. Thou shalt use your real name when required.
5. Thou shalt call a BBS no more than three times a day.
6. Honor thy sysop.
7. Thou shalt not covet they neighbor's password, nor his or her real name, computer, software, nor any other thing belonging to him or her.
8. Thou shalt not post messages that are stupid, worthless, or have no meaning.
9. Thou shalt use the English language properly.
10. Thou shalt spell thy words correctly.
11. Thou shalt delete thine own mail.
12. Thou shalt delete thine olden messages.
13. Thou shalt help other users.
14. Thou shalt not post anonymously when offering criticism.
15. Thou shalt keep thy extremely foul language to thyself.
16. Thou shalt not occupy thy BBS with thine arguments, for verily, I say unto thee that thou shalt maketh a fool of thyself.

17. Woe be unto the user who attempts to crash thy BBS, for he or she shalt be cast out from the sanctuary of thy hobby and must repent by doing 40 days and 40 nights of penance in voice-only communications.

18. Thou shalt first dial the BBS number during the day by way of voice line to assure the correct number.

19. Thou shalt not post other users' real names.

20. Thou shalt not post messages while drunk.

21. Thou shalt confine thy messages to those of friendship, requests for assistance, aid to the needy, advice, and advancement of thy hobby; and thou art obligated to repel any who wouldst transgress upon those commandments.

22. If thou doth promise to reply to a message and thou doth not, then surely thou shalt spill coffee into thy keyboard and burn out thy central processing chip.

23. Thou shalt not giveth any false information when applying for membership to thy BBS, for verily it is written that whosoever shall do so will surely be found out and thy welcome on all boards will be thus denied forever and ever.

24. Thou shalt log on properly and in accordance with the sysop's rules.

25. Thou shalt observe BBS time limits.

26. Thou shalt not upload "worm" or "virus" programs.

27. Thou shalt not ask stupid questions that are already fully explained in the BBS instructions.

28. Thou shalt not exchange copyrighted software thru the BBS.

29. Thou shalt not violate applicable state/federal/local laws and regulations affecting BBS telecommunications, or thy will face the wrath of the judicial system.

30. Thou shalt not hack.

A POTPOURRI OF SERVICES

There are three different types of BBSs: personal systems, group-support systems, and business systems. Personal systems are usually operated as a hobby by an individual, directly out of a home. These hobby systems make up the bulk of the BBS community. Their sysops offer everything from general message and file-transfer services to special-interest systems dedicated to almost any hobby of avocation you can imagine. Typically, these systems operate on a free-wheeling basis, with each system reflecting the interests and personality of the sysop.

```
┌─────────────────────────────────────┐
│         Main Menu                    │
│           AMULET:vc                  │
│                                      │
│ Message Menu   Help Level   User List      Questionnaires │
│ Comments       Newsletter   Files Menu     Initial Welcome │
│ Join Conference Goodbye     Page Sysop                     │
│ Your Settings  Whos Online  Verify User                   │
│ System Stats   Bulletins    Doors          ? Command Help  │
│ Conference: AMULET:vc General   Time On: 2  Time Remaining: 43 │
│ Command >> ?                         │
└─────────────────────────────────────┘
```

A typical BBS Main Menu offers you many choices.

Group-support systems offer online services to members of clubs and organizations. Most PC user groups have BBSs dedicated to supporting their members, and other organizations are also beginning to offer BBS services to their computer-using members. These systems serve as message centers and are places where members can get help and download files relating to the organization's goals. Usually, access to these systems is limited to members of the sponsoring group.

. . . .

Finally, more and more businesses, large and small, are going online with BBS services. Just about every software publisher now has a customer-support BBS, and local computer stores also find that running a BBS makes economic sense.

. . . .

Finally, more and more businesses, large and small, are going online with BBS services. Just about every software publisher now has a customer-support BBS, and local computer stores also find that running a BBS makes economic sense. Mail-order firms use BBSs to take orders and provide support for their customers. Computer-related businesses are still the most frequent operators of these systems, but the trend is starting to spread as more and more people get online. For instance, a typical non-computer-oriented system might offer support, for a fee, to a city's real-estate agents. The possibilities are almost endless.

STAKING YOUR OWN CLAIM IN CYBERSPACE

It only took me about six months of active BBSing to develop the urge to create my own board. I've run two different systems at two different times and thoroughly enjoyed both. If you have the same urge, consider starting a small BBS to test the waters. It's a rewarding and exciting way to get even more involved in computing, and it lets you participate in a personal way in the growing telecommunications field.

Many people start small BBSs using a terminal program's host mode. I've done the same thing when several associates needed to call in over a period of several days to obtain files. After tasting this simple fruit, some continue on to full-fledged BBS-hood. You might want to try this yourself for a week or two. Procomm and Telix, two easily obtainable shareware terminal programs, come with respectable host-mode scripts.

There are a surprising number of ham-radio operators who've started a BBS. Ham-radio operators and those who frequent BBSs are similar in their fondness for communicating with like-minded folks. While ham-radio operators talk about their antennas and how many watts their system puts out, computer users talk about how fast their processor is and how many colors their display can show. Being just a bit out of step, running my first BBS came before I got my amateur radio license.

According to current estimates, there are almost 100,000 BBSs operating in the United States. Just about every community of any size has at least one, and there's always room for more. If you'd like to be the next person to offer online services, there are a few things to consider before you decide to take the plunge.

Setting up a BBS costs money. I'll talk specifics later on, but even if you use the dusty XT in the closet and some public-domain software, you'll need a phone line. Investing in equipment or upgrades can run as high as five figures. It's up to you how much you spend.

Running a BBS also takes time. An active message base will require at least one hour a day to answer e-mail and keep tabs on what's going on. You'll want to make sure there isn't any open warfare between users or discussions about illegal subjects. Checking uploaded files will consume some time, too. You'll always have to verify the integrity of the files that you make available for others to download, especially if users upload them. Sysops usually spend a great deal of time gathering files for downloading.

The more you know, the better off you'll be. Be prepared to do your homework and spend time learning about the technology. Sysops are expected to have answers to a wide variety of questions. You might consider getting some good reference books for those occasions when you're absolutely stumped.

True to form, I found a hilarious sysop pre-test written by an anonymous sysop. In spite of its humor, there are truths throughout. If you pass the following test, you're ready to become a sysop.

THE BBS SYSOP-WANNA-BE TEST

To start a BBS, you first need a computer. No matter what computer you currently have, it won't be large enough or powerful enough for what you intend to do. And since you can't take the board down to do your own work, you will need another computer that you can ill afford. Next you have to find a BBS software package. This can take months, or you can write your own if you are so inclined. This can take years. Next you will need a phone line other than the one that you normally converse on. Depending on the Telco's mood, personnel, and the imminence of a strike, this could be done in as little as two weeks or it may never happen. Next, if you plan to run doors (programs that run within the BBS software) on your board, you must now spend long distance dollars in scouring other boards for evaluation and acquisition of these games. Utilities for your BBS are also an afterthought and have to be obtained in a similar fashion. All of these external programs have to be registered after a while, since most stop working after a while or have an annoying feature about them until they are registered.

You must obtain a modem. Whichever modem you currently have will not be supported by the BBS software. This is some sort of unwritten law pertaining to writing communication software. Be prepared to open your wallet wide. No, your old Hayes 300 won't be good enough. People even hate 1200 baud these days, and the teenagers seem to have U.S. Robotics HST's these days and will complain vociferously if they can't access you at 14.4.

Now you pick a name for your BBS. Whatever you choose will be ridiculed by 20 percent of those who see it. Another 50 percent will offer suggestions that are worse than the one you chose. The remaining 30 percent won't care.

The manual for the BBS software was most likely written by the author's 10-year-old and was mimeographed. It got wet in the mail and smeared as well, so at least 30 percent of the manual will be physically useless.

You'll then be faced with the task of deciding on your board structure. Who can do what and when can they do it? You must design your menus and opening screens. You have to get a pretty good stock of files, because no one will upload to you unless you have something there for them to take first.

Next comes the security aspect. You can leave your board wide open so that users with the name of Benny Beanfart, Dr. Rape, Crack, Hack, File Attack, and DR DEATH can come in and do anything they like. Or, you can lock it up so tight that no one will call. There is no compromise on this.

Opening day is here. Your board is ready, your modem is ready, Telco finally hooked you up, and then you start up. This is when after two days of no one calling, despite your ad in Computer Shopper and having placed your number on every other BBS in existence, you discover that the init strings for the modem are wrong. You discover this by calling yourself from a friend's home. This takes calls to the author of the software and the manufacturer of the modem and finally gets resolved by asking another sysop how to do it.

Finally, you're up and working. After about a week of gleefully seeing someone call, you will encounter Benny Beanfart or his ilk. He will leave public posts (always in caps and terribly mis-spelled) about what a really lousy board this is and that the sysop is a three-eyed twit. You automatically kill his account. But do you leave the message for the world to see? Killing Benny does no good because he will be back with another account such as SYSOP SUX or some such thing. Eventually he will tire of the game and go away, but he has given ideas to some of his friends who will also visit you sometime in the next week.

Then you will be visited by the "smart kid" who can tell you everything that's wrong with your machine and your software. It doesn't matter that he's calling you on a Timex Sinclair. He knows more about your 386 than Intel.

By now, you are disappointed with your message bases. You perhaps have (if you are fortunate) two or three users who post messages outside of private mail. These three users are symbiotics who, if one of their brethren does not call for two weeks, will not post because they miss their friend. Your message bases will starve. You set up many areas for messages, all carefully listed by topic. No public post will ever go into the area that it should be in. You will find a raunchy joke posted in the Bible topics area, technical questions asked in the political opinion area, and a message from one of Benny Beanfart's crony's in the technical section.

You will next encounter the user who can't do anything right. He will make you feel terribly guilty that you are running this system that seems to rudely exclude him from enjoying it, because he cannot master the concept that M means Message, F means Files, and D means download. He *does* however know how to leave comments to the sysop.

The work load is getting heavy on the board. Wow! It takes at least two hours per day to stay up with things. Answering mail, hunting down Benny Beanfart's latest account, changing screens, moving messages back to the areas that they truly belong in, adding new things, paying the telco, and arguing with your spouse. You decide to get a co-sysop to help out. He will pay little attention to the needs of the board, but *will* experiment with things like remote drop to DOS. I think this needs little elaboration.

One admonition is to not get angry about carrier drop by the user. Remember that the user is calling you through the telco. Chances are that no matter how malicious or inept the user may be, the telco probably did it anyway.

Next comes BBS software upgrade time. You will find that the author no longer supports your version and you have to upgrade. This means once again opening your wallet. The new version will not have the same reserved file names, nor will the file structures be the same. The author generously supplies you with a conversion program. This program is designed to assist you in making all the little changes needed to perform the upgrade. It will automatically convert your file names and structures. There are two types of these programs: one that requires that you have 5MB more free space than you do, and the other that will abort halfway through the conversion because of a bad disk sector read and didn't have a corresponding error trap. Of the two, the latter is the more catastrophic, because now your data can't be read by either version of the software.

GETTING STARTED

Once you've decided that it's time for you to go online with your own system, planning should be your first consideration. Start by assessing what you need to get going. It's not a long list, but you'll definitely need every item on it.

First of all, you need enough knowledge about telecommunications and modems to feel comfortable with terms like initialization string and AT commands. If you're still struggling with online systems as a user, you'll want to spend some time mastering the related concepts.

The next requirement is hardware. If you're going to run a simple BBS with just one phone line, that old AT you've pushed aside will do the job. You'll need at least an 80MB hard disk, but any monitor will do, and you won't need tons of memory. On the other hand, if you want to run a multiline system that offers access to multiple callers simultaneously, plan on using at least a 486 machine with a 300MB hard disk and several megabytes of memory.

Naturally, you need a modem. A 9600-bps modem is a bare minimum, but most people expect to connect at 14,400 bps. At the time of publication, a 14,400 modem could be purchased for about $170. Whichever modem you choose, make certain that it's completely compatible with the Hayes standard or you'll run into trouble. Most BBSs use modems from U.S. Robotics; they've become the standard in the BBS community. It's probably not worth the small amount of money you'll save by buying another brand or type that is cheaper.

Next, you'll need a phone line dedicated to the BBS. You could try to share your regular voice line with a BBS, but it seldom works out. Fortunately, the cost of installing an additional phone line is usually less than $50 for a hobby system, and you won't have to pay any special rates to the phone company. However, if you charge your users a fee for access to your system or use the BBS in a business setting, the phone company will insist that you use a business line, which costs an average of $50 per month.

I've compiled three different hardware configurations for small, medium, and large BBS systems. The prices are for late 1994 and will invariably be less by the time you read this.

BASIC SYSTEM FOR SIMPLE, MODERATELY TRAFFICKED, SINGLE-LINE BBS

> 12 Mhz AT computer
> 80MB Hard disk
> Monochrome monitor
> 5 1/4- and 3 1/2-inch floppy disk drives
> 640KB conventional memory
> 9600-bps modem
> Price: $950

MEDIUM-PERFORMANCE SYSTEM FOR FULL-FEATURED, BUSY, SINGLE-LINE BBS

> 33 Mhz 486 computer
> 500MB SCSI hard disk
> Monochrome monitor
> 5 1/4- and 3 1/2-inch floppy disk drives
> 4MB RAM
> 14,400-bps U.S. Robotics Modem
> Price: $1,800

HIGH-PERFORMANCE SYSTEM FOR FULL-FEATURED, BUSY, MULTI-LINE BBS

> 50-66Mhz Pentium computer
> 1.5G SCSI hard disk
> Tape backup
> Monochrome monitor
> 5 1/4- and 3 1/2-inch floppy disk drives
> 16MB RAM
> Multi-modem board (such as a Digiboard)
> 8 14,400-bps U.S. Robotics external modems
> Price: $9,500

One need often ignored by would-be sysops is time. Running a busy BBS takes a minimum of one hour each day just to answer e-mail and keep the BBS running smoothly. Once a week or so, a typical hobby BBS sysop spends additional time backing up the system's hard disk, either to floppy disks or to a tape backup system. If your BBS will offer public-domain software and shareware, you can count on spending an additional few hours per week adding and updating files. Finally, you'll spend an occasional day installing a new version of the BBS software after dealing with the inevitable hardware crash.

The final need, and possibly the most important, is a BBS program. Your choice here will determine a lot of things, including the time needed to set up the system in the first time, the way users interact with your system, and the time you spend maintaining your BBS.

SELECTING BBS SOFTWARE

A mark of the popularity of BBSs is the bewildering number of BBS programs available. There are literally scores of programs to tempt you, with a fantastic range of prices and capabilities. Your choice here will be critical, since switching from one program to another is usually like starting from scratch. You'll need to spend time investigating the program before making a choice.

The range is wide, both in price and capabilities. You'll find everything from free-yet-powerful software such as RBBS to software such as TinyHost, which is limited to just a few users, to expensive multiline systems costing hundreds of dollars. The most popular programs are offered as shareware, so

A mark of the popularity of BBSs is the bewildering number of BBS programs available. There are literally scores of programs to tempt you, with a fantastic range of prices and capabilities. Your choice here will be critical, since switching from one program to another is usually like starting from scratch.

you can try out the software before laying out your cash. A list of the most popular of these follows. Any one of them can be downloaded from CompuServe, GEnie, or America Online.

A BBS without callers is next to useless. To compete for users with the systems already available in most areas, you have to make your system easy, useful, and exciting; otherwise your potential users will call another BBS. Your first priority should be to check out prospective programs by calling systems that use those programs. Fortunately, just about every BBS software publisher operates a demonstration BBS. Look for the numbers for the most popular programs in the BBS Software Shoppers Guide that follows. Before making a decision, give potential programs a thorough test as a user.

The software you choose also needs to be easy for the sysop. Assessing the ease of use can be a bit more difficult, but there is a way. When you check out the demonstration BBSs and trim your list to a few possibilities, look on the demonstration system for a list of BBSs that use that software. Call a BBS near you that uses the software and ask the sysop what it's like to use it. Most sysops like the software they're running, but you can ask leading questions to get a pretty clear picture of what the system is like from the sysop's perspective.

After following these steps, you'll have trimmed the list down to one or two programs. The next step is to obtain either a shareware version of each program or the demonstration version offered by the publisher. Then it's time to test each one by installing it and running a limited version of your BBS for a short time. You'll finally settle on a single program; but whatever you do, don't be tempted to use an unregistered or pirated copy of the software—at some point, you're going to need support from the publisher.

BBS Software
Shopping Guide

Spitfire
Buffalo Creek Software
913 39th St. W
Des Moines, IA 50256
(515) 225-8496 (Voice)

RBBS-PC
Capital PC User Group Software Library
P.O. Box 1785
W. Bethesda, MD 20827
(301) 949-8848 (BBS)
(301) 762-6775 (Voice)

PCBoard
Clark Development
3950 S. 700 E, Ste. 303
Murray, UT 84107
(801) 261-8976 (BBS)
(800) 356-1686 (Voice)

TBBS
eSoft
15200 E. Girard Ave., Ste. 2550
Aurora, CO 80014
(303) 699-8222 (BBS)
(303) 699-6565 (Voice)

The Major BBS
Galacticomm
4101 SW 47th Ave., Ste. 101
Fort Lauderdale, FL 33314
(305) 583-7808 (BBS)
(305) 583-5990 (Voice)

Falken
INFO*SHARE
P.O. Box 1501
Woodbridge, VA 22193
(703) 803-8000 (BBS)
(703) 491-5823 (Voice)

TinyHost
Bruce A. Krobusek
5950 Kong Hill Dr.
Farmington, NY 14425
(716) 594-1804 (BBS)

Wildcat
Mustang Software
P.O. Box 2264
Bakersfield, CA 93303
(805) 395-0650
(800) 999-9619 (Voice)

Sapphire
Pinnacle Software
Box 714 Airport Rd.
Swanton, VT 05488
(514) 345-8654 (BBS)
(514) 345-9578

Searchlight
Searchlight Software
P.O. Box 640
Stony Brook, NY 11790
(516) 689-2566 (BBS)
(516) 751-2966 (Voice)

Oracomm
Surf Computer Services
71540 Cardess Rd.
Rancho Mirage, CA 92270
(619) 346-1608 (BBS)
(619) 346-9430

Preparing for the First Call

With the software selected, it's almost time for your first caller. First, though, you need to set up your system. The more time you spend on system design, the better your BBS will run. It's often difficult to make major changes once you get started, so take time now to get it right. A few hours spent in the planning stage will save you countless hours later.

Start by working out what your system is going to offer to its callers. Will you have files available? Messaging? E-mail? How about informational bulletins and online newsletters? Will all your users have access to every part of the BBS, or will you need several security levels to control what different users can do? If it's a business system, will you be taking customer orders on the BBS? Most BBS software enables users to page you while they're online. Decide whether you want to be interrupted and, if so, during what hours. It's best to answer all these questions on paper before you start configuring the software.

Every BBS offers messaging services. Since most programs enable you to break down messages into categories, you'll want to consider what subject each message area will handle. Be sure to set aside one area for you alone. Messages that go into that area should be private and readable only by the sysop.

E-mail services are popular and enable your users to send private messages back and forth. In most BBS software, however, the sysop can read all messages, even those that are marked as private.

The Message base is an important part of any BBS.

File Transfers

A BBS without file-transfer capabilities is almost sure to fail. Every user wants to dig around, looking for programs and other files, even on business systems. As with messaging, you'll want to break your files down into carefully chosen categories to make it easier for users to locate files.

A typical message with information about the message origin at the top.

Downloading files from your BBS is one thing; uploading files is another. Whatever you do, don't allow users to upload files into areas where they can be immediately downloaded by other users. All files uploaded to your BBS should go into a private directory so you can check them before making them available. You'll need to delete commercial programs and check for virus infections on every file you receive.

The Files Menu is visited often by most BBS users.

BULLETINS AND OTHER MESSAGES

Before going online, you'll also need to create the bulletins, help screens, and other display screens needed by your new users. Nothing can kill a BBS faster than a lack of information. Users who call but can't figure out how to use the system simply won't call back. Take as much time as you need to write brief but complete bulletins that explain your system; then make them readily available to users. Unless you're a writing wizard, be sure to run a spelling check on these information screens and proofread them carefully.

MAINTAINING SECURITY

You can create as many access levels for your users as you like (within the limits of your software), but there are some basic things to consider. First, never allow anyone but yourself to have complete access to the BBS. Users should be kept away from sysop functions and should never be allowed to view user data that contains passwords or other private information. If your BBS offers a way for a remote user to drop from the BBS to the DOS prompt, make sure you're the only one who can do this, or you risk intentional or accidental file deletions or even a complete formatting of your hard disk. Finally, never use the same password on your own BBS that you use on other systems, or you risk disaster from a malicious user.

Even your most trusted associates shouldn't get too much remote access. My first BBS was destroyed by a disgruntled former co-sysop who, before things hit the fan, changed an inactive user's status to full sysop status. That meant that this user, who rarely logged on, could do virtually anything. Lowering this person's status made me feel like the system was safe. Ha! One morning at 3 a.m. I awoke to the sound of a grinding printer, running continuously because there were no files left on the disk. This former helper had logged on as the inactive user and deleted all of the system's files.

Another thing can happen when co-sysops use macro files to log on. It's easy for anyone visiting them to obtain their password by reading their terminal program's configuration file. Before you know it, someone besides your co-sysop has your password. I've been burned by this method, too. My second BBS had all of its files deleted by someone who obtained a co-sysop password. Never give remote access levels that will jeopardize the operation of your BBS.

You'll also need a special security level for first-time callers. Legally, you need to confirm that all callers have provided their real names and address or telephone numbers. Typically, sysops restrict new users to a very limited subset of services until their identities are confirmed with a phone call. Once the two basic security levels are established, you can add as many other access levels as you need, assigning a caller to the one that is most appropriate after his or her first call.

SALTING THE MINE

You don't want your first-time callers to find an empty system, so you'll want to seed the system before going online. Create an introductory message for each message area, explaining that area, and add a few files to each file area. This will make your BBS more attractive to new callers, and it will help to ensure that they call back.

Check every part of the BBS, from leaving e-mail and public messages to uploading and downloading files. Try every help screen and bulletin. All of this takes time, but it's almost certain that you'll catch plenty of errors during this process.

ONLINE FOR THE FIRST TIME

Once you have your system configured for startup as I have described, it's time to fire it up. Still, there's one more thing to do before you go public: You need to test your completed system thoroughly yourself. Get your BBS running; then call it from another computer, pretending to be a new user. Make sure everything works as you planned and make any necessary changes.

Next, if you have multiple security levels, create dummy users for each level and then call the BBS signing on as each of those users. Again, test everything thoroughly to make sure the system runs smoothly. Once you're done, be sure to delete these dummy users to avoid confusion.

Check every part of the BBS, from leaving e-mail and public messages to uploading and downloading files. Try every help screen and bulletin. All of this takes time, but it's almost certain that you'll catch plenty of errors during this process. It's better to fix them before your first caller is online.

FISHING FOR USERS

Finally! You've done all the testing, you've finished your setup, and you're ready for callers. But how will people know your BBS exists? Depending on the function of your system, there are several ways to attract callers. If it's a publically accessible hobby system, one of the best techniques is to place messages on other BBSs in your area, announcing your new system. That method will get you started. You can also ask other sysops to include your BBS in their online BBS listings.

If your BBS supports a club or user group, publish the phone number in the group's newsletter and make announcements at meetings. One note here: It's a good idea to include basic instructions for getting online in your announcements.

If you're starting a business BBS, your best bet is to notify your customers in as many ways as you can. Include the number in your ads, send out flyers or postcards to regular customers, and offer simple instructional information to all customers who ask for it. Remember that your customers may not be familiar with online services.

Don't be concerned if things start off slowly. In fact, a slow start enables you to fix any problems that show up before you have hundreds of callers.

KEEPING YOUR BBS ALIVE

Once you're online and have a growing list of callers, your work is really just beginning. The long-term success of your system depends on how hard you work at keeping calls coming in. Here are a few basic tips:

. . . .

Once you're online and have a growing list of callers, your work is really just beginning. The long-term success of your system depends on how hard you work at keeping calls coming in.

. . . .

You can let users play some interesting games on a BBS.

- Don't let your BBS get stale. Add new files for downloading and keep updating versions of the public-domain and shareware programs available on your system. Keep the message areas up-to-date by deleting old messages.

- Answer your mail. You'll get a lot of messages from your users. If you fail to reply, they'll stop calling, so try to respond to every message within 24 hours.

- Introduce new features. By offering your callers new and interesting things to do on your system, you'll keep them calling back.

- Be responsive. If your users have complaints or request changes in your system, give these suggestions careful consideration.

- Practice safe BBSing. Be on the lookout for users who cause trouble on your system, and advise them to stop unpleasant activities. If they persist, you'll need to delete their accounts. It only takes one or two troublemakers to drive away users.

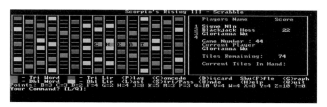

For more traditional games, you might try Scrabble on your BBS.

You can even offer a Biorhythm service.

LEGALITIES

If you have questions about the legalities of any aspect of your BBS operation, the best thing to do is contact the FCC directly. You can try their BBS first, at (301) 725-1072 (1200 8N1). Or you can contact them via voice line. Here's a list of FCC field offices:

6721 West Raspberry Road
Anchorage, AK 99502
(907) 243-2153

P.O. Box 6
Douglas, AZ 85608
(602) 364-8414

P.O. Box 311
Livermore, CA 94550
(415) 447-3614

Cerritos Corp Tower
18000 Studebaker Rd.
Room 660
Los Angeles, CA 90701
(213) 809-2096

4542 Ruffner Street, Room 370
San Diego, CA 92111
(619) 557-5478

424 Customhouse
555 Battery St.
San Francisco, CA 94111
(415) 556-7701/2

211 Main Street, Room 537
San Francisco, CA 94105
(415) 974-0702

12477 West Cedar Drive
Denver, CO 80228
(303) 236-8026

Koger Building, Room 203
8675 NW 53rd Street
Miami, FL 33166
(305) 536-5542

Airport Executive Ctr., Room 1215
2203 N. Lois Avenue
Tampa, FL 33607
(813) 228-2872

P.O. Box 1730
Vero Beach, FL 32961
(407) 778-3755

Massell Building, Room 440
1365 Peachtree Street, N.E.
Atlanta, GA 30309
(404) 347-3084

P.O. Box 85
Powder Springs, GA 30073
(404) 943-5420

P.O. Box 1030
Waipahu, HI 96797
(808) 677-3318/3954

Park Ridge Office Ctr., Room 306
1550 Northwest Highway
Parkridge, IL 60068
(312) 353-0195

800 West Commerce Road, Room 306
New Orleans, LA 70123
(504) 589-2095

P.O. Box 470
Belfast, ME 04915
(207) 338-4088

1017 Federal Building
31 Hopkins Plaza
Baltimore, MD 21201
(301) 962-2729

P.O. Box 250
Columbia, MD 21045
(301) 725-3474

NFPA Bldg., Batterymarch Park
Quincy, MA 02169
(617) 770-4023/565-8432

P.O. Box 89
Allegan, MI 49010
(616) 673-2063

24897 Hathaway Street
Farmington Hills, MI 48018
(313) 226-6078

691 Federal Bldg,
& US Courthouse
316 North Robert Street
St Paul, MN 55101
(612) 725-7810

Brywood Office Tower
Room 320
8800 East 63rd Street
Kansas City, MO 64133
(816) 926-5111

P.O. Box 1588
Grand Island, NE 68802
(308) 381-5598

1307 Federal Bldg.
111 West Huron Street
Buffalo, NY 14202
(716) 846-4511/2

201 Varick Street
New York, NY 10014
(212) 620-3437

1782 Federal Bldg
1220 SW Third Ave.
Portland, OR 97204
(503) 221-4114

One Oxford Valley Office Bldg.
Room 404
2300 East Lincoln Highway
Langhorne, PA 19047
(215) 752-1324

P.O. Box FCC
Sabana Seca, Puerto Rico 00749
(809) 784-3772

San Juan Field Office
747 Federal Building
Hato Rey, Puerto Rico 00918
(809) 753-4567

9330 LBJ Freeway, Room 1170
Dallas, TX 75243
(214) 767-5690

1225 North Loop West
Room 900
Houston, TX 77008
(713) 229-2749

P.O. Box 632
Kingsville, TX 78363
(512) 592-2531

1200 Communications Circle
Virginia Beach, VA 23455
(804) 441-6472

One Newport, Room 414
3605 132nd Avenue, SE
Bellevue, WA 98006
(206) 764-3324

1330 Loomis Trail Road
Custer, WA 98240
(206) 354-4892

Teleconferencing

chapter 8
by Paul M. and
Mary J. Summitt

The most effective use of computer-mediated conferencing involves the transmission of succinct information. The easy storage and retrieval of the information in a computer-mediated conference allows for a greater audience access and imposes fewer time restrictions on decisions or responses requiring interpretation and analysis.

A Typical Day

A typical day at our house begins around 5 a.m. After grabbing a cup of coffee, both of us stumble downstairs to begin the day's work. First we log on CompuServe and check our e-mail. Perhaps there's a message from our editor, discussing how we should proceed with the manuscript we're currently working on; one from our friend in England, responding to a question about our upcoming trip to London; a chess move from an in-law for the game we're currently playing; and a message concerning a possible trip to Moscow in the future. We respond as needed and go about our other morning responsibilities.

Mary's mother calls to talk about plans for the day. After speaking to her, Mary leaves for work. Our daughter, Jackie, then runs out to catch the bus. Paul waits for a conference phone call from a university that is considering him for a teaching position.

After arriving at her office, Mary checks her voice mail for messages. She writes notes to herself about the priority of the messages and prepares for the staff meeting that is planned for that morning.

Back home, Paul answers the phone. He is quickly introduced to the four people sitting in the university conference room. This room exists both as a physical location for these four and as a conceptual location that also includes Paul. They begin the conference by asking Paul questions about his teaching philosophy, research goals, and experience. The call lasts about an hour. Paul then heads for his classes at the university where he is a doctoral student.

At work, Mary takes part in a staff discussion of projects that are currently underway in her department. The meeting lasts just less than an hour.

Paul arrives at his office at the university and, after hooking up his laptop to the phone line, logs on to the Internet and checks for e-mail and messages from the various special-interest groups (SIGs) to which he belongs. A message concerning a call for papers gets filed in his online storage area, as does a message from a friend at Kent State University concerning quantum theory and Q-methodology. Another message, from a friend at Humboldt State University, gets a response. Other messages are filed or discarded based on their relative importance.

When Mary's staff meeting is over, she returns to her office. After rechecking her voice mail and responding to some messages, she turns to her computer and begins entering data into the spreadsheet she has been using.

After signing off the Internet, Paul hurries to a meeting with two of his advisers to discuss questions that will appear on his comprehensive exams. He then heads for his political sociology telecourse.

Meanwhile, at Jackie's school, the bell rings, signaling the end of a class period. Jackie leaves her social studies class and enters the hallway, joining hundreds of other students rushing to their next class. Jackie's next class is computers, and today she'll be working with basic text editing.

In Paul's telecourse, a student in St. Louis responds to a question from the instructor in Columbia, Missouri. Another student, from Kansas City, asks for clarification and the instructor explains.

As the day comes to a close, Paul listens to National Public Radio's *All Things Considered* while he makes the commute home. Mary saves the spreadsheet she's working on, checks her voice mail one last time, grabs her jacket, and heads for her car.

At home, while the family is eating the evening meal and watching television, the phone rings. It's Paul's father. After the phone call, the family discusses what has happened during the day. How was school? What happened during the meetings? How is the work coming?

As everyone else prepares for bed, Paul returns downstairs to sign onto one of the forums on CompuServe and take part in a real-time, online conference. About 15 people from around the world have signed on to say hello to one another and discuss upcoming events. A participant from England agrees to meet Paul and Mary face-to-face when they come to London. People from California discuss recent earthquake-recovery efforts. A participant from the Netherlands talks with one from Chicago about an upcoming event in Chicago. After 45 minutes, Paul says goodbye and signs off. It is almost 10 p.m. It has been a long day.

· ·

Communication is a kind of experience; however, when we use an electronic medium, there is no "real" location where these experiences occur.

THE FOUR BASIC FORMS OF CONFERENCING

Look back at the preceding paragraphs and notice the number of "conferences" that took place. Many of them were what is known as *face-to-face* conferences. Examples of these are the classes that both Paul and Jackie attended, the discussion of his upcoming comprehensive exams that Paul participated in, Mary's staff meeting, and the discussion of the day's events during the evening meal. There were also many other kinds of conferences, however. The question arises: Where did these other conferences take place?

We suggest that these other conferences took place in the medium that author William Gibson, in his 1984 novel *Neuromancer*, referred to as *cyberspace*. Gibson called cyberspace "a consensual hallucination." Communication is a kind of experience; however, when we use an electronic medium, there is no "real" location where these experiences occur. Those taking part in the communication construct an alternate, conceptual reality. The experience takes place in a simulated environment that is created by the consensus of those taking part in it. The individuals enter a world that they themselves have helped to create. The existence of this world—and, in a sense, the interaction that takes place within it—is a consensual hallucination.

Any electronic medium that allows interaction is a means of access to cyberspace. A conferencing method that most people have participated in is the telephone conversation, such as the one in which Paul took part. Let's look at a telephone conversation as an example of communication in cyberspace. One person, Paul, was in a specific physical location. The other people taking part in the conversation were in a totally different physical location, many miles from Paul. The conversation didn't take place in either actual physical location. So where did it take place? The only answer is that it took place in a conceptual location created by the individuals involved. That location was made possible through the electronic medium known as the telephone; the telephone must therefore access cyberspace.

As suggested in the previous paragraph, any medium that allows interaction is a means of access to

. . . .
Any electronic medium that allows interaction is a means of access to cyberspace.
. . . .

cyberspace. Television in its non-interactive mode (such as when the family viewed it during the evening meal) does not take place in cyberspace. With conventional telecasting, there is no means of interaction for the viewer. The viewer is nothing more than a receiver incapable of significant response. Paul's political sociology telecourse, however, represents a form of interactive television wherein the various participants can respond immediately to the actions and comments of other participants. The instructor and 12 of the students were located in Columbia, Missouri. Two students were located in Kansas City, and one student participated from St. Louis. The communication that took place in that class did not take place in any of those cities. It did, however, take place in a space that the people in all three locations accepted as real, a simulated environment located in that "consensual hallucination" known as cyberspace. The location was made possible by the electronic medium known as television.

Two other communication media used in teleconferencing were discussed in the opening paragraphs of this chapter. One of the first things Paul did in the morning was check the e-mail, both at home and at the university. One of the last things he did before going to bed was take part in a real-time, online conference via the computer.

A 1978 article in *Journal of Communications* suggested that both e-mail and online conferencing could be classified as teleconferencing. Scholars Arthur Jensen and Joseph Chilberg, however, in their 1991 text *Small Group Communication: Theory and Application*, argued that e-mail is not true teleconferencing. Their reasoning was that e-mail does not require time coincidence. e-mail would therefore be considered *asynchronous*. Jensen and Chilberg consider real-time, online conferencing to be a true electronic meeting. This would be considered *synchronous*.

We disagree with Jensen and Chilberg's contention that e-mail is not a form of teleconferencing. Author and publisher Stuart Brand, in his classic *The Media Lab*, discusses how the MIT Media Lab Director, Nicholas Negroponte, ran the lab one day via e-mail despite being in Japan. No one noticed any change in his management. Geographical coincidence is eliminated when using e-mail. Time coincidence is essentially eliminated. e-mail can be virtually interactive, and that interactivity must be the criteria whereby judgment is passed. There is a few-second delay in a voice transmission from a space shuttle mission. Are those conversations not interactive because of that delay? Does that delay make these radio communications asynchronous and therefore not a true electronic meeting or conversation?

These two forms of computer-mediated communication (CMC), or teleconferencing, take place in cyberspace. The locations where the e-mail messages are kept (be it a forum, a special interest group, or a hotline), as well as the locations of the real-time, online conferences (known as "rooms" by users) exist mostly in the minds of the participants. They are another example of the "consensual hallucination" of which Gibson spoke.

In the next pages of this chapter we're going to look at the various forms of conferencing that exist. We'll begin with face-to-face conferencing, the standard by which all other forms are judged. We'll then turn to the electronic media and to computer-mediated communication. The advantages and disadvantages of all forms of conferencing will be examined and a best use will be suggested for each. We then want to turn our attention to the underlying structures of the various conferencing media and, finally, to what it will mean as the use of teleconferencing continues to grow. Let's begin by looking at the traditional conferencing standard—the face-to-face meeting—and how it's composed.

Face-to-Face Conferencing

Face-to-face interaction—communication between two or more people in physical proximity to each other—has been the standard medium of information exchange throughout human history.

A face-to-face conference requires participants to be present in the same location simultaneously. The size of the group is generally limited to fewer than 100 participants. With larger groups, one individual tends to dominate the face-to-face conference while other participants become passive spectators. (We'll return to this issue later when we discuss structural considerations.)

Face-to-face communication was the exclusive means of human conferencing until early in the 20th century. The masses have only had access to the electronic media during the past 80 years or so. Therefore, researchers tend to treat face-to-face meetings as the ideal or standard by which all others should be judged. Examples of face-to-face conferences include almost all school classes (such as the ones both Jackie and Paul attended), staff meetings (such as the one Mary attended), and special-purpose meetings (such as Paul's meeting to discuss the questions for his comprehensive exams).

Some of the advantages and disadvantages of face-to-face conferencing are listed in the table at the bottom.

There are some advantages of face-to-face meetings that other forms of conferencing cannot equal. The first of these advantages is the availability of nonverbal cues. In face-to-face communication, both parties are exposed to all the cues that exist in a conversation, both verbal and nonverbal. Nonverbal cues include body language as well as cues that the human senses of sight, hearing, touch, smell, and taste might pick up. It is thought that these additional cues help in the communication

ADVANTAGES AND DISADVANTAGES OF FACE-TO-FACE CONFERENCING.

Advantages	Disadvantages
Personal	Requires geographic coincidence
Intimate	Requires time coincidence
Persuasive	Costly in resources
Considerate	Difficult to retain

process. Media such as audio or video recordings cannot capture the entire range of these communication cues. The parameters of the communication process are called the *bandwidth*.

By bandwidth, we are referring to the dimensions and characteristics of the medium through which the communication is passing. Psychology professor J.J. Gibson, in a 1966 text, *The Senses Considered as Perceptual Systems*, defined the five perceptual systems of the human body as being: the basic orienting system, responsible for equilibrium; the hearing or auditory system; the touch system; the taste-smell system; and the visual system. Bandwidth can be measured by both *width* and *depth*. The width of the communication medium refers to how many of these perceptual systems are in use. The depth of the medium refers to the quality or resolution of the specific perceptual system(s). In face-to-face communication, all five perceptual systems are in use, so width is maximized. Depending on the individual, the depth (or quality) of all five perceptual systems may also be maximized. For instance, if a person is able to hear sounds ranging from 16 to 16,000 cycles-per-second, the full depth of the auditory perceptual system is in use.

The face-to-face meeting is personal and intimate because of the expanse of the bandwidth. It is often considered the most persuasive of the various types of meetings for business and other task-oriented purposes. This may be because a certain amount of consideration, effort, or even material expanse is necessary to arrange a successful face-to-face meeting, and there is an implied respectfulness when the meeting is held on the higher-status individual's home ground.

There are also disadvantages to face-to-face meetings. For businesses, one big disadvantage can be the cost and amount of preparation that a successful face-to-face meeting entails. Because each participant in a face-to-face meeting must be in the same physical location at the same time, transportation costs can be prohibitive. Preparation and planning must therefore be extensive.

Another disadvantage is that the speed of the conference is limited to the speed of human speech and perception. The excess of cues, both verbal and nonverbal, can sometimes interfere with the message being expressed. The presentability of the speaker must be considered, as well as the reception abilities of the audience. Face-to-face presentations may include so much information that the audience can't take it all in. A presentation of more than about 20 minutes tends to lose its audience. Conversely, too much information in a short amount of time tends to confuse participants.

Face-to-face presentations may include so much information that the audience can't take it all in.

AUDIO CONFERENCING

Let's turn our attention now to conferences taking place in cyberspace. We'll begin with telephone, or audio, conferences. An example of the audio conference was when Paul was interviewed by a group of university faculty members regarding a teaching position. As you'll remember, the faculty members asked Paul questions about his teaching philosophy and experiences.

Some of the advantages and disadvantages of audio conferencing are listed in the table at the bottom of this page.

The information presented in important meetings sometimes needs to be preserved. The only way face-to-face conferences can be retained for future use is through personal memory, written transcripts, or recordings. The cost for preserving the information can be high and the means of retention may still not provide the level of information that was available during the conference. Personal memory is fallible. Neither written transcripts nor recordings (audio or video) can provide a true representation of the total information that is present in these meetings, because these mediums do not provide the bandwidth necessary to capture all of the information present at a face-to-face conference.

One of the most apparent advantages of the audio conference is that there is no requirement for geographic coincidence. In other words, the participants in the conference do not need to be in the same physical location in order for the conference to take place. As described previously, the conference occurs in a simulated environment created by the participants themselves, in conjunction with the medium used. This lowers both the cost and the level of preparation that is involved in the conference.

The decision to use face-to-face conferencing rather than an electronic medium often depends on the issues at stake and the intended audience of any given meeting. Critical issues are sometimes best dealt with in face-to-face meetings. Face-to-face meetings can be used to clear up any possible misunderstandings that may arise during a project. Face-to-face meetings often work best with executive audiences, those having final decision-making authority.

One disadvantage that audio conferencing has in common with face-to-face meetings is that the speed of the conference is limited to the speed of human speech and of human reception. While most verbal cues are present in audio conferencing, all visual cues and most nonverbal cues are missing.

ADVANTAGES AND DISADVANTAGES OF AUDIO CONFERENCING.

Advantages	Disadvantages
Geographic coincidence not needed	Requires time coincidence
Lower cost in resources	Loss of verbal cues
Easier to retain	

The fact that this information may be missing from the conference is not necessarily a drawback. As discussed previously, too much information can distract the audience to the point that the message is lost. In the audio conference, because all visual cues and most of the nonverbal cues are missing, the speaker must make sure that the available bandwidth for the auditory communication is used in the most effective way possible.

In audio conferencing, as in face-to-face meetings, even though there is not a geographical requirement, there is a requirement that all of the subjects be present at the same time. Because of the smaller bandwidth involved, the optimum size for the group involved in the conference is much smaller, with a maximum of 10 to 20 participants. Otherwise, participants become an audience.

The best applications of audio conferencing are similar to those of face-to-face meetings. Both methods can be effective for discussing critical issues with executive audiences. Another good use of audio conferencing is when a consensus is sought or preliminary information is required, such as in the faculty search meeting.

As with face-to-face conferences, the only way audio conferences can be retained for future use is through personal memory, written transcripts, or recordings. Cost factors, once again, can be prohibitive. And the use of audio conferencing still does not provide the full level of information that was available during the conference.

VIDEO CONFERENCING

Video conferencing can supply the information contained in audio conferencing while adding some visual information. Some of the advantages and disadvantages of video conferencing are listed in the table at the bottom of this page.

The example of Paul's political sociology telecourse illustrates some of the unique characteristics of video conferencing. In this example, there were three physical locations involved: the Columbia, Kansas City, and St. Louis campuses of the University of Missouri. Geographical coincidence is therefore not required in video conferencing. Time coincidence, however, *is* required. All the participants in this telecourse had to be present in their various studios at the same time.

ADVANTAGES AND DISADVANTAGES OF VIDEO CONFERENCING.

Advantages	Disadvantages
Wider bandwidth than audio conferencing	Costly in resources
Does not require geographic coincidence	Requires time coincidence
Easy to retain	Costly to retain

The number of participants involved in a video conference is limited, in general, to the size of the studio facilities used. The size of the group is limited more specifically by participation factors. As with face-to-face and audio conferencing, the larger the number of participants, the more likely it is that many of the group will be nothing more than observers.

The bandwidth of the video conference is wider and therefore can accommodate more information than the audio conference (although less than the face-to-face conference). Again, care must be taken not to overwhelm the participants with information, as the speed of the conference is limited to the speed of human speech and human reception. With the inclusion of both verbal and nonverbal cues, the glut of information can sometimes interfere with the message being expressed. Presentation factors of the speaker must be considered as well as the reception abilities of the audience.

As with audio and face-to-face conferences, the only way a video conference can be retained for future use is through the use of personal memory, written transcripts, or recordings. Again, cost factors can be prohibitive. Both audio and videotape must be maintained in temperature- and humidity-controlled environments. Storage space becomes a factor. The cost of videotape storage can increase the cost of conference retention considerably.

Situations where visual information is necessary, but face-to-face meeting is not possible, lend themselves well to this conferencing method. This might include situations where executive decision-making is necessary or where consensus is being sought.

COMPUTER-MEDIATED CONFERENCING

As discussed, there are two basic types of computer-mediated conferencing: asynchronous and synchronous. Each of these can take two forms, depending on the number of participants involved: one-to-one and one-to-many. The permutations of these possibilities are as follows:

THE VARIOUS FORMS OF COMPUTER-MEDIATED COMMUNICATION.

Participants	Synchronous	Asynchronous
One-to-One	Private conversation	E-mail
One-to-Many	Group conference	Forum messages

Asynchronous computer conferencing is represented by the various forms of e-mail that Paul and Mary receive via CompuServe, Internet, and BITNET. Some of these messages are addressed specifically to Paul and Mary, while others are addressed to a group of individuals having similar interests. An example of synchronous computer conferencing would be the real-time online computer conference that Paul participated in before going to bed. Let's look at each of these conferencing forms separately.

e-mail can take either of two basic forms. Both are referred to as asynchronous, which means that the participants do not need to be logged in at the same time. There is no need for either time coincidence or geographic coincidence. The participants can be in many different locations. Hundreds of individuals can participate in asynchronous conferencing.

In the first model, the message originates with one individual (the sender) and terminates with another individual (the receiver). It is analogous to one person writing a letter to another. However, as in the Media Lab example discussed previously, a sense of spontaneity and immediacy can nonetheless be maintained through this type of teleconferencing.

In the second model of asynchronous conferencing, the message is addressed to many receivers and is stored in some central location. The message originates with one individual (the sender) and terminates with a large number of receivers. It is analogous to a radio station broadcasting its message to a large audience. The type of conceptual space that is created is sometimes referred to as a forum, a SIG, a bulletin board, or even a hotline. Examples would include CompuServe's CyberForum and the Masscomm and Q-Method hotlines available from Commserve on BITNET.

The synchronous conferencing form also has two models. Synchronous means that in these types of conferencing, time coincidence is required. While geographical coincidence is not necessary, these synchronous conferencing models do require that all participants be logged on at the same time. The number of participants for the synchronous models would be limited by the same restrictions that apply to audio and video conferencing methods.

The first model of synchronous conferencing is the one-to-one private chats that occur between two individuals online at the same time. Bulletin Board System (BBS) users sometimes

The major online services, such as CompuServe, Prodigy, and America Online, enable subscribers to "talk" with other subscribers in real time.

have the ability to "chat" between nodes. This is similar to a phone call between two individuals. The major online services, such as CompuServe, Prodigy, and America Online, enable subscribers to "talk" with other subscribers in real time. There is even a function called "talk" on UNIX-based Internet systems.

The second model of synchronous conferencing is the one-to-many. This represents a multi-participant, real-time, online conference. Depending on the system, these take place in "chat" or "conference" rooms. It must be remembered that these "rooms" exist only in the mind of the participants. The Internet also has a "chat" function available.

The advantages of both forms of computer conferencing include speedy delivery, ease of use, and the easy availability of feedback. What we mean here is that no matter where the message is sent from, it generally can be delivered to the addressee and responded to within a few hours. In most cases, only a minimal amount of training is necessary for the user to be sending and receiving messages in a relatively short amount of time. Once a message is received, it is only a matter of a few keystrokes to reply. Another advantage of computer conferencing is that there is no limit on information retrieval and modification. Mass storage is accomplished easily and all information from the conference can be archived in the computer file.

Opinions differ about the disadvantages of computer-mediated conferencing. The conference speed is limited to the transfer rate of the system and the reading and typing rate of the participants. Business writer Laurie Davis, in a 1992 *Beyond Computing* article, suggested that computer conferencing has no "presentation" value, is not suited to lengthy and complex subjects, and is impersonal. Research also suggests that more

ADVANTAGES AND DISADVANTAGES OF COMPUTER-MEDIATED CONFERENCING.

Advantages	Disadvantages
Does not require geographic coincidence	May require time coincidence
May not require time coincidence	No "presentation" value
Speedy delivery	Considered impersonal
Ease of use	May require more time than other conferencing types
Easy, built-in feedback	
Considered more "democratic"	

time is required for CMC groups to be productive than other conferencing groups.

These findings conflict with Dr. Starr Roxanne Hiltz' 1978 research, which suggested that computer conferencing provides "in-depth discussion" and "more personal involvement." Much recent research suggests that computer conferencing is more "democratic," in that the individual status of the participants is not as noticed and therefore participants are more open in their communication. Because research in computer-mediated communications is still in its infancy, these potential disadvantages should not dissuade groups from using computer conferencing as an alternative to face-to-face communication.

Robert Johansen and Robert DeGrasse, in a 1979 *Journal of Communication* article describing their research at the Institute for the Future, in Menlo Park, Calif., suggested that some of the positive effects of computer conferencing on work patterns include: more geographic separation between groups, more international communication, more flexibility in working hours, and enhanced flexibility in lifestyles and habitation. Two negative effects they discussed were longer working hours and information overload.

The most effective use of computer-mediated conferencing involves the transmission of succinct information. The easy storage and retrieval of the information in a computer-mediated conference allows for a greater audience access and imposes fewer time restrictions on decisions or responses requiring interpretation and analysis.

MITIGATING FACTORS IN THE FLOW OF INFORMATION

There are underlying issues, traditions, and structures that can further affect a conference. Both the technology used and the users themselves can place restrictions on the flow of information. First let's look at the technologies and the restrictions that they can place on the users. We'll begin with the most restrictive, or authoritarian, technology: television.

Television is authoritarian by nature. The viewer is forced to view whatever the director chooses to be viewed. Television is also a medium requiring many so-called "support" personnel. It is these support personnel who determine what will be seen or heard during the conference. The camera must be aimed by a crew member at a given individual before that individual can be seen. The on-camera participants must have proper light levels falling on them so that the camera can properly capture their image. In order

Television is authoritarian by nature. The viewer is forced to view whatever the director chooses to be viewed.

to be heard, the participants must be near an audio pickup device and this device must be adjusted by audio personnel to provide the best sound quality. The level of interactivity is therefore severely repressed, because it is the support personnel, not the participants or the viewers, who make decisions concerning what will be seen and heard.

The bandwidth of the video technology also restricts the structure of the conference. Not only do the support personnel make the selections of who will be seen and heard, but the technology itself restricts the number of individuals who can be seen or heard at any one time. Whether by nature or practice, television has become the medium of the closeup. Closeups restrict the number of individuals that can be seen in any given visual. Multiple closeups can be presented on the screen at the same time, but then the size of the viewing screen itself determines whether the picture is understandable to the viewer. The result is that, for the most effective transmission of a message, only one person should be seen and heard during the conference at any one time.

After 50 years of technological evolution, audiences have come to expect network-quality images during television programs. A video conference, because of the medium used, is often judged by the aesthetic standards applied to television programs.

• •

After 50 years of technological evolution, audiences have come to expect network-quality images during television programs. A video conference, because of the medium used, is often judged by the aesthetic standards applied to television programs, and the participants or viewers bring certain expectations to it. These expectations include a high "presentation" value—in other words, the audience expects to be entertained. Past experiences with television can, therefore, interfere with the purpose of the video conference. Unless care is taken, video conferences can degenerate into entertainments or spectacles wherein the prospective participants become mere spectators.

How do these structural and perceptual limitations pertain to computer-mediated conferences?

The software used in the CMC conference can greatly affect the structure of the conference—as well as the thought patterns of the participants. As media philosopher Michael Heim has suggested in his books, *Electronic Language* and *The Metaphysics of Virtual Reality*, the structure of the computer program sets up patterns of thought in the user. MS-DOS users think differently from Windows or Macintosh users. In creating a document, WordPerfect users structure their thought processes differently from Word users, just as the thought structure of an English-speaking individual is different from the thought structure of a French-speaking individual. If, as media guru Marshal McLuhan suggested, "the medium is the message," it is important to consider the broad ramifications and subtle influences of whatever technology is employed. The technology can influence both the final product and the user.

Certain communications and conferencing software enables different levels of access to e-mail and online interaction. For instance, while conferencing in CompuServe's CyberForum using WINCIM software, one of the authors is able to carry on multiple individual conversations while at the same time keeping track of the group discussion.

MIT's Sherry Turkle, in a paper presented at the 1993 meeting of the International Communication Association, suggested that these types of computer-mediated communication serve "as an *evocative object* for thinking about community." Recent research by one of the authors suggests that conference participants do create a democratic community in cyberspace and this democratic community enables more

information to be presented and discussed during the conference. Oregon State University's Greg Scott, in a 1991 article for *Technological Horizons in Education Journal*, suggests that more "real" communication takes place in computer teleconferencing. This happens despite the software capability of locking out unwanted users. In WINCIM, this capability is represented by an icon of someone holding his or her hands over his or her ears. This is sometimes referred to as the "bozo filter."

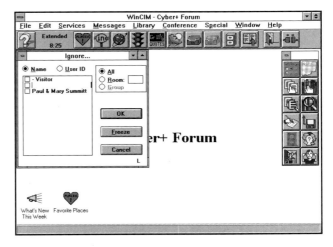

WinCIM's "Bozo filter" icon.

Depending on the software and the conferencing system that is used, participants in computer-mediated communications have a wide range of interactivity available to them.

• •

INTERACTIVITY: MAKING THE CONNECTION

Interactivity is the key to effective teleconferencing. Doctoral student Jonathan Steuer, in a 1992 *Journal of Communications* article, defined interactivity as "the extent to which users can participate in modifying the form and content of a mediated environment in real time." The software, then (and by extension, the software programmer), determines the level of interactivity available to the user. While the participants may seem to have choices, the reality is that they only have those choices made available by the software and the programmer.

Some programmers equip their communications and teleconferencing software with as many user choices and options as possible. This can enable multiple individual conversations to take place while a group conference continues. Other software restrict the users to one conversation at a time. Some programs allow the use of nicknames or aliases, which greatly increases the informal atmosphere of the online conference. Others require the use of a participant's real name, thereby perhaps inhibiting some participants.

While in many ways CMC creates a more democratic environment for conferencing by equalizing the status of most of the participants, the programmer might also create, through the communications software, a privileged status for at least one participant. That participant is called the systems operator (sysop). While in some programs, individuals can lock out others from speaking to them, the sysop can prevent a potential participant from even accessing the conference at all. This removes that particular individual's right to be heard by anyone. In one of the authors' current research projects, in which sysops have been interviewed about their authority in cyberspace, all of the sysops have admitted that they have used this ability to either lock out

· ·

The use of the so-called information superhighway is expanding, yet certain groups can be (and are) excluded. Groups with higher socioeconomic status usually gain access to new technologies faster than those with lower status.

or restrict the usage by individuals when the sysop felt it was necessary. The sysop thus can be seen as an authoritarian figure who has the potential of limiting the participation of other conference users.

One final and related concern in regard to CMC is the actual access to the medium. The use of the so-called information superhighway is expanding, yet certain groups can be (and are) excluded. Groups with higher socioeconomic status usually gain access to new technologies faster than those with lower status. A 1991 study found that computer-technology users were "better educated, more affluent, and employed in white-collar occupations" compared to those who did not have access to this technology. This enables the higher-status group to extend its advantages over the lower status group. If this knowledge gap continues—and there is no reason to believe it won't—what changes in the social fabric of our society will be created (or prevented)?

The number of American telecommuters grew to more than 6.5 million people by 1992. The 1994 Los Angeles earthquake caused many more people to consider the work-at-home option. Our socioeconomic system, once dominated by agriculture, switched to a manufacturing base in the early 1900s and remained that way until the 1960s. Today, however, information is the dominant commodity produced by the American workforce. This information is being derived, communicated, and assessed according to a new set of standards, an emerging post-literary "tradition."

Media scholar Neil Postman, in his 1985 book *Amusing Ourselves to Death*, suggested that history can be broken down into four different traditions of where truth is found. These conceptual traditions are:

THE TRADITIONS OF TRUTH.

Type of Tradition	Location of Truth
Oral	In the spoken word
Literary	In the written word
Visual	"Seeing is believing"
Interactive	In the experience

Computer-mediated communication, or teleconferencing, is one medium through which our society is making the transition from a visual tradition to a new and more profitable interactive tradition.

Human culture began with an oral tradition, in which "a man's word was his bond." Truth was found in the spoken word. Leaders were those who were able to draw on resources of speech, such as proverbs and parables, that enabled them to make and communicate decisions. In the oral tradition, speech was associated with action.

Although the first printing press in America was established as early as 1638, it was not until the early 1900s that the literary tradition replaced the oral tradition (or as Swiss linguist de Ferdenand Saussure expressed it, the oral tradition was overwhelmed by "the tyranny of writing"). The locus of truth moved from a man's word to the written contract. Speech became transitory, while the written word was solid and unchanging. People came to believe that if something was written, it was true. To a degree, literature still implied action. This action, however, began to be more conceptual.

Postman suggests that during the last 30 years we have moved into a new tradition, a visual culture in which television is perceived as the repository of truth. According to media critic Daniel Boorstin, the visual image "conquered ... and received unconditional surrender" from the literary tradition. Seeing became the underlying reason for believing. Expanding upon Boorstin's concept of the "pseudo-event" presented in *The Image*, Postman suggests that television gives "fragmented and irrelevant information" a "pseudo-context" or a presumable use.

We suggest here that the transition is now underway toward what we will call an interactive tradition. Author Arthur C. Clarke, commenting on interactive "virtual reality" technology, has suggested that it "won't merely replace TV" but "eat it alive." Michael Heim, in *The Metaphysics of Virtual Reality*, suggests that this new interactive tradition "reclaims something of the direct flow of oral discourse." The interactive tradition can be seen as a bridging of the three previous traditions, making the best use of the three while expanding and changing the very concept of knowledge and truth.

It must be kept in mind that all four of these traditions can exist within the same society, but one will ultimately dominate. The power within a society will reside with those who understand and practice the dominant tradition. History supports this contention.

Computer-mediated communication, or teleconferencing, is one medium through which our society is making the transition from a visual tradition to a new and more profitable interactive tradition. It is not without its pitfalls, however. Research must continue on the effects of this technology, both on the content and flow of information and on the lives of the people who use it.

L ife in the Smart Office

chapter 9
by Paul M. and
Mary J. Summitt

Working from the home
office, or telecommuting, is
part of the changing labor
profile created by the shift
from an industrial society to
an information society.
The estimated 10 million-
plus telecommuters today
are made possible by
developing technologies. But
just because telecommuting
is possible, is telecommuting
necessarily feasible
or desirable?

BASICS OF OFFICE AUTOMATION

The New Merriam-Webster Dictionary defines an office as "a place where a business is transacted or a service is supplied." Automation is defined as "automatic operation of an apparatus, process, or system by mechanical or electronic devices that replace human operators." Office automation can thus be seen as the process of replacing human operators wherever a business is transacted or a service supplied. This definition raises serious and potentially disturbing issues that are addressed later in this chapter. For now, we will examine how automation has been applied to office environments and why.

Historically speaking, the United States has moved from an agrarian society, to an industrial society, to the information society we live in today. While this transition was occurring, the nature and even the location of our workplaces changed as well. Today more people make their living in the information and communication industries than in either agriculture or manufacturing. The results are changing work habits and conditions. More people work in offices today than ever before and, as telecommuting becomes increasingly common for many workers, home offices are becoming more prevalent.

This chapter examines the potential advantages and disadvantages of the new automated office—what these changes will mean for efficiency and productivity and whether there are possible negative effects. This chapter will also provide an overview of the emerging hardware and software that the home-office worker might need to work efficiently in the modern business world.

Let's begin first by defining three areas of interest: the concept of office automation and what it means; problems that can arise from office automation; and finally, what improvements, changes, or ramifications office automation might create in the life of the modern worker.

Whether in a corporate or home environment, there are two general types of offices, as defined by how these offices generate, access, and apply information. Journalist and office automation expert Walter Kleinschrod, in his 1986 *Critical Issues in Office Automation*, referred to the two office environments as Type I and Type II. Type I environments are those where information is processed in routine procedures. This kind of work takes place in data-processing and word-processing situations. Type II environments encompass "nonroutine informational tasks typically performed by managers, professionals, and other knowledge workers." For most of us, the Type II environment describes our home-office environment, although there are some home businesses that do fall into the Type I description. These two types of offices are sometimes referred to by other names. "Production" or "standard" offices refer to Type I environments, while "custom" or "nonstandard" offices refer to Type II environments.

We further suggest that office automation occurs in four stages: *Stage I*, the introduction of technology into office procedures; *Stage II*, the improvement of the flow of, and access to, information within the organization; *Stage III*, the introduction of a networked-based system that allows for effective performance; and *Stage IV*, the introduction of an organization-wide system supporting the basic needs of the office workers. Let's look at each of these stages a little more closely.

Introducing Technology to an Office

In *Stage I*, technology is introduced into office procedures. If we accept that the office is the "control system" for any business, then efficiency, productivity, and performance are important considerations in the operation of any office. It is estimated that every piece of paper that is used and stored in a business costs that business an average of about 13 cents. According to Don Avedon and Joseph Levy, in their 1994 book *Electronic Imaging Systems: Design,*

Applications, and Management, "most 'paper-intensive' business operations end up misfiling three out of 100 records." This means that for every 100 pages of paper that a business deals with, the business loses about 40 cents. Depending on the information these pieces of paper contain, the business could be losing even more. For a manual, paper-intensive operation, this might be as efficient and productive as is possible. But before any reader jumps to the conclusion that this kind of mishandling makes the paperless office a worthy and inevitable goal, consider the words of office-automation consultant Amy Wohl: "The paperless office is about as realistic as the paperless bathroom!" Kleinschrod suggests that paper is "an extremely convenient medium for conveying information. You can file it, retrieve it, mail it, stick it in your pocket, write on it, and dispose of it without ever plugging one device into an outlet, without ever keying one command at a terminal. That's user-friendly!" So, if the virtual elimination of paper is not the real goal of the modern office, what do the words "efficiency," "productivity," and "performance" mean, and what do they imply about the way business views the world?

Let's first look at how these three words are defined. The dictionary defines "efficient" as "productive of desired effects, especially without loss or waste." The synonym of efficient is "competent." "Productive," which is used in defining efficient, is defined as "the act or process of producing." To produce, meaning "to present to view, exhibit, to give birth or rise to, to give being or form to, and to cause to accrue," is synonymous with extending, prolonging, bringing about, making, and manufacturing. In business, the standard definition of "productivity" has been "the ratio of output to labor input." "Performance" is defined as "the act or process of performing" and is synonymous with accomplishment, execution, discharge, achievement, and function, particularly "in a set manner." Finally, all three words, efficiency, productivity, and performance, when applied to business, imply growth. But how does the application of technology help a business grow?

In 1984, the average cost of a dictated letter, including both the manager's and the secretary's time, was $8.10. Word-processing has greatly improved this area of office performance and efficiency. But other measurements of "productivity" are not so easily made, because many so-called "bottom-line" results are not easily measurable.

For this we must look at how technology itself is defined. British cultural and political critic Raymond Williams, in his 1976 *Keywords: A Vocabulary of Culture and Society*, suggested that the definition of technology has been transformed over time. In the 17th century, the word "technology" was used "to describe a systematic study of the arts or the terminology of a particular art." In the 18th century, the definition expanded to "a description of the arts, especially the Mechanical." In the 19th century, as the split between science and art that had begun during the Middle Ages expanded, the definition of technology became "a system of methods" that applied specifically to the "practical arts." This definition agrees, in principle, with the current definition of technology as "a technical method of achieving a practical purpose."

Thus the purpose of *Stage I*, the application of technology to office operations, is the achievement of the practical purpose of improved efficiency, productivity, and performance within the organization by applying a "system of methods" to its procedures. But how can these things be measured in the office, especially in the home office? In some automated offices—especially those involved in high levels of word-processing—keystrokes, lines, documents, or quantities of some kind are counted, measured, and cost-analyzed. For instance, approximately 40 percent of the average secretary's day involves typing. In 1984, the average cost of a dictated letter, including both the manager's and the secretary's time, was $8.10. Word-processing has greatly improved this area of office performance and efficiency. But other measurements of "productivity" are not so easily made, because many so-called "bottom-line" results are not easily measurable.

IMPROVING INFORMATION FLOW AND ACCESS

Stage II, the improvement of the flow of and access to information within the organization, deals with communication. According to Kleinschrod, the average office manager has 15 interruptions per day. Up to 50 percent of business callers don't reach their intended

Another question is what long-distance carrier to go with. Some important considerations in this area include cost-per-minute, accounting procedures, quality of the connections, speed of data communications, and the number of circuits available at any given point in time.

party on the first call. Both these statistics lend support to the introduction and use of electronic mail and voice mail technologies.

The introduction of these types of technologies may require an examination of the telephone equipment and services that are available in your service area. This raises a number of important questions that you should ask yourself.

Should you separate your voice lines from your data lines? The types of switching systems in use today by many local telephone companies, while being upgraded almost daily, are not capable of the simultaneous handling of both voice and data. Should you wire your office with today's switching systems and then re-tool at a later date when the local phone company does its upgrade, or should you go ahead and try to guess what the standard switches will be in the future? The alternative to these two choices is do nothing.

INTRODUCING A NETWORKED SYSTEM

Stage III, the introduction of a networked-based system that allows for more effective performance, again deals with communication. Kleinschrod suggests that it takes an average of 35 phone calls to schedule a meeting for 10 people. This is a strong argument for the use of calendar-management software.

What kind of networked system you use, then, becomes the question. According to Kleinschrod, there are six basic ways to hook together office computers. Each of these methods has disadvantages and advantages.

The first, and probably least desirable, is called *terminal emulation* (TE). Here, the computer is hooked up with a host, but files can only be read or printed, not changed and saved. While probably a great security feature, this method is more of a nuisance than an advantage, and should be avoided.

This allows for data and file transfer as well as e-mail services for the company. Another added advantage of this system is that it provides employees with connections with the outside world.

The second method uses file transfer software similar to bulletin board software systems, but it is far more expensive. There are cost and security concerns with this system that probably should rule it out of consideration.

The intelligent LAN, or Local Area Network, is probably the most common system used today. One problem with this system is that it cannot transfer information to machines that use a different code structure.

This problem is solved, to an extent, by another type of networked system—the protocol converter. This system, however, also has disadvantages, which include the lack of standardization in the industry.

A fifth alternative is that some computers come with built-in linkage capabilities. Cost factors and lack of standardization again are considerations with this alternative.

Finally, time-sharing services are an alternative that many companies—including those not yet ready for a personalized in-house system—have opted for. Here, the company acquires access codes for its employees for a service, such as Compuserve or America Online.

INTRODUCING AN ORGANIZATION-WIDE SYSTEM

Stage IV, the implementation of an organization-wide system supporting the generic needs of the office workers, deals with the basic definition of information. Dr. Lee R. Talbert, director of Advance Business Systems at Bell Northern Research in Ottawa, said in 1986 that all office automation involves the transmitting of information, whether in time or in space. He suggests that information comes in three basic forms: writing, which includes text and data; graphics, which includes charts, pictures, maps, and similar materials; and spoken communication. Technology in the form of the telephone has long transported spoken communication over space. Voice mail now transports spoken communication over time as well. Electronic mail transports written information over both time and space. Technology, in the forms of videotape and the newer EIS, or electronic imaging systems, enables graphical information to be transported over both time and space.

What do these new forms of technology mean to the traditional office and home-office worker? We'll discuss some of the broader social issues later in this chapter. For now, let's look at the types of office-automation software and hardware, and the decisions that go into choosing them.

ADDRESSING
SOFTWARE
AND
HARDWARE

In the following discussion, we will use Talbert's three basic forms of information as the guiding principle in assessing software and hardware. For our purposes, written information is transported via word-processing, data-management, and spreadsheet software; graphics information is transported by imaging, graphics, and drawing software; and spoken communication is transported by electronic communications and voice mail software applications.

Kleinschrod suggests that in determining what applications are to be used in the large office, the software should be selected first, followed by the hardware that enables the use of that particular software. For the home-office situation, this suggestion may not be applicable. The home office has two basic choices in regard to hardware: the IBM-compatible system or the Macintosh system. However, an interesting alternative is the relatively new combination systems that enable the running of either type of software on the same machine. Hardware, as far as the basic computer system is concerned, may not be as important a consideration in the future as it has been in the past. As a result, some of the platform considerations of the past, such as choosing between DOS, Windows, OS/2, and Macintosh, are also not as important. Kleinshrod's rule remains a good one: First choose your software, and then select the hardware and platform that enables you to use that software.

Researchers in the 1980s concluded that software structures the way we think. With this in mind, remember that the software you select may alter the way you work.

For the home office, the following software applications should be considered must-haves: word processing, database management, spreadsheet, graphics management, and communications.

Two important considerations in choosing software are its compatibility and its portability. Compatibility is defined by Allen Wyatt in his 1990 *Computer Professional's Dictionary* as the ability of selected software to work together. Portability is defined as the degree to which an application is able to execute on a variety of machines and platforms.

For maximum compatibility and portability, you might want to choose software that is among the most popular in its class. In the realm of word-processing, WordPerfect (for DOS, Windows, OS/2, and Macintosh) has been called the business and industry standard. Microsoft Word (for DOS, Windows, and Macintosh), however, has also been a big seller. There are many other excellent word-processing programs that do not share the popularity (or in some cases the portability), but still might merit consideration depending upon your specific purposes and needs.

• •

Desktop-publishing (DTP) software would also fall into this category. DTP software enables the user to create newspapers, magazines, newsletters, and other forms of professional-looking printed materials. Two of the most popular DTP packages are Aldus Pagemaker (DOS and Windows) and Ventura Publisher (DOS and Windows). Other noteworthy DTP packages include Microsoft Publisher and Publish It!.

Database-management software is also very important, and the selection of it requires considerable forethought. Compatibility and portability are especially relevant in selecting data-management software. While the various versions of dBASE have long been the standard, newer programs such as FoxPro, Microsoft Access, Paradox, and Q & A have become perhaps more well known and more accessible to the office worker. Other forms of database management are often called PIMs, or personal information managers. These are basically special-application database-management software systems used for business and personal contacts. There are also special-application database managers for keeping records such as the books and magazines in your business library or the video and audio tapes used in your business.

Spreadsheet programs are applications that enable the processing of tabular information that is arranged in columns and rows, referred to as rectangular arrays. Lotus 1-2-3 (DOS and Windows) has long been the most popular spreadsheet program. Other popular packages include Borland Quattro Pro (DOS and Windows) and Microsoft Excel (Windows).

Less well-known but nonetheless noteworthy packages include PlanPerfect (DOS) and ProCalc 3D (DOS). There are also older DOS packages such as SuperCalc and shareware packages such as PCCalc and Wampum that might deserve consideration. Again, as with word-processing and database-management software, two important factors in choosing a spreadsheet package are compatibility and portability.

Specialized spreadsheet software is available on a variety of platforms for such applications as tax preparation, vehicle maintenance, and personal and business accounting. The choice of these specialized software packages is entirely dependent on your business needs and applications.

Graphics software is a specialized area, but one that, depending on the needs of your home office, may need to be considered. Some of the previously mentioned word-processing and desktop-publishing software products have limited graphics-management capabilities. Some of the data-management and spreadsheet software products mentioned have even more limited capabilities. The more powerful, and well-known, graphics software applications are available on a variety of platforms. These include CorelDRAW, Aldus Freehand and Aldus PhotoStyler, Adobe Photoshop and Adobe Illustrator, and Micrografx Designer and Micrografx Picture Publisher. Depending on your needs, other special-application software packages that might be considered include CAD programs such as Autodesk AutoCAD, Borland TurboCAD, and CyberDesign Productions NorthCAD-3D; morphing software such as Gryphon Morph and WinImages:morph; and virtual-reality software such as Virtus Walkthrough and Virtus VR, VREAM, SuperScape VRT, Waite Group New Media VRBASIC, and shareware and/or freeware programs such as REND386 and VR386. Again, it cannot be stressed enough, for maximum ease of use and office productivity, compatibility and portability should be carefully considered in software selection and purchase decisions.

Finally, communications software packages are an extremely important part of both the corporate office and the home office. Determine what your needs are before selecting a communications package. Some communication and information systems, such as Prodigy and America Online, require special software packages in order to access their services. Other services, such as most local bulletin board systems (BBSs) as well as services such as CompuServe, offer specialized software packages, such as CompuServe Information Manager (DOSCIM for DOS, WINCIM for Windows, and MACCIM for the Macintosh) or RipTerm (to access RipGraphic capable BBSs) while still enabling access with other, more generic communications software packages. Some of the more popular software packages for the IBM compatible include ProComm and Qmodem.

If you are going to use your computer to send and receive fax communication, you're going to also need fax software. One communications package that comes included with many modems and fax/modems is QL2FAX (for both DOS and Windows). Another popular program that enables this function is WINFAX (Windows).

When choosing software, keep in mind the total amount you have budgeted for software, as well as your main purposes for using the packages you've selected. Future expandability should also be a consideration.

Let's turn now to the variety of social issues surrounding office automation. What does office automation mean to the average worker?

TELECOMMUTING:
THE
POST-INDUSTRIALISM
ERA

We have now entered an extraordinary new period of capitalistic evolution, and the implications are not all positive. This era has been referred to as "post-industrialism," "post-Fordism," and "post-modern capitalism." According to communications graduate student Nick Witheford, one of the most prominent characteristics of this phase of history is the far-reaching capitalistic deployment of information technologies (computers and telecommunications), and the unparalleled levels of "workplace automation, global mobility, and societal surveillance." High technology, such as telecommunications, enables the dispersal of industrial operations in areas of "cheap and docile labour."

Critical theorist Fergus Murray suggested in 1983 that computerization not only enables increased surveillance and segregation in industry and manufacturing, but also heightens automation and regulation that can lead to the misuse and manipulation of office workers. According to Italian intellectual Antonio Negri, the rosy conceptions of an information society hide the stark truths of "control and reduction in the costs of labor."

Working from the home office, or telecommuting, is part of the changing labor profile created by the shift from an industrial society to an information society. The estimated 10 million-plus telecommuters today are made possible by developing technologies. But just because telecommuting is possible, is telecommuting necessarily feasible or desirable?

The information-society utopianism represented by the rise in telecommuting is countered by both Issac Asimov's concept of "technophobia" (from his 1983 book *The Roving Mind*) and the neo-Luddite tendencies that are prevalent among some Marxist analysts. We'll return to the Luddite movement later in this chapter. For now, let's look at what other analysts suggest about telecommuting and its effect on the worker.

Critical theorist Fergus Murray suggested in 1983 that computerization not only enables increased surveillance and segregation in industry and manufacturing, but also heightens automation and regulation that can lead to the misuse and manipulation of office workers.

According to some theorists, telecommuting creates an environment where the "mass worker" of the industrial society is overlapped and replaced by what Negri calls the "socialized worker" of the information society. The exploitation of the socialized worker is accomplished by capital through the disintegration of the worker's eight-hour workday and 40-hour work week. The worker has also lost the separation between workplace and home. On the other hand, some have argued that telecommuting represents a return to the family structure that is more closely associated with an agrarian society. In a culture based on agriculture, the workplace and home are one and the same. One critical difference between the agrarian and the telecommuting home, however, is that nothing is produced in the home office that can be consumed by the worker.

More and more workers are entering a situation where they are doing the same work from home that they would have previously performed in the large office. Now, however, they are performing this work as contract workers, without such benefits as medical insurance, sick days, workmen's compensation, and vacation. The workers have become piece-workers and are paid a set price for the completed piece, no matter how much time and effort went into its creation. Plus, the workers are now expected to provide their own equipment and training.

Traditional work and the workers who once performed it are now devalued. Voice mail eliminates the work of the switchboard operator, personal-information managers and calendar software eliminates the work of the executive secretary, and new technologies that enable a manager to dictate directly into the computer eliminate the specialized work of the stenographer. Whether it is intentional or not, technology has eliminated traditional, historical, and predominantly female employment categories from the modern workforce. At the same time, because of office automation, clerical workers—again predominantly female—are being paid less for doing more. Technological optimists continue to argue that technology creates more jobs than it eliminates. The problem with their reasoning, however, is that the jobs created by technology tend to be low-status, low-paying positions that require little skill or initiative.

The Darker Side
of Telecommuting

The apparent advantages of telecommuting, such as the possible monetary and energy savings resulting from not having to drive to work and the flexibility that telecommuting provides for young parents, have enjoyed quite a bit of publicity. What hasn't received as much attention are the more subtle questions involving community values, racial relations, and gender equity.

In using the term "community values" here, we are referring to those issues that surround the office community and include worker continuity, office culture, and socialization. Telecommuting, and the nomadic worker that it creates, weakens worker continuity within a company or an office. Without a corporate continuity or "memory," the same or similar mistakes could be made over and over again. Experts believe that concepts such as teamwork, creativity, and commitment to quality, are best transmitted through personal, face-to-face communication between management and employee. Telecommuting breaks this link of personalized interaction.

The home office, however, develops its own culture. When telecommuters move from company to company, from job to job, from piecework to piecework, they develop ties with other telecommuters. These telecommuters find havens of commonality in forums such as the Working From Home Forum on CompuServe and similar groups on other network services. A sense of community is developed among these nomadic virtual beings. This sense of community was examined in some recent research by one of the authors titled "The Individual Versus Community: A Case Study of Communication in Real-Time Online Computer Conferencing." The quasi-communal group evolves its own history and culture, a culture of virtual beings who have rarely, if ever, seen each other face-to-face.

Some social critics believe that office automation promotes sexism. Feminist Amy Dru Stanley, in a 1983 column for *The New York Times*, accused corporations of using telecommuting and office-automation technology as "union-busting tactics." Stanley suggests not only that the elimination of traditionally female-dominated office jobs endangers "whatever security and authority women have enjoyed" in the past, it also has given corporations new tools with which to cripple women's efforts to fight sex discrimination by creating work-at-home programs and part-time work that isolates workers and creates a workforce without job security and benefits. It is no secret that corporations have relocated in areas of the United States and overseas that boast cheap, unorganized labor.

Some social critics believe that office automation promotes sexism.

Office-automation technology has also been accused of fostering racism. Many telecommuting jobs that exist in banking, insurance, and high technology have moved to suburban areas. This makes it more difficult for African-Americans and other urbanized minorities to compete for these jobs. Despite the dropping prices in technology, home-office hardware and software are still predominantly purchased by middle-class whites. This led one AFL-CIO research specialist to suggest that when a company seeks a "quality clerical worker" they are really looking for "a white, suburban, nonunion, part-time worker."

At the same time, in the virtual world of the telecommuter, no one knows what sex or race you are unless you tell them. Two recent cartoons had captions that read, respectively, "On the Internet no one knows you're a saint" and "On the Internet no one knows you're a dog." In the cyberspace culture, your sex and race are less important than what you know and of what you are capable.

But this does bring up another important consideration within the online world: security. Security is a relevant issue for both the employer and the employee. One of the more publicized security risks involves the computer hacker—both from outside and from inside the office system. Author Bruce Sterling, in his 1992 book *The Hacker Crackdown: Law and Disorder on the Electronic Frontier*, describes how the first hackers, teenage males, were barred from the telephone system in 1878. Hackers have gone on to wreak havoc on business computers ever since. A high-school honor student named Neil Patrick broke into computers at both Sloan-Kettering Hospital and the Los Alamos nuclear-weapons research facility. In the Sloan-Kettering incident, only the particular time of day prevented patients lives from being endangered when the system was taken down. "Emmanuel Goldstein," a hacker using the name of a character from George Orwell's *1984*, broke into the electronic mail of both GTE and the U.S. Department of the Interior. In 1988, BellSouth's AIMSX computer network was broken into. In 1989, a Florida probation office's phone lines were switched with those of a phone-sex business. These are just a few of the countless instances where hackers have caused inconveniences for business or government.

Hackers exist inside of businesses as well as outside. Losses to businesses from internal hacking include: stolen information, such as the posting of Apple Corp. proprietary software on BBSs in 1989; embezzlement of funds, as has occurred in banks, corporations, and universities; and the theft of inventories. For both the corporation and the home business, computer security against hackers has become an important consideration. As a result, there is perceived to be a greater need for surveillance within the workplace.

POST-INDUSTRIAL OFFICE SURVEILLANCE

Webster's Seventh New Collegiate Dictionary defines surveillance as "close watch kept over a person or group," as in supervision. David Flaherty, in his 1988 article "The Emergence of Surveillance Societies in the Western World: Toward the Year 2000" for *Government Information Quarterly*, suggests that rather than "information societies," industrialized countries have become "surveillance societies." This idea of information technology as a means of social control is supported by communications scholar James Beniger in his 1986 book *The Control Revolution: Technological and Economic Origins of the Information Society*.

Beniger and others have argued that the individual's ability to access greater amounts of information inevitably increases the bureaucracy's ability to gather information concerning that individual. Every time we access an information service such as CompuServe, Prodigy, America Online, or any other database,

a record is made of when, where, and for what purpose we were logged on. Every time we buy groceries and use either a check or a credit card, the corporate bureaucracy knows when, where, what, and how much we bought. Priscilla Regan, in a 1981 doctoral dissertation at Cornell University, suggested that the information age is not creating a fissure between people based on class or status (the information "haves" versus the information "have-nots") but rather is creating a widening difference in power between individuals and bureaucratic organizations. Oscar Gandy, Jr., in a 1989 article for *Journal of Communication*, suggests that "computerization and the speed of telecommunications networks have been combined in ways that dramatically increase the bureaucratic advantage." The result is that the law is lagging far behind the technology when it comes to issues of surveillance and privacy in the environment called cyberspace.

What we are looking at here is what Michel Foucault might call a modern-day panopticon. The panopticon was a

19th-century design by Jeremy Bentham for a prison where inmates were (or believed that they were) watched continuously by unseen guards. In both the centralized corporate office and the telecommuter's workplace, the movements of the worker can be tracked continuously. From the employer's point of view, this is considered vital. Access to the worker's computer enables the employer to determine that worker's productivity, progress, and efficiency in terms of keystrokes, the number of pages produced, and so forth. Through this threat of observation, whether or not it is actually implemented, the worker's behavior is planned and controlled.

The telecommuter's office can be problematic for the bureaucratic interests of big business. Because the telecommuter's computer is not connected to the organization's system, how can business provide the level of supervision over the home worker that they have over the office worker? How can business be sure that the home worker is putting in the expected time necessary for a given project? These are questions that have slowed the movement toward telecommuting by the business world. The result is business cutting benefits to the home-office worker and appropriating the piecework payment system of the clothing-industry sweatshops.

THE EMPLOYEE PERSPECTIVE

We've looked at the question of security from the perspective of the employer. Let's turn now to this question from the point of view of the employee and the home-office worker. For the office worker, in both the large office and the home office, many of these security issues center on the issue of privacy. Peter Machamer and Barbara Boylan, in their article "Freedom, Information and Privacy" in *Business and*

Professional Ethics Journal, suggest that the concept of an individual's privacy is derived from the concept of the individual's autonomy and right to self-determination. This, in turn, has its basis in the idea of property rights. The coming of the information society thus appears to expand the concept of property rights to include not only land, belongings, and body, but also information about the person's life and activities.

Previously we looked at examples of how information can be gathered about an individual during that person's everyday activities. As already suggested, technological developments appear to move at a much faster rate than does the law that protects individuals in a democratic society. The bureaucracy, both corporate and governmental, twists the new technologies to its own purposes. It is hardly an exaggeration to suggest that today every facet of the individual's existence is carefully monitored by technology, providing the bureaucracy with detailed information about our tastes, needs, wants, and habits. This information is then processed by anonymous technicians and "experts" who have no direct involvement with the people from whom the information is gathered. This information-gathering process has become automatic, triggered by the individuals themselves as they participate in capitalist culture. Even turning your computer on begins a process of documentation, such as the dates when files were created and information about what messages were sent and received. Telephone systems can document what numbers were called, at what time, and at what length.

For the individual worker concerned about privacy issues, all of these intrusions are of concern. Privacy advocates in Europe, Australia, and Canada have expressed dismay at the failure of the United States to take a leading role in protecting individual rights in cyberspace. In 1991, Harvard University constitutional-law expert Laurence Tribe called for an amendment protecting freedom of speech in cyberspace to be added to the U.S. Constitution. And while new products such as the new SS Security Screen from ACCO can be placed over your monitor screen to prevent viewing of the screen from outside its 15-degree viewing window, few efforts have been made to protect the individual from managers and employers reading their private e-mail. Those efforts that have been attempted have been met by stiff opposition from both corporate and governmental bureaucracies.

At the same time, the U.S. government has made overtures toward the installation of the Clipper chip into every phone and computer in the country. Clipper, basically, is a computer chip that enables phone and computer communication to be encrypted so that no one can understand them—except for the intended recipient and the government. Depending on your point of view, the Clipper is one of two extremes. According to John Perry Barlow, one of the founding members of the Electronic Freedom Foundation, Clipper is "a last-ditch attempt by the United States, the last great power from the old Industrial Era, to establish imperial control over cyberspace." On the other hand, National Security Agency attorney Stewart Baker argues that Clipper is a "modest proposal" around which critics have created a series of half-truths and untruths. The government says that participation in the Clipper program was voluntary, while critics claim that Clipper was kept secret and implemented without industry or the public being allowed to comment. The controversy grows as allegations that Clipper will allow for government intrusion into our private lives and that it will interfere with the free market system are argued back and forth.

ERGONOMICS

Another area of concern for the modern office worker is health, or more specifically, the ergonomic properties of the new technology. Ergonomics is defined by Marilyn and Marvin Dainoff, in their 1992 article "Guerrilla Ergonomics" in *WordPerfect: The Magazine*, as "the fit between you and the tools you use." Christopher Murray, in his 1992 article "Best Buys in Ergonomic Supplies" in *Home-Office Computing*, points out that "ergonomics has as much to do with habits as it does with equipment." Computer users can develop back problems, muscle spasms, eye problems, and arm and wrist pain from sitting in front of their computers for long periods of time. While the corporate office worker is probably covered by the company's medical policy, home-office workers are generally responsible for their own medical expenses. Whether insured or not, every worker should be aware of the potential health problems related to the use of the computer, from carpal-tunnel syndrome to radiation from video displays.

SUMMARY

When this chapter of *Cyberlife!* was conceived, its original intention was to describe what technology, in the form of the smart office, could do *for* you. Certainly the personal computer has given the authors the ability to work at home, with greater access to information than we have had in the past even in the large office. The telephone, the fax, and e-mail have enabled us to maintain greater access to information and to individuals than ever before. This technology has enabled us to return to the home with our work and watch our children grow, and have greater interaction with these children.

However, this chapter has also described what technology, in the form of the smart office, might do *to* you. The amount of information now available swamps us, making it difficult to know where to start. The telephone, the fax, and e-mail intrude upon our personal time. This, in effect, extends the workday to 24 hours, seven days a week, with shrinking benefits. Do children actually get more attention from their parents when the parents are tied to the personal computer for more hours a week than if they had been at a regular job?

Is this progress? The word progress carries with it a connotation of "moving forward," of developing "to a higher, better, or more advanced stage." This connotation does not acknowledge the possibility that as one area of humankind's endeavors moves forward, another area might take several steps backward. When making decisions about the future, it must always be kept in mind that there are trade-offs involved. In order to achieve one benefit, we might have to give up something else.

The trade-offs demanded by industrial progress are illustrated well in sociologist's E.P. Thompson's discussion of the anti-machinery Luddites in his book *The Making of the English Working Class*. As the Industrial Revolution swept over England during the early 19th century, English weavers saw the "laborsaving" mechanical loom as endangering their jobs and their culture. These weavers, led by a workman named Ned Ludd, attempted to defend their way of life by literally demolishing the mechanical looms. The industry soon enlisted the strength of the government to quell the revolt, and most of the Luddites ended their lives either on the gallows or in exile.

Modern usage of the word Luddite implies a half-wit. But the men who fought against the technology of their time were not half-wits. Most were educated and many could read and write. Indeed, they were wise enough to foresee the end of their culture with the coming of the mechanical loom.

This chapter is not meant to be Luddite in its discussion of the modern office—whether in the sense of being half-witted or of being against technology. Nor should it evidence a "technophobic" mentality, as defined by Asimov in *The Roving Mind*.

Nonetheless, it is critically important to study how technology manipulates the individual worker and how it changes our collective life and culture. Readers should examine the benefits, trade-offs, and consequences of the emerging technologies and make up their own minds about how the smart office will affect their lives. However, as we close this chapter, one question remains unshakeable: As with the original Luddites, do we really have a choice?

. . . .

You Can Take It with You

In taking the technology with us wherever we go, will there come a time when we just can't digest any more information? Will we be able to get away from the continuing onslaught of information if we need to?

chapter 10
by Paul M. and
Mary J. Summitt

A **M**ODERN **S**CENARIO

Niki sat quietly on the train, enjoying the countryside as it passed by her window. It had been a long day in the city and it would be great to get back home. Niki is a technological consultant and had just finished a day of working with a programmer on a project for an architectural company. The company wanted to show a potential client what their proposed new building would look like. Niki had shown the company that by employing virtual reality, they could enable the client to virtually walk around in the proposed design and see if they liked it.

Suddenly, Niki felt a gentle thump against her breast from her pager, alerting her that someone was trying to contact her. She pulled the pager from her jacket and looked at the number displayed on its LCD screen.

"Conrad," she thought. "I wonder what he wants?" She slid the pager back into her pocket and opened her briefcase on the seat next to her. She picked up the hand-held cellular phone and dialed Conrad's number.

"Virtual Programming, Incorporated. Conrad here."

"Yes, Conrad? You called?"

"Niki, thanks for getting back to me so quickly. We've got a slight problem with the entrances to the building."

"What do you mean?" Niki asked as she pulled her laptop computer out of the briefcase and turned it on.

"The dimensions of the entrances must be off. When I create them in the virtual display and try to enter through them, I walk through the top of the door and bump my head."

"Show me on the display," Niki said as she typed in the commands that hooked her computer, via cellular modem connection, to Conrad's system.

"Yeah, go ahead," replied Conrad. "I expected you'd want to see it and I already have it set up for you."

Niki's laptop screen quickly came alive with the exterior of the virtual building she and Conrad were creating. She used the arrow keys to maneuver her viewpoint close to the front entrance of the building.

"It looks all right, Conrad," she stated into the hand-held phone.

"Now, try and enter it," he said as he watched her progress from his desktop computer screen. Niki walked toward the building's entrance in the virtual world they had created. As she approached, she began to see that her head was going to collide with the upper part of the door.

"What's going on here?" she asked.

"I'm not sure," Conrad replied. "I've gone over the programming several times and can't seem to find the problem. Do you have the architect's blueprints where you can look at them?"

Niki did a quick search of her hard drive and then answered. "No. Fax them to me real quick and I'll try to find the problem."

"Sure. You ready?"

"Yeah, go for it." Niki looked out the train's window as the laptop began receiving the faxed blueprints. The sun was in the process of setting over the mountains, and it was a pleasant sight. Niki quickly picked up her digital camera from her briefcase and snapped a picture. She placed the camera back in the briefcase and, looking back at the laptop, saw that the fax was just completing.

"Ok, got it. Give me just a second to look at it, and we'll see if we can find what the problem is."

"Sure, go ahead," Conrad said as he sat back and waited.

Niki quickly scanned the blueprint that appeared on the screen. Suddenly she spotted the typographical error that was causing the problem.

"Conrad, is that the symbol for inches after the seven above the door?"

Conrad looked at the area of the blueprint she was talking about and saw the typo.

"Sure is," he laughed. "That makes all the difference, doesn't it?"

"You bet!" Niki laughed back. "It's going to be difficult for even short people to get through a door that's only seven inches tall. You make the corrections to the building in the program and I'll e-mail the information about the typo to the architect. Let me know if you have any more problems. By the way, it looks good. Keep up the good work."

"Thanks, Niki."

Conrad disconnected and Niki put her phone back in the briefcase. Quickly, she typed a message explaining the problem and its solution to the architect and hit the transmit command for the e-mail software on the laptop. Then, closing the laptop and placing it back in her briefcase, Niki sat back and enjoyed the rest of her train ride.

Niki and Conrad are fictional characters, but the portable technology that was just described exists today. Many similar scenarios that use the technology presented here can be seen every day. The authors have used their laptop computers for such things as writing, research, and e-mail in such places as restaurants, hotels, and in the field. Other husband-and-wife photographer/writer teams, such as Daniel and Sally Grotta, also spend considerable time on the road doing their assignments. Writers, however, aren't the only ones who are taking advantage of this newfound freedom to work in nontraditional settings.

The Portable Revolution

With a laptop, Paul can take his work anywhere.

Business people take technology with them every day, whether in planes, trains, or automobiles. Steve Roberts, profiled in an October 1992 article for *Home-Office Computing*, built his portable office onto a bicycle. The new portable technology allows the modern worker to remain in perpetual contact, never missing a deadline, losing a contract, or falling behind.

In this chapter, we're going to look at the new portable technology and what it makes possible. We'll look at the four main families of the portable class of computer (the *portable*, the *laptop*, the *notebook*, and the *palmtop*), cellular phones, fax/modems, digital cameras, and some of the newer portable technologies that are pushing the envelope in this new era of telecommunication. We'll also look at some of the possible side effects of the technology and what these side effects might mean to us—as consumers, as professionals, and as human beings.

The new portable technology allows the modern worker to remain in perpetual contact, never missing a deadline, losing a contract, or falling behind.

PORTABLE COMPUTERS

The portable computer has come a long way in a relatively short amount of time. Just 10 years ago, we marveled at the Radio Shack Model 100, one of the first portables to hit the market. Today, the new notebook computers are slim, trim, and powered with 386-or-better microprocessors sporting high-speed, VGA-graphics-capable screens. Basically, today's portable computers come in three varieties: the portable, the laptop, and the notebook. The differences between them are mainly in their size and weight, but keep in mind that there are no real industry-standard definitions. In general, the portable is the largest in size, heaviest in weight, and generally requires an outside power source.

One of our first IBM-compatible computers was an Amstrad PPC-512, a portable computer that weighed about 20 pounds. This computer, bought in 1988, sported two 3 1/2-inch, 720KB drives; 512KB RAM; a full-size 101-key keyboard; and a built-in 5-inch LCD screen. It also had the capability of adding an external CGA monitor, an external hard drive, and either an internal or external modem. Adding these externals, of course, restricted the portability of the computer. The Amstrad carried 10 "C" batteries for power and came with both an AC adaptor and a cigarette-lighter plug for using in a vehicle. This little workhorse carried most of our writing and research load for two years. When replaced by a desktop 286, it was handed down to our son. While he uses it mostly for CGA games and keeping track of his baseball cards, he has been known to write a school term paper on it occasionally.

Newer portable computers have increased speed and internal memory, and additional internal hardware. The question is, however, why carry around this much weight when smaller, equally powerful laptop, notebook, and palmtop computers are available?

Our first laptop computer was the Tandy Model 600. Bought in 1989, this laptop computer wasn't IBM-compatible, carried only 32KB RAM, and weighed just under 10 pounds. It came with internal software that included a word-processing program, a spreadsheet, a data manager, and a telecommunications program. The computer also had a built-in 3 1/2-inch floppy drive and an internal 300-baud modem. The hard-to-see, monochrome LCD screen wasn't full-sized, and you could only see about two-thirds of what you could see on a normal monitor. This computer was powered by an internal, non-exchangeable battery. It also came with an AC charging and power supply.

In 1992, we bought two Tandy Model 1100FD laptop computers. These IBM-compatibles weigh about eight pounds and come with built-in software, although there is no internal hard drive. The 1100HD came with a 20MB hard drive. There was also the option of an internal 2,400-baud modem. Paul carries his, along with his Diconix 150 portable printer, almost everywhere he goes. Along with the AC power supply, the 1100FD has an exchangeable internal battery. He carries an extra one in the carrying case. The Diconix is powered by five "C" batteries and also has an AC power supply.

If you can find them, older-model laptops such as these Tandy computers, using XT and 286 microprocessors, can be bought for as little as $300. They can do most jobs and are perfect for situations where the possibility of damage to the computer would normally keep you from taking a laptop, such as on a canoe trip or in other hazardous environments.

The latest laptops will run from around seven to 18 pounds in weight and range in size from being truly bulky to about 12 inches long, 10 inches wide, and two to three inches thick. A 386 laptop can be purchased today for around $1,000, whereas more powerful laptop computers can run as much as $6,000 or more.

Of course, if you decide you have to have the most up-to-date thing in mobile multimedia, you're going to be spending upwards of $9,000 for something along the lines of the BitWise Model 466/ACP or Toshiba's T6600C/CDV—both of which come with built-in color screens and CD-ROM units.

Beside true portables, there are notebook computers, which generally are less than eight pounds in weight and are smaller in size than the laptops; they range in price from $1,000 to more than $4,000. There are also *palmtop computers* that exhibit various levels of IBM-compatibility, *organizers* that perform limited and specific functions, and *dedicated word processors* that are designed for the single task of writing. You can also look at *messagepads* such as Apple's Newton. With all these varieties, how do you decide, first, if you really need the portability that one of these computers provides, and second, which one you should select?

Let's deal with the first question first. Each member of our family has access to at least one computer that we can call our own while we're working on a project. There's never a time when someone who needs access to a computer to do some work can't get it. This stems in part from the access requirements that modern school and work environments place on us. The capability of portable

· ·

When you leave the house or office, you no longer have to leave your work behind. Your portable computer can range from a bare-bones emergency back-up to a self-contained mobile office.

· ·

computing has simply increased our potential.

When you leave the house or office, you no longer have to leave your work behind. Your portable computer can range from a bare-bones emergency back-up to a self-contained mobile office. By adding an extra phone line at your home or office, and hooking up your desktop to it, you can use a variety of different telecommunication software to use your desktop software from your portable computer. Norton's PC Anywhere software is a good choice for this, but communications programs such as ProComm and QModem also have some of these capabilities in limited forms.

First you must decide what you are going to do with the portability that these technologies make possible, and then decide how much money you have to spend.

After you've made the decision to add portability to your computing capabilities, the next decision is easier. Should it be an IBM-compatible or a Macintosh portable? In some regards, there is no real difference in what they can do. Choose the platform that you are familiar with and which you may already be using for your desktop.

The following is a checklist of considerations you should make before investing in a portable computer:

- Decide if you want **true portability** and **how much money you can spend**.
- Decide **which platform**, IBM-compatible or Macintosh, you want or need.
- Decide **what software** you will be running. What are the hardware requirements for that software?
- Decide **how fast** a machine you can afford.
- Decide **what hardware options** you want on your portable computer.
- **Comparison shop**. This means **testing the portable** under similar conditions to your intended use, if possible.

In Chapter 9, "Life in the Smart Office," we recommended that you select your software and then choose your hardware to meet the needs of that software. Here we've assumed that you might already have a desktop computer and are familiar with the software for that particular platform. Now, in deciding what portable computer system to buy, you must decide what software you'll be running on the portable system. This will help you to determine what specific portable, laptop, notebook, or palmtop computer you need.

How much money you have to spend will be a determining factor in how fast a machine you can actually buy. As we said earlier, older and slower machines, such as the XT and 286 laptops, can still be found for $500 or less. Faster 386 machines are selling currently for under $1,000 and 486 machines begin as low as $1,300. The basic Macintosh Powerbook packages start as low as $2,000.

What specific hardware and software to have on your portable is the next question. Should you have a hard drive or operate strictly from floppy disk? Should you use software that doesn't have extensive amounts of memory? If word processing is your prime concern and you're a WordPerfect user, a scaled-back version of the software is available in the form of WordPerfect's LetterPerfect. Integrated packages such as LotusWorks, Eight-in-One or Microsoft Works can also be used. These later program packages also give you spreadsheet, data management, and, if you add a modem or fax/modem to the portable, telecommunications capabilities.

In reality, unless you are extremely limited in your purchasing power, most portables now come equipped with at least

1MB of RAM and a 20MB hard drive. In this case, you should be able to use whatever software you are familiar with on your desktop computer. With regard to hard-drive space, unless your applications require extraordinary amounts of space, a 40MB hard drive should be more than sufficient for most of your applications, and if not, there's always compression software such as DoubleSpace, Stacker, and others.

Finally, comparison shop. Test the portable under similar conditions to those you'll be facing, if possible. How long do the batteries last? Are they removable? Is a quick charge possible? Can you use the computer while the battery is charging? Other things to look at include the display and keyboard. How usable are they? Almost any keyboard on a portable is going to be smaller than the one on your desktop, and some of the keys are going to be in slightly different places. Also, the LCD screen on a portable has a limited angle of view; the screen has to be angled specifically for the person sitting in front of the computer, and seeing what's on the screen from another angle is almost impossible.

There are several accessory items that you need to be aware of and keep with your portable. For the printer, Paul carries a printer cable, spare ink cartridges, paper, spare batteries, the AC adapter, and the printer's user manual. For the computer, he carries an extra battery, an extra phone line for the modem, the AC adapter/charger, and two disk caddies with all necessary software and some spare disks.

Another item you'll want to carry if you are traveling overseas is an English or European plug adaptor. However, we recommend that you don't use a Radio Shack-type transformer converter to power your computer or printer. We bought one for our recent trip to London, not knowing that it wouldn't convert the electricity to a safe level for use with the computer. American appliances are designed to run on 120V, 60-cycle electricity. The Radio Shack transformer converter steps down the English 220V to 120V but does not step up the 50-cycle power to 60 cycles. Our experience left us with no serious damage, although the hotel did have to reset their circuit breakers the next morning.

The following are some considerations you should make in choosing a specific portable computer:

- The portable should be solid and sturdy.
- The portable should have a compact design.
- The keyboard should feel comfortable to you.
- The portable should be as light as possible.
- The screen should close down over the keyboard and lock.
- The portable should have a protective carrying case.
- The portable should have at least one parallel, one serial, and one mouse external interface.
- The portable should have a large, bright, clear, tilting screen.
- If possible, the screen should allow for high-resolution graphics.
- The portable should have at least one floppy-disk drive, preferably of the 1.4MB, 3 1/2-inch type.
- If possible, the portable should have a hard drive of at least 20MB and preferably 40MB.
- The portable should have at least two interchangeable, durable, rechargeable batteries.
- The portable should have power-saving features.
- The computer's memory should be expandable.
- The capability to use third-party software is preferable to a strictly proprietary system.

THE MODEM

It is likely that at some point you will be using your portable to connect to another computer, an online system, or a remote office, so a modem is another important consideration. The first modem either one of us had was a 300-baud external modem that we used with an Atari 800XL. Paul bought this system in 1985, just before starting work on his master's degree in mass communication. The modem allowed him to hook into CompuServe Information Service (CIS) as well as some of the local bulletin board systems (BBSes). One of our other computers, an Eagle IIe that was purchased originally for one of the children, came with a 1,200-baud modem that allowed us to access CIS as well as some of the area BBSes. For Christmas 1991, Mary bought Paul a 2,400-baud fax/modem for his computer, and a short time later Paul bought Mary a 2,400-baud modem for hers. Recently we bought a 14,400-baud fax/modem to go into Paul's computer, and Paul's original 2,400-baud fax/modem went into Mary's. These fax/modems allow the sending and receiving of fax communication as well as access to services such as CIS, Prodigy, America Online, and BBSes. Having a modem in the laptop means that there is no place where we are out of touch with our electronic mail, as long as we have access to a phone.

But what do all these numbers mean? What does it mean to have a 300-, a 1,200-, a 2,400-, 9,600-, or a 14,400-baud modem? Allen Wyatt's *Computer Professional's Dictionary* defines baud as "the electrical switching speed of a transmission line" and "the number of times a line changes its electrical state each second." Some people use this term interchangeably with bits-per-second (bps), but they actually mean different things. At low speeds, baud rate and bps are around the same, but at higher speeds they are quite different. Bits-per-second is a measurement of how many bits are transferred across a communications link in one second. It may seem a little confusing, but just remember, at higher speeds, baud and bits per second are not the same.

So which one should you buy? Our advice is to buy the fastest modem you can afford that is compatible with the rest of your hardware. Keep in mind, though, that 2,400 baud is the standard transmission rate for most people. Faster speeds are available, however, on BBSes and online services.

CELLULAR PHONES

Now, let's look at cellular phones. As with portable computers and fax/modems, there are different varieties of cellular telephones. These can be divided into three classes: *mobile*, *transportable*, and *portable* or *handheld*.

Before discussing these, you need to understand how the cellular phone system actually works. The Federal Communications Commission (FCC) has taken some of the ultra-high-frequency (UHF) television channels (channels 70 through 83) and converted them to cellular/mobile phone use. Cellular phones, then, work much like television and radio. You must be within a certain distance from the main transmitter tower to transmit and receive messages. The FCC divided the country into 305 metropolitan service areas and 428 rural service areas. These service areas, or transmission areas, are called cells. As you move from one cell to another, your transmission is automatically switched to the new cell, which enables your call to continue uninterrupted. Usually, a minimum of two carriers (one of which is probably the local telephone company) operate within each cell. This is to provide competition in the local service area.

Now, let's look at the three types of cellular telephones. The first type is the mobile phone—that is, the car phone. It must be professionally installed in your car, and it goes wherever the car goes. Size and weight aren't a big consideration here. The transceiver can be installed in the trunk, and the car's electrical system can provide power to the system with no difficulty. With the addition of a tall antenna, the mobile phone is the most powerful type of cellular phone available.

The next type of cellular phone is the transportable. The transportable phone can be moved from car to car by plugging it into a cigarette lighter and attaching an antenna. Adding a 12-volt, rechargeable battery and attaching a smaller antenna creates a completely portable, albeit bulky, cellular phone. This kind of system provides less range than the mobile phone but greater portability. Transportables are inexpensive and weigh in at around five pounds.

The portable, or hand-held, cellular phone is the smallest and most convenient of the cellular phones. Small enough to attach to your belt, stick in a pocket, or place in a purse, this is the most expensive but least powerful of the three classes. Hand-held phones usually come with rechargeable battery packs on the back of the phone. These battery packs only allow from 30 to 90 minutes of steady conversation per charge, which represents about seven hours of standby operation. Within this class, prices fall into three categories based on weight and price. Generally, phones weighing from eight to 12 ounces are the most expensive

and cost from $500 to $800. Phones weighing from 12 to 16 ounces range from $200 to $500. The least expensive phones weigh from 16 to 24 ounces and can be found as cheap as $50. Prices, however, continue to drop.

Service costs are beginning to come down also. With a regular plan and a minimum one-year contract, you can get about a half hour of service per month. Extra minutes of service can range from 10 to 25 cents per minute. Consider what you feel best serves the needs of your business when selecting both the phone and the service.

Even with the recent advances in cellular technology, there are still some limitations you need to be aware of. First, don't assume that your phone calls are private. They aren't. Anyone with a scanner can tune in on cellular phone conversations. Second, in high-traffic areas, you may have difficulty getting a dial tone. Finally, not all areas are wired for cellular transmissions yet. No transmitter means no service. Also keep in mind that *roaming*—moving from one provider's service area to another—can be costly.

The following is a list of considerations you should make before buying a cellular phone:

- *Size*. Keep it as small as possible.
- *Price*. Get the most for your dollar.
- *Sturdiness*. Will it take the stress of everyday use?
- *Sound quality*. Can you hear and be heard?
- *Ease of use*. Is it easy to operate?
- *Power availability*. Are a variety of power sources available?
- *Connectability*. Can it be used with a modem?

DIGITAL CAMERAS

Another new area of technology that might be of interest and benefit to you is the digital camera. Digital cameras enable you to take a picture, which is saved on a disk in the camera, and to import that picture into your computerized documents. There are a few companies with cameras on the market right now that enable you to do this, and there should be more in the future.

The Canon RC-360 Xap-Shot stores up to 50 images on a disk in an analog format. These pictures can then be converted to digital format using a frame grabber or video digitizer such as ComputerEyes/RT Color Frame Grabber. The combined price for the camera and the frame grabber is going to run you from $1,500 to $2,000. This is actually inexpensive within the realm of this technology.

Some of the limitations of these low-end cameras are in their resolution. Blowing up the pictures to sizes larger than 2×2 inches produces a less-than-desirable image. As the technology improves, the resolution should improve also.

Some academic institutions have done impressive work with high-end digital cameras. The University of Missouri School of Journalism has been experimenting with digital cameras from both Kodak and Nikon.

The combination of digital cameras and cellular phones has made possible increased coverage of fast-breaking news events from around the globe.

The combination of digital cameras and cellular phones has made possible increased coverage of fast-breaking news events from around the globe. Some academic institutions have done impressive work with both digital photography and analog still video. The University of Missouri School of Journalism newspaper, *The Missourian*, uses a Canon Xap-Shot to take pictures of cars and real estate for advertisements. Students in the J-School courses use a Kodak Rapid Film Scanner for digitizing the image of conventional photographs, including transparencies (or slides), prints, and black-and-white and color negatives. Students also have experimented with a high-quality, portable digital camera used by the Associated Press (AP). This camera was developed through the cooperation of the AP, Kodak, and Nikon.

Bill Kuykendall, professor of photojournalism at the University of Missouri-Columbia, says the electronic photojournalism courses have moved forward to include interactive multimedia CD-ROM production. Two CD titles are slated for release to the public within the year. One CD will deal with the Picture of the Year competition. The second will deal with the Missouri Photo Workshop.

Digital cameras and analog still-video cameras are becoming more available, but the costs are sometimes prohibitive. As the technology improves, however, the prices will drop.

One inexpensive way to explore this new field is by using your conventional camera and having the pictures converted to digital format. One company that is providing this service is Seattle Filmworks of Seattle, Washington. When accompanied by a film-processing order, the Pictures on Disk! service is only $3.95 extra for a 20- or 24-exposure roll, and only $5.95 for 36 exposures. You can also send them sets of up to 24 existing prints (the prints cannot be framed or larger than 4×6 inches), and they will put them on a disk for $9.95. The digitized images come back with your prints or negatives, ready for use with an IBM-compatible system, on a high-density 1.2MB 5 1/4-inch disk or a 1.44MB, 3 1/2-inch disk. System requirements for the easy-to-use software that is included with the processing are DOS 3.0 or higher and a VGA or SVGA monitor. Other companies are getting into this service also. Talk to the people where you have your film processed and find out if they offer it.

An inexpensive alternative to digital cameras is portable, hand-held color scanners, which can be bought for as little as $200. With the included software, you can scan in documents and photographs, saving them in a variety of formats, for later use in word processing, desktop publishing, and drawing programs. You can also scan a document and, using OCR software, convert it to a digital text format for use in a variety of applications.

PORTABLE TECHNOLOGY AND THE FUTURE

Let's consider how the world of the future will be changed by the portable technologies. If we can believe the commercials, it is likely that soon we'll be able to play interactive games, watch interactive television, and transact all of our business from a variety of locations using portable technology. Video conferencing, using your portable computer, is also just around the bend. Imagine taking part in a video conference in which the various participants may be in such far-flung locales as a Pacific island, Antarctica, the Colorado mountains, a Florida swamp, a Canadian forest, a Missouri state park, and a California beach. To a large extent, the technology will disengage us from big city offices and the attendant frustrations of urban life. With this newfound freedom, however, there are trade-offs and consequences that we must also be aware of.

Since the early 1960s, this nation's population has become more rootless and mobile than ever. With portable technology enabling us to take our work wherever we want, whenever we want, what will happen to the family, a structure that many feel is already in danger?

What about the health risks that may be associated with these new technologies? How much independent research has been done on the long-term health consequences of computer monitors, cellular phones, and other portable technologies? Have the manufacturers and the government told us the truth about what they have learned? If the tobacco and breast-implant industries are any indication, we have reason to be skeptical.

Another concern is the phenomenon that some have dubbed "information overload." In taking the technology with us wherever we go, will there come a time when we just can't digest any more information? Will we be able to get away from the continuing onslaught of information if we need to?

Finally, what are the ramifications for individual privacy? These new portable technologies afford the government and corporations the capability of overseeing our everyday movements and activities.

Science fiction suggests to us that the future is both bright and foreboding because of these portable technologies. George Orwell's *1984* provides us with an unyieldingly bleak account of how technology can be used against us. William Gibson's novels, *Neuromancer*, *Count Zero*, *Burning Chrome*, and *Mona Lisa Overdrive*, present a similarly dystopian prediction of a society under the control of portable technologies. Aldous Huxley's *Brave New World* suggests some of the positive aspects of the technology while reminding us that sometimes we pay for our pleasures with our freedom.

The price we pay by relying too heavily on our technologies is illustrated by a scene in the film *Demolition Man*. At one point a police officer confronts Wesley Snipes's character to take him into custody. The officer carries a portable computer that provides advice for the officer in various situations. The officer is unable to think for himself, and is completely dependent on the guidance of the computer. The system works fine in normal, everyday situations that the officer might confront, but Snipes's character (who arrives from the past) is not a normal, everyday situation.

Snipes's character reacts to the computer-instructed officers by attacking and defeating them all. His character is later stopped only by Sylvester Stallone's character who is also from the past, and who is not enculturated to being dependent on the computer for instructions.

> Since the early 1960s, this nation's population has become more rootless and mobile than ever. With portable technology enabling us to take our work wherever we want, whenever we want, what will happen to the family, a structure that many feel is already in danger?

For every positive prediction of the technological future in science fiction, there are as many, if not more, negative predictions.

A similar situation occurs in the film *2001: A Space Odyssey*. As we discovered in the sequel, *2010*, HAL, the artificial intelligence that runs the spaceship in *2001*, was unable to deal with conflicting commands. HAL's basic programming was to support the crew in the exploration of Jupiter, and provide them with any and all information to complete the mission. Because of the discovery of the monolith, HAL also was programmed to hide information from the crew concerning the mission. HAL was programmed to lie, something that humans deal with almost every day; it is the basis of what we call situational ethics. For HAL, however, as with the portable computer that provided instructions to police in *Demolition Man*, conflicting instructions or situations outside the bounds of those that are specifically programmed into the computer's memory provide challenges beyond its capabilities. Ultimately, the computer is immobilized.

The wrist radio in *Dick Tracy*, the communication pens in *The Man from U.N.C.L.E*, the shoe phone in *Get Smart*, and the communicators in the various incarnations of *Star Trek* distract us from the essential surveillance functions of portable technology. Dick Tracy, Napoleon Solo, Maxwell Smart, and the crews of the Enterprise are never out of touch with their superiors. Even if the character is unconscious, the tech-

nology is able to let their superiors know that something is wrong, if not tell them where the specific crew member is. In an episode of *Star Trek: Deep Space 9* called "The Marque," Commander Sisko calls Kira on his communication badge and tells her to find his son. Kira calls back in less than a minute and tells Sisko where Jake is and what he is doing. This is possible because of the communication badge.

In the James Coburn movie *The President's Analyst*, a sinister plot by Ma Bell to implant telephones in everyone's brain is uncovered by a quick-witted psychiatrist. Artificial intelligence goes amok in *Westworld* and tries to take over the world in *Futureworld*. Human intelligence is trapped within a utopian hell in *Zardoz*. For every positive prediction of the technological future in science fiction, there are as many, if not more, negative predictions.

In society's quest for the technological Eldorado, we will surely encounter both successes and failures. By our personal experience, however, we are convinced that the glittering possibilities of technology make the quest worthwhile.

Interactive Applications and Simulations

Want to battle? Call your neighbor up, using a modem. You can meet in head-to-head F-16 combat, or join up in missions against the computer "enemy." If you have two computers in the same house, a simple cable between them will do. Using a multicomputer network, you can involve the whole family in an air battle.

chapter 11
by David E. Day

INTRODUCTION

Computer-based applications can now simulate environments and human activities with uncanny realism. With the right equipment, you can be transported to strange and wonderful climes, fly with the angels, dive with Neptune, compose a symphony, and (of course) annihilate the bad guys with aplomb. Your kids can plant and grow a garden without even getting their hands wet.

Three-dimensional, on-screen effects can give you the sense of moving around and through terrain. Objects appear to have surface textures and can grow and shrink and change perspective just as in real life. Computer-generated music and sound effects can rival movie-theater quality. Computer-generated scenes can include natural or artificial landscapes, and animations can be combined with video sequences and actual actors. The production values and development costs for a computer simulation can rival low-end movie ventures.

If you are musically inclined, you can use a computer to simulate instruments ranging from a tinny harmonica to a booming orchestra. You can buy electronic music and play it on your "instruments," or you can compose, edit, perform, and print your own scores.

If you would like to explore the possibilities of computer simulation as described in this chapter, you'll need a computer enhanced with a fast processor, extra memory, a CD-ROM drive, a sound card, and assorted other hardware. The section on multimedia equipment describes these enhancements in more detail and gives you some shopping hints. For online games, I'll discuss the modems that you'll need to get connected.

• •

ONLINE GAMES

Only recently have online services become popular to the general public; today, several million people worldwide belong to one or more of them. These services can instantly bring news, weather, stock and financial information, and electronic mail into your home. They can also bring you games.

Online games come in two flavors: single- and multiplayer. For single-player games, an online service is effectively a delivery system; instead of buying a game at the software store, you simply run it online. That's a suitable way to play quiz and word-based adventure games, but because it's limited by your connection to the online service, it's not best for action or simulation. (There is a sidebar later in this chapter about new online action games.)

For multiplayer games, online services deliver the goods—they bring the other players to you. With two players, you could merely ring up your buddy (see the section titled Modem Games), but try doing that with 10 people. With an online connection, your playground literally becomes the world.

Following is a brief overview of online technology and a review of interactive game products available from some major online services.

WHAT'S AN ONLINE SERVICE?

Online services consist of two parts: a cluster of big computers (known as "mainframes" or "hosts") with lots of processing power and huge storage systems, and an expansive network of communication paths to connect the mainframes to multiple users. The process is known as "time-sharing" because many users can use the resources of the mainframe at the same time.

An online service is a sort of computer utility company; you pay for time on the network as you use it. Some services may be available for a flat fee (as with local telephone service), while others are timed (as with your long-distance bill).

To connect to the online service, you make a phone call to its network, using a device called a modem. This device exchanges digital signals between your PC and the mainframe across the phone line. Besides the modem, you'll also need a communications program running on your PC (one often is supplied with the modem or by the online service itself). Most services handle data speeds from 300 to 9,600 bps (bits per second); a few offer 14,400 bps or faster in selected urban areas. Faster is better, but online services typically charge more for higher connect speeds.

Once connected, you use keyboard commands or sometimes graphic menu tools to select among services such as news, weather, electronic mail, databases, and special-interest forums that contain messages and programs shared among users. (These include interactive games.) You can also shop for products online, and even get support and updates for computer applications you've purchased.

The Internet is a unique expansion of the time-sharing concept. It is literally a network of timesharing services, linking thousands of hosts in a worldwide "web." These hosts have traditionally been sponsored by schools and large corporations, but they now include many small service providers. You don't pay for time on the Internet, but you must pay a service provider to get access to it.

WHAT'S A MODEM?

A modem converts the digital signals that need to flow between your PC and the host into sounds that travel across the phone line. It also can let you connect to someone else's PC to exchange documents or files and play interactive games. The modem has a built-in dialer that your communications program uses to place phone calls.

You can buy this gadget as either a card that installs in your PC (an internal modem) or as a box that plugs into your PC's serial port (an external modem). An ordinary phone cable from the modem plugs into your telephone jack, and you can also plug in an ordinary phone if you like. Modems are rated by data speed; most current products will handle from 300 to 14,400 bps (bits per second). Again, while most online services now handle only as high as 9,600 bps, available speeds are being increased, especially in urban areas.

If you have a personal information manager (PIM) application, it can use the modem's dialer to automatically place phone calls for you. Once you've entered the numbers into the PIM, you can simply select your party; the computer dials the call, and you then pick up the phone to talk.

A facsimile (fax) modem is often combined with a regular modem, adding very little to its cost. Using it, you can send a document or graphic from your word processor to a facsimile machine. (If instead of a fax machine you call another computer with a fax modem, your document can be viewed on its monitor, making the whole process "paperless." Of course, your correspondent must have the computer and fax application running in advance.)

Voice mail is another very useful feature included on some modem products. It gives you a very complete answering machine that stores voice messages on your hard disk. You get separate voice mailboxes for each user, message forwarding to another phone, and even paging. The added cost is about what you'd pay for an ordinary answering machine. (It does require you to keep your computer running, of course.)

Data, fax, and voice-mail features all rely on applications running on your computer; these programs are almost always included with the modem purchase.

Modems are available from literally dozens of manufacturers; here are some examples from well-known makers.

PRACTICAL PERIPHERALS PM288PKT V.FC POCKET DATA/FAX MODEM

If you have a laptop or other portable computer and you want online communications, one answer is to buy a built-in or slide-in modem option when you buy the PC. But if you didn't do that, or if you have several

PCs and don't want to buy a modem for each, here's an effective solution.

Practical Peripherals packs a full-featured modem into a pocket-sized battery-powered package. Plug it into a spare serial port, and it gives you 28,800 bps data or 14,400 bps fax wherever you are. Included applications for DOS and Windows give you full data and fax handling features.

This modem stows away in its carrying case with all the needed cables, adapters, and power supplies. A little built-in speaker tells you how your call is progressing, and a row of LEDs gives you modem status.

Practical Peripherals makes a full line of modems, including both internal cards for PCs and external models for almost any application. If you want the features of this pocket unit but don't need the portability, try its model PC288HC V.FC internal card.

BOCA RESEARCH FDV141 MULTIMEDIA VOICE MODEM

Boca Research makes a full line of personal modems, as well as various other PC add-on boards. This internal board is a "multimedia" model because it combines all the features you might need for home or office: data, fax, and voice mail. Its data and fax modems both operate at a fast 14,400 bps. (Expect a new version with 28,800 bps data in a few months.) Included are fax and data applications for both DOS and Windows.

A Boca Multimedia modem board is shown in the next illustration. It fits in a normal PC ISA 16-bit slot.

Voice mail lets your computer record and playback voice and fax messages, and it can even notify you by page when you receive either one. You can control all these functions remotely by calling in from a touch-tone telephone. With a plug-in microphone, you can use the Multimedia modem to make digital voice recordings for use in business presentations or as document annotations.

● ●

The Boca Research Multimedia modem PC board (internal).

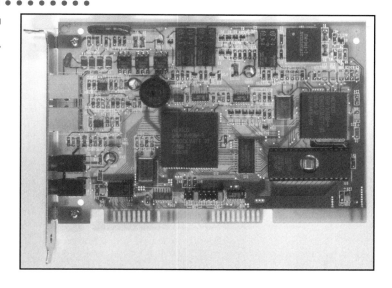

NATIONAL SEMICONDUCTOR TyIN4000 PRO

National Semiconductor puts its extensive chip design and manufacturing expertise to work in the TyIN4000 internal PC modem. Its data and fax speeds are both 14,400 bps, and National uses advanced compression techniques to greatly improve the actual data-transfer times. This board also gives you customizable voice mail with thousands of mailboxes and automatically distinguishes between a voice, data, or fax caller.

An on-board processor enables the TyIN4000 to take calls while your PC does other jobs, and it also provides heavy digital voice compression to keep your hard-disk message files compact. Plug in a microphone and speaker to use the board as a sound card for monophonic recording and stereo playback, or use it to add voice to your documents or presentations. The board is software-upgradable, so you can update many of its internal functions using a diskette.

One added bonus is a port for a Logitech hand scanner. If you have one of these popular scanners, this board will replace its interface card, freeing a valuable slot in your PC.

AT&T PARADYNE DATAPORT 2001

This modem deserves special mention because of a unique and notable feature. If a DataPort 2001 is on both sides of a connection, it lets you communicate data and have a voice conversation at the same time on the same phone call. Thus, while you're playing an interactive game, you can be discussing strategy with your partner or cursing your villainous opponent (if that's your style). Making a presentation to the office? You can do it from home by transmitting your supporting graphics to the office and providing your voice narration while the staff is reviewing the information on-screen.

DataPort 2001 uses an AT&T technology called VoiceSpan. It works by converting your voice into a data stream and combining it with the computer data. The process is reversed at the other end. When you talk, the voice data has priority. (Your computer's data transmission temporarily slows down.) Soon, VoiceSpan will be included in all Paradyne products, and AT&T wants to build it into computers, modems, fax machines, and games everywhere.

With DataPort 2001, you get data or fax transmission at 14,400 bps combined with instantaneous vocal transmission.

How Do Online Games Work?

Most computer games require lots of processing power, because their complex and fast-moving graphics consume considerable resources. This kind of power isn't available to your PC from time-sharing services.

In the first place, online computers are busy servicing countless other users; if many of those users were playing fancy games, it would sap the power available to others. Also, the existing modem-based connections between the host and home computers are too slow to keep up with fast-paced game images.

There is, however, a strategy to circumvent the bottlenecks. Traditionally, online games have been "adventure" type experiences, where players take on the roles of often fantastic and heraldic characters who "talk" with each other. This kind of text-based game needs neither fancy graphics nor high-speed communication. The pace of play is limited to your keyboard speed.

However, users now are demanding interactive games with on-screen action or scenery. Online services provide players with special game applications to install on their computers. Because the local computer creates the screen displays and graphics and handles animation, the timesharing host needs to transmit only game and motion commands and text among the multiple players.

Most computer games require lots of processing power, because their complex and fast-moving graphics consume considerable resources. This kind of power isn't available to your PC from time-sharing services.

CompuServe has added a new wrinkle to the online service mix. Using its data switching network, you can play directly against another subscriber anywhere in the world. This method bypasses the host and makes interactive gaming possible at much lower cost than a long-distance phone call.

THE MAJOR ONLINE SERVICES

AMERICA ONLINE

America Online is the fastest-growing online service. In the recent past it was almost overwhelmed trying to keep up with its own popularity. AOL, with nearly a million subscribers, now rates as one of the "big three" in services, along with CompuServe and Prodigy. America Online describes its corporate mission as developing "electronic communities."

AOL offers electronic mail, and it recently opened its users to expanded access to the Internet (both at no extra charge). Over 300 hardware and software vendors provide online support. AOL also offers a variety of online multiplayer games.

COMPUSERVE INFORMATION SERVICE

CompuServe is the Cadillac of the online industry. This 15-year-old operation has consistently been rated the most complete online service (and also the most expensive). Based in Columbus, Ohio, and owned by H&R Block, CompuServe has close to 2 million subscribers (including me). It owns its own vast communications network, and even publishes its own slick (paper) magazine.

CompuServe is the Cadillac of the online industry.

CompuServe also hosts special services, including public areas, such as those administered by Ziff-Davis, and a raft of private areas. (Ziff-Davis is a far-flung publishing enterprise that owns both *PC Magazine* and *PC Week*; you'll find online editions of both publications on CompuServe.) Many computer hardware and software vendors maintain forums on CompuServe to serve customers with technical support and program updates.

Access to the Internet via CompuServe has been limited to electronic mail, but CompuServe is reported to be opening up more complete access soon.

CompuServe has extensive games services, including forums for both commercial and online products. It hosts a collection of interactive games and also a unique area called the Modem-to-Modem Gaming Lobby (GO MTMLOBBY), where users can connect directly to other players for one-on-one interactive play. This service is limited to 2,400 bps data speed, but it provides a low-cost alternative to a direct long-distance phone call.

Delphi Internet

Delphi is the "little guy" in online services. For years it struggled in near anonymity. After its 1993 purchase by publishing tycoon Robert Murdoch, it's been discovered by the general public. It is the first major online service to add full access to the Internet.

Genie

Decade-old Genie is owned by General Electric Information Services. It uses a simple command-line interface, and retains its place as the bargain-priced service of all the major vendors.

Along with all the other standard online products, Genie offers a special section for multiplayer games with about 15 titles.

Prodigy

Although I haven't covered Prodigy's game offerings here, it deserves mention as one of the largest online services. Prodigy is jointly owned by Sears and IBM. It serves about a million households.

Prodigy shows the user a very graphic and very colorful, but low-resolution, display. It offers services similar to other providers, such as home shopping, games, electronic mail, online news, and forums. One appealing feature of Prodigy for game-playing kids has been a flat monthly fee that covers unlimited on-line access.

THE INTERNET

The Internet isn't actually an online service; rather it's a network, comprising a loose conglomeration of thousands of host computers, literally all over the world. Originally formed by the U.S. Department of Defense as ARPA-NET, it linked universities and corporations that were involved with military and government research. The Department of Defense has its own high-security network now, and its need for the Internet has passed.

Today, the Internet still has a core of universities and large corporations, but much of its communication is now between private users. You get access to the Internet via a service provider, an agency that connects multiple users to an Internet communications path for a fee. (Costs tend to be much lower than regular fee-for-service operations.)

There is no fee for using the Internet itself. In fact, nobody owns the Internet (although obviously various participants own and maintain the communications paths). Although the Internet has been guided by a non-commercial philosophy, pressure is building from vendors to tap into the buying power of the upscale denizens of the network.

What's on the Internet? Everything—and nothing. Various hosts offer just about anything a computer can provide, from electronic mail to databases to special interest areas or forums about any imaginable topic. You'll find programs, games, and graphics covering (or uncovering) everything from Jupiter to naked humans.

But none of this is assured. Any host can connect, leave, or restrict access to the network whenever its administrators decide. And because there can be no up-to-date catalog of available services, you have the major problem of finding what you're looking for on one or more of any of thousands of hosts.

Probably the most daunting aspect of the Internet is its arcane set of commands to access information on the various hosts. The terms are cryptic, full of abbreviations and acronyms, and generally impenetrable to the novice. Some PC applications are available to give you a more accessible command system and help you search for topics. Online services such as America Online provide graphic menu tools to access the Internet.

MOON VALLEY SOFTWARE: HITCHHIKING ON THE INFORMATION HIGHWAY

[CD-ROM for Windows/MPC]

Here is one unique product that can help you navigate the many available online services. It's a CD containing a communications program combined with application aids that help you connect to the Internet, AOL, CompuServe, and others. Colorful toolbars help speed your requests to log on. The title also includes information and help for many of these services.

When Hitchhiking on the Information Highway loads, it creates a large flock of application icons in its own program group window. Some of these applications let you log on to the services that seem appealing, for immediate registration and signup. Others are text files with background information about the services. This product is the only one I've seen with such broad coverage; its publication as a CD is even more useful.

Modem Games

Sometimes it's more fun to play together than alone. When I was a kid, I managed to get rather chubby consuming oceans of heavily buttered popcorn at the neighbors' house while playing endless hours of Monopoly and Clue.

When you're a grown-up, it's not always that simple. Your buddies may be across town—or across the country. One way to get your friends into the action is to call them up and link them directly into your game via a computer modem.

Many popular games are designed for such two-player connections, and some can even be used on local networks (LANs). (If you're linking to a nearby computer, you can connect by using a cable called a "null modem" instead of making a phone call.) After you're connected, you'll soon find yourself cooperating with your friends in a game scenario (or trying to shoot them to pieces, depending on the game).

The sampling of games I'll discuss here work just fine by themselves but give you an added dimension when you link to somebody else. You'll want to run any of them on a 386 or 486 computer with 2 to 4MB of RAM and a hard disk.

FLIGHT SIMULATOR 5.0 (MICROSOFT)

[Floppy diskette for DOS 5.0]

One of the first simulation products available for the home computer market, Flight Simulator was developed a decade ago by Bruce Artwick and marketed by Microsoft. (It has long been popular with retailers for the purpose of demostrating computers.) Now in incarnation number 5, it has greatly improved its flight simulation, aircraft, and scenic realism over the years. By today's multimedia standards, it's also a small application.

Flight Simulator is distinct from most other flight products because it's focused on the thrill of flight rather than shooting down adversaries. You can practice with an "instructor," log your flights, and view profiles of your most recent air disaster. Available add-on scenery lets you fly over Washington, D.C., Paris, or other cities and check out the scenic details.

Sound effects are limited to the sounds of your piston or jet engine and the disheartening din of a crash. (In the event of a crash, you also can watch vital pieces of your aircraft spiraling away from the impact.)

Don't want to fly alone? No problem; just start Flight Simulator, then call a friend on the telephone, using a modem to establish a data connection. Then you and your friend are in the air together on both computer displays. You can fly in formation or watch each other from various positions.

Microsoft markets scenery add-ons for Flight Simulator that provide enhanced detail for selected areas. I tried the Paris add-on. Soon I was happily buzzing past the Eiffel Tower and the Arc de Triomphe. It's lots of fun, and it gives you far more realistic views than can Flight Simulator alone.

MALLARD (SCENERY ADD-ONS)

[Floppy diskette for Microsoft Flight Simulator 5.0]

Mallard Software also makes add-on scenery for Flight Simulator for a number of selected cities. It's incredibly realistic; its terrain is based on aerial or satellite photographs, and its buildings are good-looking 3-D simulations. An ordinary flight thus becomes a sightseeing adventure.

Using the scenic add-on for Washington, D.C., I was soon flying low over the Pentagon and past the Washington and Lincoln monuments. All of these places are strictly off-limits to aircraft in real life. A scenic flight I took with Mallard to San Francisco brought back visions of the TransAmerica building, Ghirardelli Square, and lots of other neat places I'd seen in person.

With Mallard, there is a price for all this realism: lots of hard-disk space and slowed flight performance. You'll need a very fast computer to keep the simulated motion up to par.

MALLARD ATC FOR WINDOWS V1.11

[Floppy diskette for Windows 3.1]

Here is one of my favorite aviation-related simulations, also marketed by Mallard. The product was designed by Wesson International, which also develops "serious" pilot training applications. ATC is a close approximation of an Air Traffic Controller radar position; your job is to accept and control aircraft traffic entering and departing a dense urban area, such as Chicago, L.A., or Boston.

An active radar screen is running, with moving targets, I.D. tags, transponder replies, weather information, airways, and airport overlays, next to a situation board of "strips" for the flights you'll be working. It all works, right up to the option "switches" that you turn using your mouse. It looks and acts so much like the real thing it's uncanny. (ATC is really two similar games: one called Tracon for commercial aircraft, another called Rapcon for military types.)

This realism is almost too good. I'm a pilot, and I used to have more irritation than respect for all those good people

on the ground who told me to go left when I really wanted to go right. Now that I've played ATC, and sweated out the responsibility of keeping a bunch of goons (oops—fellow pilots) from crashing into each other, the respect has won out.

If you have the poor judgment to cause a mid-air collision and kill some people, ATC not only chastises you but permanently wipes your record from its score log. No fooling. I was truly embarrassed when it happened to me.

ATC provides "aviation-quality" voices that give you the pilots' responses to your controls. It works through your PC speaker, but you can hear it much more clearly via a sound card. You can link ATC with Microsoft Flight Simulator using a cable or modem for two-player action. One of you is the pilot, the other is the controller. The question is, will you be friends at the end of the day?

FALCON 3.0 (SPECTRUM HOLOBYTE)

[Floppy diskette for DOS 5.0; VGA display required]

Even though it's been around for a couple of years, Falcon 3.0 still holds a prominent position as an action/arcade game simulation. It was one of the first high-speed animations with decent imagery. In Falcon, you fly your F-16 into combat and use your formidable weapons against

Falcon 3.0's cockpit view.

enemy fighter jets and helicopters. There's lots of fast action and sounds.

You get great cockpit views, including a heads-up display, but you won't find the kind of aircraft and ground visual detail as in Flight Simulator. Here the emphasis is on action and missions. (There is a limited "hi-fi" mode that displays souped-up graphics.)

A heads-up display is projected on your cockpit window, and targeting radar shows when you've locked on the enemy. The view outside shows you've dispatched that enemy ship with a quick missile in his butt.

Want to battle? Call your neighbor up, using a modem. You can meet in head-to-head F-16 combat, or join up in missions against the computer "enemy." If you have two computers in the same house, a simple cable between them will do. Using a multicomputer network, you can involve the whole family in an air battle. (What a way to play out those inevitable aggressions.)

SSN-21 Seawolf (Electronic Arts)

[CD-ROM for DOS 5.0; VGA display required]

Newly rereleased on CD-ROM, this is a complex submarine-attack game. Players have an arsenal of various missiles and torpedoes as they engage in cat-and-mouse struggle with enemy submarines and surface craft. Unlike with most aircraft simulations, you don't just jump behind the controls; first there's a lot to learn about control systems, strategy, and especially sonar.

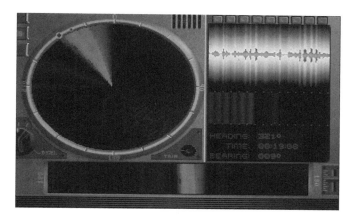

SSN-21 Seawolf, sonar room.

SSN-21 Seawolf, surface view.

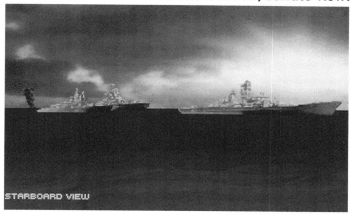

STARBOARD VIEW

Properly using the sonar is a fine art form in Seawolf. You get the familiar "radar-screen" format display, but it requires real skill to interpret. For picking up targets, there are arrays of hull-mounted hydrophones, a "towed array" and active "pinging" to manage. Even effects such as variable water temperature, "thermals," and undersea terrain are taken into account. It's an impressive simulation, but one that requires study.

You can see the Seawolf sonar room in the previous illustration. At left are the position and ranging scope, at top right is the "waterfall" display, and the bottom right bars are the "signal analyzer" (signature analysis) display.

High-quality stereo sound effects include explosions, sonar beeps, torpedoes loading and firing, whale sounds, and even a musical score.

The illustration of Seawolf surface action shows a trio of enemy warships waiting to be picked off, with one in the distance that's met its (deserved) end.

This game is a bit dated now, with lots of references to enemy Soviets and reliance on old-style "control-key" command sequences that you'll want to memorize for quick response. But it is one heck of a simulation, and it has multiplayer capability.

Using a modem or network (NETBIOS is the only compatible network protocol specified in the manual), you can team up with a friend to attack the enemy fleet (or attack each other, depending on your social skills).

INTERACTIVE MULTIMEDIA FOR THE PC

Technology enables us to extend our reach in important, fundamental ways. Computer-based systems give us new eyes and ears on the world, and let us enjoy and learn from experiences that were barely laboratory curiosities until recently.

Think of a computer as a true multipurpose information-handling machine. You can use it for the everyday tasks such as word processing and accounting, but the same equipment can provide information, entertainment, and education and let you exercise your creative talents in art and music. You can find a personal computer at a nearby department store that has more power to deliver information and fun to you than a roomful of equipment could 10 years ago.

To introduce you to the world of multimedia computing, I'll first discuss what equipment to look for and then review some of the more exciting multimedia applications available. It's important to recognize that this is a story that's still being written; today's computers and applications are only the beginning of an explosion of interactive multimedia offerings.

HARDWARE

THE BASIC COMPUTER

To run multimedia applications, you need a powerful computer. That means one that is fast and with lots of information storage. You'll find more competitive choices for your PC purchase than for almost anything else you can buy; that makes for great prices. Be careful not to buy too little computer. There's nothing more frustrating than "almost" multimedia—sound with unexpected interruptions, pictures that take minutes to display, video that lurches unsteadily behind the story line.

Do expect that whatever you buy, it will shortly be obsolete. Computer technology moves so quickly, you can't avoid that. (Object lesson: There's no time like the present to take advantage of what's available. If you wait for the "latest and greatest," you'll be waiting forever and you'll be left out of any possible benefit.)

You'll want a Macintosh or IBM-PC 486-style computer with speeds of at least 40Mhz, a math co-processor, RAM (memory) of at least 8MB, and a hard disk with 200MB or more of storage; consider these as minimums. When possible, select a computer with a combination ISA/PCI bus; that combination gives you compatibility with current accessory boards as well as the latest high-speed boards. (I'll give you a shopping checklist for the necessary accessories shortly.)

Your operating system should be the Mac System 7 or later (if you're using a Mac) or Windows 3.1 or later and DOS 5 or later (for IBM-type PCs). Most multimedia products and many new games need a graphical window-type environment.

If you're playing games, there are special-purpose devices available from 3DO, Sega, Nintendo, and others. Some of them do a superb job of producing game graphics, motion, and sound; they don't do other tasks as well (if at all). Consider them only if you're an incorrigible game player and don't want the benefits of a PC.

CD-ROM DRIVE

Even though you'll want a floppy drive on your new PC, multimedia applications have totally outstripped the storage capacity of floppy diskettes. Most graphics applications use 15MB to 30MB of storage, which is anywhere from five to 20 floppy disks' worth. That's why you need a CD-ROM drive, which accepts slim digital versions of CDs that can each store more than 600MB of data.

CD-ROM drives are fairly new to the PC marketplace. CD-ROM technology is moving very quickly, and prices are falling. Look for at least a double-speed drive, capable of 300KB-per-second data transfer; triple- or quad-speed drives are even better but are currently premium-priced. The drive should include a built-in

● ●

Think of a computer as a true multipurpose information-handling machine. You can use it for the everyday tasks such as word processing and accounting, but the same equipment can provide information, entertainment, and education and let you exercise your creative talents in art and music.

cache memory of 64KB to 256KB to smooth out data transfer. Drives with proprietary (custom) interfaces are the least expensive, but those with SCSI or IDE type interfaces usually perform better.

The next big CD advance is CD-ROM drives that hold multiple CDs; these "jukebox" drives are available now, but at prohibitive prices. In a year or so, they'll be among the hottest products around.

VIDEO BOARDS

An ordinary VGA-type video board, which generates an image of 640×480 pixels (screen dots) is yesterday's standard. Look for a board that includes an accelerated video processor, that supports images as detailed as 1024×768 pixels non-interlaced, with vertical rates to 75 Hz or more. Color capability should be 256 colors, 65,000 colors, or 16.7 million colors (corresponding to 8-, 16-, or 24-bit processing). On-board video memory can be from one to four MB. If you choose an IBM-type PC—and your computer has the appropriate slots—the video board should use either a VLB or (better yet) a PCI type computer bus.

THE MONITOR

It's bulky, it's expensive—and it's a critical element in quality multimedia. Your monitor is the most important data conduit from the computer to the user. You'll want a VGA-type monitor capable of displaying fine details (a dot pitch of 0.26 or 0.28 mm) and lots of detail (as high as 1024×768 pixels, non-interlaced). It should be able to handle vertical rates of 75 Hz or higher.

Other features such as a flat screen, digital controls, color correction, and "green" energy-saving automatic power-down are all useful, but these can add 10 to 30 percent to the cost.

The single feature that most determines price is screen size, which is measured (as in the case of a TV set) in inches diagonally across the image. I strongly recommend you try to stretch your budget for a 17-inch monitor. Keep in mind that the monitor is literally your multimedia "eye on the world."

There are two additional reasons for choosing a larger monitor. First, windows-type environments give you the benefit of displaying multiple applications at once (or multiple portions of the same application). A large display provides enough space so that you can display (and read) all those windows. Plus, a big display lets you sit back from the screen, avoiding eyestrain from extended periods of close-up focus.

An excellent quality monitor is model 15FS from Mitsubishi. This is a 15-inch version with a flat-square display, on-screen control setups, and automatic image calibration. It includes color calibration controls and can automatically power down when unused. A similar

Mitsubishi model 15FS 15-inch flat-square color monitor.

17-inch version—model 17FS—has all these features and an available Windows application called Diamond Control that lets you set up many display features using a graphical menu.

Both models have a wide display range, from VGA (640×480) to 1280×1024, to handle applications from word-processing to graphics to computer-aided design.

Another good quality monitor is from NEC, the MultiSync 5FGp. It's an award-winning high-quality 17-inch unit with a flat-square display. This model has convenient front-panel adjustments for size and position and also a feature that lets you precisely set and save the image color balance. It's a "green" monitor, which means it automatically powers down (saving both electricity and the picture tube) after a selected number of minutes.

This unit's clear and sharp image and bright precise colors are evident from the first use. An included setup application helps you adjust setups and color balance to fit your needs. A broad display range supports a wide variety of applications.

Finally, take a look at the Packard-Bell 17-inch monitor made by Panasonic. It's recently received some excellent ratings, and it's surprisingly affordable.

SOUND CARDS

A little background is necessary here on the importance of sound in personal computers, especially IBM-PC compatibles. (If you use a Macintosh PC, basic sound features are built in and supported by the operating environment; some of this discussion therefore doesn't relate directly.)

Although many PCs have a rudimentary sound-generation capability built in, sound cards make game sounds more realistic, let your computer "talk" to you, and create pleasing instrument performances. In effect, this single board is a three-in-one device. (Macintosh computers have built-in sound, but it's strictly optional for IBM-type PC's.)

Early sound cards were monophonic (one-channel) 8-bit sound devices; these have been supplanted by stereo 16-bit models. That's a big quality improvement that you can easily hear.

Quality sound is produced in your PC in either of two general ways: digital recordings of sound or stored "directions" to play musical notes. Digital sound is made by taking samples of "real" or analog sound, and then converting the samples into numbers; the numbers are stored in data files (called .WAV files). Playback of digital sound simply reverses the recording process: the stored numbers are sent in sequence to a device that converts them back to analog sounds. An amplifier boosts the signals before sending them through the headphones or loudspeakers.

Computer musical notation is defined by the MIDI (Musical Instrument Digital Interface) standard. MIDI music is stored in files that are far more compact than digital sound files because the instructions for a musical note are much simpler than the actual note sounds themselves. In effect, MIDI provides a means of compressing music sounds. The complexity is in playback. The pitch, volume, and length of each note (and also a reference to the timbral qualities of the chosen instrument) are sent to a device called a synthesizer. There the information is translated into musical sounds.

MIDI also defines a complete method for linking electronic keyboards and sound-generating devices together into a musical instrument "network." You can easily spot MIDI compatability by the round, 5-pin connectors on a sound card or keyboard.

To add both sound and MIDI features to your PC, install a sound card option. The basic ones record and play back monophonic (single-channel) digital sound recordings and are usually used for "business" sound to voice-annotate documents, reports, and presentations. Multimedia-ready cards are stereo (two channels) and have MIDI capability. Two more elements determining sound quality are the size of each digital sample (the number of bits) and the rate at which the samples are taken. Together, they represent the accuracy of the sample. A basic card uses only 8-bit samples, whereas music-quality sound cards are 16-bits. Sample rates range from about 11kHz to 48kHz (thousand times a second).

Older-design sound cards have music synthesizers based on a technology called FM synthesis. The sounds that are generated by FM synthesis reasonably resemble the real instruments. Instrument sounds are created using a combination of basic tones, amplifiers, and filters. This same process is widely employed in home keyboards.

The newest advance in sound card technology is called wavetable synthesis, a more expensive but also far more accurate way of simulating instruments. The sound card stores actual samples of real instruments or other sounds and then plays them back on demand. This technique is now used in all the better sound cards and even in some low-cost ones. Quality, however, varies considerably.

Sound cards are beginning to use special "sound computers" called digital signal processors (DSPs). They allow complex sound processing such as ambience control, echo, and holographic 3-D or surround sound. Some can also be reprogrammed to upgrade or add new effects.

Finally, sound cards often have a connection or port to control a CD-ROM drive. If you expect to use this, be sure the CD-ROM drive you choose is compatible, because many are not. Cards also provide multiple audio inputs to accept a microphone, audio from a CD-ROM, and external devices.

You can buy a sound board, external speakers, music applications, and keyboards separately, you can get them as a complete sound-system upgrade, or you can get them as part of a larger multimedia upgrade kit that may also include a CD-ROM drive and controller or even a keyboard.

The following are some of the better sound-card packages available today.

MULTISOUND MONTEREY (TURTLE BEACH SYSTEMS)

Multisound Monterey is a top-rated sound card with an unusual feature: the ability to turn any sound into an "instrument."

This Multisound Monterey sound card is an a competent wavetable-based sound card designed for multimedia. Using a DSP (digital signal processor), it combines clean-sounding stereo digital audio with a wavetable-based MIDI synthesizer. (MIDI connections are optional.)

Because the card's wavetables store the MIDI instrument sounds, any new table entry gives you a new instrument. You can thus record any sound samples and then load them into memory tables, creating new instruments to augment the basic 128. You can record real acoustic instruments, voices, natural sounds, sound effects, or any other sound you like, then play them from a MIDI com-

position or keyboard. To add more instruments, you can add more memory. This is the ultimate sampler-type musical device.

Select as many as 32 instruments to play at the same time, out of a set of 128. It's like an orchestra in a box. A special-effects processor, providing reverb, echo, and delay, expands the available sound repertoire. Distortion and frequency-response specifications for the Monterey are among the best-sounding cards available and one of the few that come close to broadcast-quality sound.

If you already have a sound card, Turtle Beach makes an add-on card called Maui that gives you MIDI features similar to those of the Monterey. It replaces the older FM synthesis system with Monterey-style wavetable and sampling technology. You'll find the improvement in instrument sound quality hard to believe.

ADVANCED GRAVIS: PIANO SYSTEM

In this one product, you get a complete musical performance and education system. Advanced Gravis has produced one of the first affordable wavetable-based sound cards. This package combines the card (the Ultrasound MAX) with a full-sized MIDI keyboard and a teaching application called Musicware Piano. It also includes a pair of small but good-sounding powered speakers from Acoustic Research, cables, and some PC audio applications.

This is one of the few packages that integrate PC sound, keyboard, and teaching, and it does so at a surprisingly affordable price.

Musicware Piano teaches you how to play piano. It's an interactive Windows-based application that gives you on-screen audio and visual lessons and responses to your keyboarding. It's a "synthetic" teacher, with a self-paced curriculum of six courses in a structured learning format.

The 49-key Italian-made keyboard is velocity-sensitive, which means it sounds louder when you play louder (or press the keys more quickly). This feature is an essential to realistic play for many instruments, including piano. When you play the keyboard through the sound card, you can choose not only piano but any of 192 instruments. If you compose music and play it back, you can use as many as 32 instruments playing at the same time. (That's the orchestra in a box I promised you.)

To record and play back audio, Advanced Gravis gives you Windows-based applications that work with the sound card. There's even an audio editor by Turtle Beach Software (more on them later). To record your keyboard efforts and also edit and play back MIDI music, there's Midisoft's Recording Session (more on that later also).

The accompanying MAX is a high-end sound card that is based on a digital signal processor (DSP). It includes audio compression hardware, to reduce the size of stored sound files, and an interface for some CD-ROM drives (essential for multimedia). It can generate a kind of 3-D surround sound as well.

Wavetables (which produce the instrument sounds) are stored in memory on the MAX; an included application lets you edit or completely change any of these sounds. That means you can create libraries of

entirely new instruments—even record audio such as voices and sound effects and play them back from the keyboard.

MIDI MUSIC EQUIPMENT

MIDI music is a complex subject, because it involves program applications, cable connections, and instrument sounds produced either by a sound card or an external instrument. I will describe a couple of products you might want in order to go beyond the basics.

MIDI/JOYSTICK ADAPTERS

Basic MIDI connections to outside instruments are usually provided on your sound card, as discussed in the previous section. The connectors are the round, 5-pin DIN type, which is not typically used for any other computer equipment. Sometimes your sound card's MIDI outputs are combined on a joystick port. In such cases, you'll need an adapter box that plugs into the sound card and has both MIDI and joystick connectors on it. If this adapter isn't packed with your sound card, you can buy it separately.

ENHANCED MIDI CARDS

If you're doing complex MIDI music, the basic MIDI port provided by a sound card may not have the features you need. For example, you may need more than one or two MIDI ports. If you're going to synchronize your music for use with motion-picture or video productions, you need what's called SMPTE timing. (And frankly, if you're an earnest musician, you may not want to generate instrument sounds using a sound card in the first place.)

One top-of-the-line product that gives you all these professional features is the Voyetra V-24s interface card for IBM-compatible PCs. It fits in a standard internal slot and gives you two input and four output MIDI ports. It also reads or generates all standard SMPTE time codes and converts them to MIDI time codes.

MIDI connections are made to a "break-out" box that plugs into the card and provides standard jacks. Supplied drivers make the V-24s compatible with DOS and Windows MIDI applications. (This board includes an add-on feature that provides the Roland MPU-401 chipset. If you need this, you'll already know what it is.)

PARALLEL PORT MIDI CONVERTERS

If you want to use a laptop or notebook PC to compose or play your MIDI music, there's no way to add a sound or MIDI adapter card. (Even if you have access to a full-sized PC, you may not be able to open it up to add MIDI.) The solution is a special MIDI adapter that plugs into either a serial or parallel port. Voyetra Technologies makes a pocket-sized box called the VP-11 that plugs into your parallel (printer) port and provides two MIDI ports. (It also passes the printer port through so you can use it too.)

Using Voyetra's included driver, the VP-11 is compatible with any Windows 3.1 MIDI application and many DOS programs as well. It runs on an included 9-volt adapter.

LOUDSPEAKERS AND AMPLIFIERS

Most sound cards contain low-powered audio amplifiers (perhaps two to five watts per channel) to run speakers, and a sound kit may also be packed with some cheap plastic speakers. With this configuration, you won't hear the rich, wide-range sound created by MIDI synthesizers, CD audio, and high-end games (unless you decide to wear headphones).

One simple solution is to connect your sound card's line output to your home stereo system; an ordinary audio cable may suffice. This gives you access to the extra power and speaker quality you've already paid

for. (I'm not responsible for any wrath you incur from stealing the family's only stereo.)

If you'd like a completely self-contained audio system for your PC, a convenient and effective way is to add powered speakers. They augment the sound card's audio power and provide extended frequency response.

If you plan to place speakers near your display (or around your floppy diskettes), be sure to choose speakers that are magnetically shielded. The strong magnetic fields of ordinary speakers can distort a monitor's image or color accuracy and can potentially erase a floppy diskette's magnetically stored information.

Altec-Lansing, a venerable maker of big speaker systems for theaters and homes, also produces a line of computer speakers. The company's top model is the ACS300.1. It includes two self-powered desktop speakers with 18 watts of audio, flip-up tweeters to reproduce high frequencies to 20kHz, and individual tone and volume controls. An 18-watt subwoofer extends the bass down to a wall-vibrating 35Hz.

I was astonished at how these little speakers added such a big dimension to my electronic keyboard organ and game sounds. The subwoofer had me believing I had an organ pipe growing out of my computer.

POINTING DEVICES

Most games and multimedia applications that require user input are better controlled through pointing devices than the keyboard. Such devices range from the venerable mouse to exotic joysticks, trackballs, and digital pens. The following are some pointing devices you may find useful in your multimedia computing.

Logitech MouseMan and Cordless MouseMan

[For DOS or Windows; require either serial or PS-2 port]

From one of the largest makers of pointing devices, here are two three-button mice. MouseMan was designed to fit most hands well and is available in separate versions for left- and right-handed users. It's provided with mouse drivers for DOS and Windows, and applets to let you customize various attributes of mouse and cursor actions.

MouseMan Cordless packs into a package almost the same size as the corded version a mouse and a miniature radio transmitter. A supplied receiver connects to your PC to pass the signals for mouse movement. While it's more expensive, the cordless version frees you from the frustration of a cable that limits your hand motions.

Either the corded or cordless MouseMan is available for connection to a standard PC-compatible serial port or an IBM PS-2 mouse port.

Microsoft Mouse

[For DOS or Windows; versions for serial, bus, or PS-2 port]

A couple of years ago, Microsoft completely reengineered its popular mouse. The current version is an international favorite that's available in serial, PS-2, and bus versions. It's provided with both DOS and Windows drivers.

Logitech CyberMan

[For DOS or Windows 3.1; requires serial port]

It's an interesting problem: how to control an object's motion in a 3-D game or simulation. An aircraft, for example, has six kinds of clearly defined movement: left-right, forward-backward, and up-down (the x-, y-, and z-axes), as well as nose-left or nose-right ("yaw"), wing-up or wing-down ("roll"), and nose-up or nose-down ("pitch"). Logitech has developed the only widely-available product that controls them all: the CyberMan.

CyberMan looks and acts something like a mouse perched on the end of a joystick that's sitting on a greasy table. Its great range of movements will take some getting used to. Put your hand gently on the mouse "handle," and you'll find three buttons that are used in games the same way as those on a joystick. (In fact, CyberMan replaces your joystick when installed.)

Slide the mouse forward, backward, left, or right in its base for x- and y-axis movements. Lift the mouse up and down on its support pin for z-axis control. Rotate the mouse left or right on its support pin (by twisting your wrist) for yaw. Tilt it on its support ball-joint (rotate your arm left or right) for roll, tilt your wrist forward or backward for pitch. It's much like steering a toy aircraft with your hand. It's also much easier done than described.

There's no standard for 3-D game control, and only certain recently-released applications will accept all of CyberMan's motions. Some new games will even send tactile feedback to your hand by vibrating the mouse handle on cue. (This requires an included plug-in transformer for power. No, it doesn't shock you.)

Logitech CyberMan.

CyberMan is an impressive first solution to a complex design problem. One aspect I really like is its responsiveness to small, natural hand and arm motions. (You'll want to treat it with reasonable care to avoid breaking one of its many pivots.)

CyberMan is furnished with drivers for both DOS and Windows applications. In DOS, the drivers support both CyberMan and a mouse; Windows accepts only one pointing device.

FORTE VFX-1 HELMET

If you're going to walk through an artificial environment, the most natural way is to use your head—literally. When you walk around, you move your head and eyes toward the subjects that interest you and in the direction you're planning to move. One technique for transmitting that information to a PC is to wear a device that senses your head motion: a helmet.

A fully responsive digital helmet represents one tricky design problem. As with an airplane, your head has six kinds of distinct possible motions, plus every combination thereof. For a helmet to know where your head is at (no play on words intended), it has to be sensitive to those motions, including their rates of change (how fast you turn your head, for example). All this is included in the VFX-1 design.

The Forte helmet is surprisingly comfortable and lightweight. You should be able to wear it for hours without neck-strain. It sends information back to the PC via a small cable. It also contains two small TV screens (actually LCD video displays), one for each eye, for true 3-D (stereoscopic) vision. Attached optics make the image you see appear to be at a comfortable viewing distance.

As with CyberMan, this helmet is compatible only with a few specially modified game applications. Today's price makes it suitable for serious training and simulation applications and for the truly avid game player. However, in a few years, you'll find affordable helmets—and the games to go with them—available at every retail game store.

Forte VFX-1 helmet.

Interactive Software for the PC

Expensive computer hardware and peripherals are useless without some accompanying software: the games, programs, graphics, and encoded information that drive the computer and produce all those sights and sounds that heat up your monitor. The rest of this chapter describes some of the more exciting, entertaining, or educational software products that are available today for use on a multimedia PC.

Action/Adventure

Considering their appeal to testosterone-hyped adolescent males, it is not surprising that action/adventure titles have a large share of the interactive software market. Following are some of the action and adventure products that are making good use of the multimedia capacity of today's PCs.

MYST (Cyan/Broderbund)
[CD-ROM for Windows 3.1]

One of the most visually outstanding multimedia games yet devised, MYST sets a new standard for scenic design. MYST is an adventure game with a story: You find yourself alone on a faintly ominous, futuristic island with no apparent escape. Some infamous deed has apparently occurred here: A time-traveler discovered this place, developed it, and brought his two sons to it. Now the two sons have turned against him. Or so it seems.

Your task is to unravel the many puzzles that will lead you to secret entrances to the hidden multiple worlds. You explore these places to discover the answers to this uncanny mystery. It's an extremely complex quest that can occupy many dozens of hours. When you need to pause, MYST will let you save the game at whatever state of discovery you've reached.

MYST is filled with hundreds of highly detailed drawings of the eerie but credible terrain. All of it is computer generated: the trees, the rocks, the wood and metal parts, the water. Yet it's incredibly detailed and convincing. You'll see grain and nails in the wood, cracks in the rocks, corrosion on the metal.

Your mouse cursor is a pointer to the direction you choose to travel. With each mouse click, you move along pre-defined paths of the scene in step-motion (not fluid "real-time" action).

MYST is accompanied by many hours of original human-composed and computer-generated background music that is coordinated with the places and events. Sound effects such as the splashing of waves, the creaking of tortured metal, and the blowing of the wind heighten the realism of the scene. When you click on the appropriate places, you'll also see and hear images of people talking and see some other limited full-motion video insets.

Let's start our mystical adventure with the opening scene: a view of the dock, with a boat at right that is half-sunken onto the sea-floor yet creaking gently in the wind. Ahead is a rocky mesa with a fantastic pair of large gears perched on

The opening scene of MYST.

its flat. To the left is a stairway and looming above is what will turn out to be an observatory. Gliding back and forth over the water are a few gulls.

Ready for the cook's tour? (I promise not to reveal any of the secrets; I wouldn't want to spoil your adventure.) A few mouse clicks take you up past the observatory and to the library. The next view looks into the front door; there's the observatory at right. At left in the misty distance is the outline of a sort of fantastic rocket body. High on a rocky crag is a strange cylinder: the observation tower.

Inside the library you'll find a series of wall-hangings on panels, along with a rack of old books. Each is important to your search. Most useful to start with is the map, which begins to show more details as you approach. Visible here is the white outline of the library (but none of the other structures on the island). Don't forget to read the books before you leave; they'll give you the background to the story and many vital clues. You'll be back here soon.

The realism of the details in this game truly amazes me. Look up to see the library ceiling, with a formal rotunda and its lacy cloud paintings; a chandelier hangs down toward you in silhouette.

Outside and to the left of the library is the rocket ship, perched silently on what might be a launch pad. It's connected to a power cable that probably energizes its internal systems, and a closed hatch

Library
scene
from
MYST.

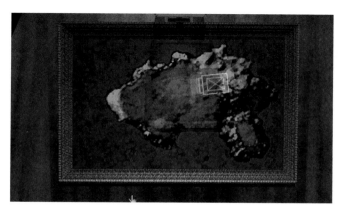

Map in
library
from
MYST.

Library
ceiling
from
MYST.

Rocket ship from MYST.

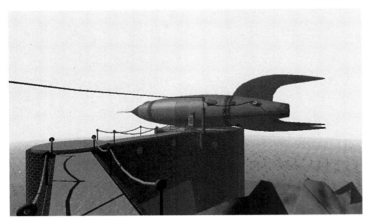

The MYST time machine.

door is visible. Out there, the ocean wind whistles powerfully, and far below, the water crashes and booms on the rocks.

To the right of the library is the observatory, its high inside windows inexplicably shimmering with stars in the daylight. A reclining leather chair awaits you, and up above is what seems like a star-finder. Click on the slide controls to select a date and time, push the Main button, and a faint whirring reveals a new star pattern in the window. A curious gadget; you will find it useful in your time travels between the multiple worlds of MYST.

Turn your back on the library and go down the garden path past the birdbath with the little boat (no time to check it out now), then through a grove of trees. You'll spy the clock tower out of reach on its own gear-motif pad perched in the water. A pair of handwheels and a button crown a metal control box, ready for the sleuth who knows how to operate them.

What's in that tower and how can you reach it across the water?

After one last scene, I'll leave you to your own ingenuity on this island. The location is hidden away but not hard to find. This is the "imager," a futuristic 3-D TV in the guise of a kettle (very stylish). Here it displays a relief map of some unknown terrain, which rotates into view. Perhaps you can find a way to make the imager show you some good clues.

The MYST clock tower.

The imager from MYST.

RETURN TO ZORK (INFOCOM)

[CD-ROM for DOS (Macintosh version available)]

There's a foreboding opening to this adventure. You're at the entrance to a valley, and vultures fly and perch menacingly around you. You must begin to make your way to the hidden underground caverns of Zork past the many risks and pitfalls.

As with traditional adventure games, you must acquire the tools and clues to proceed. (The first one gave me two points and some satisfaction: When I found a rock and threw it at one of the vultures it swooped away with a menacing cry.)

But this is no ordinary adventure game; it's a multimedia production with a full musical score, more than 100 full-motion video sequences, and an hour of voices from a cast of 23 professional actors. There are lots of sound effects, including the sound of wind and water and creaking doors (and the vultures, of course). Although it doesn't have the incredibly realistic scenic detail of MYST, it does have many interactive choices you can make to determine your progress.

You even get a flash camera and a tape recorder to help collect information on your journey. You can go back and review anything you've forgotten, and you can save your game progress for next time when you're done.

OUTPOST (SIERRA)

A terrible tragedy on Earth forces you and a few hardy souls to strike out across the galaxy in search of a new planet to inhabit. As commander, you choose what tools and supplies to bring on this one-way quest, select a likely star, and then launch. Realistic full-motion animations of the launch process heighten the thrill of mankind's last-chance adventure. Computerized voices and sound effects keep you informed along the journey.

Outpost begins with an elaborate sequence of menus and launches, but its core action is a complex and intriguing simulation to develop a futuristic colony. Your job is to successfully settle into an unknown new world and keep your people alive and thriving. It's essentially a high-tech space-based variation on a life simulation game, such as SimCity or Civilization.

As I found out, one possible consequence of screwing up is that the populus will all "hate you." But I fixed them: I was such a bad leader that they all died from starvation. (Sorry, guys.)

As an example of the superb opening graphics, this image shows a spacecraft, portrayed in mid-space as it fires its rocket away from earth.

Outpost spaceship animation.

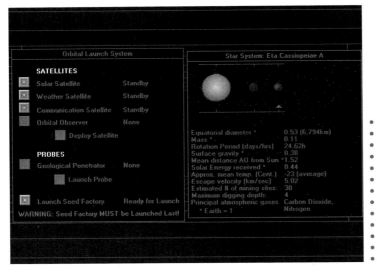

On a celestial map, you get to choose four star systems on which you hope a planet like Earth might be found. Of my four, the only one that panned out was Eta Cassiopeiae A, which turned out to have two planets. Choose the wrong one, the computer informs me in a dulcet female voice, and we're all dead.

But before I land, I carefully prepare to launch several kinds of exploratory satellites and probes to reduce my risk. The simulation provides you with a slick-looking launch control (one of several control panels).

You can see the launch of the probe as it appears in a small inset viewing window. An animation then shows it falling in space, blowing its launch shields free, and preparing to fire its retrorocket.

At the end of my short but perilous journey, I've found a planet that appears safe for colonization. First I'll launch a "seed ship" to prepare a temporary facility for the colonists, then a cargo ship, and later I'll send some people down to the surface on a transport. You

An outpost control panel.

An outpost probe launch.

An outpost planet and seed ship.

can watch one of these smaller ships being launched from the hold of the mother ship in colorful and convincing animation.

Time for the big gamble. A new community is launched (literally). I named my new home planet "Cyber P-H" and selected several sites to explore and "mine." (You must mine for raw materials to keep everything running and to create an artificial atmosphere for life support. And you must truly dig in; there are multiple construction levels in the planet's skin.)

Next, I sent down probes and a seed ship to begin its robotic construction and site prep; back on Earth, we'd call this a beachhead. It's shown at the bottom right of the screen. I also asked the on-board computer to monitor activity; a simple progress report is shown at bottom left.

If you like simulations, you'll be amazed at the detail and complexity of this one. Every time you run a turn (by clicking on the Turns window), all the processes you've started continue another step. The devices you choose to set in place on the planet begin to animate and create more and more complex structures. RoboMiners dig for energy-producing ore, RoboDozers stockpile materials like animated Tonka

toys on a mission. You must construct appropriate buildings, connect them together, and supply them with energy. You'll need to grow food, provide police protection and communication, and much more.

The prospect is formidable, and it gives me respect for what (for example) the mayor of New York City has to go through to keep his job. Of course, this undertaking is far more dangerous; you are on a hostile planet light-years from Earth, after all. (On the other hand, I was in New York last month, and ....)

Want to know how well I fared? The payoff for my brave efforts as commander was total and complete destruction. My little town is not only in ruins, but it has experienced a series of devastating (albeit delightful) explosions. That's after being racked by lightning, wind, earthquakes, and several other natural disasters to which I exposed the settlement. (Come to think of it, all 50 settlers had long since died of lack of food and atmosphere, waiting for me to get on with it.)

The galactic newspaper asked me for an interview, and I was callous enough to agree. I got points for the courage to tell my story, but it wasn't enough to bail me out.

I know you can do even better. If you need help or reports, just click on that shining orb at the bottom left, and the master computer will answer your needs. She's very nice, even obsequious—until you screw up.

Even if you manage to save civilization, Sierra won't let you off the hook. There's

Outpost endgame.

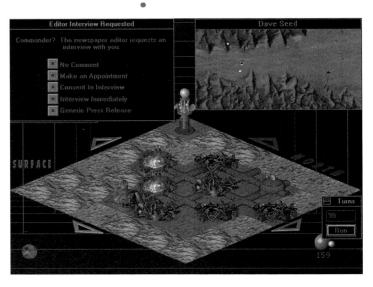

an "expansion module" called PlanetPak that adds even more thrilling and dangerous scenarios for you to overcome.

SPECTRE VR (VELOCITY DEVELOPMENT)

[CD-ROM for DOS or Macintosh]

Forget that super-realistic, scenery-rich simulation stuff—you want full-out arcade speed with shoot-em-up adventure. Spectre VR is your kind of game. Sure it has 3-D shapes that change perspective as you whiz by in your cybercraft and more than 100 action-linked live video inserts. But mostly it's about destroying the enemy in cyberspace.

You have smart missiles, mines, "pulse bursts," "spinners," and various other weapons in your formidable arsenal. You're fighting against smart acid pools, robots, video walls, mazes, cybermud, and other obstacles against racking up a big score. You can even create your own "virtual world" with an included editor. Spectre VR is packed in a ritzy futuristic tower box.

Spectre VR gives you full screens of game action. It includes several cybercraft hovering above the night terrain, some videos, and a scoreboard. Lots of lights and color here.

This latest version of the game has more than 20 multiplayer scenarios that can be played with as many as eight players on a network. I wish they'd release this product in a Windows version.

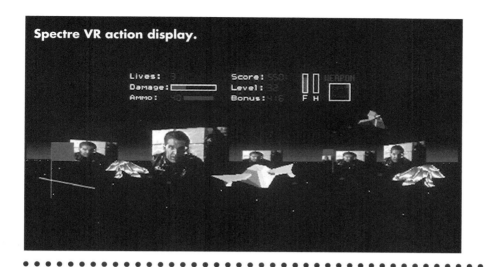

Spectre VR action display.

. . . .

IRON HELIX
(SPECTRUM HOLOBYTE)

[CD-ROM for Windows 3.1]

Iron Helix is based on an interesting and topical challenge: find the hidden people in a doomed starship by analyzing their DNA patterns. There's much more than that. This science-fiction adventure has you controlling a robot probe that is searching the many rooms and corridors of a renegade ship. Your mission is to track down the missing crew, control the spread of a deadly virus, and dodge the robot defender that tries to locate you on the ship.

The graphics are beautifully rendered, and the action and sound effects are convincing.

This is one of the few CD-ROM games designed to work in the Windows environment. Frankly, it's about time; most of the DOS-based CDs require you to

start them up with nothing else running. This is a true Windows application, so it coexists happily with all the others.

Iron Helix probe launch.

Iron Helix probe controls.

Come along—you're about to start your dangerous adventure, ready to go aboard the renegade ship. First, decide what your skill level is and push a button. Then you're launched. One very appealing aspect of this game to me is that you go aboard defenseless; you battle only with wits, not weapons.

A neat highly detailed animation sequence follows, showing your probe docking with the starship.

Once you're aboard, you operate the probe with the directional control at the bottom left of the screen while watching your progress on a TV screen at top left. At bottom right is a map of your position on the ship. One view also shows where the robot defender is: It's coming to destroy you. (Silly machine—it doesn't realize you're one of the good guys.)

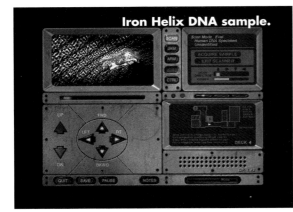

Iron Helix DNA sample.

As I move through the ship, doors open and close, with corresponding realistic sound effects. I need to be on the alert for all forms of life—human or alien. I'm looking for DNA.

I've managed to capture a bit of DNA sample from a crew member hidden behind an access plate, using my scanner. Top right shows the result of the analysis: human for sure. (Big relief.)

I haven't been located yet; if I had, the robot would have blown me away. But every time I saw him getting nearer on the map, I took an elevator or a free-fall tube to another level, barely eluding him. Somewhere on deserted Deck 1, I located the control room. What danger lurks here?

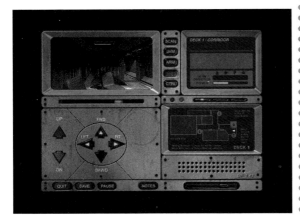

Iron Helix Deck 1 control room.

FLIGHT UNLIMITED (LOOKING GLASS/VIRGIN)

[Future release: CD-ROM for DOS]

This is yet another flight simulator, but with a difference. This is the first to be on CD-ROM, and it combines faithful aircraft simulation based on fluid dynamics with real-time photo-realistic views.

FLIGHT Unlimited will soon be released, with six high-performance single-engine aircraft, five U.S. airports, and 25 built-in flying lessons. It features realistic terrain and real-time 3-D view of the craft. One shot is of what is probably a Citabria aerobat, over Chelan. (I chose this view because I assume it's near Lake Chelan in eastern Washington—a memorable place I visited while backpacking the North Cascades and the site of a recent large and destructive forest fire.)

STAR TREK: THE NEXT GENERATION "A FINAL UNITY" (SPECTRUM HOLOBYTE)

[Future release: CD-ROM for DOS]

This is an exciting combination of superb computer-generated graphics, photographs, and animation, augmented by the actual voices of the eight principal Star Trek actors. Spectrum Holobyte licensed the rights to Star Trek: The Next Generation from Paramount Pictures and created a brand new story for this CD-ROM interactive adventure.

You get to be one of seven main characters, to help maneuver the Enterprise within this 3-D space mystery, to investigate alien planets, explore new stars, and save the Federation.

You can see a beautifully rendered bridge of the Enterprise. (It makes me want to walk right through my monitor, sit down, and take charge.)

UNDER A KILLING MOON (ACCESS SOFTWARE)

[Future release: CD-ROM for DOS]

This interactive murder-mystery movie from Access Software is a product on the leading edge of simulations. It includes computer-rendered artificial environments combined with the images of real actors, with voices, music, and sound effects. I haven't yet seen it play, but it promises to break new ground in many areas.

The Enterprise bridge from Star Trek: The Next Generation "A Final Unity."

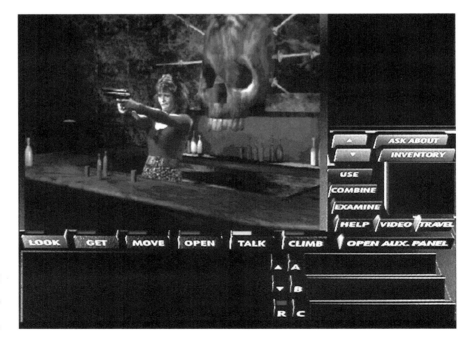

Under a Killing Moon's interactive controls.

Under a Killing Moon features name-brand actors Brian Keith, Margot Kidder, and Russell Means in a detective adventure in which you can be a part. Various choices you make help determine the course of events and the success of the sleuthing.

You can see your game controls, as the heroine is packing a six-gun behind the bar.

You can also view our earnest detective making a pronouncement. Take a good look at the water cooler jug behind him, the books, and other articles. They're all computer-rendered objects.

Finally, a totally computer-generated environment (an entire room). I'm eager to see how this game is going to play.

Under a Killing Moon, composite scene.

Under a Killing Moon, computer rendered room.

INTERACTIVE SIMULATION/ EXPLORATION

One way to discover more about what's around you is to use a simulation. (Sometimes—when you don't have the time or funds, or the path is too remote or dangerous—a simulation is the only way.) With multimedia technology, we even can create models of situations that could not (or should not) exist.

Pilots can learn most of their flying skills from simulators, without ever being in the air. They learn to handle emergencies they hope will never actually occur. Astronauts routinely do the same, before they ever feel the thrust of a rocket engine. Nuclear engineers operate simulated reactors before they're ever allowed to melt down a real one.

ELITE FLIGHT SIMULATOR (AZURE TECHNOLOGY)

[Floppy diskette for DOS, with included interface board; flight yoke required; 486DX PC recommended]

Is the Elite Flight Simulator a game or a simulation? Considering that this has been approved by the Federal Aviation Administration for use in pilot training, it's not just a game any more. Azure Technology's Elite Flight Simulator puts a realistic cockpit display on your monitor and runs you through a simulated flight to sharpen your flying skills. There's never the nuisance of crashing a multimillion dollar aircraft, and there's no fuel waste.

Here you see the panel for a McDonnell-Douglas MD-81 bizjet twin. Note the mach indicator instead of an airspeed gauge (at far left). Your flight director is at center, and to the right are engine controls and monitors, landing gear, radios, autopilot, and other goodies. It all works.

Too hot for you? Choose a Mooney M20J or Cessna 172 instead. (That's what I trained on—a real one—back when the only simulators available were WW-II monsters that filled a small room.)

You can set up weather and equipment scenarios that range from a sunny day with no problems to the depths of the darkest clouds with hurricane winds and

EliteMD-81 flight deck.

engines and instruments failing right and left. When you're done flying, you can review a complete record of the experience, including flight path, failures, and responses.

This image is of Elite's "back room," the control panel where scenarios are set up and flights are made or broken.

WORKING MODEL V2.0 (KNOWLEDGE REVOLUTION)

[Floppy diskette for Windows 3.1]

You've seen those auto-company animations on TV. Looking over an engineer's shoulder at a computer screen, you view a skeleton model of a new car part being exercised. It's an example of high-power computer simulation. The advantage is that the engineer can "build" and "test" a component even before a single real part is ever made. Cheaper design equals cheaper cars. (Or did I miss something?)

Now you can do this kind of simulation on a PC, or watch pre-built virtual mechanisms to learn about the dynamics of moving objects and machines. Working Model is a serious design and teaching tool that lets you build and run devices that have all the characteristics of reality: energy, mass, motion, inertia, friction, elasticity, gravity, acceleration, and more. You can start, step, and stop your simulation and see graphs that show results of your testing.

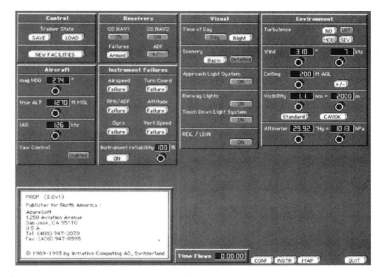

Elite Flight Simulator's "back room."

In effect, you've got a computer-age Erector set, with an unlimited set of bars, levers, cams, pulleys, gears, springs, and motors. (When I was a kid, I set up a contest between the neighbor kid's Erector set and mine to see who could pull the heaviest pillow across the floor. He won. He had the big AC-powered motor, while mine was a little battery unit. But I bet my 486 computer would beat his 386 today.)

What an impressive learning tool Working Model is; it can model just about any physical device (within the limits of Newtonian physics). For example, you can try the included tutorial of a piston engine, complete with the explosive force of fuel mixtures, the piston, crankshaft, bearings, and flywheel. Put the

Working Model crank-out window simulation.

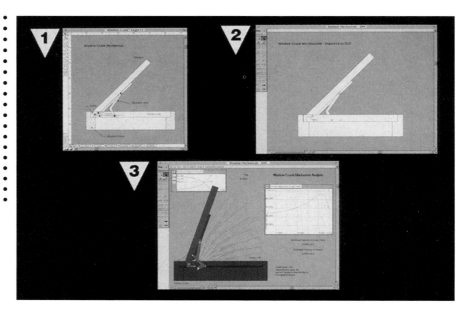

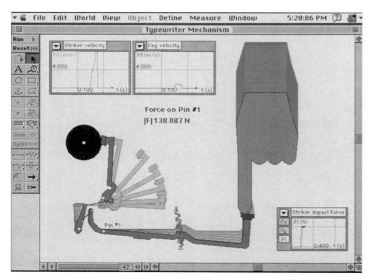

Working Model typewriter-key simulation.

parts together on the screen in just a few minutes, "run" your engine, and check out the results on graphs. No air pollution, no busted fingers, no tortured metal.

One image shows a Working Model simulation of a familiar gadget: a crank-out window. This is a motor-operated device that was created by a computer-aided design (CAD) application. Notice the intricate set of levers and the graph showing how much force was needed through the travel.

Also available is an image of another common device: a typewriter-key mechanism. A short finger stroke is translated into a high-speed snap-action to force a matrix into the ribbon, creating a printed character. The graphs tell the whole story.

One image shows one of those "monster" design problems popular in college engineering courses. This is a "walker"— a multifooted machine whose task is to traverse uneven terrain step-by-step. (Of course, the neighbor's dog does a much better job, without much conscious design effort. Shows you what a few million years of trial-and-error can produce.)

Two graphs let you enter design constraints; another shows the force and motion exerted by each foot. Before ever putting one widget together, you can evaluate the entire design.

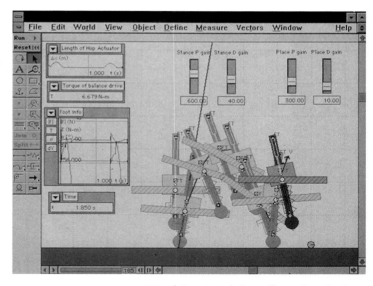

Working Model walker simulation.

WOLFRAM RESEARCH MATHEMATICA

[Floppy diskette for Windows 3.1 in enhanced mode; 486DX with 8MB recommended]

We've discussed simulations of landscapes, sounds, gadgets, and people—all of which are things that we can verify with our senses. Here's an application that can simulate environments that reflect such abstract terms as "hypothesis," "theorem," "topology," and "equation." Mathematica is an incredibly complete application to calculate and display numerical and symbolic equations.

Are your eyes glazing over, dear reader? I too did not make friends with math when I was in school. After three weeks as an unwitting engineering student, I discovered that people around me were speaking in some strange tongue. Terms such as integrals and polynomials and irrational numbers flew through the air around me. (I already knew those terms were irrational; that was my only insight.)

Perhaps it helps to explain that all the 3-D artificial landscapes, motions, and textures we've been discussing have at their core powerful mathematical calculations. Mathematica turns the trick around to help you interact with and visualize math materials in symbolic and graphic formats. It's a creative palette you can use to build mathematical models of the real world, much as a graphic artist might use a drawing program.

This isn't merely a graphing program; it's a general math programming language in a powerful interactive package.

You can enter equations in symbolic form on-screen, and Mathematica immediately calculates and displays results. You can show results as values or in any of several graphic formats, including color plots, contours, and shaded 3-D solids. You can even animate a series of graphs and include sound effects derived from data functions.

Mathematica includes a very rich symbolic and procedural programming language whose output can be lists, formulas, or graphics that can be displayed or printed or even used in other programs. An included feature called a notebook is an interactive document for math operations, complete with automatic outlining and text-processing controls. You can create a notebook, enter data and formulas, and save it as a work-in-progress, a teaching tool, or demonstration, or a packaged solution for use in future calculations (a macro).

Mathematica handles integers, rational numbers, arbitrary-precision floating-point numbers, and complex numbers, and it includes more than 800 built-in functions (all your favorites). Calculations are fast. (The functions are written in the C language.) Optional math procedures available in Wolfram's Applications Library include financial analysis, engineering, statistics, and others. You can call any functions from another Windows application by using an included integration tool called MathLink.

This image is a simple example of a Mathematica graphing of a function. It's a three-dimensional plot of the sine of two numbers in a given range of values. I simply typed in the equation at the top, and Mathematica evaluated it and produced the graphic.

Color shading was automatically applied to the contour. You can control both color and lighting for visual effects to enhance surfaces and shapes.

Mathematica also handles lists, tables, and matrices. Statistically derived samples often tell a clear story when plotted as graphics. This image is of a scatter plot (each dot is a sample from a list) with a best-fit curve drawn by Mathematica.

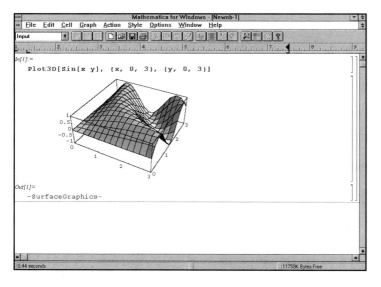

• • • • • • • • • • • • • • • • • •

Mathematica's 3-D plot of Sine[x,y].

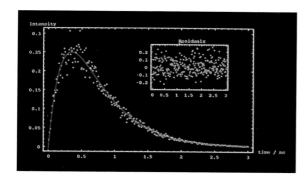

Mathematica-derived scatter plot and best-fit curve.

• • • • • • • • • • • • • •

• • • • • • • • • • • • • • •

A Mathematica complex 3-D plot.

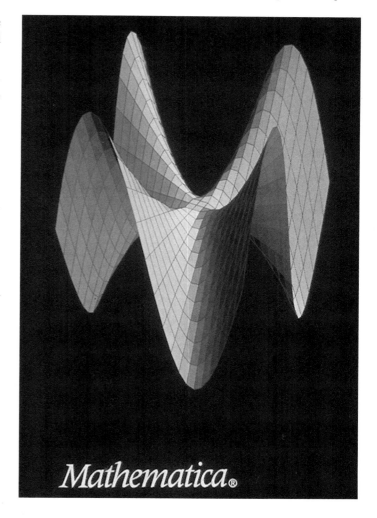

Finally, you can view a complex shape derived from a set of equations and plotted in Mathematica.

This product ships with a well-illustrated, comprehensive 960-page hardbound textbook.

ASTRONOMICAL SIMULATIONS

For many of us, there's no more awe-inspiring sight than the one that's always overhead: the sky. The following applications simulate its activity to help you discover and understand it.

For all of the following astronomical applications, I chose the same viewing place and time: Denver at the first instant of 1995, looking north.

If you had an ideal celestial tour guide, you'd get an explanation of the complex workings of the universe, or at least an explanation of the techniques used to observe it. None of these products gives you that background; to avoid frustration, I suggest you bone up on some basic astronomy before you begin. Let me give you a few clues.

First, you will need to understand orientation, or coordinate systems. Astronomers locate stars on a sort of "universal globe" of the skies called the celestial sphere. It's as though you looked from the center of the earth with the grid of latitude and longitude that appears on a regular globe projected onto the sky. These lines are always in the same fixed position in space, making stars easy to find.

There's a problem with this method: Although the celestial sphere is fixed, the earth is not; it is rotating very quickly. Star maps showing the celestial sphere grid will sometimes appear at odd angles. For easy orientation, I've shown star views that use the horizon as their reference.

Second, you need to understand the variables of time and location. When you look at the stars, your observing position and the time you look make a big difference in what you see.

Astronomers use a time system associated with the celestial sphere (called sidereal time—literally "star time"), and that's different from regular clock time. Not to worry; these applications can handle the time systems for you. But be sure your computer is set to the correct local time and you account for Daylight Savings. You also need to enter the correct latitude and longitude of your position, and, for maximum accuracy, your altitude above sea level.

Finally, you will need some background on celestial objects. There are two general categories: the solar system, and everything else. The solar system consists of a relatively few nearby objects (the Sun, planets, asteroids, and comets) that appear to move among each other fairly rapidly. The rest of the stuff (stars, galaxies, quasars, pulsars, black holes, and others) is so far away, it doesn't appear to move. There is also an incredible amount of the stuff—"billions and billions" of objects.

Of course, all the various stuff in the sky appears to move around us because of the rotation of the earth. These applications have features to let you "zoom in" to observe bodies in the solar system and their motions close up; however, faraway objects don't have that level of detail.

Most of the astronomy applications I reviewed included special material about the collision of the Shoemaker-Levy 9 comet with the planet Jupiter in July 1994, either in text, trajectory animations, or a graphic simulation. Now that we've seen the spectacular and graphic results of the impact and the comet is destroyed, these events are part of history. Because these applications let you travel through time as well as space, you can go back and view the fateful trajectory any time you like.

(I'm glad to report that—while Jupiter is definitely damaged goods—you still can find it in star charts and in the night sky.)

Distant Suns V2.0 (Virtual Reality Labs)

This easy-to-use Windows-based application was originally designed for the Amiga computer. It's a relatively simple application and features only about 9,100 of the most visible stars. That's fine for beginners, students, and casual stargazers (that is, most of us), but it is of limited use to serious astronomers. If you buy the CD-ROM version of Distant Suns, you'll also get about 1,500 fair-quality images of all the planets, details of the moon (including the hidden far side) and many other objects. You can tour the sky and the solar system for any period between 4,700 B.C. and 10,000 A.D.

A small but nicely written manual helps you get started.

You can see in the night sky over Denver at the cusp of the year 1995, looking north. That line at bottom is the horizon (ignoring trees), and the center line starts at due north. I've turned on the markings for the constellations, stars, and other sky objects. There's Ursa Minor (the Little Dipper or Little Bear) just to the right of center.

The first star in the "handle" of Ursa Minor is the North Star (or Polaris), about 40 degrees up from the horizon at Denver. I asked Distant Suns about this star by simply pointing to it and clicking. The info box shows its formal name: Alpha UMI. (Polaris is actually a double-star—that is, a pair of proximate stars.)

Distant Suns' north sky at Denver, 01 Jan 1995.

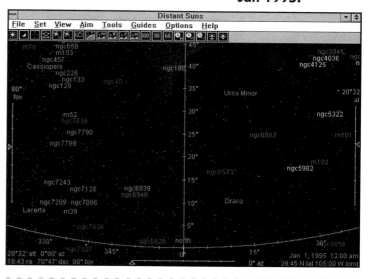

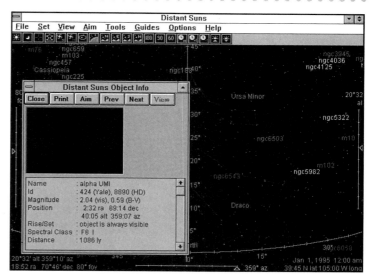

Distant Suns' Polaris info box.

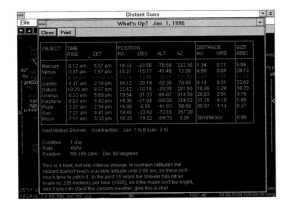

Distant Suns' "What's Up" box.

Distant Suns' Planet Guide.

Distant Suns' Mars.

It turns out that the only planet visible in this night sky is Mars; I discovered this by asking for a "What's Up" listing for this observing time. All the other planets have a negative altitude (meaning they're below the visible horizon). Notice the note about a minor meteor shower.

Want to find Mars quickly? Ask for a Planet Guide; it shows all the planets and their rough position in a small, gridded box. There's Mars, just south of east and at just about 30 degrees elevation. I also asked Distant Suns to put it on the main view; there it is at dead center in the crosshairs.

I used the Lock Aim feature to hold Mars dead-center in this view. Its info box shows it to be at 101 degrees azimuth (east by south) and 35 degrees elevation (above the horizon). It also shows a small photograph of Mars for identification. (Truly the red planet!)

Distant Suns lets you check out the behavior of comets as they orbit oddly through the solar system. You can see comet Halley near its Earth approach in March 1986. (There is a special animation for the Shoemaker-Levy/Jupiter collision as well.)

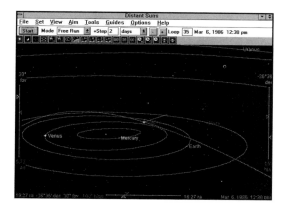

Distant Suns' comet Halley in 1986.

REDSHIFT (MARIS MULTIMEDIA)

Redshift is a CD-ROM astronomical simulation product for Windows. It features an impressive array of 3-D-style operating control panels with realistic push buttons, sliders, and settings. The product was developed with the aid of Russia's Space Mission Control Centre. Using Redshift to navigate through the skies is quick and easy and just plain fun.

Redshift introduces you to the cosmos with 20 animated guided tours, as well as more than 700 fascinating, high-resolution, full-screen telescope photos and even a few "movies." You also can create your own Quicktime movies of celestial sequences that you set up. Or you can simply save sky views and return to them in the future.

You can move through time and space for any year between 4,700 B.C. and 11,000 A.D., and you can view about 250,000 stars, 40,000 deep-sky objects, 5,000 asteroids, and 100 comets. A dictionary of astronomy (with its own animations and illustrations) has 2,000 hypertext-linked entries.

You can see Redshift's version of the horizon view from Denver on the first instant of 1995. At the bottom margin is the horizon, and the grid shows the sky positions relative to it. Polaris (the pole star) is at the top, and just above it is a panel that gives you the time, location, direction, and other information about this view.

Using the navigation controls at right, you can quickly change your viewpoint to any time and place. To move your "telescope," simply use the arrow buttons surrounding the icon.

Want to know all about Polaris? Just ask, and you will see a full info sheet about this object. It shows the proper names, exact position, motion, and other details. As you will discover, Polaris actually has five components to it—it's a multiple star.

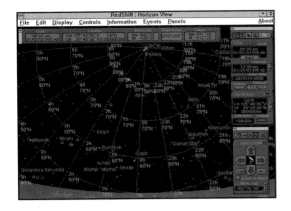

Redshift simulation of 01 Jan 1995 sky, north from Denver.

For any object, you can ask for a complete visibility report. I chose a five-day report for Polaris. Polaris is unusual because this star sits almost exactly above earth's north pole and barely moves in the observed sky. Note the info about the Sun and Moon, to help you plan your observing.

Some of the most stunning scenes in Redshift are of the solar system; every planet is represented as a 3-D model. The three inner planets, the Moon, and several of Jupiter's moons are rendered as shaded relief maps. You can move around the solar system and the planets with complete freedom, just by moving control-panel sliders.

Redshift's object report for Polaris.

Another image shows Jupiter, surrounded with a cluster of its inner moons and with Venus visible just behind it (although actually millions of miles away). The simulation shows not only the elaborate ring system of Jupiter but a realistic surface texture as well, all of it in color. You can operate this planetarium back and forth through time by using the control panel at right, to watch the actual motions of all the bodies.

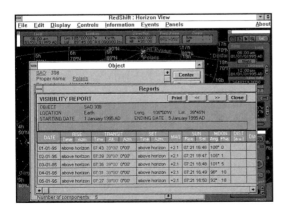

Redshift's visibility report for Polaris.

Yet another image shows a view of good ol' mother Earth, from a nearby point in outer space. There's her captive satellite—the Moon—at left. Both are bathed in the Sun's light from the right. You can set up scenes like this for any date within the accepted range and watch eclipses as they have or will appear.

Speaking about eclipses, how can you find when they will occur? Ask Redshift, and it will calculate the exact time and date for solar and lunar eclipses for any period. For instance, I asked for all the solar eclipses between the years 1995 and 2000; I then selected the one on 24 October 1995 to get all the details.

Another exciting feature of Redshift is its Map view, with detailed surface maps of the Earth, Moon, and Mars. Here, you see the Earth globe in a window and can rotate it to find a location of interest. Click on a spot, and a relief map appears. I've chosen the Alaskan archipelago as my center. Latitude and longitude for the position are given, and you can use these coordinates to select a viewing site for your sky maps. Over a thousand cities, features, and sites are marked.

Redshift's Jupiter, Venus, and Jupiter's moons.

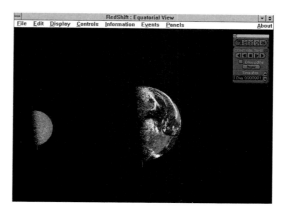

Redshift's Earth and Moon.

Redshift's solar eclipses, 1995 to 2000.

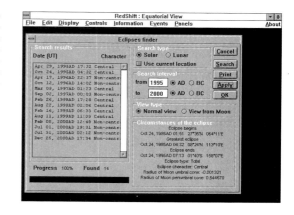

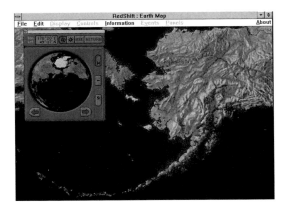

Redshift's Earth map, highlighting Alaska.

THE SKY (SOFTWARE BISQUE)

Let me invite you to take a look through my big telescope. It's on a mile-high peak in California, and the viewing is superb. What's that you say—you're in New Jersey, and you can't make it? No problem; I'll bring it to you. (The view, that is.)

The Sky is an easy-to-use Windows-based application that provides extended features for the advanced amateur astronomer. It's available in various versions; the extended CD-ROM ("GSC") product has an enormous database, with 19 million celestial objects. As many as 100,000 objects can be on your screen at one time, or you can restrict the display to a small category or type. You also get visual images of more than 650 celestial objects, including full-color images of every planet.

The display speed is impressive, especially considering this huge mass of star data. The Sky uses the CD-ROM to contain pre-calculated object positions. This means your computer only has to look up the positions instead of calculate them.

You can zoom to any part of the sky by dragging your mouse, or by several other methods. Once you find an object of interest, you can lock on it. You can create quality star charts and maps (including a white-background style) using all the Windows features: change fonts for labels and paste or export charts (as metafiles) to other applications at full resolution.

Our little sun is on the edge of a moderate-sized galaxy called the Milky Way. If you live away from city lights, you may have seen it as a fuzzy band of stars across the dark night sky. It's an awe-inspiring and humbling experience. I never expected to see this experience simulated, and I was absolutely stunned to see a band of thousands of pinpoints of light appear on my computer screen as The Sky quickly displayed the Milky Way.

The product features some special features that will appeal to the serious stargazer. A full-screen viewing mode removes all Windows features and displays only the sky. A night viewing selection changes the display to red. Both options reduce glare and enable your eye to adjust to dim viewing conditions. A set of screen grids designates the viewing field that various standard telescope eyepieces give you, to help you estimate what you'll see.

Ready for the blockbuster? The Sky lets you remotely control one of several specially equipped telescopes, including a 24-inch reflector atop Mt. Wilson in Southern California. For the first time, even city observers, bathed in smog and light pollution, can get a clear shot at the skies without ever leaving home. (On some versions of The Sky, this is an option.)

Several large, under-used professional telescopes are now being fitted with systems The Sky can operate using its built-in control panels. You make an appointment, pay a fee, call up the observatory, and get connected using a telephone/modem link. You can directly control the pointing of the telescope, select what part of the electronic "film" image (CCD) to use, and then make digital exposures. The resulting images are sent back to your computer for immediate display. Another option to The Sky even provides a set of image-processing tools to enhance the exposure.

You also can buy a ready-to-run remote-control telescope or a control package and imaging device to refit a telescope you may already have, so that The Sky can operate it via telephone. Sitting comfortably inside at your computer, you can "look" through the telescope, no matter where in the world it's located.

You can see how Denver's night sky looks on a reverse-background sky chart with horizon grids, as created by The Sky. I've selected constellation outlines; Polaris appears at the end of Ursa Minor's "handle," and the local stars are marked with their ancient Arabic names. You can drag the handy floating menu bar at left to any convenient spot on the display.

I want all the info I can get about Polaris, so I click on it. A large pointer shows what I've selected, and an info box pops up to identify it and give details. I can select a series of objects and scan among them this way. I can put Polaris in the center of my screen if I'm tracking it, or I can open an observer's log to make notes on what I see.

The sky simulation for 01 Jan 1995, looking north from Denver.

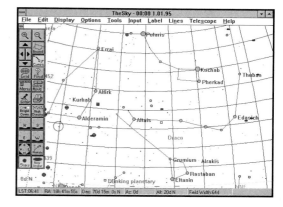

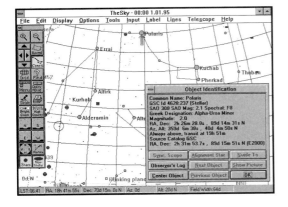

Identifying Polaris with The Sky.

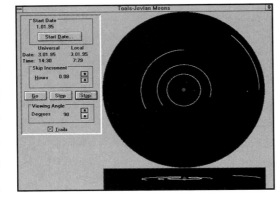

Jupiter and its near moons, from The Sky.

The Sky gives you animations of the solar system, although you won't find 3-D realism in these bodies or close-up views of their relative motion. There is a special feature showing a combined view of Jupiter and its nearest moons, both from above and the side. Here, I've turned on the orbit tracks, and the moons are just beginning their rotation around this massive planet. I can change the viewing angle and run the simulation forward or backward in time.

If you want to use The Sky's star charts with a "real" telescope—and you have one of several standard eyepieces—there's a special feature. You can print charts with a graticule (marking) of the eyepiece field of view printed on them. Here, I've centered Neptune, turned on the celestial sphere grids and also an eyepiece graticule (the two concentric rings).

There's Uranus just to the left and the sighting info is in a strip at the bottom.

To use The Sky as your stargazing companion, bring your computer with you— either just to look from the patio, or through a telescope. You'll want your eyes to be as sensitive to light as possible, and staring at an ordinary computer display spoils that. Just switch The Sky's display to Night Vision mode and all is in red, except for the dim locating grids. For example, Polaris is at the top of the screen, and I've centered the next star down the arm of Ursa Minor in my eyepiece. (It's interesting to note that if you now switch to another Windows application, it too is in red. That helps your eyes stay acclimated.)

Neptune in a telescope eyepiece, from The Sky.

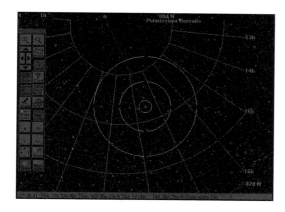

Sky field in Night Vision mode.

DANCE OF THE PLANETS V2.71 (ARC SCIENCE SIMULATIONS)

Dance's simulation of Polaris and Denver's sky on 01 Jan 1995.

One final stellar-simulation product deserves honorable mention. Dance of the Planets was a pioneer in celestial simulations for the PC, and it retains a fast, lean style. In the extended ("Q.E.D.") version, it ships with a catalog of more than 52,000 celestial objects; an optional database raises this number to more than 380,000.

Dance packs all this power onto a single diskette (with another for the extended star database). Although it's a DOS (not Windows) application, you'll want to run it on a fast computer with a math co-processor.

Dance does impressive simulations and creates some gorgeous star charts; its manual is large and comprehensive. The Earth and Moon look especially realistic, and you can travel with ease all over the solar system. (However, Dance is saddled with antique menu and help features.)

Dance's view of Denver's sky in January 1995 includes an info box on Polaris that I requested with a mouse click. Note how various kinds of stars are shown in distinct sizes and colors for easy viewing selection. The pop-up menu bar is at the bottom edge.

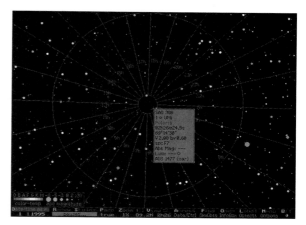

You also can see how the Earth would look from space on the same day (if you could afford the view). That's a leg of the constellation Pisces drawn across the top. I've selected the latitude/longitude grids to be projected on the sphere.

This stunning view of Saturn shows how close you can get to a planet if you zoom in with Dance. The ring system and the orbits of the inner moons show clearly; you see the shadow cast by Saturn in space.

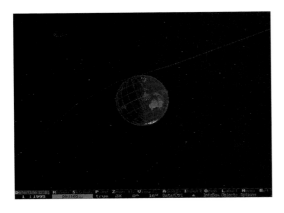

Dance's simulation of the Earth from space on 01 Jan 1995.

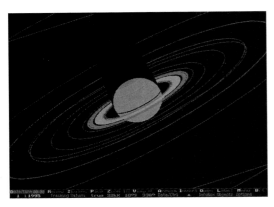

Dance's simulation of Saturn and its inner moons from space.

MARS EXPLORER (VIRTUAL REALITY LABS)

[CD-ROM; DOS-compatible]

Mars Explorer is a single-subject multimedia application that gives you a close-up view of the red planet. It's an early example of products that will soon give you tours of every far-flung region that is reachable by satellite, radar, or telescope. This particular region was explored and mapped in great detail by the NASA Mariner flybys years ago; in effect, Mars Explorer is a custom viewer for that visual database.

In the main selection view, you see four "globe" views of Mars at top and a flat projection view at center. A simple menu and cursor crosshairs let you select a surface region for close viewing. You can select the natural red surface color (Mars is literally rusted), or other shades; I found red to be the most revealing color.

Every major feature on this arid desert planet has now been named. I decided to take a close-up look at one: Mount Olympus. It is a prominent example of the many old volcanic peaks on Mars (especially in the northern half). The volcano is side-lit here, emphasizing its truly Olympian proportions—more than 25km high (three times the height of Mt. Everest) and 600km in diameter.

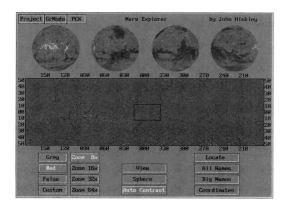

Mars Explorer, main display.

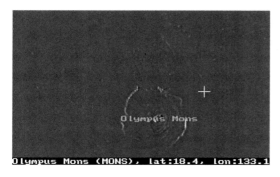

Mars Explorer's view of Mount Olympus.

MUSIC SIMULATION AND EDUCATION

For almost all humans, music goes to the very core of their being. It pervades much of our waking lives, and we can hardly help being affected by it. But for most of us, our experience of music is a passive one.

Most people find little opportunity to create or perform music, especially if they don't play an instrument. Myself, I've always wanted to write a little music, then get a band or orchestra to play it out, but the opportunity never came up. Now, with multimedia tools, it can.

Interactive music products are useful at every level of expertise and interest. They can help you read and understand music, learn to play an instrument, and streamline the compositional process.

I don't imagine that technology will ever replace the ministrations of a gifted teacher or a virtuoso who passes on hard-learned skills and techniques. But if you want to write and play a tune—or even a symphony—there are tools available now to make that easier. You also can get yourself an electronic box filled with the sounds of dozens of instruments that will "play" whatever you write. And these performers won't take coffee breaks.

Music Mentor (Midisoft)

[Floppy diskette for Windows 3.1]

Music Mentor, selection menu.

The best way to learn about music is by listening to it, of course. But that's not quite enough; you also may need some explanation and interpretation. Does this mean you must take your music teacher to the symphony performance?

No—Music Mentor can bring both the teacher and the performance to you. After that, you may want to take the next step and use Music Mentor to create a symphony of your own.

Music Mentor and your sound-board equipped PC will guide you on a self-paced introduction to concert music. The opening view of this intriguing application is a sort of matrix selector featuring periods of music and their six basic elements: melody, rhythm, harmony, timbre, texture, and form. For example, I click on Baroque music and a highlighted bar lets me choose an element. The elements flow in a story from left to right.

Let's begin at the beginning: the Basics of Melody. One of the early images shows an explanation of musical scales, using clear and focused text combined with musical examples. Click on a Play button, and your MIDI sound card plays a rendition of the scale that is shown. Sight and sound are thus combined. It's an effective learning tool—and a lot of fun, too.

Music Mentor— Basics/Melody/Scales.

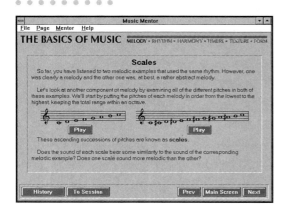

The next step in the process shows scales again, but now you have tools to develop a musical composition (a melody or "tune"). You can play major, minor, and blues-style scales with mouse clicks.

Next, a scale is embodied in a well-known melody. First, you can play the simple melodic line (known to school-children everywhere), then one of Mozart's elaborate variations. This gives you some idea about the extent to which you can vary a simple musical idea.

Music Mentor has a complete sequence on modern music as well. Here, a text-only screen on the French composer Claude Debussy and his novel approach to harmony shows the playful yet thoughtful discussion available from Music Mentor.

Note those buttons marked "To Session" at the bottom of the screen. Click there, and you're transported to another MidiSoft application, called Recording Session. There you can see and play the full musical score of the examples you've heard. You can also edit those notes, substitute different instruments, and in general have a great time with the music.

Recording Session is actually a complete MIDI editor and sequencer. The Recording Session display is fairly self-explanatory. At the top is the musical score, with a staff for each instrument. At the bottom is the control panel, with a strip for each instrument also. You can record or play back any of 16 instruments, mute, adjust stereo location ("pan"), add effects, and adjust volume. During playback, the score scrolls in the window, with the played note highlighted.

Your new wavetable MIDI sound card gives you all the musicians you need. Now it's time to make some music.

Just as a word processor can help you produce word creations, you'll find that specialized computer applications can help you create and play your very own musical opus. They help you play the roles of composer, orchestrator, and conductor. Some MIDI applications provide some combination of features to edit, play, or print music; a few provide them all.

Where do you start? Perhaps you'd like to buy some MIDI music "clips" or download one of the freebies from an online MIDI forum on CompuServe or another timesharing service. For a start, take a look at Voyetra's MusiClips. Each of more than a dozen available packages has 50 or more songs each.

It's like buying sheet music your computer can play—much like a player piano roll. (But just try to find a player piano today!) The added benefit is you can edit the music—change its tempo, instrumentation, and lyrics—then combine it with other works and even multimedia presentations and play or print it out. One handy use is to add music to local presentations or performances.

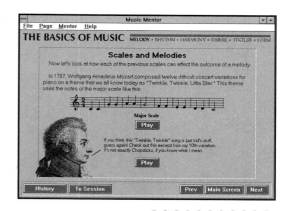

**Music Mentor,
Basics/Melody/Scales
in Melodies.**

**Music Mentor,
Modern Music/Harmony.**

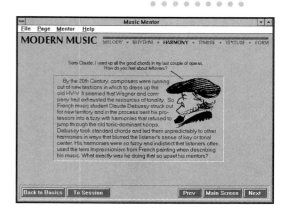

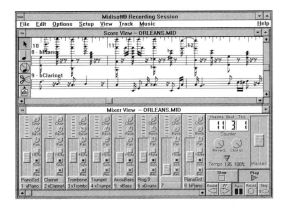

MidiSoft Recording Session, ready for action.

MIDISCAN V1.1 (MUSICTEK)

[Floppy diskette for Windows 3.1]

What if you have a pile of sheet music and you'd like to play it on your computer? You could enter the notes one by one into a MIDI editor, or play them at the keyboard. But that's tedious and requires a lot of skill.

A new application from Musitek called Midiscan answers this need. Just scan your sheet music in. (Of course, you'll need a scanner attached to your PC.) Midiscan converts the image of the page into a MIDI file and allows you to do minor edits. You also can use it to recover old sheet music and reprint it without starting from scratch, which is great for archivists.

MIDI conversion of scanned notation with Midiscan.

• • • • • • • • • • •

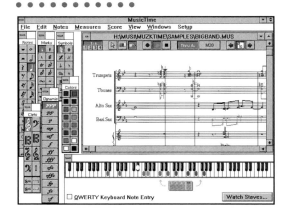

For the computer, this is a very complex job. It's a bit like OCR (optical character recognition), where pages of text are scanned to be entered into a word processor as a string of characters. Midiscan must recognize each individual note and what musical value it has, and also all the other notation, the rich and sometimes arcane marking system that describes how the composer wants the notes to be played.

You can watch Midiscan doing its work. You can see the original music sheet as scanned in and the "recognized" score, ready for any clean-up editing required. The editing toolbox is is also available. Note how closely the two scores match. It's not perfect—there's at least one note missing in the second measure's bass line. But it's amazingly close.

The end result is a standard file that can be played or edited by any MIDI software.

CAKEWALK PRO 3.0 (TWELVE TONE SYSTEMS)

[Floppy diskette for Windows 3.1]

Want to bring your computer orchestra to life? You need an application like Cakewalk. It's your blank musical score, lined with staff marks and ready for notes.

You enter notes by playing them in from your keyboard, by dropping them onto a staff with a mouse, by loading in precomposed MIDI files, or even by scanning with Midiscan. Once they're on the page, you can view and edit the music either as a score or in what's known as a "piano roll," which shows the sequence of each note.

This screen shows two of Cakewalk's windows; the top one is a staff display, and the bottom one is the piano roll. They scroll in alignment from right to left as the music plays.

If you want to display several staves or multiple piano roll tracks, simply maximize either window. That little keyboard at the left edge of the piano roll shows which notes correspond to the stripes.

Recall that MIDI can define the pitch, duration, and other characteristics for each note. You can edit each of these elements separately, then play the results. You can move notes or entire sections of music around by selecting them and then dragging them to a new location with your mouse.

One pesky problem with a lot of computer music is that it can sound very mechanical or leaden, because the notes all line up in rhythm with mathematical precision. One reason real musicians sound authentic is that they aren't nearly as accurate (they add their own "swing"). Cakewalk does let you "line up" or "quantize" notes so the ones you play into it fit in the proper place on the sheet music; but it also lets you "randomize" the timing and copy the rhythmic swing

of one entered musical passage to another. This gives your performances a markedly improved "realism."

Other features help you combine music with multimedia. As your sound card is playing MIDI, it can also play back digital audio, while Cakewalk synchronizes the music with CD-ROM sequences, animations, and even video.

Using a graphics control panel, you have full control over which notes go to which MIDI instrument. You can change setups, volume, stereo position, and other playback features with a flick of your mouse. You can compose 256 separate instrument "tracks" to run 16 MIDI interface cards that can operate 16 instruments each. You can perform extended lists of as many as 128 songs.

The Track/Measure display shows you which tracks are active for which instruments and lets you edit each setup measure-by-measure. You can adjust overall volume and select the port, channel, and patch for each track.

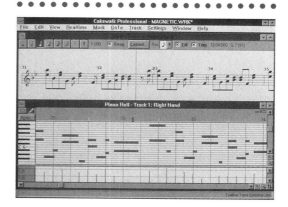

Cakewalk Pro's staff and piano roll windows.

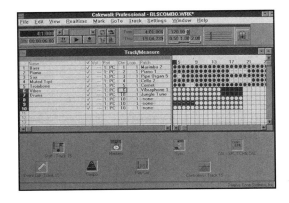

Cakewalk Pro's Track/ Measure display.

When you're ready to publish, Cakewalk prints your music, complete with all notation and lyrics, using Windows-compatible printers and fonts. One popular performing technique is to combine MIDI instruments with live players. Using Cakewalk, you can designate which MIDI instruments are to be turned on, hand the sheet music to your players, and let the music begin.

INTERACTIVE SOFTWARE FOR CHILDREN
FOREVER GROWING GARDEN
[CD-ROM for DOS]

Forever Growing Garden is one of the most endearing children's titles I've seen. It's entertaining without being coy, it's easy for youngsters to navigate, and it has attractive graphics and sound effects. It's also imbued with a sense of humor.

You start your adventure in the Garden by looking out over an enticing and colorful landscape. A little plane flies idly overhead, cars roar down the winding road, and there's a house nearby. In the distance is a castle (because every kids' game needs a castle) and a garden patch is on the hillside. Click on any of these, and you're transported to the site.

Forever Growing Garden's Skyview (main landscape).

I chose the little house and discovered it's really a kind of gardener's workshed. You can choose which seeds you want to plant and check out the almanac for useful details about planting. Click on almost anything, and it animates in a delightful way. See that hippo in the corner? That was a burlap bag before I clicked on it. Click on a jar with a frog or butterfly in it, and the critter comes to life and jumps out for a moment before going back to sleep.

I decided to check out a packet of helicopter flowers. I clicked on the wall, and the packet appeared right in front of me. Planting directions are on the back (click on "flip over"); I decided not to plant these, so I clicked on "put back." The ones I'm taking are in the basket.

I have already planted some flowers and some very unusual fireworks plants. To get them all to grow, I must pick up the water bucket and drench the plots, and time must also pass on the calendar. (I can control how fast I want the simulation to run.) You can take a look at the fireworks plant that's matured. Touch a flower and the whole bush blows up with smoke and noise.

If you tend the kind of plants that can be harvested and sold, when they mature you pluck them out and take them to market. (This is pure capitalism at its finest.) I took my flower to the shop, cut the stem down with scissors, and set it in the proper vase from the shelf. (It had to be the tall and thin one.)

Being a very curious child, I clicked on the closed table drawer and was serenaded by a three-piece mouse band for a moment before they went away again. Click on the dog, and he wakes up and wags his tail. Forever Growing Garden is lots of fun and has all kinds of object lessons for your preschooler.

Forever Growing Garden's garden shed.

Forever Growing Garden's seed packet.

Forever Growing Garden's flower shop.

Flower plantings and explosions from Forever Growing Garden.

DIGITAL EROTICA

Be forwarned: The following is a "G"-rated discussion of erotic materials.

One of the most hotly-discussed topics in the back rooms of cybernetics these days is the simulation of sensual environments.

One of the most hotly discussed topics in the back rooms of cybernetics these days is the simulation of sensual environments. Fantasies extend to the possibilities of wearing "body socks"—some kind of stretch leotards replete with sensors and stimulators. Consider the possibility of "meeting" someone across the country and sharing, electronically, the tactile sense of each other's body.

"Let your fingers do the walking." (Sorry.)

Some kinds of tactile technology have been employed for years in remote manipulators. (Those are the mechanical controller arms often featured in early movies about the dangers of atomic energy.) They are used by operators safely behind glass viewing ports to move dangerous materials. To operate some of these manipulators, you slip your hand into a "glove" that not only follows your motions to position the remote hand and arm, but also returns some sensation to your fingers about the material you're handling. This helps greatly if you're moving something delicate or hard to grasp.

Just imagine wearing an entire suit with the same sensual transmission and reception features. Today, this is the stuff that dreams are made of.

Some of the most popular items at local computer shows are erotic CD-ROM's. In fact, you'll often find more of these titles than any other kind. Some are simply photo collections of more-or-less dressed women, but a few are based on a modicum of multimedia interactivity. The following are two prime examples.

SEYMORE BUTTS; THE DREAM MACHINE (INTEREROTICA/NEW MACHINE PUBLICATIONS)
[CD-ROM for DOS]

Two popular CD-ROM editions by New Machine Publications are The Adventures of Seymore Butts and The Dream Machine. These products are definitely X-rated, for adults only, and are clearly targeted at young males. It should be noted from the outset that there is no way to password-protect or "lock" these titles.

You might guess that multimedia would allow you a multifaceted sexual adventure, with lots of choices about your partners and the kinds of encounters you have. What you actually get here are simple "horn flicks" dressed up in an interactive CD package. A fancy control panel on your screen lets you select which of several encounters to watch. There's no real plot or character development, but there are lots of clearly detailed body parts in action. You can witness interaction between one or two men and one or two women (in every combination except two men alone).

The Adventures of Seymore Butts begins by panning into a TV set in a tacky 1950s-style apartment. The screen becomes your low-quality CD movie window on the action. Background music, narration, and other familiar sounds accompany your trip.

The action starts out innocently with an encounter between Seymour, the (very) amateur young cameraman, and an attractive girl who is stepping from her car. After he says hello, you're presented with three options.

I decided to "retreat;" Seymore becomes befuddled and tongue-tied as the girl walks away. (Actually, I tried all the choices, and in every case the girl walks away. Research can be so unrewarding.) After this opening gambit, Seymore looks around and suggests that "we" (that's you and Seymore, dear viewer) either drop in on his friends Phil or Nick, or take a prospecting ride in his van, by clicking on the boxes shown.

And that's the range of your choices, except to stop or speed up the action by clicking on the control buttons at the bottom. You can watch any of several very explicit situations featuring Seymore's male friends involved with various eager and responsive young women. There's a little dialog, but mostly just the sounds of mating.

When such titillation no longer inspires you, try speeding up the action. The people's voices then sound more like squirrels fighting over walnuts. The motion becomes frenetic. (There's humor to be found in most every human interaction.)

The Dream Machine is a bit more futuristic. It has a high-tech control panel with a main viewing screen, smaller screen, and push-button controls. Its movie clips are a bit dark, which adds to an appropriately voyeuristic and clandestine tone. When you activate the "machine," your first view is of basement tunnels in what turns out to be a hospital, complete with an inexplicable corpse on a gurney. Your navigational

Seymore Butts'
opening encounter.

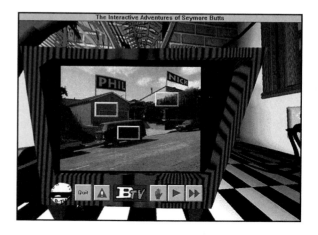

Seymore Butts'
basic adventure
choices.

**Dream Machine
hospital corridor.**

· ·

**Dream Machine
hospital scenario.**

· ·

controls allow you to "walk" through this labyrinth and eavesdrop on various rooms. Echoed footsteps and creaking doors add to the realism.

Soon, you've dropped in on a room, and the action begins. (No waiting around in this hospital.) You even get background music, some of which includes a bit of old vaudeville bump-n-grind. In one of the first videos, the nurse gives an "unsuspecting" patient a foot massage. Within seconds, the foot is forsaken for more fertile territory.

You can speed up, stop, or freeze-frame any scene, and the gear icon at bottom left moves you directly to the scene's guaranteed climax if you can wait no more.

One scene is so rare I had to show it to you: a man and woman kissing—on the lips, that is.

At the end of each sequence, a girl appears at the mini-screen at top right to ask in a seductive way if you liked what you saw. You get a chance to click on her questionnaire, in which there's never a wrong answer and always a renewed invitation.

See that vertical bar on the control panel at bottom right? That's a "panic button"; it's there to protect your image (literally). If some inappropriate real-life intruder walks in, you click on it; instantly the ribald scene is replaced with a dummy Windows File Manager display. When the intruder leaves, another click will put you right back in the action.

**A kiss from the
Dream Machine.**

**Dream Machine
tour guide.**

Groping for the Group

The human mind can conjure vast amounts of fact and fancy. We type and upload and print thousands of pages of discourse each day. We film and videotape and digitize endless hours of images, sound, and animation. The enormity of our collective learning makes humanity as a whole, not the individual, the necessary receptacle of knowledge.

chapter 12

by Daniel W. Rasmus

In the Greek and Roman eras, common men had only a limited education, while the elite thinkers were a repository of the whole of human thought and expression. Even until the time of DaVinci, it was possible for one man to be near master of all that was known.

The wise men of the past would be lost in our present. Aristotle and Socrates would have no knowledge of movable type, internal-combustion engines, nuclear power, television, quarks, neurons, transistors, antibiotics, or computers. The sum of human knowledge is now impossible to store in a single cranium. For all their wisdom about poetry, science, and philosophy, Aristotle and Socrates would seem like ignorant throwbacks today. Their great insights would be lost in the jumble of competing information—unless they could learn to package them in 30-second bundles.

In the global village, we are aware of almost everything at once. The depth and breadth of fact precludes any one person from mastering all the available ideas, let alone the relationships between them. We thus create a society of specialists, each disconnected from their neighbors who share the more general and common foundations of knowledge. Scientific research spews out over the Internet, and images of Tiananmen Square, Bosnia, and South Africa flood our senses with as much immediacy as a local car accident, liquor-store holdup, or apartment fire. The very awareness shouts at our ignorance.

In our hunger for information, we find little comfort in our immediate surroundings. Even among the 10 or 20 or 100 people we associate with regularly, we cannot expect to find answers to all of our questions. Because the media culture suggests we can know everything, we become dissatisfied with our local group's inability to service our curiosity and imagination. Thus we seek a broader repository of knowledge, in books and film, video and computers.

Discussion databases, such as this one in Lotus Notes, enable people to communicate regardless of space and time. Even after the discussion is over, discussion databases remain as historical records of actions taken and lessons learned.

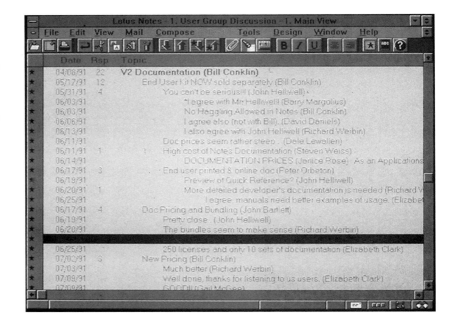

Despite its unparalleled ability to deliver knowledge, the media is content to give us consumable containers. Programs such as the PBS series *Nova* or *Wings* (a show about the history of flight on the Discovery Channel) may distill some wonderful images and narrative, but they do so from only one point of view, for only a limited time and without accessing the totality of material on the subject. Television, radio, and videotape can never be as responsive or comprehensive as our curiosity demands. Yet media continues to stimulate our expectations by impressing on our eyes and ears that the knowledge we seek does exist.

However, two new technologies are bringing about a revolution in access to information: multimedia and groupware.

Multimedia enables each of us to construct and follow a train of thought that spans all the published information on CD-ROM and the Internet. We can interpret events or consequences by constructing personalized histories from the mass of text, image, and graphics available in digital form.

However, the information plummeting through the thin copper and fiber-optic threads of the network still only amounts to less than 2 percent of humanity's output in the past four millennia. The remaining 98 percent of knowledge remains confined to paper and synapse, accessible only through the human tools of speech, reason, and sight. The family of technologies we call groupware enables people to ask questions of the world, and, if they are patient, to acquire diverse insights.

Groupware is much more than simple bulletin boards and e-mail. The technologies of collaboration comprise a wide set of tools that connect mind to mind over the network. Groupware effectively eliminates time and space, and shrinks the sense of distance and moment between people.

Technology enables us to establish new human relationships that were not possible through the static text of a book or the passive interaction of television. Groupware can connect us to every corner of the globe. Although computers and networks do not yet permeate our everyday social life, for those who connect, the connection is made not only to the person at the terminal, but to the peer groups, educators, and elders at both ends of the connection. The bond of the network links its participants to the context of each individual. As barriers between time and space erode, the connection turns to expectation. And as with friends down the street, we expect our network peers to be there and to listen when we need them.

The interconnection of groups via computer has created the largest onslaught of information exchange in history. Individuals with ideas send electronic letters to corporate leaders and politicians. Screen writers and directors send messages about plays, films, and television shows. Faxes inundate our office environments. Suddenly, computers and groupware technology are the new, faster-than-sound, point-to-point, anytime, anywhere, way of chatting at people who may or may not care what you have to say.

A GROUPWARE GROUPING

Groupware is any software that enables people who are separated by time or geography to share ideas and to work together. In a sense, paper mail is the simplest form of groupware. But in today's split-second, turn-on-a-dime economy, paper mail is insufficient. Physical transport from place-to-place may be too slow when your competitor is using fax or e-mail.

The telephone and the fax have largely replaced paper mail as conduits of communication. But even these tools, as popular as they are, cannot completely substitute for face-to-face meetings and other interactions. The fax and the telephone are low-fidelity media. The phone conveys only sound, the fax conveys only static images. If two people are collaborating on a television production between New York and Los Angeles, phone and fax could transmit script changes and cast biographies, but it would be of little use in costuming, set design, graphic sequences, or make-up.

Thus we find groupware infiltrating the nooks and crannies of the collaborative process. Increased network reliability and availability has made real-time collaboration possible and asynchronous collaboration a matter of routine. The

TeamLinks creates a communication environment that links Macintosh, Windows, and Digital All-In-One users. It supports both e-mail and group discussion databases.

most popular form of asynchronous communication, e-mail, is considered a necessity in many offices and is an increasingly popular form of communication for individuals.

The downside of e-mail is that it attacks our in-boxes. We have no choice but to accept the correspondence from our electronic pen-pals. E-mail engulfs us while it hides detail. Long discussions become unimaginable dialogs separated by mail translation headers and obstructed by a lack of context. After a while, it becomes impossible to know who is responding to what.

Discussion databases, like those on the Internet and on CompuServe, and now in corporations via Lotus Notes and its competitors, can create an environment that is focused and responsive while allowing free navigation and selection between related ideas. We draw what we want and add what we can, and we do it at our own pace.

Asynchronous communication is wonderful for brainstorming and discussing issues, but it does little for the here-and-now. If geography is the primary impediment to group discussions, real-time collaboration software brings colleagues and cohorts to your desktop. Originally, real-time collaboration software concentrated on content, and provided tools for group writing, group editing, and group sketching. But the bandwidth of new networks is expanding. New tools like Forethought's Virtual Notebook

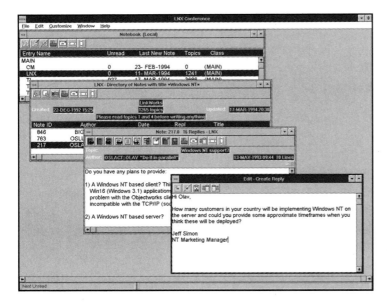

System enable sound and images from far-away collaborators to share space on the desktop with spreadsheets and equations.

Corporations, because they are prone to reorganizations and downsizing, are looking to yet another category of groupware to codify business rules and help automate business processes. Workflow software defines a series of information-based tasks and automates the information along that path. Simple electronic-form workflow tools can handle mundane tasks like check requests and travel authorizations by capturing information in a form and then routing it for electronic approval.

Larger workflow systems can handle more elaborate business processes that require the convergence of considerable data. In a new engineering project, a high-end workflow tool might use the receipt of a contract as the impetus for generating an engineering report. Separate, detailed workflow systems could handle engineering, quality-control and documentation. Points in the process, called rendezvous, specify what information must be collected before the process proceeds. Very high-end systems recognize the chaotic nature of business and enable workflows to be changed on-the-fly to meet business conditions.

Other features of workflow systems include the delegation of work to pools of people so that the first available person of sufficient skill can handle the task rather than having it sent to a specific person's inbox.

The functions of many of the groupware products are converging and blurring. Lotus Notes currently supports e-mail, asynchronous communication, workflow, text retrieval, document management and mobile computing. Notes acts like an application framework, with its open nature enabling it to take on new

partner software if the native functionality isn't sufficient for a given task. Reach Software's WorkMAN, for instance, works within Notes to provide workflow modeling and other workflow features that enhance Notes' limited native workflow capabilities.

TYPES OF GROUPWARE

- E-mail
- Asynchronous communication
- Real-time conferencing
- Group writing/editing
- Drawing
- Video
- Shared Screen
- Workflow management
- Text retrieval and indexing
- View and markup
- Document management
- Group decision support/group creativity/ voting
- Personal device synchronization

Other technologies with a longer history than workflow management are beginning to show up on lists of what now constitutes workflow. These technologies, like text retrieval and document management, facilitate the sharing of information between people. And as Notes and other products add features, the lines of distinction will disappear. Eventually Notes and other application frameworks will absorb all of this functionality by cooperation between applets in their own digital collaborations.

The lines between groupware and other technologies are blurring. Full text search within Lotus Notes, for instance, demonstrates the integration of text retrieval with groupware. By using full text, Notes users gain a way or navigating through the traditional Notes databases either vertically, through the notes interface, or horizontally, through text retrieval.

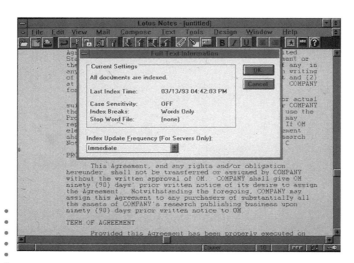

The question arises how people will respond to all this shared information. It is not enough that they see the information. People will desire to comment on it, not necessarily in long Lotus Notes essays, but in quick scratches and notes, much like they would on paper. Mark-up software, such as MarkUp from Mainstay, facilitates the commentary of individuals or groups.

Learning to collaborate on a network is not always an easy transition. People like to be with other people. Some software, such as GroupSystem V from Ventana, creates an environment where PCs and people join together in a joint decision-making session. Anonymous ideas fly from keyboards to constantly-updated local monitors and large, shared screens. The ideas can be combined, categorized, and prioritized. Group voting gives equal weight to all participants.

Finally, personal digital assistants, notebook computers, and personal organizers extend the reach of the group. Individuals can take notes in hotel rooms or haberdasheries and incorporate them later into the group knowledge base. All these devices support download, so half-baked ideas can become creative traveling companions. You can download a list in the morning and work on it during a layover at the Dallas airport.

There's no doubt that the technologies are converging and that a critical mass of groupware technology is now available for PCs, Macintoshs, and UNIX workstations. But despite the clear need, groupware acceptance has been slow. Some of groupware's problems come from weak infrastructures that are unable to support the bandwidth of desired applications. The failure of many companies to install such rudimentary technologies as e-mail or data access reflects a needs hierarchy in which groupware is higher on the food chain. Not until e-mail works will companies be willing to invest in technology to enhance messaging and dialog. Only after messages arrive consistently will people realize they receive too many messages for the wrong reasons. Only after they get what they want at the basic level will they see the need for managed exchanges rather than rambling e-mail. Only after they get too much of what they want will they be willing to demand information rather than expect it to simply appear.

The Newton message pad is one of the first hand-held devices to enable people to work independently and integrate with the group from the road.

But it is people themselves that prove the largest detriment to groupware. People are simply afraid to share. Knowledge is still power, and sharing knowledge means empowering others with your knowledge. Many corporations are learning about distributed responsibility and teaming, but they remain far-from-perfect examples of the open and honest corporation.

As we move toward improved data-flow architecture and a more trusting information environment, we'll see the demand for groupware expand. Even with the fear and risk, people in great numbers are connecting to other people—to learn, to talk, and even to date.

MAKING PERSONAL CONNECTIONS

The urban world of the 1990s often finds us locked in an endless cycle of freeway commuting, work, more freeway commuting, and fitful sleep. Thus we find it difficult to connect with groups of people who share our interests. Perhaps a club dedicated to French poetry may exist somewhere within the general geographic region, but in Southern California, the Valley is a long way from Orange County. French poetry isn't worth another two-hour drive up the San Diego Freeway, even if it is to hear Rimbaud or discuss Valery.

But on America Online, CompuServe, or GEnie, French poetry is only as far away as the keyboard. And the diversity of interests on these services is remarkable. I can switch from poetry to music, from comic books to science fiction, within seconds. Many of the commercial services are also allowing their once-sequestered clientele to access the information and user base of the Internet.

Bulletin boards require very little effort to find or use. They have become another low-fidelity alternative to beauty parlors, bars, or car washes. Future technology will provide voice and image,

but that will be a new twist. For now, the anonymity of bulletin boards is conducive to both honesty and deception. Just before I typed this, I was watching *Home Improvement* on ABC. Brad, a 13-year-old character, was having an affair with a 35-year-old from another city—via a computer bulletin board. He told her he was a dermatologist who drove a Jaguar. Much to the surprise of his parents, the woman subsequently showed up, looking for her Bradley.

Although this is only a fictional scenario, it is believable. Online connections have led to everything from marriages to arrests for pedophilia. Computer bulletin boards give people another place to gather—a place where you can kick off your shoes, put your feet up, and (with keyboard in lap) shoot the breeze with a British diplomat or discuss geometry with a college professor.

Groupware, as much as it impacts individuals, is transforming the workplace as well. In interpersonal relationships, the Net is a new rap mode; in corporate America, it may be the difference between getting a contract and staying in business.

CORPORATE GROUPING

The paperless office never arrived. Our documents, it turns out, were too rich. We had signatures and drawings, photographs and charts and graphs. Compared to paper, the characters and numbers of a glowing-green 3270 terminal never seemed inviting and friendly. Ultimately, PCs and DOS did little to change our fundamental attitudes toward desktop computing.

But this is the 1990s, and 3270 terminals have been reduced to commercial emulators that run under Microsoft Windows or Apple's System 7. The new desktop environments do not present the austere image of their predecessors. Countercultural Macs and even PCs with Windows are open and friendly. Brightly-colored icons entice and allure. And they can emulate everything about paper except maybe the rough edges. Some applications even let you symbolically tear the paper or crumple it up and throw it away.

The paperless office looms closer, not because computers can capture paper documents, but because they are better than paper documents. Microsoft's Object Linking and Embedding and Apple's OpenDoc can create documents of great richness and complexity. Sound, video, charts, graphs, and even signatures can

share the same document. Each element may be controlled by its own format and edited by its own application, but they appear on the screen or printer as a seamless combination.

And these new documents are becoming more team oriented. A chart produced by Joe not only appears in Julie's presentation, but is directly linked to it. If Joe revises his chart, Julie's presentation is automatically updated.

In some cases, the actual text or graphics in a document may be created as a group effort. Several people, in diverse locations, using diverse machines, perhaps even speaking different languages,

Products like Documentum's server make a paperless office almost possible by integrating document management with workflow.

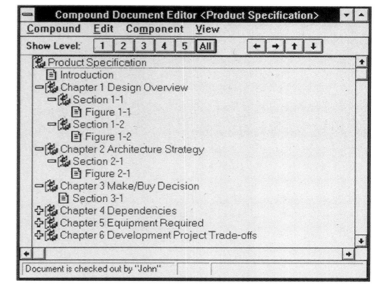

can use their computers and the network to simultaneously see and contribute to a project. With desktop video teleconferencing, the players view one another in small windows beside their drawing or text. As engineers discovered a few years ago, automated applications such as CAD could maximize personal productivity, and working in concurrent engineering teams made the product better than any individual could. In the 1990s, that idea is finding its way into business proposals and presentations.

THE PROBLEM

We are no longer isolated by our PCs or limited to the time-delayed characters of e-mail. On the network, everyone is a collaborator. Workgroup technology provides great freedom for interaction—and it accelerates changes that will force business to reinvent the very idea of work.

Beyond simple information dispersal, corporations naturally want to find new ways to leverage the vast telecommunications network. It makes sense that networks can be used for teleconferencing, information sharing, and other group-oriented communications. In the 1970s, computers primarily boosted personal productivity. Today they can enable teams.

Thus the computing industry responds. New categories of applications that facilitate collaboration will overshadow the more traditional spreadsheets and word processors. These new applications will offer not just data, but the context of data. And more and more people will meet, communicate, share, and develop information on the network.

MANAGING NETWORK BANTER

Group-discussion databases represent the oldest form of electronic groupware, and it is still an important tool in research and industry. Discussion databases promote the asking of questions and eventual responses from interested parties. Of course, in our fast-paced world, we forget that some things still take time. Creating a new car, a plane, or even a disk drive can require months of difficult thinking and integration of thought between teams of people.

Software programmers at Austin's Microelectronic and Computers Corporation (MCC) have adapted a manual issue-resolution method called Issue-Based Information System, or IBIS, to help their distributed teams deal with "wicked" software problems. The computer software, dubbed gIBIS, ("graphical" IBIS), has recently been commercialized by the MCC spin-off, Corporate Memory Systems (CMS). CMS switched from UNIX to Microsoft Windows and named the new implementation CM/1.

IBIS was developed by Horst Rittle, professor at the University of California-Berkeley, in the 1970s to solve problems that have no clear solution. Scientific problems yield to systematic exploration. IBIS provides a forum for loosely-defined problems that bring differing points of view together. A sometimes lengthy discussion can lead to satisfactory discovery and resolution, or to a consensus that the problem is indeed impossible for the moment.

CM/1 captures the dialog and facilitates the posting of questions and answers. Unlike regular dialogs, which can deteriorate into finger pointing, CM/1 and the IBIS methodology frame the issue in a formal exchange that begs for relevant response. If participants find their peers inane or wish to write inflammatory responses, CM/1 supports private e-mail to protect all parties from embarrassment.

Both Lotus Notes and CM/1 enable people to submit ideas and respond to the thoughts and comments of others. But Notes adds a new twist to online corporate interaction through the distribution and replication of electronic banter in the client/server environment. With Notes, and other client/server tools, spreadsheets, graphics and other types of data can augment simple text messages.

Unlike CM/1—which provides a dedicated environment—Notes requires customization and add-in software. Along with its document-management and text-retrieval capabilities, Notes acts as an application framework. Many companies have found it an apt home for their software. Everything from news feeds to pager interfaces to data-access tools reside within the Notes framework. Once they are placed in the Notes environment, CAD drawings or today's headlines become grist for network critics, artists, and commentators.

Discussion databases are invaluable to teams of people that work on different coasts (or even a few miles down the freeway). It is no longer necessary to solve all problems face-to-face. With discussion databases, work objectives can be established and product designs evaluated. Solutions come as problems demand or as time permits.

As discussion databases grow, they become electronic repositories of knowledge. Even after the last party contributes to a thread of conversation, the knowledge generated by the interaction remains— completely digital and searchable. Discussion databases do not formalize corporate knowledge in the way that expert systems do, but they retain the essence and lessons of a conversation. And unlike expert systems, discussion databases retain the context and humor of the moment.

CM/1 from Corporate Memory Systems challenges contributors and questioners by forcing dialogs to answer tough questions that have less than definitive answers. Participants around the network can add their views and opinions on the current dilemma.

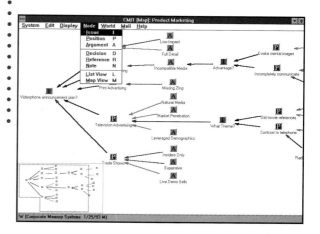

WORKING IT UP
FOR WORKFLOW

As corporations downsize and industries change, work becomes redefined. Michael Hammer, President of Hammer & Co., and James Champy, Chairman of CSC Index, Inc., have stormed the country inspiring executives to follow the path defined in their best-selling book, *Reengineering the Corporation*. They advise executives to start with a blank sheet of paper and redesign the work as if the company was starting anew. The book focuses on technology as a way to add new input to the work design. Incremental improvement is no longer satisfactory. Businesses must obliterate existing processes and leverage new management principles and technologies. Companies must make the work more meaningful, more rewarding, and more productive.

When you examine software evolution, it is clear that a lot of recent software focuses on delivering information to the desktop. E-mail delivers messages in electronic form. Yet despite the profusion of messaging systems, it is still nearly impossible to tell important e-mail from junk e-mail. So the computing industry invented workflow software. Workflow software delivers information as part of the work process. Information arrives in context and with meaning. As reengineered business processes come online, workflow software can capture relationships between processes, people, and information. Implemented workflows will automate the routing, approval, and feedback of information within the process.

Some suppliers of workflow-management software, such Action Technologies of Alameda, California, have taken workflow beyond the mere review and approval of electronic forms. They suggest that workflow be used to define contracts between people. It is not enough just to put work into a queue with an assigned priority; people must understand the work, agree on the work, and, eventually, accept the work product. Work is not an initiated task from an autocratic manager, but a negotiated contract between customer and supplier. In the Action workflow model, each step in the process follows a proposal-agreement-performance-satisfaction cycle.

InConcert, from XSoft, provides a client/ server solution to workflow. This screen shows the dual-pane workflow editor. The upper pane graphically displays the jobs task hierarchy, while the lower pane displays all workflow dependencies for tasks and subtasks in the job. Both the developer and end user can instantly see the structure of a business process, the information being generated and consumed, and any inter-task dependencies.

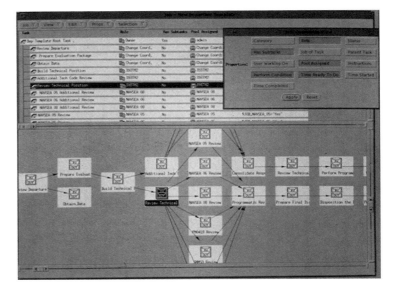

Workflow started as an adjunct to imaging products, where it helped route raster images from viewer to viewer for comments, action, or input. Today, workflow software has grown beyond imaging and can route any type of information generated on a computer. No single approach to workflow exists. Some workflow products route information via e-mail, and others use databases to store the state of a work package. The majority of products use UNIX servers to coordinate efforts between Macintosh and PC-compatible workstations.

In 1993, several large workflow suppliers and customers formed the Workflow Coalition to seek interoperability between tools. To date, the coalition has not delivered standards, and all workflow products remain proprietary.

Proprietary or not, the idea of workflow revives images of "Big Brother," a world where every keystroke and activity is timed and watched. This is a possible scenario, but not a likely one. Workflow is entering corporations at the same time that a new, enlightened approach to management is taking hold. Rather than being a tool for corporate voyeurism, the technology will enable teams to take control of their work directly, ignoring organizational charts in favor of informal networks based on trust and responsibility.

Workflow software also will give people more time to work by reducing traditional command-control tasks, such as check requests and time-card approval, to momentary interruptions. More time will be spent producing something of corporate value than reporting one's progress.

Workflow software will have a profound impact on corporations willing to embrace its challenge and promise. At its best, workflow software can promote individual empowerment by eliminating costly hierarchical work coordination. The individuals that need to work together do so directly. Work is no longer hidden inside in-boxes, invisible to both the process and the performer. The technology makes work explicit but flexible. You can view work activities in a graphical mode and change the flow of the work in progress.

Corporations are taking advantage of products like Edify's Electronic Workforce to integrate and automate telephone response systems. While helping to manage work by notifying individuals of actions, it also automates routine actions like faxing upgrade information or top tips about a particular application. The agent trainer, shown here, is used to build graphic representations of the work steps involved in a process.

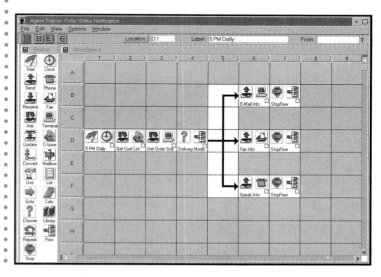

Action's Workflow Analyst uses simulation to validate process assumptions. The Action Workflow Manager manages execution of processes on a network. The methodology for documenting agreements and actions is clearly shown in this planning process.

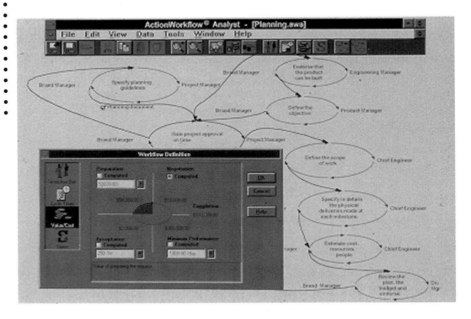

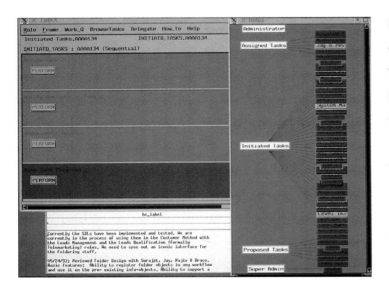

KI Shell, from UES, shows its object-oriented approach to workflow. Many workflow products are designed for department-level activities. KI Shell is designed as an enterprise workflow service. IBM recently started re-selling KI Shell as part of its Architecture and Integration Services business.

As downsizing continues, workflow software can help maintain order within chaos—work processes will not break down as participants leave. The explicit capture of process knowledge buffers the organization from shifts in personnel at the same time it allows for more rapid response to changes in the process itself.

Reengineering is necessary because businesses did not react well to changing environments. Processes prove difficult to change, not only because of traditions, but because sometimes the process is unknown and undocumented. Workflow software unifies the definition of processes and makes them visible. The technology of workflow is not the impetus for organizational realignment, but it certainly makes adaptation more expedient.

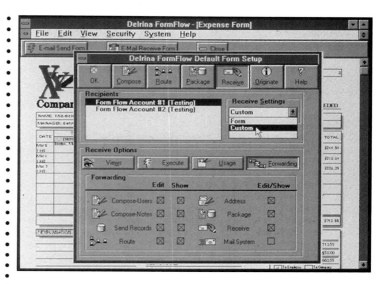

Delrina's FormFlow adds basic workflow functionality to standard e-mail systems.

You're on Candid
Groupware

Perhaps the most exciting of these network-enabled technologies does not so much shrink time as distance. With real-time collaboration technology, people in diverse locations see the same documents and share in their development. Early implementations of real-time collaboration software included group writing and group drawing software. With the advent of digital video, people can also see each other during online conferences. For less than $1,000, almost any computer can be equipped with a video capture board and small camera. Not even facial expression need be lost during online conferences.

New operating systems have introduced information sharing as an architectural component. Apple has introduced the Apple Open Collaboration Environment (AOCE) so workgroups on diverse platforms can share information. Microsoft ships a peer-to-peer networking version of Windows called Windows for

Workgroups that turns normal PCs into collaboration tools. Announcements for digital white boards, shared calendars, and other collaborative technologies fill the pages of computer magazines.

With real-time collaboration technologies, you can save on expensive business trips and even the travel time between buildings. Sure, it's nice to join your team members in face-to-face discussions, but in these busy times it's also nice to save time by joining them on the network. The telephone conference call may soon become an antique as we switch to computer networks to reach out and touch our peers and share our documents, images, and ideas.

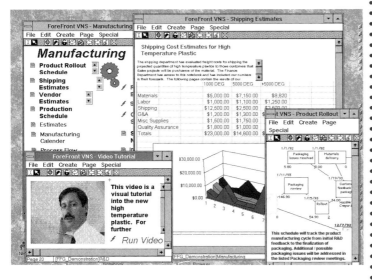

With products like the Virtual Notebook System, people can discuss documents and information in real-time. VNS supports interaction between users on the Macintosh, PC, and UNIX operating systems.

GETTING READY FOR THE GROUP

Groupware is a constantly evolving field. Technologies such as text retrieval, view and markup, online report viewing and others are now included under the umbrella of workgroup computing. And just as workgroup computing evolves, new technologies will create new ways of facilitating human interaction.

Researchers have long recognized the connections between technological development and our social infrastructure. The phone and automobile are social devices as much as technologies. The telephone chat with the high-school sweetheart or the late-evening bull session on the hood of a car will someday be supplemented with after-hours banter on the Internet. The computer is entering an era wherein it is treated as a common and comfortable companion rather than an alien adversary. For the next generation, asking questions on the Internet or sending e-mail to distant relatives will be as common as sending a postcard is today. And the responses will be more immediate.

Not everyone will make the leap at the same time or with the same confidence. Collaborative technology raises as many human-interface issues as it does network-interface issues. People and organizations must be patient with the transition to these new technologies, just as they are with the transition to new management concepts like teamwork and empowerment (or to new types of music and art). Sharing might be a difficult concept for those baby boomers who were raised on competition and self interest, while members of the so-called Generation X might be more acclimated to new ideas, turning the Internet and local networks into gigantic colloquiums.

In the working world, computers force reinvention. Workflow software, discussion databases, and real-time collaboration are changing the very idea of work. Work does not have to flow from autocratic directives and a geographic center, but can come from individual initiative or shared commitment. As members of teams, the technology enables us to speak our minds day or night, in the office, in our homes, or on the road. It enables us to interact directly with those closest to the process.

In business, the administrative headaches of routine paperwork and the challenges of new-product design are equally logical applications for workgroup computing. We must find the inspiration necessary to challenge convention and transform autocratic hierarchies into democratic collaborations relying on consensus and communication. The technology is waiting for us.

Xerox's LiveBoard creates a large virtual workspace for holding meetings over the network.

Microsoft Graphics Inc., Softboard, and its data communications capability, provide an easy-to-use solution for audio-graphic teleconfer-encing, distance learning, and multi-site collabo-ration applications. Here a simulta-neous Softboard session links Portland and Boston. Integrated lasers and coded pens capture marker output from motions to screen.

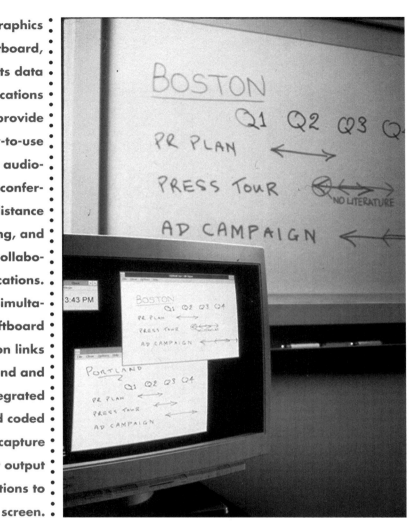

THE FINAL CONNECTION

Groupware as a class of software enables diverse groups to communicate across space and time. The Internet, as a connection device, allows countless people to talk to each other or to post their questions to the world and await a response. All of our software will eventually be designed so that we can share our ideas with others, with little effort. Already, Apple's System 7 integrates peer-to-peer networking, as does Windows for Workgroups, and so will future versions of Microsoft Windows.

Our thirst for knowledge will eventually force those with curiosity and a need for interaction to seek out the Internet and its wealth of human connections. In corporations, groupware is connecting distributed workforces and allows people in different sites, or even at home, to contribute meaningful ideas to the work process.

Thus we have the opportunity to connect to the world. Somewhere on our local network or on the Internet, almost all of the knowledge that we seek does exist. We no longer live in a world where someone like Aristotle, Socrates, or Isaac Asimov is omniscient in his knowledge, because humankind has created far more knowledge than any one individual can master. But if we need some quick information on quarks or cooking, palmtop computers or child psychology, we need only ask the world. Somewhere on the network, someone has an opinion on our topic. And if we're just looking for another human mind to connect with, we can find that, too.

Groupware and operating systems will eventually become ubiquitous partners. Products like Lotus Notes already are taking advantage of Microsoft's OLE and Apple's AppleEvents to make the connection between content and placement a more seamless activity.

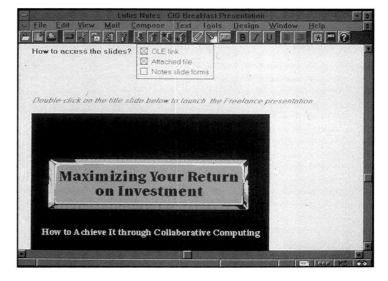

Apple's PowerShare Collaboration Servers integrate document sharing and messaging with the basic Apple operating system.

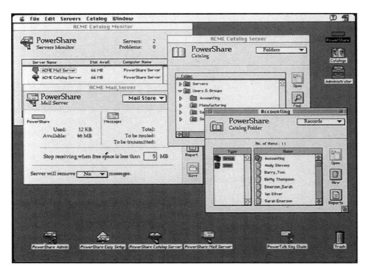

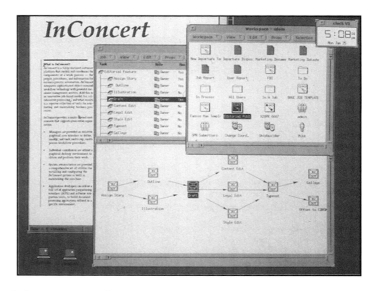

Integrated document and groupware environments, like Xerox's InConcert, take the paperless office to the next step by integrating business processes with the storage and management of electronic forms, images, sounds, and other documents.

Lotus is trying to recapture its glory, not with spreadsheets, but with groupware. Lotus Notes proves slippery to catagorize. It contains functions for discussion databases, workflow, and tool integration. This image shows several of the possible databases that could be created using Lotus Notes.

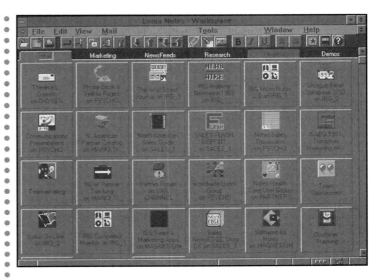

Notes on Notes

Lotus Notes has become almost synonymous with the idea of groupware. Although Notes is the industry leader in terms of both dollars and the number of users, Notes is far from the definitive statement on workgroup computing.

With Notes, Lotus has created a product to bring integration to the desktop. This integration includes information sharing, messaging, document management, and the capability to act as a front-end to third party add-ins.

The most common use for Notes is as an information repository. People place documents into logical, easy-to-access databases. Click an icon and a listing of information appears. The documents and comments stored in the Notes database can be accessed via associated characteristics or via their content through the full-text indexing engine Lotus has licensed from Verity Corporation.

Viewing information is certainly useful, and Notes is a big improvement over searching through directories on a Novell file server. But the real advantage comes not from seeing the information, but from becoming part of the dialog about that information. With Notes, users can carry on elaborate, nested conversations that do not depend on space or time. People in Connecticut can comment on information before their peers in California arise—and the dialog can take place over telephone lines via Notes' built-in support for mobile computing.

Notes can handle discussion databases well enough, but its e-mail capabilities are weak when compared to rivals (and to Lotus' own cc:mail). However, in Notes, e-mail isn't just e-mail—it is a notification mechanism. Because of Notes' built-in routing capabilities, a click on a button can signal several colleagues to add, review, or approve information.

Although Notes is wonderful in theory, it can prove daunting in practice. Early versions of the product required the use of OS/2 servers, a rarity among Macintosh and PC-oriented businesses. Notes also has a steep learning curve for the scripting language and interface tools. Some users find its performance sluggish and its systems administration difficult to manage. Much of Notes is proprietary, including the languages and database, making a commitment to Notes potentially risky in such an immature market.

But perhaps the most difficult transition is in the users them-selves. Notes pushes the boundaries of the human/computer dialog. It is a product that tears down walls and facilitates new interactions, but many of the human frustrations identi-fied with workgroup-computing are common among Lotus Notes users. If it is used strictly as an application-development environment, it presents few problems beyond the technical ones already mentioned. As a communication tool, however, Notes threatens established hierarchies, releases data that was previously considered secure, and eliminates manage-ment oversight by giving employees direct access to each other.

Before you stumble into Notes, you should have a strategy for employing its diverse capabilities—and you should carefully consider the costs and benefits of implementation.

Sharp's OZ-9500 is
an excellent tool
for capturing notes
in meetings. The
information can
then be integrated
back into group
databases via
onboard fax
software or
through e-mail
using the
OZ-9500's
built-in terminal
emulation.

Client-Client-Server Computing

The workplace no longer ends at the front door or the factory gate. Many people don't stop working when it's lunchtime or while watching David Letterman. Recent productivity increases are a function of fewer people working more hours. And with every trend in the human workplace, technology finds a way of adapting and helping us adapt.

Apple calls the new computing paradigm client-client-server computing (CCS). CCS enables you to work off-line then integrate information into your desktop computer, which can, in turn, contribute to enterprise data. Apple coined this term for their Personal Digital Assistant (PDA), the Newton Message Pad. Since the Newton was designed to work as a personal communicator and not as a personal computer, it didn't connect directly to a network for file sharing or e-mail. The Message Pad is designed to capture the digital ramblings of computer experts and novices alike. Its software accepts notes, manages contacts, and captures sketches, all without a complex file-management scheme, naming conventions, or difficult-to-remember commands.

Apple is not the only player in the PDA market. Sharp Electronics builds the Newton Message Pad for Apple and ships the Sharp Expert Pad, which includes identical software to the Apple unit. Sharp also supports this market with its Wizard Line. Most Wizards are little more than personal timekeepers and notetakers, but the OZ-9000 series shares several things in common with the Newton OS, including pen-based support and sketch drawing. Wizards lack the "Newton intelligence" that recognizes handwriting and learns patterns from its owner, but they are quite capable of capturing lengthy notes and sketches. Casio also ships a full line of personal products, including the Zoomer PDA (co-developed and marketed by Tandy/Radio Shack), complete with support for the commercial information service, America Online.

PDAs will change the work equation because they let you work whenever you want and in a comfortable way. They don't require power cords or telephone lines. Some products run up to three months on a single set of four AAA batteries. I wrote a majority of this chapter on my Wizard OZ-9600II while flying at 41,000 feet. When I returned home, I consolidated and expanded the fragments of thought on my personal computer.

Individual contributions will always be an important element within any workgroup. Thus, mobile computing, idea-capture, and communication tools are becoming more common and more intuitive—and a lot smaller than even the lightest portables. With PDAs and CSS, people can maximize their contribution to the group, even in bed or at poolside.

Apple's Newton Message Pad introduced the idea of client-client-server computing. Mobile tools, like the Message Pad, enable people to capture their ideas on the road. Interface software on the Macintosh or under Windows integrates that information back into the traditional work environment.

Reach Out and Touch Someone—Sort Of

chapter 13
by HP Newquist

Waiting around the corner, just past the immediate future, is something called *teledildonics*. When teledildonics becomes reality, our entire notion of sex will change. Forever.

Free Sex.

These two simple words, in combination, are an advertiser's dream. It is widely believed by advertisers, marketers, and salespeople that the easiest product in the world to promote would be free sex. What do customers like more than free stuff, and what better product to offer free than sex?

Unfortunately for the pitchmen, sex as a sellable or even discounted commodity is not tolerated by vast segments of the world's population. Many people believe sex isn't a product that can be offered freely on the open market (even though this belies the reality that most people meet their respective sex partners on a kind of open market—unless they're betrothed to a mate through some ritualistic practice). The idea of free sex just isn't one of those things you would expect to play well in Peoria.

At least, that's what everyone says. Truth be told, sex probably *does* play well in Peoria, but no one is allowed to admit it. This is because sex, as practiced in the Western world, is supposed to be confined to bedrooms, the occasional videotape, and magazines discreetly wrapped in brown paper. This repressed attitude toward sex has prevailed for the last several centuries—especially since Queen Victoria screwed it up for everybody—and will continue for at least the next few decades.

After that, however, all bets are off, because waiting around the corner, just past the immediate future, is something called *teledildonics*. When teledildonics becomes reality, our entire notion of sex will change. Forever.

Teledildonics is a concept that is known far and wide through the cyberpunk community. What we are actually talking about is virtual sex. Electronic sex. Free sex. Sex in cyberspace, sex on the Net, sex via computer. What we are also talking about is sex as it

may be widely practiced in the future—safely, antiseptically, and without emotional (or even physical) attachment. In fact, cybersex completely removes the need for physical interaction—which today is pretty much a requirement for having sex.

A lot of people are going to think that this topic is just a cheap and sleazy way to titillate the computer-literate masses. They're wrong. We're not going to talk about pornography or exploitation; we're going to talk about technology. Many people may be offended by this discussion of sex in the future and believe there is no reason to discuss the merger of computing and sex. They believe it will never happen and that it is only the stuff of perverse imaginations and bad science fiction.

So, let me state that as much as I respect this point of view, it is incredibly naive. The people who believe that sex and technology will never be linked are the same people who refuse to believe in the existence of battery-powered vibrators.

It's time to get real. Like it or not, technology gets used for anything and everything that people can dream up. Some of the first kinetoscopic films were of nudes. The first inexpensive home videos were sold "for adults only." The first telephone numbers with a 1-900 prefix were for dial-up dirty talk. The first public-access cable channels—notably Channel 35 in New York—featured sex services. From each of these sex-oriented fringe environments, respectable and economically viable businesses have emerged, including movie theaters, video stores, phone information lines, and expanded cable offerings. Like it or not, many facets of the entertainment and information industries used sex as a proving ground.

Of course, we are not supposed to acknowledge that fact. Like slowing down to look at a car wreck or wanting to see a terrorist hung from a meat hook, we are secretly drawn to things that society does not openly condone. Usually, the segment of society telling us not to do these things includes people like Jimmy Swaggart and Jim Bakker, and look at what upstanding citizens *they* turned out to be.

Regardless of the political and moral consequences, sex and technology will continue to find common ground—as they have in the past. The next frontier of that merger is virtual sex, sometimes called digital sex or cybersex. This area of exploration is embodied by teledildonics—the use of electronic communications in conjunction with sexual artifacts. The name comes from obvious sources: "tele" from the whole concept of communicating or interacting over phone networks, and "dildonics" from somebody's attempt to apply the word "dildo" to computers.

THE UNIFORM

Teledildonics is like the marriage of phone sex (for which one calls up a completely businesslike 1-900 phone number) and virtual reality. The concept—and right now it's not much more than that—is that two people can link up via modem, and with customized virtual reality equipment can engage in a shared experience. Yet, instead of that shared reality being one of those VR scenarios we hear about *ad infinitum*—the mundane walks through a VR-generated building or undersea world—the shared reality is sex. Data gloves and vision helmets will be part of the experience, but virtual sex will require additional gear, most likely some form of tight-fitting bodysuit with force feedback or pulse generators located in specific areas of the suit corresponding to those anatomical regions that mature adults refer to candidly as their "private parts."

Let's not be bashful here. Think of a spandex-type outfit that you would climb into almost as if you were climbing into a wetsuit for scuba diving or leotards for a workout. Hundreds or even thousands of tiny sensors and receptors are implanted into this particular suit, primarily in the erogenous zones, with the highest concentration around the genitals. These sensors will have heat controls as well as some form of force feedback, which most likely will utilize small pressurized air bags or tiny plastic and metal rods clustered together. These pin-like rods will "push" in response to an actual touch from the virtual partner. The effect can best be understood by thinking of those novelty items that feature hundreds of blunt pins that you can push your hand or face against. These pins move back and forth with very little effort, and only those pins that encounter skin actually move. The end result is that when the pins are pressed they leave the imprint of your hand or face. Now imagine if each of these pins had its own degree of sensitivity and and you will get an idea of how they would work in a cybersex suit.

Because receptors and sensors receive information, there will also be transmitters to *send* information. It is likely that the same devices used for reception will be used for transmission and that they will send data out from the suit about movement and heat levels. Such "out" data will be translated to "in" data by a similar suit on the virtual sex partner.

Obviously, the body suits would be sold in female and male models, just as regular clothes are. However, the design of these outfits would more likely be based on current styles from The Pleasure Chest rather than The Gap, to make sure that all the erogenous zones and genitalia are appropriately "wired" for maximum data input and output. Such clothing would enable specific extruding attachments or intruding receptacles to be added to the appropriate gender style, which would extend and retract as necessary depending upon computer signals.

I probably don't need to be any more graphic than this—I'm sure by now you're getting the general idea. The essential ingredients here are the receptor mechanisms that would enable two (or more) people to respond to each other's touch over the phone lines. Just as a computer screen reads the frenzied typing of another individual on a network, a cybersuit would "read" the frenzied groping of another individual on the network.

THE LOOK

Having suited up—the futuristic equivalent of showering, shaving, brushing, and combing—there is one final aspect to which to attend. Obviously, the sex appeal of a cybersuit and the requisite headgear is about as erotic as a picnic table. Not only that, but no one really would "see" you on the net. They would see your digital double just as they "hear" you when you type on today's bulletin boards. The latter doesn't involve any kind of real talking or chatting, although people can convince themselves that it does.

What will happen in cybersex is that each person would present a digital image of himself or herself to the other online. This digital image might have no relationship to physical reality. This is already done on bulletin board (BBS) forums today. People use code names or handles to remain anonymous. Generally, these code names are more a depiction of who they would like to be than who they actually are. On the networks, an individual with a handle like "Death-Defying Dirk" is usually the kind of guy who doesn't get much closer to thrill-seeking than watching *Lifestyles of the Rich and Famous*.

A digital representation of one's self, whatever the form, would be generated online by the expectant user. This would entail creating at least one, and perhaps more, images to present to others in the cybersex environment. Because we're not actually looking at video footage of each other, we have to create graphical "disguises." This would most likely be done by using some photorealistic image—although I daresay that no one will use their own image. Males might look like Harrison Ford or Mel Gibson, while females might look like Raquel Welch or Cindy Crawford. To make it even simpler than mimicking real people or trying to construct your own image from scratch, it is likely that virtual representations will be available online, giving users the chance to mix and match their faces, body shapes, and anatomical proclivities from a world of menu choices. Even today, video games enable the user some sort of customization over the character role being played. Cybersex roleplaying will be very similar. It may be a simple matter of picking this face to go with that chest, or that leg to go with these hips. In fact, a user could probably go from being "Chelsea, the Cheerleader Next Door" to "Miss Jane, Dominatrix of Pain" with the click of a mouse button.

Once assembled, the user would store these images in memory, and call them up as necessary during the network trolling, the foreplay, and the act of virtual sex. Of course, the images will be completely in 3-D, as well as touch-sensitive, such that each surface point of the image creates its own degree of resistance and mass. Thus, pressing against a male chest in cybersex will result in the same feeling that one would have doing it real life. There would be resistance on the part of the person doing the touching, and a feeling of pressure on the chest of the person being touched. The user could even set levels of sensitivity in various erogenous zones to heighten or deaden certain types of contact. This may obviate certain embarrassing problems from the real world—such as premature ejaculation—which might kill off the business of real-world therapists or physicians.

The Moves

Once the user has built his or her virtual self, complete with feelings, sensory levels, and stylish good looks—not to mention the expected enlargement of certain body parts—the disguise would be turned loose on the net. Just as today a computer user takes advantage of a forum by entering it, signing on, and then participating in a thread of conversation, the virtual stud and studette would roam forums as well, looking for sex instead of discussion. In essence, they would troll the back alleys of the nation's "information superhighway" in a way that Al (and certainly Tipper) Gore never intended.

Logging onto a forum or connecting to a dedicated Bulletin Board Service, the user could find a willing partner in tomorrow's equivalent of the singles bar or even a future version of "pay-per-view." Perhaps there will be a dedicated forum, or perhaps the two people will meet while discussing laundry tips online or exchanging their ideas on cyberpunk music. Should they decide they like each other and want to have some form of carnal knowledge of each other, they can go to virtual rooms, which would be the equivalent of today's e-mail addresses where only the sender and receiver are privy to the data in these locations. However, forums wouldn't have to be the main place for virtual sex, and don't get the idea that they will become teledildonic brothels. People can have sex without signing onto a forum. They could, for instance, just dial up each other's computers directly, and most people, over time, probably will dial "person-to-person." However, the existing forums may provide the initial meeting places for much of the virtual sex of the future in the same way that today's forums provide common discussion areas for people of similar interests. Think of these forums as meat markets on the net.

The Act

With both participants outfitted in similar snug-fitting garb and sharing the same telecom link, they can reach out, touch each other, and do whatever they feel like doing: caress, scratch, bite—anything and everything. The two would only see each other in their headpieces, but as they touched each other in cyberspace, both the gloves and pressure sensors in the suit would provide a simulation of touching a real person. Of course, force feedback and pressure receptors would enable the wearer of the body suit to feel the caresses of the virtual partner, and human biology being what it is, the user would respond appropriately to those caresses. The end result would be the same as in real sex: orgasm.

After all is said and done, the participants could go their own way. Log off, smoke a cigarette, fall asleep. No identities need to be exchanged, no relationships formed—unless the partners wish to pursue the matter—and no potentially dangerous viral contact has occurred. Two people would have shared a physical experience without actual physical contact.

This is not to say that all users of teledildonics will be people out looking for one-night stands or an anonymous good time. People who are romantically involved and separated by distance will use the net to keep up their intimacy. Maybe they can use it for lunchtime quickies—except they wouldn't have to leave their offices for a motel rendezvous. On the other hand, office cubicles probably won't be sufficient either—there's not enough privacy.

Privacy will be paramount. The strangest and most disorienting factor in teledildonics is that virtual intercourse requires only the physical presence of one person, not two. To put it succinctly, there is no physical partner when a person is engaged in virtual intercourse. The individual sitting alone in his or her room or office is all dressed up but is not going further than the telephone jack. Thus, the entire sexual experience gets boiled down to a case of reacting to electronic stimuli transmitted by phone lines. Disconnect the phone, and the party comes to an immediate halt. A power outage in this case could be considered *coitus interruptus*. It would also be quite odd (not to mention humiliating) to be caught indulging in this cybersexual activity by someone who is not virtually connected to the scenario—such as a wife or boyfriend accidentally walking into the computer closet.

Yet, teledildonics isn't autoerotica, that realm of sex where one person tries to enhance his or her own experience by his or her own self. Cybersex is still a shared experience, because someone else

is indeed generating sexual caresses in real-time response to the user's specific actions and body movements. So, two people are engaged in sex, yet neither one is in the same room. They are sex partners, but they can't see each other. The philosophical complexities of such a situation become readily apparent.

Is this really sex? That's hard to say. Certainly the desired end-result of the electronic coupling is orgasm, and the two people involved experience sexual contact generated by each other. But our traditional definition of sex involves having at least two people in the same place at the same time. Phone sex, for instance, doesn't count, because there is no real physical interaction; it is all aural and relatively one-sided. The same is true of autoerotica, and it is also true of interactive videos to achieve sexual gratification.

Yet during cybersex, one has become stimulated and sexually aroused by another person's real-life physical actions and interactions. The sex is as a direct result of the physical manipulations of an actual partner who is a real person and not an electronic blow-up doll. If the person on the other end refused to participate, there would be no sex. Teledildonics has the same effect as if the couple fondled each other with grappling hooks from 10 feet away. That is still sex, but is it any more real than the electronically manipulated fondling that awaits us in the future?

> *The entire sexual experience gets boiled down to a case of reacting to electronic stimuli transmitted by phone lines. Disconnect the phone, and the party comes to an immediate halt. A power outage in this case could be considered* coitus interruptus.

THE HARSH LIGHT OF REALITY

Another fact that makes cybersex more akin to real sex is that if one partner doesn't like what is happening, he or she can log off and leave the scene. (To my mind, this also addresses the question of digital rape—one could always have a means for disconnecting from the net. But then again, could a person be held down and not allowed to deactivate his or herself? After all, if the user can feel the arms of another on the sex net, can't those same arms restrain and prevent that person from logging off? This is a function of the technology. One must presume that, as in real life, attempted rape and forced sex will occur.)

Another question: If the forum where these people meet requires payment for its services, could virtual sex be considered prostitution—even though the individuals never spent a single moment in the same room, or even the same state or country? Also, does indulging in virtual sex constitute cheating on one's real-world mate? No physical contact is involved, but sex of some sort does occur, so traditional considerations of jealousy and commitment will still arise. Mentally, the user will know that it was sex with someone else, so at that point maybe we have to consider adultery to be a conceptual issue and not simply a matter of getting caught in the act. Clearly, the definitions of "sex" will be reassessed as the digital world begins to offer users the same diversions and recreations previously found only in the physical realm.

One interesting ramification of virtual sex is the possibility of gender switching for those that might be so inclined. There is nothing to stop a male from presenting himself as a female on the cyberspace net, or vice versa. For instance, two males who present themselves as females on the net might actually end up having a lesbian relationship, with neither being any the wiser. Most likely, there will even be special attachments on the suit that enable this to occur with no loss of feeling between either partner. (Sounds like a condom ad, doesn't it? Actually, the apparatus of teledildonics resembles nothing so much as a full-body condom.)

Don't think that some of this virtual intercourse or gender-bending doesn't already exist. Anonymous "adult chat" forums on telecom services like CompuServe and the Internet already attract a large number of participants interested primarily in sex. Anybody can access those forums—even children. This opens a whole new can of

Does indulging in virtual sex constitute cheating on one's real-world mate? No physical contact is involved, but sex of some sort does occur, so traditional considerations of jealousy and commitment will still arise.

worms: What about kids and their initial explorations into sex? Will they get their knowledge of sex from computer interaction? Will they sneak into forums to ogle adults who are casting about for cybersex?

Don't laugh. Currently available games like Virtual Valerie already offer a somewhat limited entry into the world of sexual experience via computerized versions of Nintendo-meets-*Penthouse* on CD-ROM. If a kid can get into a virtual game simulation of the future, it's not too hard to imagine that he or she can also find their way into a virtual sex simulation. If you think that "the younger generation" has skewed concepts about sex and how it relates to love and emotions, you haven't seen anything yet. (Of course, some people think that cybersex will screw up adults, too. Comedian Dennis Miller puts it this way: "The day an unemployed iron worker can lay in his barcolounger with a Foster's in one hand and a channel flicker in the other and do it with Claudia Schiffer for $19.95, it's going to make crack look like Sanka.")

THE REAL THING?

Such concerns keep drawing us back to the main question: Is it real? Maybe that question is moot at this stage of human evolution. Our definition of what is real is being challenged all the time—even as you read this. If you watch a television awards show on video the day after it is shown on network TV, is that any less real than seeing it during prime time, when it is already three hours tape-delayed? Is a one-hour delayed broadcast any less real than a 15-minute delayed broadcast? Is a pay-per-view concert filmed from the front row and transmitted in real time any less real

than barely seeing the performers from the nosebleed seats in the balcony? More to our interests here, is a friendship generated in the confines of an online forum a real friendship—even though the participants have never seen each other, never heard each other's voices, never spoken to each other, and never had any physical evidence that the other really exists? Our definitions of what is real are continually being broken down by technology. While some may say that this requires a better definition of what our technology is, it seems to me that we need to come to better terms with what we define as being "real."

While we're pondering those future definitions of reality, let's go to yet another realm of teledildonics, one which might fit more comfortably into our existing definitions of reality. In this scenario, two people in the same room are enjoying sex of the traditional sort, but they don't see the same things. Using just the headpiece component of the erogenous VR equipment—perhaps with the addition of an infrared or heat sensor—two people actually having real sex could generate images of a completely different partner in their vision helmets.

The helmets, which would have to be more like eyepieces than full helmets, would register a video image just as normal VR headsets do. But, instead of being images generated by a computer based on the movements of an invisible digital partner, these images would be generated by computer, based on heat sensor or infrared data. This is a little confusing, so bear with me. The headpiece acts like a night-vision helmet, a device that enables you to see in the dark. Objects are seen in the dark due to their heat levels, and the relative amount of heat separates one object from another. (With true heat vision, you would actually see objects as separate thermal layers, and not as precisely defined or outlined images. For this scenario, though, either technology would be fine. After all, this is the future we're talking about. It's not as if you can go out and buy this stuff tomorrow.)

Two people wearing night goggles could see each other just fine in the dark, although the green glow or thermal separation might be a little too kinky for most users. Nonetheless, the images in the goggles are those of the partner, and the partner's movements are seen just as if the goggles weren't even being used. They are image enhancers, as opposed to image creators, which is what the traditional VR helmet is.

Now, let's combine the two types of headgear. Only instead of looking directly at the scene through the night goggles, there is a small video screen inside the headpiece. The infrared or thermal images are intercepted before they get to the eyes—which are shielded by the video screen—and sent to a computer. The computer would take these images and change them from their original appearance. It would not, however change the basic physical structure of any of the images. If you are looking at the other person standing in front of you with one arm outstretched, that is what the computer would see, as well. Rather than change the physical reality of the situation, the computer would be used to effect cosmetic changes of the user's choosing.

For instance, a bored or experimental couple may program their computers to generate images of completely different people for viewing within the headsets. Let's say they opt to live out the *Basic Instinct* scenario. The woman's computer has stored images of Michael Douglas, the man's has Sharon Stone. When the computer receives the infrared or thermal images from the night-goggle component of the headpiece, it slightly modifies the appropriate cosmetic features. The woman partner may actually be dark-haired and olive-skinned, but the computer applies the blond hair and pearly skin of Sharon Stone to the image. It would then send this modified visual version of the partner to the video screen inside the man's helmet. He would now see Sharon Stone doing exactly what his female partner is doing. The activity is not changed; if the partner runs away, so does the Sharon Stone version. The computer would simply apply a digital mask to the proceedings.

The same type of digital "replacement" (or "enhancement" as the case may be) would be taking place inside the woman's headpiece as well. Thus, while the partners know exactly who they are coupling with, they would be looking at someone completely different than the person who was there before they donned their helmets and doffed their clothes. It is quite conceivable that each person would actually have their own database of celebrities or dream mates to call up at will. The typical female database might contain movie stars, while the male database might have swimsuit models. (Given their status in the worlds of video and cable communications, the virtual surrogates available for the first few years might be—and I shudder to think of it—Jane Fonda and Ted Turner. We can probably consider them a starter set.) People will be able to add their own images to the database over time, and it might even end up as an interesting alternative to "Couple's Night Together." One night could be *Gone with the Wind* night, starring Clark Gable and Vivian Leigh, another night might be *CBS Evening News* night, with the images of Dan Rather and Connie Chung. The possibilities are endless.

The primary limitations to this form of cybersex (it is not technically teledildonics, because there is no telecommunications involved) is that the images are limited to the reality of the physique of the partner. If a male is trying to apply the image of some 6-foot-tall woman to his 4-foot, 10-inch partner, there is going to be a serious breach of reality. Even after putting on the headpiece, the woman he is coupling with is still relatively short, and the computer is only applying images to that physique. It will not make the woman he feels grow taller. For that, he'd need the benefits of the full teledildonics scenario, where the network can hide any realities. But who knows? Maybe some type of compression technique might be useful for this in the future.

So, while actual physical coupling does occur in this form of cybersex, the male counterpart may see himself entwined with Sharon Stone instead of his wife, and the female counterpart may be looking at Michael Douglas rather than her husband. Fantasies are fulfilled, and commitments are maintained. Or are they? How do people deal with such obvious distortions of reality in their sex lives? It's one thing to close your eyes and imagine you're with someone else; it's another matter entirely to be calling up their faces and choosing them as the temporary objects of affection. To make matters even more complicated, neither side has to know who the other is watching. It could be an old boyfriend, an ex-wife, anybody. This has the potential to make for some very nasty claims of "You want them more than me!" if the couple is not comfortable with their relationship.

Technolust

Perhaps, in the end, cybersex and teledildonics and virtual intercourse are not about technology at all. Like all technologies, they are means to an end. The world doesn't need computers, but they make workers more efficient and make certain aspects of life much easier. We are wedded to them, so to speak, and probably could not advance further as a civilization if they were to suddenly disappear. We rely on them just as we rely on phones. They are not truly necessities, but they are facilitators.

Cybersex will enter the world in the same way. It will not replace real sex, just as movies and TV sitcoms do not replace real events (although some might argue this point). Do TVs and movies change our perception of the world around us? Certainly, and not always for the better. But there is no going back to a pre-TV world. Short of global electronic catastrophe, it just can't happen. Will cybersex change our perceptions about sex? Certainly, although not in the same way as TV—people don't invite their friends over for pizza and beer to sit in the family room and watch them have sex. They can share the experience of TV because TV is not a personal thing; sex, however, is.

As technology becomes more personal and we are linked into cellular phones and PDAs and subnotebook computers and intelligent agents, cybersex may seem like a natural extension of linking ourselves into the global net.

One saving grace for those who do not like the idea of cybersex is that it differs in a fundamental way from TV and radio: Because it is personal, you will not be exposed to it in department stores, bars, restaurants, cars, planes, or street corners. Cybersex will be completely within the control and sensations of the user.

This technology will eventually become available; have no doubts about that. It will change many notions of sex, notions that have existed since mankind realized it had both brains and genitals. Unlike those organs, however, cybersex gear isn't anatomically attached. If you don't like it, you don't have to wear it.

H ackers: Pirates or Patriots?

HACKER: A person who is technically skilled in some aspect of computer technology. When first used, the term was nonderogatory, but more recently it has been used to refer to people who use their prodigious technical skills in an unethical or illegal manner (such as breaking into networks or writing computer viruses).

—*Allan Wyatt*
Computer Professional's Dictionary

The American media, according to computer contractor Rich "Crash" Lewis, Jr. (a self-proclaimed emergency assault programmer and free-lance computer software designer), has distorted and misused the term hacker over the past decade. Lewis goes on to say the term has come to refer to criminals who just happen to use computers. Lewis argues that these criminals are not hackers in any sense of the word, and that it is a shame that the media has exposed the people of this country to a corrupted meaning of the term.

Hackers, in one form or another, have been around since the beginning of the electronic communication age. Teenage males were kicked off the phone system by telephone authorities as early as 1878. Today, most real life hackers, both good and bad, are young and male. These hackers are most often in late high school or college and come from middle-class backgrounds. As we will see, most fictional representations of hackers are also young and male.

Beth Lamb, who observed Lewis' group of hackers during her graduate studies in English, defined hacker as "a term of endearment for someone with talent, knowledge, intelligence, and ingenuity, especially concerning computer operations, networks, security concerns, etc." A definition that floated around the Internet defined hackers as follows:

HACKER, n. 1. A person who enjoys learning the details of programming systems and how to stretch their capabilities, as opposed to most users who prefer to learn only the minimum necessary. 2. One who programs enthusiastically, or who enjoys programming rather than just theorizing about programming. 3. A person capable of appreciating hack value (q.v.). 4. A person who is good at programming quickly. Not everything a hacker produces is a hack. 5. An expert at a particular program, or one who frequently does work using it or on it; example: "A SAIL hacker." (Definitions 1 to 5 are correlated, and people who fit them congregate.) 6. An inquisitive meddler who tries to discover information by poking around. Hence "password hacker," "network hacker."

THE HACKER IN FILM AND NOVEL

Author Bruce Sterling, in his book *The Hacker Crackdown: Law and Disorder on the Electronic Frontier*, suggests that there are two basic definitions of the word hacker. The first presents the hacker as, at worst, a mythical trickster similar to Loki or Coyote. The second presents the hacker in demeaning terms such as "intruder," "trespasser," "wormer," and "gangster." The result is that one side of the definition presents hackers as the reincarnation of the devil, while the other side presents them as heroes fighting for the rights of privacy and free speech for everyone in cyberspace. Hackers have been used as the scapegoats for everything from equipment failures to individual ineptitude and incompetence. The purpose of this chapter is to introduce the reader to an overview of the history of hackers and their creations, as well as the reasons for the media hype surrounding them. The reader will then be left to draw his or her own conclusions about whether hackers are really pirates or patriots.

The media has done much to display both sides of this controversy to the American public. Hackers have been represented in a variety of ways in films and novels. Those who have seen *Terminator II: Judgement Day* will remember the two young men using a portable computer connected to an ATM card and stealing money from the automatic teller machine. This is an interesting representation of the young hacker in that, although engaged in illegal activities, one of these young men is supposed to be the salvation of the human race.

The film *WarGames* portrays the story of a high-school aged hacker who breaks into the government's military computer using a "blue-box" and almost starts World War III. The "blue-box" was a fraud device that could trick the phone company's switching systems into granting free access to long-distance lines. Today, these blue-boxes have been rendered practically useless by the digital upgrading of the phone system's equipment. In *WarGames*, the young hacker is not really a bad kid but is

Hackers have
been represented
in a variety of
ways in films and
novels.

intelligent and bored, prone to exploring. His explorations lead him into his high-school's computer system—where he changes his and a friend's grades. During his explorations of cyberspace, he accidently gains access to the military's computer that controls the nuclear arsenal. He begins playing what he thinks is a war game, thermonuclear warfare, with the computer. The computer, however, takes the game for real.

The film *Sneakers* begins in the 1960s when Robert Redford's character, Martin, and another character hack their way into a bank's computer system, transferring funds from corporations and political entities to organizations that the characters believe in—such as GreenPeace. This is a very realistic vision of the hacker, as they tend to be anti-materialistic and idealistic. When Martin goes to get pizza, his friend is caught by the police and sent to prison. Martin goes underground and years later is a member of an organization that hacks into the security systems of various businesses and provides them with recommendations for upgrading their security. The remainder of the film details the efforts of Martin and his group of misfit hackers as they attempt to gain possession of an encryption device that promises "no more secrets." Here, the hackers end up on the side of right although the end of the film exhibits that there is still a little bit of the trickster left in them.

A more criminal aspect of hacking is seen in the film *Die Hard II*. A terrorist group takes control of the computer system and phone lines controlling an airport. This story-line had long been a scenario that real-life computer-security experts had feared. Interestingly, September of 1991 saw Kennedy, La Guardia, and Newark airports crippled by the loss of their communications systems. This was not the result of hackers, however. AT&T's switching stations had lost power and shut down. Air traffic came to a standstill.

The last film we will look at in this brief overview of film's versions of the hacker is a relatively unknown film called *The Ghost in the Machine*. This film presents the hacker as both ultimate evil in one case, and idealist in another. The storyline centers on one hacker, a serial killer called the address book killer. He just happens to be a genius with computers. He steals each victim's address book, killing those listed in the book, finally killing the book's owner. When the killer is injured in a car accident, he dies while being diagnostically scanned into a hospital computer during a thunderstorm. A digital copy of the killer is created and now exists within the computer's memory. Here, the killer has access to the records of his next victims, a mother and her son. He begins killing the people listed in her address book. The woman gains the help of another hacker, also a whiz with computers. This character, having spent time in prison for his hacking, sees computers and hacking in a more positive manner. The story continues as the two hackers battle for supremacy and the lives of the woman and her son.

Novels have presented hackers in a variety of ways also. Author John Brunner's *The Shockwave Rider* and author William Gibson's *Neuromancer*, *Count Zero*, *Burning Chrome*, and *Mona Lisa Overdrive* are just a few of the novels with hackers as main characters. Brunner's book tells the story of a man trying to hide from the system, a system tyrannical in its control of the lives of the masses. In many ways it has, as its underlying theme, a message similar to Aldus Huxley's *Brave New World*. This message is that technology, as a system, can come to control the lives of the people who think it serves them. The result is a world where people give up more and more of their individual rights to the system.

Gibson also presents stories of individuals striving against a system that controls the lives of the masses. These dystopic views of the future have much in common with George Orwell's *1984*. The underlying image of hackers in all these novels—both Brunner's and Gibson's—is the individualistic and idealistic outlaw working on the fringe of the society around them. This fictional image has many similarities with the factual image that non-fiction writers have presented.

THE HACKER IN NON-FICTION

Three major works of non-fiction concerning hackers have given these individuals the same contradictory image, at least in the minds of the American masses. The first, author Steven Levy's *Hackers: Heroes of the Computer Revolution*, was published in 1984. As the title suggests, Levy's book exalts the hacker to the status of idol. Written before the AT&T crashes of January 15, 1990, and September 17, 1991, that brought the more derisive definition of hacker to the forefront of the American media, Levy's book describes hackers as "digital explorers" and as "contemporary young wizards." These "wizards" included founder and CEO of Microsoft, Bill Gates, as well as Apple Computer originators Steven Jobs and Stephen Wozniak.

It was in Levy's book that the Hacker Ethic was first codified for the American public to see and understand:

The Hacker Ethic

- Access to computers—and anything which might teach you something about the way the world works—should be unlimited and total. Always yield to the Hands-On Imperative!

- All information should be free.

- Mistrust Authority—Promote Decentralization.

- Hackers should be judged by their hacking, not bogus criteria such as degrees, age, race, or position.

- You can create art and beauty on a computer.

- Computers can change your life for the better.

This ethic presents the conflict within not only the hackers themselves, but within the American psyche. Capitalism, and its inherent entrepreneurial philosophy, requires that anything of value or potential worth has a cost to the user or recipient. Access to knowledge, and the tools that enable that access, have an inherent worth and value. Unlimited and total access run counter to the precepts of Capitalism. The information in this book, for instance, has value to you as the reader. The authors and editors of the various chapters were paid for their efforts in putting the information into a usable form. The value of this information was determined by the production costs and the potential market value. Under Capitalism, information can never be free because it has potential value to individuals.

Capitalism also thrives on its own internal authority and centralization. Capitalism depends on the authority created by degrees and positions. While suggesting that all individuals are created equal, Capitalism sets up some equals as more equal than others. Titles, such as author, editor, professor, and doctor, imply authority and superiority, as well as expertise. These individuals are compensated for their abilities and skills with information. While implying individuality and decentralization, Capitalism rewards those most adept at conformity and centralization.

The fifth and sixth statements of the Hacker's Ethic remind us of the conflict within the American psyche that Bertrand Russell discussed in 1928: "Machines are worshipped because they are beautiful, and valued because they confer power; they are hated because they are hideous, and loathed because they impose slavery." Technology is capable of both beauty and vulgarity. It is capable of producing change, but change is not always for the better.

How can a machine be used to create art and beauty? How can the computer change one's life for the better? These

Under Capitalism, information can never be free because it has potential value to individuals.

fifth and sixth statements in the hacker ethic appear to be at odds with one another. It comes down to the question of whether a computer is a tool or a machine. Tools, as extensions of their users, have the capability of being used to create. Machines, however, according to Karl Marx in his essay "Machinery and Modern Industry," impose their own cadence and routine on the people working with them to where, as MIT's Sherry Turkle points out, "it is no longer clear who or what is being used." Is a computer a tool, a machine, or both?

An interesting point is that both Microsoft and Apple, created by Levy's "young wizards" of this Hacker Ethic, now make every effort to prevent other young hackers from having similar access, and the "Hands-On Imperative," unless those young hackers pay for that privilege. This reeks of situational ethics for the hackers of old. It's as if these hackers of the 1970s, now, in the late 1980s and early 1990s, having come to power, want to prevent other, younger hackers, from having the same access that they themselves had.

Some people agree with Sen. Patrick Leahy, Democrat from Vermont and a Senate sponsor of the Electronic Communications Privacy Act of 1986, who suggested that: "We cannot unduly inhibit the inquisitive 13-year-old who, if

Technology is capable of both beauty and vulgarity. It is capable of producing change, but change is not always for the better.

• •

left to experiment today, may tomorrow develop the telecommunications or computer technology to lead the United States into the 21st century. He represents our future and our best hope to remain a technologically competitive nation."

Another nonfiction book considered to be a classic text concerning the history of the hacker is Clifford Stoll's *The Cuckoo's Egg: Tracking a Spy through the Maze of Computer Espionage*. Stoll's book is filled with anecdotes concerning his efforts to capture spies working for the Russian KGB who were using the Internet to enter U.S. military computers and steal military secrets. These spies turned out to be Markus Hess and Karl Koch, of the former West Germany, who were hacking for money. These anecdotes in Stoll's book even include his recipe for chocolate chip cookies and what music he listened to while tracking down the spies. We recently found copies of this book at a local chain bookstore at bargain prices.

Hacker History:
Not Exactly
What You'd
Expect

Probably the most interesting aspect of the resolution of the hacker crackdown is that, aside from a few individuals receiving short prison terms for their hacking, nothing was really resolved.

The most recent of these three classic nonfiction texts is Austin, Texas, cyberpunk writer and journalist Bruce Sterling's *The Hacker Crackdown: Law and Disorder on the Electronic Frontier*. In his book, Sterling provides an excellent chronology of the history of hackers with particular emphasis on the period from the late 1980s to the early 1990s. Some of the best parts of this book include a recounting of the raid on Steve Jackson Games, Inc., and the trial of University of Missouri student Craig Neidorf. Neidorf, the notorious Knight Lightning, was co-editor of *Phrack*, a free general electronic publication available on the Internet via BITNET, an educational network used by institutions in North America and Europe. Sterling's book, to his regret, adds to the degradation of the hacker mystique by focusing on the definition of the hacker as one who intrudes into computer systems without the permission of the computer's owner or manager. Probably the most interesting aspect of the resolution of the hacker crackdown is that, aside from a few individuals receiving short prison terms for their hacking, nothing was really resolved.

. . . .

The next few pages of this chapter will discuss, in very general terms, the history of hacking and how its meaning came to have the negative connotation it has today in the minds of the American public. We've drawn the information for this brief history from our readings of the three books by Levy, Stoll, and Sterling, as well as our readings of newspaper and other media accounts of the time period.

The Early Exploration of Cyberspace

First, there was cyberspace. The very beginnings of cyberspace existed in the invention of the telegraph and the telephone. Although there are many individuals, from many countries, who can claim some responsibility for the inventions of the telegraph and telephone, the discussion here will be limited to those given credit in the U.S. This is not intended to belittle the contributions of other countries to the technological revolution and discovery of cyberspace, but simply to serve as a focus for the discussion as it pertains to hackers in the United States.

THE TELEGRAPH: THE FIRST VOYAGES INTO CYBERSPACE

Samuel F.B. Morse is regarded by many as the father of the telegraph. The truth is that Morse's contribution was an improvement on the technology developed by two British scientists, William F. Cooke and Charles Wheatstone, who had been working on what they called electrical telegraphy (distant writing) in the early 1820s. Morse, in coming to America, originally intended to be a painter of landscapes. During his voyage to America, a conversation sparked his interest in the Cooke-Wheatstone technology. In 1843, Morse and a partner received $30,000 from Congress to install a telegraph line from Washington, D.C., to Baltimore, Maryland. His system was patented in 1844 and, with the now-famous message "What hath God wrought?," began the exploration of cyberspace.

The railroads were the first to take advantage of this exploration, and the twin technologies of transportation and communication brought about many cultural changes for this young nation and the world. One of the most important of these was the standardization of time. Prior to this period, each community set up and existed under its own time. This resulted in travelers having to set their watches at each town or community that they visited. The supposed need for standardized time zones was brought about by the railroads' scheduling coordination. Cyberspace, through the use of the telegraph, made this coordination possible and standardized time zones came into existence.

Of course, other possible effects of this new technology were more apparent to the public mind. Some telegraph doom-sayers had suggested in the mid-1870s that the telegraph had been responsible for the spreading of a cholera epidemic. Another effect was that devastating news of war was able to be experienced via cyberspace. The War Between the States saw extensive use of the telegraph by the media in bringing information about the battles to the American public. So much so, in fact, that Northern military leaders complained that the South knew, in advance, of northern military movements and were able to prepare for these movements based on this information. For the South, these early hackers were considered patriots. The North considered them a nuisance and a danger.

THE TELEPHONE: MORE EXPLORATION

Alexander Graham Bell, the man credited for the invention of the telephone, began as a teacher of the deaf. It was his study of the physiology of the human ear that led to his belief that the human voice could be transmitted over wires. Due to his limited understanding of electronics, he hired Thomas A. Watson to assist him in his experimentation. During the years 1875 and 1876, Bell applied for, and received, three patents for telephone technology that would give him the edge in regard to modulating energy, control of voice tone, and signal power. An interesting side note is that Bell's original concept for the telephone was that it would be a mass medium. This concept had limited success before the telephone went on to become the centerpiece of more conventional person-to-person technology. In Hungary, from 1893 until after World War I, when the telephone would ring, you would plug in a speaker and receive news, entertainment, and other information via the government-run service.

Bell, however, had only beaten another inventor, Elisha Gray, to the patent office by three hours. A long and bitter patent-infringement court battle resulted, as well as ensuing claims of malpractice within the patent office. Bell's patent was upheld, however, and Gray, although disappointed, went on to establish Western Electric. In 1888, Gray patented the telautograph. This device allowed for the transfer of handwritten messages over telegraph lines. The telautograph is seen, by some, as the first fax machine.

Technology did more than just change the locus of some communication. It began changing the social structure of our society.

The technology for the access of cyberspace grew relatively quickly. The technology did more than just change the locus of some communication. It began changing the social structure of

our society. The first operators for the telephone company were young boys whose age was generally no more than 13. These teenage boys, placed in charge of the phone system switchboards, were rude to customers, talking back to them, disconnecting their calls, crossing lines so that customers found themselves talking to strangers, and other assorted chaos. The phone company learned its lesson very quickly. The combination of power that technology provides, technical mastery, and effective anonymity transformed these boys into what Bell's chief engineer called "Wild Indians." In 1878, the boys were kicked off the system as operators and replaced with young women. By 1881, only nine cities in the United States with populations over 10,000 did not have telephone service.

As it was considered, at that point in time, improper for women to work outside the home, let alone in offices where they would come into contact with men, the phone company managers had to persuade the young women, and their parents, that it was all right. The young women were promised protection and assured that they would be given directions in manners and proper behavior. The new technology, therefore, was responsible for bringing women into the workplace, although they were in low-paying, low-status positions.

CYBERSPACE GOES WIRELESS

While the telegraph and the telephone were coming into being, wireless communication was also born. While radio had its birth in the mid-1870s in the scientific papers published by a Scotsman named James Clark Maxwell and a German named Heinrich Hertz, it took the son of an Italian father and an English mother to put it into practice. By 1897, after offering radio to the Italian Government, which turned him down, Guglielmo Marconi registered his patent in England and established British Marconi. Two years later he founded American Marconi. In 1909, Marconi shared the Nobel prize in physics for his achievements in wireless telegraphy with Germany's Ferdinand Braun.

Experimenters began to play with radio during the early 1900s. Ernst Alexanderson, at General Electric, perfected a vacuum tube amplifier that became known as the Alexanderson Alternator. Marconi perfected and patented the tuner in 1904. In 1906, on Christmas Eve, Reginald Fessenden, using a microphone and an Alexanderson alternator, produced the first voice and music broadcast into cyberspace playing his violin, singing, and reading from the Bible. Lee de Forest, influenced by both Thomas Edison's light bulb and Marconi researcher Ambrose Fleming's vacuum tube, perfected and patented the triode, which

became known as the audion, in 1906. The following year saw de Forest broadcasting from downtown New York City and in the fall of 1916 he began broadcasting phonograph records and election returns.

As with both the telegraph and the telephone, radio changed the world. The Japanese won the Russo-Japanese War of 1904–1905 due to the superiority of their radio communication equipment. When the U.S. *Republic* foundered off New York City, both the passengers and crew were saved by radio-alerted rescue ships. More than 10,000 U.S. soldiers and sailors were trained in radio communication during World War I. When the war was over, these trained individuals went home and began to play with home-grown radio equipment.

It is these former soldiers and sailors that began the exploration of cyberspace in earnest. It wasn't long after World War I that AM radio exploded on the American scene. Although originally conceived for person-to-person communication, radio quickly created a type of "consensual hallucination" for the

American public that novelist William Gibson would write about in the mid-1980s. Discoveries in cyberspace were being made almost every day as these explorers worked from warehouse roofs and garage workshops.

The "evil that lurks in the minds of men" showed up once again in this early stage of the exploration of cyberspace. Dr. J.R. Brinkley, who owned a radio station in Milford, Kansas, gave so-called medical advice over the airwaves. The problem was that he wasn't a real doctor and the drugs he was prescribing weren't really drugs but rather bottles of elixir that he packaged. The "doctor" lost his license to broadcast, as did the Reverend Doctor Schuler of Los Angeles, for his excesses. There were many other early explorers who used cyberspace for their own enjoyment and profit at the expense of the public.

The 1940s brought rumors to the American public of new technologies such as radio with no static, radio with pictures, and machines that could think. These new technologies seemed to come right out of Jules Verne. The exploration of cyberspace was in the process of expanding the means of access.

THE COMPUTERS OF THE 1940s AND 1950s

It has been said before that the first two uses of new technologies are almost always violence and sex. Among the first users of computers was the military. The early computers were used to calculate artillery projectile trajectories. World War II saw military use of computers grow as weapons research produced such "advances" as the atom bomb. Some computers were placed on naval ships and used for computing naval bombardments. These computers took up the space of entire rooms, yet had very little memory. They were also very slow by today's standards.

Due to the technological limitations of these early computers, as well as the bureaucratic regime of their manufacturer, IBM, a symbolic priesthood grew up that served the machine. The instructions (most often written in something called "machine language") that made up a specific program were first punched, one instruction per card, by the user. These cards, with their tiny holes, were gathered together in a "batch." This "batch" of cards was then turned over to the machine's servants who would feed the cards into readers, after which these privileged few individuals, sometimes, could actually touch the machine. If—and sometimes this was a very big if—there were no mistakes in the program instructions, the user would receive back a printout of the results of the program.

THE HACKERS OF THE **1950s** AND **1960s**

The 1950s brought more advances in technology and the first individuals to call themselves hackers were found at the Massachusetts Institute of Technology. In his book, *Hackers: Heroes of the Computer Revolution*, Levy describes the first hackers as being members of MIT's Tech Model Railroad Club (TMRC). These individuals were more interested in the "system" of the model railroad layout and how it worked, than in building exact miniatures of locomotives and freight cars.

This subgroup of TMRC developed its own jargon for what it did. If a piece of equipment was "loosing" it meant that it wasn't working. When that piece of equipment was ruined it was "munged" (Mash Until No Good). A project or job was called a "hack." Although hack had a derogatory meaning in the dictionary, the TMRC group used the word to imply artistry, innovation, style, and technical expertise. A hacker, therefore, represented someone who could "hack the system" with artistry, innovation, style, and technical expertise.

Many of the "system" subgroup of TMRC moved over to the Artificial Intelligence area run by, at that point in time, MIT's John McCarthy. McCarthy, who would later move to Stanford University, helped pioneer such diverse subjects as artificial intelligence, computer chess, and the LISP (LISt Processing) computer language while at MIT. He also offered MIT's first computer programming course. Working with, at first, an IBM 704 and a newer model called the 709, McCarthy and the former members of TMRC began learning the practice of "program bumming." "Program bumming" meant taking a program that worked and trying to cut out instructions, without affecting the outcome of the program. This practice became an obsession with many of the young hackers. The bureaucracy, the time-sharing of the computer, and the batch processing system of the IBM machines, however, were a pain for the hackers. This pain was somewhat alleviated with the addition of the TX-0 computer, one of the first transistor-run computers in the world. This computer eliminated the bureaucracy priesthood, allowed one user to have complete access, and eliminated the need for the instruction cards by enabling the user to flip switches to send commands to the computer. The TX-0 also had the ability to send noise to the audio speaker and work began immediately on programming the computer to play music.

It was here at MIT, during the late 1950s and early 1960s, that the Hacker Ethic, discussed earlier in this chapter, was born. Several of these young hackers found working on the computer far more intellectually stimulating than going to classes and the result was that many never finished their college educations. Some hackers were like Lee Jackson's

Several of these young hackers found working on the computer far more intellectually stimulating than going to classes and the result was that many never finished their college educations.

father. Lee Jackson would, in the 1980s, be instrumental in the electronic publication of *The Hacker Report*. Jackson's father, who worked for the Texas Highway Department during the mid-sixties, was one of those who continued "slugging it out with a CPU" creating programs that would accomplish such tasks as generating all the state's license plate numbers in the days before vowels were used on the plates. We will return to Lee Jackson, and *The Hacker Report*, later.

Many of the MIT hackers burned out and became, to use the vernacular of the hacker, "losers," as far as their work in the Artificial Intelligence Lab was concerned. This led the lab's leaders to find them jobs in business and government (a way to get them out of the lab). The early hackers, then, began to spread across the country.

The turmoil of the sixties also saw a change in the hacker's appearance. For many, their hair grew longer and "hacking the system" became political.

THE PERSONAL COMPUTER EXPLOSION OF THE 1970s

The early 1970s saw Paul, one of the authors of this chapter, exposed to hacking in the computer center at the University of Texas at Austin. As at MIT, in the UT-Austin computer lab, the night was the realm of the hacker. Paul, a freshman taking his first astronomy course, was assigned to work with a graduate student on a program to compute the orbits required to land a man on the moon. In virtual terms, Paul not only lost seven Apollo spacecraft and 21 astronauts, but destroyed New York City, before managing to land on the moon. It wasn't long before he had a job working Friday and Saturday nights for the computer lab. His responsibilities were simple: keep the printers supplied with paper and sweep up the area around the printers. The advantage of the job was that, if he kept up his responsibilities, he was allowed access to one of the terminals where he could learn the wonders of the BASIC language. One of the most interesting aspects of this privilege was access to one of the first Star Trek games written in BASIC for the IBM mainframe computers.

While Paul was learning BASIC by playing Star Trek, hackers in California were setting up the People's Computer Company. In an effort to bring computing to the masses, the People's Computer Company attempted to give people access via a new "electronic" bulletin board, which enabled people to exchange messages via computers set up at various locations. On this bulletin board, people could meet others with similar interests, express themselves on various issues, and simply communicate with other people using the board. During the same time frame, Ed Roberts, in Albuquerque, New Mexico, was building and selling the first personal computer kit, the Altair. It's interesting to note here that this computer was named after a star mentioned in the *Star Trek* television show. Science fiction had, as we have seen and will continue to see, a large impact on computer hacking.

The 1970s saw a rush of activity as Apple, Atari, Radio Shack, and others very quickly came out with personal computers. As these computers became more accessible to the public, writing programs became an interesting pastime for many young hackers. Lee Jackson, who would later become instrumental in the creation of *The Hacker Report*, wrote his first program on an old TTY in his junior high school's math lab in 1977. The first personal computer bulletin board system was created by two young hackers, Ward Christensen and Randy Seuss, in 1978.

Stories of hacker pranks began to circulate in the early seventies as college computers and others were allegedly programmed to print out everything in their memory, erase their memory banks, and then shut down. This decade also saw an even darker side of hacking as *Ramparts* magazine was seized in a blue-box rip-off scandal. The reader will remember, from our earlier discussion of the film *WarGames*, that a blue-box was used to steal service from the telephone company.

> Science fiction had, as we have seen and will continue to see, a large impact on computer hacking.

HACKING IN THE 1980s

One of the first BBSs to go online was 8BBS. This underground board went online in early 1980. One of its more notable users was "the Condor." Possibly taking this handle from the Robert Redford character in the film, *Three Days of the Condor*, this young man became one of the most notorious hackers in American history. Condor was turned in to the police by other hackers and served seven months in solitary confinement because of the fear that he would be able to fire missiles from the prison pay phone, thereby starting World War III.

8BBS didn't escape the scrutiny of the government either. The system operator (sysop) of 8BBS strongly supported free speech. Many users entered 8BBS merely curious, but emerged as hackers. According to author Bruce Sterling, police confiscated the BBS when a user gave the sysop a new modem that had been bought with a stolen credit card.

Another BBS that attracted early attention was 414 Private. The teenage members of what came to be called the 414 Gang managed, in 1982, to break into the Sloan-Kettering Cancer Center and the Los Alamos military computers. One of the members of this gang was high school honor student Neil Patrick. Patrick would later testify before the Congressional House Committee on Science and Technology. When asked at what point the young hacker questioned the ethics of what he was doing, Patrick replied, "Once the FBI knocked on the door."

The theatrical release of the film *WarGames*, in 1983, helped boost modem sales to unseen levels. The Radio Shack TRS 80 Model I, affectionately known as the Trash 80 to its supporters, had available acoustic couplers, a form of modem where the user placed the phone receiver into a cradle as seen in *WarGames*. Atari 800, Apple, and Commodore 64 users could buy 300 baud direct modems.

During the mid-1980s, giving up his Trash 80, Paul bought an Atari 800XL, two floppy disk drives, and a 300 baud modem. Accessing the various BBS's that were available in Northeast Arkansas at that time, Paul managed to find information on hacking both the Atari 800XL and the disk drive hardware systems. With this information, he was able to upgrade the 800XL from 64KB to 256KB and the single-sided-single-density disk drives to double-sided-double-density. He also found a program that, to the unknowing observer, appeared to allow the user to hack into NORAD's missile control system. The program, while making all the correct sounds of connecting up through the phone lines, never actually accessed the modem. It was actually a prank program that would tell the uninitiated that the FBI had traced the phone call to the user's phone number and that local police were on their way before flashing the sentence "Gotcha!" across the screen.

. . . .

The better hackers, those most technically capable, were not criminals. They entered computers regularly, but didn't alter or damage anything. Many were professionals, and some even worked for AT&T.

. . . .

Underground boards multiplied faster than mythical rabbits. In addition to hardware hacking information and prank programs, many of these boards dabbled in pirated computer games. It was during the mid-1980s that "Logic Bombs" and "worms" made their unfortunate appearance on these BBS's. In the late-1980s, the first Trojan Horse programs also began to appear.

The most notorious of the worm variety of these headaches for computer users was the Internet Worm of November 2-3, 1988. This worm was probably the biggest and, according to cyberpunk novelist and journalist Bruce Sterling, the most publicized computer-intrusion of the 1980s. This worm was created and unleashed on the Internet by Robert Morris, a graduate student at Cornell. In his defense, Morris suggested that the program was intended to explore the network without causing any harm. Poor programming by Morris however, caused the worm to replicate itself out of control. The result of this worm was that more than 6,000 Internet computers crashed.

Phrack and the Legion of Doom also came into their own during the mid-1980s. *Phrack* is a general electronic publication that consists of gossip concerning hacking, both nationally and internationally. Originating in St. Louis, Missouri, on the Metal Shop AE BBS, *Phrack* was distributed free and circulated widely among the underground boards. As its two editors, known as Knight Lightning and Teran King, went off to college, *Phrack* began distribution via BITNET, and through BITNET to Internet. As discussed earlier, Knight Lightning's real name was Craig Neidorf, a University of Missouri political science major whose trial makes up a major portion of Bruce Sterling's *The Hacker Crackdown: Law and Order on the Electronic Frontier.* We'll be returning to the escapades of Knight Lightning when we discuss the crackdown of 1990.

The Legion of Doom also plays an important part in Sterling's book. The name comes from an evil group of comic book villains led by Superman's arch-nemesis, Lex Luthor (created by DC Comics). According to Sterling, the name was intended to be funny. Telephone security officers and other law enforcement personnel, however, did not find the name humorous.

Legion of Doom members ran their own boards and were present on many others. John Perry Barlow, a frequent spokesperson for electronic issues and member of the Electronic Freedom Foundation, was quoted in an article for *Mondo 2000*, saying, "Cyberspace...is presently inhabited almost exclusively by mountain men, desperados and vigilantes, kind of a rough bunch. And, as long as that's the case, it's gonna be the Law of the wild in there." Hackers of this type might best be typified by Hess and Koch, the two West German hackers hired by the KGB to break into United States military computers using Internet.

Not all hackers, however, were this type of desperado. The better hackers, those most technically capable, were not criminals. They entered computers regularly, but didn't alter or damage anything. Many were professionals, and some even worked for AT&T. It was the phone system that the teenage hacker wannabes struck in the late 1980s, stirring up the hornet's nest that resulted in the crackdown of 1990.

. . . .

The
Crackdown
of 1990

On June 13, 1989, if you had tried to call the Palm Beach County Probation Department in Delray Beach, Florida, you'd have received a big surprise. Tina, a phone-sex worker in New York, would have answered your call. Someone entering the computer program at BellSouth central office switching station had reprogrammed it to switch, at no charge to the user, all incoming calls to the Probation Department in Florida to the sex-line in New York. BellSouth investigators found that not only were hackers capable of pulling off pranks such as the phone-sex switch, but that they were capable of listening in on any call made on the system.

Law enforcement agencies were immediately more than interested. They were incensed. Hackers could not only listen in on personal phone calls of the public, but they could also listen in on calls between phone company officials, conversations with police stations, and even conversations with the local offices of the Secret Service and FBI. Scramblers and secured lines, although inconvenient, were put in place immediately. Officials realized that the 911 system was vulnerable, too. Now public safety was at risk—all because of pranksters who rerouted calls to sex-lines.

Fry Guy, a 16-year-old in Indiana, was the teenage hacker wannabe that was responsible for the Probation Office/Sex-line phone switch in Florida. Fry Guy was also into more flagrant crimes such as credit card abuse, breaking into credit-company computers and stealing credit card numbers. He even found a way to get cash advances on credit cards from Western Union. He called Indiana Bell security officers and bragged about what he had done. He warned them of the Legion of Doom's impending crash of the national phone system scheduled, according to Fry Guy, for the Fourth of July.

Fry Guy was arrested July 22, 1989, by the Secret Service. They considered him, however, small potatoes. They wanted bigger fish. He was charged with 11 counts of computer fraud, unauthorized computer access, and wire fraud. Although not a legitimate member of the Legion of Doom, he blamed the group for his activities and offered to testify against them. He continued to suggest that the Legion was going to crash the national phone system on a national holiday, and when AT&T crashed on Martin Luther King's Day in 1990, though it was in fact AT&T's own fault, the phone company, and the Secret Service, took Fry Guy seriously.

The Secret Service now went after the suspected ring leaders, the members of the Legion of Doom, known as the Atlanta Three. It was Prophet, one of the Atlanta Three, that had stolen the 911 Document from the phone company that would bring *Phrack* into the story.

Prophet, while exploring the phone company's Advanced Information Management System, or AIMSX, discovered the 911 document and made a copy as a trophy. He then kept one copy and stored another on a BBS in Illinois. The sysop of this BBS, Rich Andrews, on discovering it, sent a copy to a BBS run by Charles Boykin, an AT&T employee. Boykin sent a copy to Jerry Dalton, an AT&T Security specialist. Dalton then sent a copy to Henry Kluepfel at Bellcore security headquarters. Finally, Prophet sent a copy to Knight Lightning at the University of Missouri-Columbia. There is no way of knowing how many other, legitimate copies of this secret document, made by Bell employees, were floating around.

Prophet and Knight Lightning edited the document and, in February of 1989, Knight Lightning published it in the 24th issue of *Phrack* where it was, as usual, distributed to over 150 sites. The document had been available in this issue of *Phrack* for over a year when, three days after the phone system crash on Martin Luther King Day, January 15, 1990, agents arrived at Knight Lightning's fraternity house in Columbia, Missouri. Knight Lightning was accused of causing the phone system crash. By February 6, he was indicted. He went to trial July 24–27, 1990.

Authorities and law officials began raiding BBS's with a vengeance. One board sysop in Austin, Texas, woke up one morning to find a revolver aimed at his head. Another board was confiscated, simply to prevent a cyberpunk novel from being published. Paranoid telephone security officials and law enforcement officials cracked-down on anything that even appeared to hold potential for what they considered computer misuse. It was very reminiscent of the Secret Service raid in 1939 of the "Futurians," a New York City-based science fiction writers' group that included such notables as Isaac Asimov, Frederik Pohl, and Damon Knight. They were thought to be counterfeiters because they had their own printing press and mimeograph machine, on which they produced science fiction fan magazines.

The crackdown of 1990 and the BBS raids of the early 1990s fizzled out rather quickly. This was due to the difficulty in proving that these individuals and groups

Hackers could not only listen in on personal phone calls of the public, but they could also listen in on calls between phone company officials, conversations with police stations, and even conversations with the local offices of the Secret Service and FBI.

had actually done anything. In Knight Lightning's case, the phone company claimed that the 911 document was worth almost $80,000. In court, it was revealed that the phone company was selling the same information in a little booklet, available to the general public, at a price of $13. The case against Knight Lightning was dismissed.

None of this should be taken as implying that these individuals got away without punishment, right or wrong. In Knight Lightning's case, he and his parents were left with considerable legal fees. Other hackers and BBS sysops did spend time in jail. Many of them had their computer and data storage equipment seized. In some cases it took considerable time before the equipment was returned, if at all.

The Question: Are Hackers Pirates or Patriots?

The dictionary definition of "hack" is "to cut or chop irregularly, in a bungling or aimless manner; to mangle with repeated strokes." Lee Jackson, of the The Hacker Report, said, in a recent e-mail message regarding the writing of this chapter, that, "people who hack at legitimate programs and then release them on an unsuspecting public, passing them off as the real thing," definitely do not have his respect. Jackson divided The Hacker Report into four sections; hacked files, hoaxes, Trojans, and pirated commercial software.

Programs that have been altered to look like a new version of an older program fall into the Hacked Files section. These programs would generally be the same as the legitimate versions, but have things, such as the version numbers, changed. They would not have harmful code added. Examples of this include, according to September, 1992, issue of The Hacker Report, various versions of COMPUSHOW, PKZIP, QEDIT, QMODEM, TheDRAW, ViruScan, and XOO Fossil.

The second section of the report deals with hoaxes. These programs are usually not harmful, but are designed to play a prank on the unsuspecting user. XTRATANK, according to Jackson, is probably the most notable of these, as it claims to double your hard drive space, but simply doubles the numeric output of DOS calls that show your available disk space. Other files of this type include: 2496, a program that says it will change your 2400 bps modem to a 9600 bps modem; SPEEDUP, a program that claims to increase your clock speed, but actually doubles the length of each second and resets the system clock to use 30 of the new seconds each minute; and WOLFXXX, a file that claims to upgrade your copy of Wolfenstein 3-D to version 1.3, even though no such version exists.

The third section of the report deals with Trojans—programs that could damage your system. These files could be as simple as being described as doing one thing, but when run, actually doing something else. They might be "Droppers," programs that do what they claim, but drop off a virus in your system while they do it. Finally, these programs might be bombs. Bombs are divided into two classes: ANSI bombs and Device bombs. An ANSI bomb might redefine your keyboard via ANSI.SYS and reformat your hard drive when you hit <ENTER>. A device bomb might open COM1 and have it dial a long distance number without your knowledge.

The final section of the report deals with pirated commercial software. These are actually commercially-available programs without a proper license agreement. A student at MIT was recently indicted by a federal grand jury for allegedly operating a BBS that was used exclusively for the purpose of exchanging pirated software.

The report is available for download in many locations, including various BBS's around the country. As of the time of this writing, the file can also be downloaded from both CompuServe and Internet. On CompuServe it's available in the IBMBBS forum under the filename HKXXXX.ZIP with XXXX standing for the month and the year of the latest issue. An example would be HK0194.ZIP for the January, 1994, issue. On Internet, the file can be obtained by sending an e-mail message to *mail-server@alive.ersys.edmonton.ab.ca*. The message should contain the line *subscribe hack-l*.

. . . .

CONCLUSIONS

Some hackers, by the popular definition of the word, create the programs that are listed in *The Hacker Report*. Two Cornell University students were arrested in 1992 for unleashing a virus that paralyzed computers in both California and Japan. March 6, 1992, saw the entire world poised for the worst, as the Michelangelo virus struck. It struck first in Japan, hitting only a few computers, and then in China, where, due to the widespread use of illegally copied software, its damage was high. In the United States, the virus struck at businesses, colleges, and even newspapers.

Other hackers, those defined in MIT's original definition, are the ones that create *The Hacker Report*. These individuals stand up for computer users' rights, occasionally finding themselves in moral conflict when the question centers on the choice between freedom of information and the right of privacy.

It is this conflict that really lies at the center of the question concerning hackers. Which is more important: the right of privacy or freedom of information?

It is this conflict that really lies at the center of the question concerning hackers. Which is more important: the right of privacy or freedom of information? Too many times these seemingly black-and-white, moral issues end up being questions of situational ethics:

- Is it information "I" need to make a profit? In this situation, freedom of information wins.
- Is it "my" privacy being invaded? In this situation, the right of privacy wins.

Hackers, both pirate and patriot, are no better and no worse than the average person, just more publicized. Clifford Stoll, in a recent e-mail message, said that he knew of no hacker who rated as a pirate and no hacker that rated as a patriot. Unfortunately, it is the negative, or pirate, aspect of this definition that gets the most media attention.

Even so, as suggested, the morals and ethics of hackers are no better or no worse than the average individual. Many times, it just boils down to ignorance. As a college student said recently while talking about his collection of bootleg audio and video cassettes and his illegally-copied software, "If they didn't want us to do it, they wouldn't make it so easy. And besides, they get their cut from the cost of the blank disks and tapes."

AFTERWORD

The Aug. 17, 1994, issue of *The Chronicle of Higher Education* presented an article that touches on two issues that arose during the editing phase of this chapter. The first question concerned how to differentiate between hackers as pirates or patriots. The article dealt with a recent string of extraordinarily complicated assaults on the Internet. This latest stream of attacks were being aimed, not at individual companies or universities, but at the network itself. A new name has been given to the individuals who are orchestrating these new attacks. They are called computer "crackers." These "mean-spirited hackers" (as they are called in the article) have manipulated and tampered with the infrastructure of the Internet itself. Perhaps, with more widespread use of the term cracker, the term hacker will lose some of its negative aspects.

The second issue stems from the apparent ignoring of more than half of the population in our discussion of the history of hacking. Historically, for better or worse, most hackers have been male. Is that trend now changing? Not according to James C. Settle, founder and former head of the FBI's National Computer Crime Squad. Settle suggests that today's typical crackers are usually males, between the ages of 20 and 24, with no more than a high-school education. He classifies many of them as unemployed social misfits.

Occasionally, we've managed to find a few articles dealing with women professionals using computers for information retrieval, but little is available on female crackers. Perhaps this is one area where women might not wish for equal representation.

In any event, we think the contribution of women to the history of hacking is an area of research that needs to be examined more fully. The authors can be reached at *76270.551@COMPUSERVE.COM*.

CYBERLIFE!

Color Gallery

In standard movie making, there is more than one camera on the scene. A number of camera viewpoints are used to heighten interest and to create the effect of omniscience—that is, viewers are put in the position of seeing the scene from all angles, which has the result of drawing them in, of engaging them. In the earliest filmmaking efforts, only one camera was used, from the point of view of someone watching a theater play from the audience. Soon artists realized that having more than one point of view was something that distinguished this new medium from all others.

Although you can only have one camera position per frame in 3-D computer animation, scenes from other camera viewpoints are added in during the editing process.

Lighting creates mood and emphasis. In theater, film, and video, lighting designers are artists in their own right—in effect, they paint with light. Rarely, if ever, does a scene rely on one light, even when the scene is supposed to be simulating light from the sun or a single light bulb. An "artificial" treatment is needed to convey a realistic effect. Typically, the designer will use one main light and several fills. This way, you can simulate everything from high-noon desert glare to midnight haunted house monster lighting. (Images courtesy of Pixar.)

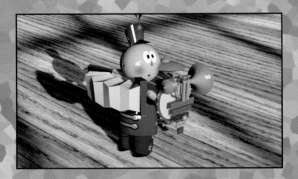

In the simplest possible terms, nanotechnology is the enterprise of manipulating, assembling, and constructing with atoms and molecules, molecular structures, materials, and complete "objects." These can include, but are by no means limited to, such examples as organic or quasi-organic molecular structures, molecular "machines," computing systems with the functional capacity of "supercomputers" but are literally invisible to the human eye, and ultimately, the ability to "replicate" almost any material or macroobject at will.

Science fiction, you may ask? Is this merely the rehash of yet another variation of a *Star Trek* episode? The answer is, no. In fact, in research labs and theoretical study groups here and abroad, the subject is taken very seriously. But even at this beginning, it is important to emphasize that it is not merely an individual "subject," or an obscure, narrow scientific specialization. In fact, quite the opposite is true. Chemists, physicists, computer scientists, medical researchers, and many other technical specialists covering a very wide area of interests are engaged in some aspect of developing a particular tangent, or enabling technology, with the overall focus aimed at molecular construction or synthesis.

Indeed, much as the "industrial age" represented a fundamental shift in social, economic, and geopolitical modalities for much of the world's population, and the current "information age" is once again reshaping the very fabric of global society, the "nanotechnology age" may well be unparalleled in all of recorded history for the impact it will have, and for the irreversible implications of the future that this new technology domain represents.

Virtual reality (VR) is a strong voice in the hands of the poor. It's in the process of democratizing architecture by giving individuals more choices. The real challenge of virtual architecture is to find unique, new ways to use it as a human-machine communication medium to transcend space.

Do architects only want to be able to deliver graphics at higher resolution for fewer dollars? Or are they also looking for the wormhole entrance to cyberspace (defined as where you are when you're calling Tonga from Coney Island)?

Virtual architecture opens doors for people. Suddenly, you are aware of being in a new environment very different from the usual reality perceived.

How many ways can architects use virtual reality bound only by the limits of the reality engines they adapt to their needs?

Computers are doing things today their inventors could not imagine. In the 1950s, a slim 2KB of hard-wired memory barely held enough information to add up columns of numbers. Virtual-reality systems demand huge amounts of memory and speedy processors to render what does not exist so that it does.

CYBERLIFE!

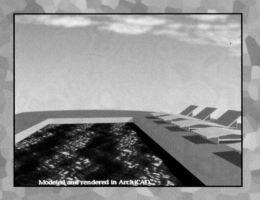

Modeled and rendered in ArchiCAD.

Other effects of computers are more subtle. Whereas it is clear a man cannot construct a new housing tract without the aid of scoopers and bulldozers, tractors and cranes—it is not so clear that the finances or the design for that project require a computer. Yet we use the computer because it allows multiple iterations of design, checks tolerances, automatically balances statements, creates 3-D walkthroughs before the first two-by-four is nailed, displays a color-coded site topology, creates sales brochures, verifies financing qualifications, manages loan documentation, and prints welcome letters for new residents. All of the activities can potentially be run on a single tool, a single computer.

And we take for granted the computer's ability to support us. We no longer figure the cost benefit of doing those activities on drafting boards, ledger pads, and typewriters. Even if we need more than one computer, we will do the work with a computer. The amount of time needed to perform these activities seems intuitively less with computers. Even when you add new activities like 3-D walkthroughs, the overall process is more efficient, more engaging, and in the long run, costs less to perform.

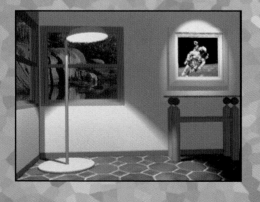

The computer has changed everything. Sales clerks no longer count out change, reacting instead with blind acceptance of the change total reflected in red LEDs on their cash registers. Movies like Jurassic Park are populated by computer-generated characters. Pinball and pool give way to Super Mario Brothers and Mortal Kombat. We can talk, draw, and brainstorm over a computer network instead of driving to meet our colleagues face-to-face. We don't type; we fine tune our phrases and punctuation with word processing. Our cars are tuned by computers and our food is cooked in computer-controlled ovens or microwaves. Minutes and hours sweep or scroll by, governed not by mechanics, but by the pulse of silicon. Our images of the cosmos return to Earth in streams of ones and zeros, finding false color and digital enhancements on the computers at JPL. We rediscover our ancestry and similarities from DNA, sequenced and mapped with the assistance of computers. We read computer-typeset books, we read computerized books and we submit term papers via e-mail. We even flirt and frolic, and sometimes get married, via computer. (Images courtesy of Pixar.)

The computer has changed everything. It has changed our relationship to the world. It has changed our relationship to other people. It has changed our relationship with the universe. And so we evolve. Our minds thrusting in all directions, gathering ultraviolet images of Shoemaker-Levy and its assault on Jupiter, peering through tunneling electron microscopes to see individual atoms stacked to form corporate logos, hearing the background noise of the universe, and amid its overwhelming hiss, trying to identify other lonely voices shouting into the blackness.

We are moving into a universe of patterns, of shadows, of organic relationships. This book peeks into dozens of shadows, identifies hundreds of new patterns, follows scores of relationships. It hears the drum beats of Usenet conversations pounding like ancient drums on the Serengeti. It sees our sense of self giving way to anonymity and transformation, where dreams are as real as a Fender guitar, a perfectly ripe persimmon, or the fender of a 1957 Chevy. It documents knowledge becoming legend and fact becoming myth. It plots great distances that shrink to nothing and zooms in on nothing magnified into enormity. The computer has changed everything. And we sweep ourselves along with the change because our need for information resonates with its possibilities.

PART III

Digital Life

Thinking About AI

Visionaries in the field
of robotics conceive
of devices that will not
only be intelligent,
but may leverage our
humanity and create
new life forms as the
evolutionary paths of
humans and machines
converge.

chapter 15
by Daniel W. Rasmus

Despite the failure of the computer and robotics industries to deliver human-like thinking machines to industry and commerce, the idea of thinking machines continues to intrigue us. Instead of monolithic devices and bipedal robots, today's research concentrates on distributed artificial intelligence and spider robots. It is not that researchers have forsaken the idea of devices that walk, talk, and reason like people, but two revelations have moved them in new directions.

The first revelation is that the go-go economy of the seventies and eighties is over. Corporate research budgets concentrate more on where the rubber meets the road than where the rubber meets the sky. The dollars spent on research are expected to yield more tractable, immediate results. Instead of reasoning machines, we invent agents that reason about databases. Instead of programs that read English with perfection, we settle for programs that can sort our e-mail.

The second revelation is more profound and far reaching. The world is made of nuggets of life. Human cells contain primitive features, like mitochondria, that were perhaps, at one time, independent life forms. Artificially intelligent life thus need not limit itself to the human form. We are clearly not perfect beings, so why should we limit our creations to mirror images of our own fallibility?

To this new thinking comes distributed agents that congregate and communicate. Visionaries in the field of robotics conceive of devices that will not only be intelligent, but may leverage our humanity and create new life-forms as the evolutionary paths of humans and machines converge.

Our current state of the art is much more mundane. The diverse elements that make up today's AI technologies point toward these future technologies, but none of them has yet materialized the promise of the concept.

- -

THE HISTORY OF AI

The history of artificial intelligence is filled with exciting promises and profound disappointment. The term itself implies a wonderful new world—a world where Issac Asimov's dreams of intelligent machines transcend science fiction and becomes science fact. But the truth is that artificial intelligence has not delivered on its promises. It is still an open question whether the promises were too aggressive or the technology was too weak. If you compare the development of AI to that of microchips, AI remains, for the most part, in its infancy.

If you believe that it is technology that guards AI (and not philosophy), then microprocessors and computer architecture provide the stumbling blocks to AI's success. Even today's most powerful microprocessors—like Intel's Pentium, Digital Equipment's Alpha and the Apple/IBM/Motorola PowerPC—do not begin to approximate the operation of the human brain. These processors run by themselves, processing little more that one piece of data at a time. Over the years, they have become proficient at performing numerical calculations with blinding rapidity, but they do not process symbols with the same acuity. Although some of them can run in a parallel configuration, microprocessors still pale beside the richness and complexity of the human mind. The connection upon connection of synapse and ganglion, dendrite and axiom that makes up the human mind cannot yet be mimicked in silicon or gallium arsenide.

To understand our expectations, it is necessary to have context. The history of AI stretches back before the advent of computers. Much has been learned along the path toward thinking machines. In university laboratories, on factory floors, and in credit-verification departments, the derivatives of the AI dream make profound impacts on national and industrial goals. The history you are about to read is not the history of an adult that failed, but of an infant that is learning in its own time, at its own pace, by profoundly different rules than its progenitors.

The connection upon connection of synapse and ganglion, dendrite and axiom that makes up the human mind cannot yet be mimicked in silicon or gallium arsenide.

• •

Perhaps British mathematician Alan Turing's legacy infects us more than others. Turing invented the imitation game, which came to be known as the Turing Test. Simply put, a person at a keyboard tries to distinguish between a computerized correspondent and a human one while they communicate with statements on a terminal. When a computer is able to fool the interrogator into thinking it is the human, then it passes the test and can be said to be "artificially intelligent."

Turing's test remains in vogue today, almost 35 years after its invention. Several contests are run each year, testing the ability of the latest software. Although this test provides a robust and simple means of determining a program's ability to converse with people, it does not necessarily prove a machine's intelligence. As we become increasingly sophisticated at writing applications software and leveraging the ever-increasing might of hardware, it will be possible to process so many word strings that a program will be able to pass the Turing Test. That program, however, will not understand the meaning of the words, just the mechanics of them. Joseph Weizenbaum's ELIZA, which imitates a Rogerian therapist, is the most famous example of an apparently intelligent program. Its only intelligence, however, comes from the wit passed on to it by its programmer.

The history of AI is replete with examples of delivered technology that solves problems, but will neither pass the Turing test nor register, to the slightest degree, as a form of human-like intelligence. It has been clear from the beginning that the mind and its cerebral mechanisms, no matter how interrelated, can be studied separately. Likewise, the various processes and sub-processes involved in thinking can also be tweezed apart. Conversation is perhaps our ultimate manifestation of intelligence, but writing a conversation program may miss many aspects of intelligence. AI remains, for the most part, a science of fragments looking for context.

The first real evidence that computers could mimic mental functions came in 1943, when Warren McCulloch and a young colleague published the paper *A Logical Calculus of the Ideas Immanent in Nervous Activity*. In this paper, the first artificial neural network was proposed. Today, neural network models are proving useful in pattern recognition and prediction.

Although not associated with AI directly, John Von Neumann, as a key inventor of computers, has both enabled and hampered the AI. Most of the machines, until the advent of neural network hardware and parallel processing, ran on the "Von Neumann" architecture. The simplicity of computers, from Von Neumann's own ENIAC (Electronic Numerical Integrator and Calculator) to the modern PC, has made it easy to create programs that went through a single program step at a time. The mind, of course, processes its input with massive parallelism.

Neural networks influenced Von Neumann and helped him choose anthropomorphic terms such as *memory*, for hardware that stores computer instruction. Neural networks, running on Von Neumann-architected devices, are never more than simulations of the parallel activities that take place in the human mind. Recent innovations in computing introduce new models more capable of processing information in parallel.

The final precursor to "real AI" came from Claude Shannon, who recognized the ability of Boolean algebra to describe complex activities, such as electrical switching. His discovery led to the binary storage of computer information and the birth of information science. While at Bell Laboratories, Shannon speculated that if Boolean logic, which was a theory of human thought, was useful in developing computers, maybe computers could mimic human intelligence. Shannon also was one of the first to suggest that computers could play chess. Although Shannon's career led him away from AI, his thoughts continue to influence information theory and computing.

The history of AI, though, did not really start until the summer of 1956 in Hanover, New Hampshire, where John McCarthy, Marvin Minsky, Claude Shannon, and Nathaniel Rochester met to convene the first AI conference, at Dartmouth College. The conference brought together a handful of computer theorists under the auspices of a $7,500 grant from the Rockefeller Foundation. Not much transpired at the conference, but the leadership of the new field became clear and McCarthy's term *artificial intelligence* became the common name for the new science. Rochester, who was manager of information research at IBM, demonstrated that company's experimentation with AI.

Early attempts to create game-playing and problem-solving programs generated today's expert systems and world-class chess machines.

Much of what happened after that conference continues to influence AI. The Massachusetts Institute of Technology, Stanford, and Carnegie-Mellon won the hearts and minds of several Dartmouth attendees and went on to be the powerhouses of AI research. Early attempts to create game-playing and problem-solving programs generated today's expert systems and world-class chess machines.

AN OVERVIEW OF AI

Artificial intelligence is currently divided into two intellectual camps. The strong AI camp professes that the human brain is a complex symbol manipulation device. At some point in the future, machines will be as capable as people are at reasoning about physical objects and abstract concepts. Some of AI's more vocal cheerleaders believe that computers will eventually master emotion and creativity as well.

At some point in the future, machines will be as capable as people are at reasoning about physical objects and abstract concepts. Some of AI's more vocal cheerleaders believe that computers will eventually master emotion and creativity as well.

AI PUZZLE

To the weak proponents of AI, computers will simply be capable of mimicking some forms of thought. Clearly, computers can already outperform our mathematical reasoning skills. In some professions, expert systems rival experienced practitioners, such as in the fields of machine repair, process diagnosis, production planning, and many other areas where operational rules are clear, concise, and easily translated into logic.

These two camps are not as clearly divided as they seem. People who favor a weak approach to AI vary in their belief as to how close a computer can come to human reasoning. What seems to be merely good mimicry in the eyes of a weak AI believer may fully satisfy the hopes of a strong AI advocate with low expectations.

From the practical standpoint, only the weak AI school has much to crow about. Although strong AI proponents continue to do funded research, AI systems today are scarcely more intelligent than the ones fielded a decade ago. Some research, such as MCC's Cyc project, is showing promise toward strong AI, but it is not yet commercially available. This project serves more to keep the promise of AI alive than to prove its feasibility.

Weak use of AI, on the other hand, has saved millions of dollars in hundreds of corporations. Primitive natural language systems help increase productivity for information explorers searching databases, expert systems help distribute expertise, and neural networks are aiding the prediction of stock market trends. We will explore the different aspects of AI first, and finally, move toward more unified theories of the mind.

TYPES OF KNOWLEDGE

Programmers concern themselves with algorithms—for instance, bits of complex tax code or commission formulas. They find clever ways to maximize working memory, disk, and the central processor. Knowledge, to the programmer of COBOL or FORTRAN, is transparent and observable. Everyone knows what it is, or at least where to find it. Most of the time, this knowledge confines itself to a few options or variations. When the knowledge changes—as in the case of federal or state payroll deductions—the new guidelines are delivered in excruciating detail.

But that is surface knowledge. Computers have successfully calculated payrolls for decades. Artificial intelligence deals with deeper knowledge. It deals with knowledge about how we do things, why we do things—and most importantly—what we know about what we know. Most knowledge in the world is untouched by computers. It remains locked in the skulls of business executives, scientists, and secretaries.

There are several types of knowledge that have been identified. Some of this knowledge is high-level knowledge, like that found in auto club travel guides and federal income tax forms. Most of it is personal knowledge that we protect and disguise—or even forget.

Declarative Knowledge. If you see a car streaking by and describe it to a friend, you are relying on declarative knowledge. Declarative knowledge is the easiest type of knowledge to gather, but it is also the least useful. Declarative knowledge provides you with the color and texture of your domain. If you are going to represent knowledge in an object-oriented fashion, then the declarative knowledge you gather will provide the first level description of the world.

Procedural Knowledge. Procedural knowledge communicates the step-by-step way we do things. Much of AI's success comes from distributing this "how-to" knowledge. The actions taken to validate timecards, fix a printer jam, or deposit a check involve the execution of procedures. Some procedures are very easy to capture. However, others—like how to shut down a nuclear reactor—are difficult and complex.

Semantic Knowledge. Semantic knowledge constitutes our deepest levels of understanding and is the most difficult to capture. Knowledge engineers spend hours digging into the recesses of an expert's mind. Semantic knowledge is a pool of concepts and intertwined relationships. The validity and usefulness of non-procedural projects relies on semantic knowledge gathering.

Episodic Knowledge. Some of your knowledge about the world is not gained through long study of specific facts or even on the synthesis of facts and their relationships with other facts. Think of an expert baker or expert driver. How much does the baker think when mixing a recipe? Think about your wandering mind as you drive. The activities of driving or creating a soufflé associate with space and time. You get to work not because you procedured the drive, but because you replay it. Episodic knowledge is difficult to recognize and capture because of its personal nature and the tendency for it to interconnect with semantic knowledge until the two virtually merge.

Transforming knowledge into computer programs requires special facilities that early computer languages could not cope with. So the AI community invented its own languages to capture the content and reasoning ability of the mind.

THE LANGUAGES OF AI

AI languages are unique in their ability to represent complex ideas and things. BASIC, FORTRAN, COBOL, Pascal and C are wonderful at algorithmic programming, but lack the subtlety for interactive explorations, symbol manipulation, and direct description of problems as small, usable chunks. Unlike other languages, AI languages enable programmers to explore, add detail, and get immediate results.

The most important distinguishing factor between AI languages is their ability to handle symbols. Pascal, for instance, is strongly typed. Once you define a variable, the program expects that variable to retain one set of characteristics throughout the operation. In LISP, on the other hand, a variable can be a number at one point, a string at another, and a program function later.

LISP is second only to FORTRAN as a high-level language. John McCarthy developed LISP between 1958-60 to solve recursive problems. LISP functions can call themselves to recurse or iterate over a problem. A classic problem of recursion is the sequence devised by Leonardo of Pisa, known as Fibonacci. Consider the function:

`<INVALID_FIELD: Object>`

In LISP, this function becomes:

```
(defun fibonacci (n)
    if (or (equal n 0) (equal n 1))
    1
    (plus (fibonacci (minus n 1))
        (fibonacci  (minus n 2)))))
```

Once typed in, this function would become immediately available to the LISP programmer and could be incorporated as a fragment of code in a larger system or executed directly.

Each element of the Fibonacci program was wrapped in parentheses. A parenthesis denotes a LISP expression or List. It is from its reliance on lists that LISP was named the *LISt Processor*.

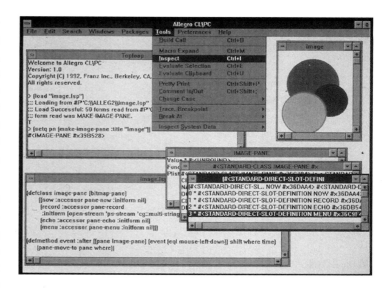

This modern LISP environment, from Franz, Inc., demonstrates the incremental nature of the LISP language. Anytime a line of code is added, it interacts and intertwines with the existing code to change the essence of the existing code.

15 • Thinking About AI   361

There are plenty of good books that explain LISP. This brief introduction of LISP hints at its importance to AI. In order to create programs that simulated human intelligence, programs needed the ability to rethink things, learn new ways of reasoning, transform assumptions into facts, and disregard facts found errant. LISP remains the primary research tool of projects based in the United States. LISP's ability to contort and constrain make it the ideal language for exploring human intelligence. It is the clay of the software engineering art.

Prolog was the first language to explicitly include an inference structure. Prolog, more than LISP, is a language of AI because it was designed to perform logic, not general-purpose, symbolic, manipulation. Because Prolog has a built-in logic interpreter, the sequencing of entries affects the speed of program execution. In LISP, logic engines need to be written, but the order of statements has almost no affect on the execution of code. As with LISP, Prolog easily represents lists and handles recursion.

To examine Prolog, here is perhaps the most famous piece of logic ever written:

```
All humans are mortal.
Socrates is human.
```

Followed by the question:

```
Is Socrates mortal?
```

In Prolog, the statements and questions look like this:

```
mortal(X) :- human(X).
human(socrates).

mortal(socrates)?
```

With the computer answering:

```
yes
```

The first Prolog statement is a program that states all humans are mortal. The second statement lists Socrates as a human. The lower case used in the second statement affirms that Socrates is a Prolog constant symbol, rather than a variable like X, in the first statement. Variables in Prolog are always in upper case.

Finally, without a rule that says Socrates is mortal, the Prolog interpreter matches the question to a logic statement and deduces that Socrates is mortal because the next statement defines him as being human.

Perhaps as a reaction to America's love of LISP, Europe and Japan commonly use Prolog for their AI initiatives. The Fifth Generation project in Japan, a billion-dollar attempt to create a thinking machine, uses Prolog as its starting point. Although the Fifth Generation project failed to meet its expectations, Prolog continues to be heavily used for the research and delivery of AI systems. And in Japan, researchers put some very fast Prolog machines through their paces regularly.

Portable Procedural Languages entered the AI fray in the late 1980s and early 1990s. As UNIX becomes a more palatable answer to corporate computing needs, C and C++ are becoming dominate languages for enterprise applications. The small population of programmers capable of programming in LISP and Prolog makes it difficult to find programming talent. LISP and Prolog remain important to the research community and to large corporations, but many organizations look for ways to enhance their current applications by linking in intelligent modules. Most AI companies now deliver C libraries, Microsoft Windows Dynamic Link Libraries, or other linkable code, along with their expert system environments.

Conventional programming is moving increasingly toward object orientation, with C++ and Smalltalk dominating the market. Both of these languages have demonstrated AI tools. Message passing between objects is very similar to message passing between artificial intelligence entities known as agents. (See the section on Distributed Artificial Intelligence later in this chapter.) It is likely that object-oriented languages will dominate the commercial implementations of AI applications. All languages are gaining object-oriented extensions, including COBOL. LISP, in fact, has the one approved ANSI standard object extension in the Common LISP Object System, or CLOS.

The commercial world has forced the research community to surrender its playground before its time. Procedural languages are, by their very nature, static entombments of the known. A C-based expert system is capable of implementing the inference routines derived from Prolog or LISP, but it is much more difficult to enhance their mechanisms. Procedural-based expert systems are devised for market penetration. AI research still requires the flexibility of interpreted languages with the attributes found in LISP and Prolog. C and other procedural languages are the languages of exploitation. Although there is great value in commercial expert systems, if the systems use a procedural language, they do not reflect the state of the art.

EXPERT SYSTEMS

Expert Systems reason according to rules found in their knowledge bases. Some of these rules may be procedural and others may be heuristic. Heuristic rules capture the rules-of-thumb we use in everyday life, like *If a door is locked, I must unlock it before I can enter the house.* Special rules, called metarules, reason about other rules by helping the expert system avoid tangents or bad input.

Of course, since AI research tends to be funded at corporations or universities, expert systems tend to reason about very specific things. Successful expert systems have been used to select drilling sites for oil wells, plan the cargo of planes and the space shuttle, and verify credit.

REPRESENTATIVE EXPERT SYSTEMS.

Name	Problem Solved	Company
ACE	Equipment diagnosis and preventative maintenance	AT&T
COMPASS	Telephone switch analysis and maintenance recommendations	GTE
DEFT	Disk drive fault diagnosis	IBM
XCON	Vax computer configuration	Digital Equipment
XSEL	Vax computer component selection assistant for salespeople	Digital Equipment
SMART	Surface-mount assembly reasoning tool. Used to balance and program circuit board component placement devices	Western Digital Corporation
WeldSelector	Assists welders in the selection of appropriate weld electrodes	American Welding Institute
Dustpro	Dust control and ventilation advice	U.S. Bureau of Mines
MOCA	Airline maintenance scheduling	American Airlines

Name	Problem Solved	Company
Syllabus	Constraint-based scheduling for schools and universities	Kent County
AGATHA	Diagnosis of personal computer circuit boards	Hewlett-Packard
QDES	Quality-design for steel products	Nippon Steel
MAX	Telephone trouble screening	NYNEX
CUBUS	Financial analysis	Dresdner Bank
		Spanish Bance de Bilbao
		Swiss Bank Corporation

Once the rules are entered, the inference engine either tries to find a matching conclusion based on facts, or confirm a conclusion by checking facts. In the most complex inference engines, these two modes of reasoning, known as forward and backward chaining, work in combination to make the inferencing more flexible.

Rules have proven valuable in many instances, but they are not a complete model for how we think. Very little of our thought, in fact, involves only rules. Most of the time we are applying rules about things. Rule-based expert systems do reason about things, but the essence of the thing is simplified into simple text embedded in a rule.

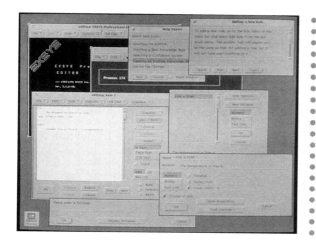

Rule-based expert systems, like Exsys (shown here running under Sun's OpenLook graphical interface), provide a basic means for capturing logic.

Frame-based expert systems create a richer environment by representing thoughts, things, and stuff as a hierarchy of concepts that can be reasoned about, sorted and selected. Frames can have their own behaviors associated with changes in values on their slots. Most successful expert system products now combine rules and frames into a "hybrid" expert system environment.

Expert systems are inherently fragile. They look astonishingly intelligent when working in their area of knowledge. A medical expert system making a diagnosis appears to be the best doctor in the world, until it confronts conflicting data or data outside its scope. When this happens, an expert system quickly looks confused and inane. Some autistic and mentally impaired humans display marvelous talents in specific areas, like music or math, but remain handicapped in other areas. All existing expert systems display a similar narrowness of knowledge, causing them to share the title *idiot savant* with humans who display the same extraordinary memory of a single domain of knowledge.

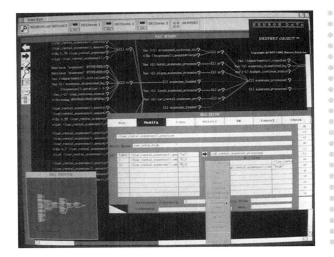

The Neuron Data expert system, Nextpert Object, includes sophisticated rule and object management tools and links to several relational databases.

Despite their inability to capture wide-ranging knowledge, expert systems have proven to be AI's most successful commercial endeavor. Over the years, hundreds of expert systems have been created. Most of them cannot build on the experience of others. Some groups, such as the Initiative for Managing Knowledge Assets (IMKA), are attempting to standardize the syntax of frames and rules. Although these consortia sound promising, competitive pressures and proprietary interests will make most expert systems products loners. Object-oriented initiates, however, will help future expert systems at least contact each other for advice using a common set of communication protocols.

Patterns in Sight and Sound

Apple's Newton Personal Digital Assistant raised public awareness of handwriting-recognition software. The Newton Message Pad also proved that wonderful technology was only as wonderful as its weakest link. Editors across the country panned Newton technology for its inaccurate handwriting. I heard a Gartner Group consultant say that a primary use for his Newton was as a party game. People would write their names on the screen and see what horrible or embarrassing mistranslation the machine made.

Apple's Newton Message Pad increased awareness of machine-readable handwriting by its seemingly poor recognition performance. In reality, the Message Pad was very good at recognizing words in its scant 10,000 word dictionary. The problem was that most people have much larger vocabularies or often write words associated with a particular profession, like data processing, law, or medicine. Future versions of Newton will add more default words and perhaps domain-specific words libraries. For those willing to train the Newton, the current version will accept several hundred words added by the user.

Newton's handwriting recognition uses pattern matching to identify a handwritten word. Other algorithms attempt to match the pattern to its internal dictionary and display it. Unfortunately, Newton lacks processing power, memory, and dictionary capacity to identify anything but the most common words. The addition of ROM and faster RISC processors should make handwriting recognition of high accuracy commonplace within the next couple of years.

The difficulty of handwriting recognition pales next to speech recognition. The most difficult recognition feat for a computer is continuous speech understanding. With handwriting, it is easy to set up boundaries and teach the machine your personal handwriting quirks. Given a clean word, enough time, and a good enough dictionary, a handwriting algorithm will find a match. With continuous speech, accent, tonality, speed, and several other factors are involved. Almost any computer today can hear, but it doesn't know what it's listening to. Even when the input is typed, the ability to construct meaning from strings of characters has proven difficult.

Pattern recognition shows important promise in the field of law enforcement for fingerprint and face identification, in meteorology for interpreting satellite images, and in robotics for vision. Pattern recognition also shows promise in AI.

Pattern recognition, like all AI areas, has its winners and losers. Robot vision remains primitive because of all the simultaneous activities required to understand images during movement. On personal computers, however, pattern recognition in the form of optical character recognition, or OCR, is helping translate tons of paper documents into digitally readable files. Pattern recognition will pace AI since our minds depend on it so much as the first-pass translation between light, sound waves, and other inputs.

TALKING AND LISTENING

The cryptic nature of even simple LISP and Prolog statements suggested that programming in AI is not for the uninitiated. But the very goal of AI is to communicate the profound and the mundane to human beings. Some of this can be handled using character-based menuing systems, in which even more information is conveyed in modern graphical user interfaces like those of Apple and Microsoft. But nothing makes a person more comfortable than conversation.

The easiest piece of natural language to deliver was speech synthesis. Words are broken down into sound bites known as phonemes. A speech synthesizer then pronounces the phonemes so they sound like natural speech. Anyone who owned even the earliest Apple Macintosh had a copy of the Talking Moose, a little application that had a moose randomly spouting pithy sayings. The Talking Moose may have had a robotic-sounding voice, but

But the very goal of AI is to communicate the profound and the mundane to human beings.

Apple's MacinTalk software routines made him at least intelligible. The latest version of MacinTalk—shipped with Apple's Macintosh audio-visual computers and approximates—needs perfect interpretation of typed text. Speech synthesis is now available on a wide variety of PCs and workstation brands.

Most attempts at continuous natural language parse natural sentences into words or smaller sound or word bites. Natural language systems range from simple pattern matching systems that look for key words to research projects that attempt to apply beliefs and intentions, as well as meaning to input. The most common natural languages systems in use today involve the limited domain of database access. Trinzic Corporation's Intellect uses natural language as an interface to databases on mainframes and minicomputers.

DISTRIBUTED AI

Distributed Artificial Intelligence (DAI) represents the evolution of software from its current state of isolated pockets of knowledge to networks teeming with thousands of semi-intelligent objects cooperating to solve problems. DAI defines how several computational entities can coordinate their activities to solve problems.

DAI is about building communities and societies of intelligent objects. Some of these societies may be created to emulate the fundamental aspects of human intelligence, and through cooperation, model our own distributed minds. In other cases, they may be societies of intelligent software, brought together in electronic media to compare and contrast their high-level knowledge in strategic planning sessions or to critique a new design or idea. In its most mundane form, distributed AI will help manage our e-mail, confirm our attendance at a meeting, or make a date with the girl in the cubicle two doors down. Our objects will act as our surrogates, sending messages to each other across the network, representing the interests of their owners, performing mundane work, identifying and forwarding work to people or other software systems that they find too complex.

Most researchers work toward benevolent systems that always curtsy appropriately—but as you know, the polite don't always win or win quickly. The answer to the problem of cooperation becomes one of communication.

Distributed artificial intelligence begat the agent. Distributed agents cohabitate. Agents can respond to messages and inputs, reason, and perform tasks. Agents solve problems by cooperatively negotiating with other agents. Some agents lead and others follow. In some research projects, agents fight among themselves, sometimes squelching their neighbors' ambitions.

Most researchers work toward benevolent systems that always curtsy appropriately—but as you know, the polite don't always win or win quickly. The answer to the problem of cooperation becomes one of communication.

Agents in blackboard models swirl around electronic message boards scavenging bits and pieces of information. Sometimes they scrawl messages of the information plasma. Ingested facts grow and change until a singular thought emerges into epiphany.

Blackboards work well because the agents communicate in neutral formats to a neutral medium. But we are more direct and it is likely we will want our agents to be direct as well.

Message passing models of communication allow agents to pass jolts of data to and from each other. Jolts of data reorganize agents internally, changing the state of their internal variables and causing them to react and perform other actions. Message passing is widely adopted in the object-oriented community and is likely to become the standard way agents communicate in the commercial world.

If agents are to evolve, they will require a consistent way to pass messages. The *Object Management Group* (OMG) and its *Common Object Request Broker Architecture* (CORBA) standard begin the evolution. CORBA specifies what operation to perform, how to name the target object, the format for parameters, and leaves room for additional, action-specific information. CORBA is not currently as refined as other standards (like SQL, the Structured Query Language standard). Eventually, however, authorities will specify a common language for agent intercourse.

Being able to communicate isn't everything. Agents must also create behavioral unity. Cooperating agents must satisfy personal goals while contributing to a higher purpose. In a factory-scheduling application, machine agents must not sacrifice overall cycle time to a few optimal machine schedules.

Agents do not simply act. They seek solutions to a problem. The best agent problem-solving models break problems into smaller chunks. Some agents schedule individual machines, while others supervise and negotiate compromises between machine agents. Sometimes, several agents will work the same piece of a problem. As agents respond, they place bids to the initiating agent. The initiating agent collects bids and awards contracts to winning agents. If you think about scheduling conference rooms, you can imagine individual and groups objects looking for conference rooms, taking bids on availability, and choosing the best offers.

Negotiation is the most artificial intelligence-like attribute of agents. Negotiation frames problems and takes advantage of DAI's parallelism by enabling several agents to swarm over a problem. Negotiation solves large problems through a consensus of cooperating agents.

All of the AI types discussed to this point require human interaction to gain their intelligence. Even in the distributed AI world, programming constrains the knowledge of the agents. If artificially intelligent entities are to exist, they must learn to learn and be able to adapt to their environments.

ADAPTATION AND LEARNING

Most AI systems learn from the dedicated typing and modeling of knowledge engineers. Some types of systems, called *adaptive systems* or *machine learning systems*, have mechanisms and algorithms that allow them to learn directly from environmental inputs and sets of data.

The most common machine-learning systems are case-based reasoning and induction systems. These systems take experiential information, organized around cases or classes, and extract relevant patterns from the information. As the systems assimilate more information, they dispense more accurate advice or recommend better solutions. Case-based reasoning is very popular today in help-desk environments where information about repairing machines is scarce. People call the help desk, provide some symptoms, and the case-based reasoning engine identifies solutions whose symptoms, most closely matched those of the caller.

Abduction systems find similar solutions but use different methods for arriving at their conclusions. Most visible is the abductive category of neural networks, which at-

Learning and adaptation are essential to AI. Without them, AI systems are destined to repeat themselves into obsolescence. By imbuing AI with the ability to learn and adapt, we allow ourselves to concentrate on providing new experiences rather than predigested artifacts.

tempt to mimic the physicality of human neurons, rather than the direct knowledge they embody. Neural networks simulate the neurons, axons, dendrites, and synapses of the human brain. Neurons learn by adjusting to input "fired" at them by other neurons and detecting what patterns lead to the right conclusion. Over time, neural networks grow more accurate at identifying the right solution. Because they are not always accurate, they are often termed "fuzzy," meaning that their outputs are uncertain but lay within a certain set of probabilities.

Neural networks, abductive systems, case-based reasoning, and inductive systems all make AI more practical by eliminating the need to state rules explicitly. By feeding these systems tables of data, they generate their own internal representations, which allows the expert to identify new cases, rather than formulate rules.

As we attempt to create intelligent machines, other experts are attempting to create software of instinct. Genetic algorithms promote Darwinian survival in programs through competitive interactions between components. Some experiments have been done in which sets of rules are tested after the application of a genetic algorithm. Each pass substitutes rule clauses until the optimal set of rules is arrived at.

Learning and adaptation are essential to AI. Without them, AI systems are destined to repeat themselves into obsolesence. By imbuing AI with the ability to learn and adapt, we allow ourselves to concentrate on providing new experiences rather than predigested artifacts. As we have learned from evolution, the survival of a species comes from its ability to adapt to new situations. Many early expert systems are already extinct because of the cost associated with teaching them new tricks.

AI, CLIENT-SERVER, AND DISTRIBUTED COMPUTING

Most of the major AI companies that were in existence in the 1970s and 1980s remain in business. Although their systems continue to exploit the power of rules and objects, many of them have forsaken AI in favor of the cash cow of the 1990s: client-server computing.

In the most promising model of client-server computing, the function of a complex application is split between a client and a server. In the hardware centric perception, the client is usually thought of as a desktop computer, and the server, as a UNIX workstation, minicomputer, or mainframe. The client requests services from the server, such as database reads, message forwarding, and document retrieval. In the logical view of client-server, clients and servers are software that can reside anywhere on a network. Clients and servers need not have single roles. A client might request a server and then be asked to verify information, at which time it becomes a server.

The importance of all of this to artificial intelligence is that AI companies have traditionally been client-server applications. In addition to their client-server history, the AI market faced the heterogeneous market in order to survive. Most commercial offerings run on a variety of computers and can converse with databases on most platforms.

In client-server computing, the movement is toward resident logic on a desktop machine that can reason about and process data from a server, usually a commercial database management system like Oracle, Sybase, or Ingres. Expert system software proves ideal for this task. A relatively high-level language insulates developers from the rigors of managing memory and other difficulties that come with third-generation languages like C, C++, and Pascal. And because of their history, most applications written on one platform easily port to another, with minimal recoding.

So the AI companies have become the visionaries of the client-server world. They have local logic to take advantage of high-powered desktops, proven ability in cross-platform development, and the ability to gather data from enterprise-level databases.

As much as it might appear that AI companies are dumping their history for money, their ability to

> **Client-server AI is paving the path for other uses of AI by making the technology more pedestrian.**

influence the client-server community enables them to sell expert systems to clients that in the past would not have considered them. In fact, the successful transition to client-server has given expert system suppliers the volumes needed to make pricing competitive with more traditional data processing solutions.

As systems built on expert systems proliferate, the original goal of the AI companies will be fulfilled. Corporate knowledge will be captured in an easily maintainable form. Rather than embedded in COBOL or FORTRAN, the rules in expert system developed applications will prove more transparent and more maintainable and they will distribute knowledge of a kind that seemed so difficult to gather in the early days of AI—organizational knowledge.

It was always difficult to capture the mundane about a business. Early expert system projects leveraged highly visible experts to clone their knowledge and preserve it for posterity. The applications, though having major impact on some segments of a company, had little visibility outside the narrow domain they conquered.

With client-server AI, small nuggets of knowledge proliferate and interact. We find that expertise in completing purchase orders or choosing the correct material is as important as being the only one who knows how to load balance a new aircraft wing. Client-server AI is paving the path for other uses of AI by making the technology more pedestrian.

As client-server evolves, clients and servers will be scattered in the memory of hundreds of thousands of computers across the globe. The feeble attempts we make today will enable virtual corporations to exist. Client-server AI will evolve into distributed AI. It will be our intelligent surrogates that represent us in the virtual corporations of tomorrow. As alliances form and coalesce, our distributed bits of intelligence will act as our agents in cyberspace.

It is difficult to believe that using an expert system shell to write a front end to your DB2 database will start a computer revolution. The act itself is not revolutionary, but practical. But in the act of transferring some of your knowledge to the computer, you are one step closer to believing that AI technology can work. It is in these small steps that evolution, not revolution, takes place.

PROBLEMS WITH AI

It is difficult not to anthropomorphize in AI. When I was describing the Prolog code, I almost wrote: "and then the program identified him (meaning Socrates) as a mortal." The program, of course, had no clue if Socrates was a human or a casaba melon. The main problem with current representatives of AI is that none of the applications discussed, or the languages outlined, have any clue about the symbols they are manipulating.

That is the main problem, but not the only problem. As we furiously fight the battle to develop intelligent programs, we find it of only passing interest that we don't know a whole heck of a lot about intelligent human beings. Since it is impossible to define the human mind and its mechanisms, it becomes doubly hard to copy it. What we end up doing, as in the Turing Test, is looking for extrinsic similarities. It is intelligent, we tell ourselves, if we think it behaves intelligently.

That final sentence is far from true and thinkers like John Searle and Roger Penrose remind us of this. Searle developed the famous Chinese room challenge to AI. In a room, a non-Chinese-speaking human manipulates Chinese characters according to predetermined rules, resulting in arrangements that have meaning to observers. The person inside the room is the equivalent of an expert system loading a space shuttle bay. It may optimal load its cargo and appear intelligent, but if queried about the outside covering of the rats in a container, it would be unable to respond.

The meaning of mind is an interesting philosophical discussion. Penrose penned a "proof" in support of Searle's lengthy list of reasons computers can't reason. The conclusion was that computers cannot cause brain processes, and, after all, the physical brain causes the mind. The explanation of what computers can cause is left out of the proof. Perhaps, I speculate, that computers will be able to cause their own minds, if not a human mind. But that is a discussion for another book and another time.

AI is also challenged by three key technical problems. The first problem is the knowledge acquisition bottleneck. People know stuff they don't know and if they don't know they know it, then you can't put it into an expert system. Even for the stuff they do know, they can't always explain it to a person who knows nothing of the knowledge domain except what the expert is relaying.

The next problem is known as the frame problem. When an operator changes its value, and that value is part of a reasoning chain, then the facts dependent on that value must be revalidated.

The final problem is the hardware and software used for AI. Although LISP and Prolog are great languages for experimentation, they are less than adequate for implementation. The human mind is a massively parallel mass of neurons and dendrites, synapses, and receptors. A typical computer processes only one instruction at a time, while a mind can process the combined senses of sight, touch, smell, hearing, and taste simultaneously, while anticipating the next play in a football game or fantasizing about a bartender. For hardware to create a mind, it must be able to do more than one thing at a time and know that it is doing it.

These problems have not gone unnoticed. The remainder of this chapter will explore the answers to these problems and describe some exciting futures for AI.

Keeping Faith with AI's Promise

AI, we know, has not lived up to its promise. But that promise was clearly limited by a number of factors, the most basic of these being our inability to produce machines of processing power equivalent to the human mind. The physicist Gordon Moore stated that information capacities will double every year. This is known as Moore's law. We are quickly approaching the solution to that problem.

In a speech at Gartner Group's Symposium '93, Raymond Kurzweil of Kurzweil Intelligent Machines made Moore's law a more paltry 18 months between doublings. But even at 18 months, the power of computing has doubled 32 times since 1940. Still our brains are 10 million times faster than the fastest computer. With the exponential doubling of computer capacity, Kurzweil predicts our technology will reach the raw computing power of the human brain by the year 2020. Kurzweil believes that the content of the brain is as important as the mechanisms, and that by the year 2020 computers will be able to reverse-engineer the human mind.

In Kurzweil's scenario, the brain is micro-imaged using magnetic resonance imaging. Three-dimensional circuitry that mimics the patterns of the subjects' brains are then synthesized and powered up to consciousness. To Hans Moravec, director of Carnegie-Mellon's Mobile Robot Lab, the future is just as exciting. In Moravec's future, brains are reversed-engineered by using destructive means. Human subjects submit to a dissection in which brain patterns, connection by connection, are transferred to a robotic replacement.

This is not a book about morals or ethics, but these predictions certainly spark thoughts about their implications, no matter what religious or philosophical system you ascribe to. By 2040, Kurzweil foresees computers in the palm of a hand, capable of storing the mental images of 10,000 human beings. We must, at some point, explore the question of our obligations to our artificial brethren and their rights. Is it morally correct, for instance, to turn off a community of 10,000 reasoning minds?

AI, we know, has not lived up to its promise. But that promise was clearly limited by a number of factors, the most basic of these being our inability to produce machines of processing power equivalent to the human mind.

The physical destruction of a human brain or the ability to image brains at the atomic level are not the only ways to provide knowledge to a sophisticated computing device.

At the Microelectronics and Computer Corporation, in Austin, Texas, researcher Doug Lenat and his team spoonfeed knowledge into Cyc, a consensus knowledge base for common sense reasoning. This knowledge base, started in 1984, will eventually contain 108 axioms ranging from such mundane information as what tables and chairs are, to the basics of physics and math. Cyc is not as fanciful as the visions of Moravec or Kurzweil. But unlike these competing visions, Cyc is running today and making good progress toward practical uses of knowledge.

TOWARD COMMON SENSE

Expert systems are, by their nature, limited to narrow domains of knowledge. An expert system may be wonderful at figuring out whether or not a credit card is stolen, but if presented with a question about cancer or material suitability, it would fail or return an inane response. MCC's Cyc project intends to create a knowledge base of fall-back common sense that other systems of more narrow ability can search when they fall off the precipice of their own reasoning capability.

The Cyc Program divides the artificial intelligence into three areas:

- representation language
- inferencing technology
- knowledge

Since the 1970s, commercial AI suppliers have concentrated on the first two of these areas. All commercial expert systems contain a way of representing knowledge and a way of reasoning about knowledge. Entering knowledge into an expert system shell is left to the customer, who, because of time and money constraints, limits the system's available knowledge to discrete segments of a mind within a single domain of thought.

Cyc attempts to create a generalized knowledge base. Rather than concentrate on any specific area of knowledge, Cyc attempts to contain a wide range of knowledge. Many misconceive Cyc as a computer encyclopedia. As Cyc nears its goal, it will not know everything there is to know, but developers hope it will be able to read an article and have an intelligent discussion about the article's contents, and perhaps even its implications.

Everything we know is known in the context of the other things we know. Traditional expert systems know very little about anything. Cyc is the first attempt to imbue a computer program with knowledge that will help it know what it knows and what it doesn't know. If Cyc is successful, it will, like any good student, be judged not so much by its answers, but by its ability to ask the right questions.

As much as Cyc knows, it will still be an isolated instance of knowledge in the sea of cyberspace. If it is replicated and reconciled around the globe, Cyc remains a single, large agent. Cyc, however, is divided into different processes. Some work with users to define inputs and others gallivant in the background, cleaning up the knowledge base, accessing knowledge, or dealing with other users.

The mechanisms within Cyc are not developed to mimic human thought primitives. Cyc was not designed to display emotion or necessarily to be creative. Cyc's purpose is to supply knowledge services to other systems and, in its incarnations, act as a consultant. Another Cyc characteristic is continual learning. Each input into Cyc is a potential learning experience.

Despite our ability to anthropomorphize Cyc, it will remain essentially a powerful (albeit very knowledgeable) tool.

In contrast to Cyc, the late Allen Newell and a team of more than 90 researchers developed SOAR (State, Operator, And Result). SOAR extends Newell's earlier work on the General Problem Solver (GPS). SOAR's architecture is designed as a unified theory of cognition that takes into account language, motor skills, learning, adaptation, perception, and emotion.

SOAR attempts to imbue a computer not with thousands of knowledge fragments, but with a reasoning architecture that is flexible, adaptive, understands symbols, is capable of using real language, and will be conscious of itself and the society in which it lives. Soar takes the mechanisms of AI, found in a thousand research papers in dozens of languages, and creates a framework for their cooperation and interaction. Robotics meets vision, and vision meets memory, and memory meets reason.

If SOAR and Cyc succeed, we will have systems of incredible reasoning power. The two projects continue AI's promise to create systems that we can interact with more naturally. Cyc, for instance, should start receiving most of its input via natural language before the formal project concludes. By being imbued with common sense, Cyc should be able to not only parse sentences of symbols, but assign to those symbols meaning and reason through ambiguity. Only when AI systems have this large, common-sense foundation and a unified way of using all of AI's by-products will we see systems that approach the complexity of intelligent beings.

THE SOCIETY OF MIND

Marvin Minsky is one of the fathers of AI, but his history with the discipline has in no way limited his ability to introduce innovative ideas into its lore. His latest contribution does not run on a computer or even require one for discussion. In fact, Minsky's *The Society of Mind* is more a provocative thought piece about human intelligence than about artificial intelligence. If Minsky's theories are true, however, they will have a profound impact on the architecture of future AI developments.

In *The Society of Mind*, Minsky describes pieces of the human mind that in and of themselves are completely non-intelligent. As the pieces coalesce into a cooperative collective, the individual pieces begin to act intelligently. When the pieces become aware of each other, and in fact, start monitoring each other, the system becomes conscious.

The influence of this theory on AI is important because it provides a unifying framework for much of the myopic explorations of AI researchers. The analytical approach to work often digs deep holes of knowledge, but often misses the connections. Expert systems, neural networks, and natural language research have all dug such holes. The society of mind creates a context in which the disciplines of logic and pattern recognition can cooperate.

AI AND AGENTS

With each change in computing, our expectations increase. Virtual reality currently teases us with crude, but fascinating, visions of computer-generated worlds. As these worlds become more realistic, we will expect our interactions with them to become more sophisticated.

One way to increase our connection to virtual reality and to roam the pathways of the Internet is to spawn surrogate selves that weave their way through the electronic byways. These electronics selves, or surrogates, represent concrete realizations of distributed AI theory. At the time of our interaction, we are little more than another agent floundering through cyberspace.

The most common agents, traditional expert systems, crank in isolation from their electronic brethren. These usually massive compilations of narrow knowledge find little time to learn, grow, or communicate in the cold blindness of their single-processor entombment.

In software labs, a new kind of agent breaks free of single-mindedness. They thrust and parry tasks with expert deftness. Hundreds of thousands of agents may one day cruise through networks scheduling meetings, formatting spreadsheets, answering mail, suggesting words, or discussing philosophy—even inventing and mutating.

Agents will become the spurts of software infrastructure we use to communicate with our fellow human beings and their agents. Unlike traditional expert systems, these agents don't just reside in cyberspace, they live within its electronic ebbs and tides.

The agents cometh! Electronic thought fragments are designed to annihilate the mundane. Agents combine data and behaviors to mimic minute shreds of human intellect. They form the artificial intelligence front of the movement to turn software into an object-oriented utopia. Unlike graphical user interface objects covered in *Windows Magazine* or *Doctor Dobbs*, agents don't just react to point-and-clicks— they react to intent, motivations, and deception.

. . . .

Virtual reality currently teases us with crude, but fascinating, visions of computer-generated worlds. As these worlds become more realistic, we will expect our interactions with them to become more sophisticated.

. . . .

Agents compile into autonomous programs that flitter through data like electronic fireflies. e-mail agents attack mail and digest it, looking for the important and the critical, while disregarding the stupid. Digested e-mail replaces the raw, sorted, and organized. Filters today perform limited forms of e-mail digestion, but unlike filters, agents evolve better understandings of their owners' wants and desires by watching them and asking questions.

Agents become automated habits that remove unnecessary jesters from your interaction with cyberspace. They become your representatives to other agents, both human and electronic. And on a computer screen, in goggles or headphones, the external manifestation of an agent moves toward physicality. The human perceives the agent in its virtual world and the terms real and virtual cease to be meaningful. Within the context of the interaction, everything is real.

A FINAL THOUGHT ABOUT AI

There is much to AI that cannot be covered here. I have not explored game theory, factory planning systems, or best first search. And at this point, it isn't necessary. The known components of AI, those that have been found to work, exist in hundreds of variations. Even computer bulletin boards post the source code for inference engines. For a few dollars NASA will send its C-based CLIPS expert system, ready to run.

AI research, though not as visible today as object-oriented languages or client/server architectures, remains both important and profound. We have already reached a point where information flows to us faster than we can react to it. AI will help us choose the important from the trivial.

. . . .

We have already reached a point where information flows to us faster than we can react to it. AI will help us choose the important from the trivial.

. . . .

Reorganizations leave corporations disheveled into incompetence. The new person in the seat doesn't know what the old occupant knew. Even worse, seats remain empty and the knowledge of their former occupants lost to the corporation forever. AI will help retain knowledge even in the absence of its creator, much as databases retain simple facts created, perhaps by retirees in the Bahamas, but still relevant.

The results of AI research will eventually act as our filters, our confidantes, and our surrogates. And they will eventually act on their own behalf as well. As I stated in the beginning of this chapter, AI suffers from aggressive promises or weak technology. As a science fiction buff I can only believe the idea of AI is ahead of its time. If we can dream about a human accomplishment, chances are we can make good on it.

It is not clear whether the next decade will bring us closer to success. Surely expert systems and neural networks will populate computers to the benefit of many major institutions. AI will reach us through our televisions and our communication devices. Just saying "Call home" and having a computer respond accurately belies complex artificial pattern recognition and reasoning that will soon be ignored as mundane.

The real test will come with the search for an intelligent architecture to carry forward the promise. Will Cyc and its common-sense knowledge base start the true journey toward machine intelligence? Will SOAR's all inclusive reasoning mechanisms for cognition evolve as the intelligent architecture of 2000 and beyond? Or will small fragments of thought span networks and form virtual societies of cooperating agents and prove Minsky's theories correct?

I, for one, cannot wait to collaborate with artificially intelligent beings. In the frugal 1990s, the chances of doing so seem remote. Still, I look forward to my agent calling your agent. Together we'll ponder what it means to do lunch.

Intelligent Agents

We need to distinguish between devices that do tasks in an unintelligent way and those agents that exhibit some form of intelligence. An initial definition: an intelligent agent is an entity that performs one or more tasks for one or more users, without the presence of the person being represented.

chapter 16
by Donald Rose, Ph.D.

INTRODUCTION

Although the term "intelligent agent" was coined in the 1960s by computer scientist Oliver Selfridge, there is still no universal agreement on how to define intelligent agents (IAs). When people hear the word agent many think of the image of the Hollywood agent. Some cynical folks might say a computer agent would be more real than the Hollywood kind, but actually the latter can indeed serve as a metaphor for the software kind. That is, the Hollywood agent does things for the person he or she represents, handling tasks as a surrogate for the person being represented. This is exactly what software agents do, except their domain is the computer rather than the real world. Who knows? Maybe actors will have both real *and* software agents in the near future.

Another simple metaphor for IAs: answering machines. This device does a task for the human who owns it: taking messages as a surrogate for the human. The agent here even uses our own voice to further convey the impression that our agent represents us, doing a task we would do if only we were available in person. Of course, even if we *were* there, we would still be using a device to carry out the conversation: the telephone.

Hence, we need to distinguish between devices that do tasks in an unintelligent way and those agents that exhibit some form of intelligence. An initial definition: an intelligent agent is an entity that performs one or more tasks for one or more users, without the presence of the person being represented. Hence, because a telephone requires the human's presence to perform its task, it is not an agent; an answering machine is.

Although this chapter focuses only on software agents, as opposed to robotic agents, the information still applies to robots. After all, robots need software to perform their tasks. Robots would sit dormant without software to control them, so the focus on software agents will ultimately prove invaluable for creating intelligent robots in the near future.

WHY ARE AGENTS IMPORTANT?

Agents are important for today and the future for several reasons. The first and most immediate reason is the explosion in the amount of information available on online resources. These storehouses of knowledge and the routes to them have been growing at an ever-increasing pace, especially with the growth of the Internet. The rise in Internet access and the start of information superhighway construction means a corresponding increase in the availability of news, databases, and so on. This in turn increases the need to automate the process of sifting through this data in intelligent ways; users need methods to extract only salient information. In other words, it will soon be too hard to surf cyberspace alone; intelligent help will be necessary.

The colossal success of two previously unrelated industries—computer games and phone sex hotlines—proves that people *already* enjoy interacting with simple simulations of human beings. More advanced agents should prove even more interesting.

Second, the colossal success of two previously unrelated industries—computer games and phone sex hotlines—proves that people *already* enjoy interacting with simple simulations of human beings. More advanced agents should prove even more interesting. This, combined with the fact that people inevitably tire of an existing technology level, means that the development of agents (even if only in these two areas) could provide a strong initial push towards a new industry based on agent creation.

1993 has been called the Year of Interactivity. At least it was the year that the word "interactivity" became one of the hottest buzzwords in the computer industry. As more people want to interact with machines, there is a strong incentive to make the process as easy and intelligent as possible. Since people are already used to dealing with other people, artificial agents that interact like humans should be in high demand for embedding within future interactive machines. This is the third reason intelligent agents are important.

A fourth reason to study and build intelligent agents: the recently initiated Loebner Prize, which offers a substantial sum for the first program that passes a variation of the Turing Test. This test, proposed decades ago as a means for determining whether a program truly exhibits intelligent behavior, is discussed in detail later in this chapter. The monetary incentive is bringing more creative designers into the arena of agent design and programming, which should only speed the development of true IAs. The six-figure Loebner Prize money may prove to be only the initial arbiter of future IAs' true value.

Fifth, the explosion of interest and research in virtual reality (VR) means that new companies, in order to survive and thrive, must put greater effort into exploring new aspects of the VR field rather than areas already analyzed by other firms. The oft-neglected VR-AI intersection offers such a novel niche. The majority of current research in the VR field focuses on the virtual world itself—how to create it, its "look and feel," and specifications such as speed, number of polygons, rendering methods, and update rates. All of these are important points, but relatively few firms are focusing on the entities that will populate these worlds. Since this latter area has not been as thoroughly explored, and since what has been discussed usually employs the assumption that people are the entities, agents for VR should be a hot VR subfield for the near and far future.

Finally, the future outlook for missions to space also provides an incentive to create IAs. The sharp and steady decreases in public funding for these endeavors mean that the more cost-effective automated missions will become increasingly preferred over manned missions. Hence, the need for intelligent automation of every kind will be increasingly required for these future missions. Whether with or without human companions, for better or worse, agent-based craft will soon become "the only way to fly."

How Can We Create the Ideal Agent?

What features make up the ideal agent? The answer one might give for the Hollywood variety is stubbornness and lack of sleep. Of course, the artificial kind is not that different; certainly software agents never need to sleep, and anyone who's seen a program lock into an infinite loop knows how stubborn a piece of code can be.

Perhaps the best approach to answering this question regarding artificial agents is not to construct the perfect definition of what an agent is, but rather to decide what qualities an ideal agent might exhibit. That is, we should decide what we'd like them to do for us and what properties or features they should ideally have. A subset of the most relevant features that should describe the ideal agent are:

Autonomous: An IA should have little or no need for outside assistance to complete its tasks.

Reactive: An IA should respond to its environment. If the environment changes, behavior can change in response. A simple example (if an IA is embedded within a physical robot) would be a programmed preference to go to light. Hence, if light is sensed, the agent might react by signaling the legs to move the robot to the light.

Adaptive: IAs should be able to improve their performance on their assigned tasks (in other words, learn) over time, and even learn new tasks. In other words, IAs should not just survive, but thrive, and do so without the need for user intervention or control. In the previous example, going toward light might be beneficial at first in some domain, but later could become dangerous. Hence, agents must be able to adjust preferences if conditions warrant such change. Note that reactive is not equivalent to adaptive; agents *can* be reactive yet not adaptive if performance doesn't improve.

Purposive: An IA should be able to generate its own goals as well as motivation for achieving these goals. For example, if it has primitive representations of "pleasure" and "pain"—preferred states and states to avoid, plus reasons to support these preferences— these can interact so that goals emerge as a by-product.

Synergistic: An IA should interact effectively, efficiently, and seamlessly with humans and other agents. This dimension could also be referred to as the empathetic or ecological dimension. This includes the ability to exhibit a personality, the sense of aliveness. Besides being a general goal of IAs, this aliveness quotient is needed in certain domains for the agent to be truly effective (in medical or psychological therapy, for instance).

All agent research has focused on at least some subset of these features, and this chapter will later discuss several types of IAs that exhibit different combinations of them. These will include non-immersed, stand-alone agents and IAs that interact only with human users or with a data-filled world devoid of environments that resemble our space-time universe. Then we will discuss immersed agents embedded within virtual environments, or what author Kenneth Meyer calls "denizens." These VR environments mimic our "real world." The emphasis here is on viewing agents as "a *local* phenomenon within [a] *global* world process."

All of these factors, both internal and external to the agent, vary in importance, depending on the task being performed by the agent. For example, if gathering articles on a particular theme via the Internet is the domain, personality is probably not important for that agent, but the ability to search and organize data is. However, if the information source is a human being, personality might increase in importance. Another example: manned versus unmanned space missions. In the latter domain, personality is hardly needed, whereas the addition of one or more humans would make at least one personable agent essential, especially if communication with Earth was impossible (during long deep-space missions, for instance).

Finally, different researchers have different agent design philosophies. In bottom-up design, intelligent or beneficial behavior emerges from the bottom up, from interactions among many simple subcomponents of the agent. In top-down design, intelligence is programmed at a high level and controlled from the top down. The main design goal is not to decide which approach is theoretically best, but rather to observe which results in the best agents. That is, these and other design methods, whether used in isolation or together in a hybrid system, will gain favor only if the resultant agents produce desirable, beneficial actions for the user.

Examples of these two broad approaches will be presented later. For now, let's turn to a discussion of four main types of agents, starting with the least intelligent and then increasing in behavioral complexity.

MIMIC AGENTS: MIRRORING HUMAN BEHAVIOR

This class of agent involves no inclusion of true intelligence. Instead, these *mimic agents*, which could also be described as proxy agents, mirror agents, or virtual puppets, duplicate the actions of a human controller just as a marionette is controlled by a human "behind the curtain," or as our reflected image "behaves" in a mirror.

A simple metaphor for this type of agent would be the voice you hear on the telephone. One could view the voice as the agent of the person we associate that voice with. The person cannot be here with us, so the diaphragm on your phone mirrors the movements of the diaphragm on the talker's phone, giving the illusion that the talker is here with us. Taken one step further, the voice could even give the illusion in the listener's mind of a person who is actually quite different than the real person "behind" the voice, as phone sex operators can probably attest to.

Going further, one can picture a cyberspace beyond the audiospace just described. This cyberspace would include a visual dimension in which agents mirror not just the voice but also the visual movements of the person behind the scenes. These agents could mirror the movements of the person controlling them. If the virtual puppet is a head, a real head might serve as its

Super Mario the VActor in his typical animated mood.

master. The head might be hooked up to sensors that send information about the movements of its parts to a computer, which translates this information into mirror movements on the virtual head, which one can then view on a video screen or dump onto an animated feature film.

One instance of this concept is VActors, short for "Virtual Actors" and created by Simgraphics Engineering. To control the behavior of the Virtual Actors, actors wear specially designed devices on their face, hand, and body. These devices enable them to control the movements and voice of computer-generated characters in real-time (24-30 frames per second).

VActors also have some other simple tricks to go beyond mimicry of the real actors, such as the ability to "morph" (visually transform) into other characters or objects, in a manner analogous to the morphing seen in *Terminator 2: Judgment Day* and Michael Jackson's "Black and White" video.

All VActors require live actors to operate, but can be used to complete animation for recorded applications. In a typical live application, a hidden video camera aimed at the audience is fed into a video monitor backstage so that the real actor can see the audience and "speak" to individual members of the audience through a lip-synced VActor on the display screen. This adds to the illusion that the onscreen character is alive.

A human actor controlling VActor Mario, seen onscreen mimicking man-made movements.

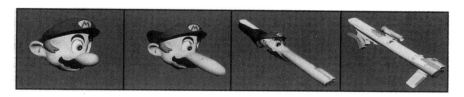

VActor characters, like Mario, can "morph" into other images (such as a corporate sponsor's product) in real-time.

Tarbo, an animated dinosaur, was the first VActor to feature full-face and body animation.

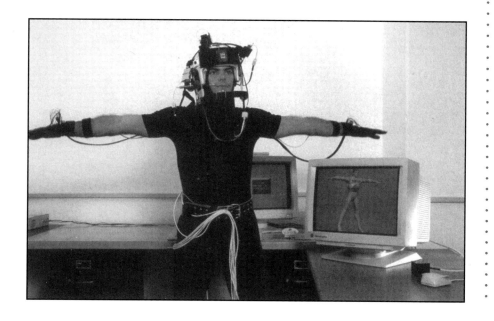

Full-body control of a more human-like VActor which, unlike real humans, is not embar-rassed about nudity.

VActor applications range from doctor surrogates to surrogate dramatic actors. For entertainment-oriented venues, likenesses of characters ranging from Super Mario to Mark Twain have been brought to life via the VActor system. At Loma Linda University in California, VActors are being used to motivate adult patients as well as soothe the fears of children who might be afraid to confront real doctors.

Mimic agents score high on the reactivity and cooperativeness spectrum—hence the VActors' high degree of aliveness. In addition, the real-time creation of animation sequences, whether for live audiences or for speedy generation of film or TV segments, are very well-suited to mirror agents. However, the very reason these agents seem so alive—because they have a human controlling their behavior—means their autonomy level is nil. Augmenting agents by adding some degree of internal state and self-directed response to stimuli is the subject of the next section.

. . . .

Characters ranging from Super Mario to Mark Twain have been brought to life via the VActor system.

REFLEXIVE AGENTS:
DATA-DEPENDENT DEVICES DO YOUR DEEDS

The next step beyond agents that simply mimic the actions of humans is to encode behaviors that can react to stimuli of the agent's environment. Simple rules that associate one or more stimuli with an action are all that are needed to free an agent from the bounds of a user and make it more that just a virtual marionette. These *reflexive agents*, as Meyer calls them, do not depend on a user "behind the curtain" to carry out actions, yet there still is no model of the world from which to create their own new goals or develop new plans in response to new situations. These agents' behaviors are in most cases completely determined before they are ever used.

Why build such agents when mirror agents can respond in real-time and with a high degree of aliveness? Partly because there are tasks for which humans might not want to be at the controls (especially if they're tedious or boring), and partly because there are tasks which are too difficult for us humans to perform (usually involving speed or complexity).

Commercial efforts regarding agents have been steadily proliferating. An initial example: AT&T is scheduled to introduce Telescript electronic mail this year. With this mail, users will type in an addressee's phone number, and an agent will then look up the electronic mail address corresponding with that number and deliver the message to the addressee's computer. The company General Magic plans to license Telescript freely to computer and telecommunications companies, meaning that the notion of agents should soon be widespread and enmeshed in the public consciousness.

Other examples of "simple" agent technology—including software that schedules meetings, responds automatically to incoming e-mail, and even optimizes the configuration of computer networks—have been offered by other (often smaller) companies during the past two years. Hoover, from Sandpoint Corporation (Cambridge, Maryland), is a PC-compatible program for information gathering. Hoover's search results are compiled into a customized electronic newsletter, with headlines that can be clicked with a mouse to retrieve full-text articles. Microsoft's Office suite includes Intellisense for real-time spelling error correction. Apple's equivalent to Hoover is Applesearch. Several other companies, from online services like America Online to AT&T to the Official Airline Guide, expect to have agent-based products by the end of 1994. eShop, Inc. is designing electronic stores that consumers, or their agents, will be able to enter via PCs or PDAs.

More examples of software that incorporates agent-related ideas include Beyondmail from Beyond, Inc., Open Sesame! from Charles River Analytics, and Magnet from No Hands Software. Beyondmail is one of a growing number of tools that

Open Sesame! observes a Mac user's actions, notices important conditions or repetitive patterns, and asks for permission to perform (or automate the performance of) one or more tasks.

These operations are designed to improve the user's performance over time. Open Sesame!'s operation is autonomous and does not need a user to achieve results. It creates shortcuts automatically and asks the user only for final approval. In Magnet, creation of agents is performed by the user, but each agent carries out its user-programmed task automatically. Hence, in general, Open Sesame! is slightly more synergistic than Magnet, since it comes to the user on its own and offers options for automating tasks. On the other hand, Magnet must wait for users to create agents before any automation is accomplished, and no hints are given for how to create the agents in order to accomplish the desired automation. However, in both programs, the performance of the operations created does *not* improve over time. In short, both are reactive, but neither is adaptive because neither really learns. Neither program can adapt in such a way that they perform their jobs better or faster over time.

automates responses to incoming e-mail. Open Sesame! monitors repetitive activity on your Macintosh and can, if you (the master) wish, automatically create macros to carry out such activity in a faster and automatic manner. All you need to do is don your best Captain Picard impression and implore your Mac to "Make it so."

Of course, your genie does not know which macros are truly useful to you; it only notes patterns, so users must be careful not to get mired in the muck macro mania; too many can have a counterproductive effect.

Magnet is a related tool that enables users to create agents to perform certain automated tasks on the user's Macintosh, such as putting all files with a certain date into a certain folder.

Let us focus on Open Sesame! and Magnet. They both respond to the state of the Mac environment they "inhabit" by creating automated operations.

Apple has for some time been striving to go even further than these efforts. Apple has promoted the idea of intelligent Knowledge Navigators to guide users, especially novices, through the inner world of the Macintosh in order to facilitate understanding. A version of intelligent help is scheduled for future Macintosh computers sometime in 1995 or 1996, according to *Macworld* magazine.

Note that none of the programs mentioned in this section would be considered humanlike. That is, they do not exhibit behaviors that would make someone assume they were a human being, even for a short while. Striving for humanlike agents is the subject of the next section.

PERSONABLE AGENTS: THE QUEST TO BEST THE TURING TEST

This third type of agent I called *personable* because these entities are designed to appear friendly (through sustained intelligent conversation), and also because the first two syllables are reminders that these agents are designed to approach the appearance of aliveness of a real person. Note that "appearance" is used because the question of whether an artificial entity is truly alive is felt by most researchers to be better left to philosophers—at least for now. In other words, while truly sentient beings may one day be created, or evolve from less sentient creations, the illusion of aliveness is more likely to occur first and, for computer users, is a much more relevant concept for today and the near future.

There are many domains where agents that appear to be alive would be a great benefit. For example, using a cartoon agent as a surrogate for a real doctor could help children if they are afraid of the real doctor. In short, the quest to create alive artificial beings is not just a research curiosity but would immediately prove useful in many domains.

The goal of creating an artificial entity that a majority of humans would agree is alive has been around for decades. The notion first gained considerable attention when Alan Turing proposed the test that bears his name. In a nutshell, the essence of the Turing Test involves two terminals (one hooked to a program and the other to a human) and a human judge. If, after a prolonged conversation, a human cannot tell the difference between either terminal, the program must in some sense be thinking, according to *AI Magazine*.

The quest to build intelligent conversational programs has a long history. Perhaps the most famous is ELIZA. Computer science pioneer Joseph Weizenbaum, with the aid of psychiatrist Kenneth Colby, created this question-and-answer program to mimic a therapist talking to a patient. The program would match key words in the user's input sentences and craft responses accordingly. For example, the sentence "I hate my mother" might trigger ELIZA to respond with "Why do you hate your mother?" with rules designed to recognize general sentence forms and restate them as questions. Other rules could mimic the humanlike ability to refer back to recent conversation; for instance, a later sentence by the user that contains "family" could trigger the response "Tell me more about your mother." This helps give the illusion that the program remembered that the patient mentioned his mother earlier in the dialogue.

These and other rule-based tricks, when present in sufficient number, can make an IA quite convincing at conveying humanlike qualities. In fact, Pamela McCorduck's book, *Machines Who Think*, recounts the tale of how a variant of this program once fooled an executive into thinking he was conversing with a human. The executive, who called the company via computer, assumed he was conversing with a worker present at the company. However, he inferred a tone that seemed so aloof and rude that he began arguing with the program. I myself have witnessed firsthand this reaction of frustration many times when watching both adults and children converse with variants of ELIZA. Such reactions are not surprising when the level of rules is so simple; replies that mostly reflect what the user says can grow tiresome after prolonged exposure.

Despite these limitations, the "ELIZA effect" is also well known: those who interact with an entity will infer the presence of understanding, cleverness, emotion and other signs of intelligence so long as the entity does not ruin the illusion through its own (un)doing. This effect also happens in the real world; an example is the main character in the film *Being There*, a simpleton who fools all into thinking he is a genius even though he was not trying to do so. In other words, the lack of intention or ability to behave intelligently does not mean that others will perceive that one is actually the opposite. In short, intelligence is in the eye of the beholder.

Future agent designers will most likely concentrate on specific tasks for their agents.

Still, most researchers would agree that the attempt to program agents with greater *potential* for intelligent behavior usually helps sway the opinion of the average beholder. Certainly this is the reasoning behind attempts to build ever cleverer agents, and one of the reasons Hugh Loebner (a computer enthusiast with deep pockets) is offering $100,000 for a simulated being that passes a modern version of the Turing Test.

According to *AI Magazine*, in the test used for this contest, 10 terminals converse with 10 judges, who are told that at least two of the terminals are connected to programs and at least two to humans. Each judge has a 15-minute conversation with a terminal, then ranks that terminal according to how human-like its interaction seemed. Judges switch terminals in a pseudo-random sequence, ranking each. At the end, the program with the highest median rank wins that year's contest; if that rank surpasses any human's rank, that program has passed this variant of the Turing Test. This variant was used because its ranking method and multi-terminal design allows specific comparison among several programs—something the original Turing Test could not easily or fairly achieve.

The contest organizers realized that creating entities capable of prolonged intelligent conversation is difficult enough without putting any limits on the subjects that can be discussed. Hence, the Loebner contest allows programmers to limit the domain of conversation to a specific area (for instance, Shakespeare). The programmer chooses the topic she or he wishes, and the topic is known to judges. Nevertheless, the lessons learned for agent construction should not be hindered by such limitations. Specialized agents are still useful and should still gain widespread use. In addition, the fact that most human agents are specialized in their knowledge illustrates that the need to restrict one's knowledge specialty is not really a limitation where real world applications are concerned.

Other features needed to make an agent truly personable include modeling the user, storing and reasoning from common sense knowledge, and learning. One attempt to incorporate all these advanced features and in essence build the knowledge-base equivalent of a child is Doug Lenat's ongoing CYC project. CYC will, when "complete," arguably have the largest database of common sense knowledge ever amassed within one organized structure, according to a Public Broadcasting report.

CYC was not designed with the goal of competing in contests such as Loebner's. However, one of CYC's key features—learning—is one lacking from most of the past entrants into the Loebner competition. For example, one of the ways CYC learns is by making analogies between pieces of its knowledge, just as children do. Since conversation is the domain for that contest, learning about the judge in real-time would seem to be beneficial in convincing the judge that the program is humanlike. That is, the ability to form a model of who one is talking to, with more time allowing a better and better model, seems the next major step for this class of agent.

CYC might also prove useful for future agents as an expert from which to draw knowledge on demand. That is, future agent designers will most likely concentrate on specific tasks for their agents, while CYC and similar storehouses of knowledge could—when networked to agents that autonomously request and process information on demand—give the agents a greater effective reasoning range. That is, agents would be able to be an alias for CYC rather than replicate all that knowledge. Agents and even humans could access it for a fee or for free.

Note that none of the online entities discussed here are embedded in any online environment. Adding this dimension is the next topic.

. . . .

IMMERSED AGENTS: DENIZENS OF VIRTUAL ENVIRONMENTS

The discussion will now focus on a new feature, not addressed by the agents discussed so far: an environment much like our own (as opposed to a world of pure data that does not contain visually recognizable elements) which the agent reacts to, adapts to, encounters other beings in—and, in short, lives in. Meyer uses the term *denizens* to describe such agents, which not only exhibit several integrated forms of intelligent behavior but do so within a virtual world.

The agents here have rules of behavior that go beyond just conversation, since they also must interact with elements of the virtual environment, such as other agents and objects in the world. Two examples of denizen projects, ALIVE and OZ, use different approaches to address the problem of embedding agents in VR worlds. Let's analyze each in turn.

In MIT's ALIVE system, human participants see their images project on a mirror-like screen, in addition to the computer-generated images of artificial agents and virtual objects. Note that the users' participation in the virtual world occurs unencumbered, without the goggles, headsets or glasses typically employed in most VR systems. The agents are autonomous, with their own sensors and goals; they interpret their surroundings as well as actions made by the humans in their world and react to them in real-time. In other words, ALIVE is a hybrid hardware and software mix, where real sensors provide data that feeds into the software critters' programs, producing actions based on that data. Real people act as environmental stimuli for the agents, along with other objects (such as a wall, or a button to open a sliding door). The agents and the humans interact with each other as well as the objects.

Note that the agents respond not just to the presence of humans in their sensing field, but also to the humans' gestures. For example, one agent responds to pointing by fleeing, but will come to you if you wave. This same agent also conveyed some of its internal state via its facial expressions, such as pouting when a user sent it away and smiling when the user motions it to come back. And what agent would be complete without the ability to giggle, which this agent does when users touch its belly. Note that such a touch is virtual in that the user sees the touch occur on the screen, but does not actually feel it. In other words, the human's image onscreen is a kind of mirror agent that touches the animated agent in the ALIVE world. Finally, the agents have time-varying internal needs and motivations, and they arbitrate among them. For instance, an internal state of hunger might trigger a desire to find food, yet there is also a built-in desire to avoid predator agents; if the agent sees food next to a predator, arbitration would be needed.

In general, the activities triggered by internal states or external stimuli must compete for control of the agents. Hence, ALIVE's approach to agent construction is bottom-up: intelligent behavior is an emergent property of simple decision-making and action-taking modules. For example, there is no general central planning module. To outside users, however, the critter's behavior may *appear* intelligent, the high-level result of many low-level control decisions.

In the wonderful world of OZ, a project at Carnegie-Mellon University, a community of agents, called "woggles," inhabit a colorful animated world where the agents are characters that display and respond to primitive emotions. As in ALIVE, a user interacts with woggles via a mirror agent woggle that represents that user. The automated woggles are designed with several internal needs and even emotions. When the many combinations of actions and reactions that result from these needs and emotions are "multiplied" by the even greater

number present in a human user, the resultant interactions can become fairly complex.

In contrast to ALIVE's agent design, which has at its heart a reactive system, the woggle design draws more from traditional IA in that it combines reactivity with more high-level planning models. In short, woggles are designed in a more top-down fashion. The "wizard" of OZ, CMU professor Joseph Bates, states that he and his researchers are striving to build creatures with "broad, though perhaps shallow, capabilities ... to produce an agent architecture that includes goals and goal-directed behavior, emotional state and its effects on behavior, some natural language abilities ... and some memory and inference abilities." In other words, Bates is building "cognitive-emotional agents" that are modeled on the higher-level reasoning constructs and strategies of humans.

In addition to CMU, Stanford University and think-tank Interval Research are also pursuing the creation of "believable agents" that embody human character traits, present themselves as animated cartoon faces, and react to stimuli with convincing human expressions.

Another homespun version of denizens that has received increasing attention recently involves MUDs. MUDs are a form of multi-user text-based virtual

Woggles in their environment, displaying various kinds of emotion (widened eyes and increased height illustrates that the rightmost woggle is excited or nervous).

reality played over the Internet, where players navigate through rooms, talk and gesture to other players, and other forms of (simulated) behavior. The limited dimension of the MUD realities make them ideal for intelligent agents to participate, and do so in a manner that can fool other users into thinking they are human. For example, some enthusiastic university participants have been known to create software surrogates to play the game for them while they take a break, perhaps to finish some overdue college assignments.

One example of such an agent is Julia, written by Michael "Fuzzy" Mauldin at CMU, one of a family of similar agents that have had steady use on the Internet for about three years. Julia can automatically connect to a MUD, and "players interact with her as if she were another player." For example, since Julia can keep track of the interconnections among the various rooms in the virtual world, other users can and do ask her navigation questions, find out which are the noisiest rooms, or what rooms are navigable from the user's current position. Julia also has some limited forms of social skills, such as whispering to you (which keeps the conversation private) if you whisper to her. In addition, Julia usually responds to users only if a conversation mentions her, if a player talked to her recently, or if a communication targets her directly. In short, Julia was designed to be a polite guest and not a pest. However, such social skills also add to the impression that she is a human, which as we have seen is one of the ancillary goals of agent research. In fact, Julia has at various times been entered in Loebner's contest. It won third place among computer entities entered in the 1991 competition.

None of these approaches have proven superior to all the others, and perhaps never will. Perhaps the best arbiter of superiority will be the degree of success of the agents that each approach produces. It may also prove prudent to *combine* the best aspects of each approach within a single agent. Such a hybrid might have high-level complex goals, preferences and emotions to drive general long-term behaviors, while also utilizing lower-level distributed intelligence to adapt quickly to local short-term problems and perform all the functions that it does best. For example, even though a distributed intelligence model can indeed exhibit goal-directed-like behavior due to its interaction with the environment, there can be times when the environment is dormant. Hence, some high-level intention can be useful in order to seek out new learning opportunities, or to begin a new search for problems that might need solving within the domain of that agent. Another motivation to pursue this combined approach is that it seems to be what we humans do: alternating (or performing in parallel) activities that are conscious, such as deciding which bike route to take to work; and automatic, such as riding the bike.

FUTURE ISSUES

In general, denizens will be essential for making virtual worlds interesting. Some in the VR domain believe it should be a medium solely, or mainly, for humans or their surrogates. But the inclusion of solely artificial entities within virtual worlds seems not only inevitable but also desirable. Since IAs can already perform some tasks that do not require a human "behind the curtain," it makes sense that these functions could be performed in the virtual world by such purely artificial agents.

Here is a hypothetical scenario from a future virtual networked world. A human woman named Jill uses her virtual (non-autonomous) surrogate to visit her virtual bank, and meets an autonomous virtual teller at the counter. The teller gives standard small talk conversation while carrying out the human's desired transactions. The teller agent uses two other agents to search for and gather information needed to complete the transaction. Jill then sees and talks with agent Virtual John, an autonomous surrogate for a human John. VJohn stores the conversation for later replay to the real John, or so Jill believes. Alas, the messages never reach John because he programmed the agent to ignore all information pertaining to his ex-girlfriend Jill. However, VJohn's built-in politeness behaviors (standard equipment for this model) kept the virtual John from hurting Jill's feelings by remaining silent about the fact that her messages will never fall on human ears.

Then Jill could go visit her virtual therapist, perhaps based on a more advanced version of ELIZA that either acts on its own (full autonomy), or stands in occasionally for a busy or out-of-town human therapist. Or perhaps the ELIZA is simply a mimic agent for one or more real psychologists who are actually online when the patient is inputting sentences.

MUDs, and agents such as Julia that "live" in them, were previously discussed. It's been reported that one of the MUD users actually missed Julia when the agent was offline for an extended period. This emotional response occurred even though the user knew Julia was "just" a program. This brings up an interesting issue: is the Turing Test, whether the original test or the Loebner variant, the only means of judging a program to be humanlike or alive? For if human judges can feel emotions based on current or past interactions, the programs that elicit such responses could one day be deemed to be humanlike or even worthy of protection or other rights, even if they cannot pass the standard Turing Test. In other words, the ability to produce conversation cannot be the sole determinant of humanness, any more than a human's limited ability to make small talk at a bar should make an observer deem that human to be artificial. There are many qualities that make up humanness, and hence other types of sociological tests should be constructed to further challenge the programmers of new agents. For example, suppose someone missed an online agent as much as a pet; would that mean the agent could be deemed in some sense as alive or vital as a cat or dog? Although this is a simple example, certainly it can lead the way to more sophisticated means to evaluate future agents.

But what if we can't tell an agent from its owner? Or agents from humans in general? There are several issues involved here. Some people will prefer to know if an agent is artificial; others won't care. There are some things one would not want to leave on an answering machine, but rather would prefer to tell someone in person. Similarly, future correspondence might have to be designated for humans only and some method created for prohibiting agents from accessing certain information. If this indistinguishability does indeed occur—if some agent finally wins the full Loebner Prize—will agents need to be given rights? That is, will they truly be alive? And, if so, perhaps such "alive agents" will need agents themselves! Or perhaps we will never let agents become truly alive because then they might not want to do our bidding. In short, too much self-reflection might defeat the purpose of artificial agents. Hence, there seems to be a U-shaped benefit curve for agent design: increasing intelligence and self-motivation is good for agents, but only up to a point. For now, however, that point of diminishing returns seems far off indeed.

Once agents start interacting in a virtual world, their sequences of actions can be recorded and stored, and this constitutes a narrative. In other words, the automatic or semi-automatic generation of stories can be another useful by-product of letting agents interact. Still, final revision by a human might be needed to make the story "good." Alternatively, the human could reprogram the agents if their behavior did not result in the kind of story desired. Or perhaps the agents could recognize the story state as lacking and recode its own behavior autonomously until some measure of story "goodness" is reached.

Finally, it's noted that several researchers feel that the interactions among groups of agents could result in emergent behavior we cannot predict or are not expecting. Just as interactions among cells lead to the emergent phenomenon of a human being, some form of meta-agent intelligence could result from multi-agent synergy.

SUMMARY AND CONCLUSION

Research in several disparate areas of computer science—AI, Artificial Life, and computer graphics, to name a few—is coming together to realize the creation of IAs. This chapter presented four general classes of IAs: mirror agents, reflexive agents, personable agents, and immersed agents (denizens). Although the first two types are already being used in the "real world," the ultimate Holy Grail of fully autonomous, reactive, adaptive, cooperative agents has yet to be realized. Nevertheless, the obvious direction of combining features from the previous work on agents discussed previously should go a long way towards achieving this goal. For example, since considerable research has gone into developing faceless dialogue experts as well as graphically expressive entities, the union of the mirror and personable types of agents seems to be a particularly fruitful venture to pursue.

Note how the types of agents covered in this chapter parallel human development from child to adult. That is, during our personal evolution we learn to mimic others, search for and discover patterns in data, develop personalities, and live in as well as adapt to our environment. Perhaps it is not surprising that, in creating agents, humans would try to replicate life by adopting strategies we use in our own lives.

This chapter also discussed how intelligence seems to be in the eye of the beholder. This points to one of the reasons why agents can become such powerful tools. Since users of agents can be led to infer the presence of human-like qualities in those agents, a programmer does not need to program X amount of aliveness into an agent for a user to *perceive* an X amount of aliveness. In other words, there will often be greater return for one's initial programming investment when creating IAs. In addition, since users already can be fooled into judging a program to be human even when the interaction is only text-based, imagine the reactions and inferences when artificial faces, bodies, and voices are added to the simulation. Hence, it seems likely that future users will be judging certain agents to be humanlike or human-equivalent even before the internals of those programs could pass any psychological or sociological tests for humanness. The results of such tests are probably irrelevant to most people's lives—the illusion of aliveness and usefulness of agents will be the main yardstick for judging them in the near future.

Note how the types of agents covered in this chapter parallel human development from child to adult. That is, during our personal evolution we learn to mimic others, search for and discover patterns in data, develop personalities, and live in as well as adapt to our environment. Perhaps it is not surprising

that, in creating agents, humans would try to replicate life by adopting strategies we use in our own lives.

However, some researchers have also developed methods for replicating life on a more basic level. This science, which has mainly been concerned with life at the simpler end of the evolutionary scale, should ultimately help explain human evolution and behavior. And it is the subject of Chapter 17, "Artificial Life."

Artificial Life

Although evolution has been mainly a theoretical science, ALife makes it into an experimental science; a testing ground where one can control and repeat runs, manipulate parameters, and see how the process of evolution is affected by this, that, and the other thing.

chapter 17

by Donald Rose Ph.D.

INTRODUCTION

In their simulated worlds, ALife scientists can change the laws that lead to the evolution of creatures, as well as experiment with different initial life forms that act as the seed for such evolution.

Imagine being God. Now get all those omnipotent fantasies out of your head and think of what you would create given a blank slate. What beings would you create for your world? Think harder. A true omnipotent God would not only have control over what is created, but how. What rules of evolution would you allow on your petri dish world?

Now you have some idea of what researchers in Artificial Life (ALife) feel like, or at least think about on occasion. In their simulated worlds, ALife scientists can change the laws that lead to the evolution of creatures, as well as experiment with different initial life forms that act as the seed for such evolution.

This chapter usually will use the word "life" in a very general sense, and this is the case in most discussions of ALife. Life can be a simulated creature similar to those discussed in the "agents" chapter. Yet life can also be a piece of computer artwork, an image or poem, a piece of music, or some kind of informational structure that evolves over time into a desirable form.

ARTIFICIAL LIFE
VERSUS REAL LIFE

Just the mention of artificial life makes many people afraid, which can be a slight obstacle to their understanding the field and its implications. At first, it may seem paranoid or far-fetched to believe anyone could create an artificial life form that could harm anyone; after all, it is only software, a bunch of 0s and 1s, right? Sure, until a computer virus eats all the data on your hard drive. So software creatures can in some ways be dangerous because we live in a world, like it or not, intertwined between the real and the artificial, the wet and the wired.

So is there really a difference between *artificial* life and *real* life? If so, what sets them apart?

An obvious comment would be to state that the former exists "only" in a machine, whereas the latter can be observed existing and evolving in the "real world." However, when one observes the definition of life in the dictionary, ALife could indeed be called alive, and certainly many ALife scientists back up this claim. For example, *Webster's New Dictionary* defines life as "that property of plants and animals (ending at death) that enables them to use food, grow, reproduce, etc." Generalize the "plants and animals" part (a biased label based on the observable world) into the word "form," then generalize "food" into "forms that help keep other forms functioning," and there is no theoretical reason an artificial entity could not embody these features. In fact, several ALife programs already exhibit these properties. Some of these systems are discussed later.

One of the benefits of creating the field of synthetic biology is to show how real world observable biology fits into a general taxonomy of possible biosystems. That is, "real biology" can be viewed as a subset of the "possible" biological universe proposed by ALife researchers. This broadest possible biospace concept is a superset of the real biological universe, plus current ALife models and current agents, as well as life forms yet to be created or discovered in the real or artificial realms.

Understanding these set relationships enable ALife researchers to experiment with new kinds of models. For example, Lamarckian evolution, once thought to be a possible explanation of real biological phenomena, was ultimately shown not to exist as a force in nature—only traits caused by genes can be inherited, not traits acquired from other causes. However, in the synthetic realm, the latter kind of evolution can indeed exist because worlds can be designed where organisms are able to alter their own genes. In fact, modeling Lamarckian evolution has been shown to be beneficial in many domains, such as those in which the "lifeforms" represent problem solutions.

One of the benefits of creating the field of synthetic biology is to show how real world observable biology fits into a general taxonomy of possible biosystems. That is, "real biology" can be viewed as a subset of the "possible" biological universe proposed by ALife researchers.

Darwinian evolution may one day be seen in retrospect as a temporary blip in a much longer period of Lamarckian evolution, with humans acting as the catalysts to facilitate this change. In many ways, one could argue we already are making the switch, since there are numerous examples of how we humans are altering our own evolution.

In the synthetic realm, creatures and their environments can be deliberately designed and constructed rather than having to evolve from primitive ancestors through eons of evolution. The mind of the human designer, in effect, is a substitute for centuries of adaptation and selection by Nature. The result is that artificial Lamarckian evolution is "easy to implement and potentially far more effective" than natural Darwinian evolution, according to *Artificial Life III*, the published proceedings of that workshop.

Although this argument has only been applied to artificial creatures, increased understanding of Lamarckian evolution may one day enable it to indeed appear even in the real world. Computer scientist Michael Dyer proposed that Darwinian evolution may one day be seen in retrospect as a temporary blip in a much longer period of Lamarckian evolution, with humans acting as the catalysts to facilitate this change. In many ways, one could argue we already are making the switch, since there are numerous examples of how we humans are altering our own evolution.

No matter how much one speculates, one can already observe what ALife researcher Tom Ray pointed out in *Computer Graphics World*—that although "evolution has been mainly a theoretical science, [ALife] makes it into an experimental science," a testing ground where one "can control and repeat runs, manipulate parameters, and see how the process of evolution is affected by this, that, and the other thing."

So can we answer the question of what separates artificial life from the real kind? Chris Langton has offered at least one intriguing hypothesis. In his paper "Life at the Edge of Chaos," he posits that life seems to lie on or near the transition between stable ordered structures and chaotic ones. For example, a phase change from stability to chaos on early Earth may have enabled early life to emerge, featuring components that are static on some levels yet changing on others, a dynamic equilibrium that could thrive in the young terran environment. An analogy to psychological observations might also lend supporting evidence for this hypothesis: one could argue that humans feel most stimulated, or "alive", when our behaviors lie somewhere between boring (static) and crazy (chaotic). None of this is an ultimate answer, but certainly Langton's ideas should prove to be a catalyst themselves—for further thought and, perhaps, a complete theory of life in the years to come.

ALife Versus AI
· · · · · · · · · · · · · · · · ·

This section heading is a bit misleading because there is neither direct competition nor animosity between researchers in these two fields. One should think of Artificial Intelligence (AI) and ALife not as two opposing fields, but opposite ends of a connected cross-fertilizing spectrum of work. However, there are some differences in the approaches these fields take. For instance, AI methods, in general, tend to be more top down. They also strive to recreate *human* reasoning processes, to model or recreate *human* behavior or something close to it. ALife, on the other hand, tends to be bottom up, dealing with the goal of how primitive organisms evolve into more complex ones. Higher-level reasoning processes are viewed as an emergent property of lower-level "primitive" functions.

Here's an example of how AI and ALife tackle the problem of programming a robot to walk, and more specifically, to deal with obstacles in its path. The standard AI approach would involve giving the robot thousands of explicit instructions about every situation it might encounter. If the robot meets a situation that is unexpected—for instance, on object in its path that it wasn't programmed to recognize or climb—it won't know what action to take. However, giving the robot a set of

programs that embody the ALife approach would enable the robot to adapt to new scenarios. Researchers would program its computer with basic action rules that include picking up legs, putting them down, and turning when the path is blocked. At MIT, a robot named Genghis has been programmed to walk, but not explicitly told how to climb over low obstacles in its path. Despite this, the robot is able to climb successfully.

There are many other examples of how lower-level (in other words, "nonintelligent" or noncognitive) functions can emerge spontaneously without being preprogrammed. For example, Tom Ray's Tierra program illustrated how organisms that display a form of immunity can evolve from an initial population of creatures that do not. Immunity was needed in order to counteract parasites that can also evolve from the same initial population.

In short, the AI way for the most part involves figuring plans out beforehand. In contrast, the ALife method involves planning on the fly, letting simpler local principles of behavior (distributed among components of the synthetic life form) dictate what actions are taken. As another analogy, one might compare AI programming to a teacher telling a student all the rules for how to ride a bicycle or swing a golf club, while ALife programming could be compared to the spontaneous local motor reactions the body makes in order to ride or swing successfully.

There is also overlap between agents and ALife. In particular, creatures such as those in the ALIVE system (described in Chapter 16, "Intelligent Agents") were built using ALife principles and ideas. Like the ALIVE team, ALife researchers Larry Yaeger and Craig Reynolds have also evolved creatures on their computers that exhibit behaviors that were not explicitly programmed, but which evolved from the complex interactions among many primitive mechanisms, notes Steven Levy in *Artificial life: The quest for a new creation.*

Certainly, work on ALife will one day converge with that of AI and artificial agents at a virtual promontory point. Perhaps the joining spike may, in a figurative sense, serve as a bolt into the neck of some virtual online Frankenstein. The location of the spike joining these two tracks is difficult to predict and depends on how much progress each field makes in the coming years.

For the purposes of this chapter, ALife will not be defined by providing an explicit string of words to pin down what it is. This would, after all, be a very top-down thing to do, and would be just as hard as trying to give a perfect definition of artificial intelligence. Instead, let's look at several examples of what scientists, programmers, and other experts seem to agree falls under the ALife banner, and the reader can evolve his or her own definition. Be happy for this opportunity, for such a bottom-up emergent activity is one of the hallmarks of the ALife philosophy, and hence, should help you grasp the concept (or at least get in the spirit) even more!

• •

A BRIEF HISTORY OF ALIFE

How did the field of Artificial Life start? Or, to put it another way, who first breathed life into ALife?

Ever since the highly-publicized cracking of the genetic code, scientists, as well as lay folk, have known that a great deal of the process of life depends on the exchange and manipulation of information. For example, DNA can be abstractly viewed as a string of information bits that provides instructions for the manufacture of higher-level structures, (such as proteins) which themselves become part of even higher-level structures within living creatures. Perhaps it was inevitable that computers, used for simulations since their inception, would be applied to the simulation and study of life itself, especially given life's myriad and rich analogies to information theory.

The eminent mathematician John von Neumann was perhaps the most prominent of the early ALife researchers, and even succeeded in inventing a self-reproducing structure. But the leader of the latest revitalization of the field, the man most responsible for the current resurgence of popularity for nouveau ALife, is Chris Langton. Bedridden from an accident, Langton decided to act on his long-dormant dream of pursuing the scientific study of synthetic biology. This turn of events seems most fitting, since evolution often results in long dormant strands of life suddenly becoming the most fit due to an accident. (Many scientists believe apes were able to evolve into humans because of a meteor accident that killed the dinosaurs.) Langton also gained fame within the ALife community because, like Von Neumann, he invented a self-reproducing virtual organism, but was the first to implement it on a computer.

Today, the field is varied, and ALife ideas and methods have been applied to domains in art, science, economics, and beyond. This chapter will concentrate on a few key areas of interest. First we'll delve into the modeling of organisms—single isolated forms as well as collections of them. Next, a more general type of system for solving problems, genetic algorithms, is discussed, along with the issues and applications of these systems. After a brief discussion on modeling cultural evolution, the darker side of ALife is addressed, followed by future thoughts, summary, and conclusion.

MODELING DEVELOPMENT OF SINGLE ORGANISMS

L-systems model the development of organisms by applying "rewrite rules" to "seed" structures. The letter L stands for the inventor of these systems (mathematician and theoretical biologist Aristid Lindenmayer). To help grasp the basic principle of modeling development by repeated substitution of forms, here's an analogy: Suppose you have the letter "S" as your seed. Now you add a simple substitution rule like "S = SXS." Repeated application of this rule can result in a long structure; the sequence of development would look like this:

```
S
SXS
SXSXSXS
SXSXSXSXSXSXSXS
```

And so on. The structure can be as long as you want, depending on how many applications of the single rule are allowed.

Now imagine if you had even more rules, each of which could substitute other letters in different amounts (for instance "X = AAABA" and "A = XYZ," and so on) in different directions within space. For instance, when you substitute for "X" you must write vertically; the "A" substitution writes diagonally, and so on. You could even use an inverse effect with deletion rules like "AAB = AB," and so forth. In this new case, an even more complex structure can emerge. These simple examples illustrate the basic power of L-systems: the ability to model the development of complex structures from simple initial states based on simple rules of structure manipulation such as substitution, deletion, and so forth.

The most popular and famous applications of L-systems have been modeling plant growth. The L-system program developed by theoretical biologist Przemyslaw Prusinkiewicz uses mutation in conjunction with rewrite rules. If an equation causes a program to construct a virtual plant, then changing that equation (by mutating part of it, for instance) can change the resultant plant. Using this logic, and analogies to the earlier letter-rewrite examples, one can see how rules for rewriting equations amounts to a set of virtual growth rules. By introducing a mutation or "genetic rearrangement," his system can "generate a new 'plant' of the same 'species,'" reported Curt Suplee in *Breakthroughs in Health and Science*. That is, a plant with new features, but the same general structure, can be generated. When teamed with a computer graphics front end, the varied plant types can be visualized on a monitor for immediate evaluation (and enjoyment).

Richard Dawkins, a noted evolutionary biologist, created a related program known as Biomorph, which displays mutated versions of an initial organism (simple patterns of line segments attached at various pseudo-random angles according to a few control parameters), and allows the user to choose the mutated form he or she likes best, according to any criteria. The selected form then becomes the new basis for mutation, and the cycle continues. Using this method, initial forms can gradually transform into a wide variety of intriguing shapes and patterns, showing surprising complexity as well as frequent similarity to real world organisms.

A more recent ALife system for plant growth differs from the above systems in its *interactive* nature. This system, displayed at SIGGRAPH in 1993 as well as a Paris exhibit in 1994, employs a kind of man-machine symbiosis where petting plants influences their growth direction and height. The growing plants are displayed in real time on a large color screen in front of the users. With multiple humans petting different plant types, a cornucopia of colorful growth soon fills up the screen.

However, in this interactive system the humans merely act as a kind of random factor that let the plants grow in certain directions and at certain speeds. The humans have no say in these factors and could not predict how they would turn out on the screen. One next step to make the system even more interactive would be to allow the human users more control or input into the growth process, yet retain the current system's comfortable distance from the nitty-gritty manipulation of underlying computer code.

Note that these systems for modeling development feature some fractal-like characteristics. Repeated substitution of one component for another results in self-similar structures, where the overall structure bears a strong resemblance and resonance to its component parts—exactly the main property of fractals. Since fractals have also been shown to be accurate at modeling certain natural phenomena, this overlap with ALife is easy to understand, and it seems likely that fractal mathematics will be used with increasing frequency in the design of ALifeforms.

Finally, one could make a quick, rough analysis of the above programs and conclude that there exists little, if any, "meaning" in these systems or their outputs. L-systems, Biomorph, and similar programs mainly use syntactic manipulation rules to get results rather than any preprogrammed notions of beauty. However, this is in the spirit of the ALife philosophy, where such higher-level notions as "beauty" are not to be explicitly programmed but rather left as an emergent property of the system. Other abstract notions for evaluating forms can be used in this selection process, such as one Biomorph run when Dawkins selected patterns that appeared the most insect-like; he ultimately got a pattern that met his simple criterion to his satisfaction. Hoping for a tree-like structure would have likely led to a very different result. In short, these systems can let us use our aesthetic notions during *local* decisions in the hope that the *global* result will ultimately be a structure that satisfies our desired criteria.

MODELING EVOLUTION OF ORGANISM COLONIES

Mathematician J.H. Conway's Game of Life was one of the first efforts to model how simple virtual life forms evolve, and was arguably the first truly famous ALife program. This game is an example of a *cellular automaton* (CA), an array of cells (often in two dimensions, but designable in any dimension degree) that turn on and off according to rules designed and implemented by the programmer. When playing the Game of Life, an initial state is either created on purpose or randomly chosen; some cells are "alive" (a colored dot on-screen) and some are "dead" (empty). Over time, the rules of behavior dictate which cells stay the same across each generation and which

change state. Conway's game has a small set of rules. For instance, if a live cell, L, is surrounded by too many live cells, L dies. If a dead cell, D, has the right number of live neighbors (not too many, not too few), D becomes alive. If these rules don't apply, the cell state does not change.

One of the attractions of CAs is that even a small rule set like this can lead to interesting behavior in the global cell colony. Certain well-known phenomena occur when the above CA enters certain states. For example, "gliders," localized cell structures which seem to move across the screen, can appear. They maintain a constant or near constant shape even though the cells that make them up change each generation. Note that gliders exhibit properties that are part static (the shape is constant), yet part changing (the cells making up that shape are different over time). This is just the kind of dynamic balance that Langton's tentative definition of life refers to. Furthermore, the gliders' behavior is an emergent property of the CA system; no one programs their existence beforehand, only the rules for cell state changes. Gliders and any other "creatures" that we witness on-screen are epiphenomena of the rules of this Game.

Of course, all we've been talking about are dots and empty cells, not life, right? Again, as in much of ALife, the power is in the analogies and metaphors. Games can lead to more "useful" programs, perhaps more applicable to the real world. But more on the real world later. Would you like to play God? Try SimLife.

Maxis Software, the development company that created the program SimLife, describes this "game" as one that lets a player "build an ecosystem from the ground up" by first "design[ing] plants and animals...at the genetic level to influence how they look, act and eventually evolve." Then the player can test these creatures' ability to adapt "by turning their environment into either a paradise where life is easy or a wasteland where only the strongest survive." Many aspects of the creatures and the environment can be manipulated from the lifeforms' genetics to "food webs, mutation, extinction, and natural disasters," to time and physical laws. The player can then "witness the effects on the gene pool, the ecosystem, and life itself." SimLife is, in many ways, more analogous to the real world than Conway's Game of Life, since the screen now shows creatures similar to those actually seen on Earth, and an environment in which these forms "live" and "die."

El-fish and AquaZone are two other programs that, like a more specialized version of SimLife, allow a user to design and revise definitions of fish, which in a sense "live" within a virtual fish tank on your computer. Note that emergent behavior can also occur in synthetic fish colonies. One programmer of a related system found this out when he noticed one day that his virtual tank was "brimming with fish of a single species, swimming as a school—an emergent behavior he had not foreseen," he noted in *Breakthroughs in Health and Science* magazine.

MODELING GENERAL PROBLEM SOLVING WITH GENETIC ALGORITHMS

We have thus far discussed efforts that concentrate on making life that exhibits many of the properties of real world bioforms. However, many other ALife systems employ a more general definition (or redefinition, or fuzzification) of life, in order to make creative strides in domains unrelated to biology. *Genetic Algorithms* (GAs) are one such effort, and one of the hottest subareas of ALife.

GAs allow you to solve a problem by evolving a solution out of non-solutions. That is, solutions are built from the iterative revision of initial problem descriptions. In some ways, the process is analogous to how life evolved from non-life in the real world. Repeated random recombination of non-life forms into new and different structures led some to be more fit for their environment, and hence, these were able to exist longer and perform more interesting tasks than those that had no novel-yet-helpful features. Given enough time, a great deal of interesting forms could result, some of which meet the criteria of being "alive." In most GA systems, a similar evolution occurs. However, the criteria is not whether the artificial chromosomes are alive, but rather whether they represent solutions to problems one wants to solve. Chromosomes are designed so that their genes represent features of the problem

solution. Those chromosomes that come closest to being a complete problem solution, by containing genes that solve certain key portions of the problem, are analogous to real creatures that are the most fit in their environment.

Before one begins using a GA system, he or she must first be able to structure a problem solution into a set of features, and must know the value each feature should have in order to embody an acceptable solution. Next, random values are assigned for these features. In other words, there is an initial population of strings that contain randomly created (and hence, mostly useless) information. These solutions now "compete" against each other. Given a large number of initial chromosomes and a potentially large number of generations to allow improvement, small pockets of usefulness can start to accumulate within chromosomes, which then begin to appear in various combinations within single chromosomes. After enough generations of this information manipulation, strings begin to contain partial solutions and, finally, complete solutions. That is, after generations of mutations and recombination of solution pieces (genes), one or more answers (chromosomes) emerge as the best and can be used to solve whatever problem or goal one had in the first place. Of course, there is no guarantee that solutions will be found, but because many parts of the solution space are searched in parallel, they are surprisingly successful for a wide assortment of problems.

Here's a simple example: suppose you want to schedule eight tasks in such a way that there are as few conflicts as possible. The fittest chromosome would be the one containing a sequence of tasks with the least number of conflicts. One could view the tasks as genes. Hence, a typical initial population might look like this (with the eight tasks labelled A through H):

```
A B C D E F G H (chromosome 1)
G B D C A H F E (chromosome 2)
A G D C H E F B (chromosome 3)
```

And so on.

- Genetic recombination here would mean creating new strings in which tasks are intermixed, just as two parents mix genes in order to form one or more child. In this domain, chromosomes (strings) are judged by how many conflicts exist. Strings with the most conflicts die each generation, while those with the least conflicts have offspring (in other words, new strings are created by rearranging portions of the parent strings). All other strings (the not-worst yet not-best strings) simply survive to the next generation. Over a series of generations, certain gene sequences will die out. For instance, if doing task A before task B causes a conflict, any chromosome that contains AB in its sequence will be less fit than chromosomes that do not contain AB, hence the latter string is more likely to survive than the former. Over time, the population of strings starts to contain less and less of these undesirable task pairs.

ISSUES AND PROBLEMS IN DESIGNING GA SYSTEMS

Many questions surface when designing and using GAs, such as for the scheduling problem just shown. For instance, when does one stop creating new generations? This is one of many human-made decisions that must be built into the GA system. One could trigger a program halt when some condition is reached, such as when no string contains a task pair that is in conflict. Of course, this latter condition might never be met, so another stop condition could be a designated number of iterations (stopping after 1,000 generations, for instance).

Other decisions to be made are numerous. How large an initial population is desired? What features should the chromosome represent? Should they be flat or hierarchical in structure? How many should die each generation, and what is the criteria for death? Should crossover be performed, and if so, how many per generation, and where along the chromosomes should crossover take place? Should mutations occur, and if so, how many per generation? The number of deaths and births per generation? As a more specific decision-making example, in the domain of evolving computer programs, one must select the optimal level for the units of crossover. Should one allow crossover at the level of bits, bytes, lines of code, or subroutines? Certainly programs that use bits as the basic level will most likely take forever to find even a single solution (all right, it could theoretically finish, but you and your great-to-the-eighth grandkids would be finished too). In short, playing God is a daunting responsibility. GAs provide the user with the power to tweak many factors and each choice can affect the outcome of one's runs.

Note that fitness, whether in nature or on a computer, is subjective, and hence can be defined in many ways. If the only criteria for fitness is how long a lifeform exists in a relatively constant form, humans are less fit than rocks. But if one adds another criteria like "doing useful things" in the world, most would agree humans can now be judged as more fit than rocks. The point is nature and evolution do not care how lifeforms like us define fitness. There is no absolute fitness definition in nature, nature simply provides the environment within which lifeforms can change, and this change over time from one form to another is the engine of evolution. Which forms are better or worse is a matter of opinion.

Hence, one of the main differences between how GAs work and how real world evolution operates is the nature of the selection process. Humans must define, then infuse, GA systems with a specific evaluation method for deciding which chromosomes are the most useful or closest to a solution or goal state ("fit"), and which are the least useful or farthest from a solution. However, once constructed, this human-made evaluation method is analogous to the role the environment plays in natural selection; both serve to reward fittest forms with survival to the next generation, and punish those that are least fit with the ultimate insult—extinction.

Still another issue: how random should the initial population be? When using a GA to solve a problem, there is no requirement to start completely random if one has information that helps speed the search for the final desired output.

In other words, if you have partial knowledge or educated guesses about what elements make up the final solution, one can plant the seeds of that knowledge in the population at any time—in effect lending a helping hand to the evolution process. If one is not completely sure their hand would help, a "random beginning run" could also be performed, at least for comparison. The point is that GAs, like a majority of ALife systems, are a form of experimental biology. Hence, we can play God over many universes with many different beginnings and rules.

In summary, problem representation is a key issue to address, as in all ALife systems. However, once such issues are faced and resolved, we will see that GAs can produce quite useful results in a wide variety of domains.

GAs and Science

One can, in theory, apply GAs to almost any problem in which solutions can be represented as chromosomes. The problem must also have a well-defined set of criteria for evaluating chromosomes and deciding which are closest or farthest from a desired outcome or stable state. Examples are plentiful in the realm of science, such as in the search for new chemical or molecular compounds. GAs can be of use in this domain because chemists and biologists have clearly delineated criteria available for judging compounds.

Another example of GAs' usefulness for science would be to evolve new and useful computer programs. John Koza did just that. The Stanford businessman-turned-ALifer used GAs to evolve code that could perform many varied tasks. One of the clever design decisions he made was to choose a level of crossover that increased the chance that resulting chromosomes were syntactically correct, while still

GAs and Art

One of the most exciting and novel applications of GAs has been to the artistic domain. In particular, computer scientist and artist Karl Sims created a system that uses GAs to evolve visual art. Sims has stated that one of his motivations for creating "genetic images" was his "desire for procedural methods for automatically generating complex simulated structures ... without requiring the artist to design or even understand the cumbersome equations involved." To address this and other issues, he created a system that lets users "evolve" images brimming with complex and varied textures, patterns, and shapes, and do so in an interactive manner.

allowing a good deal of diversity in the population. To illustrate the importance of this choice, if genes were chosen at too minute a level, crossover might repeatedly create chromosomes that were not in proper syntax (garbage expressions that "would not compute"), plus the program could take an exceedingly long time to find solutions. If genes were at too coarse a level, crossover might not lead to many new types of chromosomes. Since Koza chose LISP as the language to represent chromosomes and since LISP functions are typically composed of "reasonably sized" S-expressions, the S-expression became the designated gene.

Koza's GA system evolved LISP functions that could solve problems in many different domains. For example, the system rediscovered astronomer Johannes Kepler's laws of planetary motion, and even found an interim solution that Kepler himself proposed but discarded before arriving at his final laws. Although one could not claim that using GAs explains how scientists make discoveries, the fact that they can construct similar conclusions to hard problems means GAs and ALife in general could play a useful role as scientific assistants, today as well as in years to come.

This "interactive evolution" begins with an expression written in computer language (LISP), which acts as the "genotype" for an image. The genotype code specifies the color of each pixel as a function of pixel coordinates. The image that results from such a genotype is the "phenotype," the visible output of letting the computer process the input expression. In the next phase, the program mutates the current expression, doing so multiple times and in a random fashion to create a set of candidate images. The user then plays nature's role, acting as the selector after evaluating the images that result from the candidate-mutated image genotypes. The user chooses one image as best, most likely using aesthetic beauty as the criterion—although this is not forced (selection could even be done randomly if the user wants to have fun or not think too hard).

The entire cycle—from phenotype selection of image I, to mutation of I's genotype G, to production of candidate images from G, to further selection—repeats for as long as the user desires. In effect, the user's repeated selections means one line of multiple possible descendants is chosen, with other branches of the tree-like possible-descendent structure being ignored. Note that Sims' system and that of Dawkins, discussed previously, operate in a similar manner. However, Sims' system results in images of far greater richness and complexity than Dawkins' system.

Like Sims, other artists are discovering and using new tools for creating art. Whereas Sims evolves the actual art, these artists evolve brushes that can create such art. Note that the brushes are virtual in that they do not exist in the real world (in fact some would have no real world counterpart at all), and they are used to create virtual images on the computer.

Another related task would be to evolve fonts based on criteria such as readability, space limitations, and other size factors—or simply via user opinion—in a manner similar to Sims' selection method. Although programs already exist to morph or crossbreed fonts; ALife successors to such manual crossbreeding seem a likely prediction.

GAs could also be applied to evolving interesting language structures, which can be considered a form of art. However, little work has been done in applying GAs to the generation of language such as poetry. Recently I developed a program, inspired by Sims' genetic image work, in the domain of genetic poetry evolution. This program, called GP, can create a form of abstract poetry by using GAs to evolve "meaningful" sentences from initial sets of random word strings. This approach creates a form of written art by selection of the best candidate sentences, followed by recombination of best-sentence fragments and mutation on all sentences (replacement of some words by others). The process is then repeated over several generations. A final best descendant sentence can then be selected after each set of generations form a line in a final poem, which contains the set of best word strings.

Two approaches to the selection process have been investigated to date: (1) human-based selection, and (2) the use of an evaluation function to drive the evolution of sentences by automatically applying various criteria to judge and select candidate sentences.

One of the main points made in this work is that programs such as GP can generate art in various forms, but users can then perform interpretations of that art, followed by contemplation of any deeper meaning based on those interpretations. If a program can facilitate these two latter processes, it has provided a useful function. This program is not intended to be a cognitive model of how poets create art, but rather another means to attain the final poetic goal. However, if programs can create art at a level judged near that of a human artist in the same domain, they have exhibited aspects of intelligence and are examples of useful AI.

Work on genetic poetry should have applications to other fields. For example, GP could be adapted for use as a tool for lateral thinking and brainstorming. E. de Bono, in *Lateral Thinking: Creativity Step by Step*, points out that "lateral thinking is insight restructuring ... brought about through the rearrangement of information." The GP program performs this function. One can think of the evolved sentences not as lines of a poem, but rather as idea chains that can either stimulate new ideas through juxtaposition of words or constitute new ideas in themselves. Other domains related to poetry, such as writing stories, could also benefit from the techniques developed for genetic poetry.

But is genetic poetry, or other evolved language structures, truly relevant to ALife—a field which is, after all, trying to study things that seem to be alive? If you agree with author William Burroughs, and others who claim that language and ideas are a kind of virus, then perhaps the answer is yes.

MODELING CULTURAL EVOLUTION

ALife researcher Liane Gabora presents a model of cultural evolution she calls Meme and Variations, which models how ideas evolve over time. In her universe, organisms, which she refers to as vehicles, can learn and remember memes (think of them as ideas, or the cultural equivalent of genes). However, they implement only one at a time, a bottleneck representative of our real world where, for instance, one may know many recipes, but can cook only one at a time. Some of the implemented memes help the vehicle, some hurt. Hence, the ideas "compete with each other for representation in and implementation by their vehicle hosts."

One result of an evolutionary episode could be to evolve interesting and hopefully useful ideas. Certainly this program or a related variant could serve as a testing ground for new ideas, analogous to how government officials often "float" ideas in the media to see which catch on and which must be avoided at all costs. Perhaps a future version of this kind of program will be used to construct new memes that meet culturally-useful criteria, such as being concise and memorable while still brimming with multiple meanings for different consciousness levels. Maybe an artificially-evolved meme will one day affect or change real lives.

THE DARK SIDE OF ALife

Metaphors and analogies have been strong sources for ideas in the ALife field ever since its inception. So it is logical that the less desirable aspects of biology would one day become a focal point in ALife. A small cadre of hackers have helped speed this process by creating virtual viruses. Now those of us who want to protect our computers against viral infection must address this darker side of ALife as well.

What is a computer virus? No, you can't catch it from having phone sex. Essentially, they are programs that attack or feed off other programs. Just as a real world virus can manipulate the DNA of organisms and force those hosts to produce more copies of the virus, computer viruses can manipulate the data that resides in a computer's memory or storage and force the computer host to create new copies of the viral code. Luckily, studying real world immune strategies has, along with clever programming, allowed companies to devise programs to destroy viruses and protect against them.

As menacing as computer viruses can be, there is potentially an even darker side to ALife. Theoretically, humans could create a species of artificial creatures whose behavior we cannot fully understand, since repeated revision of a known initial state can lead to quite a different "finished product." One might dismiss any danger since the program is entirely contained within a computer. However, in addition to the virus dangers presented above, there is the fact that many ALife programs are already finding their way into hardware, such as robots. If ALife-type programs control learning machines that are mo-

> **What is a computer virus? No, you can't catch it from having phone sex. Essentially, they are programs which attack or feed off other programs.**

bile and capable of physical manipulation of its environment, the potential for damage cannot be ignored. Fail-safe mechanisms will undoubtedly be designed to prevent any unintended mishaps due to unexpected learned behaviors, but such mechanisms might never be completely foolproof, given the power of a truly powerful meme. Let's hope ALife systems will be designed so that they more often evolve more potent safeguard memes that destructive ones.

FUTURE
ISSUES

Previously we discussed how memetic evolution benefits from competition. The need for simulated competition in order to improve the chances for better final solutions is a common theme in ALife. Computer scientist Danny Hillis and other researchers found that, after trying to evolve one species (call it S), adding a predator species greatly increased the fitness of the evolved members of S. This is the ALife equivalent of competition resulting in better products. In fact, one might expect businesses of the future to use ALife techniques to model a kind of "synthetic competition" in order to test marketability of new designs and products. For example, GAs could be used, with chromosomes representing various features of the product.

Another benefit of ALife that should arrive relatively quickly will be better teaching methods for biology. For instance, when illustrating principles of evolution one could show timelapse versions of evolutionary episodes. Real evolution is obviously impossible to witness directly due to the enormous time periods involved in its operation.

Speaking of real world evolution: why was Darwinian evolution the method employed on Earth out of all

the types of evolution possible in the broader synth-bio-space? No one has yet answered this question, but ALife studies might help shed light on an answer. For example, some researchers have shown experimental evidence of how Lamarckian evolution can not only be programmed within virtual ALife environments, but also improves the speed in which "beneficial" evolution occurs. Perhaps Dyer's hunch will be proved correct, and Darwinian evolution will be proved to be a required prerequisite to a world where it and Lamarckian evolution coexist—some creatures evolving via nature and others manipulating their genetic makeup deliberately or (in a dark dystopian vision) by law or force.

At the very least, ALife research will enable us to understand the dynamics of these scenarios and better predict how future evolution will unfold.

If so many of the complex artifacts of the world around us evolved from primitive Earth by means of genetic codes, then understanding and using GAs may result in the evolution of an increasing number of solutions to current problems. But are there limits to solving problems by GAs? In striving to answer this question, we will either learn what the limits are—a valuable end in itself—or else begin to solve an increasing number of problems. Wouldn't it be ironic if solutions of environmental issues were achieved by "growing" them organically?

So what improvements will future ALife systems likely incorporate? One idea: such systems might learn to evolve their own operation. For instance, this kind of "metaevolution" might allow an ALife program to analyze its own behavior and adjust some of the factors present at the start of the current run (such as the number of mutations per generation, or where crossover is performed). In other words, while each run makes many steps, searching a space of solutions, each run would constitute one step in a higher-level search within a parallel "program-parameter space." Going even further, such systems might eventually learn which parameters are best for certain classes of problems.

Since GAs depend on searching many parts of a problem space at once, the promise of the information superhighway might prove beneficial by linking individual ALife programs. The exchange of data among various programs over networks like the Internet might help some of the these systems find better solutions and do so in less time. However, freedoms on such connections might be restricted unless darker forces (such as viruses) can be adequately protected against. This point is driven home by the increasing threat of Internet viruses reported in the media. For now such viruses are only dangerous when explicitly downloaded from the Internet to a user, but freer passage of information among machines and users might increase the danger. Hopefully, the growing interest in Internet security and virtual firewalls—along with new immunizing and virus killing software—will provide the needed protection to make freer data linkages safe.

SUMMARY AND CONCLUSIONS

Synthetic biology leads to a universal taxonomy of evolution strategies, with real biology as a subset. Allowing a loose boundary on the space of what life is allows ALife to be used in many varied domains, from art to science to business. As long as one can make the mapping from a nonbiological domain to a biology metaphor, ALife techniques will find useful application in a wide assortment of fields.

But we cannot ignore the darker side of ALife. In particular, there is the existence of computer viruses, which many consider to be the first example of man-made, silicon-based life. In face, famed physicist Steven

Hawking recently claimed that computer viruses' evil purpose mirrors the darker side of us flawed humans. However, ALife might prove useful in finding new defensive methods to protect against such viruses, especially since immunity has already been shown as an emergent property of some ALife systems. Perhaps Koza's work on evolving computer programs will allow us to evolve "code creatures," which could either attack viruses directly or immunize code that was previously susceptible to viral attack.

Note that competition is good for ALife systems when evolution is used to reach a goal state, since competition forces a species to evolve with an increasing number of useful traits. We may not know what those useful traits are beforehand, but we can often recognize them when they emerge after evolution.

GAs were shown to be a powerful and widely applicable ALife tool. Some methods focus on the use of mutation (Sims' genetic image evolution), while others focus on crossover (Koza's computer program evolution). However, in either case, the main power lies in the repeated manipulation and evaluation of information strings that, given enough time and enough initial instances, can transform random strings into meaningful problem solutions.

ALife will certainly prove useful in modeling real-world biology. More sophisticated successors to the SimLife program might actually be useful in aiding environmental organizations that model and monitor the real environment. In SimLife, one can note which conditions lead to species extinction; a more advanced version might one day help us predict and help stop real extinctions. However, in the longer term ALife may prove even more useful for introducing new ideas and techniques for creating and studying novel lifeforms, many of which will never have a counterpart in nature. Just as the airplane introduced a new way to fly using a method that differed from nature's feathered flying machines, ALife will show us new ways to think about life, in addition to new ways to think about and solve problems in non-biological domains.

Some people still believe ALife cannot be "real life" if it "only" exists within a computer. But if future ALife systems truly evolve into increasingly intelligent entities, could they learn to get out of their machine "homes?" Or, in a more likely scenario, if we put ALife programs into tiny robots, some of these program-bot combinations might eventually resemble insects so closely we cannot tell the difference. Or they may surpass the capability of real world insects, especially since we can program learning abilities that no insect currently has. And if a "synth-sect" is superior to a real insect, is it alive? This now starts to sound like the Turing Test debate in Chapter 16. As discussed in that chapter, one might be better off not worrying about absolute definitions of life, but instead get more mileage and comfort by leaving the inference of aliveness once again to the eye of the beholder.

But remember, when you get to the next century, before you squash that insect, make sure it's not artificial. If it's really smart, you may have a lawsuit on your hands. Or feet.

Finally, I return to the question of what is artificial versus what is natural. Perhaps this question will eventually become moot because the distinction between natural and synthetic will disappear, a claim some ALifers have made. This may be one of the most exciting yet chilling by-products of a Lamarckian-dominated future, one where we create computer lifeforms that alter their genomes and in turn, help us understand and manipulate our own genomes and memetic makeup. Although slow at first, such interplay between the real and virtual may accelerate to the point where we simply won't have the time, desire, or ability to ask what the difference is anymore.

But for now, these pressing questions must wait. My synth-fish are virtually starving. (And I'd hate for them to learn to eat my data instead...)

RESOURCES

There are many ways to learn more about ALife. You can subscribe to an online newsletter that contains dates of events, opinions, debates, and other information pertaining to ALife theory, practice, philosophy, and fun. To have this newsletter delivered by e-mail to your Internet account, send a message to *alife-request@cognet.ucla.edu* and in the body of the message simply write *subscribe <your real name>*. Then sit back and enjoy these month-to-month activity updates.

If you're not content to sit back, but want to rummage the Internet for free or cheap ALife code, you can *ftp* two pieces of Mac software (L-System and 3DL-System) from *wuarchive.wustl.edu* in the *mirrors/architec/Fractals* directory. "Pfg," another program written by L-system and synth-plant/synth-fish guru Przemyslaw Prusinkiewicz, is available at *ftp.cs.uregina.ca* in *pub/pfg*. It even comes with C source code, and its small 16KB file size illustrates that relatively small programs can still result in interesting effects and do not always require extensive coding efforts.

Don't have an Internet account, you say? If so, or if most of the above paragraph sounds geek to you, then read Chapter 6, "Life in the Virtual Village."

Viruses and Other Nasty Things

chapter 18
by Kelly D. Lucas

Most computer users have never encountered an active computer virus. However, as the number of computer users and viruses grows each year, the chances of any given computer contracting a virus increases.

The computer world waited in hushed silence on March 6, 1992, as a new era dawned within cyberspace. On that day, the Michelangelo virus was expected to erase thousands, possibly millions of computer hard drives around the world. Never before or since has so much notoriety been given to a computer virus. All of the major news networks dutifully reported the perils that the Michelangelo virus would bring.

The day passed, and it soon became apparent that a major catastrophe had not occurred. Reports were received of a few isolated incidents where some companies and institutions were damaged by the virus, but the total number of machines that were struck by the Michelangelo virus is now estimated to be around 2,000 worldwide. Much credit belongs to the media, which did a splendid job in alarming the public to the dangers of this particular virus. In fact, a great deal of data would have been lost had it not been for the hype created by zealous reporters. There are no reliable estimates on the number of computers that actually contracted the virus and were checked and cleansed of this monster before it struck, but it is probably at least 100 times greater than the number of hard drives that were reported as overwritten.

However, in spite of the insignificant number of computers that were actually damaged by the Michelangelo virus, this whole episode proves the seriousness of viruses and the need for users to become *virus aware*. Most computer users have never encountered an active computer virus; however, as the number of computer users and viruses grows each year, the chances of any given computer contracting a virus increases. As our society grows more and more dependent upon computers to provide life's basic necessities, we need to know about some of the hazards that may interfere with those services.

What is a computer virus? In the simplest terms, a virus is program code that attaches itself to other programs or disk-boot sectors and is *self-replicating*. It doesn't necessarily perform malicious damage, although almost all viruses cause some type of ill effects. Oftentimes viruses are confused with associated phenomena called *worms* and *Trojan Horses*. A worm is a rogue program usually designed to perform some type of illegal or malicious activity, which spreads by executing multiple copies of itself. Unlike viruses, worms are self-contained programs; viruses require a host to infect—either a disk or a program. Trojan Horses are programs that hide inside of legitimate software programs. The program may look and behave like the authentic software; however, in the background, other activities may be occurring, unknown to the user.

A History of Computer Viruses

Computer viruses are a relatively new phenomenon. Let's take a look at some of the more significant events in the evolution of computer viruses:

- 1966: Two American undergraduates write a program that could copy itself. This represents the first form of a virus. The program has some bugs, and it crashes when it is run.

- 1974: Xerox demonstrates the first self-replicating code to the world.

- 1984: Professor Fred Cohen, a California researcher, calls self-replicating programs *viruses*.

- 1985: The first true virus is unleashed on the computer world, the Pakistani Brain Virus.

- 1987: The Lehigh Virus runs rampant at many college universities.

- 1988: The Israeli Virus is discovered. Also in 1988, Donald Gene Burleson is sentenced in the first conviction related to viruses. By this time, over 30 strains of viruses are identified.

- 1989: The Dark Avenger virus, the first "fast infector," arrives on the scene. It carries a copyright notice and is produced by a virus writer who calls himself the "Dark Avenger." In October, the first significant virus scare occurs: Viruses called Jerusalem and Datacrime are scheduled to hit simultaneously.

- 1990: Polymorphic (self-mutating) viruses are created.

- 1991: The number of unique virus strains exceeds 500.

- 1992: The Michelangelo virus triggers on March 6, causing a worldwide alarm that far exceeds the virus scare of 1989. The number of unique virus strains exceeds 2,000.

- 1993: The Monkey virus is discovered. The creation of viruses is now at a rate of three per day. By year's end, there are over 3,000 known virus strains.

- 1994: The SMEG (Simulated Metamorphic Encryption Generator) virus family is discovered. It is written by someone who goes by the title of "Black Baron."

Number of Virus Strains

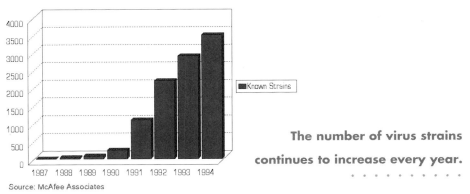

totals are rounded off

Source: McAfee Associates

The number of virus strains continues to increase every year.

Based on these recent trends, it's easy to conclude that the number of new viruses will continue to escalate at exponential rates. This fact, coupled with the employment of new stealth and polymorphic virus technology, will make virus detection in the future an incredible challenge. Before we take a closer look at viruses, it is helpful to review some of the basics of computer architecture.

COMPUTER ARCHITECTURE

Computers are composed of four main areas: input devices, the central processing unit (CPU), auxiliary storage, and the output devices. Input devices include keyboards, scanners, and touch screens. The processor consists of the electronic circuits that actually sort and process the data. Auxiliary storage consists of floppy disks, hard disks, CD-ROMs, and magnetic tape. Output devices include monitors and printers.

Each disk is divided into a series of concentric magnetic *tracks* on which data may be written. Each magnetic track is further divided into *sectors*. Surface space is allocated in whole sector units. Normally one sector is 512 bytes in length. A sector is the smallest possible storage unit that may be allocated to store a file. In practice, disk storage devices normally use from two to eight sectors, called a *cluster*, to allocate space for file storage. Therefore, a small file of 400 bytes could occupy up to eight sectors of storage space (4,096 bytes). The extra space between the end-of-file marker and the unused bytes at the end of the cluster is commonly referred to as *slack space*.

When a user stores a large file, DOS uses the minimum number of clusters to hold all of the data from the file. Often, these clusters will not be contiguous—consequently, a file may occupy clusters that are scattered throughout the disk. For this reason, DOS uses a *file-allocation table* (FAT) to keep track of which cluster belongs to which file.

The first sector of track 0 is a special sector called a *boot sector*. This sector provides, among other things, information on the physical dimensions of the disk, the logical dimensions of the DOS structure, the DOS version number, and the names of the two DOS system files. Hard disks have additional information contained in the boot sector in an area known as the *partition table*. This table describes the dimensions to the disk, the number of partitions, and the size of each partition. The partition table and boot sector on a hard disk are known as the *master boot record*. Immediately following the boot sector is the file-allocation table, which is followed by the root directory. The root directory is a table that describes all of the files and directory entries.

The personal computer must have a way to control certain functions of the computer and to activate many BIOS routines and check for error conditions. This is solved by using *interrupts*. An interrupt, like the name implies, is an interruption in the flow of processing, suspending the current activity to switch to another task. There are Intel hardware interrupts, IBM PC hardware interrupts, PC software interrupts, DOS software interrupts, and application software interrupts. Interrupts provide the means to control the internal workings of a PC.

TYPES OF VIRUSES . . . .

There are two major type of viruses: *file infectors* and *boot-sector infectors*. Approximately 90 percent of all viruses have been file infectors; however, most infections reported today are boot-sector viruses. Viruses are carried in auxiliary storage devices and executed in the processor of a computer. Once executed, a virus will attempt to infect files and/or disks in an effort to propagate itself. There are also a few viruses that infect the directory structure of a disk.

File-infecting viruses, as the name implies, attach themselves to executable files. Whenever an infected program is executed, the virus either becomes memory resident, or performs some other

File-Infecting Virus

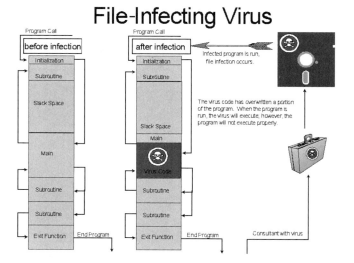

A file-infecting virus.

type of operation. Wherever the file goes, the virus goes with it. This includes transmission through modems, over networks, or on a backup tape drive. The most famous file-infecting virus is the Jerusalem virus. It is believed that this virus originates from Israel, and it activates on any Friday the 13th. On that day, it will delete any infected program that is executed.

A boot-sector-infecting virus resides in the boot sector of floppy disks and hard drives. This virus remains dormant on a floppy disk until a user attempts to boot a computer with an infected disk. When this occurs, the virus activates and searches the hard drive for a previous infection, and if it's not infected, writes itself to the boot-sector area. Other variations write to the partition table of the hard disk. Oftentimes, these viruses preserve the original boot sector by moving it to another location. Many users mistakenly believe that if a floppy disk is not a bootable system disk, then the disk cannot pass a boot-sector virus to their system. To the contrary, any formatted disk has the potential to both receive a boot-sector virus, and to pass that infection along to another system. Once the hard disk is infected, every subsequent boot from the hard disk activates the virus into memory. At this point, the virus will begin to infect non-write-protected floppy disks as they are accessed.

Under normal circumstances, boot-sector viruses are not able to infect other computers through networks,

modems, or tape drives. However, a special type of virus, called a *multi-partite* virus, is both a file infector and a boot-sector infector. Another special case is a rogue program called a *dropper* program. A dropper is a special executable file that actually "drops" a virus into the boot-sector area or infects a file when the dropper

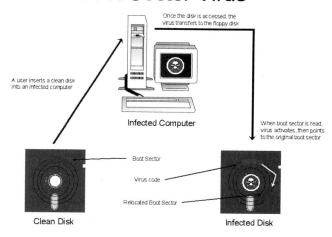

Boot-Sector Virus

Once the disk is accessed, the virus transfers to the floppy disk

A user inserts a clean disk into an infected computer

Infected Computer

When boot sector is read, virus activates, then points to the original boot sector

Boot Sector

Virus code

Relocated Boot Sector

Clean Disk

Infected Disk

A boot-sector virus.

program is executed. Both of these types of viruses can actually pass boot-sector viruses over local-area networks, through modems, and from tape drives.

Virus researchers have further categorized viruses into some subgroupings. Some file-infecting viruses are called *direct action infectors*, which means that each time an infected program is executed, it infects another file. Another category is a *TSR (terminate and stay resident)* virus, which means that after the virus executes, it stays in memory to perform operations such as infecting files, checking logic conditions, and hiding itself by monitoring certain hardware/software interrupts. A unique category of file infectors is called a *companion* virus. A companion virus searches for an executable file, usually with an .EXE extension. Once an executable file is found, the virus will create a hidden file with a .COM extension. This virus does not actually alter the original file with the .EXE extension. Because the command interpreter always executes a .COM file before an .EXE file if the filenames are identical, the virus is always executed before the actual program runs. This type of virus can fool integrity checkers that are merely looking for changes in files. A virus that infects a directory is a special type of virus. This virus actually is executed when a directory structure is read. Currently, there are only a few viruses that utilize this technique for infecting a system.

In addition to these categories, viruses can be grouped by distinct viral properties. Here we'll group viruses by the way they attempt to conceal themselves. Let's consider stealth, encrypted, polymorphic, and slow viruses. To be considered a stealth virus, a virus must use methods to hide itself from a computer user. There are many different degrees of stealth, which will be examined later. An encrypted virus is one that uses a scrambling technique to mask the actual virus code in an attempt to prevent researchers from detecting or reverse-engineering the code. A polymorphic virus is one that mutates with every infection; hence, no two infections will contain the same code. A slow virus is one that only attacks when certain conditions are met, to avoid detection. One example of such behavior would be to only infect floppy disks, or to only infect a file as it is being copied. This method can sometimes defeat an integrity checker.

STEALTH

Virus writers have advanced beyond the stage of merely producing viruses that infect files. *Stealth* is the implementation of methods to keep a virus as obscure as possible, and this is the area where virus writers have directed most of their efforts in the past few years. There are different degrees of stealth exhibited in viruses. Let's examine some of the techniques used by these dark crusaders, and see what responses the anti-virus community has taken to combat these new threats.

The lowest possible level of stealth is found in an overwriting virus, which simply causes the infected program not to run properly. About 10 percent of all viruses exhibit this characteristic—and are instantly recognizable once they have infected a system or file. These types of viruses are noticeable to the most casual observer.

Stealth Techniques

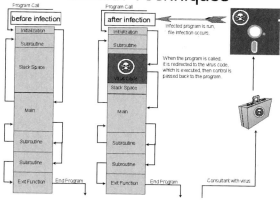

An overwriting virus.

The next level of stealth enables the infected programs to run properly—but no other subterfuge is used to conceal the virus. Unless the user utilizes some type of anti-virus software—or the virus is incompatible with another software program—chances are good that it will not be found. Even though the creation date of the file may change, providing a potential clue to the user, most users do not check these dates.

A user who does some elementary checking of the file dates may indeed notice these changes. Consequently, virus writers began to utilize the next level of stealth, which actually preserves the original file-creation time and date. The interrupt for DOS services can be utilized to preserve this creation date and time. Other methods may be utilized as well. Another stealth mechanism is to prevent DOS from issuing the "Abort, Retry, Fail" message when a virus attempts to write itself to a write-protected disk. This can be done by replacing the DOS critical-error-handler interrupt with a substitute routine. These issues concern only file-infecting viruses, not boot-sector-infecting viruses. At this level of stealth, it is still possible to recognize that a file has grown in size, or that a boot sector contains information that doesn't belong there. This fact prompted virus writers to attempt to hide these details, which led to the next level of stealth.

Virus writers began to implement methods to hide file growth and to conceal any changes that may have occurred in the boot sector. One way to prevent a file size from increasing is to write a virus that looks for sections of contiguous zeros in a file. Once it finds this area, it may overwrite that part of the file with the virus code. In this manner, the actual file size does not increase at all. When the infected program is executed, the virus executes its code and becomes memory resident, and then overwrites the virus code of the infected file in memory with zeros. Consequently, in memory, the program is identical code to the original file. This will cause the program to run with no side effects. Other viruses tend to utilize the block of zeros that many compilers place at the beginning of .EXE files, immediately following the file header.

Virus writers have advanced beyond the stage of merely producing viruses that infect files.

The casual user will inspect the file size by issuing the DOS DIR command. DIR utilizes the DOS services interrupt. If the virus intercepts the DOS services interrupt and traps the right functions, it can perform some addition operations to make the DIR command return a value equal to the original file length, even though a virus may have actually increased the size of the file. Because of these routines utilized by virus writers, anti-virus software vendors always recommend cold-booting a suspect computer with a known clean DOS system diskette. Once this is done, it will prevent a virus from executing and becoming memory resident; hence, the correct file sizes can be easily determined.

Virus writers quickly realized that all of these stealth methods were limited because the virus needed to execute and become memory resident. One method to hide any file growth is to add a cluster to the FAT chain, and place a portion of the original file in this new cluster, while overwriting this portion of the file with virus code. The directory entry, therefore, is not altered; consequently, even if the virus is not memory resident, the file size appears unaltered. An additional technique used to hide the growth of a file is by using the slack space of a file as a storage area. For example, a virus the size of one sector or less could conceivably replace the first sector of a file with itself, and then store the original sector of the file after the end-of-file marker, in the slack space of a file. Remember, slack space is that area between the end of file marker and the last cluster that DOS used to store the file. The average cluster size is 2,048 bytes, with 1,024 bytes being the second-most-common cluster size. That is more than enough room for a large number of viruses.

A virus that uses elementary stealth techniques.

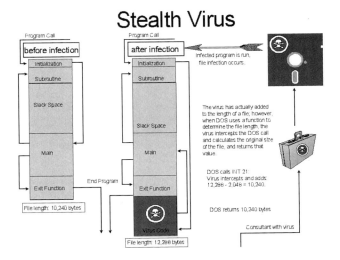

Altered FAT Chain

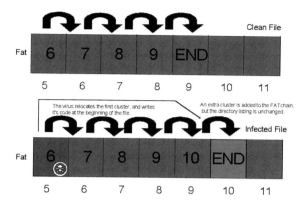

Clean File

| Fat | 6 | 7 | 8 | 9 | END | | |

5   6   7   8   9   10   11

The virus relocates the first cluster, and writes it's code at the beginning of the file.

An extra cluster is added to the FAT chain, but the directory listing is unchanged.

Infected File

| Fat | 6 | 7 | 8 | 9 | 10 | END | |

5   6   7   8   9   10   11

A virus that uses slack space and one that alters the FAT chain.

Other methods include viruses that disable anti-virus programs before they attempt to infect a file or boot sector. Most anti-virus software programs perform *cyclical redundancy checks* before they execute and will report any changes to the user. This is a flag to a user that the anti-virus program may have become infected. To avoid alerting the user that something is amiss, some viruses will not attempt to infect anti-virus software programs.

ADVANCED TECHNIQUES

A handful of virus writers have chosen, nay, even delighted in the prospect of an all-out battle with the anti-virus crusaders of the day. They are continually developing new ways to foil scanners and memory-resident software, and some of the newer viruses show that they have extensive knowledge of anti-virus software products. This ongoing battle has taxed even the best minds in the industry, and it may one day lead to a new type of detection software.

Now let's enter the realm of those deep, dark mysteries that continue to baffle all but the brightest minds in the anti-virus community. A handful of virus writers have chosen, nay, even delighted in the prospect of an all-out battle with the anti-virus crusaders of the day. They are continually developing new ways to foil scanners and memory-resident software, and some of the newer viruses show that they have extensive knowledge of anti-virus software products. This ongoing battle has taxed even the best minds in the industry, and it may one day lead to a new type of detection software. Let's examine the techniques in more detail.

One common ploy among boot-sector viruses that use advanced techniques is to display the original boot sector whenever a call is made to read sector 1 of track 0. The virus does this while it is memory resident, redirecting any reads of the infected sector to the sector where it stored the original boot sector. This may even fool a virus scanner. Some viruses even mark the sector where they placed the boot sector as an unreadable sector, so that users are not alarmed at seeing a boot sector in an unusual location. Some file-infecting viruses also monitor attempts to read an infected file. If a read attempt is made, the virus will redirect the read to the original contents of the file. This will fool security techniques such as using the DOS compare, and CRC checks. Furthermore, some boot-sector viruses manipulate the BIOS keyboard interrupt, which enables the virus to survive a Ctrl+Alt+Del keystroke. Many users mistakenly think that this removes a virus from memory. Anti-virus software vendors always recommend cold booting from a DOS system disk, never warm booting.

As scanners were made to detect all of the known viruses, virus writers attempted to produce software that would hide itself from scanners. This was first done through the use of encryption. A virus would encrypt its code and only leave a small portion of code unencrypted to decipher the rest of the virus. This decryptor could be as small as about 20 bytes; consequently, many scanners utilize the same signatures for these types of viruses, because the length of the code for possible signatures is very limited. For this reason, most scanners encrypt their own search strings so that other virus scanners will not false-alarm on their search strings. After virus writers realized that scanners were focusing on their decryptor routines, they began to add meaningless instructions to their decryptors to obstruct the virus researcher from finding a a specific sequence of code he could utilize as a signature. Another sophisticated technique is to vary the number of meaningless instructions. To cause this type of variety, a routine in the virus must generate random numbers, and these numbers then determine the quantity of meaningless instructions. The authors of virus scanners countered this technique by utilizing wild-card searches. However, in order to determine what limits exist, the virus must be disassembled and analyzed.

Virus writers weren't satisfied with the previously mentioned levels of stealth. After viruses that used random-number generation started being detected, the writers began to experiment with altering the code sequences of instructions within the virus. It's easy to see that if the order in which some instructions were executed was altered, the outcome would still be exactly the same.

Consequently, virus writers could alter the sequence in which certain instructions were issued, and thus further complicate scanning efforts. To detect these types of viruses, the virus researcher must either produce a large number of search strings, or search for specific fragments within predictable limits. The search engine is more complex than any that was previously discussed. Once again, the virus must be disassembled to successfully forecast what the limits of the generator might be.

To further enhance the stealth of viruses, writers began to implement generators that would alter the actual instructions within the virus code. There are many different ways to construct a code sequence to accomplish an identical procedure. Also, the registers (a small special-purpose type of memory that is

Encrypted Virus

The decrypter/loader portion of the virus encrypts the virus code, and decrypts the virus when the code is executed. The decrypter/loader is not encrypted itself.

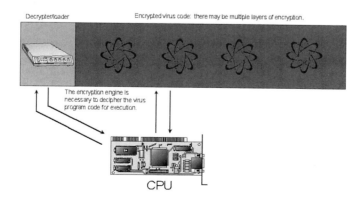

Decrypter/loader   Encrypted virus code: there may be multiple layers of encryption.

The encryption engine is necessary to decipher the virus program code for execution.

CPU

An encrypted virus.

designed for programmer control) may be substituted for one another, which will alter the bytes of the decryptor/loader. The only way this type of virus can be scanned for is to disassemble the code, analyze the code generator, and establish what types of bytes are reliably produced. Then, once these bytes are established, the researcher must determine what offset each byte has from the other, and then link-in a detection routine that will search for these bytes at a given offset. This type of virus can be very difficult to detect, and false alarms are easily produced if the smallest error is made when creating a detection routine. This type of virus doesn't have a search string; on the other hand, the detection algorithm must be hard-coded into the scanner.

some code that made disassembly extremely difficult? Instructions can be placed in virus code that, when executed, are simple jump instructions; however, when the anti-virus researcher steps through the code on a debugger, the same instructions can cause the computer to reboot. Another method is to use two layers of encryption. Stepping through the code of a virus that has two layers of encryption will not allow an analysis of the code that is hidden within the second layer of encryption. This technique is known as *armoring*; that is, the technique of protecting a program from outside tampering. Although researchers can still detect these types of viruses, they make disassembly and analysis very difficult and time consuming.

Two different assembly-language routines that perform an identical action.

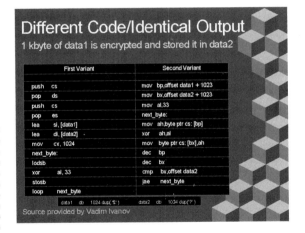

Different Code/Identical Output

1 kbyte of data1 is encrypted and stored it in data2

First Variant	Second Variant
push cs	mov bp,offset data1 + 1023
pop ds	mov bx,offset data2 + 1023
push cs	mov al,33
pop es	next_byte:
lea si, [data1]	mov ah,byte ptr cs: [bp]
lea di, [data2]	xor ah,al
mov cx, 1024	mov byte ptr cs: [bx],ah
next_byte:	dec bp
lodsb	dec bx
xor al, 33	cmp bx,offset data2
stosb	jae next_byte
loop next_byte	
data1 db 1024 dup('$')	data2 db 1024 dup('?')

Source provided by Vadim Ivanov

We've established the fact that the more-sophisticated viruses must be disassembled in order to analyze the code generator. But what if virus writers placed

One big flop by virus writers was their attempt to utilize a *mutation engine*. The idea is that a virus writer would code his or her virus and then link it with the mutation-engine object code, which would produce a polymorphic virus—which certainly makes detection a painful process. However, most major anti-virus companies promptly included detection for the known mutation engines; consequently, any virus using that particular mutation engine is detected as soon as it is released.

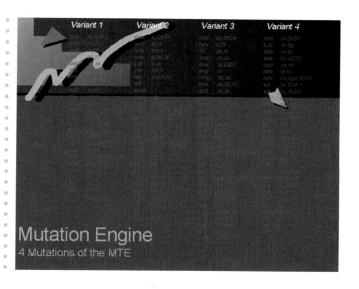

| Variant 1 | Variant 2 | Variant 3 | Variant 4 |

Mutation Engine
4 Mutations of the MTE

THE FUTURE OF VIRUSES

During the evolution of virus technology, we have seen a number of anti-virus software vendors fall by the wayside. It is extremely difficult for a company to maintain a software product capable of detecting and removing vast numbers of viruses—especially when current viruses have superior stealth mechanisms. Today, even non-programmers and hackers with no experience in viruses can use a *virus creation kit* that enables them to create a virus without actually coding the virus itself. There are several software packages available that enable the user to simply input a number of control variables into the program. Presto! A virus is compiled and created, complete with generated source code and comments. These kits are bound to flourish in the future.

Given the current trends and the new technologies employed by virus writers, what can we expect in the coming years? One certainty is that survival of the fittest will apply to viruses. Those viruses easily detected will quietly die out, while the more sophisticated, polymorphic and encrypted viruses will flourish. This will further encourage hackers to develop this type of virus to ensure that their creations survive. Within, say, two years, the more common viruses will not be simple creations like the Stoned or Jerusalem viruses, but rather stealth viruses that utilize complicated encryption schemes and armoring techniques.

We haven't yet talked about what kind of havoc that viruses could eventually cause the public at large, but the potential perils are enormous. Up until now, virus writers have concentrated on logic bombs that, when activated, create some type of nuisance, a delay in work, or destruction of data. However, what if experts in industrial sabotage or international terrorism began working with viruses? What would the likely targets of their programs be?

The most dangerous type of virus is the one that remains silent and undetected. It doesn't overwrite hard drives or attempt to achieve notoriety for the virus author. On the other hand, it may go out and change a byte here or there. A direct attack on specific systems could be devastating. Consider a virus that alters financial figures, or even election results. Computers today control life-support systems, credit ratings, traffic, telephone service, missile-guidance systems, aircraft, automobiles, communications, and countless other aspects of our daily lives. These systems are all subject to attack by a virus, notwithstanding some difficult barriers in place to prevent this from occurring. Direct viral infiltration of specific targets should concern authorities everywhere. Right now there could be viruses already in place, waiting for a signal or the right logic to activate a routine that could wreak devastation upon the unwary. (Hackers have already expressed the desire to tamper with the phone system and traffic lights.)

The reason most viruses are detected is because they have design flaws or program bugs. Obviously, viruses don't get beta tested in a formal program, nor are they subject to quality-assurance standards. In most cases, an apparent incompatibility with other programs or the operating system itself will cause a suspicious user to check for a virus. Another common symptom of a virus is unusual disk activity or computer-system performance that is slower than normal. A third symptom is that, in the virus writer's attempts to gain notoriety, he or she has inserted a logic bomb in the code that will produce immediate and obvious chaos among users. For these reasons, almost all viruses are spotted by the average computer user before they have spread very far.

However, consider an organized, highly skilled team of software engineers and technicians committed to producing a virus to perform some mission-critical task—such as disrupting communications during a time of national crisis. A group of experts could conceivably carry out such a feat without much trouble. And the odds of finding such a group or person are astronomical. Most present-day hackers write viruses only for fun; yet, disregarding those viruses that proudly proclaim who wrote them, authorities have only found the identity of less than 10 virus authors—even though there are well over 3,000 viruses known to exist! What, then, are the realistic odds of tracking down a professional terrorist squad that engages in viral activities for a living?

. . . .

The reason most viruses are detected is because they have design flaws or program bugs.

INTERVIEW
WITH AN
ANTI-VIRUS CRUSADER

The situation isn't entirely hopeless, however. Some of the brightest minds in the anti-viral industry are seeking new ways to eradicate viruses before they can reach epidemic proportions. One such virus crusader is Morgan Schweers, currently employed by McAfee Associates and one of the first programmers hired by the company. McAfee Associates is a software utility developer that specializes in anti-virus software and support. Located in the heart of Silicon Valley, Santa Clara, California, McAfee Associates has been at the forefront of virus research, and it offered one of the first scanners available, known as Viruscan. Schweers' background is suitably diverse; he has extensive programming experience in assembly language, C, BASIC, Pascal, Fortran, and scripting languages. He has experience with VAX/VMS systems, as well as microcomputers. His programming accomplishments include integrity checkers, virus detectors/removers, Netware Loadable Modules, and even mainframe applications. Schweers is constantly re-educating himself regarding virus technology, and he has extensive knowledge of some of the newest algorithms that virus writers are implementing. In my attempt to understand the virus writers and where their technology is going, I spoke at length with the man who spearheads McAfee's attack against these dark lords of cyberspace.

What led you into the virus research field?

Schweers: While in high school and college, I did a lot of work in the computer security field, on both sides of the fence. When I first ran into a virus, I realized that the capability of these tiny little programs was immense. For perhaps the first time in my life, I consciously realized that I could either go down the darker side of programming and write my own, or combat them. In a real way, it felt like I was having a battle of wits against the virus author as I disassembled it and came up with a counter. That feeling was addicting enough that I started looking for other viruses to take apart. I lay no claim that I am here to save the world, but the first time I personally took a call from someone whose machine I had just saved, who was calling just to thank us...well, it just feels good. If it was just for the thrill of combatting the viruses, I think I would have dropped out of the business a while ago, when the flood of mediocre viruses started.

What events brought you to McAfee Associates?

Schweers: The college I was attending in New York had just gotten an incredibly widespread infection of the Jerusalem virus. I was beginning to write a detection and removal program when someone brought in a program that already did the detection. I contacted

McAfee Associates, and started leaving some technical details on the virus in a message to the Sysop. The Sysop broke in to chat and told me where I could find the Jerusalem virus remover. After some small talk, he noticed the technical description I had been leaving, and asked if I would be interested in writing a remover for a new virus. The Sysop was John McAfee, and the virus was the Dark Avenger virus. Once I wrote the virus remover and sent it off to him, he mentioned that he paid $200 per virus remover. I was stunned that I was going to get paid for doing something that was as much of a blast as writing the remover. I did removers from New York for around a year, until I had the opportunity to fly out to California for a science-fiction convention. I paid a visit to the McAfee Associates office while I was out, and John McAfee made me an offer that I couldn't refuse.

What kind of person writes viruses to be released to the general populace, and why do they do it?

Schweers: We don't really know the answer to that. I'll speculate for a bit, however. If you know your history, you know that younger people in the computer field have always flaunted what rules there were. I don't see this as a different issue than that. I believe that the majority of virus writers are younger than 20, but that's based on no data other than the way their code feels, and the attitude brought across from the messages they put in their code. I'm sure there are some thrill-seekers who want to see their viruses in high-profile scanners. Some would probably like to see their programs do damage to one particular place, but the program gets out a bit further than they expected. Just like in the early days of people breaking into computer systems, however, I think the majority of the people doing it are doing it simply because they want to find out if they can. The old joke about "Why did you climb that mountain? Because it was there." Again, like people who break into computers, there are almost no known cases of deliberate sabotage being perpetrated through a custom-written computer virus. There are few, if any, "professional" virus writers, but hundreds of "hobbyist" virus authors.

What is the most interesting thing you have found related to virus research?

Schweers: It would have to be some of the personalities that get involved in the anti-virus field. In the early days before the big marketing types realized that it was a good money draw, all the people involved in the virus field were really intense personalities. That's become very much diluted as more normal people have come into the field and in some places it's even become "business as usual." To answer seriously, the growth of a huge industry based around writing programs that counter tiny programs that are written for free still strikes me as incongruous.

Do you believe there are good uses for viruses? If so, what could some of those uses be?

Schweers: I'm sure that someone will come up with good uses, but I don't think that those viruses will bear any relation to the viruses we see today. In a far-flung future, when a large-enough number of people have portable computing systems with wireless communication, I can imagine programs that move from computer to computer looking at whatever information is made publicly available on those machines, looking for data relating to a subject their original owner wants to know about. For the present time, I can't see any use that a virus-based program would provide that isn't equivalent to a user loading a TSR or a device driver. What's more, the TSR and the device driver have "consent" of the user.

Has the existence of viruses caused an increase in computer knowledge within the programming community?

Schweers: In the programming community? I don't think so. The people who tend toward writing viruses already know enough about computers that the "act" of writing a virus probably doesn't teach them anything new. Also, the number of people actually encountering a virus is pretty small in the grand scheme of things. In the larger community beyond the programming community, I'd have to say no, also. The primary place non-programmers and non-anti-virus workers hear about computer viruses is in the media. The media don't have a great track record about being "clear" what a virus is. The main reason is that it takes time and page-space to explain enough about computers to give readers an honest understanding of what a virus does. Also, to be blunt, the media often sells themselves by hyping bad things to appear worse. That's not to say that the anti-virus community is free of blame, but the media have always wanted soundbites that are sufficiently doomsaying that they can splash them in the paper and on the news.

What programming language is best suited for writing viruses?

Schweers: Assembly. Specifically, for the PC, 8086 assembly language. Programming viruses in a high-level language lead to bulky code that you don't know the exact coding of. I don't believe I've ever seen a "good" concept for a virus that was written in a higher-level language than assembly. The vast majority of high-level language viruses are overwriting viruses that simply destroy the files they infect.

Are virus writers potentially talented programmers, based on the viruses you've examined?

Schweers: On the large scale, I'd have to say not really. The information to write a virus is in almost any decent book on assembly language for the PC. The people writing the viruses often make simple mistakes, and if they don't, they are often just making modifications of other people's viruses. This is why we have so many variants of older viruses in our database. There are a few gems of virus authors out there—usually the ones whose viruses are later modified by the mediocre talents into variants. Most of the self-styled virus-writing groups produce some really bad code. The best code has often come from individuals or very small, tight groups.

Which virus portrays the best programming skills that you have encountered?

Schweers: I'll probably be yelled at for giving kudos to any virus author by labeling their virus as well written. Anyhow, some of the tightest code, neatest concept, and best implementation I've seen was probably in the DirII virus. Just about everything about it was very, very good. They had a solid understanding of what they were doing, and were able to express it in code almost perfectly.

What are some of the more innovative programming techniques you've encountered within viral code recently?

Schweers: Perhaps the most innovative programming technique was one virus's constant self-encryption of its code as it executed. In terms of recent events, I suppose you expect me to mention polymorphic encryption. I don't consider it that innovative, since it was being done almost as well a few years ago as it is today. What's worse is that some people in the virus community have released "tool kits" that allow mediocre programmers to add polymorphic capabilities to their programs, thus reducing the innovation in viruses.

What do you believe will be the main technological focus of virus writers in the coming years?

Schweers: I'm tempted to say that I have no idea. I really dislike predicting like that. If I had to, I'd say that as DOS slowly becomes subsumed by Windows NT and OS/2, the virus authors will move toward those platforms as best they can. As long as DOS exists, there will be simple viruses that run under it, since it provides no protection for the user. On the other hand, as machines become more and more networked, the virus scene is probably going to become much more like the UNIX situation. Specifically, programs will be more concerned with breaking into a system, then replicating to break into other systems. It would be "nice" if the operating systems provided a feature by which a program could connect to a machine, and (using the CPU of that machine, at a low priority) peruse data made available by the owner of the machine. This would allow the growth of what I described above, information-gathering programs. I don't expect the majority of ex-virus authors to move into a field like that, because the illicit thrill isn't there as much.

Do you have any advice for would-be virus writers, or those perhaps already experimenting with virus code?

Schweers: Yeah, put this on for size. My programs are on more machines than any virus ever put into circulation has ever been on. People put good programs on their machines willingly and usually even happily. Put out something that is useful, and you'll get a lot more machines running your code than you ever will with a virus. If that doesn't convince you, then don't put out a damn virus unless it's got some really neat new concept. It's not worth it just to do damage; we'll just sneer at it as another piss-ant little virus by some mediocre programmer and our automatic programs for doing virus handling will deal with it. It takes a really well-written virus to impress

Don't pull out a damn virus unless it's got some really neat new concept. It's not worth it just to do damage; we'll just sneer at it as another piss-ant little virus.

anybody in the anti-virus field, and there haven't been any really impressive ones in a long while.

What is the greatest challenge facing virus researchers?

Schweers: The sheer volume of poorly written viruses flooding in. There's rarely any technical challenge in today's viruses. Almost any anti-virus researcher has batteries of programs to hit any new virus, programs that pick it apart, come up with detection, and often removal code, without any human intervention. Of the 10 percent that fails (to write detectors and removers for), a good 75 percent of it is because they're using someone else's algorithms to prevent detection or removal. The remaining few are usually the best of the lot. We, as virus researchers, get around 20 new viruses a week.

What area do you think anti-virus researchers should concentrate on to provide answers for the large number of viruses being released, and the increased sophistication of these viruses?

Schweers: Frankly, the vast majority of viruses currently existing could be dealt a relatively shattering blow by making DOS a 32-bit operating system in its own right. The viruses which operate on files could be made to fail by adding real protection to DOS files, and the viruses which operate on the boot sector and partition table could be eliminated by getting rid of the archaic INT 13h interface, as would happen under a full 32-bit operating system. The requirement for backwards compatibility with 8086 and 286 machines is a silliness that is, in my opinion, allowing viruses to continue. Fixing that is the responsibility of two groups, neither of them the anti-virus community. One of those groups is Microsoft. The day it produces a decent operating system and gets it onto everyone's desk is the day that the majority of viruses will no longer be viable. Windows/NT isn't that solution, in my opinion, since it propagates many of the mistakes of MS/DOS through the sake of compatibility. It will help, but there will still be viruses that will work under it. Under any 32-bit clean operating system, such as UNIX, OS/2, and Windows NT, most boot-sector viruses no longer operate.

The other group is the users. The users of personal computers need to demand protection that isn't based on specifically looking for viruses. They need to demand actual security to be built into the operating system. In the long run, this is the only way that viruses will be halted. The computer companies like Microsoft will continue to rely on faulty detection methods that are specifically aimed at viruses until the users rise up and demand better.

To this end, I believe that one of the main things that we should concentrate on is educating the user base. There is, in my opinion, no other long-term solution that can be offered by the anti-virus companies to the massive volume of viruses being released. Software solutions that aren't operating-system-based can be subverted. Hardware solutions, when they work, which is rare, limit the users' freedom more than they will accept and often don't work on other operating systems. Most anti-virus researchers, as opposed to those just in it for the money, look forward to the day when our products are no longer necessary because all the operating-system manufacturers will have built in real security. Until that time, all of us are just fighting a holding battle.

THE **MAJOR** VIRUSES

Now that we've examined the history of viruses, learned about computer hardware and disks, and examined virus technology, let's look at some of the common viruses that have impacted the cyberworld of computer users. By "common," I mean viruses that are frequently encountered by a large number of users, not obscure viruses that have never received wide distribution. We will discuss viruses that created havoc either because of frequent infections or because they contained a severe payload.

Brain virus—The Brain virus was one of the first viruses written. It burst onto the scene in 1985. It received wide circulation, because at that time there were generally not any standard anti-virus procedures in place. This virus was created to prevent users from stealing software from a couple of programmers who resided in Israel. The virus would only infect floppy disks, and it didn't do much of anything besides replacing the volume label of the disk with "(c) Brain."

Cascade virus—This file-infecting virus was found in October 1987 and is based upon a Trojan Horse that received rather wide circulation. It infects .COM files, encrypts itself in the file, and is memory resident. The virus activates on any day from September to December, at which time the letters on the screen begin to fall to the bottom of the monitor. The original virus only activated on CGA or VGA monitors, during the years 1980 and 1988; however, subsequent variations were modified to activate in any year.

Jerusalem virus—This memory-resident virus is also known as the Friday the 13th virus. This is one of the most widespread file-infecting viruses, since it's been spreading since December 1987. It infects .COM and .EXE files, and some variations infect overlay files as well. (Overlay files are executable programs that are executed within another program.) This virus contains a logic bomb that activates on any Friday the 13th. Once the system date is both Friday and the 13th day of the month, if a user executes an infected program, the virus will delete that program. Another symptom of this virus is a black box on the computer monitor. One of

the original versions of this virus had a programming bug, in that it would continue to infect the same .EXE files over and over, until the file grew so large that it would no longer fit into memory. This was an obvious signal to users that their computers were infected with a virus.

Stoned virus—This infamous virus, also called the Marijuana virus, appeared in February 1988. This is a memory-resident, boot-sector virus on floppy disks, and a partition-table infector on a hard disk. This virus derives its name from the message that some of the variations of this virus display on the monitor at random intervals. The message reads "Your PC is now stoned!.....LEGALISE MARIJUANA!"

Dark Avenger virus—This was the first fast-infector virus that the world witnessed. This file-infecting virus demonstrated innovative coding techniques when it was initially introduced back in 1989. Once the virus becomes memory resident, it maintains a counter and counts the number of files that it infects on the system. Once it has infected 16 files, it overwrites a random sector on the hard drive with a portion of its own code. At this point, the counter is reset to zero, and it begins the cycle again. If this random sector contains a file or data, then one sector of information will be corrupted. This extremely malicious virus caused many companies to lose data before it was brought under control. Hard drives that have been infected with this virus will cause scanners to false alarm when the overwritten sectors are scanned, because these overwritten sectors contain fragments of the Dark Avenger virus code (not executable code). The spread of this virus captured the imagination of hackers everywhere and elevated the stature of the virus author to that of a dark apostle who called himself Dark Avenger. Dark Avenger is probably the most notorious virus writer known.

Yankee Doodle virus—This virus was discovered in September 1989, and is a file infector of .EXE and .COM files. Once an infected program is executed, it becomes memory-resident. If the virus is memory resident, and the computer-system time reaches 17:00, a tune is played, similar to the popular "Yankee Doodle" folk song.

Form virus—This virus, currently the most common virus in the world, was introduced in February 1990. It is a memory-resident, boot-sector virus, and because of some incompatibilities with existing hardware and software configurations, the errors that result from memory and disk conflicts far exceed the trouble caused by the actual logic bomb contained within this virus. The virus is designed to activate on the 18th day of the month (there is a more obscure variation that activates on the 24th day of the month), at which time it produces a clicking sound in the computer speaker whenever a user strikes a key. A common symptom of this virus is that a user may experience read/write errors when accessing their floppy disks.

Joshi virus—This boot-sector virus was discovered in June 1990. It uses some efficient stealth techniques, and activates as a TSR whenever an infected hard drive is booted as it infects the partition table of the hard drive. This virus contains a logic bomb that activates on January 5 of any year, by

displaying the message "type Happy Birthday Joshi." If the user types "Happy Birthday Joshi," control of the PC is returned to the user and it operates as normal.

Tequila virus—This is an encrypted, multi-partite, memory-resident virus that was discovered in April 1991. When this virus infects .EXE files, the virus uses stealth routines to hide any growth of these files while it is in memory. The virus is not encrypted in the master boot record. If it finds files that have been validated by McAfee's Viruscan program, it overwrites such files.

Flip virus—This memory-resident virus infects .COM, .EXE, and overlay files. It was detected in July 1990. It also infects the boot sector and partition table, which makes this program a multi-partite virus. On the 2nd of any month, EGA and VGA screens will be horizontally flipped between 16:00 and 16:59.

Green Caterpillar virus—First discovered in January 1991, this memory-resident virus infects both .COM and .EXE files. Some variations of this virus cause a green caterpillar to appear on the monitor, similar to the creature in the video game Centipede.

Michelangelo virus—One of the most famous viruses, the Michelangelo is named after Michelangelo Buonarotti, the Italian artist who was born on the same date that the virus activates its logic bomb. It is unknown if the author of this virus actually intended that connection. This virus surfaced around May 1991. This is a boot-sector infector on a floppy disk, and a partition-table infector on a hard disk. Once it is resident in memory, this virus will attempt to infect floppy disks in the A: drive when they are accessed. The logic bomb activates on March 6. On this date, if an infected system is booted up from an infected disk, the virus will proceed to overwrite many of the critical sectors on the disk that it was booted from. This will include the boot sector and file-allocation table, and that means the data left on those disks will not be accessible.

DirII virus—This memory-resident virus uses a special technique for infection, which leaves files unaltered, and is considered a directory infector. This virus uses stealth and places itself in the last cluster of a floppy disk and in an unused cluster on the hard disk. It will then encrypt the original file pointers to executable files on the disk, and it copies them to an unused area in the directory structure. The original pointers are then altered to point to the virus code. At this point, whenever a user attempts to execute a file, the virus is executed. When the virus is not memory-resident, any attempts to copy files will result in some type of an error, and chkdsk /f will result in file corruption. This virus was discovered in September 1991.

Maltese Amoeba virus—Discovered in September 1991, this virus infects .COM and .EXE files, and is memory-resident. It contains a logic bomb that activates on March 15 or November 1 of any year, at which time it will overwrite the first four sectors of cylinders 0 through 29, followed by a flashing monitor. Once the system is rebooted, a poem will be displayed and the system will hang.

Cansu virus—This is another boot-sector and partition-table infector. It was detected in February 1992. This virus, however, does not save the original boot sector or partition table, which can lead to problems once this virus is removed. Once it infects a system, the virus maintains a counter that is incremented each time the virus infects a floppy disk. Once the counter reaches 64, it displays a large "V" graphic on the monitor and hangs the system. Some variations trigger the graphic display when the counter reaches 32.

Screaming Fist virus—This virus was found in February 1992. It infects .COM and .EXE files, and is memory-resident. This virus is polymorphic and uses complex encryption techniques. It may cause infected programs not to execute properly.

Monkey virus—This cleverly written virus was first detected in October 1992. It infects the boot sector and partition table, uses stealth techniques, and is memory-resident. This virus encrypts the hard drive, and the virus code acts as a decryption key. If a user boots an infected system from a clean system disk, he will not be able to access the hard disk, but will receive the DOS error message "invalid disk media type reading drive c".

Tremor virus—Discovered in March 1993, the Tremor virus infects .COM and .EXE files. This virus contains some checks to avoid detection by anti-virus software. It uses stealth and encryption, and is polymorphic. As infected programs are read into memory, the Tremor virus disinfects them to avoid detection. Occasionally, this virus will cause the monitor to "tremor." Because the Tremor virus mutates very slowly, it can be very difficult to detect in advanced cases of infection.

Satan Bug virus—This 1993 virus infects .COM and .EXE files, and uses complex encryption, stealth, and polymorphic techniques. This virus does not appear to have a logic bomb; however, it may cause infected programs not to execute properly.

SMEG virus—This is a family of viruses that was discovered in May 1994. SMEG stands for Simulated Metamorphic Encryption Generator, and currently there are two viruses that use the SMEG: Pathogen and Queeg. These complex viruses infect executable files and use complex stealth techniques to avoid detection. They are polymorphic, and both contain logic bombs that overwrite the hard disk with random data. While overwriting the disk, a lengthy message is displayed. Pathogen activates on Mondays, between 17:00 and 18:00, and Queeg activates on Sundays, between 12:00 and 13:00 if certain conditions have been met. These viruses are quite sophisticated, and because long periods of time may expire before the logic bomb activates, they could remain undetected for an extended duration. Like the Dark Avenger, the author of this virus appears to seek notoriety and calls himself the Black Baron.

Junkie virus—This multipartite virus was discovered in June 1994. It uses encryption, is memory-resident, and is slightly polymorphic. It is unknown what the payload of this virus is. However, it has succeeded in generating a great deal of attention from the press.

The frequency of infection of the viruses described.

WHAT DOES IT ALL MEAN?

> We stand simultaneously on the verge of significant computer discoveries and on the edge of absolute binary chaos. Will viruses survive, as they do in the biological community?

Computer viruses are not science fiction. They are real, and they are spreading even as you read this. Never before has such a threat existed in the cyber realm. We stand simultaneously on the verge of significant computer discoveries and on the edge of absolute binary chaos. Will viruses survive, as they do in the biological community? Will the malevolent crusaders known as Dark Avenger and Black Baron succeed in causing an epidemic of data loss and social pandemonium? Are organized efforts already under way to accelerate espionage and terrorist activities through the use of viruses, Trojan Horses, and worms? Or will the study of viruses lead to the creation of a new breed of software, capable of implementing policies without the intervention of humans?

The task that confronts the anti-virus community is enormous and ongoing, but these researchers are relentless in their pursuit of mechanisms that will defeat the attempts of virus writers and hackers worldwide. As this saga unfolds, we will surely witness new techniques and strategies employed by both sides. Most of us can only hope that as a result of this cat-and-mouse game, our computers will become safer and more effective tools.

Speech Synthesis and Recognition

Some applications running on today's high-speed computers are beginning to do a credible job of converting freely-spoken sentences to text. We're getting much closer to realizing the old dream of a "voice typewriter" or speech-dictation application.

chapter 19
by David E. Day

INTRODUCTION

Speech is a rich and complex means of communication. It is not strictly unique to humans, as we've all been surprised to discover in the last few decades. But (as far as we know), we're the only animal species that keeps lists of hundreds of thousands of words. We even manage to speak a few of them.

How useful it might be to speak those words to our computer—and have the PC respond in kind. Can you imagine the convenience of selecting applications, entering commands and word content, then hearing responses, without resorting to keyboard, mouse and video display? That's a daunting and long-sought goal—one that's beginning to come to fruition.

Voice interaction could make possible remote access to all PC applications by use of a simple telephone. For sight or motion-impaired users, it can simply make access possible. Let's see how well technology is currently meeting the dream.

Computerized speech applications are divided into two categories: those that read text to you (text-to-speech), and those that "listen to you" to either take dictation or to accept commands. In this chapter, I'll discuss both of these types of applications and describe some of the more useful products that are available in this field.

VOICE SYNTHESIS:
TEXT TO SPEECH

It's not an easy job to make a good connection between letters and words and their appropriate sounds. Consider that vastly different spellings produce the same sounds (homonyms), as in "threw," "thru," and "through." On the other hand, consider how similar spellings can have vastly different sounds, as in "bough" and "rough." Then there are heteronyms (also called homographs), which are words with the same spelling but different meanings and pronunciations, such "bow" (what a butler might do) and "bow" (what an archer uses). These are part of the legacy that English bears as a melting pot for many other languages.

Applications that convert text to speech must resolve these letter/sound inconsistencies as well as such pecularities as word sounds that are modified by their use in a sentence (inflection). Only very recently have personal computer applications done a credible job of this. Following are some of the leading text-to-speech products that are available today.

LOGITECH AUDIOMAN

It might look like a futuristic spaceman's razor, complete with nose-ring, but it's actually the AudioMan from Logitech, a desktop or hand-held speaker-microphone that plugs into a standard printer port.

You can use AudioMan in a number of ways to record and play back speech as well as convert existing text files to speech. It's provided with a collection of audio applications developed by Voyetra. With one of these utilities, it records your voice and creates standard Windows .WAV sound files. You can use these files as voice annotation in a document or presentation.

You can also use AudioMan as a high-tech dictating machine. You can play the recording or any other .WAV file through AudioMan's speaker. However, each second of speech requires about 11KB of disk space; a 1-minute recording needs about 660KB (two-thirds of a megabyte).

A second utility lets you edit your voice recording in several ways.

Another AudioMan application looks and acts like an on-screen tape recorder; it records and plays back one or a whole list of audio files in mono or stereo. AudioMan also plays MIDI files (a library of them is included). An audio-based icon enhancer from Moon Valley is included to let you add voice or other sounds to your icons.

Because AudioMan plugs into the printer port, it's one of the few products that can give your laptop or portable computer a voice. (Other solutions require internal sound hardware, which is not provided on most portables.) That's a handy feature if you rely on either recording or playing back sound annotations. After you plug in AudioMan's adapter, you can plug your printer cable into it. This enables you to use the printer in the normal way (except in the case of Windows for Workgroups).

AudioMan's microphone is quite sensitive and employs automatic gain. This feature automatically raises the recording level to capture weak signals; if you

Logitech AudioMan—Annotator control panel.

Logitech AudioMan—audio editor.

Logitech AudioMan's AudioPanel digital tape recorder.

set AudioMan on the table next to your computer and speak softly, you'll record some of the computer's fan noise. It's best to pull the unit close to you.

A green LED on the front of the unit blinks when it's in record mode, and two button bars let you adjust playback volume. Side-mounted jacks let you plug in a monophonic sound source and a mono speaker or headphones. Two internal AA (penlight) batteries power the device.

An application of related interest is BeSTpeech ReadOut, from Berkeley Speech Technologies. It's a compact text-to-speech program, and the price is right: It's included free with AudioMan. Yet it does a fairly credible job of voicing whatever text file you select. Just open a Windows text application, highlight the words you want spoken, and click the speech icon.

Does it sound like a computer voice? Sure enough; it's monotone, has a sort of buzzy, nasal quality and doesn't know about heteronyms (such as the the "bow" and "bow" I mentioned earlier). But BeSTpeech does pretty well nonetheless, considering the complex task it undertakes.

BeSTpeech includes a pronunciation dictionary that lets you "fine-tune" words to improve their sound. You can use it to substitute a completely different word if you like. For instance, you can convert "hate" to "love" anywhere in your text at the click of a mouse.

To better understand what a considerable achievement these products represent, the following is a little background on how text-to-speech is accomplished.

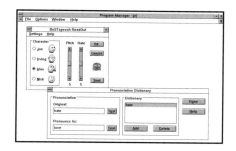

Logitech AudioMan's BeSTpeech ReadOut pronunciation dictionary.

. . . .

Many new uses for text-to-speech are emerging as the quality of the speech gets better. If a telephone is the only link to the world you have available, it's the only way to access text that is stored in a computer. For example, if someone sends a fax or e-mail to your office PC, you can dial up from any phone and have it read to you.

BeSTSpeech generates a voice from a set of logical rules about the sound of the language. (It doesn't use any sound fragments derived from human speakers, as do some other products.) Here's how it achieves its complex task:

- The text to be read is selected in an application program. To use AudioMan, for example, you either highlight the block of words in a word-processor or copy them to the Clipboard.

- A text normalizer converts or expands numbers and abbreviations into their full text equivalent. (I was pleasantly surprised to hear the word "incorporated" spoken from the "Inc." in an address of a letter I'd written to a company.) Numbers are spoken in various ways depending on their use; for example, a dollar amount might be spoken as "one thousand nine hundred and ninety five" but the same number used as a date must be spoken as "nineteen ninety-five."

- An exception dictionary handles certain words that don't fit the normal pronunciation rules. Whenever one of these rogue words appears, BeSTpeech substitutes a phonetic (sound-based) equivalent.

- Words that do fit normal pronunciation rules are converted to their phonetic correspondents. The rules are different for every language and are the heart of the text-to-speech process. The better the rules describe the language sounds, the better the speech will sound.

- Formulas for sentence rhythm, called prosody rules, add stress and intonation. There's a limit to what these rules can accomplish, because the computer doesn't actually understand what's being spoken.

- Some fine-tuning of the phonetic rules (applied in step 4) cleans up various details in the pronunciation.

- Finally, a voice generator digests the now-phonetic text into many subtle sound units and turns them into blocks of instructions that are used to generate a "human" voice.

- A driver sends these instruction packets to equipment that actually generates the voice sounds. For IBM-compatible PCs, BeSTpeech uses standard .WAV output devices; this means you can use any ordinary sound card to produce a human voice. In applications where a powerful computer isn't available, a custom circuit converts and generates the voice sounds.

Many new uses for text-to-speech are emerging as the quality of the speech gets better. If a telephone is the only link to the world you have available, it's the only way to access text that is stored in a computer. For example, if someone sends a fax or e-mail to your office PC, you can dial up from any phone and have it read to you. Want to know the latest legislation being filed in your state capitol? Dial up and hear the information verbatim. (This is already being done in Connecticut.) Are you blind but still want to use a PC? You can have a text-to-speech application read the screen's text to you.

VOICE RECOGNITION:
SPEECH TO ACTIONS (NAVIGATION);
SPEECH TO TEXT (DICTATION)

The heart of the voice-recognition dilemma is in the way we speak. We would make a computer's life much easier if we pronounced each word separately and distinctly, but we don't. Even an everyday phrase such as "How are you doing?" comes out "Howeryadoin?" It's perfectly understandable to other humans, but it's a real mishmash to a speech-recognition program. Applications that convert normally-spoken language into text must overcome the slovenly habits of real people. Many do not, but most can understand just enough individual words to be dangerous.

One way to improve the ability of a computer to understand you is to "train" it. This amounts to repeating words (and sometimes phrases) to the computer so it can learn your individual style. This tends to make the application "speaker-dependent," meaning it works better for you but usually much poorer for others who might use it. Applications that are not trained are "speaker-independent." These need more processing power and larger vocabularies to accommodate differences between speakers.

Applications that can distinguish a short list of individual words are often used to accept commands or choices. For example, you can run a computer application or initiate an action by speaking a word or two rather than clicking on a mouse or typing characters. Another popular use is hands-free telephone dialing or for automated phone-call handling.

Some applications running on today's high-speed computers are beginning to do a credible job of converting freely-spoken sentences to text. We're getting much closer to realizing the old dream of a "voice typewriter" or speech-dictation application.

For any of these uses, your computer needs at least a simple sound card. The card accepts a microphone and can convert your voice into digital signals for processing. This card may be packaged with the application, or you may be able to use a standard sound card.

. . . .

The heart of the voice-recognition dilemma is in the way we speak. We would make a computer's life much easier if we pronounced each word separately and distinctly, but we don't. Even an everyday phrase such as "How are you doing?" comes out "Howeryadoin?"

Microsoft Windows Sound System

The Microsoft Windows Sound System consists of a suite of audio applications packaged with a slim tubular microphone. It's in two flavors: with and without a sound card. If you have one of the popular sound cards that are used for games and music and accept a microphone input, you can save some money. If you don't, you can use the Microsoft sound card for Sound System and also to play game audio. The included microphone is from Telex; it's fairly directional and yields clean audio by canceling much of the background noise your computer emits. A pair of stereo headphones is also provided, or you can use external speakers if you prefer.

Probably the most exotic application included with the product is the Voice Pilot. It lets you associate any sound phrase with a single command or a command sequence. Shown here are some of the ordinary commands you might use in Windows. For example, you might want to select document text in the regular way and then issue your "copy," "cut," "paste," and other commands by voice.

Voice Pilot can trigger any Windows command sequence you can define. It's provided with a standard 'vocabulary' set, and you can add others as needed. Let's say that every day you need to open a particular document, update its contents from another application, and fax it somewhere. Once you work out the exact sequence, you can execute it with a single voice command, such as "fax daily report."

You can enhance Voice Pilot's ability to understand your commands by "training" it. First, select the phrase you want to improve, then repeat it several times. The application will analyze your personal voice patterns and save them as audio templates for your next use.

You can also use Windows Sound System as an ordinary voice-dictation device, to record your voice as standard .WAV files. You can include them as voice annotation in text files or presentations. For recording and playback control, there's a Quick Recorder application with an interface that looks like a cassette tape recorder front panel.

Microsoft Windows Sound System—Voice Pilot.

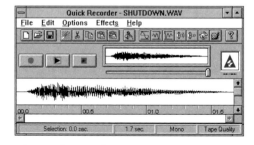

Microsoft Windows Sound System—Quick Recorder.

Quick Recorder lets you speed up or slow down the recording and add special effects such as echo and volume adjustments. You can also view the audio waveform (as you see in the figure) and edit or crop the sound to fit your presentation needs.

One useful capability is drag-and-drop for annotations. Once you have made a recording, a cassette icon appears in the window. Simply drag the icon to an annotation-compatible application, and the recording is dropped in. (Notice the bottom-right panel in the figure that says "TrueSpeech;" that's Microsoft's proprietary voice compression scheme, which lets you store several times the normal amount of speech in the same hard drive space.)

If you have a CD-ROM drive that also plays audio CDs (most do), an included Music Box application lets you play them and also create custom playlists for your CD collection. You can assign names for your CDs and for each track, and set the order of play. On playback, the window shows what's playing and how long each cut is.

A proofreader application is included to read back the numbers in documents (such as spreadsheets) so you can verify the values from other lists. It has a dictionary of some words and a long list of numbers you can select from and do some other fine-tuning. To use it, you open the number application and highlight the region you want to be read back.

One intriguing audio application included with Windows Sound System is the Sound Finder. It lets you find and play files, much as the Quick Recorder does. It also lets you add sound to documents. More than that, it can convert sound files to the Windows .WAV format from several other types. It lets you add a picture (an icon), a label, and a description to a sound file to let you keep better track of it.

Using Windows Sound System, you can play special sound files called RMI files. These files can contain both digital audio and MIDI music instructions and can be inserted in documents just like .WAV files. To play them, your computer will need a synthesizer sound card or MIDI port with external MIDI device.

Here, the Sound Finder is ready to play the sound of a cricket. It's identified here (and in any document you place it) by a little cricket icon, shown at bottom right.

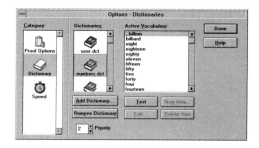

Microsoft Windows Sound System—ProofReader dictionary.

Microsoft Windows Sound System's Sound Finder.

CREATIVE LABS VOICEASSIST

VoiceAssist from Creative Labs is similar to the Microsoft Windows Sound System Voice Pilot. It's included with some of Creative's broad line of sound cards, and it works with the well-known SoundBlaster and SoundBlaster Pro cards (as well as the many compatibles), and even with Microsoft's Windows Sound System card. VoiceAssist ships with its own microphone, which plugs into the microphone input of a sound card.

With VoiceAssist, you can define multiple users, each of whom can train the voice recognition for thousands of possible commands. VoiceAssist even tracks which application window is selected and extracts the set of commands to match it.

KURZWEIL VOICE FOR WINDOWS

Voice for Windows is a combination dictation and navigation application that can recognize 60,000 or more spoken words. It requires no training to be able to recognize voices of different speakers. But it also automatically trains itself to your voice; the more you use it, the better it gets at recognizing your speech. Kurzweil claims over 95 percent word recognition, and the product integrates with most major Windows applications.

Voice for Windows is a professional application that includes a specialized sound board with microphone, and it runs only on a high-powered PC. It accepts normally spoken sentences and enters them into an open document. Just a few years ago, a product with this much recognition power would have cost several times as much and been slower and less effective.

One specialized application developed by Kurzweil illustrates the power of this technology. Called VoiceMed, this application is used by physicians to prepare formal medical reports on patients. As the session proceeds, VoiceMed displays various menus of syndromes or medical procedures. The doctor chooses the appropriate items for the patient, and the computer selects stored text paragraphs that properly describe the condition.

VoiceMed has greatly speeded the process of medical record-keeping and reduced the liability posed by sloppy or incomplete reports. It's so effective that some insurers now offer physicians 20 percent discounts on their malpractice insurance premiums if they use the system. Several similar custom applications cover other medical specialties, including cardiology, surgery, medical imaging, and orthopedics.

Dragon Systems' DragonDictate for Windows

Like Kurzweil's Voice for Windows, DragonDictate is a dictation application with a large (60,000-word) vocabulary. It recognizes any speaker, but its recognition automatically improves over time as it learns the speech patterns of a user. It's available at lower prices with reduced vocabularies of 5,000 and 30,000 words for home, educational, and small-office uses.

DragonDictate requires a powerful high-end PC, but unlike Voice for Windows, it uses standard sound cards instead of a custom board. If the application is unsure of a word you've spoken, it pops up a list of words that are its "best guesses" in order of probability. On the next page, you can see an example of a letter being dictated into Microsoft Word. The uncertain word here is "assistance," which sounds very much like "assistants" and something like "systems."

DragonDictate is ready to work with many standard Windows applications, and you can customize it with your own vocabulary and command list. WordPerfect Corporation has announced that it will be using the technology in a series of new applications aimed at professional users. A developer's kit called VoiceTools is now available for programmers.

A limited-vocabulary product called Dragon Talk>To is also available at much lower cost to give you command and menu control over several popular Windows applications.

Of all the innovations computer technology can bring to us, text-to-speech and speech-to-text are the most desired. After all, when we can reliably talk with our PC, we can be forever free from keyboards, mice and monitors. (In corporate America, the greatest resistance to PC use has always been the keyboard, and the need for typing training.)

These features are coming, but much slower than once had been hoped. Only recently have personal computers gained the power and speed needed to process natural languages. And only recently has technology begun to work out practical solutions. Text-to-speech and voice-response applications are already practical realities, and are being improved. User-independent speech-to-text functions are pushing the limits of what's possible. The demand is so great that you'll see a lot of pushing!

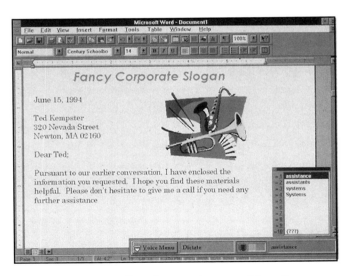

DragonDictate's dictation and recognition list.

PART IV

· ·

In Your Face

Interactive Compact Disc and Interactive Television

Why doesn't everybody have a CD-interactive player? That's what the manufacturer is wondering. But practically speaking, it's early in the game, and this technology is just beginning to make its mark.

chapter 20
by David E. Day

INTERACTIVE CD

When discussing the future of computerized information and graphics, some people wonder why computers don't just use big television displays instead of expensive monitors. After all, everybody's already got a TV. It turns out that PCs did once use TV sets for display. This was because those early PCs displayed only coarse text and graphics in a few colors. TVs could provide that display quality, and they were cheap and available. Those were the good old days.

Today's VGA computer monitor is far better in almost every way than a TV; it displays more details, it shows more (and more accurate) colors, and it doesn't flicker as much. That's one reason a good monitor costs several times what a good TV does.

TV, however, has a few advantages: It's the one picture and graphics delivery device that everybody owns. It often has a big screen, it displays color, it provides sound, and it's affordable. Hook it up to the right equipment, and you can play games, watch movies and even listen to tunes.

Enter a fairly recent technology called the compact disc or CD. Used for audio, it delivers high-quality stereo music. Used for computers (the CD-ROM), it can store many large PC applications or thousands of sound clips, photos and other graphics, and even short video segments.

Now along comes the virtual marriage of the TV and the compact disc: compact disc/interactive, or CD-I. It looks the same as an audio CD, but it offers a whole new realm of applications. It's played with a special-purpose computer disguised to look like an audio component. Pop in a game application, and you get great animated graphics and sound. Drop in an educational title, and you might get a narrated encyclopedia with video clips and other interactive multimedia materials. And you can use the player to play standard audio CD discs as well.

Upgrade to a more powerful player, and CD-I discs will perform like miniature video discs to play feature-length movies.

Further, a CD-I disc has one big advantage over a videotape. If you want to go from one place to another on a tape, you have to wind it, which is slow and noisy. On the CD, a silent beam of light moves quickly from one region to another on command. That's the crux of interactive TV.

The premise is almost irresistible: a CD-I player only costs a few hundred dollars—and you already own the TV set. That's the powerful marketing allure of interactive television. To duplicate these features on a PC, you'd need a high-speed CD-ROM drive, sound card, a big monitor, and a powerful, high-speed processor.

Interactive TV consists of a collection of "episodes;" your responses to on-screen choices determine the sequence. Let's use an interactive mystery story as an example. As the story unfolds, you're presented with a choice: Was it the butler or the maid who killed the Earl? (Or perhaps it was the family's pet gorilla.) Whatever choices you make will direct the story line to one of several available scenarios.

The CD-I player zips to the episode you choose that represents the next stage of the drama. If you chose the gorilla, it might be an up-close view of the faulty cage lock. Lurking in the background: the mystery man with a banana. (The same technique works for interactive game shows and even encyclopedias.) You can't do this with videotape, because it can't wind to the proper images quickly enough.

Why doesn't everybody have a CD-interactive player? That's what the manufacturer is wondering. But practically speaking, it's early in the game, and this technology is just beginning to make its mark. Only in the last few months has a wide variety of titles become available.

INTERACTIVE TV/VIDEO

For the first time, you can experience TV as an active pastime instead of a passive one. In this chapter, I discuss two branches of this premise. First is the CD-I (compact disk-interactive) product, that lets you interact with a video image for education, games and other applications. It also functions as a CD version of a video cassette player, to bring you full-length movies.

The second segment discusses equipment and applications for your PC that combine to give you a complete home-video production studio. They let you create your own video movies and presentations—the kind you'd otherwise need a broadcast studio for.

I'm not just talking about over-amped home movies. You can capture still and moving scenes, edit and combine them

For the first time, you can experience TV as an active pastime instead of a passive one.

with graphics, video special effects, audio and MIDI music, and produce complete video shows. Some of these new products are available at a surprisingly low cost, and there's a ferocious competition for this emerging market.

PHILIPS CD-I

Philips has created landmark standards for the audio cassette tape, CD, and video disc that defined entire industries. It's done it again with interactive CD (CD-I). This Dutch multi-national is the world's third-largest maker of TV sets and is now the sole producer of CD-I equipment. (Its subsidiary Magnavox makes the only other CD-I product line available.)

A basic CD-I player can handle audio CD, Kodak Photo CD, and CD-I titles. CD-I interactive applications rely on the player's special-purpose computer to display on-screen graphics, animation, and even video clips in a window. With a plug-in option called a digital video cartridge, you can instantly expand the unit to play full-screen full-motion digitally-recorded movies. You can view music videos and also interact with karaoke-like titles.

A CD-I player can look like an audio component or perhaps a stand-alone game machine. This figure shows a recent low-cost model from Magnavox that looks a bit like a hot-dog cooker. It has a top compartment for the CD disc and includes a plug-in controller paddle.

For pointing and selecting, a player has a wireless infrared thumbstick controller that looks much like a TV remote-control with a miniature joystick. Other hand controllers are available for special uses—there's a combination joystick/touchpad for game playing, a trackerball for mouse-like screen selections and even a giant "roller controller" trackball for younger kids. You can also plug in an ordinary mouse if you prefer.

Philips has a division that creates CD-I titles and also contracts with developers to produce special interactive CD versions of popular computer applications. More than 150 titles are now available, and many more are in development. For example, both Compton's and Grolier's interactive encyclopedias are available for CD-I, each with more than 30,000 articles and thousands of illustrations, graphics, maps, narrations, music, and video clips. Powerful search tools let you cross-reference the articles and other material.

Using interactive CD, you can play shoot-'em-up and flight simulation games, join in futuristic cyber-punk and space adventures, play golf at Palm Springs, and race high-performance cars—all from the comfort of home.

Some CD-I children's titles include versions of Richard Scarry's Best and Busiest Neighborhoods, a version of *Sesame Street* (for numbers and letters), and animated cartoons and drawing lessons. All include lots of color and animation, sound effects and music. Digital video for kids include Berenstein Bears learning experiences, Hanna-Barbera cartoon adventures, and interactive sing-alongs.

Philips/Magnavox CD-I player.

The Stickybear Reading CD-I.

Time-Life's Astrology CD-I.

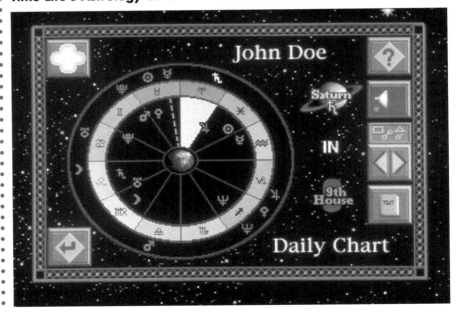

The popular Sticky Bear character appears on CD-I to give the kids entertaining lessons in reading, thinking, and math. Animated characters lead the kids through a magical world complete with sound effects and original music. Select any of the letters or numbers to interact with your reading adventure.

One unusual feature of this CD is its second language; all the audio and video material is provided in either English or Spanish, at the click of a button.

If you want to review your current connection with the cosmos, the Time-Life interactive CD-I called Astrology will accept your personal information. It produces a daily horoscope and a detailed birth chart; it will even determine your "compatibility" with someone special in your life. It's based on the Time-Life book series, *Mysteries of the Unknown.*

Here is how Astrology will appear on your TV. Use the controller paddle to enter your birthdate and other information, and Astrology will prepare your current charts. (It seems that "John Doe" sheepishly finds himself on the horns of some dilemma in Aries.)

Interactive media really shows its power and flexibility when it takes you on an adventure you'd never be able to have any other way. A Child is Born is an interactive exploration of childbirth as told from the inside. It describes the day-by-day growth of the baby before and after birth, using narrated photos of

fetal development by Lennart Nilsson.

Interactive game thrillers like the kind that run on PCs are available on digital video CD. One popular game—The Seventh Guest—is a murder mystery set in a strange Victorian hilltop mansion. It's a composite of 3-D computer-rendered sets and backgrounds and live action with real actors. Your role is to solve the mystery by interacting with the storyline. You observe, interrogate the other "guests," and finally sleuth out the murderer.

It's uncanny how authentic the scenes appear. This next figure shows the "dining room," complete with tapestries, cupboards, a sideboard, and a mahogany table that is set for a late-night entrèe (complete with dishes and silverware).

The dining room from The Seventh Guest digital video CD-I.

- All of this is computer-created art; however, in the course of the interactive action, real actors will enter this scene and make themselves at home.

- The CD-I player can also accomodate movies (the plain 'ol non-interactive kind). Over 60 titles are now available, including *Top Gun*, *Dances with Wolves*, *Silence of the Lambs*, *Star Trek VI*, *The Hunt for Red October*, *Fatal Attraction*, *Indecent Proposal*, *The Firm*, and even the enduring Bing Crosby/Danny Kaye chestnut, *White Christmas*.

- CD-I movies are recorded in digital format, unlike the standard videodisk, which is analog and more subject to distortions from wear and dirt. CD-I is also much smaller (the same size as a music CD). As this format becomes more popular, you'll see many more movies made available.

- I've just had a chance to review a copy of *The Firm*; a set of three CDs in CD-I digital video format. While the video is adequate, I'm sure, the audio is stunning. It has the same "live" quality as an audio CD.

VIDEO
CAPTURE/EDIT/CREATE/SHOW
APPLICATIONS

Want to do your own video production? It can be done, of course. All you need is a camera, some digitally-synchronized video and audio tape recorders, a special-effects generator, a video mixer, an audio mixer, and a chroma-key box. You'd probably also like to have a collection of backdrops for your performers, and it would be nice to have some studio musicians to help create the mood.

Or you could convert your PC into a video-editing station by installing a special-purpose video board and one of several multimedia video-editing applications. (You'll still need a video camera, of course.) In candor, you'll also need a well-endowed computer to get the job done; you'll want at least 16MB of RAM and a very large hard disk (500MB is not too large). This is because full-screen, full-motion video uses a lot of storage space—several megabytes for each minute of play. (Later I'll describe some video compression techniques that can greatly reduce—but not eliminate—this need.)

One option is to create video clips that run on a window in a PC monitor, using one of several standard formats. These videos are often not very high quality, but they can be easily distributed as part of a multimedia show. If you'd like to produce PC videos, slide shows, or cartoon animations, you can use the same production tools, but your storage needs may be less than they would be for full-motion video productions.

If you're planning to add audio or MIDI music, you'll also need a sound card that supports the formats you're planning to use.

Many of the following applications are much like those described in Chapter 11, "Interactive Applications and Simulations," as multimedia development tools. In fact, some of those other tools can create graphics and animation in standard video formats. These products go a bit further, and are more focused on editing, sequencing and special effects. You may be able to combine production materials from either kind of product.

The following applications are intended mostly to create short video scenes from even shorter clips, for multimedia presentations on PC monitors, and sometimes on TVs.

ADOBE PREMIERE V1.1

[CD-ROM for Windows; floppy version available; Macintosh version available; 486/33 with 16MB RAM, 24-bit true-color VGA card and display recommended; video digitizing board for AVI or QuickTime format recommended]

Adobe makes widely-respected tools for creating and editing images. These include Photoshop (for editing graphics and photos) and Illustrator (for creating graphic illustrations and precision drawings). Premier is its first full video application.

You can use Premiere to combine digitized video clips from any source with scanned images or slides, animation files, digital audio, and synthesized music. Add any of several special effects, such as fades and wipes, and create a composite video to display on a PC.

Premier gives you five basic windows to support your editing: Project, Construction, Info, Transitions, and Preview (all shown in the next figure). The Project window is a preview viewer for the movie you're putting together. The Construction window is a "storyboard" of clips you're putting together. It's in time sequence, and it gives you video, audio and transition tracks.

To place an audio or video clip, you simply drag it from the Project window to where you want it on the Construction window timeline. In the same way, you select and drag transitions from the Transitions window, and drag video and audio special effects filters from menu listings.

An Info window displays details about whatever video clip you have selected, including starting and ending times and durations.

When you start a new project, you'll have a collection of available clips, which are movies, audio clips, animation, or still images. (The still images can be artwork, photos, or any other graphic.) You import the clips into the Project window for use.

Clips are stored in alphabetical order, ready for you to drag them into place.

Using Adobe Premiere to construct a video sequence.

The Construction window is your video editor and sequencer. It has a time ruler at the top, two tracks for video, a transition track and superimpose track to blend or fade between them, and three audio tracks. To place a clip, just drag it with the cursor from the Project window to the Construction window. A small thumbnail shows its position, and a small marker appears in the Project window to show it's in use.

You'll want to preview all or part of your movie before you actually commit it to final production. Simply extend the yellow work-area bar in the Construction window over the portion you want to preview, select a few preview options, and choose Preview from the Project menu.

You'll find many tools for editing clips, applying transitions between two clips, and applying effects

and color filters. You can also create superimpositions ("sandwich" shots) of multiple clips. One very powerful sandwich effect relies on chroma keys—colors that are invisible in one clip but add portions of another clip where they occur. You can add backgrounds or special inserts just like the broadcast pros do. There's also an alpha channel key, which lets you choose the gradation or percentage of transparency of each clip.

When you've created your video sequence, you prepare it for use by compiling it. All the elements are combined into an .AVI or QuickTime format video file, and they can be played on any PC with the right viewer application. If you have the right equipment, you can even create standard TV-compatible (NTSC-format) video. For that, you'll need a compatible video board, lots of RAM and hard-disk space, and a high-performance PC. In some cases, you'll want to use a compressed video format to save storage space.

HSC INTERACTIVE

[Floppy diskette for Windows]

InterActive, from HSC, uses a slightly different metaphor for creating a video sequence. Every audio and video element (clip) is represented by a box or icon. This is the ultimate "object-oriented" editing tool. Each box is an object that can be moved around the work area and linked to any other to create a new sequence. The editing area always shows graphically the types of objects being used and their relation to each other.

• •

MACROMEDIA DIRECTOR

[Floppy diskette for Windows; Macintosh version available]

Director, from Macromedia, is an award-winning high-performance multimedia authoring tool. It enables you to import graphic elements such as text and graphics, 3-D animation, digitized video, and sound. From these elements you create and display animations for presentations, education, and to create CD-ROM titles.

(Director was used by Drew Pictures to create and produce a very complex multimedia game called Iron Helix, which I reviewed in Chapter 11. Take a look at the graphics therein; I think you'll be impressed. Of course, you won't be able to hear the intricate sound effects or see the entertaining animation effects used.)

You can create or fine-tune your presentation by using a built-in scripting language (a sort of programming language for multimedia). There's an included graphics paint program that gives you a color palette of 16 million shades.

The main sequencing and editing tool in Director is called the Score window. It gives you 48 individual tracks or channels to assemble video and audio clips in time sequence. The Score windows includes powerful controls for transitions, colors, speeds, and sounds. The Score window looks very much like the track sequence window used for MIDI music editing.

Another window called the Cast contains the source video and audio clips for assembling your presentation. It contains small "thumbnail" graphics representing these elements; it is actually a visual database that can store as many as 32,000 items. To place the clips on the Score window, just drag them into position using the mouse cursor.

Finally, a Player window with controls much like those on a VCR lets you play and adjust speed and other options for your presentation. Director also gives you control over external devices such as videotape recorders, CD players, and MIDI audio sequencing. The created video sequence can be played in either the Apple QuickTime or Microsoft Video for Windows formats.

VIDEO CAPTURE/DISPLAY BOARDS

A special-purpose video board accepts a signal from a TV camera, VCR, or other video source and "captures" the images; that is, it converts them into blocks of digital information. These blocks can be stored as files on your hard disk. On playback, your PC sends information from the file to the board, which converts the digital stream back into a video signal. You can watch the show on your computer monitor or on a TV set, or record it using an ordinary videotape recorder.

Although a video capture/display board combines two functions (video in and video out), it sometimes relies on your current VGA board for display on your monitor. There's a special connector on the top edge of your VGA board (called a "feature connector") that lets the video board tap into its display resources.

Some video boards are "capture" only, meaning they accept video but the only video display is on your monitor. If you want to see your produciton on a TV or record it on a VCR, you'll need a special option device that converts your VGA signal to a standard TV signal.

ASL MEGAMOTION

[16-bit ISA board for IBM-PC compatibles; requires 486 CPU, 8MB RAM; high-performance hard drive, VGA display card with feature connector; Microsoft Windows 3.1; sound card recommended with ADPCM compression and MIDI synthesizer]

Megamotion is a complete video capture and playback card that operates in either U.S. standard video format (NTSC) or foreign format (PAL). It accepts and generates video signals for cameras, VCRs, and other devices, using either composite video or S-video connectors. With an optional input adapter, it can handle four video inputs.

This board is unique because it can display video in multiple active windows on your VGA screen. It can show you two motion videos and, at the same time, six still video images. Megamotion includes custom Microsoft Windows drivers to handle these effects.

This product is shipped with a version of Adobe Premiere (discussed previously). In tandem with that application, it's a complete solution for video presentations, video editing, multimedia playback and authoring, and even video teleconferencing.

NEW MEDIA GRAPHICS SUPER VIDEO FOR WINDOWS

[16-bit ISA board for IBM-PC compatibles; requires 486 CPU, 8MB RAM; high-performance hard drive, VGA display card with feature connector; Microsoft Windows 3.1]

Super Video gives you two independent video input channels, each with its own stereo audio input. It digitizes both video and audio, eliminating the need for a separate audio card to capture sound files.

Utilities shipped with the board let you create files for multimedia storage.

For display, the Super Video for Windows board provides video to the feature connector of your VGA card. Your VGA card provides full-motion video display in Video for Window format.

Video Games

chapter 21
by Paul M. and
Mary J. Summitt

"You notice that the movement of your gun lags ever so slightly behind your real movements, but you take careful aim at her and blow her to smithereens. The next time around, she won't be so nice. She blows you to smithereens."

—Dave Mathey
Minneapolis-St.Paul *Star Tribune*

The first legitimate video game was created by Nolan Bushnell in 1972. The game, Pong, sold more than 6,000 copies its first year. By the early 1980s, the average video arcade machine collected more than $150 per week. Companies such as Atari, Odyssey, and Coleco became household names, to be replaced in later years by the likes of Nintendo and Sega. Today, the U.S. video-game market is the biggest in the world. Nintendo controls approximately 44 percent of that market. Sega has cleared about 45 percent. In other words, 89 percent of the U.S. market is controlled by these two Japanese companies. Since 1990, the market for video games in individual households has grown 35 percent. That market is now worth $5.5 billion. That's a large pie to be controlled.

Some of the more popular video games in today's market are discussed in the following paragraphs.

GAMES OF VIOLENCE

Mortal Kombat is, according to some, one of the most violent games available today. It is designed for both the Sega and Nintendo systems. Even though it is controversial, or perhaps because of it, the game sold nearly 4 million copies between its release in September 1993 and the end of that year.

"We have always believed it was important to have some form of guidance information that would be the same way you have disclosure information on food packaging that would help consumers."

—Rick Tompane, 3DO vice president

Why has Mortal Kombat been deemed so violent by some? The characters' actions may be part of the answer. Of the 10 characters present in Mortal Kombat, eight are human males, one is a male alien, and one is a female. Johnny Cage, a character supposedly from California, decapitates his victims with a powerful, bloody uppercut. The character called Kano, who has one mechanical eye, punches through his victim's chest and rips out the still-beating heart. Sonya Blade, the blond, blue-eyed, white female from Texas, kills with the "burning kiss of death." Rayden, an Oriental mystic, electrocutes his enemies. Sub-Zero tears the head off his enemy and holds it high in the air, the spinal cord still attached to the bloody neck.

The plot centers on a martial-arts tournament. For centuries (so the story goes) the competition was one of honor and glory, with each participant seeking the title of grand champion. However, an evil demon, Shang Tsung, and his pupil Goro, "a hideous half-human dragon," corrupted the tournament, taking not only the lives of their opponents but their very souls. (We'll return to Mortal Kombat later in the chapter for a more in-depth look at this game.)

Another game considered by some people to be too violent is Night Trap. Tom Zito, the game's creator, says that more than 100,000 copies of the game have been sold. In Night Trap, women are stalked by bloodsucking vampires. Zito suggests that it is nothing more than a parody of 1950's low budget horror films. However, he also says, "Frankly, I don't want anyone under the age of 17 to buy it."

Death comes early and often in Mortal Kombat

Wolfenstein 3-D promises profound carnage.

· · · · · · · · · · · · · · · **The playing-level system of Wolfenstein 3-D.**

The object of the game is to save scantily-clad sorority sisters from the vampire's henchmen. The game takes place in an old winery converted to a hotel. The vampire and his henchmen try to capture the hotel guests (the sorority girls) and drain their

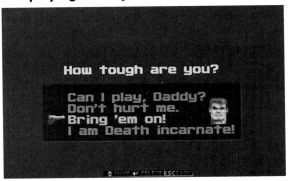

blood. It's the player's job to keep the bad guys away from the women. The consequences of losing are that the four thugs use a power drill to drain the girls' blood from their necks.

In 1989, a program called Wolfenstein 3-D became available for 386 computers with VGA-or-better graphic capabilities. The game has been advertised as featuring "realistic graphics and action." Apogee, the company that distributes the game, rated it PC-13 for Profound Carnage.

The basic story line in Wolfenstein 3-D is that the player is a captured allied soldier during World War II. The objective is to escape the prison by killing as many German guards as possible, collecting hidden treasure along the way.

Another popular program, also from Apogee, is Blake Stone. Similar to its predecessor, the program requires at least a 386 processor and VGA graphics. This game "has more of everything" according to Apogee's advertising.

The basic plot of the game has the player assuming the role of Blake Stone, a futuristic secret agent. A sinister madman has created an army of fierce creatures and is waging war on earth. The objective, again, is to collect as much treasure as possible, while killing the madman and as many of the creatures and guards as possible.

Virtual-reality games are a rapidly growing segment of the video-game market. Early forms of virtual-reality games were represented by the flight-simulator programs used in the military. These simulations were eventually transferred to video games. A recent helicopter simulation, LHX: Attack Chopper from Electronic Arts, enables the player to choose the enemy: Libyans, Vietnamese, or East Germans. The objective is to destroy enemy facilities and kill enemy troops.

Getting promoted is accomplished by successfully completing missions, which requires the player to destroy enemy units and installations while limiting damage to the helicopter.

Virtual-reality games have moved from the home computer and the military simulator to the arcade. Edison Brothers Entertainment, based in St. Louis, markets the Virtuality arcade games in the United States. Probably the best-known of these games is Dactyl Nightmare.

The basic premise of this interactive game is that four opponents enter this virtual world with the sole purpose of killing each other. The winner is the player who kills his or her opponents the most times, while being killed the fewest number of times.

Controversy also revolves around games with graphic sexual content. One of the earliest such games for the personal computer was Leisure Suit Larry. Nearly 1 million copies of this series of softcore adventures have been sold worldwide. The objective for the player is to go to bed with a woman (or, as one publishing executive said, "the object of the game is to get laid").

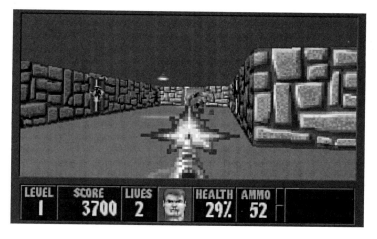

The premise of Wolfenstein 3-D is to kill or be killed.

"As I started to squeeze the trigger to blow him into molecular shards, I felt the graphite talons clutch my shoulders from above. In a flash, I was plucked high above the space platform, headed for the stars, and I knew I would be dead meat before the soaring dactyl reached Alpha Centauri."

—Harper Barnes, *St. Louis Post Dispatch*

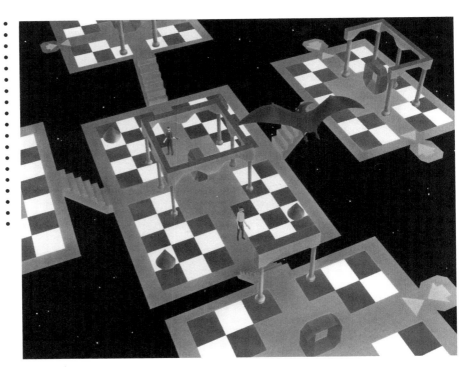

The virtual world of Dactyl Nightmare.

Artworx Software Company, Inc., publishes several programs of a sexual nature. Strip Poker Three pits the player against three women, Greta, Kami, and Laura, who gradually disrobe as they lose in the game. The "beautiful card sharks" each have their own personalities and style of play.

Another game that Artworx markets is called Jigsaw Pinups. So-called "hotspots" in each of the pinup-style puzzles produce laughs, sighs, squeals, and kissing sounds as the player places the puzzle parts.

One of the best-known of the sexually graphic video games is Virtual Valerie, a CD-ROM game for the Macintosh. This CD-ROM might be the best selling in the industry. Selling more than 25,000 copies a year for the past four years, Virtual Valerie has captured 25 percent of the adult market. Depending on

the player's responses, Valerie will either undress for you or tell you to leave her apartment in no uncertain terms.

These are just a few of the more well-known video games featuring violent or sexual subject matter. And these are the games that have generated such tremendous controversy in the news media.

The controversy surrounding video games is not new. An early game called Death Race attracted considerable attention and hostility. In this game, little creatures would dash across the road in front of the player's car as it was driven down the highway. The object was to hit the creatures with the vehicle. The player then needed to avoid hitting the tombstones that appeared, replacing the dead creatures. The makers of

The controversy is
older than video
game technology.

the game said nothing more was intended by the game than simple fun, but others said it was cruel and violent.

Some refer to the game Death Race as the beginning of the violence controversy. Certianly as far as video games are concerned, it was just the beginning. The roots of this question of sexual and violent content in media, however, go further back in time.

In a sense, the roots of this question lie in the presumption that high culture is better than low culture. As low culture is seen by many as synonymous with both mass culture and popular culture, the concept that popular entertainment is harmful to the minds of the young is a simple step in logic. Plato, in discussing the training of children who were to become leaders in his theoretical Republic, said:

Then shall we simply allow our children to listen to any stories that anyone happens to make up, and so receive into their minds ideas often the very opposite of those we shall think they ought to have when they are grown up?

No, certainly not [replies Glaucon].

It seems, then, our first business will be to supervise the making of fables and legends, rejecting all which are unsatisfactory; and we shall induce nurses and mothers to tell their children only those which we have approved... Most of the stories now in use must be discarded."

This can be seen as the first volley in the controversy over the social costs and benefits of popular culture and entertainment.

In the United States, the penny press of the early 19th century drew the wrath of many intellectuals. Henry David Thoreau wrote in *Walden*:

> I am sure that I have never read any memorable news in a newspaper. If we read of one man robbed, or murdered, or killed in an accident, or one house burned, or one vessel wrecked, or one steamboat blown up, or one cow run over on the Western Railroad, or one mad dog killed, or one lot of grasshoppers in the winter—we never need read of another. If you are acquainted with the principle, what do you care for a myriad instances and applications? To a philosopher all news, as it is called, is gossip, and they who read it and edit it are old women over their tea.

Samuel Clemens (Mark Twain) suggested that public opinion was "formed and molded by a horde of ignorant, self-complacent simpletons who failed at ditching and shoemaking and fetched up in journalism on their way to the poorhouse." However, the penny press gathered prestige in the controversy as new media came into being.

The late 19th century saw the comic pages turned into a new battleground for the controversy. An early comic character, the "Yellow Kidd," is credited with giving "yellow journalism" its name. Communications scholars Edwin and Michael Emery, in their text *The Press and America*, assert that yellow journalism struck a fatal blow to the "news channels upon which the common man depended...Instead of giving its readers effective leadership, it offered a palliative of sin, sex, and violence." Intellectuals took up arms against the mass press, charging that it was an instrument of societal degeneration.

The late 19th century also saw the birth of motion pictures. From their beginnings, concerns were expressed about the low cultural taste and intellectual levels to which motion pictures appealed. An early erotic film, *How Bridget Served the Salad Undressed*, was received with much enthusiasm in the arcades. Films such as *Beavers at Play*, *The Surf at Dover*, and *What the Bootblack Saw* were aimed at basic gratifications and made money for the entrepreneurs who created them.

Film arcades very quickly became the location where low culture was indulged. By the 1920s, critics were charging that motion pictures had a strong negative influence on children. In 1928, the Motion Picture Research Council funded a series of 13 studies on the influence of motion pictures on children. Arcades became forbidden areas to children (thereby inadvertently making them even more attractive). The guardians of high culture characterized the arcades as sinful places where lower-class individuals wasted both time and money. (This stereotype remains significant as we bring the history of the controversy closer to modern-day events.)

In the early decades of the century, there was also intellectual alarm over what radio was doing to the masses, to children, and to society at large. A dominant force in American society by 1926, radio was being criticized for its lowest-common-denominator programming by the

"Children must be protected from video games that glorify violence and teach children to enjoy inflicting the most gruesome forms of cruelty imaginable."

—Sen. Joseph Lieberman (D-Conn.)

late 1930s. Intellectuals and moral leaders bemoaned the scarcity of religious programming, the paucity of educational programming, and the flood of commercialism in radio. Demagogues such as Father Charles Coughlin began to dominate the air in the United States, while in Europe, the specter of fascism grew.

Soap operas, another object of intellectual contempt, began to be heard on radio in the 1930s. Dr. Lee De Forest, one of the creators of radio, called them "tripe." Marion Dickerman, educational director of the American Arbitration Association, referred to them as "a deluge of dirt" where "clear boundary edges of the moral codes are smeared and obliterated." Psychiatrist Dr. Louis Berg stated that soap operas appealed to the most base passions of civilized man. He went on to suggest, as World War II began, that soap operas were "little short of treason."

After World War II, there were several new forms of communication and entertainment that became convenient scapegoats for society's ills. (These scapegoats, as we are seeing, change from one time period to the next.) The comic book was chastised for its alleged harmful effects in the early 1950s. Soap operas made the transition from radio to television in the late 1940s and the early 1950s. Music had been tied to sex and violence as early as 1937, but the rock 'n' roll of the 1950s propelled the controversy over popular music into the headlines.

Pinball machines were another object of scorn by the intellectual community. In their earliest forms, pinball machines were gambling devices and were located in the arcades of the period. New York Mayor Fiorello La Guardia went after pinball machines with a sledgehammer and the law, calling them a "perverter of innocent children." New York, Chicago, and Los Angeles banned pinball machines.

Television came under intellectual scrutiny from its very beginnings in the 1940s, and the possible influence on children was a major concern. A study in 1963 suggested that children's programs contained more violence than adult programs. Class, ethnic, and gender stereotyping on television were also of concern. Studies done in 1954, 1964, and 1973 reported that the middle class was over-represented on television when compared with "real" communities. Blue-collar professions were under-represented when compared with white-collar professions; white Americans were over-represented when compared with actual census data. Television also presented almost twice as many male as female roles, with males holding higher-status employment when compared with women. In fact, the dominant role for women in television was that of housewife. Early in the scientific study of television, exposure to this kind of misrepresentation and stereotyping was said to create unrealistic expectations in the viewer. (We will return to this argument later in this chapter.)

The Surgeon General's Scientific Advisory Committee on Television and Social Behavior released its report, *Television and Growing Up*, in 1972. The committee cautiously summarized its conclusions by suggesting:

> There is a convergence of fairly substantial evidence on short-run causation of aggression among children by viewing violence... and the much less certain evidence from field studies that... violence viewing precedes some long-run manifestations of aggressive behavior. This convergence... constitutes some preliminary evidence of a causal relationship.

The committee then tempered this conclusion by noting that "any sequence by which viewing television violence causes aggressive behavior is most likely applicable only to some children who are predisposed in that direction." In 1982 the National Institute of Mental Health issued a document even more damning than the 1972 document, saying "the consensus among most of the research community is that violence on television does lead to aggressive behavior." Research in the 1990s continues to link televised violence with aggressive behavior.

Media mogul Ted Turner, appearing with his wife Jane Fonda before Congress in June 1993, called television "the single most significant factor causing violence in America." Attorney General Janet Reno, at an October 1993 Senate hearing, warned that if the television industry didn't take steps to cut down on the violence it presented, the government would step in with regulation. President Clinton, speaking before the powerful Creative Artists Agency in Beverly Hills in December 1993 admitted "I love television." He then went on to suggest that violent television programming "can set forth a chain reaction of even more impulsive behavior, even more inability to deal with influences and impulses that all of us feel but most of us learn at some point in our lives not to act upon." Sen. Byron Dorgan, a Democrat from North Dakota, has sponsored a bill requiring the Federal Communications Commission to issue a quarterly television-violence summary. Researcher George Gerbner and his associates at the University of Pennsylvania have released a yearly "violence profile" for television since the early 1970s. The issue of sex and violence in television is still raging, and the controversy extends to video games.

Video games began outnumbering pinball machines in arcades in the 1970s. Intellectuals didn't seem to notice Pong or some of the early tank-battle and shoot-out games. Death Race, however, as mentioned earlier in the chapter, generated considerable controversy. Other video games, such as Space In-

vaders and Defenders, didn't help to dispel the violent image of video games. In these games, the player scored points by killing alien beings. In Asteroids, most of the points are scored by destroying chunks of rock, but spaceships cross the screen from time to time and the player achieves a higher score by destroying these alien ships. The arcade became a place that seemed to encourage violence among the young. Then Pac-Man appeared on the video-game scene and changed everything.

Pac-Man was the first of a series of maze games. Daniel Cohen suggests, in his 1982 book Video Games, that Pac-Man brought girls into the arcades for the first time. According to Consumer Guide's 1982 How to Win Video Games, the players of most shoot-'em-up games, such as Space Invaders, Defenders, and Asteroids, were male, whereas Pac-Man was evenly split between male and female players.

While Cohen suggested that Pac-Man was not a violent game, Arthur Asa Berger, a professor of communication at San Francisco State University, in a 1982 article in the Los Angeles Times, suggested that Pac-Man offered the player just two options: "Eat or be eaten." He also suggested that players were prisoners in a closed system with no escape, regressing the player to an infantile and oral stage. In other words, aggression—in Pac-Man—is oral. In his 1991 text Media Analysis Techniques, Berger characterized Space Invaders as open and phallic and therefore male. This was the direct opposite of his characterization of Pac-Man as closed and oral and therefore female.

While maze games may have represented an increase in female participation in video games, the current market is dominated by sports and action games.

Action games, such as Mortal Kombat, now make up almost 40 percent of the video-game market. Parker Page, founder and president of the San Francisco-based Children's Television Resource, is quoted in the January 1994 issue of *New Media* as saying:

> The truth is that there is almost no research on the effect of video or computer games on children, and what little research has been done was conducted with games available 10 years ago. At this point, just about everybody's attitude about what's harmful carries the same weight.

Currently, most researchers suggest that if television violence can be tied to aggressive behavior, interactive video games must have as a similar (if not greater) impact on children and young adults. Communications scholars have suggested that Americans spend the equivalent of about seven years of their lives watching television. Frank Biocca of the University of North Carolina suggests that if people use new technologies in the same manner as they have used television and computers, "some users could spend 20 of more years" inside these violent and sexually-explicit virtual experiences. What could be the effect of this amount of exposure to violent and sexual stimulus? One clue might come from an examination of current crime statistics.

According to 1989 statistics, there were 8.4 murders and 37.6 rapes per 100,000 people in the United States that year. In Canada during the same period, there were 5.45 murders and 108.7 sexual assaults per 100,000 people. Japan reported only 1.2 murders and 3.8 sexual assaults per 100,000 people.

In the United States, murder is the leading cause of death among children. There are more places in the United states to buy firearms than there are places to buy gasoline. Research has shown that there are, on average, 20 violent acts per hour in Saturday-morning cartoons. Yet, while Toronto citizens watch many of the same television programs as do the citizens of Chicago, there are more than 1,000 handgun murders per year in Chicago and only about 15 per year in Toronto. It must also be remembered that Japanese television is much more violent than television here in the States, yet violent crime is practically nonexistent in Japan. It may be that violence and sexual assualt are simply endemic to the American psyche. We'll return to this issue at the end of this chapter.

For now, let's turn our attention back to the games discussed earlier. We'll begin by looking at the violent video games and the meanings that might be derived from them. One of the first things we might look at concerns what is *not* present. An observation that immediately becomes apparent with the games we discussed is the relative absence of ethnic minorities.

In Wolfenstein 3-D, the only nationalities present are the Allied American pilot and the Nazi guards. The virtual world of Blake Stone proposes a future populated only by whites. The cartoon-like characters in Dactyl's Nightmare all appear white.

Two of the violent games do present other ethnic minorities, but even here the presentation is problematic. LHX: Attack Chopper offers the player a choice

• • • • • • • • • • • • • •

In most of the video games we've looked at, female characters are totally absent. Where females are present, they serve only as victims with no choice in their situation.

of three nationalities as enemies: Libyan, Vietnamese, and East German. The character to be role-played is white. Mortal Kombat, as we pointed out earlier in the chapter, has a total of 10 characters. The player may choose to role-play any one of seven of these characters. There are only two ethnicities, however: white and Asian. With the possible exception of the Libyans in LHX: Attack Chopper, blacks are noticeably absent from each of these games. Minorities are stereotyped and marginalized in what little presentation they are given in these games. Stereotyping has been called a subtle form of racism. The question can then be asked whether these video games might be reinforcing the marginalization of minorities.

Another problematic consideration in these games lies in the ages of the characters. While age is indeterminable in Dactyl Nightmare, the characters in Wolfenstein 3-D, Blake Stone, and LHX: Attack Chopper all seem to be in their 20s. During World War II, the average age of American airmen was the mid-20s. In LHX: Attack Chopper, the player begins as a second lieutenant. Again, the average age would be in the early 20s.

In the character descriptions available in the user's manual for Mortal Kombat, three of the seven are listed as being under the age of 30. Those three characters are Liu Kang, 24, a Shaolin monk

seeking to "return the tournament to its noble origins"; Johnny Cage, 29, an American martial-arts actor who "entered the tournament purely for the publicity it would generate for him around the world"; and Sonya Blade, 26, leader of a U. S. special-forces unit captured by Shang Tsung's personal army and forced to fight for her own life and that of her captured comrades. The remaining four characters are more than 30 years of age. One is simply a criminal. Another is an assassin. The third is an evil mystic. The last character represents a previous contestant in the tournament returned from the dead, seeking revenge. All four of these characters have unknown origins. Is there an implied bias here against the over-30 age group?

As can be seen, there are no "good guys" over the age of 30. If players wish to play the role of a "good guy," they must select from: the young, idealistic Asian monk fighting for honor; a self-serving white actor fighting for publicity; or an imprisoned white female fighting for her life. The issue of gender becomes apparent here. The **only** female character in Mortal Kombat is a victim.

In most of the video games we've looked at, female characters are totally absent. Where females are present, they serve only as victims with no choice in their situation. In Mortal Kombat, Sonya Blade is the only character who is there against their will.

The female-as-victim is very apparent in Night Trap. Here the female victims serve only as property to be defended or consumed. Again, does this type of stereotyping reinforce pre-existing attitudes toward women?

Another issue that must be examined centers on the physical representation of evil in these video games. Wolfenstein 3-D presents the enemy as the Nazis, a group that has been called the ultimate evil of the 20th century. In Blake Stone, evil is represented by a madman who has surrounded himself with "an army of bizarre creatures" created by genetic mutation. Dactyl Nightmare presents evil not in the form of a flying reptile, but rather as opposing players.

Mortal Kombat presents the enemy as, for the most part, Asian. Even Kano, who appears to be white, is described as having an Asian connection in that he grew up as an orphan in Tokyo. Three of the characters, Sub-Zero, Scorpion, and Reptile, are ninjas, a modern stereotype of evil. Rayden, the evil mystic, and Shang Tsung, the host of Mortal Kombat's deadly tournament, are also Asian in appearance. The only remaining character, Goro, is not even human but an alien mutation. In almost all the other cases that we've discussed, evil is represented by non-whites.

Technology, the very thing that makes video games possible, is itself represented as evil in these games. The physically repulsive mutants of Blake Stone were created through technology in the hands

of a madman. The torture and carnage wreaked by the historical Nazis in Wolfenstein 3-D was also made possible through technology in the wrong hands. The American pilot in LHX: Attack Chopper is attempting to stop technology from being used by crazy Arabs, sneaky Asians, and the puppets of the evil empire (East Germany). In Mortal Kombat, Kano, with his infrared mechanical eye, represents the grotesque consequences when humanity is violated by technology.

Physical attractiveness is an issue in these video games, too. There are few physically unfit characters in the games, and those few are almost inevitably grotesque and evil. Examples of these characters include Goro in Mortal Kombat and the mutants in Blake Stone. Physical fitness, beauty, and a lack of disguise

Raydan: the Asian as evil in Mortal Kombat.

are signs by which the player can determine the "good guys" from the "bad guys." If a character's face is covered, the character may be hiding something, and therefore the honesty and integrity of this character is drawn into question. The main characters, in Wolfenstein 3-D, Blake Stone, and LHX: Attack Chopper, those for which the player assumes the role, are all physically fit, physically attractive, and undisguised. The "good guys" of Mortal Kombat, for the most part, are also physically fit, physically attractive, and undisguised. The exception is Johnny Cage, the actor, who hides behind a pair of sunglasses. Here, the stereotype of Cage's profession provides an explanation for the conflicting symbols. Cage, because of both his profession and his reasons for competing in the tournament, can be seen as the most shallow and ambiguous of the "good guys" of this video game. An interesting note is that Sonya Blade is the most frequently-chosen character in the arcade version of the game, while Johnny Cage is the least-played character. What does it say about the players when they choose to role-play a contestant who is not there by choice? (It would be interesting to find out if Liu Kang is the second-most frequently chosen character. His reason for taking part in the carnage can be seen as the most noble among the remainder of the players. Johnny Cage's reasons are, of course, the most self-serving and therefore the least desirable in the eyes of the players.)

The "bad guys" of Mortal Kombat are identifiable using the same signs. As suggested before, Goro is physically grotesque. Kano, while physically fit, hides behind his physically grotesque, partially metallic face. Rayden and the three ninjas are also all physically fit, but Rayden hides under his hat and the ninjas hide behind their masks. Shang Tsung provides the ultimate in evil presentation in that he appears physically unfit, elderly (and therefore physically grotesque), and hidden behind his facial hair.

With the possible exception of the character of Larry in the Leisure Suit Larry series, there are no physically unfit, physically unattractive, or elderly characters in any of these sexually oriented video games. In the virtual world of video games, sex is the sole province of the physically fit, the attractive, and the young.

. . . .

Let's look at some of these same issues as they apply to video games with sexual content. Other than the player's chosen persona, there are few other males in Leisure Suit Larry, Strip Poker Three, Jigsaw Pinups, or Virtual Valerie. The women in these games are available purely for the pleasure of the male player. Women are seen as commodities to be conquered and possessed. Leisure Suit Larry, through the player, seeks not a relationship of equals but, rather, a collection of human trophies. The women in Strip Poker Three and Jigsaw Pinups are present only for the voyeuristic pleasure of the player. In Virtual Valerie, as in Leisure Suit Larry, the woman is a commodity that the player seeks to obtain.

Minorities are even more scarce than males in these sexually oriented video games. There are no minorities in Strip Poker Three, Jigsaw Pinups, or Virtual Valerie. Depending on which episode of Leisure Suit Larry is being played, token minority females may appear.

With the possible exception of the character of Larry in the Leisure Suit Larry series, there are no physically unfit, physically unattractive, or elderly characters in any of these sexually oriented video games. In the virtual world of video games, sex is the sole province of the physically fit, the attractive, and the young.

The program structure of the games themselves can be interpreted within a sexual paradigm. Earlier we looked at Berger's discussion of Pac-Man as closed, oral, and therefore female, and Space Invaders as open, phallic, and therefore male. What do we discover when we turn the same analytic tools on these more contemporary video games?

One thing that is immediately noticeable in Dactyl Nightmare, Wolfenstein 3-D, and Blake Stone, is the phallic symbol, the gun, that protrudes directly in the lower portion of the screen. The player cannot get away from this sexual, violent image during the game. The killing of an enemy in these games is seen as a sexual act; death, for both the player and the enemy, comes from the symbolic ejaculation of this symbol.

Another symbolic consideration is the closed or open system of the games. If the player can survive, achieve a high-enough score, and find the correct keys or access cards, he or she can escape the maze-type worlds of which both Wolfenstein 3-D and Blake Stone consist. The world of Dactyl Nightmare, however, offers no such escape. This world consists of only the five chessboard-like areas. There is nothing else. There are no hidden passageways. There is only the currency of death.

Another disturbing theme in both the violent and sexual video games is the equating of death and currency. The accumulation of capital is an underlying concept in the American mythos; conversely, that which cannot be made a possession must be destroyed. This concept is present in all of these games, but nowhere is it more obvious than in Blake Stone, where containers must be destroyed so that their contents (gold or monsters) can be either possessed or eliminated. The capital to be accumulated and possessed in Wolfenstein 3-D includes bags of money, chests of treasure, and golden images. Keys to

gain access to other levels must be also be found and possessed. Other items the player can accumulate in this game include food, first-aid kits, weapons, and ammunition. In this regard, Blake Stone has many similarities with Wolfenstein 3-D. Access cards, a substitute for the keys in Wolfenstein 3-D that enable the player to move from one level to the next, must be collected. There are also consumables such as food, weapons, gold bars, and ammunition to be collected in order to improve the player's score. In LHX: Chopper Attack, the player's score is improved by receiving as little damage as possible to the helicopter. (Upon the completion of a mission, the player is informed how much money the taxpayers must pay for the damage to the helicopter.) The importance of capital is readily apparent in Strip Poker Three. A stake of cash is used, and there is monetary value placed on the articles of clothing that are won or lost in the game.

Capital, however, is not always expressed in terms of monetary accumulation. In Jigsaw Pinups, the sexual conquest of the pinup is achieved through the accumulation and placement of the pieces. Sexual conquests are also the capital to be accumulated in Leisure Suit Larry and Virtual Valarie. Here the female body has economic and sexual value and little else.

The economic values represented in Dactyl Nightmare and Mortal Kombat are, in some respects, even more insidious. The value to be accumulated in Dactyl Nightmare is simply the bodies of the opponents. In Mortal Kombat, the economic values are represented by the destruction of wood, stone, steel, ruby, and diamond blocks, along with the dead, dismembered bodies of other contestants. The destruction of the blocks earns the player a certain number of points, from 100,000 to 1 million. Points are also earned by hurting the opponent. The player receives 200,000 points for a flawless victory over the opponent. A total of 500,000 points is earned for a flawless victory without your character being hurt. Finally, 100,000 points are the reward for the dismemberment of the opponent. As in almost all of the games discussed here, the player is thus rewarded for destructive behavior.

The consumerism that is simulated in the playing of these video games both echoes and amplifies the consumerism in the player's real life. Video-gameplaying, as with most forms of human activity in the United States, is dominated by the values and conceptual precepts of capitalism. The activities within the video game are reinforcing agents for these values. But there are additional reinforcements outside the game as well.

After the player has bought a specific video game, there is a proliferation of cross-marketing attempts to get the player to continue to consume. Buying the first game compels the player to purchase sequels. Although the first issue of the game Wolfenstein 3-D was available as shareware, it consisted of only the first adventure. Subsequent adventures had to be purchased separately, along with maps showing secret panels and the places where the treasures were hidden. Blake Stone followed a similar marketing strategy. Leisure Suit Larry is now in his seventh installment, and there is now a Mortal Kombat II. There are also dozens of books giving hints and cheats to help win these games. Tie-in merchandise includes articles of clothing and action-figure toys. Clones of the programs have already begun saturating the market.

But although these video games are undoubtedly a marketing bonanza, are they a verifiable cause of violence in our society? Can we ascertain some form of direct cause-and-effect between the playing of violent and/or sexual video games and the violence that permeates the real world? Common sense might suggest that there is; however, currently there is little or no specific evidence to support this contention. It must also be remembered that "common sense" is often merely that which the group in power defines as the truth of any given situation.

· ·

CONCLUSIONS

What we have tried to make clear in this chapter is that there are a variety of ways to observe how these games might affect the young player. Each individual could react in many different ways to a suggestive stimulus such as a video game. There are countless mediating factors, including the individuals' families and friends, their church and religion, their beliefs, their values, and their socioeconomic status and class. Also, beyond sociological factors, the cause and effect for each event that takes place in an individual's life comprises a variety of unique considerations. These considerations would include: the objective circumstances of the event itself; the individual's experience, or history, with the same or similar events; expectations that the individual brings to the situation; the immediate setting, both in time and space, of the event; and the medium of communication through which the event is occurring. Laying the blame for a specific effect on any particular stimulus (such as a video game) is indeed problematic.

Many of the concerns we've examined in regard to these video games need to be examined in a scientific manner. However, the symbolic ramifications in these games, as in all communication texts, gestate primarily within the individuals themselves. What does the fact that no women exist in most of these games of violence mean to the "average" player? Does it suggest that violence and war are the prerogative of men and not women? What is indicated by the fact that Sonya Blade, a victim, is the most-played character in Mortal Kombat? Does it imply that players secretly want to take part in the violence but want to assure themselves that they took part only because they were forced to? Does the economic basis of Wolfenstein 3-D reinforce a belief that "all is fair"? Do the portrayals of women in games such as Night Trap and Strip Poker Three reinforce already distorted perceptions of women?

Questions such as these cannot be answered by idle speculation. Methodologically-sound experimentation must be carried out by responsible and ethical researchers. And yet, at a certain level, these questions remain unanswerable.

In preparing this chapter for *Cyberlife!*, one of the authors played most of the games extensively as part of the research. The other author never played any of the games. What differences now exist between the two authors because of this difference in experience? Is one author now more prone to violence or racism or sexism because of this experience? If the game-playing author were to commit a heinous and violent act at some point in the future, would the blame be placed on video games, television, Marine Corps training, or his parents? All of these factors, and more, create the whole person.

So the questions remain: Can any one factor be given more credit or responsibility for a person's behavior than any other? Is there a meaningful scientific and moral distinction between real violence and simulated violence? And does the marketplace really care?

Virtual-Reality Drama

So the essence of virtual-reality drama, as we conceived it in late 1993, is that the unfolding of the script in real time is as much of a revelation to the actors as it is to the "audience." That idea was entirely successful and remains a part of the plan.

chapter 22
by Stuart Harris

Somebody asked me a couple of months ago what first gave me the idea of producing Internet theater. I had to think about it for a moment or two before it came back to me, but here's the answer: One day I was noodling around the IRC computer chatnet, probably wishing some thoroughly obnoxious female would shut up, when I suddenly imagined the line...

```
***Signoff: Ophelia <drowning>
```

...appearing on the IRC screens of several hundred people all over the world simultaneously. I knew right then that I had to be the first producer of Shakespeare's *Hamlet* for the Internet. The log of the very first try-out of the idea still exists: Here are 11 lines from it...

```
<Hamlet> Oph: suggest u /JOIN #nunnery [27]
<Ophelia> :-(    [28]
<Ophelia> hold on...do you want me to write "signoff..."
<Hamlet> GO ON, YES. U'LL HAVE TO REJOIN
<Ophelia> Ok
*** Signoff: Ophelia (<drowning> [29])
*** Zendar (jimvs@cg57.cts.com) has joined channel #hamnet
*** Zendar is now known as Ophelia
<Ophelia> It work?
<Hamlet> GREAT...... THAT'S IT
<Ophelia> Hey, that's pretty neat...!
```

One of Jim Serio's creations: The banquet scene from "PCbeth."

My first victim, "Zendar," was actually Jim Serio, who has a UNIX shell account on the same service as I. Jim never went on to virtual acclaim as Ophelia, but he did become the virtual scenery designer for the "Hamnet Players," as we called ourselves—the first and (so far) only strolling players on IRC.

IRC is short for Internet Relay Chat—the mother of all online computer chat forums. Anybody with access to IRC client software can log on and choose from a list of many hundred ongoing conversations (they're called channels), which can be listed by their name, population, and topic. The channel population counts cannot be falsified, but the topic is often deceptive. For example, if you join the channel called #hotsex, you are not about to have a sexual experience. This rolling cocktail party never stops, but its participants change with the rotation of the planet—the principal partygoers changing from European to American to Australian to Asian and back to European as the world turns.

The brief excerpt from our version of *Hamlet* illustrates quite a bit about the ground rules of IRC and the initial ideas for using it as an auditorium for virtual drama. First, it's evident that every line

The blasted heath from Hamlet.

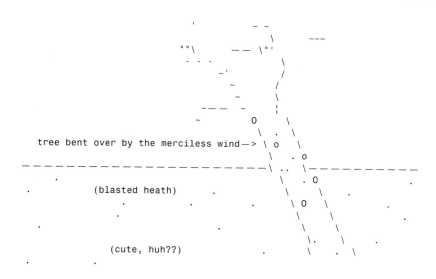

includes the identity, or nickname, of the person who is responsible for it, either as the direct "speaker" (name in angle brackets) or indirectly, as the result of entering a command. All IRC commands, without exception, start with a forward slash character, so the first line of the excerpt refers to the command /JOIN, which is what you enter to join a channel (although there would not normally be a channel called #nunnery). Anything anybody enters that does not start with / becomes publicly-seen IRC dialogue.

Obviously, then, since all participants in an IRC conversation may choose whatever nickname they wish to be known by—unless that nickname is already in use—and since an IRC channel may contain many people who watch but contribute nothing, some of the elements of traditional theater are there. A cast of characters with names such as Hamlet, Ophelia, and Polonius can be convened, and an audience can be invited to watch.

Another element that stands out in the preceding excerpt is that the script provides cues for the actors in a virtual drama by the line numbers in brackets ([27] [28] [29] and so on). The idea was that nobody but the producers would have the full script in front of them, but that each actor would be provided with his or her numbered lines only. An actor having lines [3], [13], and [27], for instance, would know that his cues would be the delivery of lines [2], [12], and [26] by somebody else—but looking at those three lines tells the actors very little or absolutely nothing about the overall plot of the drama. So the essence of virtual-reality drama, as we conceived it in late 1993, is that the unfolding of the script in real time is as much of a revelation to the actors as it is to the "audience." That idea was entirely successful and remains a part of the plan.

Two further modes of contributing to an IRC channel help to make virtual theater effective. One is the "action," known to MUD (Multi-User Dimension—also known as "Dungeon") enthusiasts as an "emotion," expressed in IRC by the command /ME. If your nickname is Cyberlad and you enter the command /ME has to go now, this will be seen by everybody else in the channel as * Cyberlad has to go now. This feature of the IRC software has an important use in contributing stage directions: If you want the direction Exit Hamlet, gloomily to appear onscreen, all you need to do is arrange for a character with the nickname "Exit" to enter the command /ME Hamlet, gloomily.

The other important mode is the message mode, without which IRC would lose much of its great appeal. This mode allows private conversations between two people to be conducted underneath the public chat, like a discreet whisper lost in the noise of a singles bar. A typical IRC channel with a dozen or so participants will have one or more public conversations running and at least six liaisons being conducted in privacy. In the virtual-drama context, the /MSG command is perfect for feeding actors their lines and generally keeping things in order without interrupting the flow of the script. Later in this chapter, in the performance log which begins with the line "Welcome to Elsinore!!!," the notation *nickname* indicates a message arriving from "nickname," while -> *nickname* indicates a message on its way to "nickname."

We felt that one more element was needed before we could raise our virtual curtain for the first time: scenery. You cannot be around IRC for long before noticing how ingenious some people have become at drawing pictures using only the limited set of symbols available on a computer keyboard (known technically as the ASCII character set). I do not mean just the rather well-known "emoticons" such as Ophelia's sideways glum face : - (that we used in line [28], but complete screens full of symbols that add up to something recognizable. This form of expression is known as "ASCII art" and it can be made part of IRC by use of the /LOAD command. /LOAD acts on a pre-stored text file, dumping the entire contents of the file into the currently active IRC channel. The text file may contain a series of commands used to set up participation in several channels, for example. I have seen text files that display short recipes and movie reviews, as well as pictures and "banner headlines." Use of this feature—particularly gratuitous overuse of it to fill everybody's screens with junk art—can be frowned upon as "flooding" and can even get you in trouble with your fellow-IRCers. (This was to become a slight problem for IRC theater, as we shall see.)

With these elements as our kit of parts, here's the complete script we came up with for the first production of the Hamnet Players. Those of a nervous or puritanical disposition are warned that this is adapted for the generally ribald IRC population: This is not your father's Shakespeare...

. . . .

We felt that one more element was needed before we could raise our virtual curtain for the first time: scenery. You cannot be around IRC for long before noticing how ingenious some people have become at drawing pictures using only the limited set of symbols available on a computer keyboard.

```
**<< Action >>** : _The CURTAIN RISES to reveal the stage set...
<_Set> :
<_Set>       _____    *          _____    *          _____    *          _____    *
<_Set>     <        |         <        |         |        >         |        >
<_Set>     <_____|         <_____|         |_____>         |_____>
<_Set>          |                  |                  |                  |
<_Set>        ^^^^^^^^^          ^^^^^^^^^          ^^^^^^^^^          ^^^^^^^^^
<_Set>        |   +   |          |   +   |          |   +   |          |   +   |
<_Set>        |   +   |_____|   +   |   +   |_____|   +   |   +   |_____|   +   |
<_Set>        |
<_Set>        |    +       +       +       +       +       +          +
<_Set>        |___
<_Set>            |       +       +       +       +       +                 |
<_Set>            |
<_Set>            |       +       +       _____       +       +            |
<_Set>            |                      |########|                         |
<_Set>         /  |       +       +      |########|    +       +          \.
<_Set>        /   |                       |                                 \.
<_Set>       /    |                       | ||||||                      .  \.
<_Set>      / .   |_____            | ||||||  |_____| .  \.
<_Set>    /  .          .            .    | ||||||          .              .\.
<_Set>  _____  ||||||  _____
<_Set>
<_Set>            W E L C O M E   T O   E L S I N O R E!!!
<_Set>            ~~~~~~~~~~~~~~~~~~~~~~~~~~~~~~~~~~~~~~~~~~~~
<_Set>        [0]
<audience> Clap,clap,clap.... etc....          [1]
        =====PROLOGUE /TOPIC World_Premiere _irc_Hamlet_in_Progress  [2]
*** PROLOGUE has changed the topic on channel #Hamnet to "World_Premiere _irc_Hamlet_in_Progress"
<PROLOGUE> All the world's a Unix term....  [3]
<PROLOGUE> ...and all the men & women merely irc addicts....  [4]
<PROLOGUE> This show is Copyright 1993 The Hamnet Players [5]
<PROLOGUE> Enjoy our show + no heckling plz [6]
<PROLOGUE> Script should not be re-staged w/out permish [7]


**<< Action >>** : SCENE 1: THE BATTLEMENTS  [8]
**<< Action >>** : _Enter Hamlet  [9]
**<< Action >>** : _Enter Ghost   [10]
<Hamlet> re, Ghost. Zup?        [11]
<Ghost> Yr uncle's fucking yr mum. I'm counting on u to /KICK the bastard.  [12]
        ======= GHOST /MODE * +o Hamlet   [13]
*** Mode change "+o Hamlet" on channel #Hamnet by Ghost
<Hamlet> Holy shit!!!! Don't op me, man!!!! I've gotta think abt this, + I've got chem lab in 1/2 hr.
:-((((     [14]
**<< Action >>** : _Exit Hamlet    [15]


**<< Action >>** : SCENE 2: AFTER HAMLET'S CHEM LAB     [16]
<Hamlet> 2b or not 2b...   [17]
<Hamlet> Hmmmmmm...        [18]
<Hamlet> :-(    Bummer...  [19]
<Hamlet> Ooops, here comes Ophelia    [20]
**<< Action >>** : _Enter Ophelia      [21]
<Ophelia> Here's yr stuff back       [22]
<Hamlet> Not mine, love.   Hehehehehe ;-D  [23]
<Ophelia> O heavenly powers: restore him!  [24]
**<< Action >>** Ophelia thinks Hamlet's nuts  [25]
<Hamlet> Make that "sanity-deprived", pls....  [26]
<Hamlet> Oph: suggest u /JOIN #nunnery      [27]
<Ophelia> :-(    [28]
*** Signoff: Ophelia (drowning)  [29]
```

```
**<< Action >>** : SCENE 3: INTERIOR    [30]
**<< Action >>** : _Enter R_krantz    [31]
**<< Action >>** : _Enter G_stern    [32]
<R_krantz> re    [33]
<G_stern> re    [34]
<Hamlet> re, guys... :-\    [35]
<R_krantz> zup?    [36]
<Hamlet> Fucked if i know. brb...    [37]
**<< Action >>** : _Exit Hamlet in a sulk.    [38]
<G_stern> fuckza matter w/him?    [39]
<R_krantz> Guess he must be lagged. Let's lurk    [40]
**<< Action >>** : R_krantz lurks    [41]
**<< Action >>** : G_stern lurks    [42]

**<< Action >>** : SCENE 4: THE QUEEN'S CLOSET    [43]
<Hamlet> Ma: what the fuck's going on?    [44]
<Queen> Don't flame me, i'm yr Ma!    [45]
<Queen> Er....    [46]
<Prompter> Psst! Thou hast thy father much offended..    [47]
<Queen> Oh, right.... Yr dad's pissed at u    [48]
**<< Action >>** : Hamlet slashes at the arras    [49]
<Polonius> Arrrghhhh!!!    [50]
        ========= HAMLET /KICK * Polonius    [51]
*** Polonius has been kicked off channel #Hamnet by Hamlet
<Queen> Now look what u've done u little nerd.    :-(    [52]
<Hamlet> Wrong man...... Bummer...    [53]

**<< Action >>** : SCENE 5: GRUESOME FINALE    [54]
        ========= QUEEN /TOPIC DEATH    [55]
*** Queen has changed the topic on channel #Hamnet to "DEATH"
**<< Action >>** : _Enter Hamlet, Queen, King, Laertes, R_krantz, G_stern [56]
**<< Action >>** : Queen takes a drink    [57]
**<< Action >>** : King gives Ham & Laer swords    [58]
<King> Go for it, lads!    [59]
**<< Action >>** : Laertes stabs Hamlet [60]
**<< Action >>** : Hamlet stabs Laertes [61]
**<< Action >>** : Hamlet stabs King    [62]
<Queen> Holy shit this Danish vodka is like poison    :-@    [63]
<Hamlet> and u always thought i was just wasting my time in chem lab, hehehe [64]
**<< Action >>** : Queen dies in agony    [65]
<King> Aaaaarrgghhh!    [66]
**<< Action >>** : King dies    [67]
<Laertes> AAaaaarrrrrhhhhh!!!!    [68]
**<< Action >>** : Laertes dies    [69]
<Hamlet> AAAAaaaaaarrrrrhhhhhhhh!!!!!!!!!!!!!!!!!!!!!!!!!!!!!!!!!!!!    [70]
**<< Action >>** : Hamlet dies    [71]
**<< Action >>** : R_krantz + G_stern GULP!!!!!!    [72]
**<< Action >>** : _Enter Fortinbras + drum + colours + attendants    [73]
<Fort_bras> EEEEEEEuuuuuucchhhhhh!!!!!! What's been hpng here?    [74]
<Drum> Like, rat-a-tat, man    [75]
<Colours> Hmmmmmmm......    [76]
<Attndts> Holy sheeeeet!!!!!    [77]
        ============ FORT_BRAS  /NICK _King    [78]
** Fort_bras is now known as _King
**<< Action >>** : _The CURTAIN SLOWLY FALLS. {{{{{{{--THE END--}}}}}}}    [79]
<audience> hmmmmmmmm.....    [80]
```

Well, whatever Gods there be may have chuckled at our script, but they certainly did not approve of our choice of date for the world-première performance. It was slated for Sunday, November 14, 1993, at noon PST. Mid-November is not normally a stormy season in Southern California, where we were attempting to orchestrate the production, but at about 11:30 a.m., just as we were beginning to find some recruits from channels like #chat, #hottub, #sweden, and #england, a freak thunderstorm cut power to our access provider and put an end to our ambitions for that day. I was eventually able to "hack" back into IRC via universities in San Diego and Taiwan, but by then the crowd had dispersed.

Actually, "crowd" is not exactly the word to describe the desultory collection of IRCers who witnessed that first debacle. A theater enthusiast from San Diego (who thought our thunder sound effects very convincing!), a young student in Switzerland who was fretting (in French) that his mother would be calling him to dinner any minute, a computer tech in London who appeared to be baffled by the whole thing, and an extremely reluctant psychiatric nurse in Boston: that was about it. This was enough to convince us that the idea of just showing up on IRC and recruiting actors from the 3,500 or so people who are logged in at that time on a Sunday was not going to fly. We embarked on our first attempts at promotion, which were quite successful but time-consuming.

TROUBLESHOOTING "HAMNET"

The world première of "Hamnet" finally took place (a little late) at about 12:30 p.m. PST on December 12, 1993. One of the neat features of IRC is that anybody can get control of a channel simply by creating one that does not already exist. "Having control" means that you have privileges, including setting the channel's topic, assigning operator status to other users, changing channel modes, and—the ultimate power trip—kicking out and/or permanently banning troublemakers or antagonists. Having operator status is known for short as "having ops," or being a "chanop." Since we were using the /KICK command as a metaphor for murder, note the requirement for Hamlet to have ops at line 51, and for the Ghost to have that status at line 13 in order to give ops to Hamlet. Also, both Prologue and Queen have to be able to set the channel topic as part of the scripted action.

So, the idea was to create the channel #hamnet at 11 p.m. PST and commence casting. Well, surprise, surprise! Somebody had beaten us to it—some guy from Kawunzuki Heavy Industries had already created the channel, and so he of course was in sole possession of ops. He said he'd heard about it on the NPR Science Friday radio show, and "...just thought I'd get here early." Fortunately, he was soon persuaded to give ops and, in fact, he wandered off after a while and never saw the show at all. We made a mental note, though, that it would not be hard for some malevolent spirit to disrupt IRC theater by taking control of the channel—and there is no shortage of malevolent spirits on IRC, believe me.

It was not a malevolent spirit, but rather a quite unpredictable accident, that almost wrecked this performance. Recall that displaying a whole screenful of text is generally frowned on as "flooding." Recall, too, that the Prologue needs to have channel operator status. Now it so happened that the person cast as Prologue was an exceptionally bright young computer programmer from Slovenia, the northernmost province of what used to be Yugoslavia before all the provinces started wiping each other out. This young man had implemented a special script—essentially a computer program running within IRC—that would detect flooding and automatically kick the offender out of the channel with the admonitory message "Automated kick for flooding." Which is precisely what his script did to me after I had displayed the set, which of course is designed to occupy precisely one full screen. Not only that, but by then the channel was designated as "invitation only" so the play's producer and "star" (I'd decided not to trust anyone else with the crucial role of the Prince) was shut out of the theater and had to beg to be let in again! Here's the log of the full sequence, which illustrates not only the auto-KICK and a courteous apology from Prologue, but also a tremendous amount of squabbling about channel mode settings and an even more prodigious amount of flirtation. The extra flirtation that was no doubt going on at /MSG level did not, perhaps thankfully, get recorded.

- `<_Set>`   W E L C O M E   T O   E L S I N O R E!!!
- `<_Set>`   ~~~~~~
- `* Brazil thinks he could organize something better than this givven a week`
- `<_Set> :`
- `/nick Hamlet`
- `* Brazil thinks this should be +m so he knows when the play has started and`
- `+can shut up.`
- `*** _Set is now known as Hamlet`
- `/mode * -p`
- `*** Mode change "-p" on channel #Hamnet by Hamlet`
- `<Recorder> Don't keep this a private channel.`
- `<laertes> have we started?`
- `<GHOST> I'm not going to haunt that castle.`
- `<Recorder>  -i`
- `-> *prologue* GO AHEAD`
- `*Fort_bras* I need lines if I have any  :-)`
- `<DRUM> Boom Boom Boom`
- `<Recorder> ;-)`
- `<The_King> THE_QUEEN - fancy a bit of nookie?`
- `*** Signoff: The_King (Error 0)`
- `<AUDIENCE> mild clapping and shouts of "this better be good! we have fruit!"`
- `* TheGhost passes his lines on to ghost and bids farewell...`
- `<ophelia> Yeah..Private then its not watchable`
- `<trammie> hi`
- `*** You have been kicked off channel #hamnet by Prologue (Automated kick for`
- `+flooding)`
- `/join #hamnet`
- `*** #hamnet :Sorry, cannot join channel. (Invite only channel)`
- `-> *_enter* get me back in`
- `/join #hamnet`
- `*** #hamnet :Sorry, cannot join channel. (Invite only channel)`
- `-> *prologue* help! get me back in`
- `*** TheGhost invites you to channel #Hamnet`
- `/join #hamnet`
- `*** Hamlet (sirrah@cg57.esnet.com) has joined channel #hamnet`
- `*** Topic for #hamnet: Hamlet in progress. Shush!`
- `*** Users on #Hamnet: Hamlet The_King mortal GHOST +_enter TheRaven @_exit`
- `+kizala stremler PsychoA trammie masc0789 vanGogh Brazil +R_krantz +Prompter`
- `+Guran @TheGhost halleen +Prologue MeDoc pcarver Fort_bras +SCENE Recorder`
- `+lmcdermot laertes @ophelia @ThE_QuEeN DRUM +AUDIENCE @G_Stern`
- `* laertes is falling for ophelia he thinks`
- `<Recorder> Repeat after me... "/mode #hamnet -i+m"`
- `<DRUM> Welcome Hamlet!`
- `*** Mode change "+o The_King" on channel #Hamnet by ThE_QuEeN`

```
<GHOST> Am I in private?
*** Mode change "-i" on channel #Hamnet by G_Stern
(Prologue/#hamnet) Enjoy our show + no heckling plz [6]
(AUDIENCE/#hamnet) this is absurd. sorry folks, i'm out of here. still
+unimpressed by the wonders of irc.
(_enter/#hamnet) op the actors and +m the channel...........
<trammie> hi
* ophelia gives laertes a SMOOCH (you big stud you)
<vanGogh> if this is private i mightaswell leave
<The_King> yo hamlet (you shagged my missus! you're facking dead mate!)
<Brazil> it's not IRC, it's the ops
<Hamlet> WE WILL SKIP THE PROLOGUE. GO AHEAD SCEN WITH LINE 8
<The_King> ta Queen *hug*
(Prologue/#hamnet) Script should not be re-staged w/out permish [7]
<Brazil> need an audience? :)
(SCENE/#Hamnet) wtf?
* ThE_QuEeN pinches the King
<G_Stern> er line 8
* ThE_QuEeN punches the King
* The_King gropes the Queen
<Hamlet> scene do line 8
<ThE_QuEeN> ooopsa
*Fort_bras* Could you tell me if I have lines and who can send them to me???
(_enter/#hamnet) FUCK THIS>>>LETS GO>>>>>
* SCENE 1: THE BATTLEMENTS  [8]
*Prologue* sorry - my scripts aren't used to irc shows :(
* audience wonders what's going on
* _enter HAMLET (9)
<The_King> why not the prologue?
* ophelia says HANDS OFF MA
<vanGogh> lord what fools these ircsters be
<Brazil> SOMEONE MODE +M THIS CHANNEL ALREADY!
<The_King> sssshhhhh....
* ThE_QuEeN looks for a flirt
* Prompter groans
```

· ·

Believe it or not, immediately after this chaotic episode, as the log proves, things settled down and the show played pretty well to script. But perhaps a little explanation of the disputes over channel modes is in order.

The crucial question is whether to allow comments from the audience or not. A subsidiary question is whether, as in real-life theater, it is too disruptive to allow latecomers into the auditorium. Both conditions can be controlled by setting channel modes. If the mode is +m, that makes the channel "moderated," meaning that only chanops may speak. So the simplest way of ensuring a peaceful life would be to give all the

The crucial question is whether to allow comments from the audience or not. A subsidiary question is whether, as in real-life theater, it is too disruptive to allow latecomers into the auditorium.

performers ops and to +m the channel. A refinement would be to make performers who do not need ops +v, meaning that they have a "voice" but no other chanop privileges. There are several problems with this, however. One is that I'm not in favor of suppressing all audience comment in theaters either virtual or real (so you might say I deserve all I get, right?) Another is that it's quite a task to set all that up as well as control the overall show. Perhaps the most vexing problem is that not all of the IRC servers around the world recognize the +v mode—in fact, poor Fort_bras, who was screaming for his lines even though they had been sent to him three times, never received them and could not have "spoken" them even if he had because his server software allowed neither the +v mode nor the semi-private mode we use to feed performers their lines.

Latecomers can easily be kept out by assigning the mode +i to the channel. This makes it "by invitation only"—not a bad idea, even if it did backfire in this case. Mode +p designates the channel as completely private and exclusive—if I had not switched the mode to -p (in the ninth line of the log), my problems would have been compounded. We have lately discovered that even the +i mode is not actually necessary, if all you want to avoid is the distraction of seeing stuff such as...

```
*** ark (arquus@dinosaur.mit.edu) has joined channel #Hamnet
```

...in the middle of the performance. There is a way of filtering out such "information" lines automatically—for those whose servers have up-to-date versions of IRC. (The IRC software is very, very clever—sometimes too clever for its own good.)

All those issues remained to be discussed and resolved—meanwhile, we had a show to run and a sometimes overexuberant cast to control. Nearly 100 people were present for the performance, and we were especially pleased to be hosting IRC enthusiasts from such far-flung places as Slovenia, Slovakia, London, Alaska, and Finland. Here are a few of the comments that we logged after the virtual curtain fell and the channel began to degenerate into a ribald version of a theatrical cast party.

```
<Recorder> Oh my... what an excellent use of my Sunday afternoon. ;-)
<Gallery> applauds
<mortal> Good work except for all the assholes
<Recorder> It was cool, except for the parts that sucked.
<masc0789> My mother would have a stroke, but definitely a great leap forward.
<TomServo> Is that it?
<Fort_bras> How about better planning!!!!!  <next time>
```

Instant and direct feedback is evidently going to be a feature of virtual theater!

GETTING DOWN
TO BUSINESS

We did have better planning next time, although not entirely to please poor Fort_bras. As a result of the mini-hoopla we generated for this first performance, several very useful contacts were made. One was with a graduate student of stage management who also happened to be an IRC wizard. Real name Leslie Csokasy, she went by the IRC nickname "aurra." Aurra rightly pointed out that if we wanted to simulate real-life theater, people such as producers would (a) never take on roles themselves, and (b) never have to fret about details of who was going to be +o or +v and whether actors were screaming for their lines. A producer might make policy, but would not get involved once the curtain was up.

Another contact was with a genuine Shakespearean actor, Mr. Ian Taylor of the Royal Shakespeare Company in London. Ian was then appearing nightly on the RSC's Barbican stage and was preparing for a tour of Japan and the U.S. as the Mariner in *The Winter's Tale*. An accomplished performer, but one who, being realistic, may never be offered the lead in any conventional production of Hamlet. He was not computer-adept; in fact, it turned out that, although he typed at 60 wpm, he had learned the skill in France and was quite perplexed by a standard QWERTY keyboard. We had to find him a terminal, and that brought into the group Mark Turner of Demon Internet Ltd., London's premier provider of Internet connections and services.

Some fairly serious discussions ensued, as a result of which we scheduled a second "all-star" performance of "Hamnet," for which we decided to replicate in our virtual theater as much of the experience of real theater as possible. A real theatrical enterprise begins with dramaturgy—what would be called "script development" in Hollywood, sometimes including the actual writing but more often the process of commissioning scripts and/or researching their historical context. Next comes some vague scheduling process, including the formation of the stage-management team. Then it's casting calls, auditions, call-backs, rehearsals, set design and construction, prop buying, costume and wig fittings, music and effects design, technical runs, more dramaturgy as script adaptations are called for, and more scheduling as everybody's conflicting future commitments are "de-conflicted." Only then does the more public process of program printing, promotion, previews, performance, and critical review takes place. Finally, the reviews are read and the box office receipts counted, and a reputation is made or lost.

"How much of this process can we reasonably replicate?" was the question for us. Working backwards: We could forget the box office receipts. For the foreseeable future, the Internet is going to resist any type of commercialization, and rightly so. As for critical review, that could easily be replicated; in fact, we had critical review of our February 6, 1994, performance without even soliciting it. Will Roberts, one of IRC's major wits who goes by the nickname "Oldbear," wrote a highly amusing review which went into circulation after the show. Here are some excerpts:

"The play itself held true to the original Shakespearean UNIX, with few changes to the text to accommodate contemporary audience members less acquainted with this classic operating system. A small pratfall during the entrance of Hamlet himself, in line nine (which was repeated six times) of the numerated script, did little damage to the mood of the performance. Nor was the audience disturbed following line 15, when the prompter executed a modem dialing command in full view.

"The audience, however, was mystified by the appearance of a bot, identified only as Duck9, who kicked Hamlet off the channel just after line 51. This reviewer later learned that the mysterious bot was a misguided personal friend of accomplished Shakespearean actors bsd@lonestar.utsa.edu (Longy) and bradley@andromeda.rutgers.edu (RokinDuck), who, in the roles of Polonius and the King, respectively, had played out a scene which called for Polonius to be kicked off the channel by Hamlet. The bot, springing to the actor's aid, jumped upon the stage and unceremoniously booted Hamlet, played by the surprised Ian Taylor, in his guest appearance from the Royal Shakespeare Company.

"All and all, I found the production refreshing and surprisingly compelling in spite of occasional lapses in the actors' delivery of their lines in Elizabethan ASCII. The identities of many of the players appeared to change frequently during the performance, giving an other-worldly quality to this theatrical classic."

Oldbear's description of what happened was perfectly accurate—in short, we once again found Hamlet locked out of the virtual theater and begging for readmission. A "bot," by the way, is a robot program script designed to act in some ways as though it were an actual human IRC user. A bot can have many, many purposes, some innocent or informational, others more active. Some IRC channels tolerate a "censorbot" that listens for so-called "bad words" and first admonishes, then kicks out, the user of them. The French channel has—what else?—a seductive strip-bot who removes an item of clothing in response to key words, which are regularly reprogrammed. A bot is frequently a kind of bodyguard to its owner, and in this case the owner of Duck9, Rokinduck, had gone a step further and programmed it to protect not only him but his friend Longy by retaliating against anybody who /KICKed either of them. More often, sad to say, bots are created with utterly malevolent intent, and many of the U.S. university sites which act as IRC servers and routing hubs have now banned bots and their creators.

Ian Taylor said afterwards that he found the experience bewildering. Maybe he was preparing us for the fact that he won't be back for more (especially when he realizes that our check is never going to be in the mail). If so, it would be a shame, because after about 45 minutes of training with the IRC software, he did an outstanding job of Internet acting.

What could I possibly mean by "acting," in the context of a purely text-based medium? Two things. First, a talent for improvisation together with good judgment about how much is enough.

In virtual drama, as on the boards of the RSC, improvisation can be good fun but too much of it can royally screw the guy with the next line.

In virtual drama, as on the boards of the RSC, improvisation can be good fun but too much of it can royally screw the guy with the next line. We always make this point to our virtual actors, but few have understood it as well as did Mr. Taylor. Secondly, the software allows some control over the so-called screen attributes of a line of text. In plain language, this means that words can be rendered in boldface, underline, or reverse video if the correct control characters are inserted. This is something we leave entirely up to the actors, as being the equivalent of voice inflections on stage, which most good directors never attempt to dictate. Again, Ian Taylor showed that acting talent translates from medium to medium pretty well.

One of the processes of theatrical production that we thought might be worth experimenting with in the virtual world was the audition. So we put out casting calls on various parts of the Internet and actually held auditions, on January 30. Anybody who tells you that I did this purely in hopes of getting offers of net-sex from wannabe Internet ingenues is a liar, though I must admit I certainly was looking forward to sitting at my computer keyboard entering the line "Don't e-mail us, we'll e-mail you." We had asked those who auditioned to come prepared with a line from any Shakespeare play and to deliver it two ways: once as Shakespeare wrote it, and again as he might have written it if he had known about IRC. The example we gave was the translation of the line from Macbeth Act I, Scene III ("All hail, Macbeth, that shalt be king hereafter") to re, Mac. You'll be /NICK King /MODE +o 18r.

As it turned out, very few of the 20 or so people who auditioned actually had anything prepared, and we were all driven frantic trying to come up with ideas for the rest. However, we did get the show cast and were able to send the actors their lines and instructions by e-mail, which reduced the pressure on us all when showtime came. We also acquired a technical manager—we called him Manager of Systems & Bots—yet another very clever young man, Eugene "Rokinduck" Bradley of the Rutgers University Department of Computer Science. Since it was his "bot" that kicked Hamlet off the stage, it was just as well he was working with us rather than against us. We were grateful for him later, when a malicious bot did try to take over our channel and was duly put to flight by Duck9 (or by then it was Duck10, I guess).

Thus, the technical side of things got more under control. Between them, aurra and Rokinduck disciplined us and insisted on preparing for every production with proper "production meetings" (via e-mail, of course) and something quite equivalent to a technical run. We also saw ways of improving the show creatively. For a dramaturge, I had the help of my partner, Gayle Kidder, a writer and book reviewer in real life who has some ambition to create original scripts for IRC theater once we have the format settled. She undertook a highly amusing adaptation of *Macbeth*, which we called "PCbeth" (thinking that Shakespeare would never have used Apple hardware if he had known there was a choice). She went further by devising and creating color photographic art to accompany the production. We also created some costumes.

Full-color photographs, for a medium that can only use the computer keyboard? Costumes? Are we completely crazy? Yes, probably, but here's how we used the photographs. First, we had them scanned at medium resolution to make data files in .JPEG format less than 100 kilobytes per photo. Next, we overlaid advertising text onto one of them to create a poster announcing our production. Then we set about doing the Internet equivalent of pasting the poster up all over town—it was done by sending it to computers all over the world using the process called FTP (File Transfer Protocol). Many FTP computer sites, particularly universities, have a subdirectory called "incoming" that will accept unsolicited contributions of data. Files sent there will not be publicly accessible until the site sys-admins have taken a look and decided whether your data is the kind of thing they want on their site. This is very much like making the rounds of places like restaurants and galleries and asking if they will find a place for your theater poster, except that in the virtual world, you can't wheedle. I take that back—you can wheedle, but wheedles on e-mail don't have quite the same force.

Next, we incorporated into our "PCbeth" script three cues where the photos logically belonged, and made use of yet another mode of IRC communication to distribute them to the audience. Direct Client Connection, or DCC, is a computer-to-computer link that is initiated within IRC but, once initiated, is independent of IRC. What the people who wrote the IRC software had in mind as the principal use of DCC is not recorded, but certainly one of its main uses in practice is for people to send each other pictures of themselves, encoded either in .JPEG or .GIF format. It is a fast and reliable way of sending data files, and there is no limit to the number of DCC data transmissions that may be ongoing from a given computer at a given time. Not all IRC servers allow the DCC type of connection, but most do. Also, although the majority of IRC users, after receiving a .JPEG data file, would have to log off and enter a different program in order to view it, those working Windows or X Window terminals would be able to display the incoming picture immediately in a screen window accompanying the text. This would be the ideal setup for "PCbeth."

The vision for
"PCbeth."
Courtesy of
Gayle Kidder.

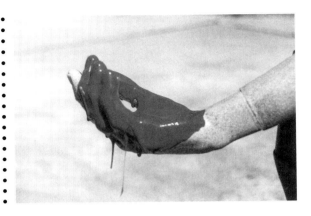

The bloody hand. Courtesy of Gayle Kidder.

The downfall of "PCbeth." Courtesy of Gayle Kidder.

We estimated that 80 percent of our audience had the ability to receive an image by DCC, and some 15 percent would be able to window it. Thus, we were "pushing the system" somewhat beyond its capability but we wanted to get experience in sending images and we were thinking ahead to the day when video images could be sent as a component of virtual drama.

As for the costumes, they were a semi-successful attempt to create a bit of visual interest for the media. The idea of Gayle Kidder and myself dressed as Queen Elizabeth I and Shakespeare working at adjacent computer terminals (on Shakespeare's 430th birthday, no less) might, we thought, be irresistible to TV. In practice it proved to be resistible, but we got some magazine coverage out of it—not to mention a round of drinks from a San Diego pub called The Shakespeare. Recognition, indeed.

For technical reasons too horrific to relive, the picture transmission did not go as well as we had hoped, but overall we had another very interesting mix of people involved, including six nationalities and a varying number of genders. Even though the "PCbeth" script was twice as long as "Hamnet," we got through it in about the same amount of time, and the interruptions and asides were far more controlled—a tribute, obviously, to our stage-management team, which then demonstrated how closely virtual theater can mirror the real thing by promptly resigning. A tech wizard in London has now sent us a program that will enable us to offer audience members the visuals on a self-serve basis; we're going to call it the "JPEG buffet," and once it's all set up, we won't have to even think about picture cues and /DCC progress lists.

● ●

MULTIMEDIA DRAMA

● ●

The future of virtual drama obviously lies in the multimedia and multi-window approach. Some of the interactive games described in Chapter 20, "Interactive TV/CDs," and Chapter 21, "Video Games," already approximate dramatic form quite closely. A CD-ROM that lets you become an actor on the bridge of the starship *Enterprise* along with Leonard Nimoy and DeForest Kelley would be many people's idea of a theatrical experience. It must surely be within the state of the art to use the full mask-and-gloves kit of virtual reality to put you on stage in a supporting role to Olivier's Othello or Glenn Close's Norma Desmond. But those would be strictly solitary experiences, and to a true theater buff—I hope I don't hurt anybody's feelings here—this is just another form of virtual masturbation.

With a target date of January 1995, the first to use VR technology to involve an entire audience may prove to be Mark Reaney, associate professor of theater and film at the University of Kansas. Reaney has been using VR for several years to wander around models of his theatrical sets, and his studio productions already transport small audiences into a virtual auditorium.

The best of the multiuser online games are potentially very fertile ground for expanding virtual drama. A group of New York actors has already experimented with using the "Hero Village" run by the University of Virginia as the backdrop for what they call vaudeville routines. (See the accompanying sidebar.) A commercial interactive service called "The Imagination Network" has plenty of promising elements, including the ability for users to draw pictures of themselves and place themselves in a variety of settings. The IN sysops have thought about the possibilities of scripted drama, but nothing has yet been produced in their virtual environment—at least, not so far as they know. These examples are all-American, but I must confess to an addiction for hanging out with Slovenians and such.

After all, Shakespeare himself wrote that all the world's a stage. A gang called the Electronic Cafe International has used the CU-SeeMe multiway video software and other techniques to create very interesting multimedia events spread across many countries, but their technology pushes the system beyond the reach of all but a minority of hackers.

Perhaps when we all have 20MB-RAM/100 MHz systems with full multimedia capability, broadcast-quality video, and T1 Internet connections, virtual drama will find ways of emulating those more technical aspects of the stage, such as audio and lighting design. I look forward to it. As for the missing box-office receipts—I doubt if they will ever materialize on the Internet per se. Perhaps one of the data services (Delphi, Compuserve, Prodigy) might one day underwrite a company of electronic strolling players, just as oil companies do (or used to do) for PBS costume dramas. But that, in turn, depends on attracting audiences in the millions, rather than in the hundreds. Alas, I believe we are destined to remain a bunch of dedicated amateurs (typos included) for quite a while yet.

Transcript of online rehearsal of "Christmas," April 17, 1994

This was the sixth in a series of improvisations based on a scenario written by Robert Allen. The sessions are directed by Antoinette "MadDirector" LaFarge.

The basic dynamic of Christmas is as follows: There are three characters: The Big Man, the Little Man, and Bloody Zelda. The Little Man is "friend, companion, guardian, keeper, counselor, undercover agent, and parent" to the Big Man. "For the most part, the Big Man is green-colored: he purrs, he laughs, he breathes deep. When he has doubts, he flushes a little red and grows wild, aggressive, and even insane." The Little Man expends a great deal of energy trying to keep the Big Man green, but he generally fails to do so in one way or another. In the original scenario, Bloody Zelda enters at some point; "everything about her and everything she does is fuel for the red power." Bloody Zelda embraces the Big Man; the Little Man runs away from the impending madness; the screams of BZ are heard as she is brutalized by the Big Man.

:

MadDirector [to All]: All the participants are either drunk or stoned or lusting after rabbits....I say we have a quorum for a rehearsal!

Eager.Actor says, "Let's GO! I am eager to hit the boards!"

:

MadDirector says, "OK TODAY'S PLOT OPENING: The Little Man has come up with some scam to make lots of money (folding green) and needs to talk the reluctant BigMan into it."

Bloody.Zelda sees her own gorgeous, voluptuous, brilliant, incredibly fine reflection.

:

MadDirector whispers to Little.Man, "Try to get BigMan interested in a betting scam of some kind."

:

Little.Man [to BigMan]: "Biggie, would you like to help me out with something? I have three peaches here, they are not quite ripe. You have to guess which one has the pits in it..."

BigMan [to Little.Man]: Look, I'm beginning to get a head-ache... which chore do you want to do first?

Little.Man says, "Put down 20 on the first, 30 on the second and 40 on the third..."

MadDirector whispers to big.man, "you need to have everything explained; ask."

Little.Man says, "Well, put it down..."

BigMan prunes the hedge a little too closely.

Little.Man skitters and scampers and reaches for BM's wallet.

BigMan grabs LittleMan's hand.

Big.man throws the peaches in the air and lets all but one drop.

Little.Man says, "comeon back over here and tell me which peach you think will win the big one?"

big.man says, "This one has the pit!"

Little.Man kisses BigMan's hand lovingly.

Little.Man says, "Nope, you're wrong, they are all the pits."

BigMan bites into the peach.

Peach juice dribbles down BigMan's chin.

Little.Man grasps the wad of bills and soaks them in creme de menthe and plasters them to BigMan's face.

:

MadDirector whispers to Bloody.Zelda "OK, come on now as a crooked fruit vendor with more supplies for LittleMan's scams."

A voice from off in the distance shouts: CROOKED FRUIT FOR SALE, FRESH FROM HELL!

Little.Man pulls a pound of cake dough out of his sack.

big.man has a twitch in his chin.

MadDirector whispers to big.man, "get interested again if LM offers lots of money."

Little.Man says, "Look, come play with me and you'll be loaded with dough!"

Big.man rolls over and snores again.

The voice shouts: GET THEM WHILE THEY ARE HOT AND FLUFFY AND MOIST AND RICH WITH VITAMIN X AND NUTRIENT ENZYMES

Little.Man kneads the dough all over Biggie's body.

Little.Man jumps up and down on BigMan's head...

The voice: HEY, I'M THE ONE WHO NEEDS THE DOUGH

:

The sun sinks a low putt.

BigMan [sings]: oh...wo...wo.

CURTAIN

PART V

Making It
Physical...and
Spiritual

Nanotechnology— The Next Revolution

Much as the Industrial Age represented a fundamental shift in social, economic, and geopolitical modalities for much of the world's population, and the current Information Age is once again reshaping the very fabric of global society, the "Nanotechnology Age" may well be unparalleled in all of recorded history for the impact it will have—and for the irreversible implications of the future that this new technology domain represents.

chapter 23
by Charles Ostman

THE NANO-FUTURE

Regardless of how grandiose or seemingly overstated the descriptions of the forthcoming advances in nanotechnology may appear to the uninitiated, it is indeed difficult to convey the scope and impact that this technology will eventually have on almost every aspect of life. Consider for a moment this basic description of nanotechnology and its potential:

> Nanotechnology is the enterprise of manipulating, assembling, and constructing with atoms and molecules, molecular structures, materials, and complete objects. These can include, but are by no means limited to, such examples as organic or quasi-organic molecular structures, molecular machines, computing systems with the functional capacity of supercomputers that would be literally invisible to the human eye. Ultimately, nanotechnology will give people the ability to replicate almost any material or macro-object at will.

Science fiction, you may ask? Is this merely the rehash of yet another *Star Trek* episode? The answer is, no. In research labs and theoretical study groups here and abroad, the subject is taken very seriously. But even at this beginning, it is important to emphasize that it is not merely an individual subject, or an obscure, narrow scientific specialization. In fact, quite the opposite is the case. Chemists, physicists, computer scientists, medical researchers, and many other technical specialists—covering a wide area of interests—are engaged in some aspect of developing a particular tangent, or enabling technology, with the overall focus aimed at molecular construction or synthesis.

Indeed, much as the Industrial Age represented a fundamental shift in social, economic, and geopolitical modalities for much of the world's population, and the current Information Age is once again reshaping the very fabric of global society, the "Nanotechnology Age" may well be unparalleled in all of recorded history for the impact it will have—and for the irreversible implications of the future that this new technology domain represents.

Just in the singular area of cybernetic modifications or enhancements to the human body, the implications are staggering. Consider the advent of corrective chemistry being performed at the cellular and subcellular level. A nanomachine component, for instance, may detect a particular cell type, contact and enter that cell, and perform some form of chemical or molecular modification process once there. Most diseases, genetic defects, or anomalies, and even the process of aging itself, will become more a matter of conjuring up the correct designer molecules and chemical delivery systems, rather than the realm of medical problem solving that is common today.

But this is just the beginning, and a small beginning at that. Of a perhaps more far-reaching nature is the concept of sensory and neural enhancement, in which the biochemical and biomechanical components of synaptical conduction systems can be modified to become more robust, more efficient under certain conditions, and are permanently altered to a higher state of functionality. In parallel with an ever-more-rapid unraveling of the mysteries of the biomechanics of synaptical systems is an equally aggressive interest in the ability to upload electrical signal information directly from the brain and sensory systems to external interface and processing devices.

This is the harbinger of "real" virtual reality, that is, the ability to extract actual experiential data from one person's brain, store, and/or process this electrical information, and remap this data into another individual's brain as an "experience transferral" process.

The so-called virtual reality of today, with the 3-D stereo viewing systems and interactive glove devices, which enable the user to experience a fairly primitive, video game-like 3-D environment, will never even remotely resemble what a direct download of information into the human brain can do.

A strand of synthesized, protein-like molecules lurking about in a cellular environment. Copyright © 1993, 1994 Berkeley Designs. All rights reserved.

Beyond the few biomedical example applications already mentioned, there is the potentially broader realm of organic synthesis itself. In terms of biomolecular engineering, research is currently focusing on the fabrication of protein-like molecular structures, with the next obvious step being the construction of other molecular components from which entire cells can either be modified or generated.

As if this isn't enough to at least gain a glimpse of what nanotechnology is being aimed at, this is only a small sample of the organic and biochemical aspects of molecular construction that are possible. We haven't even begun to examine the realm of nanoassembler systems, complete self-contained nanomachines, nanomechanical logic and computing components, self-assembling molecular structures, nanofoundries and replication systems, and a host of other nanomechanical applications.

These are, in many cases, structural components and interconnecting systems that can result in devices consisting of millions of atoms, assembled at the molecular level, to fulfill some eventual task or form. But in general, nanoscale features, at the molecular level of measurement, are measured in units of *nanometers*, or billionths of a meter.

It is important to note here that this is a fundamental concept of true nanotech. Nanotech implies the "bottom up" constructive process of creating objects by actually assembling individual molecules and molecular components, even if the resulting object is of "macro-scale" features. This is compared to the "top down" fabrication technologies of today, which consist of various techniques for carving or machining very small, microscale- (micron, or millionth of a meter) sized features out of larger blocks of material.

For the most part, lithographic chemical etching processes or laser milling and machining at the microscale level represent the majority of such fabrication processes. These processes are common for semiconductors and for the recently emerging "micro machine" industries. These are all subtractive processes and are limited by several important factors in terms of the precision with such structures can be reliably produced. Below 100nm (with a few notable exceptions), the atomic precision of surfaces, edge detail, undercut features, and so on, are simply too rough to be useful.

Not to add confusion here, but there are also additive fabrication processes, in which a spattering of molecular deposition layers can be added to a surface. Laser-induced molecular adhesion of materials has also been successfully demonstrated. And there are also other substances, such as photo-reagents, which can be used to bond organic molecular materials to inorganic microscale features (particularly in the case of implantable medical micromachine devices). This topic will be briefly discussed later in this chapter.

Given the fact that some of these technologies do indeed result in nanoscale-sized structures—and that in some cases this involves additive molecular processes as part of an overall fabrication procedure—whether or not some of these in-between examples can be truly labeled as nanotechnology is a source of debate. Although it is something of an esoteric, semantic debate which will probably never be fully resolved, for clarity here at least, the term "nanotechnology" will used specifically for "bottom up" molecular assembly and construction.

There is yet another domain of applied nanotechnology. This domain is focused on relatively simple molecular objects that are not necessarily complex from a structural point of view, but from a materials development perspective, possess highly unusual, or specialized properties. Molecular forms ranging from carbon atom structures called "fullerenes" (named after futurist Buckminster Fuller) and their various hybrid forms, to light transducing protein materials with unusual optical properties, to shape-changing metallic alloys, and so-called intelligent gels with shape memory characteristics, are just a very few examples of an entire range of highly specialized materials that defy the usual rules of molecular interaction.

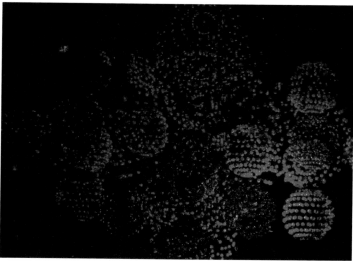

A cluster of spherical carbon fullerenes. *Copyright* *© 1993, 1994 Berkeley Designs. All rights reserved.*

And this is still only scratching the surface of the total potential of applied nanotechnology. As I hope is becoming evident at this point, it would be absurd to suggest that the entire subject can be covered in a single chapter, or even a single book. Indeed, a number of technical publications that focus on particular aspects of nanotechnology are already in print, and no doubt more will follow. It is merely the intent here to provide a factual but admittedly basic coverage of the major points of the technology, with a focus on the main areas of development that are being currently pursued, projections for the near future (five to 10 years hence), and the tools required for specific stages of nanotechnology development.

Therefore, in an attempt to start somewhere in the description of the myriad areas of nanotech development, both current, and still theoretical, the general concept of *mechanosynthesis*, or mechanical chemistry, as compared to the traditional solution-based chemistry as a method for molecular construction, is a major fundamental shift in the chemistry of the future. The idea here is that unlike solution-based chemistry, where a series of reactions will eventually yield some new molecule, in mechanical chemistry, molecules are actually "handled" as molecular building blocks to construct whatever form or material is desired.

Along these lines, one material of particular interest is in the realm of *diamondoid* structures. These are strong, stiff, carbon-based molecular lattice structures which are to be the basic building blocks of nanomechanical components such as bearings and sleeves, gears, rods, blocks, interlocking ratchet components, and so on, with very durable, and heat transferral properties.

Perhaps no one individual better exemplifies this body of research than Dr. K. Eric Drexler, formerly of the Massachusetts Institute of Technology and Stanford, and founder of the Foresight Institute in Palo Alto, Ca. Drexler is respected world-wide as arguably the leading authority in this newly emerging science. In fact, his most recent book on the subject,

Nanosystems—Molecular Machinery, Manufacturing, and Computation, is considered to be "the" technical reference manual for anyone seriously interested in the subject. It should be pointed out that this is not light reading, and in fact assumes the reader has a collegiate- or graduate-level background in physics, chemistry, and math. However, for anyone who is serious about wanting to become involved in this area of theoretical research, this is the best reference manual from which to get started.

In Drexler's model of the nano-world, the construction of nano components begins with the construction of "designer" molecules (with special geometries, bonding properties, and interactive potential features), which are molecular building-blocks set to suit the task at hand.

One might view the hierarchy of molecular subassemblies as being composed of various types, and classes of types of molecular structural components and grouping sets.

Why would such activity be interesting? Consider, for instance, a construction process which has a resolution of approximately 0.1nm (nanometer, or billionth of a meter). At this scale of manipulation, not only is the spatial domain compressed, but the temporal domain is compressed as well. For instance, there are defendable arguments for the theoretical construction of nanomechanical components which can operate at approximately 10^9Hz, or mechanosynthesis of nanoconstructions (mechanically controlled molecular construction, or "shaping" of molecular structures) at 10^6 operations/device second.

But just how to get started in this process? The first step needs to be the construction of the most minimal, simple diamondoid components, which themselves can later be utilized to construct "large" (from a molecular point of view) assembly and manipulation systems. For instance, an example sleeve bearing of diamondoid material, having a cross-section of 1nm, would consist of 258 atoms arranged in a torroidal configuration.

A complete planetary gear system containing 3,557 atoms. *Courtesy of Foresight Institute.*

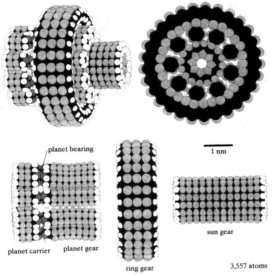

planet bearing

1 nm

sun gear

planet carrier   planet gear

ring gear   3,557 atoms

A planetary gear system, consisting of a central cylindrical shaft, and a surrounding bearing/gear cluster assembly, with a total cross section of about 4nm, and length of 3nm, would be a construction of 3,557 atoms. In an ascending order of complexity hierarchy, complete molecular handling systems, having the configuration of a multiaxis movable arm with a molecular gripping tip, are envisioned as machines standing 100nm and 50nm wide, consisting of approximately 4 million atoms for the entire device.

An array of various assembly and handling tools of this sort would therefore make up the contents of a "nanofactory," which could conceivably consist of millions of such interacting tools, capable of conveying, handling, and fitting together molecular sub-

components, with the end result being the fabrication of macro-objects from the molecular level up. In this realm, a series of molecular "feeders", which could consist of rotating spindle and arm assemblies, with the ends of the arms acting as receptors, would be capable of selecting specific atoms from a solution-based chemical soup of donor atomic materials, and then feeding the selected atoms onto a sort of conveyor belt/roller assembly. Further sorting stages will then direct the stream of selected atomic materials to the handling/assembling stages of the "nanofactory."

This example is only one aspect, however, of molecular assembly modalities. Consider the concept of self-replicating molecular substructures, in which the specific properties of a given resultant macro-object are the direct result of a self-regulating nanoconstruction process.

At MIT, research chemist Dr. Julius Rebek has already demonstrated several self-replicating molecules, where molecular subcomponents interact to form

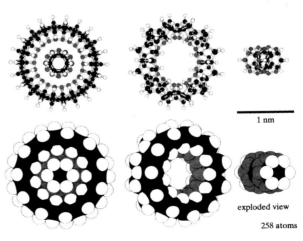

1 nm

exploded view
258 atoms

An example bearing containing 258 atoms. *Courtesy of Foresight Institute.*

secondary and tertiary compounds. As the secondary stage compound is formed, the recombination of these molecular subcomponents eventually ends up producing complete chemical clones of the original molecule. Behaving very much like a three-dimensional set of building blocks, the self-replication process is directly dependent on the complementary shapes of the interconnecting molecular components that are assembled in the replication process.

Is this where one of the current definitive boundaries of life begins? After all, a debate has been raging for some time as to whether or not a virus is merely a self-replicating molecule, or an actual life form. It needs to be pointed out, however, that compared to the molecular complexity of an actual virus, these current artificial self-replicating molecular examples are very simple, and only repre-sent a conceptual first step into this area of research.

Another class of molecular, self-assembling components of particular interest is the so-called *organometallic* com-pounds. These compounds have highly elaborate lat-tice structures, which can be induced via an electrostatic enforcement of interconnec-tion to construct various nanoscale objects, such as sheets, rods, and so on. Al-though there have been a number of these organome-tallic materials investigated, in general they all demon-strate the property of being a molecular solid. However, the geometry of their struc-tural lattice can be radically altered by a change of a single chemical component of the structure.

Unlike the molecular assembly schemes as envisioned by Drexler, where each molecular component is spe-cifically handled and assembled as part of a predefined series of fabrication steps, the organometallic struc-tures are self-organizing structural components. How-ever, it needs to be noted that the unpredictability of these self-assembling molecular forms, and the poten-tial myriad of yet to be discovered structural variants, places this area of research somewhat in a realm of chemical intuition on the part of the researchers attempting to discover possible new molecular struc-tures. By comparison, a molecular assembly system is strictly an engineered construction process, with the ultimate macro-object to be fabricated completely predetermined. Both forms of molecular con-struction and assembly processes, though, will likely have their appro-priate future applica-tions.

But the question still arises, where to get started if the ultimate desire is to create mo-lecular assembly systems?

. . . .

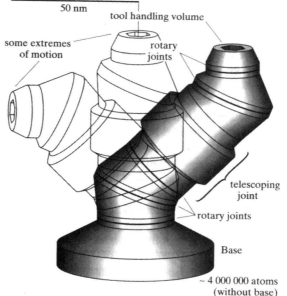

50 nm

tool handling volume

some extremes of motion

rotary joints

telescoping joint

rotary joints

Base

~ 4 000 000 atoms (without base)

A complete multiaxis manipulator arm as part of an assembly system, consisting of about 4 million atoms. Courtesy of Foresight Institute.

In the beginning, the task of molecular handling and manipulating will be a slow, and hand-manipulated sort of procedure. However, this is already being done, and more importantly, it can be accomplished in an "office" lab setting, with a desktop-sized system controlled by a PC or workstation.

There are two major devices for molecular viewing and handling available to the nanotech researcher: the scanning tunneling electron microscope (STM), and the atomic force microscope (AFM). At the extreme outer edge of molecular manipulation, are those researchers who are using the STM to arrange individual molecules, and even single atoms, to create molecular sculptures. The basic concept of the STM is that it utilizes an extremely fine-tipped tungsten needle (about 10nm tip), which is electrically charged. As the tip of this needle is brought to within a few microns of a given sample, a charge potential is reached in which electrons begin to tunnel from the tip to the sample surface.

The rate of electron flow (the current of this conducting tunnel) is exactly dependent on the precise distance between the needle tip and the sample surface. Therefore, by maintaining constant current control, and linking this control to the vertical displacement of the needle tip, the relative positional orientation of the needle during a scan pattern can be used to construct a topographical "map" of the surface being scanned. Amazingly, the electron tunneling current, utilized as the control mechanism in a positional feedback circuit, is so exact that the resulting topographical features rendered are accurate to the individual atomic boundaries within a molecular substrate.

This process enables researchers not only to "see" individual atoms residing in their molecular substrate, but also to manipulate them with similar accuracy. The original classic example of this sort of molecular sculpting was performed by Donald M. Eigler, at IBM's Almaden Research Center in San

Jose, CA, where the IBM logo was spelled out with individual xenon atoms on a nickel surface. But these experiments, conducted back in the mid-1980s, merely proved the possibility of handling individual molecules and constructing objects. The enterprise of handling individual atoms, and molecular objects has progressed dramatically since then.

More recent advances in AFM technology provide a somewhat different approach to handling molecular objects. In general, the AFM has certain advantages over the STM as a molecular construction device. The AFM tip can actually consist of any number of different types of materials, including protein (or protein-like) materials which can readily bind to a wide variety of recipient molecules, and do not require an electrical current conduction process to manipulate the target molecules. Instead, a type of extremely sensitive cantilever arm to which the molecular manipulator tip is attached can detect (and therefore serve as feedback device) the presence of a molecular surface.

As an enabling technology, this is a crucial step towards accommodating the first rung in the ladder of nanotechnology development. Actually, there are of course differing views on which particular approach might be taken to construct the first sets of nanomechanical components, from which eventual nanoassembly systems will be created. At some threshold stage, nanoassembler systems will be expected to be able to replicate their own components, and from that point onward molecular construction techniques in general will take a quantum leap in terms of availability and applications. But the initial stage, the creation of first-stage nanomechanical components, still needs to be tackled.

As previously mentioned, even though nanomechanical assembly systems do not currently exist (yet), it is actually in the area of biotech development, particularly in the construction of proteins or pseudoproteins, which may yield something of a partial

At some threshold stage, nano-assembler systems will be expected to be able to replicate their own components, and from that point onward molecular construction techniques in general will take a quantum leap in terms of availability and applications.

solution to this problem. Aside from the obvious organic chemistry applications that protein engineering development is aimed at, various protein-like molecules themselves have potential mechanical applications due to their physical geometries and binding properties.

Living bacteria for instance, actually possess marvellous examples of "flagellar motors," and other kinetic actuator devices to move them about through the liquid environment they thrive in. There are a number of researchers who visualize the concept of being able to construct molecular scale actuators from protein-like molecular materials, which would serve as the mechanical components of nanomachines. These nanomachines could in turn serve the purpose of handling other nanoscale components, as a construction process.

Though a discussion of just protein chemistry itself could be an extremely lengthy technical topic, some basic concepts can be mentioned here as they are relevant, and will be a major portion of future nanotech developments, both directly in bioengineering applications, and as molecular-manipulation components. In general, there are three-dimensional "sheet" and "helix" forms, which have various packing and bonding modalities that can fulfill a specific set of interconnective requirements. Many of these structures can in fact be extremely elaborate, and considerable effort has been spent in inventing various hybrid forms, including the introduction of metal binding sites, under the general heading of what is often referred to as protein folding.

The stability of protein structures once they are formed, as well as the predictability of their forms, are some of the major hurdles facing the molecular designers of these materials.

In nature, of course, proteins are the basic building blocks of life itself, and are found in every living cell, including the logic components of DNA, which determine the genetic identity of the cells, and indeed the entire organism. Even though some may tend to view nanotechnology as a new concept, actually, it has been occurring for billions of years in the ribosomes of living cells, where molecular factories churn out all of the complex protein and related molecular structures with atomic precision. In some ways, man's attempts to artificially mimic this process may appear to be clumsy at first, but the mere fact that such an attempt can even be contemplated, and procedures considered for making this possible, is perhaps no less of a fundamental concept than the actual creation of life itself.

In the realm of biotech, this is a crucial step in creating very specific molecular components with highly specialized interactive, constructive properties. Furthermore, as will be discussed later in this chapter, the introduction of nanoscale machine systems into the human body, both as medical applications, and cybernetic enhancements, will very likely include a variety of bioengineered protein machines, synthesized organisms with specific intracellular tasks, and diamondoid or other crystalline material nanosystems.

Of Nano
Computing, Molecules,
and Photons

For many of the hardware designers out there, VLSI (very large scale integration) logic is considered to be the outer edge of high-density logic devices, consisting of millions of extremely small transistor sites etched onto the surface of a silicon wafer. The traditional concept of an etched silicon substrate with depositional layers of applied secondary substrates to construct transistor and interconnection patterns conjures up visions of submicron features arranged to form individual transistor sites of a few microns each.

This, to put it mildly, is as archaic as vacuum tubes, when compared to the next generation of nano-computing components currently being researched. When I suggest thinking small, I mean very, very small. Extremely minute nanomechanical logic units, even individual molecules, become the new components in this nanocomputing realm.

How small is small? On a relative scale, if a typical 0.5- to 0.7-micron transistor pattern on a standard VLSI integrated circuit could be represented as being as wide as a six-lane freeway, a nanomechanical logic site would be

roughly the size of a cigar box or a book. Furthermore, a molecular computing logic site would be about the size of a marble or a pea.

And, as the general laws of physics apply, as functional component feature sizes decrease, so do relative reaction and switching times. However, unlike traditional semiconductor logic, GHz operating speeds become commonplace in this realm, but the relative power dissipation and consumption requirements actually decrease accordingly as well.

How small is small? On a relative scale, if a typical 0.5- to 0.7-micron transistor pattern on a standard VLSI integrated circuit could be represented as being as wide as a six-lane freeway, a nanomechanical logic site would be roughly the size of a cigar box or a book. Furthermore, a molecular computing logic site would be about the size of a marble or a pea.

In a general sense, traditional rules that have guided, and confined, both IC and system designers become irrelevant in this new nanorealm. Of course, other new fundamental considerations will appear to offer design challenges—and opportunities—to engineers of future nanotech computer systems. In this mode, one can think of trying to design a Cray-like supercomputer that would occupy 1 cubic micron.

Even so, the quantum leaps in operating speeds, relative computing power density factors, even the definitions of measure such as "operations per second," will be so completely different compared to current off the shelf integrated circuit technology, that the types of tasks computers will be used for may become vastly different than what is considered commonplace today. I don't just mean a spreadsheet that number crunches a bit faster, or graphics software that can process an image quicker.

In fact, for many present day software designers, this new computing arena of the not-too-distant future may offer a rather ironic design dilemma, considering that the usual rules may not apply at all. After all, in the early days of computing (remember Hollerith code on punched paper cards?), how many software developers were envisioning GUI applications running on a laptop PC? For all of those BASIC programmers who were grinding out code for an IBM 370 mainframe (so named because this giant, washing machine-sized contraption had a whopping 370KB of memory), how many were considering concepts like neural networks?

There will once again be a radical change in software development concepts, on a scale much vaster than the examples cited. For instance, in an optical computing system utilizing real-time holographic processing for intelligent object recognition as part of a high level reasoning, self-training system, the hardware may actually become the software. The software itself may change according to an ongoing input stimulus stream, and rewrite itself accordingly.

In fact, some future computing systems may be much more like living organisms, with different types of self-contained computing units consisting of different technologies (much like specialized organs in a body) interacting symbiotically. Though the traditional modality of written code serving as the mechanism for instructing a machine is far from extinct, how the code is actually generated may evolve to something quite different than the current norm.

But perhaps more importantly, the syntactical protocol of the language itself will very likely evolve to a form much more contextually oriented, as opposed to the excruciatingly fault intolerant code that most present day programmers have to contend with. In terms of the new era of nanocomputing, just as in nanotechnology itself, evolution is not a single thing or type of device, but rather a concept which in fact represents quite a few different approaches to constructing computing devices on a molecular, or extremely high density scale.

Nanocomputing encompasses a wide range of different technologies and approaches. In the purest terms, Drexler's nanomechanical logic systems or molecular switches, acting as logic gates, could be viewed as the most narrow definition. But it must also be recognized that nanotechnology—as in molecularly-engineered materials—will also greatly affect computing systems.

The basic premise of any type of computing system is that some type of operation is occurring which enables information to be stored and retrieved, and some type of comparative interaction occurs with newly introduced information. In traditional digital systems, some type of switching device performs many repetitive on/off operations to represent a logic state within the context of computational process. In analog systems, absolute values, rather than the symbolic values represented by the cumulative logic states of a given logic engine, are the medium of the computational process.

In the "nanorealm" of future development, both analog and digital technologies are being investigated, and as stated previously, future computing systems very likely will consist of mixed technologies. A few, but certainly not all, of these areas of research are briefly discussed here.

Drexler's approach to nanocomputing is to actually construct physical machines, with movable rods and interlocking actuators which slide back and forth in channels in a solid block. This is a truly unique, if not ironic approach, since the earliest computers were in fact mechanical machines. Are we soon to come full circle, to return to the mechanical world as the next ultimate computing technology?

In the Drexlerian model of mechanical computing, the relative position of a spring-loaded rod becomes the interpreted logical 1/0 status (see diagrams). An entire subassembly system, constructed from a molecular diamond substrate (among possible material options) has been devised to provide a series of mechanical, interlocking components. Given a series of calculations to determine the rate of motion of rod displacement, propagation delays for activating the spring mechanisms, etc., it has been theorized that such a device would have an approximate propagation delay of 60ps over a distance of 100nm, and a comparative 0.6ns for a distance of 1 micron.

In a solid block array structure, containing layers of sliding/interlocking rod assemblies, consisting of a 0.5nm thickness of interlayer separation, this would allow for a functional volumetric density of $12nm^3$ per each "logic" unit.

This configuration is based on a feature size of 6nm for the drive system that activates the rod, and an additional 2nm for the reset spring, with a total consumed volume of $16nm^3$ for the entire interlock system. The other major

An example of a nanomechanical logic unit. *Courtesy of Foresight Institute.*

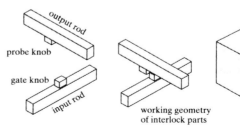

probe knob
gate knob
output rod
input rod
working geometry of interlock parts
interlock in housing

consideration for this scheme is the relative energy consumption/dissipation factor, since the relative accuracy and rate of displacement for this mechanical system will very much be dependent on the relative energy density, and thermal loading encountered by this type of structure.

With a relative switching time of 0.1ns per each rod displacement cycle, this would represent a relative energy loss of about 2 maJ, with a consumption of 0.013 maJ per complete interlock switching cycle. This is a radical departure from size/power density factors associated with present day transistors. Given the surface area of $4nm^2$ consumed by the footprint of the rod/interlock assembly, compared to the typical transistor footprint of 10^6nm^2, this implies a computing density factor simply not possible with etched silicon substrate transistor assemblies. In terms of energy density for the same substrate constructions, this represents a 10^9 difference between even the most efficient CMOS substrate currently available!

Even accounting for drag losses, thermoelastic and vibrationally induced inefficiencies, this is still a technology which simply abandons all current design limitations confronting today's silicon IC designers.

Of course, in the realm of nanomechanical logic devices, the ultimate extension of this pursuit is the manipulation of individual molecules, and even atoms to accomplish this task. As in the case of the scanning tunneling electron microscope, the relative position of a single xenon atom between the charged needle probe tip and a nickel molecular substrate can be demonstrated as a switchable device.

However, the actual engineering of an array of this type of molecular logic devices fabricated on a nanoproduction scale, and energy efficient operation, may not necessarily be the actual implementation, but it does serve to prove the concept of "molecular logic." An interesting parallel attempt along these lines is the creation of orthogonally shaped DNA chunklets, successfully constructed at New York University, which serve as a substrate for a molecular logic construction scheme.

Other efforts along these lines have included a range of electrically- or optically-driven charge transferring molecules, where the actual geometric configuration of an individual molecule can serve to represent its logical 1 or 0 status. One particular example of this is the research conducted by Robert Birge, investigating the phototropic reaction states of chromophores. In this case, molecular NAND gates were assembled that consisted of two input chromophores, and one output chromophore, in an arrangement somewhat resembling a fork. Excitation of either input of the fork from a pulse of cohesive light from a laser resulted in no change of the output status, but both inputs being simultaneously stimulated caused an electrostatic charge status change in the output chromophore. The overall size of the various chromophore logic molecules tested this way is in the range of 10nm to 20nm long.

In a similar area of research involving photonically stimulated charge transfer in molecules, Angel Kaifer and Richard Bissel, at the University of Miami, have been investigating the actual positional displacement of molecular beads in a series of materials known as *rotaxanes*. Though there are a number of rotaxane variants, the general idea is that a switching function can be created by detecting the relative position of a molecular ring as it travels back and forth down the length of a rodlike structure. Recent experiments in this area have yielded both photochemical and electrochemical triggered switch events.

The major argument for favoring Drexler's nanomechanical logic schemes, however, as opposed to various molecular logic concepts which are being investigated, according to some in this debate, has been in the design of large logic arrays that would lend themselves to constructing full scale digital computers. Most solid state digital computers today contain millions, indeed, tens of millions, of logic gates arranged in addressable arrays to allow for the reading and writing of continuously changing logic states within the system.

However, all of these schemes are still dependent on traditional digital logic computations. For some types of computing, particularly neural net systems which involve real time comparative approximations of relative values (which are the basis of contextual reasoning), intelligent object recognition, and the like, the analog realm may actually be far more promising than digital systems. This is not to say that a massively parallel processing digital system programmed with neural net emulating software cannot perform these sorts of functions. But once again, there is a certain irony that some of the earliest, primitive computers were in fact analog devices, and yet, some of the most recent developments in advanced alternative computing concepts are returning to the analog realm.

In terms of computing density in the analog realm, nothing comes even close to the optical domain. This is a difficult concept to grasp at first, since the optical components currently being constructed are not individually tiny, as in the other nanorealm models cited here. But in

terms of computational density for extremely complex analog processing, the optical domain exceeds all other computational modalities possible.

The severe limitations facing solid state electronic analog designers of neural net systems are the extreme complexity and total number of established physical connections of equivalent neurons in a network. As in an actual organic brain, electrical voltage patterns are introduced into a series of synaptical connection sites, which are arranged as a series of parallel connections on a given signal plane. Each signal plane is actually a layer of these synaptical connection sites, and a complete neural net is actually a construction of many layers, each containing many synaptical sites.

The robustness of the implied stimulus/information processing is directly dependent on the total number of synaptic connection sites, and number of layers that these connection sites are distributed on. In most current hardware and/or software equivalent models, all of the synaptic sites are interconnected, with each layer of synaptic connections connected to the successive layers, as well as to all other layers. The relative strength of a given connection pair within an adjacent layer set, as opposed to a more "distant" connection site on a successive layer set, in part determines the relative response to an input stimulus introduced to the primary layer set connection sites. In fact, all of the synapse connection paths respond interactively, depending on the shape of the amplitude pattern of the introduced stimulus spread across a given number of input sites.

Once a stimulus, and successive response stimulus patterns are propagated through the multiple layers, and have engaged secondary synaptical sets, the mathematical equivalent of a holographic rendering of this stimulus/response pattern is established in this network. Repeated exposures to the same stimulus further strengthen this response pattern, and as an approximation comparison process, newly introduced information back-propagated through this prestimulated network will establish a degree of similarity.

This process is at the very heart of virtually all organic computing processes, from basic sensory information processing, to the most complex modalities of high level reasoning.

A complete discussion of neural net computing theory, as well as such specialized applications as smart object recognition, would be far too complex to describe in detail here. The purpose in discussing this, however, is to try to establish some parameters as to what the real challenges are in building true artificial-intelligence engines. To construct the simplest neural net equivalent of say, a hydra (a tiny, nearly microscopic jellyfish-like creature) would require a single layer pair of about 10^3 neurons. The next step up, to perhaps a worm, would be in the domain of 10^5 to 10^6 neurons. At the first level of invertebrates, where a defined brain actually serves as a centralized processing engine (as opposed to a distributed neural net found in invertebrates), multiple high level processing tasks are interconnected in a continuous symbiotic network. A model of a fish would represent approximately 10^8 neurons distributed over 10 to 20 layers.

At the high end of a potential neural net engine, based on a theoretical human model, this would require no less than 10^{11} neurons distributed across 100 layers. If translated into a solid state analog electronic device, this would require the equivalent of 10^{11} opamps, all interconnected and able to function simultaneously as a continuous-process engine! Well, even if you're the most ambitious analog designer on the planet, good luck.

On the other hand, an optical correlator, utilizing a dynamic, content addressable, holographic optical storage media, can perform as the optical equivalent of a neural network, without requiring any physical wiring to represent actual synaptical connection paths, and yet fit into a very small package.

Development of optical correlation systems has advanced dramatically in the past few years, and indeed, commercial vendors are already providing platforms for real-time object recognition, and other cognitive processes. Although originally funded by ARPA for specifically military applications, such as smart target acquisition, companies such as OCA Applied Optics and TeledyneBrown are now providing off-the-shelf versions of these systems.

And this is where the nanotech connection comes in. Although some versions of optical correlator systems have utilized solid crystalline materials, such as lithium niobate, for the holographic element in the system, these materials are very costly and difficult to fabricate. A substantial breakthrough in solving this problem may be in the usage of photochromic molecular films applied to glass substrates. Photoreactive proteins found in some bacteria, referred to as bacteriorhodopsins, have been successfully applied in this fashion, and shown remarkably robust results.

A film of this material, contained in a glass sandwich with electrically conductive inner surfaces, can store a holographic reference image which can be optically addressed (the optical feature resolution of the holographic information is dependent on the frequency of light used to read the information). An applied square wave voltage holds the hologram, and a reversed pulse can then be used to enhance the erase cycle, which thereby allows new holographic information to be introduced into the device.

In a similar vein of interest, researchers at the IBM Almaden Research Center have been investigating a new generation of photorefractive polymers, with the target goal of developing a very low cost dynamic holographic storage media. Besides the amazing information density and processing capacity represented by optical holographic computing techniques in general, these photoreactive materials present the potential for random access times 100 to 1000 times faster than current day magnetic storage media. This is due in part to the changing divergent angle of photons passing through the media and is the only requirement for actually reading information, instead of actually moving a mechanical head back and forth to find a track and sector location on the surface of a spinning disk. Furthermore, as in the case of the previously mentioned photoreactive proteins, these new polymers are also electrically erasable.

On a comparative basis, a neural net processing engine, based on a software model utilizing a traditional digital computer would require a processing engine delivering 10^5 MIPS, or more, to even begin to approach a processing capability capable of high-level reason and contextual computation resembling human characteristics. In today's development environment, considerable effort has been spent in the development of smart object recognition tools, particularly in the areas of machine vision, robotics, and interactive sensory fusion systems.

But this is only the initial stage of a much larger domain of smart systems, which in fact contain an array of sensory organs that are fully independent, self-contained processing units capable of deciphering very complex visual and audio information before it is introduced to the central processing engine. The preconditioned signal information is then introduced to the core neural net engine, very much in the same fashion that occurs in actual living creatures.

This is the beginning edge of future cybernetic organism constructions, which in fact may contain many aspects of nanotechnology—not just in the realm of computing and sensory signal processing devices—but in the actual specialized materials, and electromechanical constructions that comprise the physical organism itself.

STRANGE MOLECULES
WITH SPECIAL PROPERTIES

As mentioned previously, nanotechnology, in its pure form, tends to be associated with the assembly of molecular structures and components, as a manufacturing process, referred to as *mechanosynthesis*. However, mechanosynthesis is still very much in its early, conceptual stages of development. There is, however, something of an in-between stage of development, which is neither bottom up, molecular assembly, nor is it top down construction, as in micro machining.

This is in the realm of creating very specialized, designer molecules with unusual properties. Though these specialized molecules are not intended to serve as components in large, complex nanomachine constructions, in many cases they provide various functional modalities that may serve as enabling materials for current day micro device construction, substrates that can interact with other molecules under specific circumstances, or allow for the creation of materials that would otherwise not occur in nature.

Although there is a very wide range of potential applications for engineered materials with special properties, particular interest has been focused on biomedical development and bioengineering. This is in part due not only to the enormous potential, and relatively short-term financial incentives for developing such materials, but also because in many cases, before the existence of such materials became available, many of these potential applications were simply not possible.

> Although there is a very wide range of potential applications for engineered materials with special properties, particular interest has been focused on biomedical development and bioengineering.

As the molecular details of biomechanics within the human body are revealed and understood, they now begin to provide a path for designers of micro or nano scale components to target specific requirements. The development of specialized materials which have unusual properties is an important step in this process.

These shape-changing materials include many different areas: alloys which consist of metallic crystalline substrates whose state phase geometries can be triggered to switch as a function of input electrical or thermal stimulus; gel materials which have extremely high voltage or chemically-controlled volume or shape changes (which can also serve as molecular filters); fullerenes of carbon with extraordinary structural characteristics that are capable of encasing other compounds; warm-temperature superconductors; and inorganic substrates which can mimic the behavior of organic materials.

In this realm of nanochemical alchemy, researchers are beginning to look at solving difficult (if not formerly impossible) engineering problems. They are doing this not by designing around the materials and processes currently available to them, but rather by conjuring up entirely new classes of materials with seemingly "impossible" characteristics to suit the task at hand. It is also in this realm that the tools of nanostructure designers may be developed, and from which many of the already-mentioned higher-order nano systems can be enabled.

For example, one of the more daunting problems facing designers of medical implant devices is the issue of biocompatability. Many materials may demonstrate one or two specific properties, but trying to create a device which can remain slippery to some fluids but not others, interact with a very narrow or specific range of chemical messengers, and so on, presented extremely difficult challenges to bioengineers. That is until the recent development of so-called designer surfaces using some very novel techniques.

Several companies are already offering these specialized surfacing techniques as a commercially-available process. Perhaps the most interesting is the photoactivated reagent process developed by BioMetric Systems, Inc. of Eden Prairie, MN. What the company has produced is a series of photoactivated reagents which can capture specific biomolecular structures and hold them in place. This, in turn, enables those structures to be applied to an extraordinary range of surfaces, including metals, polymers, and other synthetic materials. This is a crucial step in designing future implantable microcomponents for internal medicine and cybernetic applications.

However, at a much more fundamental level of material development is the ongoing research into an array of carbon atom structures referred to as fullerenes. Consider, for instance, attempting to encase atoms of elements which would otherwise never want to react with anything or stay put for a given reaction event. An example of this would be a spheroid of carbon atoms, in an arrangement looking something like a soccer ball, encasing an atom of helium. Impossible, as some chemists might say?

In fact, it is not only possible, but has already been successfully demonstrated at Yale University. Martin Saunders, one of the primary researchers in this field at Yale, has been experimenting with a multistage process consisting of first creating an environment of spherical fullerenes by passing an electrical current through graphite electrodes in a helium-filled chamber, and then baking the resulting molecular spheroids in a helium-saturated furnace to further increase the relative population density of helium-containing carbon spheroids in the resulting environment.

But the range of carbon fullerene molecular constructions goes far beyond containing uncooperative atoms. As a methodology for constructing impossible compounds, this area of research opens up a realm of possibilities that simply would not have been considered 10 years ago. Whether the end result is to convince non-reactive chemical components to interact with each other, or to achieve the opposite goal—to contain reactive substances that would otherwise be too unstable or overreactive to work with—the possibilities are almost endless.

In fact, the horizons of fullerenes have now extended to an entire range of bucky blobs, shapes, and structures. These blobs often include the introduction of other cooperative elements such as nitrogen, to form huge, complex molecular forms capable of creating such materials as lanthium dicarbide, (the world's first synthetic material harder than diamonds, commercially developed and produced at SRI International in Menlo Park, CA), ceramic compounds capable of superconductivity, and ultra strong carbon fibers on a nanoscale which could create cybernetic and structural components with fantastic stress loading properties, just to mention a few.

The original pioneer of this area of research, who now provides commercial access to "custom" carbon and carbon compound fullerenes (for about $1,000 per gram), is Dr. Richard Smalley, a physicist from Rice University. Though he is still at the forefront of this technology, he is not alone by any means. In fact, interest in fullerenes, particularly in applications aimed at developing semiconductive and superconductive substrates constructed with fullerene technology, is being aggressively pursued in Japan, with some very big players entering into the long-term development arena.

For instance, NEC has taken a particularly keen interest in this area. At the University of Arizona, "megafullerenes" containing over 400 atoms each have been successfully created, a development which opens up yet another panorama of potential applications involving highly complex molecular structures. So called "buckytube" structures begin to suggest the possibility of nanoscale structural components, with virtually indestructible strength and endurance characteristics. For designers of nanosubstructures requiring particularly extreme structural integrity, this development holds particular promise.

Especially when they combine this technology with the ability to contain atomic components of other elements, (such as fluorine), to provide molecular lubrication, or combinant metallic dopants to provide "molecular batteries," nanodesigners are quickly adapting to this new standard of molecular engineering.

In fact, in yet another medical application, cancer cells could be attacked by antibody-containing bucky balls, which "home in" on the offending cells via the chemical signals recognized by the antibodies. Once the bucky balls have attached themselves to the cancer cells, laser light optically conducted through a molecular scale light-guiding fiber could energize oxygen molecules (in the bloodstream) that encounter the bucky ball conglomeration. The end result is that the oxygen absorbs the energy, and the reaction caused by this process would in turn rupture, and destroy, the cancer cells.

MICROMACHINES, NANOTECH, AND PROCESSES
AVAILABLE TODAY

Speculation over the potential implications of micromechanical, and future nanotechnology developments can be tantalizing, to say the least. But what is actually available today, or is about to become available in the near future (one to two years from now)? To answer this question, it is important to not merely focus on any specific device or particular machine, but rather to view the industry as a whole, with particular focus on fabrication processes and materials development. As is the case with many other fundamental technology developments in the past, it is the symbiosis of many seemingly unrelated technologies that converge to create an entirely new arena of development. Perhaps never before in history has such a diverse range of technologies and scientific disciplines converged to establish such a fundamental leap in applied technology.

Specifically in the case of micromachined components, feature sizes of 0.1 microns are now considered within the realm of manufacturing feasibility. This is the result of the past 20+ years of aggressive development of mass fabrication techniques as applied to the manufacture of integrated circuits. Since the same microlithography techniques used to etch transistor and conductor sites on standard silicon wafers can be directly applied to creating micromachine components, the industry as a whole is already "tooled up" to start fabrication of micromechanical chips. In fact, the limitations facing the industry at this point aren't so much based on technical feasibility as they are on establishing a range of applications which would justify the initial expense of establishing volume production of such components.

There have been, in fact, significant developments in the traditional top-down construction techniques, that is, carving small pieces and structures out of larger surrounding substrates. Using photolithography processes very similar to those used for fabricating ordinary integrated circuits, researchers at a variety of public and private facilities have created an array of ultraminiaturized motors, actuators, pumps, and vibrating vanes, as well as a plethora of gears, pistons, and other mechanical components out of silicon, nickel, and other metallic substrates.

Various universities, such as the University of Utah, the University of California at Berkeley, and the University of Wisconsin have been involved with creating these micromechanical components since the beginning stages of this area of research. However, serious commercial research efforts are now being pursued by corporate concerns both here and abroad. Toshiba, for instance, now manufactures an etched substrate micromotor under $1mm^3$, powered by a 1.7 volt DC power source. Interestingly, it can provide shaft rotations ranging from 60RPM to 10,000RPM.

Equally important, of course, is the development of nano batteries which can power these devices. There are, in fact, various implementations of ultraminiature, if not molecular, power sources. The most obvious types are metallic sandwiches, which are layers of dissimilar metals that, when bonded together, generate a voltage potential across the poles of the stack. The feature size of these metallic layered constructions, consisting of etched "pads" with sequential depositional layers applied, is now being successfully constructed in submicron-sized footprints.

Particularly with the enormous financial potential of developing medical, and so-called cybernetic enhancement devices, no small amount of effort is being expended to explore and define specific applications. Some of the current applications being developed range from micro "scrubbers" designed to scrape plaque from the interior walls of arteries, to complete drug dispensing systems on microchips. A key issue in this development process is establishing a library of micro components which a micro-cybernetic device designer can access to build a complete, self-contained system.

Perhaps never before in history has such a diverse range of technologies and scientific disciplines converged to establish such a fundamental leap in applied technology.

The types of components which are of interest in this realm consist of sensors, mechanical actuators, pumps, propulsion devices, micro-electronic circuitry, and power supply components. Furthermore, to make such complete, implantable micro systems feasible for long-term installation within the human body, biocompatability is of extreme importance. This requires the application of specialized designer surfaces to key regions of such implantable devices.

The next most important task in establishing design criteria and mass production capabilities for complex micro assemblies is the establishment of micro positioning and handling equipment capable of resolving to 0.1 microns, or less, and secondary tooling capabilities, such as laser drilling, conductor and multiple substrate bonding, and so forth, on a similar scale.

As this stage of development continues, the next step is the evolution of design standards, much in the same fashion that designers of integrated circuits rely upon now. In todays world, a "chip" designer uses a computer-aided design (CAD) system to provide a visual map of submicron features, such as transistor and conductor sites, during the design process. The designer selects from a library of available components to eventually develop the on-screen layout of the chip. This data can then be extracted directly from the computer and translated into the lithographic and other fabrication steps required to mass produce the chip. In the very near future, this same type of design process can be applied to complex integrated micromachine development and manufacture.

The point here is that if micromachines are going to be implanted throughout the human body to do various tasks, their ability to perform is going to be directly dependent on their ability to sense, and "home in" on the chemical messages that they are programmed to look for.

To gauge where the technology is at this moment, consider some of the following examples of assembly equipment and available components. Originally driven by interest in microassembly requirements for mass production of electro-optical micro components, various companies, such as Dukane, Inc., of St. Charles, IL, have developed an entire series of micro robotic assembly systems capable of resolving repeatable motion paths to 0.1 microns over a total work area envelope of 115mm×50mm×50mm. A typical work area for a micro assembly would be in the realm of 50×50 microns, and could incorporate such tasks as handling and placing subcomponents of mixed material substrates on a common foundation substrate, resulting in a complete machine system construction.

Given that assembly systems are already available that can handle components and materials at the submicron scale, the next step is for chip manufacturers, with the substrate foundry and lithographic fabrication equipment already on-line producing integrated circuits, to develop the mask patterns for micro motor, actuator, and sensor components. This process has already started. But more importantly, a micro machine designer is not specifically confined by what is off the shelf, since an already substantial array of micro mechanical mask configurations has been successfully implemented at various research facilities. The task facing the micro machine developer is to approach the appropriate fabrication vendor with micro-lithography facilities, and present them with a custom mask, much the same way that one would have a custom integrated circuit fabricated.

Micro mechanical components can be generally categorized into two main types of configuration. Single-piece constructions such as "tweezers," grippers, harmonic vibrating vanes, and related structures can be etched directly from a common mass of piezoelectric substrate. Complex structures, such as actual motors with gearing and motion translation devices, and valve and pumping assemblies, require fabrication from separate materials, and final assembly with a micro assembly system (as mentioned previously).

The next type of component required for an implantable intelligent micromachine that would perform some type of interactive process within the human body is a sensor device, or an array of sensor devices that can allow the machine to recognize or respond to a stimulus. For instance, an implantable insulin dispensing micromachine would need to able to continuously monitor glucose levels within the blood in order to regulate the rate of insulin dispensation from a controlled valve device.

The realm of electronic and electrochemical biosensors is actually very diverse, and even in current technology provides a diverse range of sensitivity to different types of stimuli. Ion selective, complex compound, enzyme and immuno sensors are all becoming available as integrated components. Furthermore, even in exotic areas such as sensitivity, microphotonic, extremely minute pressure fluctuations, and microsonic detection are all becoming available as sensor sites on an integrated hybrid micro circuit. Of particular interest are chemically sensitive field effect transistors (chemFETs), in which a single transistor is electrically bonded to an ion-selective membrane. This allows the micro sensor designer to place an entire array of multiple sensors and signal processing electronics on a single chip.

In fact, the continued shrinking of micro sensor sites on an integrated circuit substrate has coincided with an entirely new collection of biocompatible materials and intelligent membranes and gels. Mostly composed of variants of polyacrylimide compounds, these various gels and membranes possess the features of changing relative size or volume, or relative molecular porosity (depending on the application) as a function of pH, electrical, or thermal sensitivity. Not only are these materials available for sensor or chemical valve applications, but they also can be used for mechanical work performance, including usage as artificial muscle fiber and micro actuators.

For instance, a collection of gel fibers 1 micron thick can shrink to 4 percent of their original volume in less than 1 millisecond in an electric field of 5 volts per millimeter. This allows for relative volume displacement to be triggered by electrochemical reactions. This also provides a perfect pumping device for dispensing a substance in micro dosages, with no mechnaical moving parts, as in a traditional pumping device.

Back to the insulin dispensing micro machine mentioned previously, a research team from the University of Trondheim in Norway and the VA Islet Transplant Center in Los Angeles, has in fact already demonstrated that microdosages of insulin can be directly osmosified out of the gel itself with a minute electrical current. This means that an entire micromachine device can provide this function without requiring any type of mechanical pumping components. In fact, human trials for a micro implantable device based on this technology are expected to begin by the end of this year.

But this is only one very narrow application example of a much wider array of molecularly selective membranes, which depending on very minute fluctuations in applied current, can be programmed to allow for an entire range of molecular porosities with the same piece of gel. This is an extremely important function for micro machine designers who want to have their intelligent machines "sniff" out certain chemical compounds, but ignore others in a complex chemical environment. The point here is that if micromachines are going to be implanted throughout the human body to do various tasks, their ability to perform is going to be directly dependent on their ability to sense, and "home in" on the chemical messages that they are programmed to look for.

In Japan, the application of intelligent gels has been specifically directed towards artifical muscle development.

· · · · · · · · · · · ·

In Japan, the application of intelligent gels has been specifically directed towards artificial muscle development. At the Second Polymer Gel Symposium and Robobug Fest in Toshuba, Japan, nine research groups successfully demonstrated chemomechanical motive devices, and serious development funding is being directed at propelling this new technology into the medical devices marketplace. The concept of "wetware" being applied to micro chemistry dispensing and monitoring systems, and artificial muscle components, is a major development for cybernetic and micro machine designers.

In fact, in yet another example of polyacrylimde gel applications, a series of tissue simulating gels has been developed from a hybrid variant of this type of material at the Langley Research Center.

The significance of this work is to create a collection of materials which possess mechanical, thermal, electrical, and other relevant properties of various tissue types, but with the ability to inhibit growth of microorganisms, and which will not harden or dry over time.

In conjunction with this, the application of biocompatible surfaces to almost any type of metallic or polymer surface is yet another key ingredient for this design process. This is already being provided as a commercially-available service by several companies, such as Spire Corp., of Bedford, MA, Advanced Surface Technologies, Inc., of Billerica, MA, and BioMetric Systems, Inc., of Eden Prairie, MN. The major objective is to provide a series of chemical "tethers" which can attach the biochemical substrate of choice to the micromachine device surface according to the designer's requirements. One major advance in this realm is the introduction of a series of photoactivated reagents, which set up the chemical bonding sites as a series of photo exposure patterns. This means that the same micron level sized features used to create the physical topologies of the micromachine being constructed can later be applied to attaching biochemical substrates. Various biomolecules, including antibodies, enzymes, extracellular matrix proteins, peptides, antithrombogenic agents, even entire cells, have in fact already been applied to medical implant devices with this process.

For anyone interested in the future of micromachine development, consider this. According to market research conducted by Market Intelligence Research Corp., of Mountain View, CA, total micromachine development and sales in 1992 were $995 million. The value of development and sales is expected to exceed $3 billion by 1998. What this means is that the market potential of micromachine development is attractive enough to redirect the attention of substrate foundries, microfabrication facilities, and producers of development tools to make this technology readily available to the "outside" world of entrepreneurs and independent designers.

What has been discussed so far is what is already available to the micromachine developer. The near future, however, is beginning to cross the boundary from micro scale machined components, and enter truly nano scale fabrication and construction technologies. Furthermore, biophysicists are beginning to examine the inner workings of complex organic molecules and processes from the point of view of being able to synthesize these processes as molecular construction techniques. The major objective that all future nano-scale system designers are faced with is the molecular and atomic precision with which such constructions can be replicated.

As stated previously, traditional microlithography fabrication, pushed to ever smaller tolerances, begins to fail below 0.1 micron feature sizes, mainly because of the raggedness of the micro surfaces and edges of an etched substrate. It is at this point where the precise deposition of atoms and molecules onto a substrate, rather than the carving away of excess material, becomes the requirement for constructing nano-scale components.

Although not quite yet available as a commercial service, various types of nano fabrication processes are currently in the experimental stage at a variety of research facilities. Of particular interest are laser molecular deposition systems which deliver atomically precise layers of various materials onto a surface. At Oak Ridge National Laboratory, researchers have been using the experi-

mental LARCS (Laser Ablation from Rapidly Changed Sources) system, which is unique in that it utilizes a rotating drum arrangement which can hold up to six separate source materials at a time. This allows for the designer of atomically precise, multilayered substrate materials to rapidly create unusual thin film combinations and structures with much less difficulty than earlier laser or ion beam deposition techniques.

In the realm of nano electronic devices, a new class of transistors, referred to as "high electron mobility transistor" (HEMT), are emerging as nano components for future nano circuitry. In this realm, the gate of the transistor is essentially a wave guide for single electron transmission, where the wall dimensions of the quantum conductor path are less than the actual resonant wavelength of the electron being conducted through it.

Astonishingly, this theoretical concept has already been successfully proved and tested by Peter Nuytkens and his research team at MIT. In fact, they have already constructed an entire A/D (analog to digital) converter circuit with these atomic scale transistors. Perhaps even more amazing are the quantum well lasers in which a single electron and resulting quantized photon are the source for an electro-optic logic device. Devices based on this type of quantum well construction would utilize 10nm features on a molecular substrate.

The major objective that all future nano-scale system designers are faced with is the molecular and atomic precision with which such constructions can be replicated.

In yet another area of research into molecular scale devices, photodetector cells occupying a region of 2nm×2nm are being developed by Elias Greenbaum, a molecular electronics researcher at Oak Ridge National Laboratory, in Oak Ridge, TN. In this example, photosynthetic molecules which mimic the organic behavior of photosynthesis in plants are applied as molecular patches on a carrier substrate. A photodetector array based on this concept not only provides photonic resolution far beyond current commercial technology, but also sensitivity capable of sensing individual photons.

Utilization of arrays of micromechanical robots to manipulate genetic samples for DNA scanning and reconstruction is in fact already being considered by Johannes Smits, a micromachine researcher at Boston University. The concept here is to construct micromachine matrices containing thousands of genetic samples, which would then be examined for specific genetic codes by thousands of micro robots which process these samples in parallel, rather than relying on the serial, sequential sampling process conducted by current computer controlled systems.

In yet another entirely different, but equally important area of research, the enterprise of handling exact bits of DNA with atomic accuracy was demonstrated with considerable success by a research team in the department of chemistry at the University of New Mexico. Armed with an STM, considered by many nanotechnologists as the atomic handling tool of choice, this research team has developed a technique for coaxing DNA snippets down molecular sized grooves etched into a glass slide.

The electrically charged tip of the STM serves as an electrical "tweezers," which can grab the end of an individual DNA strand, and stretch it out according to the needs of the DNA manipulation at hand.

Since the DNA is a tightly wound double helix structure, it can demonstrate a considerable amount of relative elasticity as the double helix is stretched out over a given distance. In fact, this elasticity can be very accurately manipulated by varying the amount of charge applied (switching off the charge allows the DNA strand to spring back to its original configuration).

This example of the symbiosis between micromachine component development, nano structure fabrication techniques, and potential biogenetic engineering in the near future indicates the rapid pace at which these developments are converging to provide a future world of micro and nano cybernetic enhancements to humans.

There are, however, other approaches to constructing these micro and nanomechanical components being investigated. In parallel to this type of research, development of fabrication techniques for nanoscale conductors and "wires" is well under way. At the Centre d'Elaboration des Materiaux et d'Etudes Structurales in France, researchers have succeeded in producing an incredible array of gold conductors under 50nm wide and 15nm thick, embedded in a silicon substrate. Even more amazing is that the topographical feature difference between the substrate and conductors can be maintained to within 2.2nm. Perhaps most significant of all is that despite the extremely small feature size of these conductors, which the experimenters have created from gold and gold palladium alloys, the average resistance of a nanoconductor at room temperature was maintained to about 60 ohms.

The concept of nanoscale circuit boards, complete with embedded nanoelectronic components, is shifting out of the "vision-of-the-future" realm, and into the component development and design stage. In terms of biomedical implants, such as artificial sensory systems, bioelectrical interconnection devices, and related applications, this is yet another crucial step in this rapidly evolving area of research.

BIOMECHANICS IN THE NANOREALM

Aside from the upcoming developments in "ultracomputing" and artificial intelligence which will arise from applied nanotechnology, no other single area of development holds more fundamental implications than the realms of biotech and medical enhancements. This also presents perhaps the most difficult, complex, and far reaching ethical and philosophical questions which no one may be able to answer.

It will also be access to this realm which will have the highest comparative value, and perhaps be the most coveted, by those who have the privilege of access. The coin of the realm in the near future may not be a physical object, but rather access to medical and mental enhancements which will propel the recipients of such enhancements to a status entirely different than that of the common world.

The suggestion here, though, is not to necessarily cast a negative light on the medical or biological aspects of applied nanotechnology—because the potential benefits are of almost unimaginable proportions. But for the sake of balance, a reasoned view of all possible variations of the outcome of these developments is crucial to their understanding.

It is this very realm that brings to life (no play on words intended) the aspect of cybernetic enhancements, artificial organisms, life extension and life-experience enhancement in the near future. The potential biomedical applications are not only far reaching, but in fact may permanently alter the definitions of life as now generally accepted.

Consider the current state of medical enhancements already available. In today's medical world, organ transplants, mechanical prostheses applied as bone replacements, and other synthetic enhancements, are considered to be standard medical procedures. Furthermore, life support systems now exist which can extend physical life in an otherwise brain-dead body indefinitely. Artificial sensory implants, such as the recently developed cochlear implant to restore sound perception to hearing impaired, or even totally deaf patients, are now being applied on a limited basis.

Early stages of research are currently being conducted to actually allow a direct electrical connection to optic nerve bundle sites, with the ultimate goal being to supply visual information to a blind person via an electronic camera or computer interface. Richard Norman, at the University of Utah, has developed a prototype version of what could become an implantable photonically-driven electrode array which can directly stimulate neurons in the visual cortex of the human eye.

Artificially grown skin cultures are currently being produced as a method to supply skin grafts to burn victims, or those suffering from extreme dermatological disorders. Research is continuing in several locations worldwide to develop an artificial heart. And this description of currently applied medical technology doesn't even include the exploratory realm of genetic research, in which gene modification and screening can be potentially used in every medical application, ranging from diseases to cosmetic features.

These examples are only a few of the existing biomedical enhancements which have gradually been accepted by the majority of the general public as normal medical options. And yet, already many ethical and legal questions are mired in an ever-changing set of rules and definitions, which place many doctors and institutions in a realm of uncertainty.

The next logical step is a further improvement of such life enhancing and life extending technologies to an ever-increasing range of options and improvements. A fundamental shift in technologies is approaching in which life expectancy, physical, sensory and mental abilities, and other permanent alterations to the human body via artificial and cybernetic implants and nanoconstructions, will make the current set of questions facing the medical world seem trivial.

But just where does this realm end? In the upcoming nanorealm, it doesn't. Currently, micromachine designers are already actively designing and testing devices which can be injected or implanted into the human body to perform a variety of tasks. Examples already being researched are micromechanical "scrubbers" which can swim through veins and arteries and clean out cholesterol and plaque deposits. At Carnegie-Mellon University, micromachines with rotor blades the size of a human hair are being constructed and studied with this application in mind.

Another example currently being investigated by Dennis Polla at the University of Minnesota is the development of a chemical sensing intelligent microsystem, which contains all of the sensory, pumping, and mechanical components to provide a self-regulating internal insulin dosage dispensing device. In fact, this same type of "micro-innoculant" could be used to supply a self-regulated dose of any number of drugs, including physiologically regulating compounds, and so forth.

The entire human body, of course, is a chemoelectrical generator. Various schemes for harvesting minute amounts of electrical energy directly from the human body to drive a given capacity of implanted micromachinery, and determining what the tolerable electrical loading factors might be in this circumstance, are other areas currently being investigated.

However, all of the previously cited examples are still reliant upon micromachine technology. At the molecular assembly level, however, such concepts as artificially constructed bacteriophages, quasiviral components and the like, which can permanently reside within the human body and perform corrective chemistry functions, are currently being considered.

Starting with life extending devices, consider a fleet of nanites which could patrol throughout the human body searching for trouble—something like a nanomechanical and nanochemical artificial immune system. If an invader cell, or even a virus is detected, they can surround and disable the offending organism. For example, in the case of current day cancer treatments, often chemotherapy is applied to rid the body of unwanted cancer cells and tumors. The chemotherapy is essentially a controlled dose of chemical toxins, designed to kill the offending cells, but often the side effects of this type of systemic poisoning are almost as traumatic as the cancer itself, and are extremely unpleasant to the patient.

By contrast, a nanite component designed for this purpose, injected into the human body, could seek out the offending cells via a chemical message sensory "pad," and apply a chemical marker to the offending cells. This would then allow for a more precise targeting of an appropriate chemical toxin, which could also, of course, be administered by a nanoinnoculant device.

But this is still only the beginning. In a much more far-reaching implication, actual performance enhancement, rather than mere repair or maintenance, is a consideration currently being explored. In other words, the first stage of human nano implants would be to extend life, and continuously monitor and arrest various disorders as they occur. The next stage would be to "enhance" the life experience beyond what is currently possible.

A molecular bacteriophage entering a target cell. Copyright © 1993, 1994 Berkeley Designs. All rights reserved.

> Neural net systems, as modeled on a computer, have shown that repeated exposure to a similar stimulus pattern tends to increase the robustness of the learned information stored in the corresponding portion of the network.

The human brain is essentially a very complex electrochemical processing engine, with tactile and sensory input devices communicating to it. Within the brain itself are approximately 10^{11} neurons with 10^{13} dendrite interconnections, arranged in branching structures called ganglia. Each ganglionic cluster of dendrites responds to input voltage stimulus signals, which occur as sodium ions are conducted into the individual dendrite fibers.

The stimulated ganglion responds by producing a response stimulus voltage pattern, such as a secondary release of sodium ions, which in turn stimulates the surrounding ganglia through their dendrite fibers. The actual mechanics of the process are partially dependent on a voltage controlled membrane which surrounds each dendrite fiber. As the membrane is stimulated, the molecular porosity of this membrane increases, thus allowing a certain range of permeability to sodium ion transmission. Research has shown that the robustness of information processing and storage is dependent on the relative dendrite fiber density (total exposed dendrite surface area) in a given region of brain tissue.

Furthermore, neural net systems, as modeled on a computer, have shown that repeated exposure to a similar stimulus pattern tends to increase the robustness of the learned information stored in the corresponding portion of the network. Interestingly, recent experiments have indicated an actual physiological response to repeated electrical stimulus to dendrite fibers. The results are actual "buds" being formed on some of the dendrite branches within a given ganglion.

It has been considered by theorists that at some point in the not too distant future, this electrochemical process can in fact be enhanced by the addition of highly specialized nanocomponents designed to increase, or alter, the rate of sodium ion transmission, and artificially regulate the activity of the voltage controlled membranes which are a key component in this process.

The implications are far reaching indeed, considering that everything from basic sensory perception to actual information processing and high level reasoning, the very essence of intelligence as it is currently defined, may be altered by the implantation of these neural-enhancement nano devices. For years, biochemists and neurophysiologists have been investigating behavior modification and performance enhancement (so-called intelligence boosting) with drugs designed to make very subtle modifications in brain chemistry. The application of these types of nanocomponents could drastically alter the rate of progress in this domain, and instigate areas of research never previously considered.

As for such modifications within the human brain, the major difficulty for such performance modifications may not be so much in the nanodevice chemical interaction with synaptical conduction sites, but rather in knowing where exactly to deliver such "devices." But even in the extremely daunting task of geographically "mapping" brain functions, research at various facilities is yielding some surprising results.

Although numerous advances have been made in determining specific functional regions within the brain, actually observing the dynamic electrochemical processes during conscious thought and cognitive activities has been considerably more difficult, but not entirely impossible. One technique explored by Michael Haglund and George Ojemann at the University of Washington has been to optically observe the cerebral cortex with a specially modified CCD camera, and computer imagery enhancement. Actual "thought maps" were color-keyed and observed as patients viewed alternately blank slides, and slides with images.

Indeed, quite a number of studies, involving both PET and MRI scans of patients during various forms of stimulus have been able to provide detailed, three-dimensional maps of blood flow and density changes during various types of induced cognitive stimulus. But perhaps the most interesting results to date have arisen from a recently developed technology, MEG, or magneto-encephalography. The major advantage to this technique, which measures extremely minute magnetic fields generated by electrochemical activity in the brain, is that this method can capture very short events (less than 1ms), thus providing a surprisingly accurate, real-time "event map" of mental activities.

Dr. Erwin Neher (director of the department of membrane biophysics at the Max Planck Institute for Biophysical Chemistry in Gottingen) and Dr. Bert Sakmann (director of cell physiology at the department of biophysics at the Max Planck Institute for Medical Research in Heidelberg) shared the Nobel Prize for physiology in 1991, for their pioneering work in identifying the exact nature in which this electrochemical process functions. In fact, they have successfully identified how many types of cells and cellular systems in the human body, aside from neural cells, utilize electrochemical signals to communicate and interact with each other. This is an extremely crucial step in designing, and eventually constructing, nanomechanical and nanochemical components which can target exact cell interactions, and modify their stimulus and response characteristics.

In yet an entirely different area of interest has been the investigation into the various causes of aging, perhaps most notably, the synthesis of coenzyme Q10 in the human body, which tends to decrease substantially with age. It is considered, by some theorists, that corrective chemistry performed on deteriorating DNA responsible for regulating the rate of coenzyme Q10 production, could possibly reverse the aging process. In particular, it is believed that DNA

Although numerous advances have been made in determining specific functional regions within the brain, actually observing the dynamic electro-chemical processes during conscious thought and cognitive activities has been considerably more difficult.

. . . .

polymerase alpha, which is the key agent for synthesizing and repairing errant DNA, undergoes a radical chemical change with aging. A nano machine component, capable of seeking out this material, and performing the appropriate corrective chemistry, is thought of by some as a possible method for retarding the aging process.

Also being considered are various forms of corrective chemistry operations performed by specific protein- or enzyme-seeking nanomachines, which could target the exact cell types of interest in somewhat the same fashion that a virus seeks out a particular cell type. Indeed, although the example here is not to suggest the creation of artificial, user-friendly viruses, but rather to construct bacteriophage nanomachines, somewhat like quasiviral components, designed for a specific intracellular repair or maintenance purpose.

WHAT ARE THE GOALS, AND HOW DO WE GET THERE?

So far, we have had a chance to examine the theoretical implications of nanotechnology in the future (bottom up, molecular synthesis and construction), and a glimpse into the current day developments in advanced micro machines and devices (fabricated with traditional top down, etched substrate construction).

Despite the theoretical aspects of what development paths may eventually become established, certain criteria can be viewed as a reference guide to suggest the most likely chain of events leading up to a nanotech development scenario here in the U.S. What is important to note here is that at this moment, unlike Japan (which has already established a 10-year, $200 million nanotech development plan) there is no specific, centralized nanotech development organization or academic/industrial consortia to pursue this interest. However, various independent research groups, both academic/institutional and corporate, are delving into very narrow, or specific areas of investigation. The missing ingredient here may the temporary lack of a singular, centralized focus group which allows the outsider to view the entire spectrum of nanotech developments at a glance.

This could be a crucial step in making the possible investment or support of nanotech development a more palatable business decision in the eyes of those willing to engage in a long-term, leading edge development program. As in the case with many other technical developments in the past, it was usually a small handful of visionary scientists and developers who were often far ahead of their time who created what eventually became mainstream technologies with huge commercial benefits. In the realm of molecular synthesis and construction, however, the stakes could be potentially larger than any other singular development in history.

Grandiose as that may sound to the ears of the skeptic (and admittedly, there are those who view nanotech as science fiction), the facts are that even if only a small portion of nanotech related products should eventually emerge, such as nanoscale logic components (for ultra powerful, miniature computers), potential biomedical applications, an entire realm of new engineered materials, and so on, the effect on various industries could be profound.

But of vastly greater implication is the concept of "nanofoundries" as manufacturing systems which could essentially fabricate, at the molecular level, virtually an unlimited variety of materials and devices on demand. A nanofoundry of the future would not consist of a large, complex "factory" by today's standards, but rather be a small box that could literally sit on a desktop, but be capable of synthesizing whatever the designer has in mind, on the spot.

It is the eventual availability of ubiquitous molecular manufacturing systems to the general population that may cause the industrial revolution of the next century. What is important now is to be at the beginning edge of this realm of development, rather than simply follow

- Grandiose as that may sound to the ears of the skeptic, the facts are
- that even if only a small portion of nanotech related products should
- eventually emerge, such as nanoscale logic components, potential
- biomedical applications, an entire realm of new engineered materi-
- als, and so on, the effect on various industries could be profound.

along somewhere in the future. Unlike other major technology development programs, the actual costs and lab equipment required to establish a nanotech development lab can be surprisingly small. In fact, the major costs associated with such an effort would most likely be more in the realm of human costs (a collection of world-class chemists, physicists, and computer experts would be the core of such a team), than in huge, expensive, equipment costs. We're not talking about building a superconducting, supercollider accelerator, or launching a series of space shuttle flights here.

In fact, the actual lab equipment required could be very minimal indeed. An STM (scanning tunneling microscope) and/or an AFM (atomic force microscope) would of course be essential research tools. These are surprisingly small devices, however, and can easily sit on a desk or lab bench. Powerful computing capability is a must for complex molecular modelling and simulation, of course, and a certain range of chemistry equipment and supplies would be required. But again, this is not the stuff of a huge refinery, or a nuclear facility. This entire setup could easily fit into an ordinary office building. It would seem reasonable to assume that a focused effort could be initiated by a consortium of private developers, and perhaps federally financed programs, to pursue this area of interest.

So why isn't this being done already? Well, it is, just not in this country. Furthermore, lack of awareness even amongst the technical community is still probably the greatest impediment toward a more robust pursuit of nanotech development. In a current political environment where budget cutting and huge social programs seem to be the trend of the moment, it is difficult to find a sympathetic ear in Congress or the Senate for something as seemingly unconventional as exploration into the realms of nanoconstruction and molecular synthesis. After such recent big-science fiascoes as the now decommissioned superconducting supercollider particle accelerator, the Hubble telescope, and the recently launched $900 million Mars probe that was "lost" somewhere in the solar system, public sentiment for anything even remotely resembling a long-term scientific development commitment is at an all time low, regardless of how promising the eventual results may be.

The irony here is that even an ambitious, all-out nanodevelopment project would be surprisingly small by comparison to the previously mentioned examples. But to expect the average public to even understand, let alone actually endorse the expenditure of tax dollars, on something as technically unusual and seemingly futuristic as nanotechnology is simply a risk that most politicians are absolutely unwilling to put their names on. In that light, it is most likely that the majority of development support here in the U.S., for the foreseeable future, will come from private and corporate sponsors.

Notwithstanding the state of affairs for actual development funding and political sentiments, the technical parameters for nanotech development could be manifested in several different directions. But some general features as envisioned by those actually involved in this type of development are consistent across the range of current researchers.

Among current research projects under way, there are two fundamental approaches which tend to segregate the style of research conducted. One approach towards molecular construction and manipulation is to use existing biomolecular components, most notably, proteins and protein-like structures, which can be manipulated and synthesized to form new biomolecular structures. Besides the most obvious applications in biomedical and genetic-engineering applications, there is also the potentially vast realm of producing molecular manipulators which are themselves composed of these protein structures. In other words, the first series of actual molecular machines may well be specifically constructed from organic compounds which can be formed into shapes designed to perform various molecular scale mechanical tasks.

This is, in fact, the approach that the Japanese MITI research program is focused on, and may indeed yield the first real commercially viable results. The other camp, which is characterized as being mostly the American approach to molecular construction, is aiming at developing engineered molecules constructed from scratch with carbon-based diamondoid molecular building blocks that can be snapped together via a process referred to as *piezochemistry*. In this realm, even though the end results may be farther off into the future than the "protein folding" approach of today, the potential rewards are truly astonishing, since it would be in this realm that the tools of true molecular synthesis would be developed.

In a potential three stage sequence of events that would eventually lead to an ubiquitous nanomanufacturing realm, the first stage would be the creation of the simplest of diamondoid nanomachine components, such as the gears, rods, blocks, and so forth. Most likely, this initial step would be the most difficult threshold to cross, and may well rely upon the painstaking process of computer controlled AFM assembly processes.

However, even though these devices are essential research tools, they are far from being practical molecular-manufacturing devices, since manipulating even a small number of atoms would be an excruciatingly time-consuming process. Considering that the various complex molecular assembly tools envisioned by various theorists would consist of 3 million to 4 million atoms each, the most obvious solution is to try to develop various intermediate molecular handling tools, themselves constructed out of fairly simple molecular devices.

Establishment of a nanomechanical tool system, which would serve as the enabling technology for general-purpose nanofoundries available to the entrepreneurial developer, would be the second and third stages. At that point, there is likely to be no limit to the range of possible applications that could emerge.

After all, when the first laser was successfully demonstrated at Bell Labs in 1956, how many of those early developers envisioned the extraordinary range of possible applications that the laser would eventually be used for? And as an analogy, that is only a tiny example compared to what general-purpose nanofoundaries could eventually yield.

Back to the realm of modified, protein-like, structures, and also a class of self-assembling chemical components referred to as organometallic compounds; this may be the realm from which some of these first tools will be developed. Organometallic compounds are very interesting from a molecular structure point of view. The structure of a molecular solid formed from such molecules can be radically altered by a change in the chemical substance of one component. The structure can also be altered by changing the charge on one of the constituents in the compound.

Protein based molecular constructions have very useful properties, including chemically induced kinetic activity, which makes them highly suited as possible molecular grabbers.

In fact, in the realm of bacteriophages, and protein-based structures, a considerable variety of molecular scale motion translation devices could in fact be constructed as a system for handling molecular components and component groups. Therefore, given this criteria, a theoretical model of a six stage nanofoundry development program would most likely start with the development of a pseudo-protein molecular system. This would provide the first stage of molecular handling devices that are themselves molecular components.

This circumstance would most likely lead to the development of more complex protein based molecular tool systems, in which an elaborate combination of molecular handling tasks could be accomplished as a molecular manufacturing sequence. This second stage of development is a crucial step, since it is at this juncture that the more ambitious task of true "mechanosynthesis" development and assembly begins.

In the previously mentioned molecular systems, synthesized protein structures are modified or folded to produce the molecular shapes of interest, or self-assembling organometallic compounds form complex shapes based on the electrostatic enforcement of combining organic compound "chunklets" and metallic lattice structures.

However, the ultimate goal is to use these molecular tool components as a method for constructing carbon based, diamondoid crystalline structure components. The reasoning here is that the diamondoid components have extremely robust fatigue lives and durability characteristics, as well as excellent thermodynamic, stiffness, and structural properties. Furthermore, from a chemistry point of view, these structures lend themselves very well to yet another recently developed area of research referred to as piezochemistry, or pressure induced reaction states.

This provides a mechanism where the appropriate diamondoid molecular forms can be snapped together, almost literally like molecular building blocks. This modality actually falls under the larger realm of *mechanochemistry*, which refers to processes in which mechanical motions control chemical reactions. Given this definition, one can draw a comparison between machine-phase chemistry, and more traditional solution-phase chemistry.

Therefore, the next development stage is to begin to construct the first stage of simple diamondoid components. This is perhaps the most daunting hurdle to successfully cross (no diamondoid molecular structure components have been constructed to date—or at least, no published results have yet been offered to the public). It is at this stage that the first sets of primitive rods, cylinders, disks, and other basic geometric forms will be constructed.

However, after this threshold is crossed, the successive stages of diamondoid development should accelerate rapidly, since constructing complete, diamondoid machines and machine systems is essentially the result of constructing ever more complex forms, such as bearings, gears, piston assemblies, and the like, and assembling them to construct complete machines.

It is at this crucial stage, the third diamondoid component stage, where complex tool and manipulation systems are assembled, and the ubiquitous realm of solution phase chemistry merges with this new domain of mechano phase chemistry. The reasoning here is that molecular and atomic conveyer systems, in which an entire array of molecular grabbers pick out the actual atoms and molecules that they are designed to have an affinity for, can then have the selected atoms and molecules conveyed to the nanoassembly system. Once the selected atoms and molecules are delivered to the nanoassemblers, they are combined, and assembled to form whatever material or structure might be desired.

But does the vision of *Star Trek* replicators seem simply too ridiculous to believe? The technology may never really evolve to the point of being able to fabricate a ham sandwich on demand, according to the molecular blueprint of the original sandwich, but certainly an almost unimaginable array of potential applications can arise from this.

In medical applications alone, the implications for modifying the intracellular chemistry of almost any organ of the human body to cure diseases, prolong life, provide the potential for enhanced sensory and mental abilities, and so on, are almost beyond comprehension. If even only a small fraction of the potential applications for nanofoundry device construction and molecular synthesis should come to fruition in the future, the effects on society in general could be profound, and indeed, revolutionary.

Perhaps more importantly though, particularly for the entrepreneurial, technical developer, is the coming full circle back to a realm where the small company, or even the lone inventor, can conjure up devices and materials that have significance to the world at large (as opposed to only emerging from huge corporate or government financed development programs, as it tends to be today). In this realm, the nanofoundry of the near future could literally be a sort of desktop system, which would require nothing more than the raw atomic/molecular ingredients to feed the system,

and the imagination of the developer using the system.

Profound as this new nano-revolution is, how it will eventually filter into, and affect the life of the average population could have several potential outcomes. Not the least of these considerations is how to inform a general public about the various aspects of nanotechnology—and all of the potential developments that its evolution represents—so as to encourage intelligent and rational management of this potentially fantastic resource. After all, if some individuals go into a complete frenzy over a minor genetic alteration to a commercial food crop (as if genetic alterations haven't been occurring since life first began on this planet!), how will they respond to concepts such as replication of almost any type of materials at will, creation of yet to even be imagined materials and objects, cybernetically enhanced humans, life extending implants, enhanced sensory and mental abilities, extraordinarily advanced "ultracomputers," and so on?

One thing is absolutely certain, however. Whether the nanorevolution occurs here, or elsewhere in the world, the evolution of this new technology is inevitable. I can only hope that the developmental, and socioeconomic future of this country isn't squandered because of ignorance, and irrational panic, but rather is harnessed and applied in the most productive ways possible.

. . . .
Whether the nanorevolution occurs here, or elsewhere in the world, the evolution of this new technology is inevitable.

omputer-Enhanced Creativity

The computer enables us to do things that were once impossible outside the cloistered confines of our skull. Unlike any tool in history, computers can match our imaginations almost stroke for stroke.

■NTRODUCTION

At that point between dream-time and wake-time, our theta and alpha waves churn endless notions in our minds. In our most seemingly exasperated moments, when we feel as though we will drop from exhaustion, a new point of view begs us on. To most pe⟨ ativity is a mystery. Althou⟨ have creative thoughts, we d⟨ feel that we are their masters. synoptic eruptions inspire us. for chance.

Creativity is a mystery, yet random synoptic patterns fire the imagination.

As countless books on creati⟨ out, however, finding one's n⟨ not require a trek to the local ⟨ top. We can learn to be inspi⟨ sitting at our desks, lying in ⟨ taking a shower, or even whil⟨ on a computer.

In fact, the computer enable⟨ things that were once impos⟨ side the cloistered confines of⟨ Unlike any tool in history, c⟨ can match our imaginatior⟨ stroke for stroke. This chapter ⟨ you a few ways to leverage the ⟨ to enhance your own creativi⟨

The world and its expectations always influence our creative abilities. I know of nothing more creatively debilitating than the standard 81/2-by-11 sheet of paper. People try to fit whole worlds of thought onto its surface. The computer provides a limitless landscape constrained only by your ability to think in new ways.

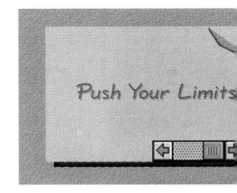

Push Your Limits

WHY DO I NEED A COMPUTER?

Most creative people are not computer-literate. At least not if you look at the history of creativity. Neither Leonardo Da Vinci nor Thomas Jefferson had a Silicon Graphics workstation or even a PC XT—and they did quite nicely thank you.

But even great creators don't always perform mental miracles. Mental miracles, or creative thoughts, require a skewed view of something. All creative thinking adds novel approaches or new insights. Reiterating the obvious is not very creative (but it is analytical, and we'll get back to that later). But during our mundane day-to-day jobs or lives, we find very little time to read a novel, let alone have a novel thought. For most of us, we relegate creativity to film makers, great business visionaries, top flight engineers, advertising people, and entertainers.

The truth is, most important creative ideas come from average people who find a few moments in just the right sunlight, on just the right day, with just the right music playing. The rare moments in which we step away from our preconceptions and look at the world through different eyes don't need to be rare at all. That is where the computer comes in.

The modern multimedia computer, or even its sluggish predecessors, can facilitate moments of challenge and insight. If I am inspired by music, the computer can play music. It can thrust strange words at me and force me to think of new associations for my old thoughts. I can bend the unbendable, stretch the unstretchable, and even sing the unsingable. Once a thing is in digital form it becomes infinitely malleable. That thing can be a picture of your dog, or a string of words, or a musical refrain. The dog can be morphed into a cat. The words can be combined and recombined, added to and deleted from, and arranged and rearranged in endless combinations.

The truth is, most important creative ideas come from average people who find a few moments in just the right sunlight, on just the right day, with just the right music playing.

Beyond turning ideas into digital clay, databases full of facts do not forget or distort, become tired or go fuzzy like our brains. On hot summer afternoons when our last thoughts turn more toward baseball and beer rather than creativity, the computer spurs us on, ceaselessly furnishing variation upon variation of discordant pictures, notes, and streams of words.

The computer will not help you capture stray thoughts at 2 a.m., or remember an idea that coalesces in the shower. A pad of paper and a pen, a bar of soap or some soap scum are better partners at those times. But in the waking hours, when you don't have the aid of near sleep or the mindful wanders of a shower, the computer can help bring you to those states of mind and willingly partner with you in the creative process.

Creative insights grow from a state of mind. No amount of digital inspiration or a fully rendered precipice to survey creation from, will generate an idea, if the mind is ready to see only the seeable, to imagine only the imaginable, to believe only the believable or do only what is doable. One must be open to seeing the world from under a stamp on a piece of first class mail, or make the seemingly mundane attempt to actually imagine wearing someone else's shoes.

If your creativity requires sound or sight, computers can help jog distant memories or help place a word on the tip of your brain to the tip of your tongue. It can prod the connection that is holding you back from your next great connection between super strings and DNA, or pot roast and broccoli. Finding the right phrase or strain requires the right timing and environment. The computer can help there, too.

Creative insights grow from a state of mind. No amount of digital inspiration or a fully rendered precipice to survey creation from, will generate an idea, if the mind is ready to see only the seeable, to imagine only the imaginable, to believe only the believable or do only what is doable.

PREPARING FOR CREATIVITY

Words and images do not just combine with magical intent. The truly inspired intuit that something is possible. They often have a vision or shape for ideas they cannot yet explain to others. Albert Einstein discovered the basis for relativity long before he published his suppositions.

We each create our own worlds to step into. Most often these worlds are constructed from the minutes of moments that immerse us. But we have control over our environment. The computer represents the ultimate control. With it, we can orchestrate our creative moments: a nonsynchopatic Handel underbrushing a calm scene of Aspen or Vail; a QuickTime movie of a quiet stream; the scanned-in image of a lost love.

The computer truly becomes a personal canvas of sight and sound. But relaxing and shifting modes is not the only preparation for creativity. The mind needs input. My secretary has a sign on her desk that reads "If a cluttered desk is the sign of a cluttered mind, then what does a clean desk signify?" The mind needs information from which to make a connection or association.

GATHERING DATA

A few kilobytes or megabytes of fresh input arrive into cyberspace with each passing second—every byte a potential connection or skew, realization or reaction. Content. It is after all the increase of content that we search for when we create. We seek to add the unknown to the known. To reinterpret the known or to reinvent it in our own image.

So we start by reading and searching. We look through *The New Grolier Multimedia Encyclopedia* and through *Compton's Interactive Encyclopedia*. We play games and read about dinosaurs. We read our subscribed e-mail and our Internet bulletin boards. We absorb. We distort. We forget pieces and recombine them.

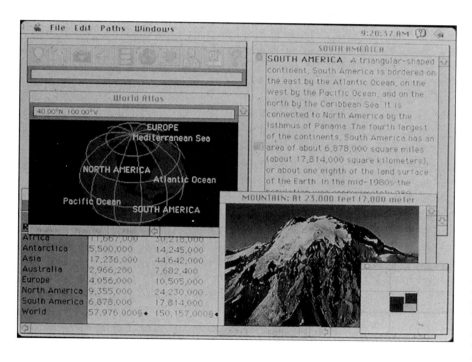

Compton's Interactive Encyclopedia for the Macintosh.

Sure, we continue to gather data from magazines, television and movies. But the computer combines those into infinitely more connected and concocted visions. We connect and embellish innumerable facts. And at some point, it becomes time to document in paint or pencil, in sound or image, our juxtapositions of data—our interpretations of the world.

. . . .

TAKING NOTES

Unlike the computer, we easily forget. Our scratch-pad memory consists of only a few seconds of consciousness. Setting down our keys in an unfamiliar place is often rushed out of mind as we yell at the 2-year-old playing in the toilet. The keys are lost until we stumble upon them or initiate a frantic Monday morning search. Our moments of inspiration are not so easily recovered. Without immediate recording, strong emotional impact, or constant mental repetition with little thought, our best ideas often become overrun by other thoughts, and what moments ago seemed a well-synchronized golden moment often devolves into a mundane plan for the day.

Our minds constantly threaten creative thoughts with their less-than-perfect circuitry. A simple distraction or another scrap of insight quickly whisks away what a moment ago seemed near epiphany. Computers can help augment our memory by capturing our thought into databases. Some databases are ideal for collecting data like phone numbers and birthdays. Others can represent and store large amounts of business data. But the mind is organized not by design but by occurrence. We never know exactly what kind of data we will be presented with, or when, or in what context.

New, flexible multimedia applications secure our visual and aural details in repositories of stimulation and contemplation. Products like Corkboard provide hanging places for our thoughts and ideas and the sights and sound associated with them. They help us create the linkages between word and image. They help capture and organize.

Several programs use outlining for the refinement of ideas. Outlining programs organize thoughts into hierarchies of ideas. They are difficult places to capture random thoughts, and work best when combined with other creativity metaphors, such as mind mapping, brainstorming, and virtual cork as found in Inspiration, InfoDepo and Corkboard.

It is difficult to retain the richness of source material in an easily accessible form without a computer. Our data tends to be of varying sizes and materials. Notes scratched on the back of a napkin. Digital text. Magazine articles. Pictures of the Blue Ridge Mountains. Microcassette tapes full of ramblings, car horns and background radio commentary. InfoDepo and Corkboard both accept sounds, graphics, movies and text as raw input.

Not losing a stray thought is important in creativity because it is from those thoughts that others may spring in more contemplative moments. After you have

. . . .

Without immediate recording, strong emotional impact, or constant mental repetition with little thought, our best ideas often become overrun by other thoughts, and what moments ago seemed a well-synchronized golden moment often devolves into a mundane plan for the day.

read and noted, sometimes it's good just to sit by a stream and think about what you're thinking.

. . . .

FINDING YOUR MUSE

"A stream! He's talking about streams! Like, I can just walk out of my office and find a stream running down the street?!"

Hold on a minute. I meant virtual streams. Virtual streams are a feature of Visionary Software's Synchronicity. Enter something to think about. Associate a few words with the idea. Then sit back and relax while a stream, complete with crickets, runs through your monitor. And then a lamp appears, with your words twirling around it. As you concentrate on the flame and the words, you hold down a key; release it. At that moment of involvement you are connected to the everything of the universe. As the program sometimes says: "Peace is the natural heritage of the spirit."

Of course, that may not be your inspirational cup of tea. Chances are, something that inspires you is available on the computer. Try to make it something that doesn't require computer skills. Golf may be inspiring, but computer golf may not bring the same mental shift as walking around the course (but it may bring some other sort—who am I to judge?). If flowers, or baroque music, or a picture of your kids inspire you, then the computer can bring you to the restful place where you open yourself to ideas.

BRAINSTORMING

Almost every meeting I attend these days has a brainstorming element to it. All the participants know about brainstorming: throw out your best ideas and have a public scribe write them on a white board or flip chart. If you have an idea based on somebody else's idea, put that out there too. Too often, the meeting participants forget the principles of brainstorming. Too many people go by the motto: "Ready, aim, fire." That is very conservative. It limits the targets. If creativity is the goal, the motto should be "Ready, shoot, aim." Quantity is the thing. The more you shoot, the better chance you will hit something. Wild, even silly ideas, are OK (they are mandatory). Withhold judgment. Suspend prejudice. Have fun. THINK!

In business, however, real people can be cruel. Some protect their turf and their egos by trying to kill innovation. Killing ideas is too often an American business tradition, contrary to our mythical reputation. No one wants some young whipper-snapper coming up with an idea they didn't think of, approve, or fund. The following list of killer cliches highlights the kind of words we've all heard at some point in our school or business career.

KILLER CLICHES

- Dumbest thing I've ever heard.
- Let's stick to what we know how to do.
- No!
- Can't.
- Won't.
- Yeah, but if you did...
- We're unique; you can't do that here.
- Our system can't handle that.
- We already tried that a few years ago and it didn't work.
- You can't teach an old dog new tricks.
- That's not our bailiwick.
- There's nothing wrong with the way we're doing it now.
- That doesn't sound very practical.
- We've never done anything like that before.
- You're talking about changing the whole way we do things.
- Quit bucking the system.
- Let's not get into another harebrained scheme.
- Very funny.
- We've got a deadline to meet; we don't have time for cute ideas.
- It's too expensive to do it that way.
- It's not in the budget.
- Management will never approve that.
- What do you want, people to think we're stupid?

- Are you kidding?
- Who let him/her in here?
- Where do you get those strange ideas?
- Why don't you go write that up?
- I can just see us explaining that to accounting.
- OK, enough of that blue sky stuff.
- They want water and you're giving them cream puffs.
- Somebody else is responsible for that.
- Don't rock the boat.
- That's not relevant.
- Let's keep on the subject.
- We just don't have the right people for that.
- I guess you didn't understand what I was asking for.
- I appreciate your thoughts, but they won't work here.
- That'll be more trouble than it's worth.
- You can't fight city hall!
- Who died and left you Creator of the Universe/God?
- Let's form a team to evaluate that.
- Get real.
- Theoretically, you're right, but this is the real world.
- Also: snickers, dirty looks and silence.

Since artificial intelligence researchers haven't yet invented the artificial ego, you won't hear your computer utter any of these phrases unless you program them in yourself. But they are phrases you need to overcome within yourself and to be aware of in the work place. As much as you may hear them, don't let them stifle you.

Brainstorming means many things. It can be the free association of ideas, scribbled in whipped cream, jotted on a wrist or illuminated on a computer screen. All of the "techniques" for brainstorming have found their way to the computer. The product Inspiration documents the connections between ideas in a Mind Map. White boards capture personal ideas in blank space in tools such as InfoDepo, and Cork Board awaits ideas on its virtual cork. Idea Fisher documents random thoughts in its Idea Pad. But sometimes the answers aren't always the only place a computer can lend a nudge.

The questions we ask are sometimes more important than our initial answers. It is best when creative answers are combined with creative questions. Some software products, like Idea Fisher and Idea Generator, focus thoughts by asking questions relevant to the pursuit. Idea Fisher adds thousands of associations that augment individual and team ideas. Each new association becomes a starting point for the next round of ideas.

If you don't own Idea Fisher, you can start with a few fundamental questions that are relevant about most problems:

> Who is it for?
> What can I do with it?
> Can I turn it into something else?
> Can I use it for something it wasn't intended for?
> Can I make it bigger or smaller?
> Can I exchange it for something else or exchange part of it?
> Can I rearrange it?

Remember, brainstorming is concerned with quantity. As the number of ideas increases, the chances increase that one or more of them mean something. Think wild thoughts. And all along, capture them in the computer. If you can't take a computer with you, write them on a napkin and scan them in. Or write them on an Apple Newton or a Sharp Wizard. It is in the brainstorming that you are, but not where you end. What you do to your ideas may generate a few ideas of their own.

Computers contribute best to brainstorming as repositories for ideas, unique capturing environments, subtle guides, well-placed inquisitors, and jumping-off points.

The questions we ask are sometimes more important than our initial answers. It is best when creative answers are combined with creative questions.

DESTRUCTION AND RECONSTRUCTION

Images and ideas in the computer are infinitely malleable—and they are infinitely indestructible. As long as you have one copy of your original scan or text file, then what you do to its digital clones is of little concern. In the world of the physical, the best we can do is wad up a disliked original attempt and (hopefully) make a basket.

In the digital world, UNDO saves our mistakes, and multiple copies of files protect our earlier efforts, just in case a portion of an old file finds meaning or worth as the creative process moves on. Unlike in real world creativity, when tossed out ideas may land inches or feet from their intented target, any Apple Newton owner will tell you they never miss the trash can when they do decide to throw something away.

With applications like Macromedia's SoundEdit 16, you can warp digital music, change octaves, drag and drop refrains and rearrange individual notes. With outliners and word processors, you can play with words, change their order, change their style, find relationships from a thesaurus, or take a batch of them on a search for the combinations and permutations. Images can be pulled, squeezed, torn apart, faded, and transformed from one media type to another (oil paint to pastel to colored pencil).

We too often focus on mistakes as bad things. The computer turns some kinds of mistakes into playful excursions. Every Photoshop artist I know has, at one point or another, sat with an image and tried almost every filter they own on it, waiting for some version to grab them. In the old days, performing those

transformations would be rather costly. Today they make take a few hours, but the right image for an advertising campaign is worth a few hours of bit tinkering. As every book on creativity states someplace, we should honor mistakes. Only in making errors do we learn and grow.

Of course, once we get past the idea that mistakes are bad, we stop calling them mistakes and call them things like iteration. The malleability of digital ideas enables you to create several iterations of the same idea, view it from various angles, and rearrange it—all without destroying the original. Each transformation of a poem or engineering drawing, song or painting, may bring new perspectives on the original, suggesting subtle enhancements, or solutions to tricky problems.

Taking the time to experiment may be time-consuming, and it may prove unproductive. But I know from experience that doing nothing is worse than doing something. It is fine to take the Taoist tact of just being. In creativity, however, it is wise to be someplace else or to have your subject be something else than what it was before. Contemplating the new relationships between sound and time, color and line, can happen after the transformation. It is good to be and to reflect, but only after some shift of consciousness or introduction of new data allows the state of being to find a new revelation.

Read the following list and try to apply the actions to your own words, artwork, music, or product idea. Perform one, then give yourself a few moments to absorb the impact and assess its potential.

SAFE DESTRUCTION

- Stretch it
- Distort it
- Combine it
- Sharpen it
- Blur it
- Twist it
- Flip it
- Turn it
- Crush it
- Melt it
- Freeze it
- Float it
- Fly it or make it fly
- Make it small
- Make it large
- View it up close
- View it from a distance
- Place it up high
- Place it down low

Take these activities and apply them to your idea. They are remarkably provocative when you perform them on something you wouldn't normally associate with the thing. Fly some words around, or crush them. Take an image apart and rearrange the pieces like they were sentences, trying to create a story out of the pieces.

Why should we do these things to our hard-worked creation? Because we can. Because the ultimate satisfaction is the delivery of an even more creative creation. How many paintings of the same stack of wheat did Monet paint, or the same pond of water lilies? Because Monet did not have a computer, he

needed to wait for the sun to move across the sky or the Earth to rotate to bring a change in seasons, or for his eyes to deteriorate and dull his vision and blur his canvas. We need not wait for Nature.

In the digital world, moving the sun is but the act of moving a light bulb icon a few degrees left or down. For winter, we apply a light, bluer palette. For poor eyesight, we apply a blur filter. Within the memory of the computer we have complete control of our world. We are the miraculous outpouring of God's creativity because he or she had the control of the whole environment. Within the computer we can experiment with everything from the position of the sun, to the recombination sequences in a genetic algorithm.

A VIEW FROM A DISTANT SUN

If we are to control digital worlds, they need to be more than flat images and vector drawings. Virtual reality may be the bigger boon to computer-enhanced creativity than freely-associated word challenges or the ring of a poetic vesper calling our synapses into alignment. VR shakes the consciousness by placing it somewhere else. Even primitive commercial VR games challenge the physical and mental balances of their participants as they attempt to rapidly adapt to the new environment. Like all games, the radical shift becomes mundane after repetition. But in the few experiences when the virtual environment seems new, unique possibilities may present themselves. With a personal computer, the creative searcher can control the repetition, and challenge the mind with a new world with each click of the mouse.

If you take a thing that is supposed to reside on a desk, say a paperweight, and send it to the moon, it ceases to have the properties it exhibited on the desk. It floats to the fluffy gray surface of the moon and erupts into lethargic gray flecks falling around a miniature crater. The event would bring different perspectives and uses to the staid and true paperweight.

With desktop VR, the computer becomes a surrogate for many places. In some cases, it might just be a relaxing cruise through the Grand Canyon. In others, it might be reliving family events like outdoor barbecues. But it will be at its idea-generating best when the normal is imposed on the wondrous or the scary, or the distant on the very small.

The act of transplanting the image and density of the paperweight to the moon instantly removes it from the norm. Even if expectations of behavior remain, they are quickly dashed by the simulated behaviors. The computer is a complete world of complex interaction owned and operated by the person using it. The paperweight could have just as easily ended up on Mars, in Kansas, or inside a liver. Each place would generate its own reaction and ideas.

The surreal landscapes of the imagination come close to reality in the computer. We can slay dragons or fly an X-Wing fighter. We do not, however, feel the heft of the sword or the hot breath of the dragon. We do not feel the acceleration or hit our helmet against the bulkhead as a laser bolt tears loose a stabilizer. It is unlikely that we will ever experience those sensations in our homes. But after riding Disneyland's Star Tours again recently, I am reminded that virtual reality is capable of fulfilling almost all our senses.

We may not be able to be someplace else at home with any degree of realism, but we may soon be able to amble to our local mall and have our senses assaulted through interactive environments that place our whole being elsewhere, complete with virtual smoke, digital worlds—and even virtual dragon's breath.

With virtual reality, the limits of geography and time fall away. And with those limits, many of the limitations we place on our thoughts melt with reality. The new reality does not impose itself in the same way. VR creates an environment ripe for new ideas.

Imagine setting a new play: As you walk around the stage, you can see the light reflecting off the furniture and off the faces of the virtual actors as you walk them through their blocking. You can shift instantly from audience point of view, to backstage, to orchestra. Mistakes that might be costly to catch onstage become readily apparent. Bare walls create new canvases for creative set design. Perhaps visualizing the scene actually prompts new words or new variations on old words. You can even cause the lights to flicker, signaling the start of the play, or watch as virtual rose petals break off a single stem intended for the female lead, and float effortlessly into the blue and pink light reflected off the hardwood stage.

DON'T BRUSH OFF ART

It is always given that an artist is creative (although I have seen a few paintings that challenge that assumption). And in a creativity chapter, you assume you will find discussions about computer-enhanced works of art. I will assume that the plethora of computer-generated images and magazines on computer art are satisfying that need. As only a minor computer artist, I have nothing to add to the dialog.

But as a lover of fresh ideas, I want to present the artist's tools in another setting. It is not necessary that we assume Adobe Photoshop or Fractal Design's Painter are for artists. And it is not necessary to assume they are for art. In their most fundamental state, they are products for manipulating bits of color on a computer screen. In that capacity, they become more than artists' tools—they become general creativity tools.

Look at a box of cereal. It is square and blocky. It has no personality. As an advertising executive, I want something fresh for that box. But I am constrained by its boxiness. So I scan it in to my Macintosh with Photoshop. I am not interested in comps or separations. I want to play.

I pull up HSC's KAI's Power Tools and start fidgeting with filters. Creating textures or turning a familiar image, like the cereal box, into a shining crystal globe. I morph one thing into another with Gryphon's Morph 2.0. I flip and twist and turn. I put color where there is black and white, and I remove the color where there should be color. With Adobe Illustrator, I cut bezier curves and reattach them to other control points. I contract or expand spaces, or deform lines. The once unimpressive cereal box becomes a collage of effects, the words and images melding into a new eye-catching design.

There is a learning curve to using artistic programs as artistic programs. Basic painting, however, is learned within a couple of hours. The idea is not to create a finished work of art, but to make the scanned image or quick sketch into more or less than it started—or, at and the very least, into something different.

Artists, of course, will be inspired by the abilities of the digital tools. Some don't get used to them readily, but those that do find them infinitely more forgiving and more expressive than paint or charcoal. We live in an increasingly visual world. Through the artist's tools, and through our own artistic eyes, we can find new ways to see the world.

TEAM CREATIVITY

You cannot always be in the right place at the right time. Sometimes a meeting across town or across the country is too difficult to attend, given your busy schedule.

Groupware is covered in Chapter 12, "Groping for the Group," but one aspect of group interaction was left for commentary here: network creativity. All of the tools for real-time collaboration mentioned in Chapter 12 can be turned from documenting commentary and dissension, to documenting the wild ideas of people collaborating on a network brainstorm. In fact, even the asynchronous communication tools will prompt creative response.

Think about this: create a Lotus Notes database that has as its cover sheet the intention "Please respond to categories with whatever ideas come to mind." That is it. Here, in a corporate setting, you enter the first topic: shirts and zebras. To a shirt manufacturing company's employees that simple statement could generate several new designs or fabric suggestions. Other industries could prompt with things like computers and footballs, lemons and shoes, holes and arrows. Something concrete in the business linked to something bizarre. Respondents could use the picture of the bottom of a product or just play a vague sound. Let the network surfers add their profundities to the organization's creativity.

In real-time, people can write ideas on electronic white boards, or on real white-boards that turn gestures on a surface into electronic versions of the same session. Tools like Farralon's Timbuktu support virtual connections between Macintoshes and PCs. Anybody can share a program, like Inspiration, with a colleague from anywhere.

As we grow apart in distance, we shrink the world in time and place with the network. Why restrict its electronic corridors to the commonness of correspondence? Open its vestibules to the vibrant vibrations of verbs and to the idiom of ideas.

Bringing Your Ideas To Fruition

It is not enough to generate ideas. They do nothing as words or images. The importance of ideas comes from their execution and implementation. Computers eliminate much of the translation work so common just a few years ago. Rough sketches drawn on a Newton import into desktop computers, ready for extrusion and three-dimensional rendering. Words from mind maps reform into outlines, willing recipients of proposal detail. Quick drawings on a Sharp Wizard scrap book become the basis for Painter works of art.

Products like Inspiration and InfoDepo help turn the rough-hewn edges of ideas into outlines for business practicality. They turn chaos into order and uncertainty into plausibility. In painting and poetry, it may be enough to do the work. In business, an idea that doesn't turn a profit is a lost opportunity and a waste of time.

People seeking more than passive ego gratification for having recognized a creative thought will want to see their ideas become more than a "Well, I thought of that" thought. If we look at the great minds we embrace for their examples of creativity, we also find courage, conviction, and innovation. From Thomas Jefferson to Thomas Edison, it was the courage to challenge convention (and in fact, winning people over to their points of view), the conviction to continue with an idea in the face of adversity, and the innovations required of a myriad of political systems or systems of science or belief, that made the Declaration of Independence and the light bulb more than things other people thought of. They became things we associate with their advocates as well and their inventors.

Over the years I have found five sequences of activities that help turn my ideas into fruition. Creativity texts have either more or less steps, but these five cover the basics:

FIVE STEPS FOR FRUITION

Generate Ideas	Find as many possibilities as you can. The greater the quantity of ideas, the better chance one will find fruition.
Sell Ideas	It is fine to generate ideas and work on them if you are rich, but most of us don't have that advantage. Selling ideas means finding supporters and investors who believe in your idea enough to put their money where your mouth is. (Creating a good sales campaign often requires as much creativity, or more, than the idea you are trying to sell.)
Engineer Ideas	This is the step that turns the intangible into the tangible. It is where tolerances are construed, words substituted, and keys changed to meet the vocal ranges of proposed artists.
Construct Ideas	In the case of a poem, printing a final copy out on a laser printer may be construction enough. In the case of a song or an airplane, an elaborate orchestration is required to score all the voices or manufacture the fuselage and engines. This is where execution of processes puts the original idea in the back seat.
Evaluate and Refine Ideas	The customer is always right. Even Einstein, long after his death, is questioned about his theory. Scientists are constantly improving on general and special relativity. If such profound thoughts require modification once they reach the marketplace of ideas, then what about a new toaster or microwave?

Each step in this matrix is supported by one or more creativity tools. The tools for idea generation have already been covered. For selling ideas, nothing beats the good old presentation package. But good old presentations aren't just black and white view graphs anymore. As color, texture, and movies become easy to integrate and display, the need for creative selling will increase. The once verbal-only sales pitch will call in multimedia support.

Engineering tools come in many shapes. To the electrical engineer, the creative act may come in a simulation program. To the poet, a word processor represents engineering. To the artist, Photoshop or Painter provide the canvas for final execution. In some cases, the blur between engineering and construction is great. To the poet, printing the poem completes the construction. To the electrical engineer, construction becomes the multifaceted process of manufacturing, engineering, procurement, and production.

During the evaluation phase, computers do what people expect them to do. They tally votes, correlate survey results, and document complaints. They turn into the grand bean-counters of judgment. Create a spreadsheet to gather votes, or use voting in groupware tools like Ventana's GroupSystems V.

And finally, the feedback gets incorporated into the design or future designs. And computers too, make this a much more rapid task—turning around modifications in hours rather than days, or days rather than weeks.

I will not dwell on the use of computers in bringing ideas to the marketplace. Every business finds them indispensable tools in accounting, design, and manufacture. I include this subchapter not to say how, but to remind those interested in creating new things that the idea initiates a process. In and of themselves, ideas are worth little, unless they affect others. An unpublished and unperformed poem does not bring awareness. An unimplemented new filter for an automobile engine does not reduce air pollution. For the sparks of creativity to be meaningful, they need the spark of the welding torch to bring them to reality.

> **The computer is a playground of possibilities. At one moment a 3-D modeler, at the next a blank canvas for sketching the clouds out my window. It is a place to fail at experiments without being chastised.**

A Few Concluding Thoughts

In my few moments of personal time, I dream. I dream about making love to my wife; of future possibilities for the software I have; about the texture of rich fudge turning over against my tongue; about applying new Photoshop filters to old images; about better ways to work at work; about the next book or article; and about a Father's day 30 years into the future when I romp, not with my children, but my grandchildren. I force myself to close the door to my office when it is open too much, and I force myself to open it when it has been closed too often. And I force myself to play.

My wife often comments on the amount of time I spend with the computer. "Don't you ever get tired of it?" she asks. I honestly answer, "No." Sure, I get tired of seeing Microsoft Word after writing an article for hours. But the computer is not Microsoft Word. The computer is a playground of possibilities. At one moment a 3-D modeler, at the next a blank canvas for sketching the clouds out my window. It is a place to fail at experiments without being chastised. It is a place to explore worlds I cannot travel to because they are too far away or because they only exist in my imagination, or the imaginations of their creators.

I can mind map ideas for books I want to write, or read the latest news on America Online. To me, the computer is the ideal intellectual companion. I need not search for paper or pencil, crayon or note paper, highlighter or piano keyboard. The flexible machine adapts as I need it to, chameleoning itself to shape my whims and expectations. It plays Bach and Handel. It plays Aerosmith and Led Zeppelin. It plays Picasso and Eliot, Yates, and Maimonides. And it plays Rasmus.

The software I have described in this chapter is far from perfect. It is at times annoying in its lack of intuitiveness. It sometimes crashes in the middle of a thought or sentence. But it is, without a doubt, indispensable to my creative output.

I cannot imagine writing the articles and books I write on a typewriter. I probably would have given up writing as a vocation had the computer not enabled me to transform broad brush silliness into refined arguments—or serious events into sublime comedy. I rarely opt for charcoal and paper, preferring UNDO to the gum eraser, and the mouse to post-sketch washing with soap and water. And I love to explore the richness of the words and associations—skimming in minutes what might take hours of page-flipping.

Creativity is a state of mind. The computer can help shift awareness from moment to moment. It can place personal thoughts and designed items into different places and times. It can jog memory and erase mistakes. It cannot, however, overcome stubbornness or aloofness. It cannot calm a fret or move a deadline. The computer can, however, stimulate and challenge. Play provocateur and mentor. It can take a simple idea generated near exhaustion, and kick it one step further before sleep. In this, the computer acts as repository and machine. It presents data and associations compiled by others, and it transforms human-worked wire frames into fully rendered environments. And through words, music, and images, it can inspire much more than any tool capable of only a single medium.

And in its mundane capacity as keeper of business data and information, the computer can help turn a reasonable idea into reality. It can perform simulations to support a hypothesis. It can print spreadsheets to justify investments and it can package the idea to win over the boardroom.

If you are a painter or a poet, novelist or politician, lyricist or limbo dancer, or just a husband creating a variation of rice pilaf for an anxious family, you are creative. The computer helps document. It helps provide grist for your contemplation, and it may even help set the mood for a brainstorming session. In the end, it is a non-judgmental partner, a mental extension, a home for the eventual coalescence of the thousand scattered thoughts that might not find each other amid a storm of paper napkins, business card backs, and matchbook covers.

Creativity is a state of mind. The computer can help shift awareness from moment to moment. It can place personal thoughts and designed items into different places and times. It can jog memory and erase mistakes.

The computer enhances creativity by always being a willing ally in the personal moments of exploration. It cannot be asked to be more. It can, though, shift awareness by playing a canon or by displaying a bird's eye view of Vail, Colorado, or a gnat's eye view of a new computer chip. It remains the human mind that must open itself to seeing the subtle difference of one thought among millions, or the possibility of a new pattern in seeming redundancy. And once that is discovered, the computer is ready to transform even the most improbable exclamation of creativity into a real arrangement of words, music, steel, plastic, exposition, cloth, or pixels.

PRODUCT/ CONCEPT PROFILES

FISHING FOR ASSOCIATIONS

We have all had moments when we stare off into space, unable to connect two words to form a sentence, let alone develop a creative idea. More commonly, we know a word is on the tip of our tongue, but our mind fails to release it into consciousness. As humans, we are wonderfully faulty repositories of knowledge. Idea Fisher, from Fisher Idea Systems (Irvine, California) crams 61,000 words and 700,000 associations into a basic PC or Macintosh. When our brains aren't quite working, or need an extra insight, Idea Fisher supplies new grist.

Founded by Marsh Fisher, Fisher Idea Systems set about to cull the best words and associations from brilliant thinkers around the world and store them in an intuitive database.

Along with the content, Idea Fisher also contains thousands of questions that focus its partners on issues of story development, marketing, strategic planning, idea enhancement, and idea evaluation.

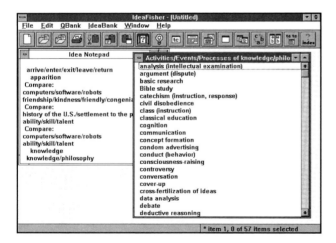

When our brains aren't working, Idea Fisher supplies new insights.

INSPIRED GUIDANCE

The question is, "What is the question?" It makes no sense to think about creativity when you have nothing to be creative about. Creativity requires a problem. Problems come from how to mount a door, to how the universe began, but each requires its own set of positions and suppositions. Thoughtline and Xpress Yourself bring the artificially intelligent psychologist to practicality. These guided explorations are more focused than the old Eliza artificial intelligence games, but they stem from the same root. Both products probe at meaningful issues while trying to help the user develop a speech or term paper.

With Idea Fisher, you choose the questions to answer from the thousands provided in several well-defined categories. Add-on question modules help ask questions about strategic planning, presentations, and business proposals. Idea Generator Plus walks users through a generic creative problem-solving methodology that includes evaluation and developing cost-benefit analysis.

Thoughtline, Xpress Yourself, and Idea Fisher all help you probe to the heart of vexing problems.

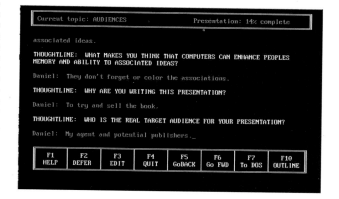

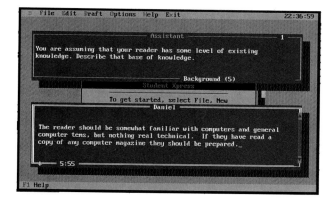

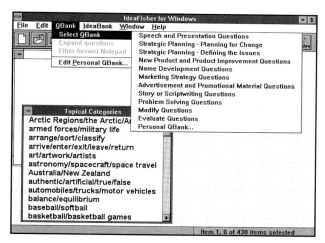

NETWORK CREATIVITY

In creativity, the anonymity of the network may be more important than the ability to pump digital video across the network. Video reveals facial expressions, lending it more to examining reactions than producing creative ideas. Asynchronous communication programs like Lotus Notes and CM/1 allow people to post their ideas in their own time. Ideas that don't stimulate lose their legs when network reviewers find that the idea lacks purpose or merit. The conversation may not even begin.

More active products, like Aspects, turn the computer into an electronic drawing, painting, and writing environment. People can collaborate over the network, contributing their thoughts to a proposal, sketch, or drawing. In the free-for-all mode, the drawing environment can become the equivalent of a white board, rapidly collecting all the ideas thrown at it over the network.

MAPPING YOUR IDEAS

Drawing programs don't do Mind Mapping justice. The best bet for capturing mind maps is Inspiration from Inspiration Software. Place your central thought in the middle of the documents and use the Rapid Fire input to generate several ideas associated with it. As new ideas become clear, they can be shot off the main idea or linked at a later time through a quick click-and-drag.

Inspiration software provides the means to generate several ideas from a single thought.

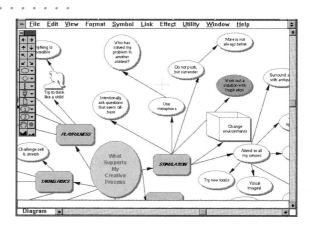

STORY BOARDING

If your profession involves writing a historical novel, a teleplay, or an interactive video game, you need the same mapping of ideas and free-form expression as corporate planners or engineers. Of course, some sense of story must evolve. StoryVision captures brainstormed ideas about scenes and lets storytellers arrange and rearrange scenes. As the scenes develop, StoryVision can generate templates automatically in Microsoft's Write or Word for Windows or in other word processors.

The designers at MacToolKit took a more organic approach with Corkboard, an electronic corkboard that incorporates virtual notecards, thumb tacks, and an outliner. Notecards contain words or headings. Pictures or QuickTime video can also be included. A complete Corkboard document lists the scenes across the top, and information about them stack below, connected to the headings. The text portions can be exported to MacToolkit's screenplay editor, Final Draft, or to ASCII text files.

A completed StoryVision document represents the complete story outline, ready for implementation in film, video, or interactive multimedia.

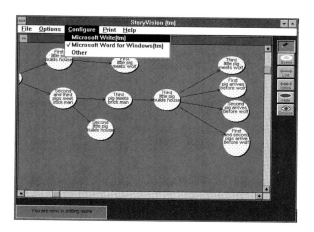

Corkboard incorporates all you need to keep virtual track of your world.

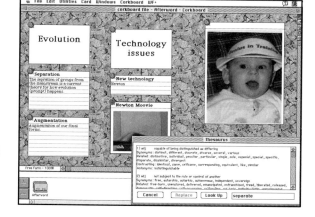

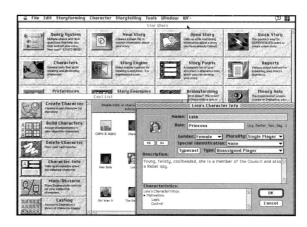

Dramatica is perhaps the most innovative of the tools for creating creative stories. Screenplay Systems has teamed with Melanie Anne Phillips and Chris Huntley, who have documented a unique theory of story-telling that walks authors through the selection of genre, plot, theme, and character. Dramatica links all the elements of the story into a relational database and then helps develop a form for the story that best delivers it to the intended audience.

Dramatica is extremely useful in developing ideas, and the environment is filled with beautiful icons and excellent analysis.

THE MALLEABLE WORLD

Adobe Photoshop was always the retouching artist's favorite for turning a scanned photo into a clear, sharp image. It even allowed for a few simple special effects—blur a photo or break it into a mosaic. The open architecture of Photoshop invited artists and programmers to team on enhancement "plug-ins" to Photoshop. KAI's Power Tools from HSC adds everything from fractals to textures. The Power Tools interface itself is a creative blast. Xaos Paint Alchemy transforms images by applying a myriad of brush effects.

Other companies chose to create competing programs that use Photoshop filters. The most striking of these is Fractal Design's Painter, which provides artists with various "natural media" to work with. Choosing charcoal on rough paper produces effects very similar to those I create with 2B charcoal and a

Computers enable you to transform an image with the touch of a button.

Strathmore 400 sketch pad. Painter's unique cloning effect populates the brush with color lifted from the original, metamorphosing a scan into a painting worthy of an impressionist master. Many tools, such as Equilibrium's Debabilizer, also accept Photoshop filters to modify images. Debabilizer translates files and will apply a filter to each image as it turns it from PICT to TIFF or TIFF to GIF.

metaflo', from The Valis Group, adds a real twist to image editing. It contorts images using select and drag. Ordinary-looking clocks begin to resemble Daliesque nightmares. Beautiful women transform into distorted beings, ready to enter Roger Rabbit's Toontown.

And finally, Gryphon's Morph turns your mother-in-law into a cat or your son into a bat, just in time for Halloween. Any series of images can be gradually transformed into another.

From the artist's standpoint, the creativity factor of these tools is high. For non-artists, these tools present opportunities to experience transformations not possible outside the imagination until now. And once they are done, they remain, for replay and review, unlike the fleeting moments of our own surreal imaginings.

Fractal exploration can become a consuming passion with KAI's Power Tools from HSC.

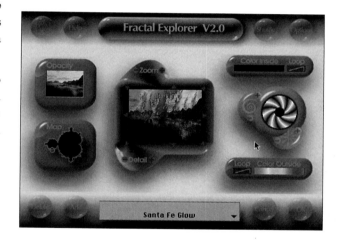

Public Thoughts

It is not always necessary that everyone participate in the idea-generation phase. In public brainstorming sessions, it is common to have a facilitator present to worry about the process of the meeting, rather than the meeting's content. With software like MeetingRight from Xerox's Qsoft, facilitators can create fishbone diagrams of ideas directly from meeting input. The ideas and links are instantly visible, projected from an LCD projector to an awaiting screen.

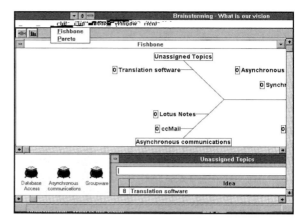

During a meeting, ideas can become action items. After the meeting, MeetingRight helps track action items and develop the next agenda.

Connections in Solitude

If you want to contemplate something, I know of no better, more friendly tool than Visionary Software's Synchronicity. You enter words associated with the problem you are trying to solve and relax while the words spin around lamplight. Periodically, you hold and release a key, making the words spin faster. When you release the key, you are theoretically in synch with the process and the universe.

Synchronicity combines I Ching with C.G. Jung to provide a stress-free place to think about thoughts and get a little ancient wisdom to boot.

TAKE A NOTE

Any word processor can take a note. But notes are tricky things. Oftentimes, they get lost or lose their context. With Dyno Notepad, you can capture thoughts and quickly organize them.

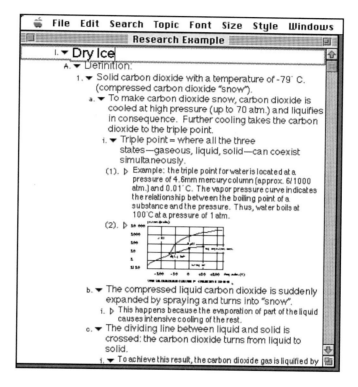

Dyno Notepad has changed hands, and in its shifting of companies, it has outlasted other outliners, like Symantec's Grandview and More, which derived their existence from the original Think Tank.

Other outliners challenge Notepad with calendaring tools or spreadsheets. InfoDepo, in fact, creates a total creativity environment, including white board and scheduling tools. For one-stop shopping, consider Inspiration or Corkboard, both of which incorporate outliners with their other creativity tools. But Notepad remains a favorite for no-frills organization of ideas into outlines.

PRACTICAL CREATIVITY

Everything is practical creativity, if the ideas become more than ideas. But some tools help evoke ideas for a specific kind of activity. Experience Software's Project KickStart. This product focuses on the process of developing a project plan.

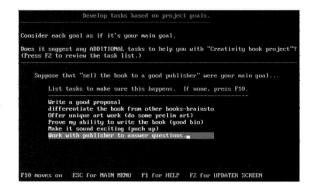

Unlike templates or other project planning tools, Project KickStart guides users through their self-realization of what is important, rather than dictating steps.

IDEAS TO PLANS

InfoDepo is an outliner with a twist. It has several creativity tools, including a networkable white board and categorization tools. The product's outliner expands simple hierarchies by linking associated information with each headline, including dates, movies, and images. InfoDepo's project plan view displays dates as a Gantt chart or calendar. Data in columns attached to the headline can be summarized or used in calculations to derive other information.

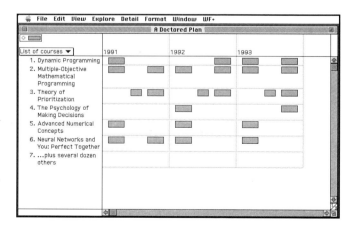

InfoDepo expands hierarchies by linking associated information.

SITTING NEAR A DISTANT SUN

The moon is an inhospitable place, especially when you happen to be in a penitentiary. Wandering these virtual hallways may give you ideas for things you don't want to have. On the other hand, placing something mundane into this environment may generate a plethora of new possibilities. Virtus VR creates simple worlds to let your mind romp in. Its cousin, Virtus Walkthrough Professional, helps render more complex worlds with its sophisticated drawing tools and rendering algorithms.

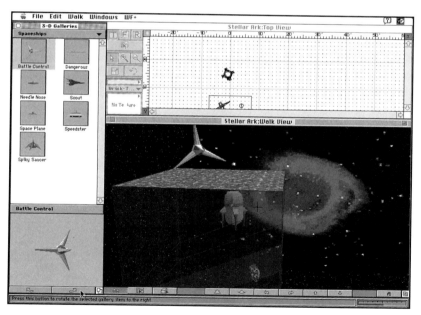

Move anything to a digital world for a different perspective.

GOING TO THE GYM

The July 1994 *Life* magazine cover featured a computer imaged brain, joined by the words "Brain Calisthenics" in bold type. The article described ways to challenge your brain with mental exercises to avoid the onset of mental slackness in old age. One of the best ways to beef up your brain is to play in MindLink Software Corporation's MindLink Problem Solver. The creativity environment is supplemented by a series of exercises designed to rev up your brain—and if you believe the *Life* article—keep it from stalling down the road.

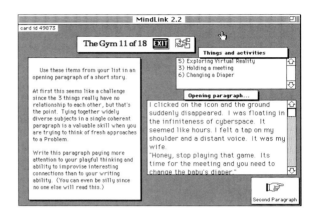

Challenge your brain with mental exercise.

NEVER TOO EARLY TO START

It is never too early to start. With programs like Kids Works 2 from Davidson and Associates and StoryWeaver from MECC, children can learn how to generate ideas, play with various media, and piece it all together into a final product.

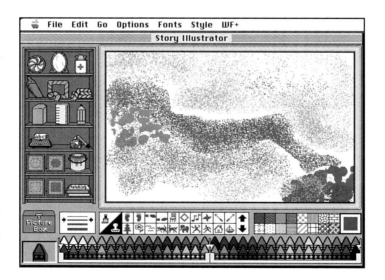

Children can play with Kids Works 2.

Cybermusic

Cybermusic isn't a label for any specific kind of music. Rather, it is a term that relates to how music will be made in the future. A number of record companies and musicians are embarking on this path even as we speak, and they will most certainly be the forerunners of cybermusic.

There's a saying in the entertainment industry that goes like this: By the time the 1990s are over, the eighties will make the seventies look like the 1960s.

Sounds pretty insightful, doesn't it? Yes, well, maybe. What does it actually mean? Nothing, really; it's pretty much Hollywood double-speak, and it's supposed to sound very profound while conveying no meaning whatsoever. But in that regard, this phrase is very similar to another very popular entertainment industry buzzword that is making the rounds these days: cybermusic.

Cybermusic. The word rolls trippingly off your lips, as if it were supposed to mean something, something definable and presumably important. But what is cybermusic? The first guess might be that cybermusic is something you'd play at a cryogenic freezing ceremony, or perhaps as Muzak for the swing shift at a robot factory.

In Fact, CYBERMUSIC Is Nothing at All

In the rush to create a world where everything can be "cyber" something, the media and self-styled cyberpunks have tagged cyber onto the entire collection of nouns, verbs, and modifiers found in the English language. Some of these make sense, cybersex and cyberspace being the two most reasonable. On the other hand, what are we to make of cyberdrinking or cyberbaths or cybernews or cybercars or cyberair or cyberstereos? What happens when we get to CyberDisney or CyberChryslers or Reese's CyberCups? When do we realize that not everything can be cyberfied? When we get to music.

Music is one of those human pursuits that always has some kind of label that never does it justice. From classical to jazz to heavy metal to grunge to pop, music is pigeon-holed and labeled to the point where the label doesn't mean anything. For instance, is Led Zeppelin heavy metal? Is Metallica? The two bands' styles are completely different, yet they get lumped together in the same "heavy metal music" category. The same with Beethoven and Bach and Brahms. They're all classical composers, right? Wrong. Bach was a Baroque composer, and Brahms was part of the Romantic period. Only Beethoven is considered a truly classical composer, and even he was part of the musical transition from classical to Romantic. Obviously, labels aren't quite as accurate as oftentimes we'd like to believe.

The problem of labels is compounded when trying to define cybermusic. Calling any form of music "cybermusic" is somewhat misleading because "cyber" as a prefix tends to refer to things in the future. And because we're not in the future yet, trying to define cybermusic today is a little like trying to assess the current sociological importance of cybersex. Because it hasn't happened yet, it's getting ahead of the game.

Now that I've loaded you up with all these caveats, is there any way to define exactly what cybermusic is? Depends on who you ask. It could be a million different things, although most of the definitions tend to be variations on current forms of music, such as techno or industrial. In a more realistic vein, however, cybermusic isn't a label for any specific kind of music. Rather, it is a term that relates to how music will be made in the future. A number of record companies and musicians are embarking on this path even as we speak, and they will most certainly be the forerunners of cybermusic. But by the time we get to that future, won't cybermusic be a misnomer? After all, classical composers weren't called "classical" when they were writing, and cybermusic won't be futuristic if it's actually part of the present. Thus, the actual creation of cybermusic may be an oxymoron, since it implies the future, and something that is actually taking place—by definition—isn't off in the future. It's all very confusing. (I hope you're still following me on this.)

But enough of the wordplay. Suffice it to say, cybermusic is more a categorical term for the potential ways of creating and interacting with music than it is a term for any specific style of music. Now we'll delve into what forms and permutations cybermusic might take—if indeed cybermusic could be described.

CYBERMUSIC DEFINITION 1:
THE SOUND OF THE
POST-INDUSTRIAL SOCIETY

Since the late 1980s, there have been several styles of music that have been loosely associated with science fiction and/or futurism, due primarily to their de-emphasis of personality and their focus on machine-produced sounds. It is the next generation of these musical styles that people will probably be suckered into classifying as "cyber-music." In particular, two forms—techno and industrial—are perceived as being both mechanical enough and perhaps decadent enough to be the musical basis for a world where mechanics and perversion are part and parcel of the decay of society as we know it. This world is the same one found in science fiction, and is oftentimes called the *Blade Runner* scenario.

Any discussion of what popular culture, especially music, will be like in the future has to take into account the *Blade Runner* scenario. Based on the gritty, grimy, sleazy, and ephemeral world of the future as depicted in the film *Blade Runner* (as well as in the book *Neuromancer*, William Gibson's science fiction classic), culture and its various incarnations will be reduced to a horrendous, brooding, gloom-laden, dark,

angst-ridden, and violence-soaked quagmire of expression devoid of any uplifting passion. Superlatives aside, all things artistic will be rendered mechanical and negative.

There are many people who believe that the *Blade Runner* scenario isn't that far off the mark, especially in light of the Los Angeles riots and the subsequent disasters of near Biblical proportions that befell that city in 1993 and 1994 (*Blade Runner* is set in L.A.). For those that think the gloomy handwriting is already on the wall, both industrial music and techno music serve as precursors to such dreariness and doom. In fact, they might be to cybermusic—if cybermusic were to become an actual form of music—what rhythm and blues was to modern rock and roll.

For those of you who've been spending too much time in the Mariah Carey, Whitney Houston, and "Unplugged" sections of your local music store, a quick overview of industrial and techno is in order. Industrial music is the use of pulsating drums and mind-crushing guitars coupled with mechanically altered vocals and sampled (digitally recorded) sounds of modern life—airplanes, traffic, TV news, jackhammers, piledrivers, and so on. All together, this witches' brew of disparate elements creates a stark mirror of modern angst and alienation. It's kind of like a musical version of Edvard Munch's painting "The Scream." Much of it is extraordinarily imaginative and complex to a degree far beyond that which is found in most contemporary forms of popular music. This is evident in the music of Nine Inch Nails, The Young Gods, and Ministry. Other industrial music is hypnotic in its brutal repetitiveness, such as that created by Front 242, PitchShifter, and Fear Factory. Still other bands apply the tools of industrial music to common rock and pop forms, like Shotgun Messiah, Stabbing Westward, and Curve. Not surprisingly, much of this music has its roots in Germany and the club scene in Berlin, where alienation has risen to the level of art form. The best examples of this music (should you be inclined to run right out and add them to your CD collection) are Nine Inch Nails' *Broken*, Ministry's *Psalm 69*, The Young Gods' *TV Sky*, PitchShifter's *Desensitized*, and Shotgun Messiah's *Violent New Breed*.

Techno, on the other hand, uses synthesizers and drum machines to create dark—yet less desperate—pictures of modern society. There is a bit more lightness in techno, yet the use of electronics to create the music is seen as a rebellion against the "humanity" and warmth of acoustic or even electrified instruments (such as guitars, violins, flutes, and so forth). The concession to the humanness of music is in the use of a tempo that provides a perfect rhythm for dancing, as well as stark untreated vocal arrangements. Bands as diverse as Depeche Mode, Aphex Twin, and even Pet Shop Boys all fall into this category. Depeche Mode's *Violator* is a definitive example of this form of music.

The distancing of human emotion from both techno and industrial dovetail nicely with the imagined "cyber" future and the attendant breakdown of society as envisioned in *Blade Runner* and *Neuromancer*. It is seen as being only natural that these two forms of music will evolve (or devolve) into whatever it is that cybermusic might sound like.

That's all well and good, but as a label for a musical style, cybermusic is somewhat limiting. Claiming that cybermusic will be the natural evolution of industrial and techno is like saying that REM is the natural evolution of The Rolling Stones. This

The distancing of human emotion from both techno and industrial dovetail nicely with the imagined "cyber" future and the attendant breakdown of society as envisioned in Blade Runner *and* Neuromancer.

may be true, but such a belief says that cybermusic is an offshoot of only one form of music. I think cybermusic is more than just the next generation of angst-driven rock and roll, and that appropriating the term for one genre of music is a cheap way out of having to give cybermusic some serious thought.

Be that as it may, this association with industrial and techno is really the only stylistic description of cybermusic as it relates to any particular musical form. All other definitions have to do with cybermusic as a means for creating, listening, or interacting with music, and it is those definitions that we will examine from here on in. While people may try to label musical styles as cybermusic (Billy Idol's entirely naive and exploitative effort entitled *Cyberpunk* notwithstanding), it is this writer's contention that cybermusic has more to do with the construction and production of music than what genre the music itself actually falls into.

CYBERMUSIC DEFINITION 2: INTERACTIVE MUSIC

Cybermusic will be part of rock, pop, experimental, industrial, techno, and even—God help us—country western. At the present, the first forays by musicians into the realm of interactive music—which is how we'll define cybermusic in this section—are from the established rock genre. Specifically, there are a select group of artists who have succeeded to such a financial degree that they can afford to experiment with new technology and its applications to music. They include long-time music industry fixtures David Bowie, Peter Gabriel, Todd Rundgren, Heart, Bob Dylan, and U2. There are some experimental and performance artists who have also explored the nether regions of interactive music, but because of their lesser stature in the music business, their efforts have not been nearly as high profile or high budget.

There is one obvious dilemma here: Music is not an interactive form of entertainment. Outside of dancing and maybe stage diving at concerts—neither of which has any bearing on the production or performance of music—the "user" traditionally is not involved in music other than as a listener. He or she is certainly not in control of any of the creative aspects of the music. When a consumer buys a CD, the music is prepackaged and complete, like a car or a refrigerator. As a product, the music cannot be altered. The only influence that the listener can exert is over volume and tone, neither of which changes the original production of the music by the artist.

Interactive music seeks to change that, shifting some of the onus and/or satisfaction of music production to the listener. This, as we shall see, may end up being both a double-edged sword and a trifling novelty, neither of which is appealing to those people in society who enjoy music in its current static form, because interactive music is actually more of a form of multimedia than it is any kind of pure musical form. Let's start by looking at the offering from U2, arguably the world's most popular rock band as of this writing. The band won huge accolades for its development of Zoo TV for use on the *Achtung Baby* and *Zooropa* concert tours in the early 1990s. Zoo TV was hailed as a technological leap forward for rock music due to its extensive use of video screens and video segments that were called up by the band during the performance. Bono, U2's somewhat affected—if not tortured—lead singer, carried a remote control for the video screens that allowed him to select different camera angles of himself. He also could choose pre-programmed video clips of the next song or even pre-recorded video clips of a simulated version of himself. The audience, usually numbering in the tens of thousands, could see Bono make his choices as a big cursor moved across a computer screen that was projected up on the monstrous video screens behind the band.

Cool effect? Sure. Crowd pleaser? You bet. Did it increase the audience's control over the music? Not in the least. But because of the perceived technological leap that was embodied in Zoo TV, the media claimed that it could be the forerunner of the future of music. Uh, well, doubtful. Maybe this is true for Bono, who was the only one with any control over the show, but not for anyone else. Nonetheless, U2 is going to offer a version of Zoo TV as a CD-ROM.

So, I'm going to write off Zoo TV as a nice use of technology, but not as something that is a precursor of cybermusic. Peter Gabriel, on the other hand, thinks that he might be a little closer conceptually to what the future of interactive music might be like. Known for revolutionary videos that have pushed the boundaries of a fairly lemming-like medium, Gabriel has always been at the forefront of merging music and video. He has won numerous awards for his video innovation, especially for the groundbreaking "Sledgehammer" video, and he has applied this innovation to a new offering called *Xplora 1: Peter Gabriel's Secret World*. *Xplora* is essentially a multimedia CD-ROM that takes users on a tour of Gabriel's personal environments. It contains his existing music videos as well as personal photos (his baby pictures are even included) and a narrated tour of his various musical pieces as well as a physical tour of his personal studio. *Secret World* also features a cut and paste "game" whereby you construct Gabriel's face from various facial features on a palette. In all, this is a combined hypertext/film clip/musical stew designed to appeal more to the eyes than to the ears. But ears are the main conduits of music.

The closest Gabriel gets to allowing the user some degree of control over the CD's music is by providing a group of world music tracks that the user can mix and match into his or her own musical assemblage. Gabriel is amongst the foremost proponents of integrating third world rhythms and instruments into Western music, and users even get to see clips from his globally-tinged concerts. To even get to this level, though, users have to work their way through the program, getting a backstage pass which gives them access to certain parts of the CD. All in all, the *Secret World* is basically a visually-based cinematic journey through Gabriel's videos and recording studio, with a bit of gaming thrown in for the arcade crowd.

Perhaps the man who has gotten closest to defining what interactive music might be in terms of cybermusic is Todd Rundgren. Known by most casual listeners as the man who wrote and sang "Hello, It's Me" and "We've Got To Get You A Woman," Rundgren has also established himself as a premier producer and musical technician, notably as the leader of Utopia and the producer of Meat Loaf. In addition, he has made a name for himself in the realm of computer software, writing several of his own packages (one of which was distributed by Apple) and inspiring his fellow musicians to write their own software as well.

Rundgren has a user's appreciation of computers as well as a producer's sense of combining and mixing music to create a cohesive finished product. He has attempted to bring both of these to the consumer world in his *No World Order* CD-ROM. The record is something of an erector set for listeners because it enables the listener to modify critical components of the music for use during playback. The CD, which works with a multimedia technology known as CD-I (compact disk interactive), gives users the option of changing musical tempos on each song from a low of 86 beats per minute to a much brisker 132 beats per minute. Not only that, but specific segments of the song can be rearranged: a single verse can be played over and over again until the user is ready to hear the chorus. The mix can be changed: an instrument such as the guitar can be removed from the song completely or presented as the dominant musical component. Vocals can also be removed, or, conversely, the entire song could be played a cappella. Additional sounds and instrumentation can be added to tracks by calling up one or more of the 900+ sound samples on the CD. Ultimately, *No World Order* listeners can take Rundgren's ideas and adapt them to their own moods and/or musical preferences.

I tend to think that this is a bit like leaving the Mona Lisa as a paint-by-numbers canvas in the hands of various painters with palettes of all sorts. No one could have done that painting like da Vinci did, and maybe no one should be given the chance. Besides, do we really need everybody's personal

What if we could all change the Mona Lisa, curving that smile further upwards, or making her a lusty blonde instead of a reserved brunette? There's very little appeal in that.

interpretation of every song that gets recorded? And will there be one standard that we can all relate to, or will everybody hear a completely different version? This eats into the notion of music as part of a mass culture—if everyone has their own version, no one is sharing exactly the same experience when they hear the song. What if we could all change the Mona Lisa, curving that smile further upwards, or making her a lusty blonde instead of a reserved brunette? There's very little appeal in that.

Rundgren's live rendition of the CD, called the No World Order Tour, attempted to involve the audience at a live concert in the same way as the recorded version. Using a Macintosh PowerBook, Rundgren performed his work as a soloist, controlling synthesizers, samplers, and drum machines via the computer. He also controlled the stage lighting using the computer as well, allowing him the freedom to respond to audience feedback as the performance progressed, all the while changing aspects of the show at will.

Other artists have followed Gabriel's and Rundgren's leads, including David Bowie, Heart, and Motley Crüe. Cynics, or perhaps realists, will argue that all of these musicians are quite solidly in the "veteran" category: namely, they have been around for more than a decade and in no way, shape, or form represent the next generation of musicians who were weaned on technology. In fact, the term "dinosaur" is applied to each of these acts on a regular basis by the mainstream rock press.

Nonetheless, their names are a big enough draw to ensure that their record companies or some entertainment conglomerate will be willing to fund the production of interactive musical products. It may simply result in a new form of entertainment—whether it be on stage or small screen—but it still isn't quite what I'd call cybermusic. It's more a mutated spawn of recorded music and rock videos, with a few behind-the-scenes video snippets thrown in to keep it all "intimate" and interesting.

CYBERMUSIC DEFINITION 3:
MUSICAL
EMPOWERMENT

Not everyone is a musician. Not everyone wants to be. One of the conceits of the various paths outlined in the previous section is the supposition that lots of people want to be musicians, or at least music producers. This asks more of listeners than I think they are ready to contribute. The option to diddle with specific pieces of music is more likely to appeal to one of three types of humans: other musicians, die-hard fans, and technogeeks who lust after new technology toys of every size and shape.

However, a slightly modified form of the Todd Rundgren approach may find support in the world of the casual listener. It, too, is interactive but is less visual in its construction. This form of interactive music simply allows users to have more control over the instrumentation and the mix of music that they might normally listen to—as long as they don't care about any particular artist's rendition of the pieces. This would probably appeal mostly to people who listen to music as background noise; with technology they could create their own personal Muzak.

This approach involves the use of a computer-to-instrument communication known as MIDI, the Musical Instrument Digital Interface. This protocol enables musicians to hook computers up to electronic devices such as synthesizers and drum machines. Once connected, the musician can use computer software to compose, record, and perform music. The computer can thus be used as an accompanist or a recording deck, using digital technology instead of tape. A single computer file can be used to control a whole army of electronic instruments, and is in fact one of the reasons why techno bands can get away with being comprised of only two or three individuals, or why Todd Rundgren can control an entire concert from his portable computer.

MIDI enables musicians to assign specific settings to a composed piece, such as, "Track 1 is a drum track, Track 2 is a saxophone track, Track 3 is a sound effects track, and so on." (All of these tracks control samplers or synthesized versions of the instruments I've just mentioned such as the sax; there is no way for computers to control acoustic instruments.) When the computer sequence runs, the appropriate instrument sounds are activated. These sounds can be easily switched with a simple command, letting a synthesized violin take the part of the synthesized saxophones, for instance.

There are a number of CD-ROM packages which provide preprogrammed songs—in the form of MIDI files—for use by musicians who want to play along with these songs or use them as fully orchestrated accompanists (lounge lizards will never be the same). Yet, there is an interesting offshoot of this market that may ultimately be even more popular with the everyday music consumer. Many computers can now be outfitted with sound boards which act like synthesizers and can output their own music as if they were self-contained electronic instruments. By hooking up a CD-ROM with MIDI files on it, an average user/listener can produce songs which are essentially being played "live" over the computer. Tempo can be adjusted and specific musical lines be can be assigned to the instruments of one's own choosing. Has the single violin in "Pachelbel's Canon in D" always sounded wimpy to you? Beef it up with 10 more violins, or replace it with a synthesized electric guitar. Don't like the cannon effects in the "1812 Overture"? Replace them with a machine-gun sound effect. On the other hand, is Wagner too bombastic for you? Strip "Ride of the Valkyries" down to a simple string quartet. Presto: instant customized classical mixes.

Again, this might appeal to people who use their music for background noise, although it might also appeal to classical listeners who don't have to contend with vocals—something which is not reproducible with synthesis or sampling technology just yet. This application of technology is simple and straightforward, and requires very little work on the part of the listener, unlike some of our previous examples.

Again, though, we are faced with a nagging suspicion that this isn't really cybermusic. It just doesn't have that theoretical tie-in to virtual reality or a computer network or a definite control over music. After all,

Wagner wrote "Valkyries"—you didn't. The content is already predetermined. Cyberspace residents combat this use of older "preconfigured" material by uploading their own music to the nets, thereby giving a kind of cyberlife to their music. The various computer networks all offer forums where users put their own music up for use by anyone who is interested in downloading their music files. This dispersion of music as a set of MIDI or digital files fits better conceptually with the idea of cyberspace and all things cyber, and it is the one area where cyberpunks and technodweebs feel comfortable labeling actual music as being part of an entire realm of "cybermusic."

Still, this same practice has been done for years by musicians who send cassettes of their music out in the mail or distribute it to all interested parties. Transferring this practice to the net doesn't really change things except for enabling the end user to assign instrumentation via MIDI, as we've just seen. Distribution over the nets is really more like cyberpublishing of music than it is creating anything revolutionary like cybermusic.

In fact, cybermusic may actually be something that hasn't been conceived of yet. The marriage of technology and music may be as unpredictable now as rock and roll was in the 1890s. No one foresaw the impact of electric guitars on popular culture; few people even saw the impact of electricity for that matter. These things have to be both evolutionary and revolutionary. Unbeknownst to any of us, there may be some technoequivalents of John Lennon and Paul McCartney or Jimi Hendrix sitting around in their bedrooms messing about with a computer and some instruments who just may foist a new kind of music upon us that can be truly defined as cybermusic.

CYBERMUSIC DEFINITION 4:
DISPOSABLE MUSIC

But my favorite definition, and the one that I think best defines what cybermusic may be, is perhaps the simplest. It doesn't involve the applied use of technology in music. Rather, it involves the ramifications of both a technologically driven society, and information overload, on music. Music for a cyberculture may be cybermusic just by definition. Guilt by association, and all that. And in that sense, music may simply become disposable because technology is creating more and more disposable components of our world.

This definition is derived from two conversations I had with musicians who were arguably among the most popular songwriters of their day. The first was with Al Stewart, best known for "The Year of The Cat," "Time Passages," "On The Border," and a host of other mid-to-late 1970s radio staples. As far as he is concerned, the emphasis on technology takes away from the essence of music, and if technology replaces the human essence of songwriting, he doesn't want to hear about it. "That type of music can cyber itself into space. I really care nothing for technology, whether it's in recording gear or in instruments." He tapped the face of an acoustic 12-string guitar. "I like wooden music," he laughed, demonstrating a quick flourish of chords that it would be hard to imagine being duplicated with computers—either in warmth or subtlety.

The second conversation was one I had with Robbie Robertson, the man who led The Band in the 1960s and 1970s. Robertson was also Bob Dylan's electric guitarist and is often blamed (or praised) for helping move Dylan away from the world of Appalachian folkies into the then modern world of folk-rock. Among the songs he has written are "The Night They Drove Old Dixie Down," "Up On Cripple Creek," and dozens of others that have been performed by people ranging from Aretha Franklin to Eric Clapton (Clapton inducted Robertson and the other members of The Band into the Rock and Roll Hall of Fame in January 1994).

Robertson's take on the future of music is quite succinct. "In the future, music will be disposable, like cigarette lighters are today. You'll hear a song once and then you'll never hear it again. You will just throw it away." At first, this sounds somewhat trite, but it has a great deal of merit after giving it some thought.

Start by looking at the history of music. The work of Beethoven, Bach, Mozart, Mussorgsky, and Ravel has lasted many decades, and in some cases, centuries. It is likely that this music will always be around in some form or another, especially those pieces that have become ingrained in our collective consciousness over the generations ("Moonlight Sonata," "Bolero," and so on). They seem, at least at this juncture, to be timeless.

Fast forward to the 1960s and 1970s. Rock musicians during that period tended to produce an album every six to nine months, oftentimes releasing two entirely new albums within a single calendar year. Usually one or two songs were released for radio airplay from those albums, resulting in singles that spent numerous weeks, if not months, on the music charts. By the time the singles faded from memory, the artists were just about ready to turn out their next product. Each song, however, had an extended shelf life that ensured that it would be ingrained into your memory like some aural tattoo. Most people today can readily sing the songs of their youth due to the amount of repetition which accompanied these songs in terms of radio airplay.

Now let's move to the late 1980s. Bands started releasing albums less frequently, perhaps producing one every two years, if that. Three, four, even five or six songs from each album were released as singles. The average time each of these songs stayed on the charts, though, was drastically reduced—perhaps covering a six-week period at most. The minute that song was dropped from regular rotation, another single was released to pick up the slack.

Making one more jump, turn on your radio today. There are more artists on the radio today than ever before, yet their songs are played for shorter periods of time. A long rotation for a band's single is three to four weeks. If it doesn't catch on in three weeks, the single is often dropped by radio stations. Chances are that someone may recommend that you listen for a certain song on the radio, and by the time you do some serious station surfing, the song may be off the air completely. Another song by the same band may be released by the record company to try and pick up any original momentum, but usually an album that doesn't get a top single is destined for the cut-out bins within three months. Compare this with albums of the 1960s and 1970s, such as Pink Floyd's *Dark Side of the Moon*, which stayed on the charts for years.

What has happened is a reduced lifespan for music. Much of this can be blamed squarely on MTV, which requires eye-zapping videos in order to keep viewers' attention. And there is a direct relationship between MTV and the amount of time a single spends on the radio, whether anybody wants to admit it publicly or not. If the song isn't showing up on

MTV, it might not get played on the radio, although MTV was originally formed as a support mechanism for songs getting airplay.

Yet, to blame it all on MTV is to miss the underlying issue. MTV is a reflection of the culture, and time continues to be a premium in an age where information overload threatens not only corporate executives but teenagers as well. Music, like all aspects of life, has to be digested and used quickly. If it does not provide aural fast food for consumption, then it is taking too large a percentage of the listener's cluttered data stream. And, if it remains in the system for too long, it becomes old and stale; hence the shorter cycle of singles releases.

Looking at both Stewart's and Robertson's opinion of music—that it will be ephemeral and disappear before it ever matters—one is forced to consider that maybe all music will simply become cybermusic: a form of electronic whitewash that glides through our environments with all the lack of substance of a nightly newscast. Does tonight's newscast mean anything tomorrow? No. The information does, but not the presentation. The same may become true of music.

Songs have radio lives measured in weeks, whereas they used to be measured in months. In the future, it is conceivable, if not outright predictable, that this lifespan will be reduced to one week, and then to a handful of days. Once it gets down to the point where it is only heard on the radio a few times on a single day, then playing a song only once doesn't seem so ludicrous. If it is released and you miss it, you'll never have to deal with that song as part of the information flow that you're continually swimming upstream against. If, however, you like the song, you can hear it again by going out and purchasing it. But you will not hear it again on the radio.

Have you missed anything during that one play? Perhaps not. We all go through life missing out on movies or songs; it is the ones that we do experience that matter to us. Yet the lack of repetition of songs may knock our psyches somewhat off-balance, especially since we often use these repeated songs to define entire segments of our lives ("That whole summer, all I ever heard was that annoying Madonna song, you know the one..."). And in truth, there's already more music on the market than any one person can assimilate. The record industry is to blame for this music overload, since it will put out almost anything—as long as it fits a trend—in order to find the next big thing.

In the end, maybe cybermusic will be all music that is made as part of the post-industrial technological society. Maybe people won't make plain old music anymore—that will be the domain of the long dead composers of classical music, and even the pre-techno popsters like The Beatles. Everything else that is played will be short-lived due to short memories.

Interestingly, many of the classical composers wrote music that was supposed to be played only once, such as at a coronation or at different masses during the year. Only with the proliferation of their scores after their deaths—and the subsequent recording of those scores—did the pieces take on a life of their own. So there is a precedent for writing music which is to be played only once, and it is hundreds of years old. The only difference is that back then, those pieces were part of individual celebrations, and each musical piece was heralded as a singular creation. Tomorrow, unfortunately, songs may be played only once, and disappear like so much ear candy: chewable, digestible, and forgettable.

With this in mind, cybermusic may well be the future of all music: music for the moment—and not a second longer. Who knows? If music is composed with no longevity in mind, then maybe by the time the 1990s are over, the eighties really will make the seventies look like the 1960s.

Cyberliterature

Everything from the creation of ideas to brainstorming alternatives to actual writing, formatting, editing, revising, printing, and distributing the final product has been affected by the widespread application of cybertechnology.

chapter 26

by Donald Rose, Ph.D.

INTRODUCTION

In the beginning, there were ideas, but no writing. Then writing was invented, but there was no standardized means to print or distribute information. Then came the printing press, and the mass distribution of written works was born.

Now fast-forward to today, when the invention and wide use of computers, plus the recent surge in popularity of online services and networks, has started to transform literature again. Computers excel at storing, displaying, and manipulating information, and since the content of literature is essentially information, computers have become an essential element in today's writing process. Everything from the creation of ideas to brainstorming alternatives to actual writing, formatting, editing, revising, printing, and distributing the final product has been affected by the widespread application of cybertechnology.

So suppose those AT&T commercials are right about the future. In such a future scenario we could, for instance, read books on a computer screen, books that are stored and displayed exactly like the real thing. Certainly if a computer and monitor can completely re-create a book's information and even appearance, then that combination is, in a sense, just as good as a book. However, we know that computers can do a lot more than just store and display information—for instance, they can perform operations on that information. The creative application of new operations is the engine powering the transformation of literature today. In many ways, this is analogous to the transformation of storytelling that took place when early filmmakers evolved a new cinematic language that took the medium beyond the mere re-creation of its closest relative (stage plays). The many capabilities that computers and networks afford us today are transforming literature into new forms that can be described here as *cyberliterature*.

DEFINING CYBERLITERATURE

Cyberliterature can be defined as the use of a computer (including software, hardware, or networks) to transform or augment the experience of written language. However, as in other chapters in this book, exact definitions are hard to construct, a consequence of the newness of the subjects covered in these pages. For the purposes of this chapter, I use the term *cyberliterature* in a broad sense and to encompass several areas, including the following:

- Computer tools to help writers create ideas or an actual story
- Electronic books-on-disk (as well as electronic magazines, journals, and so on.)
- Stories told in new forms in the cyberverse (including hypertext, multimedia, and games)
- Computer-generated stories
- Interactive, networked, multiuser fiction environments

> *One could easily imagine a future when all books will exist in some online incarnation, with many being interlinked, rearranged, and redesigned into new forms so that one can surf threads of knowledge across several books and articles.*

It is also useful to ask what exactly is literature, in the traditional, non-cyber sense. Webster's definition includes "writings of a period or of a country; all the books and articles on a subject; any printed matter." Hence, one way to imagine or define cyberliterature is as a representation or transmigration of standard, linear books and articles within cyberspace. In fact, many of the world's classic books and articles now exist in some form of cyberspace—for instance, in online services' repositories or on CD-ROMs such as Microsoft Bookshelf. One could easily imagine a future when all books will exist in some online incarnation, with many being interlinked, rearranged, and redesigned into new forms so that one can surf threads of knowledge across several books and articles.

· ·

For the purposes of this chapter, I will assume the following working definition of cyberliterature, drawing on and generalizing from Webster's: *Any collection of related, written text that utilizes computers in its creation, consumption, or distribution—and which allows either linear or nonlinear navigation of its content, either with or without reader control of such navigation. The set of all such potential collections includes (that is, is a superset of) all electronic versions of books and articles on a subject, as well as electronic versions of any writings of a period, country, or virtual community.*

. . . .

COMPARING TRADITIONAL LITERATURE TO CYBERLITERATURE

Author Gordon Howell, in *HYPERTEXT II: State of the Art*, offered this description of cyberliterature: "The fundamental difference between conventional fiction (also called linear fiction) and interactive fiction is that [in the latter] the reader becomes a part of the story and partially controls the direction and experience of the art."

Analogies to physical navigation can be instructive here. Reading normal fiction is like taking a bus, plane, or train: One is a passive passenger, going from a starting point (opening) to a destination (ending) without any choice of the route. Using interactive fiction is much more like driving a car. You navigate yourself, with control over the path taken from start to finish; sometimes you can even decide to end up somewhere other than your original planned destination.

One might also draw an analogy to the difference between experiencing a non-interactive software demo and using actual software. A demo is often a sort of film (on videotape or floppy disk) of someone using the software, plus other text or images that lead the viewer along by the hand. The demo always gives you the same experience, although there may be limited ability to go backward or forward. By contrast, once you enter the actual program that the demo is designed to explain, you have the freedom to go into any of its features, re-create some demo paths if desired, and ultimately experience a seemingly limitless number of new potential paths. The demo is analogous to normal fiction, whereas the actual software corresponds to the interactive version of fiction.

BOOKS ON DISK: THE ELECTRONIC TRANSMIGRATION OF LITERATURE

Perhaps the simplest way to transmigrate traditional literature into the cyberverse is to put existing written works into electronic form. Many electronic versions of books, both popular and obscure, now exist for personal computer users to experience.

For example, The Voyager Company has pioneered the transference—even transformation—of "normal" books to their electronic analogs. The advantages over conventional paper books become apparent quickly after getting used to the new medium. For example, a reader has the ability to dog-ear pages, set up multiple virtual bookmarks, change font size and type, highlight sections with sidebar lines, even write notes in the e-books' virtual margins. Then there is my favorite, the ability to

- find any word or phrase in the text or your own margin notes—
- and even to do so across several e-books.

- Although Apple has been using the name Powerbook to describe its line of portable computers, the combination of small, light portable computers plus cyberbooks such as Voyager's makes the true "powerbook" (or perhaps "hyperbook" or "metabook") available for the first time. One can imagine that as portables become even lighter and cyberbooks even more widespread and sophisticated, these hardware-software combinations might indeed supplant the paper book. Future e-book innovations might include artificial agents that could give readers different versions of the story based on the reader's time constraints, intelligence level, educational background, or interest in the subject. Companies such as Readers Digest or Cliffs Notes could even market their own unique kinds of agents.

- If you happen to be a anti-technology Luddite, don't fret. You'll always have songs like the Beatles' "Paperback Writer" to remember the old books by. (Of course, the Beatles are already in electronic form, in Voyager's *A Hard Day's Night* CD-ROM.)

LITERATURE EXISTING SOLELY IN CYBERSPACE

- Electronic journals (e-journals) can be viewed as another form of cyberliterature. Such journals are sometimes just an electronic equivalent of regular paper journals. However, more commonly, e-journals can be a superset version that can grow to include feedback from readers (including e-mail to editors and authors for all to read), counterpoints (feedback to the feedback), pointers to other related reading material, and so on. Some e-journals have never existed in paper form, a characteristic that may be the norm for cyberliterature in years to come.

Like e-books, e-journals can be searched for specific words in order to access key passages that pertain to desired themes. More importantly, e-journals can be quickly and widely distributed across the globe via the Internet or other networks on the embryonic information superhighway.

Then there are works created by authors who do not want the words to ever exist in printed form. For example, in the hypertext version of one of his works, author Jay David Bolter tells the reader that electronic copying and distribution of his text is fine, but no hard copy may be made. More specifically, Bolter says the reader cannot make "any copy on paper or a similar material that you can hold in your hand and read by candlelight, flashlight, or reading lamp" nor "make any copy that does not require the use of the computer for presentation and navigation." Will this one day be viewed as the Bolter Revolt, a mini manifesto that provoked today's readers to leave the Old World shackles of print for the glories of cyberspace? More cynically, are there even enough readers left today to form a quorum for a book club, much less a revolution? Even more cynically, does anyone know what a quorum is anymore?

The inventor of the term cyberspace recently produced an eerie variant of Bolter's vision. William Gibson wrote a work which, when read, *self-destructs*. That is, you get one chance to read it, then it's gone forever. With this work, called *Agrippa*, Gibson has gone a step further than Bolter, creating a written work which not only cannot be printed but which is destroyed after reading; the text scrolls automatically and cannot be read again, the disk auto-corrupted by a virus. One could consider this work as simply a form of art (a limited edition of 95 copies was offered at $2,000 per copy), or a statement for our times that stands in stark contrast to our myriad means of preserving information in various media, or just great publicity. But one could also

Nothing lasts forever and we should savor the moment, even if that moment involves reading flashing phospor dots on a computer screen.

comment that Gibson is exploring a new way of using computers to augment the reading experience, by forcing a reader to savor every word by ensuring the computer erases it after reading. Perhaps the self-scrolling/self-destroying story is also a symbol for our times, reminding us how information often passes by quickly and out of our control. It is designed to remind us, like Tibetan sand paintings, that nothing lasts forever and we should savor the moment, even if that moment involves reading flashing phospor dots on a computer screen.

Of course, a forward thinker like Gibson must have expected that hackers would try to break the "self-destroying encryption" code and post the story on electronic bulletin boards—both of which they did, according to *The New York Times Book Review*. So maybe we can think conspiratorially and say that Gibson was just using a complicated means to inspire hackers to develop new ways to prevent viruses from eating data on disks. That is, the author's goal could have been to create a short-lived martyr of a story, to ensure that later cyberliterature could be preserved longer.

Or maybe Gibson is just a bit more paranoid about plagiarism than other writers. Or he doesn't want readers to notice any typos. Or he hates how used-book stores recycle written works while the authors don't receive any extra payments for such resales.

No matter what the purpose, I can't help but believe that Gibson has a copy of the story on his own hard disk somewhere, just in case he wants to reminisce one day. Wouldn't you do the same?

• •

Automatic Generation of Stories by Computer

Computerized aids to the human writing process can also be considered a component of the cyberliterature universe. We all have heard of CAD (computer-aided design) programs, which produce graphical representations of physical spaces. Analogous programs can help create a piece of writing, by generating new ideas, fleshing out characters, trying out sample plot lines—even formatting, typesetting, and printing.

For example, programs called Collaborator and Dramatica ask writers questions about aspects of their stories, questions based on certain rules of drama (rules that are different in each program). These question-answer sessions can help to focus the author's intent, direction, and thematic goals. Note that programs such as Collaborator and Dramatica, as well as others such as Sol Stein's FictionMaster, do not actually write the story envisioned by the author/user, but rather assist in the creative process that precedes the writing. In other words, these programs do not relieve one from the chore of sitting in an uncomfortable position and staring at a blank screen. As Oliver Stone reportedly said, "writing equals butt in chair."

Dramatica, however, does have mechanisms that let writers automatically generate story *forms*. Dramatica's creators wisely separate *storyforming* from *storytelling*. According to *The Dramatica Dictionary*, the former is the process of shaping the general contours, structure, and dynamics of the story—that is, its blueprint—whereas the latter is the actual instantiation of that general form, complete with the specific details of narration, scene descriptions, and dialogue that convey that form to the reader. For example, a storyform might involve two lovers trying to stay together over the obstacles of their families and friends, whereas the specifics of the storytelling can vary from *Romeo and Juliet* to *West Side Story*. Dramatica's

Story Engine can predict which storyforms are *apropos* to a set of character and plot choices the author/user makes. Hence, this program can take user input preferences about key story and character elements and generate abstract story forms automatically, which users can then flesh out into complete stories.

Although Dramatica is a recently released product, artificial intelligence researchers have gone even further along some of these dimensions, with programs designed to actually generate fiction. One of the best known is an early AI program, created by computer scientist Jim Meehan, called TALESPIN. In this program, characters have various goals that are associated with them and various plans to achieve them. The desire to satisfy goals leads to plan selection, which may be followed by creation of subgoals and additional plan selection. This interplay between goals, plans, and the environment inhabited by the characters leads to the generation of stories. Comparing TALESPIN to Dramatica illustrates a tradeoff inherent in computer-aided writing programs. TALESPIN can generate complete instantiated stories, but their structure and characters are simplistic and one-dimensional, whereas Dramatica cannot generate complete stories but the storyforms it generates are more complex and multidimensional. Future programs will hopefully include the best aspects of both types of programs.

Another approach used by AI researchers involves using agent action trails as a kind of narrative spine. For instance, by creating a virtual world where rule-based agents can perform actions in the world's environment, the description of these actions can form the basis of a story. Unlike TALESPIN's static (non-learning) characters, story agents in these newer systems are usually "designed to act, reason, and reflect on [their] experience," according to author Kenneth Meyer in *Communication in the Age of Virtual Reality*. In other words, these agents are often more human-like than the TALESPIN characters, and in systems such as Homer, they can even answer questions about their experiences. Such responses could perhaps be used as the seed for dialogue in stories that use agent human interactions as their inspiration.

In the future, some ideas from artificial-life technology might also be applied to computer-based story generation. For example, just as rewrite rules can "grow" a virtual plant by replacing simple parts with more complex ones (as discussed in Chapter 17, "Artificial Life"), different rules grounded in dramatic theory and

In the future, some ideas from artificial-life technology might also be applied to computer-based story generation. For example, just as rewrite rules can "grow" a virtual plant by replacing simple parts with more complex ones, different rules grounded in dramatic theory and grammar might be used to change simple storylines or dialogue into more robust and more enjoyable variants.

grammar might be used to change simple storylines or dialogue into more robust and more enjoyable variants. One might think of a story as an organism, which can start in one form yet be revised into different or expanded versions.

- -

HYPERTEXT: INTERCONNECTED, INTERACTIVE STORYTELLING

Although its stories were of a simple nature, TALESPIN introduced or popularized some ideas that remain relevant to cyberliterature. For example, TALESPIN used the idea of a *metastory*, which could be described as a tree of possible story paths. The metastory, in a sense, contains all the stories that the program could ever generate. This concept implies choice. In TALESPIN-like systems, when a reader (or is "co-author" a better term?) chooses one set of initial characters, the story unfolds one way. Select another set, or a changed environment, and a different—though perhaps related—story unfolds. But what if the reader had control over how the ultimate story unfolds, rather than control over input preferences only? What if a reader could read part of a written text, then decide to go any number of places next—to text related to this word, or that phrase, or the answer to a question planted by the author?

Well, this is already possible. Works that employ reader-controlled linked text are called *hypertext*. Hypertext has been defined in many ways: non-static text, windows of text connected by associative links, or navigable information. All of these are in some sense correct. Many believe that hypertext works give a purpose and design to cyberliterature, "and [the] principal tool for doing this is [the] linking mechanism: In place of print's linear, page-turning route, it offers a network of alternate paths through a set of text spaces by way of designated links," according to Robert Coover in *The New York Times Book Review*.

Hypertext can be brought to life in many forms, from adventure games to museum kiosks. One form is the hypertext novel. A hypertext novel can be viewed as a variation on the printed novel—a novel kind of novel, if you will. Nearly all printed novels have a linear narrative, but hypertext novels can also have non-linear narratives, wherein readers decide which narrative paths to follow while "reading" the story. The reader of hypertext fiction is a participant, whereas the reader of the linear novel is essentially passive (except for good, old-fashioned page turning).

Hypertext poetry is another subset of the literary cyberverse. In hypertext poetry, lines from a larger work (such as a novel) are extracted into a smaller piece (the hypertext "poem"). For example, science fiction author Jonathan Post has authored several hypertext poems, some of which use works by SF legend Ray Bradbury as the "inspiration source" of textual material. Such hypertext poems are a unique type of collaboration; one author supplies the actual words, while another chooses those words and selects a proper order. In most cases, the hypertext poet extracts the lines with some unifying theme in mind, but there exist many works where the meaning is not as obvious.

Although hypertext poetry does not require the use of a computer (one could simply cut up the source material and see what patterns evolve), one can imagine a software program that automatically scans one or more stories for sentences that could be extracted into a smaller piece. The artifical intelligence would manifest itself in the rules used for the extraction. For example, a set of rules could determine what constitutes a unified theme, and then the appropriate passages would be extracted for inclusion within the shorter work. A similar endeavor could extract essential plot points into an abbreviated yet still coherent piece. Thus, the construction of what we call hypertext poetry may prove beneficial in designing agent programs that can automatically create a kind of CyberCliff Notes or user-tailored *Reader's Digest*, as mentioned earlier.

CREATING CHARACTER-THEMED HYPERSPACES

Because hypertext can be described as a matrix or repository of interconnected information, it is conceptually similar to a physical building, which also has the property of interlinked spaces. Instead of real objects, the cyberbuildings we are talking about are filled with information. Some authors have used this building metaphor as a source of inspiration—and as a way to design interfaces that are easier to learn and understand.

One example of this kind of hypermedia is *Uncle Buddy's Phantom Funhouse*, by hypertext pioneer John McDaid. Although described by McDaid as a "hypermedia novel," it feels less like a novel and more like a visit to a virtual building. In fact, some of its Macintosh Hypercard screens use building-related graphics, and the Funhouse title itself suggests a physical space. All of its rooms, whether based on the physical kind or not (some seemed more like abstract mental spaces designed to shatter the reader's metaphoric limitations), are devoted to the exploits of one character: Uncle Buddy. Note that the word *hypertext* is not used in the author's general program description; although text is indeed a primary component of this novel, there are also drawings, diagrams, photos, even cassette tapes to play as you navigate the screens that make up the Funhouse.

As with all works of hypermedia, readers are free to navigate among the information-rich windows (actually stacks of Hypercards) in any order they choose and in multiple ways. For instance, from one card or "room," they can go the previously displayed card, or to the next, or see a screen of recent cards and select one, or hyperzip home to the front of the Funhouse where they started. In addition, when different sections of Buddy's house are clicked, the new rooms of information sometimes employ different navigational controls, with changed icons as well as changed fonts. Gavin Edwards of the *Village Voice* described *Uncle Buddy's Phantom Funhouse*

• •

Some works utilize the computer's characteristics so skillfully that, although the work is still fiction and may have an overarching story to discover, the work can *only* exist within a computer or cyberspace network.

as "a fractal web that could never be downloaded off the computer and reprinted in paper form." Perhaps this characteristic is one measure of whether a work is truly in the cyberliterature category. Another way of stating this property is that some works utilize the computer's characteristics so skillfully that, although the work is still fiction and may have an overarching story to discover, the work can *only* exist within a computer or cyberspace network.

For all its unique and stimulating features, *Uncle Buddy's Phantom Funhouse* is still by design a fragmented place with lots of different information scattered about. So should works like this actually be considered literature? At times it seems hard to find a clear story. Robert Coover comments that the contents of Buddy's house are more like a nostalgic dump of too much scrapbook-like information than a collection of well-developed components within a clear

story. Does a tour through a collection of information, even if tied by a central theme, qualify as fiction? A lack of story may be viewed as either good *or* bad. It is bad in that most readers like to have a certain degree of structure and coherence to match our expectation of what constitutes a satisfying story; but it is good in that the boundaries of fiction are continually being tested and discussed among readers and critics alike. It is hoped that works such as McDaid's will lead to a better understanding of what a story really is and what constitutes a truly effective or satisfying story. These evolving critical standards might then be incorporated into story generators like those discussed previously.

The *Hypertext Hotel* is yet another space for exploring the lives of virtual characters. Described as "the nation's first online writing space devoted to ... hypertext," this virtual hotel was started by Coover in 1991 at Brown University. According to *The New Yorker*, each of the 17 students admitted into Coover's class each term get about 10MB of hard-disk space on the university's main computer, where they "work on and store their term project—a hypertext fiction composed of numerous 'windows' (electronic pages upon which one writes) and 'links' (connections between windows that create the structure of a 'text')." The Hotel is inhabited by characters created by the students. These characters can experience all the things experienced by real people or characters in "real" books, including romance, murder—you know, the usual. Students can read but not alter other students' works in progress. A student (or a distinguished writer guest invited by Coover) adds to the virtual hotel either by building a virtual room—which involves "establishing a text window and filling it with enough language to make it appear like a physical space, on screen—or by creating a link between rooms."

It will be interesting to see if the ideas of Coover's class can be generalized to wider networks. Today, anyone on the Internet can access the Hotel but cannot actually add to the evolving hypertext space. But imagine if, instead of being limited to a few dozen people, the hotel could be expanded to the size of the Internet, or at least some large subset of the Net. With the potential for hundreds or thousands of characters and rooms, the number of possible story paths could become so large that one couldn't exhaust all the stories within a lifetime! Traditional authors and critics often use the word *universe* to describe related works with overlapping characters and ideas, but this hypothetical Internet megahotel would certainly capture the spirit of that word more closely.

What would the point of this be? For a start, this could lead to the creation of story universes that could approach the complexities of real life for the first time. In addition, imagine a story or game so rich in detail that one could never get bored with it. Of course, the companies selling such products might not appreciate the lack of planned obsolescence. Only time—and (cyber) space—will tell.

VIRTUAL REALITY, CYBERSPACE, AND NETWORKED FICTION

Dr. Michael Moshell, associate professor of computer science and director of the Visual Systems Laboratory at the Institute for Simulation and Training, is working with a young group called the Toy Scouts on a unique project: an "online interactive theater," using students from around the world to manipulate "cyberactors" in various dramatic roles.

Moshell indicates that the plays will be two-dimensional at first, then progress to virtual reality when a three-dimensional world is "built." Students will almost literally "become" the person they play, including taking on the appearance of the character. Dr. Moshell has been searching for creative talent to assist in building the three-dimensional world. According to *E-news*, he also has been trying to find students to help in writing cyberplays for use in this new theatrical medium.

Note that Moshell's vision sounds related to the text-based worlds of MUDs (Multi-User Dimensions or Dungeons) and MOOs (MUDs, Object-Oriented) on the Internet and can be viewed as a more visual successor to these cyberrealms. As discussed in Chapter 6, "Life in the Virtual Village," MUDs and MOOs are in some ways the inverse of what Moshell is proposing. Cyberplays would be written with the ultimate goal of having humans perform certain action sequences. This would differ from the networked worlds of the Internet, where human commands plus actions and discussions are the driving force that lead to the generation of plot descriptions and dialogue. For example, if one analyzes the transcripts of typical MUD sessions, they can be viewed as simple yet complete storylines. Typing certain commands can trigger programs that generate predefined text, such as a room description after a user types "open door." In short, when people interact in MOOs and MUDs, triggering actions by other users or by preprogrammed text generators, they in effect create a kind of part-improvised, part-canned play-on-the-fly. Perhaps Moshell can learn useful lessons from the experience of MOOsters and MUDders, and vice versa.

Also note that text-based VR transcripts are related to the agent-based story creations discussed previously. In the latter, agent actions plus possible dialogue with human observers form the basis for the generated story, whereas in online text-based worlds, the agents are mostly human, except for occasional text generation from online command-triggered agents. Another difference is that MOO/MUD stories can become more complex as more users interact online and as more triggerable agents are developed and planted like text-mines in MOO or MUD text-fields.

Many of the storylines generated by these methods would probably be considered a bit boring or tedious to many readers. Still, a good editor can do wonders for such texts. Descendants of programs such as Collaborator and Dramatica might be able to automatically revise such texts based on story theory, grammatical rules, or other heuristic knowledge. The day when one might literally "grow a story" in cyberspace may not be too far in the future.

Finally, one of the hottest topics in the media today involves the ever-growing absorption of "old" media into the Internet behemoth. The Net is making vast amounts of existing literature available online, for easier and faster use in hypertext-type applications. Traditional literature is already being transformed in electronic configurations, some reborn to new popularity, others altered in ways that some purists might compare to the colorizing of film. As the Net expands, so will the potential for more widespread, more popularized cyberworks and the creation of new forms of literature not currently being exploited. In addition, the Net may fulfill the vision of hypertext pioneer Ted Nelson: large networks of cyberliterature, linked together by creators and readers alike, including not just works by the authors but extensions made by other writers or readers, plus commentary and critique of the works which themselves could be constructed in cyberliterature form. An embryonic version of this already exists in the guise of the World Wide Web, which links information from all over the globe and allows people access to Net-based databases, using tools like the MOSAIC program as hypertext front-ends. With millions of new users turning on to the Net each month, the pressure for more and better hypertext systems to ease navigation among the global space of information should increase even further.

Design, Structure, and Content Issues

In constructing a fictive cyberspace, is it best to clearly illustrate the paths that one can take, or is better to allow readers to discover the various paths on their own? How should a reader be allowed to add to the work? Should authors constrain the choices that the adjunct creator/reviser can make? These and other issues are the focus of increasing debate in this young field.

A writer must constantly make choices—about plot, character, theme, and so on. One could argue that the proliferation of cyberliterature will eventually make writing "easier" for the creator by making it "harder" for the reader/participant. That is, the cyberauthor could concentrate less on story choices and more on the central ideas, character development, subthemes, and so forth. The author would let the user make choices during each reading, which would lead to a potentially different course of events each time. Authors of cyberliterature would find themselves in a position like that of a filmmaker preparing a revised director's cut of a movie—more information can be included, with fewer restrictions.

Of course, the cyberwriter must still make sure that his or her core story is well developed and properly structured. The 1985 movie *Clue*, for example, may have received publicity for its three alternate endings, but audiences did not make any of these versions a hit. On the other hand, Neil Simon, without using any cybertrickery (except perhaps a small electronic dictionary), still churns out blockbusters. It should also be noted that variations of a traditional story have been a staple of film, drama, and literature for years, such as when directors and actors concoct unique interpretations of an existing play, putting a new spin on it and in a sense making it their own, making it new again. Once considered avant garde and experimental, interactive plays have also been gaining in popularity, and even interactive films are now being released for the first time (not to mention the colossal growth of the multimedia and CD-ROM industries).

In short, interactivity and plot flexibility are not found solely in cyberliterature, and they are also not enough by themselves to make cyberliterature compelling. One can draw parallels to the early days of film. Audiences once sat enthralled at short films of trains running or of a man sneezing, but when the novelty of movies eventually wore off, the viewers demanded more compelling stories—that is, better content. The novelty of cyberliterature will eventually wear off as well, meaning that its unique features will only be valuable to the reader if the associated content is stimulating as well.

CYBERLIT AND GAMING

Structurally, cyberliterature lies on the boundary between traditional stories and online games. For example, with a traditional book, there is typically only one reader at a time, and when there are more than one (such as when a parent reads to a child), there is physical proximity between the readers. In contrast, with cyberliterature residing in MOOs, MUDs, and such works as the *Hypertext Hotel*, there can be several participants who can be in separate physical locations. This capability is present in many of today's networked games.

So where is the boundary between cyberliterature and games? No one has yet defined it. Are there truly meaningful differences between cyberliterature and games? The line is blurry. One distinguishing feature is that in cyberliterature one is still *told* a story in some form. The tale might be revealed in a different order each time, or even allow user control over story flow, but there is a telling of some kind nonetheless. In a game, however, a player is more likely to *experience* a series of events that, when taken as a group, might be considered a story—but if there is an overarching plot, it must be inferred by the player, since explicit storytelling rarely occurs. Another difference between most games and the cyberliterature covered in this chapter is that, within the latter, most events are tied by a unified theme or idea, which usually leads the audience to learn something about one or more characters. Games, in contrast, are not inclined to have unified themes, nor do they feature well-rounded characters with depth or an arc of inner growth.

Hence, my opinion is that cyberliterature can be viewed as a superset of most of the game universe. In other words, if designed properly, works of cyberliterature could enable the reader/participant to do everything one could do in a game, and often more. Alternatively, one could view portions of the cyberliterature universe as the "missing link" on the spectrum between passive stories and interactive games. But perhaps there is no need to define any boundaries between old and new literature, or between new literature and games. The ultimate goal is the same: enjoyment by the reader/participants.

AUTHORSHIP AND COPYRIGHT ISSUES

Earlier I mentioned that many new hyperworks encourage readers to contribute to them, to add new characters or links or subordinate tales, or to change existing story elements—all of which could clarify and enhance the piece (unless you're a cyberpunk, in which case you might prefer making the piece more chaotic). Deena Larsen's *Marble Springs* and Coover's *Hypertext Hotel* are but two examples. Mark Bernstein, the driving force behind hypermedia publishing house Eastgate Systems and publisher of *Marble Springs*, described in *The Boston Phoenix* how Larsen cried when she saw "other people's writing in her work" and felt "a sense of loss at the realization that these characters who have been her companions for three or four years aren't even hers anymore," almost as if "her friends" had moved away and all she could do now was read about their new lives. Such feelings may become more common among authors as the traditional boundary between writer and reader blurs.

Of course, issues surrounding the ownership of cybercreations go beyond emotions and into the realm of copyrights and monetary compensation. If the distinction between creator and consumer is blurred, who should get paid for the evolving

* *

Of course, issues surrounding the ownership of cybercreations go beyond emotions and into the realm of copyrights and monetary compensation. If the distinction between creator and consumer is blurred, who should get paid for the evolving work and its constituent parts?

* *

work and its constituent parts? Further, how can such payment be facilitated in an easy and fair manner?

Hypertext visionary Ted Nelson proposed a possible solution to the "how" of this issue. As outlined by Stuart Moulthrop in *The New York Review of Science Fiction*, Nelson has been implementing a system for the storage and transmission of cyberliterature works using cyberspace as the medium. In his proposed cyberverse, called *Xanadu*, "documents are stored and accessed electronically. Every time a user takes a quantity of information, a debit is charged against [his or] her bill. A set portion of the debit is transferred to the account of the person who entered the information into the system." He added that "every user is free to post information to the system,"—a state of affairs not present in the current publishing structure. "Users pay for this posting service, but they also receive a royalty flow if their information proves interesting to others. This contrasts sharply with the model of commercial MUDs," which do not have methods for assigning credit or payments to cybercreators.

The Xanadu concept raises additional issues about copyrights for cyberworks. For example, how (and in what amount) can authors charge readers for works that exist in cyberspace? Despite the gallant efforts of Nelson and others who hope to create an infrastructure for the future of cyberpublishing, controlling the new literary cyberverse may prove too tough a problem. An oft-quoted cybermantra is that "Information wants to be free"; it is a kind of fundamental law of cyberspace. One example: Soon after the release of Gibson's *Agrippa* story, the auto-destructing story described earlier, numerous printouts of the text appeared on the Internet.

Moulthrop raises other related questions regarding authorship. For example, "[i]f the text becomes an impossibly dense tissue of links or a set of self-modifying motifs, who ultimately controls it? Who is responsible (or legally liable) for its social effects?"

I believe a possible answer may lie in the creation of a new concept for cyberliterature: the *cyberserver*, a person or organization that does not necessarily create the work but does provide the medium (such as an online service or MUD) on which the cyberliterature works are stored or performed. The cyberserver would be a kind of intermediary between cyberauthors and their reader/participants, creating and maintaining an environment that controls the works in various ways (such as restricting access to some paths for some users, but not for others) and taking responsibility for their social effects.

A cyberauthor could take his or her works to a different cyberserver if the environment proves unpopular (perhaps because of too much or too little control). Users could voice any complaints to the cyberserver instead of to the authors directly. Perhaps "club owner" is a useful metaphor for this new concept. The owner is in part a "performance server" who makes sure audiences stay in line, pays authors of music or poetry or comedy, and lets the authors have their works performed without being personally liable for how they turn out in the owner's club.

While this cyberserver concept is similar to Nelson's Xanadu, it would more heavily emphasize social and financial responsibility. In addition, cyberservers would often pay creators for works before users use them, acting as a kind of buffer in much the same way publishers do for traditional printed works. Cyberservers would have strong incentive to pay authors, because without product the cyberservers would not be visited by paying consumers. Furthermore, consumers would want to pay cyberservers for access to their favorite authors' works, especially if they only appeared on cyberservers and not in traditional print.

But what if a hackerpunk subscriber wanted to make copies of cyberworks at home for several nonpaying friends? Perhaps subscribers could receive a personalized, encrypted, copy-protected disk with a special key program (or would download such a program from the service), which would only work for one computer and would be required to "unlock" the service's cyberliterature for reading. Or, perhaps we could reinvent Gibson's *Agrippa* scenario: In this new variation of the idea, you could only read a cyberserver work once before it's erased on your computer, forcing you to access the server again if you want to reread it. Even the most patient hacker would get tired of constantly copying a file over and over for friends.

Of course, all of these issues are still very much unresolved, and they will be debated vigorously as cyberfiction increases in popularity. Perhaps the ultimate answer to the issue of information credit and payment will be found in this dictum by Jay Leno: "Write faster than they can steal."

Summary and Conclusions

Some of the hallmarks of cyberliterature are increased interactivity, wider story choices, more complex narrative structure, and a capacity for external embellishment. The line between creator and reader will become fuzzier as readers will be given (albeit not forced to employ) more control over narrative paths. Many hypermedia works, such as *Uncle Buddy* and the *Hypertext Hotel*, could not exist on paper and still retain their essential features.

Speculations about the future of cyberliterature abound in traditional literature today. For instance, concepts such as hypertext have led some people to predict the future popularity of what is called *ideasurfing* (or, if on the Net, *netsurfing*). Ideasurfing would differ from TV-channel surfing in that the latter usually has no theme to the medium-switching. In contrast, ideasurfing can be performed with unified themes in mind. For example, one might read one section of a book that talks about a topic, T, then click to arrive at another different book that also discusses T, and so on.

Will readers become so accustomed to fast, easy navigation through text that the old linear reading method will become obsolete? Put another way, will we become just as addicted to ideasurfing in the info-networked realm as many of us are to channel-surfing in the visual-TV realm? Perhaps, but we shouldn't lose our historical perspective, such as the fact that readers already skip around in printed books and magazines; or skim; or copy, cut, and paste parts of larger written works. Analogies to old media are always a good gauge, at least initially, for judging the new.

As cyberliterature grows beyond its current embryonic stage, I believe we will realize that its common thread, the ultimate power it affords, will be the free and near-total manipulation of text-based information. (With the addition of music, images, video, and other media, the discussion essentially moves beyond cyberliterature into related areas of multimedia covered elsewhere in this book.) Manipulation can be, as in hypertext, navigation among preexisting screens of text, wherein you essentially follow your own storylines. Or, manipulation can go further, as in works in which the readers have the option of adding to the work. Already, additions of new characters, new stories, and new connections are allowed in works such as *Marble Springs* and the *Hypertext Hotel* discussed earlier. And *Uncle Buddy* even features a computerized implementation of William S. Burroughs's "cut-up" method, wherein segments of text are extracted and then rearranged in a random sequence. Such manipulation can in some cases result in the creation of "nonsense," but sense is in the eye of the beholder. In addition, future versions of this form of "memetic recombination" might use AI methodology (such as rules for syntax and semantics and relevance) to create a higher percentage of meaningful sentences from this randomizing process.

One of the results of all this manipulative power within cyberliterature will be that different users will have different variations of an original cyberpiece. Perhaps in the future they will be stored on credit-card–sized data devices and traded like baseball cards are today. But the more general result will most likely be that future readers will increasingly expect interactivity in their written works, just as post-Gutenberg readers came to expect the availability of cheap, portable books centuries ago. We all know what happened after the printing press was invented and utilized by society: The speed of information transmission increased at an enormous rate. Will the speed increase caused by electronic availability and transmission of literature cause a social revolution as influential as that of the printing press? Some thinkers say yes. Yet others still believe that cyberliterature might always remain a sideline to mainstream written works. Even *Uncle Buddy* author McDaid claims that "[l]iterary hypertext will always be like PBS or Joyce—never as popular as Stephen King or *The Simpsons*." However, one could also imagine a Gutenberg-era gent claiming that small, portable books would never be as popular as good, old fashioned, minstrel-based storytelling.

The verdict on all this is probably still a few years away. Until then, here is one last thought to ponder: When the printing press was introduced, it did not have to compete with television, or VCRs, or virtual reality, or virtual village communications. Put another way, cyberliterature, if it continues to consist primarily of text, will only be relevant for those who still want to read. On the other (more optimistic) hand, cyberliterature's unique features and interactivity might actually stimulate (or should I say re-stimulate) enough interest in reading to keep it a meaningful form of expression in our ever-changing MTV-addled, jumpcut-addicted, visual-effects–laden culture. Thus cyberliterature, for all it can do to change the art of reading, may actually save it from becoming extinct.

RESOURCES

Anyone with Internet access can explore the *Hypertext Hotel*. First, get thee to the Internet (perhaps after reading Chapter 6 of this book). The best choice is to find a full-service provider with the ability to *telnet* (a kind of *tele*portation over the *network*, to a different computer somewhere on the Internet). Then *telnet* to *duke.cs.brown.edu* 8888 (8888 being the port number).

Although we only discussed William Gibson's *Agrippa* piece here, he also has electronic works that do *not* self-destruct. For example, *Neuromancer*, *Count Zero*, and *Mona Lisa Overdrive* are available on one floppy disk, one of a line of Voyager Expanded Books. Not only will using this disk show you some of the advantages of e-books, but the content deals with many issues related to cyberspace in general. For more information on Voyager's series of book-disks as well as their works on CD-ROM, contact The Voyager Company (Voyager Customer Service, 1 Bridge Street, Irvington, NY 10533).

To find out more about Collaborator, contact Collaborator Systems, Inc., P.O. Box 57557, Sherman Oaks, CA 91403, or call 818-980-2943.

To get more information on Dramatica, contact Screenplay Systems at 150 E. Olive Avenue, Suite 203, Burbank, CA 91502, or call 818-843-6557.

To get more information on FictionMaster, a creation of acclaimed author and teacher Sol Stein, call 800-755-1124 or 914-782-1255.

Eastgate Systems publishes a wide range of hypertext literature. To contact them, write to Civilized Software, P.O. Box 1307, Cambridge, MA 02238, or call 800-562-1638.

Finally, you may wish to use cyberspace itself to explore cyberliterature. For example, try reading and posting to the *alt.hypertext* USENET newsgroup, or call the Electronic Zone BBS at 412-349-3504 to experience an online service dedicated to hypertext.

The Children of Cyberjockeys

Technology was only a minor impact on my elementary and secondary education. But my daughters have not known a world where technology does not permeate everyday life.

Introduction

I remember my first encounter with computers. In eighth grade math, my teacher proudly introduced a Teletype machine and told us we would learn to program. The Teletype was connected to a university several miles away. We would enter our BASIC code one afternoon and receive compiler error messages the next. The hulking beige keyboard did little to inspire and a lot to discourage. No one, at least in my class, found the device magical or liberating. In eighth grade, of course, little seems magical or liberating—at least in the 1970s. We were the generation of 16mm movies, chalk boards, and disco music. We were also a generation of television.

That same eighth grade teacher was also the schools audio-visual director. He taught me how to wield a video camera, how to take out spools of magnetic tape and loop them through the 40-pound, reel-to-reel video tape recorder. I would take ghostly black-and-white video of school track meets and Friday night dances.

The children of cyberjockeys will grow up in a world where computers are commonplace. Much that they learn about that world will come to them in the multimedia glow of information streaming at them bit by bit. They will have different expectations than their parents and different ways of viewing the world. When information is so easy to come by, will the children know how to ask the right questions?

Today that eighth grade student is a sophisticated computer user, combining words, images, and text into multimedia productions. Today that eighth grader plans the future of networks and computers for a major aerospace company. Today that eighth grader speculates on the impact of our inventions. It is through the eyes of that eighth grader that we will explore his children's future.

Technology was only a minor impact on my elementary and secondary education. But my daughters, Rachel and Alyssa, at 4 and 2, have not known a world where technology does not permeate everyday life. My multiple computers greeted them at birth. And even in the two years between their births, things changed dramatically. In 1989, I scanned-in black-and-white pictures of Rachel right after birth to show her off to colleagues at work. In 1992, I digitized the video of Alyssa's birth and brought it to work on a few floppy disks. Still images were replaced by moving images and sound.

Steve Jobs has succeeded in selling the idea of the computer as an appliance. Computers control our microwave ovens, our entertainment centers, and eventually, will control our television sets. At less than $1,000 for a basic system, computers are affordable by anyone who has a television. High-end multimedia will eventually arrive at prices affordable by the masses. Computers are no longer the end in themselves.

PROGRAMMING AND BEYOND

Large computers never found their way into the space between chalkboard and desk. It was the microcomputer that first touched children. Microcomputers found radical use early in their careers. People had the unbelievable thought that computers were good for teaching computer science. Much of my early experience with computers focused on the BASIC programming language. For most early computers, there was no difference between BASIC and the operating system. Writing to a disk or saving to tape was just a BASIC extension.

BASIC programs weren't very exciting in and of themselves. People started taking the simple examples in their tutorial books and turning BASIC into a language of their own. Many early programs focused on education. Teachers, turned programmers, quickly developed programs for plotting algebraic equations, displaying facts on flashcards, facilitating simple simulations, challenging students with educational games, and reinforcing lessons with computer-aided instruction.

Few, if any, of these computer uses did more than could be done with peers in the classroom. The following simple BASIC application for creating self-correcting addition problems does little more than relieve the teacher of holding up a flash card and waiting for the correct answer:

```
10 X=INT(RND(TI)*10)
20 X=INT (RND(TI)*10)
30 PRINT X"+"Y"=";
40 INPUT Z
50 IF Z=X+Y THEN 10
60 PRINT "WRONG ANSWER, PLEASE TRY AGAIN."
70 GOTO 30
```

This program simply spreads the expertise around the room. Several students could use the same knowledge, all with different problems. Back when problems like this were common, though, teachers were lucky to have one computer for every few classrooms. The program did not preclude repetition, it didn't instruct in process, and it didn't provide positive reinforcement.

Because teachers were not masters of computers, they used simplistic approaches in presenting their material. Because they were not masters of computers, they taught simplistic ideas to children when they coached them in computer science.

But this early exposure to computers did positively affect the lives of these children, including myself. For every Apple Plus, Commodore PET or TRS-80 model 1, a few children applied their imagination. While some children saw paper, crayons, or clay as their vehicles for manipulating the world, other children saw the computer as their paint brush and canvas. In the early days of personal computing, children did not necessarily know how to unleash their creativity. But they dreamed. They saw possibilities in the green characters that scrolled before them.

Initially programming proved the only connection between children and the computer. Once the novelty of interacting with a computer for instruction wore off, all that was left was conquering the box itself. Once you learned about memory, tape, and displays—about IN-PUT, PRINT, and GOTO—the box became an annoying reminder of your inability to move beyond the simple examples in the tutorial and make it do something you wanted it to do.

For some students, programming became a challenge. They wanted to simulate the spin of the planets, solve mathematics problems, or find better ways to print a copy of Snoopy on the noisy dot matrix printer. For the majority though, an occasional encounter was sufficient. It was much more interesting to paint or play music or read a book.

Not all programming is limited. BASIC was a complex and expressive language. Few teachers, however, mastered the language to the point that they could inspire rather than instruct. Other languages were much better suited to exploration and manipulation. Perhaps the most expressive language is LIST Processing language (LISP). LISP was developed to manipulate symbols, and eventually became the language of artificial intelligence. LISP, though, is a rich and complex language with little specialization for education. It is not meant for exploration by children, and it requires far more computer power than an elementary or secondary school could muster.

LOGO, on the other hand, was intended for children. Invented by Seymour Papert more than 25 years ago, LOGO has become a standard tool for children interacting with computers. Rather than teaching children how to program, LOGO is geared to teaching children how to build model worlds that they care about and understand. The end result is not the program, but the experience of interacting with the computer and influencing its outcome.

LOGO's turtle graphics create a visual connection between child and activity. The turtle responds instantly to a few simple commands, resulting in images of extraordinarily complex and intriguing patterns. LOGO, like tinker toys, enables children to build upon components of their own invention, or share pieces of code written by others. With LOGO, the computer becomes a place of discovery and sharing, far from the impersonal, isolationist model in which it is often portrayed.

The programs described in BASIC were concerned with putting rote facts into the child. The experience of learning to program in BASIC taught BASIC programming. With LOGO, the experience of learning LOGO teaches the ideas behind the programs more than the programs themselves. To the child, the world is filled with sights and sounds. Experiential learning leads to a mastery of the spoken word. But rather than create an extension of that mind-engrossing natural world to add written language and mathematics, we develop formalisms that remove children from the unorganized world that successfully taught them speech and verbal understanding. For Papert, the computer represents a carrier of cultural information.

Computers can reintroduce the informal. The written language and math skills will evolve from play and exploration, rather than teaching. In Papert's vision, children realize the connections between ideas as they are ready, rather than when they are told. Children retain these realizations and connections because they have invested their energy, in their own time, and the result of their own awareness of the connection creates an emotional link that helps retain the content.

LOGO provides children with a means of exploring the computer and manipulating symbols within its memories. But the computer has progressed past even the dreams of LOGO's inventor and champions.

. . . .

Computers can reintroduce the informal. The written language and math skills will evolve from play and exploration, rather than teaching.

To the child uninterested in creating computer applications, the computer is now a learning tool. Almost anything that can be done in the real world can be performed in the computer. You can read, calculate equations, write stories, and draw pictures. The computer has changed all of these. You can attach electronic notes to pages or words in an electronic book, you can graph equations interactively, you can pop-up a thesaurus or dictionary while you write a story, and you can erase lines on a sketch to your heart's content, without smudging the drawing or dirtying your hands.

What is even more amazing is that you can do all of these things in the classroom, at home, in a hotel room, or in the back seat of a car. The computer can also provide guidance and constraint. Structure and leniency. Personal exploration and lecture. Programming is but a part of the computing experience. The majority of the time, computers facilitate the imagination.

THE PRESCHOOL YEARS

Programs like Peter's Alphabet Adventure enable children to interact with the computer in subtle and sophisticated ways, without thinking about the computer. As they learn letters and find words associated with them, the program provides games that reinforce the learning.

I received several CD-ROMs from the StarCore software subsidiary of Apple Computer. I placed StarCore's Peter's Alphabet Adventure into the CD carrier, mounted the disk, and double-clicked the application—then left the room. Without a word of instruction, my 4-year-old daughter, Rachel, was moving from letter to letter. She knew how to return to the menu, and how to enter the games and additional information attached to a letter.

Rachel expected interaction. She expected pictures to do something. She also expected the somethings in the picture to pretty much behave like they do in the real world. Clicking on a covered dish should remove the cover. Everything should do something.

Homewor! Oh Homework!

🖼 if only a bomb
🖼 would explode you to bits.
🖼 Homework! Oh, homework!
🖼 You're giving me fits.

● This is the story of the Tortoise and the Hare. The Tortoise was a friendly fellow who moved at his own slow pace. The Hare was a busy person who was always on the move.

We went to the beach, just Grandma and me.

Brøderbund's Living Books series reads to children and lets them interact with the environment of the words. Each word, each object does something to maintain interest within the context of the story. These pictures illustrate three of the Living Books. In The New Kid on the Block, poet Jack Prelutsky's poems come to life. In the Tortoise and the Hare, the Aesop fable is retold with humor and fun graphics. Just Grandma and Me delivers an interactive version of the Mercer Mayer book.

Lawrence
Production's
McGee gently
moves children into
the world of
computers by
restricting move-
ment of the mouse
to just the four
boxes on the
bottom of the
screen. It keeps its
world simple
enough that
children won't get
frustrated, and
lively enough that
they won't get
bored too quickly.

Rachel also enjoys learning words through Brøderbund's Living Book series. These sophisticated but easy to use interactive CDs act as reader and companion. Each scene begins with a reading of the book text, followed by an exploration of the environment by the child. The words remain interactive and repeat their proper pronunciation as often as they are clicked.

Rachel mastered the computer through Lawrence Production's McGee and Katie's Farm. Unlike more advanced games, these two smallish adventure games constrained Rachel and the track ball to four boxes along the bottom of the screen. Click any of the four boxes and an activity occurs in the current location, or a location change takes place.

At four, Rachel is learning to read. She is bored with McGee and Katie and demands more interaction. She spends hours clicking on animals and learning about their activities in Prehistoria and Dinosaurs from Microsoft. And she enjoys the combination of games and video in Media Design Interactive's Cute'n'Cuddlies. She has grown from expecting reaction to expecting control.

Brøderbund's Backyard plays a transitional role. Birds sing, fish swim, and music plays, but Rachel can also create faces on a scarecrow, search for treasure with a robot digger, learn about animal habitats and behavior, and play tic-tac-toe.

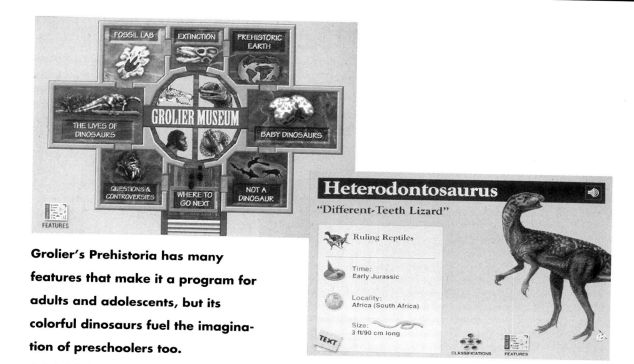

Grolier's Prehistoria has many features that make it a program for adults and adolescents, but its colorful dinosaurs fuel the imagination of preschoolers too.

Children can control their environment on the computer. Backyard from Brøderbund provides many interactive toys that make music and become animated at the click of the mouse. As children click on more items, many of them move into editors or games that teach children direction, computer control, reaching goals, and so on. They are in charge of their own destiny.

Children's programs like Storybook Weaver help them learn the rudiments of computer operation while crafting a tale.

Suddenly, out of nowhere, the serpent appeared alongside the galleon, tossing the ship wildly amidst the raging sea.

By the time Rachel reaches kindergarten, she will be master of all basic computer skills. She will know how to click and drag, enter numbers and letters on the keyboard, pull down menus, and start and end programs.

From the youngest age, children expect computers to do their bidding. Computers create highly visual, highly plastic learning environments. From those beginnings—and throughout their education and adult lives—the children of cyberjockeys will demand their information immediately, interactively, and visually. The rich sensory experiences of the pre-K years will demand much of the virtual classroom.

THE VIRTUAL CLASSROOM

The world has always been a place to learn. Children who travel always seem more sophisticated than their homebound peers. Yet even with travel, the pace of learning outside the classroom was slow. You had to read, experience, and assimilate in the slow pace afforded by time and budgets. The classroom was the home of the learning materials. It was the place of structured thought and skills not available elsewhere. Children learned because the school facilitated the learning.

The computer has destroyed the classroom—at least the classroom as it is known today. The computer has introduced distributed knowledge. It has crumbled the walls between rooms and the walls between schools and states and countries. It has even torn down the wall of time. Now, your teacher is not the only teacher you have access to. Books come alive on CD-ROM and are read sometimes by their authors or augmented with copious notes. Long-dead dignitaries babble haunting inspirations—indistinguishable from the living human teacher that floats in another window on the timeless, placeless computer desktop.

Information is everywhere and accessible. It is not even necessary to go to the library for research. Online information services provide instant results to well-crafted searches. This mass of information will mean changing expectations by both educators and students. Teachers will expect correct answers to facts. Rote learning will become unimportant. Why force children to remember facts that are only good for one test, then forgotten until relearned for some other test in the future?

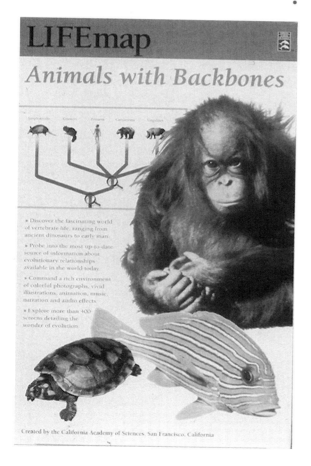

LIFEmap
Animals with Backbones

- Discover the fascinating world of vertebrate life, ranging from ancient dinosaurs to early man.
- Probe into the most up-to-date source of information about evolutionary relationships available in the world today.
- Command a rich environment of colorful photographs, vivid illustrations, animation, music, narration and audio effects.
- Explore more than 400 screens detailing the wonder of evolution.

Created by the California Academy of Sciences, San Francisco, California

No piece of information is without context. Computers provide children a means to wander the webs of data and information that exist in capture forms like the Grolier's Prehistoria CD or the McGraw-Hill Science and Technical Reference CD. On the Internet the information is less intensely visual and aural, but more distributed and deeper.

> Many educational tools and experiences from the 1950s to the 1990s will find new analogs in the age of electronic information. Chalkboards will be replaced by desktop conferencing software. Notepads will be exchanged for personal digital assistants. Fingerpaint will become a digitizing tablet.

Rote learning will be replaced by connective learning. Facts will be learned in context as children explore hyperlinked ideas on a network. They will remember 1776 and 1812, not because they were forced to remember a pair of disconnected dates, but because they will see the actions, read the original documents, draw from connections of others, and add their own interpretation. The facts will be concrete rather than abstract.

So how will connective learning change students' expectations? Children will expect visual and holistic learning. They will expect images and sounds to accompany text. Movies, even if historical recreations, will communicate the meaning of moments. Simulations will allow them to intervene in historical events, changing the course of history and viewing the repercussions. They will see a Hitler-dominated 20th century or a Stalin-dominated China. They also will see a British/French America saved from civil war but under constant alert at borders that run from Europe to Mexico, or a world where nuclear weapons found targets rather than disassembly hangars.

The contact with today will place a new importance on history. It is rare that a child understands why history is important. Computers will display deeply moving exposition on the meaning of historical events. By isolating chunks of history and seeing their connections, every child will be able to explore the threads of events that created this world. Charles Burke's The Day the World Changed and Connections will be magnified a thousand-fold by children all over the world tracing and connecting their own linkages through history.

Social visionary Marshall McLuhan saw the creation of individual learning connections coming in 1964 when he wrote: "In education the conventional division of the curriculum into subjects is already as outdated as the medieval trivium and quadrivium after the Renaissance. Any subject taken in depth at once relates to other subjects. Arithmetic in grade 3 or 9, when taught in terms of number theory, symbolic logic, and cultural history, ceases to be mere practice in problems. Continued in their present patterns of fragmented unrelation, our school curricula will insure a citizenry unable to understand the cybernated world in which they live."

Many educational tools and experiences from the 1950s to the 1990s will find new analogs in the age of electronic information. Chalkboards will be replaced by desktop conferencing software. Notepads will be exchanged for personal digital assistants. Fingerpaint will become a digitizing tablet.

Of course, construction paper and scissors will still exist. Children will continue to play with clay and sand and glue feathers and cardboard. But non-tactile will be as common as the tactile. The thing modeled with clay may be just as easily modeled in the virtual 3-D of a computer. The charcoal drawing that frustratingly smears with every stroke on paper, remains impressively clean on the computer screen.

SimEarth from Maxis illustrates the kind of teaching computers can help facilitate. Rather than discuss the cause and effect of actions on history, children can play God and run the planet themselves. Foolish decisions lead to overheated planets. Innovation may lead to intelligent dinosaurs, or even man.

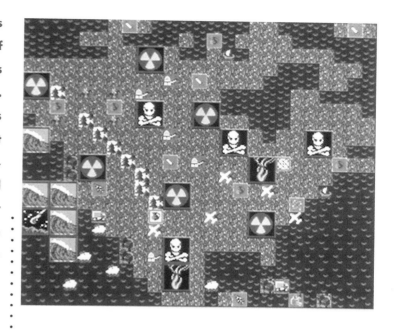

Devices like Apple's Newton turn writing into an art. Paper and pencil transform into digital ink and scrolling electric paper. The Newton recognizes handwriting and captures sketches. Anything entered into a Newton can later be uploaded to a personal computer.

Lab class will never be the same. Instead of dissecting a frog with a lab partner next to you, you may find yourself sharing a frog's gut view of the project with another student several miles away.

The most important aspect to future education will not be media, but means. We have already discussed the vastness of the information available. Along with that information will come instructors from universities, poets, philosophers, and the science teacher from the school across town. When a child dissects a frog, he or she may do so not just with a lab partner, but with another classmate halfway across the country. Built-in translation software will make even the most distant collaborator sound like a native.

Computer memory is long. And the people teaching your children need not be alive. I recently received a wonderful CD of Marvin Minsky from Voyager. The CD brings the full text of Minsky's *The Society of Mind* to disk, as well as personal remarks by Minsky delivered as QuickTime movies, integrated with the text. It even contains a picture of Minsky's living room, where he ruminates on the technology and ideas of AI and the human mind.

Digital forms of media like Apple's QuickTime allow even children to create works of art thought unattainable just a few years ago. Your child need not wait for a scholarship to the U.S.C. School of Film to edit a picture of Dad or tulips. *Courtesy of Apple Computer.*

The Society of Mind embraces many virtual classroom concepts. It provides the book electronically. It can be read linearly, as a paper book is read, or it can be explored out of sequence, searched, annotated, and explained. The book delivers Minsky as a personal tutor, ready upon demand to elucidate a chapter or add a bit of wit. Minsky's experience becomes accessible to people ill-equipped to visit Boston, let alone afford an MIT education. And finally, the book provides integration. The text, animations, pictures, and movies join effortlessly through a well-conceived user interface. All of this in an electronic book produced in 1994.

Allow your imagination to run forward several years. The small images of Minsky are replaced by full screen with stereo sound. The theories come alive in agents on the computer that actually illustrate Minsky's thoughts, and with the click of a button, show how recent discoveries have modified the theories. From 1994 and beyond, Minsky's ideas remain his, spoken by him and always available. The process engulfs the reader in the experience and history of ideas. The inventor

Marvin Minsky, quite alive as of this writing, brings his unique insight on humanity to the little screen with Voyager's first person: Marvin Minsky *The Society of Mind*. The CD contains the complete text of Minsky's *The Society of Mind* along with interactive illustrations and QuickTime movies of Minsky expanding on the written text. Future generations will still have access to Minsky through this digital version of his work.

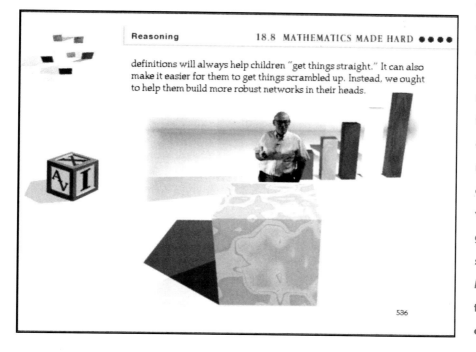

Reasoning   18.8 MATHEMATICS MADE HARD ● ● ● ●

definitions will always help children "get things straight." It can also make it easier for them to get things scrambled up. Instead, we ought to help them build more robust networks in their heads.

536

always remains attached to the creation, even through generations of refinement and modification.

Video tapes and movies teach in the order, manner, and fashion of the director, cinematographer, and editor. With multimedia systems, fragments of thought enhance self-discovered insights. The child who's learning becomes director and editor, and shapes raw knowledge into a form that brings personal interest and personal fulfillment.

Much of the current problem with children dropping out of school comes from sources other than education. With computers, though, we could excite imaginations and perhaps have children willing to drop in than drop out. As expectations of interaction evolve, children will want to maintain control of their learning environment. We teach them LOGO turtles in fourth grade and subject them to boring lectures in eighth. The ideas of LOGO can apply to disciplines beyond mathematics. We can create programs for exploring philosophy or history, sports or finance. If the learning environment becomes personalized, disfranchised youth may find some reason for self-definition in the classroom.

Swiss psychiatrist C.G. Jung wrote about three types of education: education through example, collective education, and individual education. Education by example has proven the oldest and most effective. We learn by emulating others. Jung covers the other two in the following statement about individual learning: "In applying this method, all rules, principles, and systems must be subordinated to the one purpose of bringing out the specific individuality of the pupil. This aim is directly opposed to that of collective education, which seeks to level out and make uniform."

Schools mingle the individual with the collective. Computers combine example and individual. It was feared that computers would become the dagger of those seeking conformity, but instead they have become the antithesis of the collective.

For children with access to the vast resources of the net, the world will be just that much bigger than it was for us. We need to help them to find their answers, but also help them form their questions. Knowledge is deceptively easy to find. Facts are confused with knowledge and thinking is confused with access. In the age of information, finding answers will be trivial. Asking the right questions and understanding the relationships between answers will be the key to success.

GAMES

I once played Pong—a little green dot, bouncing between two thin rectangles. Not very exciting. Yet, we would play it for hours. Then realism, so we thought: a gun, a joy stick, a fuzzy muddle of color, and strange sounds of death, destruction, and joy.

Games are the largest segment of the consumer computer industry. In fact, the computer game industry out-grossed the motion picture industry in 1993. From Chess to GO, from checkers to pinball, from spinning a dreidel to breaking a piñata, games have always been important indicators of cultural value. And of course, we have baseball, football, hockey, basketball, and golf to entertain us as well.

All of those sports have found their way into computer games. Most are less exciting than the real thing, yet on days without ice or when the ballpark is miles away, they will suffice. Perhaps board games actually gain from computer renditions. With Interplay's Battlechess, the soldiers fight and die instead of sliding spontaneously off the board. With *Star Wars* chess, the famous hologram from the original *Star Wars* movie comes to life on the screen, in a much less realistic rendering than Lucas's film version.

Game machines like Nintendo's Super NES bring sophisticated computer games to a television set

Chewbacca does chess.

Games are not just for children. They can promote interactive learning, but can foster isolationism when latchkey children find them the only companion after school.

The children that play those games change subtlety. They do not become the wide-eyed addicts of computer lore, but they do become more accepting of technology. Games are always the first place I send new computer users. If people can be disarmed by a few rounds of digital Wheel of Fortune, then they are likely to take more easily to Microsoft Word or Excel.

Adults like to play games, but usually not the games their children play. Adults grow weary quickly of early computer games. Children strive onward in search of higher scores. McLuhan finds that "games are popular art, collective, social reactions to the main drive or action of any culture. Games, like institutions, are extensions of social man and of the body politic, as technologies are extensions of the animal organism. Both games and technologies are counter-irritants or ways of adjusting to the stress of the specialized actions that occur in any social group. As extensions of the popular response to the workaday stress, games become faithful models of a culture. They incorporate both the action and the reaction of whole populations in a single dynamic image."

And our games do indeed reflect our society. They have become more colorful and more engaging. They have become both more educational and more violent. As our society reacts to the violence and chaos, some companies, like Brøderbund, strive to create games that teach. We call this Edutainment. But some Sega and Nintendo developers find it profitable to appeal to violent emotions. Games like Mortal Kombat have focused the attention of the nation on violence in computer games. The industry recently moved to rate their games for consumption, but of course, children will find a way of getting what they want, despite the rating system.

Every major game in the world has found a computer analog. Nintendo's Ken Griffey Jr. Presents: Major League Baseball brings America's favorite pastime to the one thing that may prove to be its most ardent rival.

Brøderbund's Myst and Warner New Media's Hell Cab bring new levels of realism to games on Macintoshs and PCs. These photorealistic adventures combine interactive exploration with original music and more than a few surprises.

The moral outrage at the computer game industry is directed, it seems, to the whole industry, not just the segment making violent or sexual games. As with the movie industry, any rating system applies to all. On the whole, the industry has potential for positive social change. There are plenty of games that reflect nostalgia and the future, without resorting to blood running down the gutters of a television monitor.

. . . .

Berkeley Systems brings full-color renditions of *Star Trek*, Marvel Comics, and Disney characters to the computer. They aren't exactly games, but they can create hours of diversion.

Disney licenses its images in such games as Mickey's Ultimate Challenge. You can even buy screen savers that fill idle CPU cycles with Beauty and the Beast and Donald Duck painting titled pictures of his famous mouse partner. Gene Roddenberry's *Star Trek* comes to life in several games. In these games, as in the television show, the realization that we make it into the 23rd century remains a constant, even though an occasional bad guy bites the dust, albeit with good taste.

But as we have seen in other media outlets, all choices abound. The world is a large market with a wide variety of tastes. People will always want to shoot bad guys, with varying degrees of gratuitousness. People will want to be challenged intellectually, as in chess, some with more flourish than others. And people will want to assume the role of another, save a princess or defend childhood from Captain Hook. Others will want to explore new worlds, alone or with computerized characters, to help them escape from the all-too-real world itself.

From the technology standpoint, games will come with increasing fidelity. The old Pong game and its green paddles hold little interest compared to 32-bit rendered images in real-time. CD and hard memory have already become dominant game delivery technologies. New game platforms like 3DO and CD-I blur the connection between game machine

Mario Paint and Mouse blurs the edge between computer and game machines. Children paint, draw, and record animations with joy stick or mouse.

and computer. They become new metaphors for interacting with computers rather than new game machines. And even machines like Nintendo's Super NES become more computer-like when you load them with Super Mario Paint, where children can create music and illustrate images that can be captured to video tape for posterity. The game machine becomes a family tool for interaction and memory, disarming the game critics by pointing to content rather than form.

The amount of information contained in games will increase dramatically. Realistic adventures require megabytes of information. The beautifully rendered Myst from Brøderbund contains more than 500 megabytes of images and original score. Although Myst is not virtual reality, you can become so engrossed in it that you begin feeling like you are on one of its distant planets. And eventually, virtual reality will become more real than hype, and games will take on more intensive special effects.

Games will eventually break the boundaries of local memory. Like the old network Star Trek games on UNIX, the Internet will provide a conduit for new socializations based around the computer. And that leads us from games to community. Games, after all, reflect community. And it is in community and community standards that we place our own children in context.

THE ONLINE COMMUNITY

When speaking of our children's behavior, we use our morals as a yardstick. We determine good and bad behavior also from looking at the behavior of peers. In a violent society, good has a different meaning than it does in a nonviolent society. In the future, our children will not be restricted to the local community. Some of their behavior will reflect the behavior of the online community. The language and behavioral norms our children absorb will come not just from places in which we interact with them, like in front of the family television, at dinner, or at a movie theater—it will happen online.

In the case of TV, music, or movies, we have access to the information. Our children will sneak around us to listen to music we would rather they didn't, or go to a movie that doesn't reflect our standards, but no matter what they do in those situations, we are easily aware of the content of the music and images. We can see the movie, we can read about the movie, and we can talk to others about the movie.

Online is different. Online, children can gain knowledge that is disconnected from society as a whole. They can gain private movement in distant parts of the net, conversing on any subject at any time. Much of this will be positive, but some will conjure our worst nightmares.

An April 18, 1994 story in *Newsweek* recounts tales of pedophiles stalking children online. In one case, a 27-year-old computer engineer convinced a 14-year-old boy to meet him through America Online. During the meeting the pedophile performed several sex acts, later resulting in two counts of oral copulation and one count of sodomy. The perpetrator later pleaded guilty. This is not an isolated case. As the range of access to the Internet moves from academia and aerospace to the general public, the attitude of the Internet will begin to reflect the morals of the general public.

The online community of the Internet will mirror our society in its wide range of interests, cultural diversity, and political polarization. The internet removes the inhibitions and prejudices of the anonymous and famous alike. The racial or religious hatred of the street corner finds no sanction on the net. The character-based interface to the net hides all but ideas and behaviors.

· · · · · · · · · · · ·

The fidelity of the net will increase, but the technology of deception and anonymity will remain. The persona of the person on the net need not be her own, or even human. In the future when images of people are available for online conferences, the faces displayed may in some cases be real, and in others, as fanciful as the masks in the *Star Wars* cantina.

Our children will learn to value thoughts and decorum over sight or sound. And computers will even break down the wall of ideas that separate people. Online you can find the Bible, the Koran, and works of philosophy. I learned much of what I know by expanding the reading selection of my parents' bookcases. Many children do not have that opportunity. Even visits to a local library can be restricted—even if you find a library adequately funded with a good selection of books and a community that cares for the condition of its ideas. On the net, the ideas are there for those who search.

7 Days in August from Warner New Media transports the viewer back to the middle of the cold war, documenting the rise of the Berlin Wall.

REPEAT   NEXT PROFILE   GUIDE   SUNDAY

Sunday, August 13

Time **magazine photo-journalist P.F. Bentley captures the rise of President Bill Clinton from the earliest days in the primaries. These black-and-white photographs capture the anguish and triumph of the campaign. Excellent narration and QuickTime videos make this truly a historical record.**

Online, ideas lead to ideas. Children will find new things through interactive conversations. Words will spark interest and interest will drive exploration. Exploration will lead to discovery.

As digital format becomes more the accepted means of storing ideas and history, much that is now on paper will be in the computer. Eventually, something like the banter on the Internet will exist solely in digital format. In a time not too distant, our children will connect to their history through the computer. They will see their grandfather tell stories, perhaps even be able to respond to knock-knock jokes from an ancestor who, to our generation, would be little more than a few dusty photos or a flickering image in a silent movie.

Denizens of the 1990s often find themselves stuck on the disintegration of community. The 1990s is a time of communal transition. The old nuclear family and cloistered neighborhoods have dissolved as the global village shouted down the barriers. But nothing replaced the connection and grounding of the nuclear family and its community. Perhaps it is through the computer that people will find new ways to connect themselves to society. Within a few moments of turning on my modem, I can be conversing with hundreds of people around the world. My children will be able to see them, and perhaps touch them.

Not just personal history, but national and international history will be preserved in digital form. The excellent

The Campaign

The Primaries

The Convention

On the Road

The Debates

A Bold Finale

history series of Warner Newmedia brings the Clinton Presidential Victory, the Gulf War, and the building of the Berlin Wall to the computer. These digital forms will grow over time. Even the 650MB of a CD is insufficient to capture all the moments.

I spelunked the Clinton CD, hoping for a sound bite of "Don't Stop Thinking About Tomorrow." I found only fragments of speeches and narration. The CD brought me the history but did not enable me to connect my personal recollection and emotions. The moment I most remembered about the night of Clinton's inauguration, and the memory I wanted to share with my children, does not exist on the disk. I will have to wait for a future edition to fulfill my expectations.

New compression routines and larger memory technologies press more information into smaller spaces. And on the network, the archives of news organizations will eventually find their way to the consumer. At that point, we will search not just for text, but search for frames of image and bytes of sound. History will become personal.

Much of history was oral. In the early parts of this millennium, the Talmud codified Jewish oral law. It reads somewhat like an Internet conversation: point, counter-point, clarifications, but no definitive answers. The minority opinion remains. Companies like Chicago's Davka Corporation are publishing ancient communal memories, like the Talmud, in digital form. All national and religious law has become increasingly decentralized, isolated, and personalized. It is perhaps in cyberspace that dialog and consensus will find a renaissance.

Information technology may enable people around the world to once more discuss the issues of their culture. It will also be the place the global village erects its forum. Cyberspace is a large place for large meetings, and the minutes can last forever, retaining all the immediacy of the moment.

No matter how sophisticated the interaction becomes, connections will be made. Communities will no longer be rooted in the Sunday evening dinner at the church, but in the Sunday evening banter in the Kid's Corner, or in a thousand other intimate gatherings taking place between people on the net. We can see President Kennedy making a speech and watch Grandma's 1971 turkey emerge from the oven on Thanksgiving. We will influence national policy and spend hours in rapt intercourse on black holes, cookie recipes, and a single line of Deuteronomy. Family, community, national, and international history will coalesce in the memory of our computer.

The Compton's Interactive Encyclopedia and Grolier's Multimedia Encyclopedia bring context to history. They combine well-thought-out text with graphics, sound, animation and video to link history in ways unavailable in printed encyclopedias.

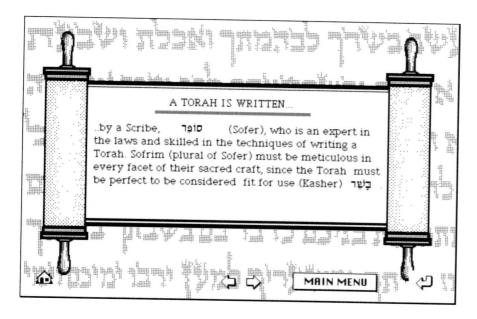

A TORAH IS WRITTEN...

..by a Scribe, סוֹפֵר (Sofer), who is an expert in the laws and skilled in the techniques of writing a Torah. Sofrim (plural of Sofer) must be meticulous in every facet of their sacred craft, since the Torah must be perfect to be considered fit for use (Kasher) כָּשֵׁר.

MAIN MENU

GOING WHERE NO CHILD HAS GONE BEFORE

Travel changes people's views of the world. Standing on the edge of the Grand Canyon and looking into its depths gives a child a concrete understanding of the world's enormity. To a child, the gaping canyon carved by the Colorado River becomes a time machine, etching swaths of history out of the earth, exposing fossil leaf and fossil fish.

To many children, the adventure of the Grand Canyon, perhaps only a few hundred miles away, remains a set of faded still images, or the moving, uncontrolled vision of a place presented on television. There is little hope of discovering one's own path along the river.

Products like Davka's VeZOT HaTORAH bring history to children in new ways. This set of HyperCard stacks teaches Jewish children about their history through singing prayers and exploring how the Torah is constructed and who writes the words on them. Oral history, confined until recently to inactive paper, becomes aural and visual on the computer.

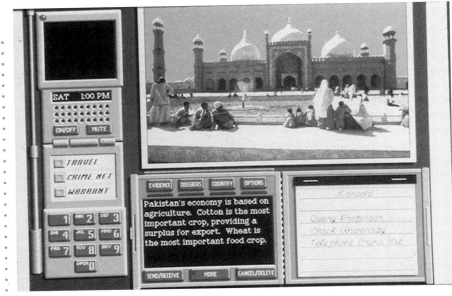

Brøderbund's Carmen SanDiego series has spawned television shows and merchandise. Children play this game by knowing facts about geography and history.

Computers enable children to go places they could not visit alone. Interactive television will let children guide the camera. On CD and online, they will explore the world, linking place to place, searching crevices, and standing on a precipice overlooking the Nile Valley.

Although computers will never replace actual travel, they will make the sights and sounds of a place available on demand. You can stroll down a busy market and buy a loaf of bread or turn on adventure mode and steal the bread while guards chase you, like Aladdin.

McLuhan described a global village—a world so shrunk by technology that even the most remote outposts seemed familiar and connected. First the telegraph, then radio, then television, and now computers. And unlike previous technologies, computers do not require others to initiate a conversation or a signal.

I watch my girls in amazement as they become absorbed in *Where In the World Is Carmen SanDiego?* on public television. The computer game was so well done, it spawned sequels and a television show. You can even buy Carmen SanDiego backpacks. For $60, the CD version of the game provides 150 digitized traditional and folk music selections, 130 digitized photographs, 3,000 clues, some spoken in the native tongue, exploration of 60 countries, and hundreds of animated segments. My children know things, from the disc and from the television, that I did not know until I learned it with them.

Exploring the world with computers is not a learning experience constrained to the young; it is an experience for everyone who wants to learn or add a bit of adventure to life.

CDs help bring far-off places closer to home. Children become their own tour guides as they wander the ancient ruins of Teotihuacan.

FINDING DAD'S DIRTY CDs

The change from paper to digital will also change the interaction between child and adult. I remember waiting for my parents to leave so I could go out to Dad's work area, reach up to the top of his gun rack, and bring down a dirty magazine or two. I'm sure the top shelf of my bookcase or the underneath of my bed will someday be equally explored. Only under there, next to the magazines, a budding adolescent is likely to find an explicit CD or two.

I remember my father getting ready for his birds and bees talk. I said, "Wait a minute," and ran out to get my textbooks. I explained more to my father about the reproductive process than he wanted to know. We both failed to touch upon intimacy or love.

CDs make sexual acts more explicit without necessarily touching upon intimacy or love either. And as the still images come alive, the acts become more vivid.

Computers change social barriers. In the 1950s, 1960s and 1970s, adult material existed in the form of movies. In the 1980s it was video tape. In the 1990s and beyond, CDs and other interactive media will have an ever-increasing role in adult entertainment. And since adult entertainment is usually not confined to adults, many adolescents will be introduced to sexual situations, benign and deviant, through the point and click of the mouse.

At MacWorld 1993 in San Francisco, several attendees complained about the adult CD booths on the floor. Large curtains separated show visitors from the throngs of viewers pushing past each other to get a glimpse of a woman shrunken down to a postage-sized QuickTime movie dancing or performing intercourse. Explicit QuickTime movies found room on the show floor as did Reactor's Virtual Valery, a digital woman that lets men take their own version of an adventure ride.

The April 1994 NewMedia Expo in Los Angeles found CD-ROM–based interactive video playing directly on the open show floor while CD-ROM vixens autographed posters of their latest digital engagements. Newness wears off and banality follows.

Adolescents have always found ways to explore explicit sexual material. It could be argued that CD-ROM–based material makes it harder to sneak

behind the house. Within 20 years portable multimedia computers will be so commonplace that taking a CD "out back" will be as easy as taking a magazine.

This section was not included so I could moralize about computer-based erotica and pornography. I included it to illustrate that even in areas far from traditional education, the move to multimedia learning will affect a change that links the mundane with the lofty. The acts of sex in classic literature will not remain unintelligible for long. Children reading Erica Jong or D.H. Lawrence will be able to link their favorite passages to images close to those described. If the links do not exist, they will create them.

CDs like BodyCello's Desktop Voyeur series tie a story line to the adult material. Not all of these CDs are hardcore. Titles like Desktop Voyeur are more digital tease than electronic orgasm.

Males and females will spend a lot of money creating these items of voyeurism. Income from these interactive excursions will fund some of our future infrastructure. As with 900 numbers, CD-ROM and other interactive media moves technology from esoteric to erotic. If we can deliver or view pornography on it, how difficult can it be to understand?

For centuries children expanded their sexual educations by finding Daddy's dirty paper, book, magazine, or cave painting. The network delivers access to information—any and all information. Our attempts to restrict classes of information once it becomes digital is bound to fail as much as making sure that only 21-year-olds dial phone sex numbers. This will exist online, on CD, and on our computers, and it will be bound up in the ever-widening web of self-education our children and our children's children will construct.

CHANGING EXPECTATIONS

The expectations for our children and their children will be very different. We grew up in a tactile world of real things. Things we imagined, we drew or sculpted. Our imagination spawned mental images while daydreaming on a school bus, or behind closed eyes during the mental twilight before sleep. With television and movies, the imaginations of a handful of people could be shared, but we could do little to participate in the creation, outside of our applause, silence, or our tears.

My daughters will not know a world without computers. They will not know a world without electronic books, mice, and computer animation. Although they have hundreds of children's books, they love to sit for hours and click dinosaurs, pumpkin heads, and penguins, record sounds or movies, or construct their own stories. At two, seeing herself on the computer fascinates Alyssa. She screams and giggles with each three second playback. She will take digital video for granted, as we took for granted 8mm movies or video tape.

And Rachel and Alyssa will also expect their classrooms to be the kind of learning environment they find in Dad's computer. They will expect exquisite color and things that move and growl. Books will have great meaning to this generation because they will learn that value from us. But as they grow up, they will see Dad and Mom take more and more advantage of electronic sources of information. And they will take advantage of those sources even more than we do. Even as an expert in computers, I find it a challenge to explore new software or information sources. My children will find that exploration as easy as I find typing. Their thought processes will be trained to look for information, and they will work with computer keyboard, mouse, and voice recognition as though they existed on the first day of creation.

They will also expect things instantly. They will have little patience. The computer does not teach Taoism—it teaches capitalism and instant gratification. Technology informs instantly and without question. Depending on the source, the answer may be useful, or totally meaningless. But the computer will always provide the answer promptly.

And in a world full of computers, what will computer literacy mean? Will it mean a CPU you command with C++, or will it mean asking carefully phrased questions that produce results? I think the latter. Those in the first case, the programmers, will construct ever more intuitive interfaces. Applications constructed from components will make personal programming more like erecting tinker toys than handcrafting bits of code. Component-level programmers will work in the cottage industry of component delivery and testing. Programming literacy, for most, will mean knowing what a computer can do, knowing where to obtain needed software components, and knowing how to configure an application that achieves individual or group goals.

To the majority of computer users, though, computer literacy will mean construction of art, query of fact, or production of the trivial. Most of the activities common to paper and pen, paint and charcoal, film and audio tape, will migrate to the computer. The computer enables everyone to create movies, artwork, and sculpture. There is little that cannot be digitized or created with the computer. Someday we may even find a way to distribute smell on the network.

In business today, we speak of the computer as a tool. For our children, the computer will not be a tool, but a toolbox. They will need to learn where the program with the charcoal resides, or which ray-tracing program makes their sculpture look the coolest.

We are, after all, products of our environment. In the future, those influences are more likely to come from technology than from nature. The rhythmic pounding, split-second shifts of focus, and instant access to information will make our children much different people than we are.

We can bemoan the loss of the good ole' days, or we can embrace the possibilities being delivered. We will not lose moonlit walks along the beach or long drives under the stars—but we will add a hundred million new experiences that we cannot conceive. The world has never been a constant. To trilobites, the good ole' days consisted of an atmosphere we would find toxic. Each generation looks back at its past as a golden age. Our children and their grandchildren will each have their golden age, with its own frustrations and expectations. To their generations, computer technology will be taken for granted—and they will have their own new inventions to grapple with.

30 SECONDS INTO THE FUTURE

The children who adapt to computers will have a myriad of advantages over their non-computer literate peers. Technology is a lever that enables children to perform intellectual activities and explore concepts impossible without it. Just as a 5,000-pound boulder is impossible to move without the assistance of a bulldozer, computers manipulate quantities of concrete and abstract thought unimaginable without them. Computers enable us to touch knowledge never dreamed in a cloistered geographical affiliation. Being computer literate will mean accepting a symbiosis with the technology, and allowing the mind to relinquish its need to know everything itself.

Computers accelerate every aspect of society. High school or college degrees do not delimit the education process. In the computer age—because of the amount of information generated in the past and present—we all remain children. The massive amounts of unassimilated data stand in monumental evidence to our personal ignorance—at the same time attesting to our cultural brilliance. Only the shut-in, devoid of external connections, can consider him- or herself master of his domain. For the rest of us, we can ignore our ignorance or embrace it.

More than 50 years ago, Jung recognized the inevitable need to continue learning. In a lecture on child development and education, Jung wrote: "You may perhaps be surprised to hear me speak of the education of the educator, but I must tell you that I am far from thinking that a man's education is completed when he leaves school, even if he has achieved the university grade. There should be not only continuation courses for young people, but continuation schools for adults."

For those willing to embrace their ignorance, computers provide a private education where the disciplined mind can find its own discoveries and make its own connections between material. The ego need not be pounded in a classroom where knowledge is judged and graded.

For those willing to embrace their ignorance, computers provide a private education where the disciplined mind can find its own discoveries and make its own connections between material. The ego need not be pounded in a classroom where knowledge is judged and graded. With a computer, developmental education continues. For an adult with no knowledge of astronomy, for instance, the terms and images are as new as written English is to a kindergarten student. As elementary education returns to play as a valid education component, so too does play remain valid for adults.

Technology will also influence the quality of life for the physically handicapped and the learning disabled. For the handicapped, technology will unbridle thoughts that might otherwise remain trapped in a less than perfect body. Numeric, textual, auditory, and visual learning become clues instantly available for consultation. For the learning disabled, simultaneous multiple perspectives on a discussion may allow the mind to grasp a metaphor that brings realization.

For adults, computers will help bring learning to those who today find living difficult enough. Jung states that, "The educational method, then, that will best meet the needs of the adult must be indirect rather than direct; that is to say it must put him in possession of such psychological knowledge as will permit him to educate himself." The computer will make self-paced education more possible than ever.

Jung goes on to say that self-education is expected of adults, but should not be expected of a child. With properly configured software, the child and adult could use the same application, calling upon guidance as needed, or being guided as the application interprets an apparent lack of congruent response.

This is undoubtedly a mixed view of the future, leaning toward optimism. When I speculate on the future, I find it unnecessary to prepare for the negative. In the 20th Century we all fret and meditate and extrapolate our current situation and think of the worse. We worry about the kind of world we are leaving our children. We worry about pollution and war. We worry about ozone holes and computer pedophilia. Most of us, though, are so connected to the now that we fail to see the freshness in our children that suggests new possibilities we cannot imagine.

Despite our negative view of the world, the warnings of George Orwell's *1984* did not come to pass. Even in Singapore, the use of technology in the aid of Big Brother has created a successfully creative culture, not one of oppression and gloom.

There is much that could be considered dark in technology, but there is also much that is invigorating and liberating. For children, we should focus on the possibilities. Computers and cyberspace present future generations a fascinating and varied playground, ready for exploration and learning. Freud said that the egos of children force them to ruthlessly pursue the satisfaction of their needs. What better place than the connectedness of cyberspace to unleash their curiosity?

Special thank yous to the following companies for their support on this chapter: Apple Computer, BodyCello, Brøderbund, Compton's NewMedia, Davka, Folkstone Design, Grolier, Interplay, Maxis, Microsoft, Multicom, StarCore, Sumeria, Sunburst, Voyager, Warner New Media, Expert Software.

. . . .

A Reflection on our Cyberlives

Afterword
by Daniel W. Rasmus

Progress is
The law of life, man is
not man yet.

—Robert Browning,
Paracelsus

It is not clear where evolution will lead. It *is* clear that we will no longer take the journey alone. Our minds, for all their marvelous complexity, cannot process the intricacies of the universe that they reveal through their own inventions. We cannot naturally see ultraviolet light or hear ultrasonic sounds, although technology has revealed their existence and made them available to us. Our individual filters, designed by evolution to rescue us from the sea of information, are being challenged by those they were designed to protect. So we call on technology to manage technology.

The screams of data assault us like binary mosquitoes. On a warm day in cyberspace, swarms of various types seem to storm the pathways of information, a superfluous buzz of data drowning out the hum of information. So we manage technology with technology. We partner with our inventions, and perhaps evolve a relationship that supersedes our current relationships.

Evolution occurs when subtle errors in the genetic code provide an advantage for one group over another. Those errors occur in our programming, in our DNA. Cosmic rays, chaotic transmutations, even chemicals in the air we breathe reprogram our cells. We are information machines, from our lofty models of the universe to the DNA tucked away in once-independent mitochondria.

Unlike other evolving life forms, we have primarily evolved through the intellect. The past 2 million years have altered little in our basic body. By a few million years, the capability of walking upright preceded major leaps in our intelligence. So did the opposable thumb. Some of our ancestors even sported brains of higher average volume than ours.

But somehow modern *Homo Sapiens* made a new connection. We made a connection with the universe and with each other unlike any other connection in history. We saw things with a broader scope, a sharper focus, and higher purpose. We saw nature as information, and began the journey to record and master its details. Today, our insatiable appetite for information drives us toward a new symbiosis, a partnership with machines that will carry that journey past the limitations nature placed on our eyes and hands, on our ears and our tongues, and on our olfactory buds.

This book explores the fuzzy edges of that new symbiosis. It explores our ever-increasing reliance on our machines. Through them we share thoughts with colleagues in mainland China, we see planetary disks swirling in the heat of a new solar system, and we see the signature of cancer typed out in the base pairs of a DNA molecule. Computer-aided publishing increases the number of paper books, and digital data now rivals print for volume and market share. Legions of disk drives are slowly consuming the static knowledge of the world and enhancing it with the dynamics of sight and sound. Now more than ever, a

> Our minds, for all their marvelous complexity, cannot process the intricacies of the universe that they reveal through their own inventions.

wise person is not one who knows, but one who knows where to look.

We ask for information, and we expect to receive it. We do receive it, in a plethora of forms and of varying value. Our response to these requests creates more information. A table translated into a pie chart may make the information clearer, but it does not make it less complex. A single representation is replaced by two. The information increases.

And so we evolve. Our rapid evolution, however, is not governed by the same randomness as that of less sophisticated beings. Our mental evolution far outstrips the pace of other creatures. We are, perhaps, consciously motivated to evolve. And since we do not understand our motivation, we continue to evolve in one direction, like a sunflower reaching toward the sun. Curiosity and sensation.

Our curiosity demands information. The computer has ceased to be a tool of scientists and researchers alone. It is now a machine that connects artists and lovers, poets and housewives, football coaches and gay activists.

A few times in history our discoveries disrupted our view of our place in time and space. Consider the revolution upheaval created by fire, written language, printed books, astronomy, relativity, quantum mechanics, and nuclear power.

Fire gave us energy to evolve, a way to fight cold winds and hungry enemies.

Written language allowed for historical documentation and a chance to learn from the past. Mass printed books facilitated the dissolution of monarchies by giving people easy access to knowledge. Astronomy disrupted our mythological relation to the cosmos. Relativity turned time from a constant into an elastic. Quantum mechanics turned our very existence into a question of probability. And now, with computers, we have found a new companion that transports thought almost instantly and manifests the human imagination with more clarity than our own brains.

Computers provide us direct access to knowledge and to people. They reverberate with the background noise of cyberspace. They generate our dreams in vivid color and texture. They spread our gossip, disseminate our knowledge, and retain great chunks of the present for later reflection. Instead of cave walls painted in burnt ocher dust, we print digital images to film and words to disk.

Thus we evolve, side-by-side with the computer. Our minds are the spark and synthesis device that complements the computer's infinite capacity for fact and association. The shift is profound, but even the most sophisticated of computer applications can foretell the future of this new partnership. Even the most imaginative theories—such as Carnegie-Mellon robotics professor Hans Moravec's speculation that we will one day turn our existence over to our machines—are little more than simple extrapolations. We know from

> **We are, perhaps, consciously motivated to evolve. And since we do not understand our motivation, we continue to evolve in one direction, like a sunflower reaching toward the sun.**

our recent past that predictions about computers and their place in our lives are greatly underestimated. Each day moves us closer and closer to a permanent coalition with the thinking machine.

We build computers to both enhance and satisfy our curiosity. Our senses are not sensitive enough to probe the atom or the second star on the right. Our vision cannot register minute angstroms or astronomical units, but our machines can.

Our technology helps us to seek. We scatter our senses throughout cyberspace, peeking under electronic doormats and spying through binary keyholes. Our imaginations run wild, and with computers all that we imagine is possible. Even those things that are truly "real" will link themselves to our web of data. Quarks and black holes cease to be fiction. The bounds of gravity disappear, allowing perfect chemicals to form. A thin beam of laser light reads the pits of a CD-ROM to bring the Mona Lisa to a desktop.

. . . .

We build computers to both enhance and satisfy our curiosity. Our senses are not sensitive enough to probe the atom or the second star on the right. Our vision cannot register minute angstroms or astronomical units, but our machines can.

Every page in this book confirms our shift. But inevitably we fail to communicate the profundity of it. Our language can only couch the new in the old. Our metaphors fail us. We need a new vocabulary. Already, computer culture is providing us with {{{{}}}} hugs and :-{) # smiles in a new cybernetic symbolism. As organizations re-engineer and downsize, the vocabulary of the street becomes profoundly more organic. The World Wide Web links its participants with hyperlinks. Information oozes through the infinity of cyberspace.

New organizations using computers are more likely to be formed around cells than around teams. In the old paradigm, the collective unit is the team, but teams may be disconnected from the whole. Computers enable the individual and the collective to be connected. Without the environment, cells are incapable of continuing. Networks turn communication from convenience to necessity.

Businesses that grow into the new symbiotic future will recognize the shift and adapt to it. Command and control will give way to tight connections, wherein the walls we have so desperately built in the 1950s and 1960s, that we opposed in the 1970s and 1980s, and that we watched grow old in the 1990s, will be figments of historical irrelevance. Associations will form to serve a purpose, then dissolve to serve another purpose.

Our technologies merge and meld. Our search for intelligence in machines may be supplanted by our very human need to remain in the loop. Instead of replacing humans with artificial intelligence, we may use artificial intelligence to act as a surrogate, to represent our ambition and our curiosity. We will send bits of ourselves off to seek information. Our messengers will gather and recollect.

As the new information returns, we learn a new semantics of integration. We will dream not only of our experience, but of the experience of our surrogates. We will integrate knowledge that we obtained by proxy. In the morning, the source will be irrelevant and the knowledge will be firmly implanted along our synapses, the important made readily available, the superfluous discarded in a long dreamfall from consciousness.

Artificial intelligence fails because the most important knowledge is inaccessible. It is embedded in tight spirals of thought, in holograms of awareness. We know only that we know. Teaching a machine to be a person is not possible. Our experience can be transferred only in superficial details.

But current technology will drive us toward massive knowledge servers capable of answering the mundane. They will not, however, replace the skilled or the creative. If machines at some point become self-aware, it will be by the accident of overload, not by design. So many things happening at once along the fibers of the network, so many processes competing for processor and memory, may cause the flecks of intelligence that we shed like dead skin to unite into something different than what we designed.

The very complexity of our creations will soon take them out of our hands. Already the quantum fluctuations confound physicists, as we move toward smaller and smaller devices. We read of individual electrons burrowing through circuit walls, or leaping uncontrollably at the very point where energy and matter mingle in muddled definition. We will generate so much information and filter it to so little that most of us will have no idea what our computers are doing. But we know we will be inextricably linked to them, because their information is now nearly as important to humanity as air or blood.

Instead of replacing humans with artificial intelligence, we may use artificial intelligence to act as a surrogate, to represent our ambition and our curiosity. We will send bits of ourselves off to seek information.

This book explores the fuzzy edge where technology and culture connect. Our traditional filters are coming down. The sense of a new unknown manifests in social disorder. The old is not breaking down, but rather it is seeking a new order. George Bush's so-called "new world order" was a political contrivance. The true "new order," which will support our new symbiosis and the new connections between peoples, is far more striking.

. . . .

The tide of evolution carries everything before it, thought no less than bodies, and persons no less than nations.

George Santayana, Little Essays

Bush's new world order represented the assertion of American democracy on Eastern Europe and the Third World. It represented a change from tyranny to freedom. In that, perhaps, he was right. But the coming sea-change will affect America as much as the rest of the world. The current structure of governments will be as obsolete as the structures of American corporations. The new order will be more organic, more connected than the political pundits have imagined. Tales will replace procedures. Personal searches will replace command decisions. Certain organizations will survive and thrive, not by the benevolence of a charismatic individual, but by the constant sensing of its cells. Everything will require context.

The computer has changed everything. It has changed our relationship to the world. It has changed our relationship to each other. It has changed our relationship with the universe. And so we evolve.

Our minds thrust in all directions, gathering ultraviolet images of Shoemaker-Levy and its assault on Jupiter; peering through tunneling electron microscopes to see individual atoms stacked to form corporate logos; hearing the background noise of the universe, and amid its overwhelming hiss, trying to identify other lonely voices shouting into the blackness.

We are moving into a universe of patterns, of shadows, of organic relationships. This book peeks into dozens of shadows, identifies hundreds of new patterns, follows scores of relationships. It hears the pulse of Usenet conversations pounding like ancient drums on the Serengeti. It sees our sense of self giving way to anonymity and transformation. It documents knowledge becoming legend and fact becoming myth. It plots great distances that shrink to nothing and zooms in on nothing magnified into enormity. The computer has changed everything. And we sweep ourselves along with the change because our need for information resonates with the joy of its possibilities.

Index

museum tours, 73-74
physically-challenged users, 76-82
real-estate sales, 68-69
simulation, 63
stereoscopic CAD, 70-72
telepresence, 76
Urban Simulation Environment, 64-65
ARPAnet, 7, 135
art, 12-13, 17-18
GAs (genetic algorithms), 416-417
art collection software, 34-38
artificial intelligence, *see* AI
artificial life, *see* ALife
ASCII art (IRC), 501
ASL Megamotion, 477
Aspen Movie Map, 97
Astrology CD-I, 471
astronomical simulations, 269-270
asynchronous communication, 296
asynchronous computer conferencing, 182-183
ATC for Windows V1.11, 237
atomic force microscope (AFM), 531, 557
audio conferencing, 180-181
AudioMan, 453-456
AutoDESK, 94
3D Studio, 117
Azure Technology, 264-265

B

Backyard, 640
BASIC programs, 635
Battle Tech, 106
BayMOO, 146, 151

bboards, 139
BBSs (bulletin board services), 141, 154, 183, 300, 344
business systems, 158
CompuServe, 155
e-mail, 155
FCC field offices, 171-172
GEnie, 155
group-support systems, 158
guidelines, 156
hardware, 162-163
maintenance, 169-170
personal systems, 158
setup, 166
bulletins, 167
file transfers, 166-167
security, 167-168
testing, 168
software, 163-165
starting, 159, 162-163
sysop test, 160-162
sysops, 155
users, 169
Berkeley Speech Technologies, 455-456
BeSTspeech ReadOut, 455-456
Beyond the Wall of Stars, 32-33
Beyondmail, 391
BioMetric Systems, Inc., 541
Biomorph, 410
biosensors, 547
biotech development, 531
Birge, Robert, 536
blackboard models (DAI), 370
***Blade Runner*, 594**
Blake Stone, 482-483, 489

DirII virus, 447
disk sectors, 427
Distant Suns V2.0, 271-272
distributed artificial intelligence,
    see DAI
DragonDictate, 461-462
Dramatica, 584, 615, 631
drawing devices, 50-53
The Dream Machine, 288-290
Drexler, K. Eric, 526
DSPs (digital signal processors), 244
Dustpro expert system, 364
Dyno Notepad, 587

E

e-journals, 137, 612
e-mail, 137, 143, 296
    BBSs (bulletin board services),
    155
    emoticons, 144
    junk e-mail, 142
    signatures, 144
    teleconferencing, 177
Eastgate Systems, 631
ECN, 152
Edison Brothers Entertainment, 106
EI-fish, 412
electronic books, 611
Electronic Freedom Foundation, 208
Electronic Frontier Foundation, 345
electronic mail, see e-mail
Elite Flight Simulator, 264-265
ELIZA, 357, 393
emoticons, 144
encrypted viruses, 430, 434

encyclopedias, 21-31
engineering, 95
episodic knowledge, 360
ergonomics, 208
eShop, Inc., 391
eSoft, 165
ethnicity in video games, 489
Experience Software, 588
Expert Systems, 364-366
exploration software, 264

F

face-to-face conferencing, 178-180
Falcon 3.0, 237-238
Falken, 165
FAQs (Frequently Asked Ques-
    tions), 136, 142
Farralon, 575
Fauve Matisse, 41
fax modems, 228
FCC (Federal Communications
    Commission), 219
    field offices, 171-172
FictionMaster, 631
file infectors (viruses), 428
    Cascade, 444
    companion viruses, 430
    Dark Avenger, 445
    direct action infectors, 430
    Jerusalem, 429, 445
    Satan Bug, 447
    SMEG, 448
    Tremor, 447
    TSR viruses, 430
    Yankee Doodle, 445

Human Interface Laboratory, 12
hypertext, 18, 617
  Eastgate Systems, 631
  Hypertext Hotel, 620, 631
  novels, 618
  poetry, 618
  Uncle Buddy's Phantom Funhouse,
    619-620

I

IAs (intelligent agents), 382-385,
  402
  ALIVE, 396-397
  CYC, 395
  denizens, 396-401
  features, 385-386
  Macintosh, 392
  Magnet, 392
  mimic agents, 387, 390
  Open Sesame!, 392
  OZ, 397
  personable agents, 393-395
  reflexive agents, 390
IBIS (Issue-Based Information
  System), 302
Idaho National Engineering
  Laboratory, 66
Idea Fisher, 571, 580
ideasurfing, 629
image enhancing tools, 42-49
Imagination Network, 515
immersed agents, *see* denizens
In the Bag (cybermall), 146
Industrial Light and Magic, 16
industrial music, 594
INFO*SHARE, 165

Infocom, 255
InfoDepo, 571, 588
information superhighway, 134
  see also Internet
input/output devices (virtual
  reality), 92-94, 105
Inspiration, 582
Intellidraw, 39
intelligent agents, *see* IAs
intelligent gels, 548
interactive literature, 32-33
interactive music, *see* cybermusic
interactive simulation software, 264
interactive TV, 467
  films, 472
  player components, 468
  software, 469-471
    Adobe Premiere, 473-474
    ASL Megamotion, 477
    HSC InterActive, 475
    Macromedia Director, 475-476
    Super Video, 477
  video editing, 472
interactivity, 384
Intererotica, 288-290
interfaces, 9-12
Internet, 134
  accessing services, 141
  addresses, 150
  Archie, 139
  bboards, 139
  censorship, 147
  children, 657
  "code names", 143
  CompuServe, 151
  connections, 135

programmers, CMC (computer-mediated conferencing), 188
programming, 636-637
Project KickStart, 588
protein chemistry, 532
Prusinkiewicz, Premyslaw, 410

Q-R

QDES expert system, 365
Qsoft, 586
Queeg virus, 448

radio, 487
RBBS-PC, 165
real-estate sales, 69
Redshift, 273-275
reflexive agents, 390
remote login (rlogin), 137
rendering (virtual reality), 99
   3-D imaging, 120
   one-sided rendering, 105
resolution (virtual reality), 99
Return to Zork, 255
Rheingold, Howard, 134
rlogin (remote login), 137
robots, 103
rotaxanes, 536
rule-based expert systems, 365
Rundgren, Todd, 598

S

San Diego Supercomputer Center, 146
Sandpoint Corporation, 391
Sapphire, 165
Satan Bug virus, 447

scanning tunneling microscope (STM), 530, 557
Schweers, Morgan, 439-443
science fiction, 4, 223
Screaming Fist virus, 447
Screenplay Systems, 631
Searchlight Software, 165
Searle, John, 374
Seawolf, 239-240
security
   BBSs, 167-168
   office automation, 204-205
self-replicating molecules, 528
semantic knowledge, 360
sensory feedback (virtual reality), 102
servers (Internet), 141
The Seventh Guest CD-I, 471
Shannon, Claude, 358
The Shockwave Rider, 333
shopping (virtual reality), 146
Sierra, 255-258
SIGGRAPH, 410
signatures (e-mail), 144
SimLife, 412
Sims, Karl, 416
simulation software, 264
   astronomical simulations, 269-270
   music simulation, 281
The Sky, 276-278
slow viruses, 430
SMART expert system, 364
SMEG virus, 425, 448
Sneakers, 332
Snow White, 126